Object-Oriented
Common LISP

Stephen Slade

To join a Prentice Hall PTR internet mailing list, point to
http://www.prenhall.com/mail_lists

Prentice Hall PTR
Upper Saddle River, New Jersey 07458
http://www.prenhall.com

Library of Congress Cataloging in Publication Data

Slade, Stephen
    Object-oriented common LISP / Stephen Slade.
        p.   cm
    Includes bibliographical references and index.
    ISBN 0-13-605940-6 (alk. paper)
        1. Object-oriented programming (Computer science). 2. COMMON LISP (Computer
    program language).   I. Title.
QA76.64.S576   1997
005.13'3—dc21   97-22732
                                                          CIP

Editorial/Production Supervision: *Kathleen M. Caren*
Acquisitions Editor: *Gregory G. Doench*
Cover Design Director: *Jerry Votta*
Cover Design: *Design Source*
Manufacturing Manager: *Alexis R. Heydt*
Marketing Manager: *Stephen Solomon*
Editorial Assistant: *Mary Treacy*
Cover art: Anni Albers. *Red Meander I*, 1969, silkscreen.
Courtesy The Josef and Anni Albers Foundation. Photo credit: Tim Nighwander.

ISBN 0-13-605940-6

Prentice-Hall International (UK) Limited,London
Prentice-Hall of Australia Pty. Limited, Sydney
Prentice-Hall Canada Inc., Toronto
Prentice-Hall Hispanoamericana, S.A., Mexico
Prentice-Hall of India Private Limited, New Delhi
Prentice-Hall of Japan, Inc., Tokyo
Pearson Education Asia Pte. Ltd., Singapore
Editora Prentice-Hall do Brasil, Ltda., Rio de Janeiro

Contents

*The body of Benjamin Franklin, Printer (like the cover
of an old book, its contents torn out and stripped of its
lettering and gilding), lies here, food for worms;
but the work shall not be lost, for it will (as he believed)
appear once more in a new and more elegant
edition, revised and corrected by the Author.*

◇ BENJAMIN FRANKLIN, *Epitaph on Himself (1728)*

iv

List of Figures

List of Tables

Preface

True science teaches us to doubt and to abstain from ignorance.

◊ CLAUDE BERNARD, *Bulletin of New York Academy of Medicine (1928)*

*A modern poet has characterized the personality of art
and the impersonality of science as follows:
Art is I: Science is We.*

◊ CLAUDE BERNARD, *Ibid.*

In recent years, academic computer scientists have debated the role of programming in introductory computer science courses. Many have argued that an introductory science course should expose the student to the great ideas of the discipline. Thus, an introductory biology course should cover topics such as evolution and molecular genetics, but not how to build a microscope. Accordingly, a computer science course should emphasize the major intellectual issues of computing, not how to write programs.

We do not agree with this position. First, programming *is* a major intellectual issue in computer science. Second, the comparison of programming to building microscopes misses the point. Writing programs in computer science is more like building a living organism in biology. If biology had advanced to a stage that permitted introductory students easily to construct amoebas and clams and roses and rabbits, there would be little debate over the intellectual content of such exercises.

Programs are the organisms that populate the world of computing. This book presents some of these creatures and shows how to build them.

This book is not an introductory programming text. Rather, it is for students who have already learned to program in some language other than LISP. Given the ready access most students have to computers these days, it is rare to find a college student interested in computers who has not previously been exposed to programming. The odds are pretty good that a student's first programming language was not LISP, but C or C++ or spreadsheet macros or database programs.

Furthermore, we recognize that people who study a new programming language usually do so to apply it to particular problems. That is, the language should be a useful tool. LISP was originally developed for artificial intelligence programming. However, over the years it has been applied to a range of applications, including data structures, computer systems, and compiler design. The present book is suitable as a companion text in such courses – a programmer's guide to a powerful software tool.

The complete source code from the book is available without charge through the Internet. The online version of appendix A, a World Wide Web document, explains how to access the code, as well as additional information about this book and Common LISP.

Common LISP is available on a variety of machines from a number of vendors. The online version of appendix A explains how to get a public domain copy of LISP and also discusses some of the differences found among various versions of LISP.

Programming is for participants, not spectators. This book is replete with examples and exercises. These sample programs demonstrate fundamental programming principles in familiar domains. The reader should execute these programs. The answers to most of the exercises will be found in appendix B (page 681).

For the benefit of C++ mavens, appendix C (page 735) provides a comparison between C++ and the object-oriented features of Common LISP.

Acknowledgments

As an undergraduate at Yale, I had a conversation with a senior faculty member who had just published a book – probably his tenth or so. He had completed the manuscript the previous summer, which had been particularly hot in New Haven. He described the rigorous craft of writing in simple terms. "Every day after lunch," he said, "I would sit at my desk, strip to the waist, open a bottle of Wild Turkey, and write a new chapter." As I now recall, this professor particularly admired the literary work of Hunter Thompson.

I must confess that I found this job description attractive. However, it happens that I became a computer scientist, not a humanities professor. Computer workstations require strict environmental controls. Thus, I never had an office that was not air conditioned. The reader may safely infer that the present book was written by a fully clothed author. In the spirit of complete candor and disclosure, I can also state that I prefer scotch to bourbon.

Another professor and inspiration was Alan Perlis, who was one of the pioneers in computer science in general, and programming languages in particular. I took Alan's "introductory" undergraduate course in computer science in which we covered hardware, machine language, Algol, and APL. In graduate school, I was a teaching assistant for Alan in another introductory course in which the students were expected to derive an APL one-liner to perform Gaussian elimination.

Whenever you felt you had accomplished something, Alan could be counted on to go you one "meta." I remember demonstrating for Alan an artificial intelligence program comprising over 20,000 lines of LISP code. Alan nodded with approval at the program's performance and then stated, "What would really be interesting is a program that would generate this program." Of course, I had to agree. The spirit of Alan appears throughout this text in the epigrams at the end of each chapter.

I appreciate the support and encouragement of Ted Stohr and my colleagues at the Information Systems Department of the Stern School of Business at New York University. I am grateful to Drew McDermott and Martin Schultz of the Yale Computer Science Department who provided me a *pied-à-terre* where I could prepare this manuscript in pastoral tranquility.

I am grateful for the constructive comments of many reviewers, particularly Natan Borshansky, Will Fitzgerald and Henry Lucas.

This book is dedicated to my two favorite autonomous agents, my daughters, Francesca Emily Marie and Alexandra Elizabeth Helene. Out of respect and love, I shall consistently use the feminine form of the indefinite third-person pronoun.

Stephen B. Slade
New Haven, CT and New York, NY
June 1997

> *Perhaps if we wrote programs from childhood on,*
> *as adults we'd be able to read them.*
>
> ◇ ALAN PERLIS, *Epigrams in Programming (1982)*

Chapter 1

LISP

High thoughts must have high language.

◇ ARISTOPHANES, *Frogs (405 B.C.)*

Brekekekex, ko-ax, ko-ax.

◇ ARISTOPHANES, *Ibid.*

*Since our concern was speech, and speech impelled us
To purify the dialect of the tribe.*

◇ T. S. ELIOT, *Four Quartets (1935)*

*From the beginning, the new artificial intelligence community
accepted list processing as the programming tool for A.I.
That is still largely true today, more than thirty years later. The
rest of the programming profession, however, did not greet the
innovation with open arms. ... To conventional programmers these
languages seemed ridiculous, if not suicidal.*

◇ HERBERT SIMON, *Models of My Life (1992)*

All computer programming languages are alike, at least from the machine's perspective. In theory, it is possible to take a program written in one language and create an equivalent program in another language. The computer may execute exactly the same sequence of commands for both programs − depending on the actual implementations.

A programming language is a notation by which human programmers communicate with computers as well as with other programmers. This communication is most effective when the programming language permits the programmer to express

1

Concept	Arabic	Roman
Integer	7	VII
Negative	-109	$-CIX$
Fraction	3/7	III/VII
Decimal	7.109	$VII.CIX$
Exponent	3^7	III^{VII}

Table 1.1: Arabic versus Roman Numerals

herself in a natural and perspicuous manner. The notation can directly influence a programmer's ability to convert thoughts and intentions into working programs.

By comparison, consider two numeric notations: Roman and Arabic numerals. Presumably, any Roman number can be converted to a corresponding Arabic number, and vice versa. Two thousand years ago, Roman numerals were popular because of the political influence of the Roman empire. However, over time, Arabic numerals have gained universal acceptance and have been extended to include negative numbers, fractions, decimals, exponents, and other notational variations.

Theoretically, Roman numerals could have embraced the same extensions. Table 1.1 provides examples of such possibilities.

As systems of numeric notation, both are equally expressive. However, Arabic numerals, with their place-value notation, facilitate a graphic representation of various mathematical properties and operations, such as magnitude, addition, subtraction, multiplication, and division. With Arabic notation, adding two 20-digit numbers is not significantly different from adding two 2-digit numbers. One can perform arithmetic with Roman numerals as well, but Arabic numerals have a form and structure which reflect basic mathematical ideas. The very expression *2-digit number* is not a useful concept with Roman numerals, as it denotes the set

$$\{2, 4, 6, 9, 11, 15, 20, 40, 51, 55, 60, 90, 99, 101, \dots\}$$

(See exercise 7.9.5 on page 265.)

It is simpler to perform complex mathematical operations using Arabic numerals. It is simpler to think about numbers and math in general using Arabic numerals. Arabic numerals provide a natural notation for math.

The Roman empire needed an accounting system. Roman numerals were useful as a notation for commerce. However, Roman numerals proved not to be satisfactory as a descriptive language for mathematics. Arabic numerals were. In the long run, Arabic numerals found their way into the accounting systems as well.

A programming language is a notational system. Today, programming languages are used to solve many problems. The choice of language is affected by many factors, but the most common reason is tradition. Programmers usually use the language that other programmers usually use. However, innovation is not the common use. Some programming languages support innovation, others support proliferation. LISP is a language of innovation.

LISP is not only one of the oldest programming languages, but it is also one of the newest. LISP makes it easier for the programmer to think about computation and to extend the language to implement innovation.

1.1 History of Common LISP

This book presents the Common LISP programming language, which is a modern version of LISP, one of the oldest computer languages in current use. Originally developed in the late 1950s by John McCarthy, LISP evolved as the primary language for research in artificial intelligence (or AI) and has matured as a general-purpose language for a wide variety of applications.

LISP, which stands for LISt Processing, was developed as a language for manipulating symbols. LISP's symbolic manipulation can be contrasted with other languages, such as FORTRAN, which are primarily used for numeric calculations. There were other list processing languages developed in the 1950s, most notably IPL, *Information Processing Language* [Newell et al., 1964]. (References appear in Appendix E, page 751.) There were a series of IPL releases, IPL I through IPL V. However, LISP proved to be the AI language of choice.

LISP has been used for many AI applications, including programs to perform tasks such as natural language understanding, game playing, learning, planning, theorem proving, problem solving, and speech recognition. As the performance of LISP implementations has improved, LISP has been adopted by computer scientists outside AI.

From its inception, LISP had several features which recommended it as a desirable programming language:

- *Simple syntax.* The canonical form of LISP is the same for both programs and data — they are both lists of items enclosed by parentheses. This seemingly trivial duality of program-as-data has significant ramifications that set LISP apart from other languages. LISP programs can directly analyze, modify, and generate other LISP programs. This is important not only for automatic programming research but also for many other complex artificial intelligence applications where dynamic program manipulation comes into play.

- *Extensible.* LISP can expand. One consequence of the program-as-data property is that the programmer can easily extend the language. She can add new functions and even make syntactic alterations through macros. This allows the programmer to develop special-purpose tools that are well integrated into the normal LISP environment. Over the years, numerous utilities have been developed and added to various LISP implementations, including in-core editors, database retrieval systems, window packages, cross-reference packages, spelling correctors, and undo facilities. LISP is a programmable programming language.

- *Adaptable.* Not only can the programmer extend the language by adding new functions and macros, but she can redefine existing ones. This ability to tailor the language can be useful in translating code from one LISP dialect to another.

- *Automatic memory management.* LISP (like most interpreted languages) performs dynamic memory allocation and reclamation, commonly known as *garbage collection.* The programmer does not need to allocate or free storage explicitly, although primitives are available for such explicit control in the rare case where the programmer feels it is appropriate.

- *Functional arguments.* LISP allows functions to be used as arguments to other functions and returned as values. This feature can be viewed as a higher-level mechanism for using programs as data.

- *Functional programming.* Functions in LISP return values. LISP programs can be streams of functions calling other functions, without side effects.

As LISP evolved into Common LISP, other features became incorporated into the language.

- *Debugging and error checking.* LISP functions can perform extensive argument checking. Furthermore, Common LISP provides the programmer with a variety of error-checking routines that can be incorporated into the user's own programs, thus facilitating the debugging of code. For programmers more concerned with speed of execution, Common LISP allows the programmer to turn off the error checking.

- *Data abstraction.* Common LISP provides direct methods for implementing and manipulating new data structures. Abstract data structures allow the programmer to focus on the conceptual aspects of programming, without regard to the underlying representation and implementation.

- *Object-oriented programming.* Under the Common LISP Object System or CLOS, every data type in Common LISP can be viewed as an object — numbers, lists, symbols, and so on. In addition to the approach of having functions act on data objects, CLOS allows the programmer to create objects that themselves respond to methods. This object-oriented programming methodology was pioneered in the languages Simula [Dahl and Nygaard, 1966] and Smalltalk [Goldberg and Robson, 1983]. CLOS provides the programmer with a seamless combination of functional and object-oriented programming.

Over the years, LISP's extensibility has lead to the creation of a variety of LISP dialects. The main predecessors to Common LISP were the following. [Steele and Gabriel, 1993]

- *LISP 1.5.* McCarthy and his colleagues at the MIT Artificial Intelligence Lab implemented this progenitor LISP. [McCarthy et al., 1962]

- *MacLISP.* The MIT AI Lab developed MacLISP to run on the PDP-10 computer. [Moon, 1974] One of the main applications of MacLISP was the Macsyma symbolic mathematics program. [Bogen, 1973] The importance of high-quality mathematical operations led the MacLISP group to pay particular attention to matters numerical. For example, MacLISP included `bignums` for arbitrary precision integer arithmetic. MacLISP also introduced the `readtable` to LISP.

- *InterLisp.* A version of LISP developed at Bolt, Beranek, and Neuman (BBN) in Cambridge was known as BBN LISP. When its implementor, Warren Teitelman, moved to the Xerox Palo Alto Research Center (Xerox PARC), the dialect was renamed InterLisp. [Teitelman, 1974, Teitelman, 1978] InterLisp was designed as a complete programming environment and included many novel features, such as a structure editor and breakpointing. Additional features, such as *undo* and *do what I mean* (or DWIM), did not become a standard part of LISP but can be found in modern desktop applications.

- *Lisp Machine Lisp, aka, Zetalisp.* In the mid-1970s, a research group at the MIT AI Lab developed a personal computer based on LISP, known as the Lisp Machine. [Greenblatt, 1974] Subsequently, companies began to produce commercial Lisp machines. The main Lisp Machine dialect was Zetalisp, which introduced a number of new features to the language, including complex lambda lists, `defmacro`, backquote, multiple values, `defstruct`, `setf`, and flavors − an object-oriented programming extension. [Weinreb and Moon, 1981]

- *Franz LISP.* In conjunction with a major project porting UNIX to the new DEC VAX machines in the late 1970s, computer scientists at the University of California at Berkeley developed a LISP for the VAX known as *Franz LISP.* [Foderaro and Sklower, 1992]

- *Portable Standard LISP (PSL).* Researchers at the University of Utah had a symbolic math program called REDUCE, which was written in LISP. In an attempt to port REDUCE to different computer platforms, the researchers developed a portable version of LISP: PSL. They demonstrated the utility of having a common, portable LISP dialect. [Griss and Hearn, 1981]

- *Scheme.* Gerald Sussman and Guy Steele at the MIT AI Lab developed a minimal version of Lisp as an experimental planning language. [Sussman and Steele Jr., 1975, Steele Jr. and Sussman, 1978] They demonstrated the benefits of lexical scoping, closures, and tail recursion.

By the early 1980s, it was all too apparent that the proliferation of LISP dialects resulted in a serious problem: lack of compatibility. A LISP program written in one dialect would not run under another dialect of LISP. LISP programs were not portable.

The answer was Common LISP, which was effectively the union of the major existing LISP dialects. Common LISP today has all the features of regular LISP listed above. It attempts to achieve the following goals. [Steele and Gabriel, 1993]

- *Commonality.* Common LISP implementors share the core language description.

- *Portability.* The language design focuses on features that can be implemented across a range of hardware, ensuring that a Common LISP program can run on different platforms. Thus, no language feature requires a graphical user interface or special microcode.

- *Consistency.* Code should run the same under the interpreter and the compiler.

- *Expressiveness.* The language should include the best features available from all LISP dialects.

- *Compatibility.* The language design should be compatible with Zetalisp, MacLisp, and InterLisp (in that order).

- *Efficiency.* The language design should make it possible to produce an optimizing compiler. That is, the language should avoid constructs that cannot be implemented efficiently.

- *Power.* The language should provide support for systems programming, permitting the construction of useful programming utilities.

- *Stability.* The language should change through gradual evolution, not sudden revolution.

Most desirable features in software can be described as *abilities*, or at least with words ending that way. Common LISP was intended as a language of outstanding ability. In addition to portability, compatibility, and stability, we have reliability (consistency), affordability (efficiency), versatility (power), and extensibility (expressiveness). The result is a language of great desirability.

1.2   The Religion of LISP

Many LISP programmers can be classified as true believers. For them, LISP embodies computational truth, light, and revelation. LISP is a manifestation of divine will. Other programming languages, which may share some of the attributes of LISP, fail to satisfy the broad tenets of programming purity found in LISP. Advocates of other languages are heretics.

The present volume is intended to provide a comprehensive and comprehensible introduction and indoctrination to the Common LISP faith. However, the LISP universe is vast, and the author recognizes that the reader may later need additional information. As with any great world religion, there are many LISP texts which provide exposition and exegesis of the critical ideas and beliefs. It is recommended that the programmer who wishes to pursue Common LISP in greater detail refer to other sources of documentation, including the following:

- *Common LISP: The Language (Second Edition).* [Steele Jr., 1990] This is the bible − the revised standard version. It informs implementors of the language exactly what features to support and why. It is the blueprint for the language.

- *Common LISP: The Reference.* [Franz Inc., 1988]. This book provides brief discussions and examples of the language features. It is an annotated parts catalog for the language. Note that the 1988 edition does not contain the updated material found in [Steele Jr., 1990].

- *Paradigms of Artificial Intelligence Programming: Case Studies in Common LISP.* [Norvig, 1992] Norvig presents a panoply of great AI programs implemented in Common LISP.

- Local system documentation. Religions have schisms which lead to separate denominations. Different LISP implementations share a common core set of beliefs but diverge at the fringes. Your own version of LISP will have certain peculiar features and capabilities. The local documentation will complement other sources.

- Internet bulletin boards, ftp and web sites (discussed in appendix A, page 679). LISP is always changing. The LISP community of users and developers are plugged into the Internet. That is the best source for late-breaking LISP news.

The programmer should appreciate that LISP is a living language. Common LISP continues to evolve. In that spirit, we have made arrangements for this book to evolve as well. Appendix A is available online as a World Wide Web (WWW) page containing updates, errata, and additional hypertext references to the great Internet LISP community.

Finally, it is most important that the reader of this book also write programs. At the risk of pushing our metaphor beyond redemption, programs are the sacraments of LISP. Only by writing programs will the reader attain enlightenment.

Throughout this text, we provide examples of LISP programs in a variety of generic areas, such as text formatting and spelling correction. These examples illustrate both basic and advanced programming techniques using LISP. The examples are chosen to focus on programming issues, not theoretical concerns. Thus, the reader is not expected to have special knowledge of artificial intelligence, mathematics, or molecular biology. On the other hand, the reader should not expect to gain any major insights into those topics, either.

In spite of the fact that Common LISP represents a great unification of LISP dialects, there remain a few areas where the LISP community, shall we say, agrees to disagree. The reader will occasionally encounter a notation in the outside margin, $\infty \Rightarrow$ such as found here. The symbol "∞" indicates that the item under discussion may vary across implementations and, like infinity, there may be no known limit to the number of variations. Moreover, given the dynamic nature of LISP, these differences may change over time, which is why we have provided a dynamic appendix for this book. The online version of appendix A discusses some of these differences.

The reader should have access to a computer running LISP and try the examples and exercises given in the book, which are also available online (see appendix A). Learning a computer language requires practice and application. Fortunately, this practice should not prove onerous. Given the fervor with which LISP programmers extol and defend their chosen language, for many programmers learning LISP is a spiritual experience.

1.3   Object-Oriented Programming

Disputes over the merits of various programming languages are chronic in computer science. The outside observer or programming neophyte is often bewildered by the arguments. Why should one programming language be different in kind from another? Don't all languages do the same things?

A programming language is a means for constructing programs. When we build a program, we create an artifact. The choice of programming language can determine the nature of that artifact. By comparison, consider the construction of a more tangible artifact: a building.

In designing a building, an architect is aware of numerous goals: function, capacity, aesthetic appeal, efficiency, stability, and the time and cost required for the design, construction, and maintenance of the building. There may be optimal ways of satisfying these various constraints. For example, Aladdin's genie from the lamp could construct the world's most glorious palace instantly, at no cost to Aladdin. Outside the land of imagination, however, the architect must recognize the practical limitations of her resources and abilities. Still, she strives to satisfy as many of the design goals as possible.

In each decision, the architect faces trade-offs between competing goals. The architect has a variety of construction materials among which to choose, such as concrete, wood, glass, brick, and steel. The choice of material constrains many factors, such as cost, stability, and appearance, which will then affect the way the architect makes other decisions. Some materials are good for skyscrapers, and other materials are better for homes. Certain materials may be well suited for very specific applications. Asphalt is terrific for paving but not for walls. Concrete can be used for both. Which is better? It depends.

Which programming language is best? It depends. Computer languages differ on many dimensions:

- Speed of program development and speed of program execution often depend on the programming language.

- Program cost is commonly measured in terms of time (speed of development, execution, and maintenance), and space (size of the program).

- Efficiency is the inverse of the cost of time and space.

- Capacity for a programming language might refer to the size of programs and problems for which the language is practical.

- Stability in a programming language is reflected in a program's ability to accommodate changes or unexpected events.

- Appeal and function are related properties. A programming language that is well suited for function X will have many supporters among those who require function X.

Many of these factors are often more related to a language's implementation for a specific machine than to any intrinsic property of the language.

LISP is one of the older computer languages and has become the primary language for artificial intelligence research. To continue with the construction analogy, the languages BASIC and Pascal might be viewed as the bricks and lumber languages for the do-it-yourselfer, due to their popularity and availability for microcomputers. The home hobbyist can build the equivalent of a deck and patio in her backyard. LISP was rarely used for mundane applications because it required the more elaborate hardware found in artificial intelligence labs. Who would want to build a picnic bench out of titanium? However, as the price of more powerful hardware has declined, there is greater demand for more powerful computer programming languages. LISP has proven to be a language of great power and sophistication. Common LISP implementations typically include an optimizing compiler to produce fast, efficient code.

One major dimension of modern programming languages is support for *object-oriented programming.* Languages such as C++ [Stroustrup, 1986] and Eiffel [Meyer, 1988] have been developed to exploit the advantages of object-oriented software engineering techniques.

What makes a language object-oriented? There is some modest consensus here.

- *Classes.* An object-oriented language supports the creation of classes, from which the user can create object instances. In our architecture world, there are standards for windows and doors, according to which specific instances of windows and doors can be created.

- *Generic Functions.* The programmer can use the same function name to specify operations on many different types of objects. For example, the addition function could operate on integers and floating point numbers. This feature is sometimes called *polymorphism*, suggesting that a function has "many shapes."[1] The architecture world might have a generic function `install` that would mean something different for a sink or a doorbell. The first would require a plumber and the second an electrician.

- *Class Inheritance.* Over the years, computer science has revealed the unshakable truth that software is DHTW (very hard to write). To tame the hideous software monster, programmers have been encouraged to reuse code rather than write new code from scratch. Object-oriented inheritance provides a principled method for code reuse. In particular, if a programmer has to create an object Z that is sort of like an X and sort of like a Y, she can specify that Z *inherits* from X and Y.

  As is the case with real inheritance, the object who does the inheriting does not have to work as hard anymore. In the architecture world, inheritance is like ordering prefabricated windows, doors, staircases, and cabinets. The resulting objects need only be painted and installed, not created from scratch.

- *Data Encapsulation.* Traditional programming languages permit any part of the program to access any other part of the program. The danger here is that one function cannot always trust another function to do the right thing. In the real world, you would be reluctant to hand over your wallet every time you made a purchase. The solution is *encapsulation.* The data, like the money in your wallet, is accessed only by a few trusted functions.

The Common LISP Object System comes with a number of standard prefabricated classes, which are shown in figure 1.1 on page 11. For the sake of pictorial convenience, the hierarchy is depicted here from left to right, rather than from top to bottom. At the left, T is the name given to the root class, from which all other classes are derived. Moving to the right, the `number` class has three derived classes: `float`, `rational`, and `complex`. The `rational` class itself has two derived classes: `ratio` and `integer`.

The numbers in parentheses following a class indicate the chapter in which that class is introduced. Thus, the focus of the first part of this book is on the native constituent classes of Common LISP.

We introduce generic functions in chapter 12 and class inheritance in chapter 13. CLOS does not have any special data encapsulation provisions because LISP already supports encapsulation through closures, discussed in chapter 5, and packages, described in chapter 15.

For those programmers who may already be familiar with C++, we provide a comparison between CLOS and C++ in appendix C.

---

[1]Cf. *politics*: "poli" (many) and "tics" (blood-sucking parasites).

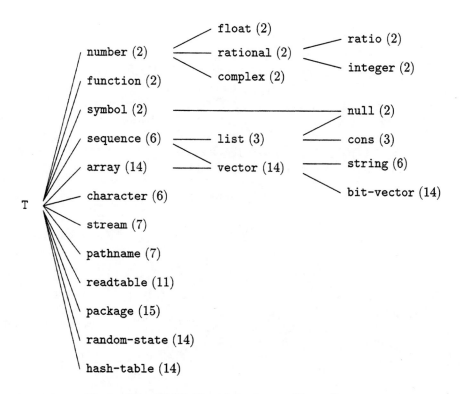

Figure 1.1: CLOS Class Inheritance Hierarchy

In one important regard, Common LISP, as an object-oriented language, is closer to Smalltalk than to C++, namely, the size of the standard library. The class hierarchy depicted in figure 1.1 has no counterpart, per se, in C++. C++ has no string class or vector class or rational arithmetic class. The C++ approach is to allow implementors to create divergent class libraries. The language does not specify the contents of those libraries. It is up to the authors of component libraries to design the classes and their related methods.

By contrast, Common LISP specifies both the classes and the dozens of related functions. This approach has three consequences. First, it increases portability. LISP programmers can rely on the fact that other LISP programmers will have the same set of standard functions. A C++ programmer cannot make any such assumption.

Second, Common LISP increases productivity. The Common LISP classes and functions comprise a vast collection of programming utilities. A C++ programmer gets a hammer and a screwdriver. The Common LISP programmer has an entire shedful of tools. Most of these tools could be built with C++, but the Common LISP programmer gets them from the beginning.

Third, Common LISP increases the size of the documentation. Common LISP is huge. Most of the size is due to the libraries — the standard classes and utilities that are included as part of the language definition. If Common LISP were smaller, so would this book.

1.4   Chapter Summary

- LISP is a computer language developed in the 1950s for manipulating symbols.

- Common LISP is a modern version of LISP, incorporating the features of many previous LISP dialects. Common LISP was designed by a committee of computer scientists and has been implemented for a wide variety of machines, from PCs to supercomputers.

- LISP's key features include:

    - simple syntax
    - extensibility
    - adaptability
    - automatic memory management
    - functional arguments
    - functional programming
    - debugging and error checking
    - data abstraction
    - object-oriented programming

- Common LISP had the following explicit design goals:
  - commonality
  - portability
  - consistency
  - expressiveness
  - compatibility
  - efficiency
  - power
  - stability

- The reader of this book should use a computer to try the examples and exercises. The code is available through the Internet.

- Object-oriented programming languages support the creation of classes, generic functions, class inheritance, and data encapsulation.

- The Common LISP language definition includes a large number of utility classes and functions that would be part of external libraries in other languages.

> *Over the centuries the Indians developed sign language*
> *for communicating phenomena of interest. Programmers from*
> *different tribes (FORTRAN, LISP, ALGOL, SNOBOL, etc.) could*
> *use one that doesn't require them to carry a blackboard on their ponies.*
>
> ⋄ ALAN PERLIS, *Epigrams in Programming (1982)*

> *Giving up on assembly language was the apple in our*
> *Garden of Eden: Languages whose use squanders machine cycles*
> *are sinful. The LISP machine now permits LISP programmers to*
> *abandon bra and fig-leaf.*
>
> ⋄ ALAN PERLIS, *Epigrams in Programming (1982)*

Chapter 2

A Tutorial Introduction

> *"Reeling and Writing, of course, to begin with,"*
> *the Mock Turtle replied, "and the different branches of*
> *Arithmetic – Ambition, Distraction, Uglification, and Derision."*
>
> ◇ LEWIS CARROLL, *Alice's Adventures in Wonderland (1865)*

> *As yet a child, nor yet a fool to fame,*
> *I lisp'd in numbers, for the numbers came.*
>
> ◇ ALEXANDER POPE, *Epistle to Dr. Arbuthnot (1735)*

> *The imagination ... gives birth to a system of symbols,*
> *harmonious in themselves, and consubstantial with the truths*
> *of which they are the conductors.*
>
> ◇ SAMUEL TAYLOR COLERIDGE, *The Statesman's Manual (1816)*

LISP is primarily an interpreted language. By comparison, the languages BASIC and APL are also interpreted, and FORTRAN, COBOL, C, and Pascal are compiled.

One important difference among languages is the manner of programmer interaction. Interpreter-based languages are *conversational*. They assume that the programmer has a computer terminal or personal computer and is able to type interactive responses. With compiler-based languages, there is a delay between entering and executing a program.

From the programmer's perspective, the difference between an interpreter and a compiler is like the difference between a conversation and a correspondence. An interpreter provides more immediate feedback, like a dialog between two people. A compiler leads to a delay between action and response, like an exchange of letters through the mail.

One might also contrast interpreted and compiled languages with interactive and batch computer systems. With interactive systems, such as personal computers or time-sharing systems, the programmer has frequent contact with the computer. The computer can prompt for more information or print out error messages. The programmer can respond and often proceed from error conditions. With batch processing (dating from the Jurassic period of computing), the programmer prepares a program and then submits it to be processed without any further intervention. The batch job can be submitted on punch cards, magnetic tape, or from disk. The important distinction is that the program will execute without any additional feedback or data from the programmer. Interactive systems are then more similar to interpreted languages, whereas batch processing seems to parallel compiled languages.

Interpreted languages are most useful for developing and debugging program prototypes. They allow the *programmer* to interact quickly and easily with the computer. Compiled languages are most useful for the producing the application version of a program to be used by someone else. The *end user* of an application program is more concerned with speed of execution than with ease of modification.

Common LISP is typically both interpreted and compiled. This means that the programmer can develop a program very conveniently, using the interpreter, and then, when the program is complete, the programmer can compile the program to produce a more efficient, production version of the program. When it is executed, the compiled version of the code will still require the interpreter itself as an execution environment. That is, the interpreter for compiled code acts like a run-time library found in other languages, such as C.

For most of this book, we will focus on the interpreted side of LISP. The compiler is discussed in chapter 16.

2.1 Running LISP

To use LISP, the programmer invokes the LISP interpreter at the operating system shell by typing LISP or `lisp`[1] or `cl` or whatever name is given to the dialect of LISP   ⇐ ∞
on your computer. With a graphical user interface, such as found in the Apple® Macintosh® or Microsoft® Windows™, the programmer might double-click the LISP icon to launch the interpreter.

At this point, the LISP interpreter will begin execution. It will typically print a greeting and a prompt. The greeting displays information such as the name and version number of the interpreter. The prompt is a character or a set of characters printed to indicate that the interpreter is awaiting input from the programmer.

Below is a sample invocation of LISP. The programmer types `lisp` at the % shell prompt, which starts up the LISP interpreter, printing a greeting and the prompt `>`. Throughout this text, computer examples will appear in `typewriter font`. In this chapter, characters typed by the programmer will be <u>underlined</u>.

---

[1] ∞ denotes implementation-dependent features; see the online version of appendix A.

∞ ⇒   `% lisp`
       `Allegro CL 4.1 [SPARC; R1] (4/7/92 13:06)`
       `Copyright (C) 1985-1992, Franz Inc., Berkeley, CA, USA.`
       `All Rights Reserved.`
∞ ⇒   `>`

At this point, there are three basic actions the LISP interpreter will take:

1. `read`. It will read each form the programmer types. A form is a LISP statement, such as "Add the numbers 1 and 2."

2. `evaluate`. It will determine what the given form means and calculate its value.

3. `print`. It will print out that value for the form.

Most forms yield values that are printed, though sometimes these values may be undefined. There are three type of forms:

- *Self-evaluating.* These are forms, such as numbers, which return their own values.

- *Symbols.* These are variables, which have an associated value.

- *Lists.* These are expressions, such as functions, which compute a value. Lists are delimited by parentheses.

This basic cycle of the interpreter is often called the read-eval-print loop or simply REPL (pronounced *"repple"*). You might think of this as a conversation with the LISP interpreter: you ask a question, which it READs; it determines the answer to the question by EVALuating it; and then it responds to the question by PRINTing its answer. We do not wish to personify the computer — however, it seems natural to understand this process as being a dialog. In fact, many LISP implementations refer to the interpreter as the *LISP Listener*.

2.2   Arithmetic

We will now use LISP to do some arithmetic and then review some of the principles of how LISP works. Here are examples of addition, subtraction, negation, and multiplication. The programmer input appears to the right of the prompt and the LISP output is below the prompt. Thus, in the first example, the prompt is >, the input form is (+ 1 2), and the output value is 3. The addition function "+" is applied to the arguments 1 and 2. You should try these examples yourself. Generally, you must type a carriage return after the closing right parenthesis.

```
> (+ 1 2)
3

> (+ 2 3 4)
9

> (- 5 1)
4

> (- 30)
-30

> (* 12 4)
48

> (* 2 3 4)
24

> (exit)
; Exiting Lisp
%
```
⇐ ∞

The last form, (exit), terminates the LISP session and returns the programmer to the shell, indicated here with a % prompt. In a window-based LISP, the programmer would choose exit or quit from a menubar selection.

We shall continue with some more arithmetic examples. This time we intersperse comments with the examples. LISP, like most programming languages, allows programmers to place comments in the midst of programs by preceding the comments with a special character, often called a *comment character*. In LISP, the semicolon is the comment character. All text to the right of a semicolon on a line is disregarded by the interpreter.

```
> (1+ 8)            ; Addition of 1;
9                   ; equivalent to: (+ 8 1).

> (1- 100)          ; Subtraction of 1;
99                  ; equivalent to: (- 100 1).

> (/ 48 12)         ; Division returning quotient.
4

> (rem 49 12)       ; Division returning remainder.
1
```

```
> (rem -49 12)
-1

> (mod 49 12)              ; Modulus arithmetic.
1

> (mod -49 12)             ; Always returns non-negative integer.
11

> (max 1 3)               ; Maximum value.
3

> (min 1 3)               ; Minimum value.
1

> (sqrt 144)              ; Square root.
12.0

> (expt 144 .5)           ; Exponent: 144 to the power one half.
12.0

> (expt 12 2)             ; 12 squared.
144

> (expt 2 5)              ; 2 to the 5th.
32

> (gcd 12 24 52)          ; Greatest common divisor.
4

> (gcd 234 345)
3

> (gcd)                   ; Does not require any arguments.
0

> (lcm 8 12 15)           ; Least common multiple.
120

> (lcm 2)                 ; Requires at least one argument.
2
```

```
> (abs -17)              ; Absolute value.
17


> (abs -17 4)            ; Example of a mistake.
Error: ABS got 2 args, wanted at most 1.
  [condition type: PROGRAM-ERROR]
[1]
> :res                   ; The number in brackets [1]  indicates a      ⇐ ∞
                         ; break loop (see chapter 10, page 360).
                         ; In this LISP, :res resets the normal
                         ; read-eval-print loop.


> (sqrt 144 25)
Error: SQRT got 2 args, wanted at most 1.
  [condition type: PROGRAM-ERROR]
[1]
> :res


> 45                     ; Numbers evaluate to themselves.
45


> -7
-7
```

These examples exhibit some major points about LISP.

- LISP uses prefix notation. The function name appears to the left of its arguments. Thus, in LISP, one writes (+ 1 2) instead of (1 + 2).

- Parentheses are used to delimit list forms. A left parenthesis precedes the
  function name in these examples. The last argument to the function is followed by a right parenthesis, which matches or balances the opening left
  parenthesis.

- Some LISP functions accept a variable number of arguments. The addition
  and multiplication functions, as well as the gcd function, take zero or more
  arguments. The functions -, min, max, and lcm, each take at least one argument. Other functions, such as abs (absolute value), sqrt (square root), and
  expt (exponent), take a fixed number of arguments.

- In LISP, functions will produce an error message if given the wrong number of
  arguments. The second absolute value and square root examples demonstrate
  this.

- Each LISP dialect allows you to recover from errors. LISP provides a facility that enables the programmer to correct a mistake from a breakpoint caused by an error in the middle of execution. This is useful for debugging and is discussed in chapter 10.

∞ ⇒
- Some functions have no arguments. One important function that takes no arguments is (exit), which is used to terminate a LISP session. exit is not actually defined as part of the Common LISP language, but each implementation provides some equivalent form.

- Numbers evaluate to themselves. This feature is quite intuitive. The last two examples demonstrate this.

Here are some other examples.

> (min 1 (min 3 0))   ; Another way to calculate (min 1 3 0).
0

> (max (+ 3 5) (abs (* -2 5)))
10

> (sqrt (+ (* 3 3) (* 4 4)))
5.0

> (- (sqrt (+ (* 5 5) (* 12 12))) (sqrt (+ (* 3 3) (* 4 4))))
8.0

These examples show that functions can have other functional forms as arguments. Notice that each list form is surrounded or *delimited* by its own set of parentheses.

This nesting of parentheses can lead to a large number of closing right parentheses, as seen in the last example. Four right parentheses match the left parentheses in the *, +, sqrt, and - expressions, respectively. The proliferation of parentheses in LISP has led some to suggest that the LISP acronym should be interpreted as *Lots of Irritating, Silly Parentheses*.

A misplaced parenthesis in a LISP form can dramatically alter its meaning. Consider the following.

> (min (+ 1 2 3) (* 2 3 4))
6

> (min (+ 1 2 3 (* 2 3 4)))
30

Many errors in LISP programs can be traced to parentheses. In view of this common pitfall, most LISP implementations and text editors for LISP programs (such as emacs [Camerson and Rosenblatt, 1991]) provide facilities for automatically matching or balancing left and right parentheses, as well as automatic indentation tools to facilitate the detection of misplaced parens. emacs itself is written in LISP and is probably the world's most widely used LISP program.

2.3 Objects

As we stated earlier, programming languages allow you to build programs. This process of construction involves materials and techniques. Just as buildings are composed of elements such as bricks, lumber, and nails, LISP programs are made from language elements. LISP also provides techniques for combining elements. In LISP, we refer to the components used for building programs as *objects*. Some objects are primitive, and others are composed of other objects.

In the preceding section, we saw examples of several LISP objects, including numbers and functions. These objects can be combined to create other forms. Throughout this book, we shall see examples of many kinds of objects, such as characters, strings, streams, structures, and files, and ways of manipulating these objects. From this perspective, a program is a tool for manipulating some object.

Common LISP, through the Common LISP Object System (CLOS – pronounced *see-loss*, or *see-loase*, or *kloss*, or *cloase*), supports object-oriented programming, which provides a means for objects to manipulate themselves, in a manner of speaking. In an object-oriented building, a wall might know how to paint itself, a roof might know how to shingle itself, and a window might know how to open and close itself.

Object-oriented programming provides a unifying framework and perspective for LISP programming. In the course of this book, we shall introduce a wide variety of objects and ways in which those objects can be combined and exploited.

2.4 Symbols and Variables

Like any other computer language, LISP allows the programmer to create symbolic names for identifying and referencing variables and functions. Unlike some other languages, LISP allows these names to be arbitrarily long. The normal rules for creating symbols are these:

- You may use a sequence of letters, digits, and punctuation marks, including:
  + - * / @ $ % ^ & _ = < > ~ .

  The use of the period "." in symbols is slightly restricted, in that you may not have a symbol consisting only of one or more periods, as this will conflict with the use of the period in list notation, discussed in the following chapter.

- You should not use the space character or other punctuation characters, including:

? ! [ ] { } ' ' ; " \ | # , :

because these characters are reserved for other purposes in the language.

- The identifier should not correspond to an existing LISP symbol, such as min, max, or rem, unless you intend to redefine that symbol, which your LISP dialect may or may not permit. If you redefine a LISP function, it will not necessarily do what it did previously. *Caveat programmer.* (See section 2.10.1, page 45.)

- You may use both uppercase and lowercase letters. LISP will automatically convert to upper case. This means that VAR and var and Var are the same symbol in LISP. Unlike C and C++, LISP is not case-sensitive. .

- You should not use a number as a symbol. FOUR-POINT-OH is a symbol, but 4.0 is a number.

Here are some acceptable symbols.

```
x
y
Variable-1
3RD-BASE
ANSWER.592
*GOAL*
Just-try-to-type-this-the-same-way-twice-without-an-error
john_loves_mary
love+marriage
365+
```

And here are some unacceptable symbols (with reasons following the semicolon).

```
3              ; Number
3e10           ; Number
.700           ; Number
"Symbol"       ; Contains "'s
(x)            ; Contains ( and )
slot:filler    ; Contains :
```

It is possible for a programmer to create symbols that violate these conventions, for example, contain lowercase letters or special characters. The programmer may either (a) precede the "illegal" character with a backslash "\", which serves as an escape character, or (b) delimit the entire symbol with the vertical bar character "|". For example, the preceding illegal symbols can be sanitized as follows.

```
\3              |3|
\3e10           |3e10|
```

```
\.700              |.700|
\"Symbol\"         |"Symbol"|
\(x\)              |(x)|
slot\:filler       |slot:filler|
```

Note that \"Symbol\" will print as |"SYMBOL"|, whereas |"Symbol"| will print as |"Symbol"|. In the first example, the lowercase letters are converted to upper case, but in the second, the lowercase letters are protected by the surrounding vertical bars.

2.5 Defining Variables and Functions

Now that we can create symbols, we can use them to identify objects, such as variables or functions. A variable is created and its initial value specified by means of the LISP macro `defvar`. The `setf` macro can be used to assign a new value. To the naked eye, a macro looks like a function. However, unlike functions, macros do not always evaluate their arguments. For example, `defvar` and `setf` evaluate their second argument but not their first.

```
> (defvar a 7)      ;  The symbol a is defined and given the value 7.
A

> (defvar b 4)
B

> a                 ;  The read-eval-print loop returns the value of a.
7

> b
4

> (+ a b)           ;  We can use a and b as variables.
11

> (- a b)
3

> (setf a 5)        ;  We can assign a new value, using setf.
5

> (- a b)
1
```

```
> (setf a 3 b 9)    ;  We can assign several values at once.
9
```

```
> (- a b)
-6
```

```
> (defvar c)        ;  Creates a variable c with no initial value.
C
```

As the last example indicates, you can define a variable name without specifying its initial value. You can create your own functions, using **defun**. The simplest function is the **identity** function, which returns its argument.

```
> (defun simple (x) x)
SIMPLE
```

```
> (simple 4/5)
4/5
```

```
> (simple 'simple)
SIMPLE
```

```
> (simple (simple (simple 5)))
5
```

```
> (identity 4/5)    ;  LISP already has the function identity.
4/5
```

```
> (identity (identity (identity (* 8 8))))
64
```

```
> (identity 'symbol)
SYMBOL
```

The function **simple** is virtually useless. We shall define a function with a little more ambition.

```
> (defun square (x) (* x x))
SQUARE
```

```
> (square 4)
16
```

```
> (square -5)
25
```

```
> (defun square-sum (x y) (+ (square x) (square y)))
SQUARE-SUM

> (square-sum 3 4)
25

> (square-sum 5 12)
169
```

We have defined three new functions: `simple`, `square` and `square-sum`. There are several things to notice.

- The names of the functions, `simple`, `square`, and `square-sum`, are LISP symbols.

- The single quote prefix inhibits evaluation of a symbol or form. Thus, `'simple` and `'symbol` return their respective symbol names as values.

- `defun`'s first argument is the name of the new function, and the second argument is a *list* containing the names of the parameters to that function. We shall discuss lists at length in the next chapter. For now, we observe that a parameter list comprises a left parenthesis, followed by zero or more symbols, terminated by a right parenthesis.

- A parameter is a name used in defining the function, and an argument is the value used when calling the function. Thus, the function definition of `square-sum` uses the parameters x and y. The first example of `square-sum` uses the arguments 3 and 4, which are bound to the parameters x and y, respectively.

- The parameter names in the new function are *local* to that function. Thus, the x in `simple` is not related to the x in `square` or in `square-sum`. Local and global variables are discussed in chapter 5.

- A new function can have as many or as few parameters defined as necessary: `square-sum` has two parameters, x and y, and `simple` and `square` have only one, x.

- A new function can call any function, including another programmer-defined function: `square-sum` calls `square` twice.

- The value returned by `defun` is *undefined*. Some value may be returned, but   ⇐ ∞
  the language does not specify what that value is. The implementation used to generate the examples in this book prints the function name to represent the data structure that holds the function.

The terms *parameter* and *argument* are often confounded. They are distinct, but in practice refer to the same object. By analogy, in a given baseball game, the player parameters would be positions, such as *pitcher* or *first baseman*, while the player arguments would be names, such as *Koufax* or *Mattingly*. In a specific game, we can use either a position parameter or a player name to refer to a particular player. Similarly, in a specific function call, we can refer to either the parameters or the arguments.

One other feature of LISP is that, unlike languages such as Pascal, the order in which functions are defined does not matter. What is important is the intuitive notion that a function must be defined before it is actually called. So, in the above example, we could have defined the function `square-sum` prior to defining the function `square` which it called. However, we have to define `square` before we call `square-sum`, since `square` is called by `square-sum`.

LISP distinguishes between functions and macros, such as `defvar` and `defun`. Macros are discussed in detail in chapter 11. Closely related to macros are special forms, which also may not always evaluate their arguments. We will identify macros and special forms as they are introduced.

2.6   File Input

By this time, you may have discovered that typing function definitions to the interpreter is a tedious and error-prone task. This is especially true if you wish to use some function in more than one terminal session. You want to avoid having to type the same definition repeatedly.

The solution to this problem is simple: disk files. You can use a text editor to create a file containing LISP function definitions. Then, you start up LISP and tell the interpreter to load in the function definitions (or other LISP forms) from the file.

∞ ⇒ There is a convention that LISP files have particular file extensions, such as `.lisp` or `.cl` (for *Common LISP*). So, suppose that you created a file named `convert.cl`, which contains the definitions of two functions for converting Fahrenheit and Celsius temperatures. That file might look like this:

```
;;;     convert.cl

;   (f-to-c ftemp)   returns the corresponding Celsius temperature.
;                    The formula is:  C = (5/9) (F - 32).
(defun f-to-c (ftemp)
   (/ (* 5
         (- ftemp 32))
      9))
```

```
;  (c-to-f ctemp)   returns the corresponding Fahrenheit
;                    temperature. The formula is:  F = (9/5 C) + 32.
(defun c-to-f (ctemp)
  (+ (* 9
        (/ ctemp 5))
     32))
```

There are several things to note at this point. First, the semicolons that appear in the file are comment characters. LISP ignores everything else on that line (including other comment characters) and skips to the next line. It is a good idea to add comments for every function that you define. The comments do not make the code run faster (or slower), but they do help the humans who have to read the code.

Second, the functions are formatted in the file with progressive indentation to indicate the levels of nesting. This indentation, like the comments, is solely for the benefit of the programmer — not the LISP interpreter. LISP would work just as well if the functions in `convert.cl` were written:

```
(defun f-to-c (ftemp) (/ (* 5 (- ftemp 32)) 9)) (defun c-to-f (ctemp)    ⇐ Bad Idea
(+ (* 9 (/ ctemp 5)) 32))
```

but chances are that you would have more difficulty understanding the code.

The basic issue here is one of programming style. As a programmer, you need to realize that sooner or later someone will have to read your code and try to understand how it works (or why it doesn't). That someone could be you, six months after you first write the program. Therefore, you should take pains to make your code, as it appears in a file, as comprehensible as possible. Clarity of exposition is sometimes more important than getting the program to work in the first place.

Your program should be visually clear and clean. The file should be broken up into a series of function definitions, each with appropriate comments. Each function definition should be formatted in the file in a consistent and logical way. Here is a set of guidelines for formatting a function definition.

- Start function definitions at the left margin.

- Try to put a function definition all on one line if it is less than half a line long (40 characters), for example,
  `(defun plus2 (x) (+ x 2))`

- If the function will not fit on one line, put the function name and parameter list on the first line, and then one expression per line thereafter until the end of the function definition.

- Increase indentation on a new line if the previous line has an open left parenthesis. You may wish to indent to the second left parenthesis on the preceding line. Otherwise, two to four spaces provide adequate indentation.

- Decrease indentation on a new line if the previous line has a right parenthesis that closes a left parenthesis from an earlier line.

- Otherwise, align the new line with the previous line.

These guidelines should help make the appearance of your function definitions reflect the logical structure of the function. Consider the following function for calculating profit on sales.

```
(defun profit (volume unit-price unit-cost tax-rate)
  (- (* volume unit-price)
     (+ (* volume unit-cost)
        (* tax-rate
           (* volume unit-price)))))
```

By virtue of the indentation and meaningful variable names, one can easily deduce that profit is revenues (volume times price) minus expenses (cost of goods sold plus taxes). The LISP interpreter would have no trouble with the unindented code.

Bad Idea ⇒
```
(defun profit (volume unit-price unit-cost tax-rate) (- (* volume
unit-price) (+ (* volume unit-cost) (* tax-rate (* volume
unit-price)))))
```

Similarly, LISP assigns no particular connotation to the choice of variable names. The following code, which uses meaningless parameter names, would work just as well.

Bad Idea ⇒
```
(defun profit (x1 x2 x3 x4)
  (- (* x1 x2)
     (+ (* x1 x3)
        (* x4
           (* x1 x2)))))
```

The reader should appreciate the value of proper indentation, perspicuous variable names, and comments.

We can now return to the convert.cl file example. We enter LISP and read in this file, using the load function:

```
> (load "convert.cl")
; Loading /server/u18/homes.ai/slade/a/mss/l/convert.cl.
T
```

```
> (f-to-c 32)
0
```

```
> (c-to-f 100)
212
```

The function load, with a filename in "double quotes" as its argument, enters a read-eval-print loop, taking its input from the given file. It READs in each form, it EVALuates the form, and it PRINTs the resulting value. To instruct load to print the value of each form in the file, use the following.

```
> (load "convert.cl" :print T)
; Loading /server/u18/homes.ai/slade/a/mss/l/convert.cl.

F-TO-C
C-TO-F
T
```

The arguments :print T tell load that you want to see the values printed.[2] In this case, we see the names of the two functions which are defined in the file.

load also prints the name of the file being loaded if the *load-verbose* variable is not NIL. The load keyword :verbose can override *load-verbose*.

```
> *load-verbose*
T
```

```
> (setf *load-verbose* nil)
NIL
```

```
> (load "convert.cl")              ; Does not print file name.
T
```

```
> (load "convert.cl" :verbose t)   ; Prints file name.
; Loading /server/u18/homes.ai/slade/a/mss/l/convert.cl.
T
```

If load does not find the designated file, it usually signals an error. The programmer can use the keyword :if-does-not-exist with a value of NIL to disable this feature.

---

[2]The colon : prefix in :print signifies *keywords*, which we discuss in the next chapter. T is the LISP symbol for truth, discussed in the next section.

```
> (load "myfile.lisp")
Error: "myfile.lisp" does not exist, cannot load
  [condition type: FILE-ERROR]

Restart actions (select using :continue):
 0: retry the load of myfile.lisp
[1]
> :res

> (load "myfile.lisp" :if-does-not-exist nil)
NIL
```

When load successfully reaches the end of the file, it usually returns the value T. Generally, load is used for its side effects, not the value returned.

The programmer should realize that read, eval, and print are actual LISP functions. We discuss read and print in chapter 7, and eval is presented in chapter 15.

∞ ⇒   When LISP starts up, it looks for a user initialization file, such as .clinit.cl, and automatically loads that file if it exists. Thus, it is convenient to put function definitions that you use frequently in your initialization file. Appendix A provides a table containing the names of common initialization files for various implementations.

Files can also load other files. So, you could have your initialization file load other files, by including the appropriate command. For example, if you wanted LISP automatically to load a special file containing utility programs, your initialization file might look like this.

```
;; .clinit.cl
(load "utilities.cl")
```

If you find an error in a function after you have loaded it into LISP from a file, you can leave or suspend LISP, modify the function definition in the file, and then return to LISP. In a windowing environment, you can simply switch from the LISP interpreter to the editor window, edit your file, and then return to the LISP window. At this point, you can reload your modified file into LISP or cut and paste the redefined function from the file to the LISP interpreter.

2.7 Predicates and Numbers

Predicates are functions that answer *yes/no* or *true/false* questions like the following:

- Is the argument a number?

- Is the argument greater than zero?

- Is the first argument equal to the second argument?

- Is the argument negative?

Predicates, in answering such questions, will return the value *true* or the value *false*. In LISP, *true* is given as the value of the special symbol T. That is, the letter T is a symbol that has the value of true. The value *false* is indicated by the special symbol NIL, which is also the value of the empty list: (). In most situations, anything non-NIL will be equivalent to true.

```
> T                          ;  T evaluates to true: T.
T
```

```
> nil                        ;  The value of nil is NIL.
NIL
```

```
> ()                         ;  The value of () is NIL.
NIL
```

There is a morphological convention in LISP for predicates: many predicates are named by symbols which end in the letter P. Here are some examples of numeric type predicates. Their names are perspicuous.

```
> (numberp 9)                ;  Is 9 a number?
T
```

```
> (numberp 3.5)
T
```

```
> (numberp T)
NIL
```

```
> (realp 9)                  ;  Is 9 a real number?
T
```

```
> (realp 9/2)
T
```

```
> (rationalp 9)              ;  Is 9 a rational number?
T
```

```
> (rationalp 3.5)
NIL
```

```
> (rationalp 7/2)
T
```

```
> (ratiop 9)              ; Is 9 a ratio?
NIL


> (ratiop 7/2)
T


> (numerator 7/2)         ; A ratio has a numerator
7


> (denominator 7/2)       ; and a denominator.
2


> 14/4                    ; The ratio is simplified, if possible.
7/2                       ; This is rational canonicalization.


> (numerator 14/4)
7


> (denominator 14/4)
2


> (/ 14 -4)               ; The denominator is always positive.
-7/2


> (integerp 9)            ; Is 9 an integer?
T


> (integerp 3.5)
NIL


> (floatp 9)              ; Is 9 a floating point number?
NIL


> (floatp 3.5)
T
```

Common LISP has several types of numbers, with associated predicates as indicated above. Figure 2.1 on page 33 depicts part of the hierarchy of numeric types.

We note that the category of numbers includes the real numbers. Real numbers are either rationals or floating point numbers (floats). Rationals are either integers or ratios. Integers are either small integers (fixnums) or large integers (bignums). The differences among numeric types are largely a matter of the effi-

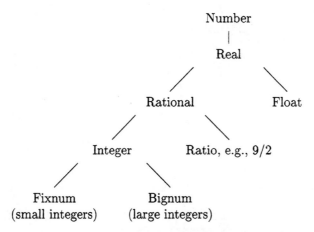

Figure 2.1: Some Common LISP Numeric Types

ciency and accuracy of the underlying computer representation. For certain numeric calculations, there may be trade-offs between efficiency and accuracy.

For example, it takes less space to represent a fixnum than a bignum, and the associated arithmetic operations are generally faster for fixnums than for bignums or floats. Ratios are often more accurate representations of fractional numbers than floating point numbers, which may be subject to rounding errors.

```
> (- 1/3 1/3)            ;  This looks reasonable.
0
```

```
> (float 1/3)            ;  float converts its argument to floating point.
0.33333334
```

```
> (- 1/3 (float 1/3))    ;  What is going on here?
0.0
```

```
> (- 1/3 0.33333334)     ;  This is equivalent to the preceding.
0.0
```

```
> (- 1/3 0.333333334)    ;  Add another significant digit.
2.9802322e-8
```

When you ask LISP to perform arithmetic with numbers of different types, LISP will try to change one of them to the type of the other. In the preceding example, the ratio 1/3 is converted to a floating point number by the float function. This conversion results in a less accurate representation of 1/3 after the eighth decimal place.

LISP actually provides four types of floating point numbers, in increasing order of precision: `short-float`, `single-float`, `double-float`, and `long-float`. LISP also provides the `type-of` function, which is useful for identifying object types.

```
> (type-of 9)              ; type-of is as specific as possible
FIXNUM                     ; and does not respond INTEGER or REAL.


> (type-of 9.0)
SINGLE-FLOAT


> (type-of 9/2)
RATIO


> (type-of 'x)
SYMBOL


> (type-of nil)            ; NULL is a special type for NIL.
NULL
```

We will later use type information to detect errors in our programs (see chapter 10) and to permit the compiler to produce more efficient code (see chapter 16). Below are some additional useful numeric predicates.

```
> (zerop 9)                ; Is 9 equal to 0?
NIL


> (zerop (- 9 9))
T


> (plusp 9)                ; Is 9 positive?
T


> (plusp (- 8 9))
NIL


> (minusp 9)               ; Is 9 negative?
NIL


> (oddp 9)                 ; Is 9 an odd integer?
T


> (evenp 9)                ; Is 9 an even integer?
NIL
```

Another common variety of numeric predicate is the comparison predicate, which takes two or more arguments. These are represented with normal arithmetic symbols, with /= used for "not equal." (The symbol /= is meant to resemble the normal arithmetic symbol for *not equal*, namely, ≠, which is not included in the LISP character set.)

```
> (= 4 4)                    ;   Is 4 equal to 4?
T


> (= 4 5)
NIL


> (< 4 5)                    ;   Is 4 less than 5?
T


> (> 4 5)                    ;   Is 4 greater than 5?
NIL


> (/= 4 5)                   ;   Is 4 not equal to 5?
T


> (>= 4 5)                   ;   Is 4 greater than or equal to 5?
NIL


> (<= 4 5)                   ;   Is 4 less than or equal to 5?
T
```

These functions can take more than two arguments or even a single argument.

```
> (= 4 (+ 2 2) 16/4 (* 2 2))
T


> (> 5 4 4 2)
NIL


> (>= 5 4 4 2)
T


> (> 9)
T
```

The differences among types of numbers can be exploited by the programmer on occasion. However, LISP allows the programmer to ignore the differences. As shown earlier, LISP will convert one type of number to another type if needed. Here are some more examples.

```
> (+ 9 .5)                        ; integer + float
9.5                               ; float


> (+ 9 1/2)                       ; integer + ratio
19/2                              ; ratio
```

This process is called *contagion*. The LISP generic arithmetic functions use contagion rules to determine the type of the result when the arguments have different numeric types. The underlying principle of these rules is to preserve accuracy and precision.

∞ ⇒   Different implementations may have different rules of contagion, which might actually lead to different results, due to rounding errors. Fortunately, the programmer can obviate implicit contagion through the use of explicit *coercion*, with the functions `float`, and `rational` or `rationalize`. (The terminology is most confusing. Both *contagion* and *coercion* smack of the Middle Ages, while *rational* and *rationalize* suggest the Renaissance.)

```
> (float 5/2)                     ; Converts to floating point.
2.5


> (rational 2.5)                  ; Converts to rational.
5/2


> (rationalize 2.5)               ; Synonym for rational.
5/2
```

Converting numbers into integers is more complicated. What is integer equivalent of 2.6? Is it 2 or 3? LISP provides four different functions for integer coercion: `floor`, `ceiling`, `truncate`, and `round`. Table 2.1 on page 37 illustrates the values returned by these functions for a number of different arguments (cf. [Steele Jr., 1990, p. 354]).

Their coercive behavior is easily explained.

- `floor` truncates toward negative infinity.

- `ceiling` truncates toward positive infinity.

- `truncate` truncates toward zero.

- `round` truncates to the nearest integer, choosing the even number when halfway between.

The programmer needs to be mindful of these differences.

There are analogous truncation functions that return a floating point result, as illustrated in table 2.2 on page 38. These functions are roughly the same as applying the `float` function to the respective integer coercion function (and the prefix `f` to the respective function name.)

Argument	floor	ceiling	truncate	round
-98.6	-99	-98	-98	-99
-98.5	-99	-98	-98	-98
-98.4	-99	-98	-98	-98
-0.6	-1	0	0	-1
-0.4	-1	0	0	0
0.4	0	1	0	0
0.6	0	1	0	1
98.4	98	99	98	98
98.5	98	99	98	98
98.6	98	99	98	99

Table 2.1: Integer Truncating Function Examples

```
> (truncate 98.6)
98
0.5999985
```

```
> (float (truncate 98.6))
98.0
```

```
> (ftruncate 98.6)
98.0
0.5999985
```

Just as some functions take more than one argument, some functions may return more than one value. Both `truncate` and `ftruncate` return two values. The second value is the discarded remainder. By default, only the first value is used. In section 9.9 on page 312, we will see how to handle multiple values.

2.8   Conditionals

Predicates are normally used in tests in computer programs for conditional execution of code. For example, IF `predicate-1` is true, THEN execute `expression-1`, ELSE execute `expression-2`. This IF-THEN-ELSE conditional construct, which prevails in computer languages, corresponds to LISP's special form `if` and the more general `cond` macro.

The `if` form takes two or three arguments. In either case, the first argument is a predicate (or an implicit predicate). If the predicate is true (actually, just non-NIL), then the second argument is evaluated. What objects are non-NIL? Numbers, symbols, functions — anything except `nil` and `()`. If the predicate is false, then

Argument	ffloor	fceiling	ftruncate	fround
-98.6	-99.0	-98.0	-98.0	-99.0
-98.5	-99.0	-98.0	-98.0	-98.0
-98.4	-99.0	-98.0	-98.0	-98.0
-0.6	-1.0	0.0	0.0	-1.0
-0.4	-1.0	0.0	0.0	0.0
0.4	0.0	1.0	0.0	0.0
0.6	0.0	1.0	0.0	1.0
98.4	98.0	99.0	98.0	98.0
98.5	98.0	99.0	98.0	98.0
98.6	98.0	99.0	98.0	99.0

Table 2.2: Float Truncating Function Examples

the third argument, if present, is evaluated. If the predicate is false and the third argument is missing, then the value of if is nil.

```
> (if t 1 2)
1
```

```
> (if nil 1 2)
2
```

```
> (if (oddp 3) 1)
1
```

```
> (if (oddp 4) 1)
NIL
```

The if form has the virtue of brevity. However, programmers often write chains of IF-THEN-ELSE statements to distinguish among many alternatives. The cond macro is a more general version of if. The syntax of cond, with its paired predicate-expression clauses, is a bit different from other LISP expressions. Here is a syntactic outline of cond:

```
(cond  ( <predicate-1> <expressions-1> )
       ( <predicate-2> <expressions-2> )
       ...
       ( <predicate-n> <expressions-n> ) )
```

The semantics of cond is an elaboration of if. Predicate clauses are evaluated in sequence from top to bottom until one of them is found to be true (actually, just non-NIL) or until there are no more predicate clauses. For the first predicate clause

with a non-NIL value, the corresponding expression clauses are evaluated and the
rest of the predicate and expression clauses are ignored.

There can be any number of expression clauses (including zero) following a
predicate clause. If a predicate is evaluated to be non-NIL but has no expression clause following it, then cond returns the value of the predicate clause itself.
Otherwise, cond returns the value of the *last* expression clause.

```
> (cond (t 1) (2))              ;  These are the cond versions
1                               ;  of the previous if examples.


> (cond (nil 1) (2))
2


> (cond ((oddp 3) 1))
1


> (cond ((oddp 4) 1))
NIL


> (cond (nil 1 2 3) (t 4 5 6))  ;  Returns last expression of (t 4 5 6).
6


> (cond (1 2 3) (4 5 6))        ;  Returns last expression of (1 2 3).
3                               ;  1 is non-NIL.


> (cond (1) (2) (3))            ;  Returns value of predicate 1.
1
```

The cond construct is a general form of the normal IF-THEN-ELSE constructions
found in most programming languages. The IF-THEN-ELSE form of cond would be

```
(cond  ( <IF-PREDICATE> <THEN-EXPRESSION> )
       ( T              <ELSE-EXPRESSION> ) )
```

The T beneath the IF-PREDICATE above indicates a predicate that always evaluates
to true. So, if IF-PREDICATE is true, then the THEN-EXPRESSION will be performed.
If IF-PREDICATE is false, then the ELSE-EXPRESSION will be evaluated since T is
always true.

Here are two examples using cond. We shall define a signum function that
returns 1 for positive numbers, -1 for negative numbers, and 0 for zero.

```
(defun signum (x)
  (cond ((plusp x) 1)
        ((minusp x) -1)
        ((zerop x) 0) ))
```

```
> (signum 5)
1

> (signum  -23.67891)
-1

> (signum (+ 1 -1))
0
```

The function `interest-rate` shows how return on investment might be indexed to the size of the investment.

```
(defun interest-rate (money)
  (cond ((< money 0) 0)
        ((< money 1000) 2)
        ((< money 10000) 5)
        ((< money 100000) 7)
        (t 10)))

> (interest-rate 99)
2

> (interest-rate 5000000)
10
```

In addition to the IF-THEN-ELSE conditional construction afforded by `if` and `cond`, LISP provides several other basic conditional constructs, including `and`, `or`, and `not`, demonstrated below.

```
> (and 3 4 5)                 ; If no argument is NIL, and returns the
5                             ; value of the last argument.


> (and 3 (evenp 5))           ; and takes a variable number of
NIL                           ; arguments.


> (and)
T


> (or 3 4 5)                  ; or returns the first non-NIL argument,
3                             ; evaluating from left to right.


> (or (evenp 3) (+ 2 1))
3
```

```
> (or)
NIL
```

```
> (not (or 3 4 5))          ;  not returns the opposite truth value
NIL                         ;  of its argument.
```

```
> (not (or (evenp 3) (equalp 2 1)))
T
```

```
> (not (not (or 3 4 5)))    ;  not takes one and only one argument.
T
```

The behavior of and, or, and not is fairly plain:

- and returns NIL if any argument is false; otherwise, it returns the value of the last argument. If there are no arguments, and returns T.

- or returns NIL if all arguments are false; otherwise, it returns the value of the first non-NIL argument. If there are no arguments, or returns NIL.

- not negates the truth value of its argument, returning NIL if the argument is true and T if the argument is false. not must have one and only one argument.

There is one additional feature of which to be aware. Both and and or are macros and differ from regular LISP functions in one important respect: they do not always evaluate all their arguments. In this respect, they are like defun and cond. In fact, one could simulate most of the behavior of cond by and and or as follows.

cond construction:

```
(cond  ( <predicate-1> <expression-1> )
       ( <predicate-2> <expression-2> )
       ...
       ( <predicate-n> <expression-n> ) )
```

and/or version of cond construction:

```
(or    (and <predicate-1> (or <expression-1> T ))
       (and <predicate-2> (or <expression-2> T ))
       ...
       (and <predicate-n> (or <expression-n> T )) )
```

This example bears some analysis. In the cond case, each predicate clause is evaluated from top to bottom until one of them yields a value that is not false. At that point, the respective expression clause is evaluated, after which its value is returned and no further clauses are evaluated. We see the analogous behavior with the and/or version. If <predicate-i> has a non-NIL value, then the corresponding expression clause, <expression-i>, is evaluated. The clause (or <expression-i> T) will always return a non-NIL value; thus, the surrounding (and ...) clause will return a non-NIL value, which will then satisfy the top-level (or ...) clause. At that point, none of the subsequent clauses are evaluated. The reader should note that this definition of cond does not always behave like the true cond. See exercise 2.11.8 on page 61.

This example demonstrates a significant property of and, or, and for that matter, cond, namely, that they sometimes avoid evaluating some of their arguments. By virtue of this important property, they are macros and not functions. They act as syntactic keywords. The LISP interpreter treats these constructs differently from functions such as min, abs, or not, which always evaluate all their arguments. The functions which you create with the macro defun will evaluate all their arguments. In chapter 11, we shall see how to create new macros.

Here is another example of creating a conditional function, this time without the use of the cond construction. The predicate go-to-moviep, defined below, shows how and, or, and not might be combined.

```
(defun go-to-moviep (age cash)
    (or (and (< age 12)              ; Child rates.
             (> cash 3.00))
        (and (>= age 12)             ; Adult rates.
             (< age 65)
             (> cash 7.00))
        (and (not (< age 65))        ; Senior citizen rates.
             (> cash 4.50))))


> (go-to-moviep 8 4.00)              ; An 8-year-old with $4.
T


> (go-to-moviep 16 4.00)            ; A 16-year-old with $4.
NIL
```

Note in the above example that (>= ...) and (not (< ...)) are logically equivalent.

2.9 &rest Notation

In this chapter we have covered a lot of ground: the LISP interpreter, arithmetic, symbols, function definition, file input, indentation, comments, predicates, and conditional expressions. We now offer one more topic: &rest notation.

As mentioned above, some functions and macros take an indefinite number of arguments. For example, the addition and multiplication functions will work for any number of numbers. To notate a parameter in a function which may occur zero or more times, we use the keyword &rest before the name of that parameter. Thus, the addition and multiplication functions, which take zero or more numeric arguments, may be notated as follows.

```
(+ &rest numbers)
(* &rest numbers)
```

Other functions, such as subtraction, min, and max, may require a minimum number of arguments but permit any number beyond that.

```
(- number &rest more-numbers)
(min number &rest more-numbers)
(max number &rest more-numbers)
```

We note that (- number) indicates negation, not subtraction.

Moreover, defun uses this notation to allow the programmer to create her own functions having an indefinite number of arguments.

```
(defun biggest (&rest numbers)
  (cond ((not numbers) 'no-input-given)
        (t 'use-max-function)))
```

```
> (biggest)
NO-INPUT-GIVEN
```

```
> (biggest 1 2 3)
USE-MAX-FUNCTION
```

This notation for defun indicates that there may be zero or more arguments to the function biggest. If no arguments are given to biggest, the argument numbers is NIL. Otherwise, numbers will contain a list of numbers. We discuss lists in the following chapter.

The &rest notation can be used to communicate both to the LISP reader and to a human reader. There are additional expository specifications of an indefinite number of arguments intended solely for the mortal reader. (You may infer that LISP is immortal.) The following are equivalent, though only the first form can be interpreted by LISP.

```
(min number &rest numbers)
(min number {number}*)
(min {number}+)
(min [numbers])
```

The notation {number}* indicates that number may occur zero or more times; the notation {number}+ indicates that number must occur at least once and, optionally, more. For example, using this notation, we can describe the syntax of cond as follows.

```
(cond {(test {form}*)}*)
```

We interpret this expression to mean that a cond form contains zero or more clauses, each of which is a list comprising a test expression and zero or more other forms.

The square bracket notation, [numbers], indicates that the numbers parameter is optional. This method is less precise in the present case and is usually reserved for a parameter whose respective argument may occur at most once. For example, we can use this notation to indicate the optional third argument to if.

```
(if test consequent [alternate])
```

Thus, every if form must contain a test and a consequent but may omit the alternate. In section 3.8 on page 88, we describe how to define functions with single optional arguments.

A final notational variant is the use of double square brackets to refer to a collection of options, each of which may occur at most once. For example, the syntax of the load function could be described in two ways.

```
(load file [:verbose verb] [:print pr] [:if-does-not-exist idne])

(load file [[option]])

option ::= :verbose verb
         | :print pr
         | :if-does-not-exist idne
```

The vertical bar | indicates alternatives.

2.10 Advanced Subjects

In each chapter, we attempt to present the programmer with a thorough exposition of the topics at hand. However, there is often a conflict between the two cardinal scholarly virtues of clarity and truth. That is, we sometimes find it necessary to lie in the interest of narrative grace or perspicuous generality.

However, such overt mendacity makes it difficult for the author to fall asleep at night. Therefore, in the interest of truth, justice, and editorial honor, we shall occasionally conclude chapters with a section in which we reveal some of the dirty details that had been obscured or ignored.

We recognize that many readers may find such esoteric discussions cures for their own insomnia. Thus, realizing that these sections could be classified as non-narcotic sleep aids, we have attempted to ensure that none of the regular material in the book in any way depends on topics discussed in these *Advanced Subjects* sections. Readers may skip these sections with impunity.

The advanced topics for the current chapter are as follows.

- Redefining System Functions

- Numerical Limits

- Complex Numbers

- Transcendental and Trigonometric Functions

2.10.1   Redefining System Functions

Some LISPs let you redefine system functions but provide you with warnings.

```
> (defun abs (x) (if (plusp x) x (- x)))
warning:
Redefining function ABS visible from package COMMON-LISP
ABS

> (abs -9)
9
```

Here is another LISP that permits redefinition but provides a less than lucid warning message.

```
> (defun abs (x) (if (plusp x) x (- x)))
;;; Warning: Redefining FUNCTION ABS whose source-file was not recorded
ABS

> (abs -9)
9
```

Other LISPs try to prevent you from redefining system functions and provide you with stern lectures. In this case, we ignore the warning.

```
> (defun abs (x) (if (plusp x) x (- x)))
Error: Attempt to make a FUNCTION definition for the name ABS.
       This name is in the COMMON-LISP package and redefining it
       is a violation for portable programs.  Replacing the current
       definition of #<Function ABS @ #x72b4d6> may be dangerous.
       The package COMMON-LISP has PACKAGE-DEFINITION-LOCK set,
       which causes the system to check for this violation.
   [condition type: PACKAGE-LOCKED-ERROR]
```

```
Restart actions (select using :continue):
 0: Set the FUNCTION definition of the name ABS anyway.
> :continue 0
ABS

> (abs -9)
9
```

As an experiment, the programmer can check to see what her LISP does when system functions get redefined. The preferred way to provide alternatives to system functions is with packages, discussed in chapter 15.

2.10.2   Numerical Limits

When discussing the various types of numbers, we indicated that the main reason for different numeric types was the trade-offs between the efficiency and the accuracy of the representations. For example, there are two types of integers, fixnums (small integers) and bignums (large integers). By LISP's definition, a bignum is an integer that is not a fixnum. Thus, any integer must be one or the other.

$\infty \Rightarrow$ When does an integer stop being a fixnum and start being a bignum? The answer to this question depends on the particular implementation of LISP. However, Common LISP does provide some standard constants that can answer the question for a given implementation.

```
> most-positive-fixnum
268435455

> most-negative-fixnum
-268435456

> (type-of most-positive-fixnum)
FIXNUM

> (type-of (1+ most-positive-fixnum))
BIGNUM

> (type-of most-negative-fixnum)
FIXNUM

> (type-of (1- most-negative-fixnum))
BIGNUM
```

For this implementation, the biggest fixnum is $268,435,455$, and the smallest positive bignum is $268,435,456$.

Just as there are different types of integers, LISP also provides different types of floating point numbers: `short-float`, `single-float`, `double-float`, and `long-float`. These floating point numbers have associated implementation dependent limits as well, which are specified by a standard set of constants.

```
> most-positive-short-float
3.4028232e+38


> least-positive-short-float
1.4012985e-45


> least-negative-short-float
-1.4012985e-45


> most-negative-short-float
-3.4028232e+38


> most-positive-single-float      ; Same as short-float.
3.4028232e+38


> most-positive-double-float
4.494232837155787d+307


> most-positive-long-float        ; Same as double-float.
4.494232837155787d+307
```

There are also `least-positive`, `least-negative`, and `most-negative` forms for `single-float`, `double-float`, and `long-float`.

To convert a number from one floating point format to another, the programmer can use the `float` function with a second argument, which contains a number of the desired floating point type.

```
> (defvar f 1.0)             ; The default float type is single-float.
F


> (type-of f)
SINGLE-FLOAT


> (defvar fl (float f most-positive-double-float))
FL


> fl                         ; double-floats print with a suffix of d0.
1.0d0
```

```
> (type-of fl)
DOUBLE-FLOAT
```

We can access additional information about the internal representation of floating point numbers by using `decode-float` and related functions.

```
> (decode-float f)          ;  decode-float returns three values:
0.5                         ;  a floating point number less than 1;
1                           ;  the exponent for the first value;
1.0                         ;  the sign of the result, either 1 or -1.


> (scale-float .5 1)        ;  scale-float reverses decode-float.
1.0


> (float-radix f)           ;  Returns the integer radix of the argument.
2


;  scale-float performs the following function.
> (* .5 (expt (float 2 .5) 1))
1.0


> (float-sign f)            ;  Returns the sign of the float.
1.0


> (float-digits f)          ;  The number of digits representing the float.
24


> (float-digits fl)         ;  double-floats use more digits.
53


> (float-precision f)       ;  In general, the same as float-digits.
24


> (float-digits 0.0)
24


> (float-precision 0.0)     ;  However, it is different for zero.
0
```

The function `integer-decode-float` is analogous to `decode-float`, except that all of its values are integers.

```
> (integer-decode-float f)
8388608
-23
1

> (* 8388608 (expt 2 -23))
1
```

In addition, for each floating point type, Common LISP provides constants that specify the smallest, positive, floating point number, epsilon, that satisfies the following expression.

```
> (not (= (float 1 epsilon) (+ (float 1 epsilon) epsilon)))
T

> short-float-epsilon
1.1920929e-7

> single-float-epsilon
1.1920929e-7

> double-float-epsilon
2.220446049250313d-16

> long-float-epsilon
2.220446049250313d-16
```

That is, if you add a positive floating point number *smaller* than epsilon to a given floating point number, the resulting number is considered equal to the original number.

Common LISP also provides implementation-dependent constants for the smallest, positive, floating point number in each format that satisfies the following form.

```
> (not (= (float 1 epsilon) (- (float 1 epsilon) epsilon)))
T

> short-float-negative-epsilon
1.1920929e-7

> single-float-negative-epsilon
1.1920929e-7

> double-float-negative-epsilon
2.220446049250313d-16
```

```
> long-float-negative-epsilon
2.220446049250313d-16
```

In our LISP implementation, the negative versions of `epsilon` are the same as the respective positive versions.

By this point, the programmer should appreciate that LISP provides exceptional support for arithmetic computation. The successful LISP programmer will be able to exploit the precision and accuracy of `double-floats` to calculate her salary, bonus, commission, stock options, and, no doubt, income taxes.

2.10.3 Complex Numbers

In recognition of those programmers for whom exponential salaries are purely imaginary, Common LISP provides the numeric data type: `complex`.

A complex number has two components: a real part and an imaginary part. A complex number in LISP similarly has two parts.

```
> (defvar i (complex 0 1))    ; i is the square root of negative 1.
I                             ; complex creates a complex number.


> (type-of i)                 ; complex is a LISP object type.
COMPLEX


> (complexp i)                ; complexp is a predicate.
T


> i
#c(0 1)                       ; This is how complex numbers print.


> (* i i)                     ; Complex arithmetic works fine.
-1


> (complex 1 0)               ; Complex numbers are simplified, if possible.
1                             ; This is complex canonicalization.


> (realpart i)                ; realpart gives just the real part of i.
0


> (imagpart i)                ; imagpart gives just the imaginary part of i.
1


> (defvar x (complex 1))      ; If you leave out the imaginary part,
X                             ; you just get the real part.
```

```
> x
1
```

```
> (sqrt -1)              ;  The square root function sqrt can
#c(0.0 1.0)              ;  produce complex results.
```

```
> (sqrt -4)
#c(0.0 2.0)
```

```
> (isqrt 2)              ;  isqrt returns the integer root.
1
```

```
> (isqrt -1)             ;  isqrt requires non-negative arguments.
Error: -1 is illegal argument to isqrt
[1]
> :res
```

```
> (conjugate i)          ;  We may calculate the conjugate
#c(0 -1)
```

```
> (complex (realpart i) (- (imagpart i)))
#c(0 -1)
```

```
> (sqrt (conjugate i))       ;  and even the root of the conjugate.
#c(0.7071067811865475d0 -0.7071067811865476d0)
```

The absolute value of a complex number is based on the Pythagorean theorem and relies on the fact that a complex number may be interpreted as Cartesian coordinates.

```
> (setf x (complex 3 -4))
#c(3 -4)
```

```
> (abs x)
5.0
```

```
> (sqrt (+ (expt (realpart x) 2) (expt (imagpart x) 2)))
5.0
```

2.10.4   Transcendental and Trigonometric Functions

We move from the imaginary to the irrational. LISP provides the normal exponential and logarithmic functions.

> (exp 1)   ; exp returns e raised to the given power.
2.7182817

> (exp 2)
7.389056

> (log (exp 2))   ; log returns the natural logarithm.
2.0

> (expt 10 5)
100000

> (log 100000 10)   ; You can specify an optional base for log.
5.0

LISP includes a variety of trigonometric functions, starting with sine, cosine, and tangent. Remember that decimal double float numbers have the suffix d0.

> pi   ; pi is a LISP constant.
3.141592653589793d0

> (setf 2pi (* 2 pi))   ; We define 2π.
6.283185307179586d0

> (setf pi/2 (/ pi 2))   ; We define $\pi/2$.
1.570796326794896d0

> (setf pi/4 (/ pi 4))   ; We define $\pi/4$.
0.7853981633974483d0

> (sin pi)   ; The sine function.
0.0d0

> (sin pi/2)
1.0d0

> (sin 2pi)
0.0d0

> (sin pi/4)
0.7071067811865475d0

> (cos pi/4)   ; The cosine function.
0.7071067811865475d0

```
> (cos pi)
-1.0d0
```

```
> (cos pi/2)
0.0d0
```

```
> (tan pi)                    ;  The tangent function.
0.0d0
```

```
> (tan pi/4)
1.0d0
```

```
> (tan pi/2)                  ;  The value returned is implementation dependent.
#.EXCL::*INFINITY-DOUBLE*                                              ⇐ ∞
```

The arguments to these functions are expressed in radians. If we wish instead to express the results in degrees, we can use the following conversion function.

```
> (defun degrees-to-radians (d) (* d (/ pi 180)))
DEGREES-TO-RADIANS
```

```
> (degrees-to-radians 90)
1.5707963267948966d0
```

```
> (degrees-to-radians 180)
3.141592653589793d0
```

```
> (sin (degrees-to-radians 45))
0.7071067811865475d0
```

The cis function computes $e^{i\theta}$, which is equivalent to $cos\theta + isin\theta$; hence, the name, *cis*.

```
> (cis 0)
#c(1.0 0.0)
```

```
> (cis 1)
#c(0.5403023 0.84147096)
```

```
> (setf i (sqrt -1))
#c(0.0 1.0)
```

```
> (exp (* i 0))
#c(1.0 0.0)
```

```
> (exp (* i 1))
#c(0.5403023 0.84147096)

> (+ (cos 0) (* i (sin 0)))
#c(1.0 0.0)

> (+ (cos 1) (* i (sin 1)))
#c(0.5403023 0.84147096)
```

We can define the secant, cosecant, and cotangent functions. These are not native
LISP functions.

```
(defun secant (n) (/ 1 (cos n)))
(defun cosecant (n) (/ 1 (sin n)))
(defun cotangent (n) (/ 1 (tan n)))

> (secant 0)
1.0

> (cosecant pi/2)
1.0d0

> (cotangent pi/4)
1.0d0
```

LISP provides the arc sine, arc cosine, and arc tangent functions.

```
> (asin pi)
#c(1.5707963267948966d0 -1.8115262724608532d0)

> (asin 0)
0.0

> (acos pi)
#c(0.0d0 1.8115262724608532d0)

> (acos 0)
1.5707964

> (atan pi)
1.2626272556789115d0

> (atan 0)
0.0
```

```
> (atan 1)                    ;  (atan 1) is π/4.
0.7853982

> (* 4 (atan 1))
3.1415927
```

These functions can be defined as follows. The `let` form creates local variables, which we discuss in chapter 5.

```
(defun arc-sine (x)
  (let ((i (complex 0 1)))
    (* (- i)
       (log (+ (* i x)
               (sqrt (- 1 (* x x))))))))

(defun arc-cosine (x)
  (let ((i (complex 0 1)))
    (* (- i)
       (log (+ x
               (* i (sqrt (- 1 (* x x)))))))))

(defun arc-tangent (y)
  (let ((i (complex 0 1)))
    (/ (- (log (+ 1 (* i y)))
          (log (- 1 (* i y))))
       (* 2 i))))
```

```
> (arc-sine pi)
#c(1.5707963267948966d0 -1.8115262724608532d0)

> (arc-sine 0)
#c(0.0 0.0)

> (arc-cosine pi)
#c(0.0d0 1.8115262724608536d0)

> (arc-cosine 0)
#c(1.5707964 0.0)

> (arc-tangent pi)
#c(1.2626272556789115d0 0.0d0)

> (arc-tangent 0)
#c(0.0 0.0)
```

LISP provides the phase function, which returns the angular part of a polar coordinate when expressed as a complex number.

```
> (phase -1)
3.141592653589793d0

> (phase 1)
0.0d0

> (setf x (complex 1 2))
#c(1 2)

> (phase x)
1.1071487177940904d0

> (atan (imagpart x) (realpart x))    ;  an identity for phase
1.1071488
```

To wrap up the trigonometric functions, we have the hyperbolic sine, cosine, tangent, arc sine, arc cosine, and arc tangent.

```
> (sinh 0)
0.0

> (sinh 1)
1.1752012

> (cosh 0)
1.0

> (cosh 1)
1.5430806

> (tanh 0)
0.0

> (tanh 1)
0.7615942

> (asinh 0)
0.0

> (asinh 1)
0.8813736
```

```
> (acosh 0)
#c(0.0 1.5707964)

> (acosh 1)
0.0

> (atanh 0)
0.0

> (atanh 1)                     ;   Causes division by 0.
Error: Illegal argument to atanh: 1
[1]
> :res

> (atanh pi)
#c(0.32976531495669914d0 1.5707963267948966d0)
```

These functions can be defined as follows.

```
(defun hyp-sine (x)
  (/ (- (exp x) (exp (- x))) 2))

(defun hyp-cosine (x)
  (/ (+ (exp x) (exp (- x))) 2))

(defun hyp-tangent (x)
  (/ (- (exp x) (exp (- x))) (+ (exp x) (exp (- x)))))

> (hyp-sine 0)
0.0

> (hyp-sine 1)
1.1752012

> (hyp-cosine 0)
1.0

> (hyp-cosine 1)
1.5430806

> (hyp-tangent 0)
0.0
```

```
> (hyp-tangent 1)
0.7615942

(defun arc-hyp-sine (x)
  (log (+ x (sqrt (+ 1 (* x x))))))

(defun arc-hyp-cosine (x)
  (log (+ x (* (+ x 1) (sqrt (/ (- x 1) (+ x 1)))))))

(defun arc-hyp-tangent (x)
  (log (* (+ x 1) (sqrt (/ 1 (- 1 (* x x)))))))

> (arc-hyp-sine 0)
0.0

> (arc-hyp-sine 1)
0.88137364

> (arc-hyp-cosine 0)
#c(0.0 1.5707964)

> (arc-hyp-cosine 1)
0.0

> (arc-hyp-tangent 0)
0.0

> (arc-hyp-tangent pi)
#c(0.3297653149566991d0 1.5707963267948966d0)
```

2.11   Exercises

At the end of most chapters, the reader will find a set of exercises which employ the concepts presented in that chapter. Following the heading for each exercise is a number in brackets, such as [5], with an optional asterisk, such as [7*]. The number indicates the relative difficulty of the exercise on a 10-point scale, where a [1] is trivial ("What color is an orange?") and a [10] is quite challenging ("Write a LISP predicate, haltsp, that returns true if a given LISP function halts; otherwise, false.") The asterisk indicates that the answer to the given exercise appears in appendix B.

2.11.1 Expression Drill [2]

Evaluate all of the following expressions by hand (or by head). Then check your answers with the help of your LISP interpreter.

```
(+ 5 (- 7 2))
(+ 5 (+ 7 2))
(+ 5 (+ 7 (+ 1 1)))
(* (+ 1 6) (* 2 3))
(* (* 3 2) (+ 6 1))
(/ 30 (- (+ 7 3) (max 1 (max 2 (max 5 (max 3 4)))))))
(/ 30 (+ (+ 7 2) (min 1 (min 2 (min 5 (min 3 4)))))))
(rem 25 (- (+ 7 3) (max 1 (max 2 (max 5 (max 3 4)))))))
(rem 25 (+ (+ 7 2) (min 1 (min 2 (min 5 (min 3 4)))))))
(abs (rem -7 (min 1 (min 2 (min 5 (min 3 4))))))
(+ (truncate 4.4) (truncate -3.5))
(truncate (+ 4.4 -3.5))
```

2.11.2 Defining New Functions [2*]

Write definitions for the new LISP functions demonstrated below. Then, check your results with the LISP interpreter.

For these and subsequent exercises, you should create a file, using a text editor, and define the appropriate functions, using proper indentation and comments. Then, start up LISP and read in the file by using load.

```
> (add2 5)                    ; Adds 2 to argument.
7

> (add5 5)                    ; Adds 5 to argument.
10

> (double 7)                  ; Doubles argument.
14

> (min-abs4 3 5 -2 -8)        ; Finds the minimum of the absolute value
2                             ; of four numbers.

> (max-abs4 3 5 -2 -8)        ; Finds the maximum of the absolute value
8                             ; of four numbers.
```

2.11.3 Foreign Function Names [2*]

It is possible to give new names to existing LISP functions. Define the foreign language versions of LISP functions as demonstrated below. For simplicity, assume that the functions take a fixed number of arguments.

```
> (ajoutez 2 5)           ;  French addition.
7
```

```
> (retranchez 7 2)        ;  French subtraction.
5
```

```
> (hochstmas 4 7)         ;  German maximum.
7
```

```
> (multiplizieren 5 3)    ;  German multiplication.
15
```

```
> (njia-ya-kutokea)       ;  Swahili exit.
%                         ;  Shell prompt returned after exiting LISP.
```

2.11.4   Zeller's Congruence [3*]

We shall now ask you to write a more complicated function, based on a formula called Zeller's congruence, which computes the corresponding day of the week for a given date after the year A.D. 1582. For a date, such as September 1, 1996, one breaks the date up into five separate numbers:

- N – The number of the day of the month. Here, $N = 1$.

- M – The number of the month, *using March as the first month*. This is used to allow for the extra day in February on leap years. Here, $M = 7$ for September.

- C – The hundreds of the year. Here, $C = 19$.

- Y – The year of the century. Here, $Y = 96$.

- L – 1 for a leap year; 0 otherwise. Here, $L = 1$.

The formula returns a number, d, between 0 and 6, corresponding to the day of the week, where $d = 0$ is Sunday, $d = 1$ is Monday, etc.

Here is the formula:

$$d = (N + [2.6M - 0.2] + Y + [Y/4] + [C/4] - 2C - (1 + L)[M/11]) \, mod \, 7$$

- where $[x]$ indicates *greatest integer not greater than x*, so $[3.14159] = 3$

- and where $mod \, x$ indicates *remainder after division by x*, so $29 \, mod \, 7 = 1$

Write a LISP function that calculates Zeller's congruence, given the five numbers.

> `(zeller 1 7 19 96 1)`   ;   1 September 19 96, a leap year
0   ;   0 = Sunday

Optional thought exercise. To convince yourself that this formula actually works, you might try an inductive proof. First, show that if the formula is correct for any given date, then it is correct for the next succeeding date. For example, if it correctly identifies some date as occurring on a Wednesday, then it will accurately identify the next date as a Thursday. Second, show that it is correct for some date. Given these two features, you may conclude that the formula is correct for all dates because the formula (1) accurately cycles through successive dates and (2) is correct for a specific date.

If you are more ambitious, you might try a derivation of the formula.

Note: Depending on your LISP implementation, you may need to represent the number 2.6 in the formula as the ratio 13/5 to get the required accuracy.

2.11.5   signum and interest-rate Redefined [3]

Redefine the `signum` and `interest-rate` functions given above, but use the and, or, and not constructions instead of cond.

2.11.6   signum Redefined Again [3]

There is an indigenous Common LISP `signum` function that has a slightly different definition from that given earlier in this chapter:

```
(defun signum (x)
  (if (zerop x) x (/ x (abs x))))
```

Give an example in which this definition of `signum` would provide an answer different from the earlier definition.

2.11.7   go-to-moviep Redefined [3]

Redefine the `go-to-moviep` predicate given above, but use cond instead of the and, or, and not constructions.

2.11.8   cond vs. and/or [4*]

On page 41, we simulated cond by using and and or. Under what conditions will the and/or version behave differently from the real cond? Give specific examples.

2.11.9   and/or Redefined [3]

Rewrite the following expressions, using only cond instead of and and or, respectively.

```
(and predicate-1 predicate-2 predicate-3 predicate-4)

(or  predicate-1 predicate-2 predicate-3 predicate-4)
```

2.11.10   My floor and ceiling [3*]

Define your own versions of the two functions, floor and ceiling. floor returns the largest integer less than or equal to its argument, and ceiling returns the smallest integer greater than or equal to its argument. Here are some examples.

```
> (my-floor 5)
5

> (my-floor 5.2)
5

> (my-floor -5.2)
-6

> (my-ceiling 5)
5

> (my-ceiling 5.2)
6

> (my-ceiling -5.2)
-5
```

2.11.11   Leap Year [3*]

February 29th appears in years that obey the following conditions: the year is divisible by 4 and the year is not divisible by 100, unless the year is also divisible by 400. Thus, 1996 is a leap year. 1900 is not a leap year, but 2000 is.

Write a predicate leap-yearp that answers the question: *Is this year a leap year?*

```
> (leap-yearp 1995)
NIL
```

```
> (leap-yearp 1996)
T

> (leap-yearp 1900)
NIL

> (leap-yearp 2000)
T
```

2.11.12   Zeller Revisited [3*]

Rewrite the function to evaluate Zeller's congruence (exercise 2.11.4, page 60), using the `leap-yearp` function described above. The function `son-of-zeller` will take only three arguments: day, month number (using the Zeller numbering of months), and year.

```
> (son-of-zeller 1 7 1996)    ;  1 September 1996.
0                             ;  0 = Sunday.
```

2.12   Chapter Summary

- The following LISP object types are introduced in this chapter. Indentation indicates subtypes.

```
number
    real
          float
    rational
          ratio
          integer
                fixnum
                bignum
    complex
function
symbol
    null
```

- LISP is an interpreted or conversational language, that may also be compiled.

- The LISP interpreter cycles through a read-eval-print loop.

- LISP arithmetic functions:

```
+           ; addition
1+          ; addition of 1
1-          ; subtraction of 1
-           ; subtraction and negation
*           ; multiplication
/           ; division
rem         ; remainder from division
mod         ; modulus arithmetic
truncate    ; integer division
max         ; maximum value
min         ; minimum value
sqrt        ; square root
isqrt       ; integer square root
expt        ; exponent
gcd         ; greatest common divisor
lcm         ; least common multiple
abs         ; absolute value
```

- Other LISP functions and macros:

```
defvar      ; creates a variable
setf        ; assigns a new value to a variable
defun       ; creates a function
identity    ; returns its argument
load        ; inputs a file to the interpreter
```

- LISP uses prefix notation with parentheses as delimiters.

- LISP allows the programmer to recover gracefully from errors.

- The generic type in LISP is the *object*. Objects encountered so far include numbers (integers, ratios, and floats), symbols, and functions.

- Symbolic names can be arbitrarily long, allowing for meaningful identifiers.

- Symbolic variable names can be defined and initialized by defvar, and modified by setf.

- Functions can be defined by defun.

- LISP forms can be read from disk files with load.

- It is important to indent and comment your programs to make them easier for humans to understand.

- Predicates are functions that answer true/false questions. LISP predicates commonly end with the letter P.

- True and false are specified with the symbols T and NIL, respectively.

- LISP numeric type predicates include the following:

```
(numberp object)
(realp object)
(rationalp object)
(ratiop object)
(integerp object)
(floatp object)
```

- The elements of a ratio can be accessed with the numerator and denominator functions.

- LISP provides four types of floating point numbers: short-float, single-float, double-float, and long-float.

- The type-of function reveals an object's data type.

- LISP provides the following basic numeric value predicates:

```
(zerop number)
(plusp number)
(minusp number)
(oddp integer)
(evenp integer)
```

- LISP comparison predicates include the following:

```
(= {number}+)
(< {number}+)
(> {number}+)
(/= {number}+)
(>= {number}+)
(<= {number}+)
```

Note that each can take one or more numeric arguments.

- Generic LISP arithmetic functions use contagion rules to convert numeric types. LISP also permits explicit coercion of numeric data types, using the following functions:

```
(float number)
(rational number)
(rationalize number)     ;;  Same as rational.
(floor number)
(ceiling number)
(truncate number)
(round number)
```

- LISP conditional constructs:

```
(if test consequent [alternate])
(cond {(test {form}*)}*)
(and {test}*)
(or {test}*)
(not object)
```

- Special forms and macros are different from functions. Special forms and macros might not evaluate all their arguments. The only special form we have seen is `if`. Examples of macros encountered so far are `cond`, `setf`, `defvar`, `and`, `or`, and `defun`.

- LISP uses `&rest` to indicate a parameter that may occur zero or more times. We also use the following alternative expository notation.

```
{object}*      ;  Zero or more objects.
{object}+      ;  At least one object.
[object]       ;  At most one object.
```

Only the `&rest` notation is understood by LISP itself.

Make no mistake about it: Computers process numbers - not symbols. We measure our understanding (and control) by the extent to which we can arithmetize an activity.

◊ ALAN PERLIS, *Epigrams in Programming (1982)*

Chapter 3

Lists and Trees

> *As some day it may happen that a victim must be found,*
> *I've got a little list – I've got a little list.*

◇ WILLIAM SCHWENCK GILBERT, *The Mikado (1885)*

> *I reckon – when I count at all –*
> *First – Poets – Then the Sun –*
> *Then Summer – Then the Heaven of God –*
> *And then – the List is done –*

◇ EMILY DICKINSON, *No. 569 (c. 1862)*

In the previous chapter, we introduced the basic read-eval-print cycle of the LISP interpreter, using familiar arithmetic functions. We saw how to define functions and load function definitions into the LISP interpreter from disk files.

We now turn our attention to the fundamental motif of LISP: the list data structure. Lists have an unpretentious notation: sequences of objects, such as numbers, symbols, or other lists, enclosed by parentheses. A tree is a list of lists. Here are some examples of lists and trees.

```
(1 2 3 4 5)
(this is a list)
((this) (is) (a list) (of lists))    ;  A tree.
()                                   ;  The empty list, also known as NIL.
(defun add1 (x) (+ x 1))
(+ (abs (rem 29 7)) (* 17 8))
```

The last three lists could also be evaluated directly as forms, demonstrating that lists can represent either programs, data, or both. This is one of the most important properties of LISP. It allows one easily to create programs which can create and modify other programs.

3.1   List Operations: car, cdr, and cons

One can perform numerous operations on lists. Most involve *accessors* and *con-structors*. An accessor returns a specified part of a list. A constructor makes a new list from other lists or objects. The primary accessors are car, which returns the first element of a list, and cdr (pronounced *COULD-er*), which returns all *but* the first element of a list. The car of a list is often called the *head*, and the cdr is called the *tail*.

The names car and cdr are vestigial artifacts. They come from the machine language acronyms used in the initial implementation of LISP: car was the Contents of Address part of Register, and cdr was the Contents of Decrement part of Register. One might expect that such arcane argot would fade over the years and be replaced by more appealing and perspicuous terms such as head and tail. This has not happened. The terms car and cdr are alive and flourishing and likely to outlive the author of this book, and perhaps the readers as well.

The primitive list constructor is cons, which joins two arguments to form a new structure, notated as a list indicated by a surrounding pair of parentheses. The first argument to cons becomes the car of the new structure, and the second argument becomes the cdr.

Another very useful function for dealing with lists is the special form quote, which merely returns its argument without evaluating it. Thus, the value of (quote x) is the symbol x, regardless of what the value of x is. A programmer will often want to suppress evaluation of certain arguments, such as when passing data to a function. In these (frequent) cases, the programmer can use quote to keep the data from being evaluated.

LISP provides an abbreviation for quote, namely, the single quote mark: ', so 'x is the same as (quote x). Note that the single quote mark (') is different from the backquote mark (`) and from the double quote mark ("), which is likewise different from two single quote marks (''). The backquote is used in macro definitions, discussed in chapter 11, and double quotes delimit strings, discussed in chapter 6.

Here are some examples. Note that we hereby discontinue the practice of underlining user input. At this point, the reader should be able to comprehend raw LISP transcripts.

```
> (quote (a b c))
(A B C)                        ; Note: LISP converts symbols to upper case.

> '(a b c)
(A B C)

> '()
NIL
```

```
> (defvar x (+ 2 3 5 7 11))   ;  The + form is evaluated.
X

> 'x                          ;  The value of 'x is X itself.
X

> (symbol-value 'x)           ;  Get the value associated with the symbol.
28

> x                           ;  REPL calls symbol-value on symbols.
28

> (defvar y '(+ 2 3 5 7 11))  ;  The quote prevents the evaluation
Y                             ;  of the + form.

> Y
(+ 2 3 5 7 11)

> (car y)
+

> (cdr y)
(2 3 5 7 11)

> (car (cdr '(a b c)))        ;  You can nest cars and cdrs.
B

> (cdr 'a)                    ;  car and cdr require the argument
                              ;  to be a list.
Error: Attempt to take the cdr of A which is a non-cons.
  [condition type: SIMPLE-ERROR]
[1]
> :res                        ;  Leaves break loop.              ⇐ ∞

> (cons 'a '(b c))
(A B C)

> (cons (car '(a b c)) (cdr '(a b c)))  ;  A list is just its
(A B C)                                 ;  car cons'd to its cdr.

> (cons 'a '())
(A)
```

```
> (cons 'a ())                   ;  () evaluates to itself.
(A)                              ;  Thus, '() is the same as ().


> (cons 'a 'b)
(A . B)
```

The last two examples demonstrate the difference between a *list* and a *proper list*. A proper list always ends with the empty list. That is, the final `cdr` of a proper list is always NIL. If the final `cdr` of a list is non-NIL, then it is printed using the dot notation of the last example above. The list in the last example is called a *dotted pair* or an *improper list*. The dot indicates that what follows is the final `cdr`. In the other examples, it was implicit that the lists ended with the empty list.

The preferred predicate to test for the end of a proper list is `endp`, which returns true if its argument is the empty list, and NIL if its argument has a `cdr`. Otherwise, `endp` signals an error.

```
> (endp '(a))
NIL


> (endp (cdr '(a)))
T


> (endp (cdr '(a . b)))
∞ ⇒   Error: Illegal argument to endp: B
         [condition type: TYPE-ERROR]
```

`cons` creates a new list without modifying the values of the `car` or `cdr`. That is, the expression `(cons x y)` yields a new result without changing either x or y, just as `(+ x y)` produces a new value without modifying x or y.

By convention, the `car` and `cdr` of `nil` are `nil`.

```
> (car nil)
NIL


> (cdr nil)
NIL


> (car '())
NIL


> (cdr '())
NIL
```

3.2 Type Predicates and List Predicates

LISP distinguishes among numerous types of expressions: symbols, numbers (such as integers, ratios, floating point numbers), lists, and others. We have already used some predicates for detecting different types of numbers, such as `integerp`, `ratiop`, and `floatp`. There are similar predicates for lists and symbols. Also, just as there are predicates for comparing numbers, such as > and =, there are predicates for comparing lists.

```
> (symbolp 'x)          ;  True if argument is a symbol.
T

> (symbolp 34)
NIL

> (symbolp '(x))
()

> (symbolp 'nil)        ;  NIL is a symbol whose value is NIL.
T

> (symbolp ())          ;  () is the empty list, which is a synonym for NIL.
T

> (numberp 'x)          ;  True if argument is a number.
NIL

> (consp 'x)            ;  True if argument has a car and cdr.
NIL

> (consp '(x))
T

> (atom 'x)             ;  (not (consp 'x)).
T                       ;  An atom is any object that is not a pair,
                        ;  including symbols, numbers, and ().

> (consp '())           ;  () is not a pair — it doesn't point to a car and cdr.
NIL                     ;  () is a list (see below).

> (listp '(x y))        ;  True if argument is a list.
T
```

```
> (listp ())          ;  () is a list — the empty list.
T
```

```
> (null ())           ;  True if argument is the empty list.
T                     ;  null is logically equivalent to not.
```

The above predicates are all *type* predicates. That is, they check the data type of the given object. Type predicates take only one argument. There are also *comparison* predicates, which check to see if some relation holds between the two given arguments. The arithmetic predicates > and < were examples of comparison predicates. Here are the important equality comparison predicates for lists and symbols.

```
> (eq 'a 'a)          ;  eq is a comparison predicate that returns
T                     ;  true if arguments are *exactly* the same objects.
```

```
> (eq 1.5 1.5)        ;  Use = for comparing numbers.
NIL
```

```
> (eq '(a) '(a))      ;  Two lists have different memory addresses, but
NIL                   ;  may point to some of the same objects.
                      ;  See Section 3.7, page 85.
```

```
> (eq (car '(a)) (car '(a)))   ;  A symbol points to exactly
T                              ;  one memory location.
```

```
> (eq (cdr '(a b c)) '(b c))
NIL
```

```
> (tree-equal '(a b) '(a b))   ;  True if the trees have the same
T                              ;  structure and the leaves are eq.
```

```
> (tree-equal '(1) '(1.0))
NIL
```

```
> (equalp '(a b c) '(a b c))   ;  True if arguments have elements which
T                              ;  are equivalent but do not necessarily
                               ;  have the same memory locations.
```

```
> (equalp '(+ 2 2) 4)          ;  The list (+ 2 2) is not the same
NIL                            ;  as the number 4.
```

Arg1	Arg2	eq	eql	tree-equal	equal	=	equalp
1	1	T	T	T	T	T	T
1	1.0	NIL	NIL	NIL	NIL	T	T
1.0	1.0	NIL	T	T	T	T	T
A	A	T	T	T	T	NA	T
A	B	NIL	NIL	NIL	NIL	NA	NIL
(A)	(A)	NIL	NIL	T	T	NA	T
(A B)	(A . B)	NIL	NIL	NIL	NIL	NA	NIL
(1 1)	(1 1.0)	NIL	NIL	NIL	NIL	NA	T

Table 3.1: Equality Predicate Examples

```
> (equalp (+ 2 2) 4)              ; The value of (+ 2 2) equals 4.
T

> (eql (+ 2 2) 4)                 ; The value of (+ 2 2) equals 4.
T

> (equal '(a) '(a))              ; equal values are isomorphic.
T

> (equal 1 1.0)
NIL

> (equalp (cdr '(a b c)) '(b c))
T
```

Table 3.1 illustrates the differences among the Common LISP equality predicates. In later chapters, we apply these equality predicates to other data types.

- eq is true for identical objects.

- eql is true if objects are eq or are numbers of the same type with the same value.

- tree-equal is true if two trees have the same structure and their leaves are eq.

- equal is true for objects that are structurally congruent, that is, if they look the same when printed.

- = is true for numbers with the same value, even if they are of different types. = applies only to numeric arguments. *NA* signifies *Not Applicable.*

- • equalp is the most general equality predicate. Like =, equalp is true for numbers that have the same value, even if they are of different types.

One other list comparison predicate is `tailp`, which indicates if one list is a sublist of another, using `eq` for matching.

```
> (setf x '(1 2 3 4 5))
(1 2 3 4 5)

> (setf y (cddr x))
(3 4 5)

> (tailp y x)
T

> (tailp '(3 4 5) x)
NIL
```

3.3   More Accessors

We now have a set of basic predicates and operations for dealing with list expressions. There are more advanced list operations that we can use for manipulating lists.

First, LISP provides a shorthand for nested `cars` and `cdrs`.

```
(car (car x))      =   (caar x)
(car (cdr x))      =   (cadr x)      (Pronounced CAD-er)
(cdr (car x))      =   (cdar x)      (Pronounced cuh-DAR)
(cdr (cdr x))      =   (cddr x)

(car (caar x))     =   (caaar x)
(cdr (caar x))     =   (cdaar x)
...
(car (cadar x))    =   (caadar x)
(cdr (cadar x))    =   (cdadar x)
...
```

The letters a and d are embedded between c and r to reflect a sequence of nested `cars` and `cdrs`. It should be apparent how one would define these functions. They are supported at up to four levels of nesting, for example, `(cadddr x)`, but not five.

There are additional operators for picking out specific parts of lists.

```
> (nth 2 '(a b c d))        ;  (nth i list) picks the ith element
C                           ;  of list, starting with 0 from
                            ;  left to right. (Pronounced enth)
```

```
> (nth 0 '(a b c d))
A

> (nth 4 '(a b c d))        ;  If i is greater than or equal to the
NIL                         ;  length of the list, the result is NIL.

> (defvar x '(a b c d e f g h i))
X

> x
(A B C D E F G H I)

> (first x)                 ;  first is the same as car.
A

> (rest x)                  ;  rest is the same as cdr.
(B C D E F G H I)

> (second x)                ;  (second x) is the same as (nth 1 x).
B

> (ninth x)                 ;  (ninth x) is the same as (nth 8 x).
I

> (tenth x)                 ;  (tenth x) is the same as (nth 9 x).
NIL
```

The functions nth, first, second, third, fourth, fifth, sixth, seventh, eighth, ninth, and tenth select individual elements from the top level of a list.

Below are some additional accessor functions.

```
> (setf x '(1 2 3 4 5))     ;  Creates a simple list.
(1 2 3 4 5)

> (ldiff x (cddr x))        ;  ldiff takes the difference between
(1 2)                       ;  the first list and the sublist.

> (ldiff x '(3 4 5))        ;  The sublist must be eq, as with tailp.
(1 2 3 4 5)

> (ldiff x x)
NIL
```

```
> (nthcdr 2 '(a b c d))        ; (nthcdr i list) picks the ith tail of
(C D)                          ; of list, starting with 0 from left
                               ; to right. (Pronounced ENTH-could-er)


> (nthcdr 0 '(a b c d))
(A B C D)


> (last '(a b c d))            ; (last list) returns the last
(D)                            ; cons of list.


> (last '(a b c . d))
(C . D)


> (butlast '(a b c d))         ; butlast is the complement of last.
(A B C)


> (butlast '(a b c d) 2)       ; An optional argument indicates how many of
(A B)                          ; the last elements to exclude.


> (butlast '(a b c . d))       ; However, butlast expects a proper list.
```
∞ ⇒   Error: Expected a true list but got a dotted list that ends with D.
      [condition type: SIMPLE-ERROR]

It is important to notice that these functions index the top-level elements of the list from left to right, starting with 0. So, a five-element list, either simple or complex, would be indexed as shown below.

```
        (a b c d e)
         0 1 2 3 4


        ((a) (b b b b) ((c) c) (((d))) e)
         0    1         2       3      4
```

So, if the latter list were bound to x, then (nth 0 x) would be (A), (nth 1 x) would be (B B B B), and so forth.

3.4   More List Constructors

LISP also provides more constructors in addition to cons. The main ones are list and append, demonstrated below.

```
> (list 'a 'b 'c)              ; Returns a proper list of its arguments.
(A B C)
```

```
> (list)                        ;  list takes a variable number of arguments.
NIL

> (list 1 2 3 4 5)
(1 2 3 4 5)

> (list 'a)
(A)

> (cons 'a (list 'b 'c))       ;  Contrast with next example.
(A B C)

> (list 'a (list 'b 'c))
(A (B C))

> (list '(a b) '(c d) '(e f))
((A B) (C D) (E F))

;  append constructs a new list whose elements are from the argument lists.
> (append '(a b) '(c d) '(e f))
(A B C D E F)

> (append 'a '(b c))
Error: 'A' is not of the expected type 'LIST'
  [condition type: TYPE-ERROR]
[1]
> :res                                                          ⇐ ∞

> (append '(a) '(b c))
(A B C)

> (list 'a '(b c))
(A (B C))
```

Both `list` and `append` can take a variable number of arguments. Using the `&rest` notation introduced in the preceding chapter, we can define the function `list` as follows.

```
(defun list (&rest objects)
    objects)
```

That is, `list` merely returns a list consisting of its arguments.

The definition of **append** requires recursion and the **apply** function. We present the function definition in section 8.3, page 280.

There are two variants of list and append: list* and revappend. The list* creates a dotted list from its arguments, and revappend appends two lists, reversing the order of the first list.

```
> (list* 1 2 3 4)           ;  Creates a dotted list.
(1 2 3 . 4)

> (list* 1 2 3 '(4))        ;  The last list is spliced into the result.
(1 2 3 4)

> (list* 1)                 ;  A single argument is returned untouched.
1

> (revappend '(1 2 3 4) '(5 6 7 8))
(4 3 2 1 5 6 7 8)

> (revappend '((1 2) (3 4)) '(5 6))
((3 4) (1 2) 5 6)          ;  Just the top level elements are reversed.

> (revappend '(1 2 3 4) ())  ;  If the second argument is NIL, we get
(4 3 2 1)                    ;  the reverse of the first.
```

Two other functions create lists.

- (make-list length) builds a new list of given length. The initial element has a default value of nil. The programmer can specify another value, using the parameter keyword :initial-element. (We discuss keywords later in this chapter.)

- (copy-list list) creates a new list that comprises a copy of the top-level elements of the given list.

```
> (setf x (make-list 6))
(NIL NIL NIL NIL NIL NIL)

> (setf y (copy-list x))
(NIL NIL NIL NIL NIL NIL)

> (setf z (make-list 10 :initial-element 'indian))
(INDIAN INDIAN INDIAN INDIAN INDIAN INDIAN INDIAN INDIAN INDIAN INDIAN)
```

3.5 Other List Operations and Predicates

Often, we want to determine certain properties of a list or its elements and also to modify the list. Here are some other useful functions for list examination and manipulation. Many of these functions take predicates as arguments, which perform tests on the elements of the lists.

Functions are objects in LISP. We can refer to a function explicitly, using the special form `function`, which returns the function associated with its argument. The function `funcall` can be used to call functions explicitly.

```
> (function +)              ;  The value varies with implementations.     ⇐ ∞
#<Function + @ #x72c776>
```

```
> (funcall (function +) 1 2 3)
6
```

```
> (funcall (function list) 1 2 3)
(1 2 3)
```

Just as the single quote prefix (') is an abbreviation for the `quote` special form, the prefix `#'` is an abbreviation for the `function` special form.

```
> (funcall #'+ 1 2 3)       ;  Equivalent to (+ 1 2 3).
6
```

```
> (funcall #'list 1 2 3)    ;  Equivalent to (list 1 2 3).
(1 2 3)
```

The functions `length` and `reverse` take a single list as an argument.

```
> (length '(a b c d))       ;  (length list) returns the number of
4                           ;  top-level elements in list.
```

```
> (length '())
0
```

```
> (length '((a b) (c d) (e f)))
3
```

```
> (length '((a b c d e f g )))
1
```

```
> (reverse '(a b c d e))    ;  (reverse list) reverses the order of the
(E D C B A)                 ;  top-level elements of a copy of list.
```

```
> (reverse '((a b c) (d e f)))
((D E F) (A B C))
```

```
> (defvar x '(1 2 3 4 5 6))
X
```

```
> x
(1 2 3 4 5 6)

> (reverse x)
(6 5 4 3 2 1)

> x                          ;  The value of x has not changed.
(1 2 3 4 5 6)                ;  reverse produced a reversed copy of x.
```

The functions some, every, notany, and notevery take a predicate function and a list as arguments.

- (some predicate list) returns true if predicate is true for at least one top-level element of list.

- (every predicate list) returns true if predicate is true for all top-level elements of list.

- (notany predicate list) returns true if predicate is false for all top-level elements of list.

- (notevery predicate list) returns true if predicate is false for at least one top-level element of list.

```
> (some #'numberp '(a b c d))
NIL

> (some #'numberp '(a b c 3))
T

> (some #'zerop '(1 2 3 4 0))
T

> (some #'numberp '(a b c d (3)))
NIL

> (every #'numberp '(1 2 3 4 5))
T

> (every #'numberp '(a b c d 3))
NIL

> (notany #'numberp '(a b c d 3))
NIL
```

```
> (notany #'numberp '(a b c d))
T

> (notevery #'numberp '(a b c d))
T

> (notevery #'numberp '(1 2 3 4))
NIL
```

The functions `member` and `remove` take an object and a list as arguments.

- `(member object list)` returns the tail of `list` beginning with `object` using eq test; otherwise, NIL.

- `(remove object list)` returns a copy of `list` with all top-level elements eq to `object` removed.

```
> (member 'c '(a b c d))
(C D)

> (member 'c '((a b c d)))
NIL

> (member '() '(a b c d))
NIL

> (member '(a) '((a) (b) (c)))          ;  Because '(A) is not eq to '(A).
NIL

> (remove 'c '(a b c d))
(A B D)

> (defvar x '(1 2 3 4 3 2 3 4))
X

> x
(1 2 3 4 3 2 3 4)

> (remove 3 x)
(1 2 4 2 4)

> x                                     ;  The value of x has not changed.
(1 2 3 4 3 2 3 4)
```

The function `mapcar` applies a function (the first argument) to the elements of a set
of lists (the other arguments). This is an extremely powerful procedure. It is useful
for applying another function over an entire list or set of lists. `mapcar` returns a
list of the results of applying the given function to the respective elements of each
list. The length of the result is the same as the length of the shortest list. In the
first example, each element is negated.

```
> (mapcar #'- '(1 3 4 5 6 -9))
(-1 -3 -4 -5 -6 9)
```

The next example adds the respective elements of each list and returns the results
as a list.

```
> (mapcar #'+ '(1 2 3 4) '(5 6 7))
(6 8 10)

> (list (+ 1 5) (+ 2 6) (+ 3 7))          ;  An equivalent form.
(6 8 10)

> (mapcar #'equal '(1 2 3 4) '(5 4 3))    ;  Compares respective list
(NIL NIL T)                               ;  elements for equality.

> (mapcar #'< '(1 2 3 4) '(2 3 4))
(T T T)

> (mapcar #'list '(joe mary sue) '(22 34 23))
((JOE 22) (MARY 34) (SUE 23))
```

The function (subst new old tree) returns a copy of `tree` with all occurrences
(not just top-level elements) eq to old replaced by **new**.

```
> (subst 5 0 '(0 1 2 0))
(5 1 2 5)

> (setf x '(learn c to be a c programmer))
(LEARN C TO BE A C PROGRAMMER)

> (subst 'lisp 'c x)
(LEARN LISP TO BE A LISP PROGRAMMER)

> x                            ;  x has the old value.
(LEARN C TO BE A C PROGRAMMER)

> (nsubst 'lisp 'c x)    ;  nsubst is a destructive version of subst.
(LEARN LISP TO BE A LISP PROGRAMMER)
```

```
> x                        ;  x now has a new value.
(LEARN LISP TO BE A LISP PROGRAMMER)
```

Note the subst uses a copy, whereas nsubst destructively alters the original tree. We discuss the pros and cons of destructive functions in section 16.1, page 639.

The mapcar and remove functions are very useful for performing an operation repeatedly for all the elements of a list. Here is an example that combines these two functions in a new function, div-by-3. The argument is a list of numbers, and the result is the subset of the given list whose elements are divisible by 3. Notice that a second function, div-by-3-single, is defined and can then be applied directly by map in div-by-3. It is very common in LISP to define secondary functions to handle some sub-problem. It is often desirable to break up a program into several modules, each of which is a separate function.

```
(defun div-by-3 (number-list)
  (remove nil (mapcar #'div-by-3-single number-list)))

;; Returns number if it is divisible by 3; otherwise, ().
(defun div-by-3-single (number)
  (cond ((zerop (rem number 3))
         number)
        (t nil)))

> (div-by-3 '(1 2 3 4 5 6 7 8 9 8 7 6 5 4 3 2 1))
(3 6 9 6 3)

> (div-by-3 '(2 4 8 16 22))
NIL

;; Here are the results without deleting the NILs with remove.
> (mapcar #'div-by-3-single '(1 2 3 4 5 6 7 8 9 8 7 6 5 4 3 2 1))
(NIL NIL 3 NIL NIL 6 NIL NIL 9 NIL NIL 6 NIL NIL 3 NIL NIL)

> (mapcar #'div-by-3-single '(2 4 8 16 22))
(NIL NIL NIL NIL NIL)
```

3.6 Using Lists as Stacks: push and pop

The *stack* is a pervasive data structure in computer science. As its name implies, a stack allows you to add things to or remove them from the figurative top of a set of objects. It is a form of *last-in first-out* (or *LIFO*) data storage and retrieval. That is, when you remove something from a stack, it is guaranteed to be the most recently added element in the stack.

The two basic stack operations are *push*, to add something to the top of the
stack, and *pop*, to remove the top item. You can use a list in LISP as a stack and
use the macros push and pop to manipulate the stack. Both macros change the
actual value of the stack, as shown below.

```
> (defvar x '())
X

> x
NIL

> (push 'c x)              ; Pushes the value C to the front of x.
(C)

> (push 'b x)
(B C)

> (push 'a x)
(A B C)

> (push 'd x)
(D A B C)

> x                       ; The value of x has been modified by push.
(D A B C)

> (cons 'e x)
(E D A B C)

> x                       ; cons does not modify the value of x.
(D A B C)

> (pop x)                 ; pop returns the car of its argument.
D

> x                       ; pop also has modified the value of x.
(A B C)
```

Both push and pop result in *side effects*. That is, not only do they return a value,
they also modify an existing value. The defun macro and load similarly perform
side effects. In fact, we usually do not care at all about the values returned by
defun or load. We look at push and pop again in chapter 11, where we discuss
macros.

CAR pointer	CDR pointer

Figure 3.1: CONS Cell

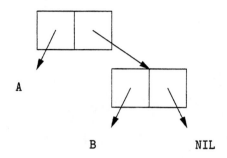

A

B   NIL

Figure 3.2: The List (A B)

3.7 List Representation

We have seen numerous instances of lists and ways of manipulating lists. We now describe how those lists are represented, both schematically and in the computer.

The primitive building block of a list is a pair of pointers, or addresses. One address points to the head of the list (the car), and the other address points to the tail (the cdr). Since the constructor function cons is used to create these pointer pairs, the pairs are often called *CONS cells*.

Figures 3.1, 3.2, 3.3, and 3.4 illustrate the structure of lists in LISP.

```
> (cons 'a (cons 'b nil))      ; See Figure 3.2, page 85.
(A B)

> (cons (cons 'a nil) nil)     ; See Figure 3.3, page 86.
((A))

> (cons 'a 'b)                 ; See Figure 3.4, page 86.
(A . B)
```

For those readers who are curious about how lists might actually be implemented in a computer, we now briefly discuss the internal representation of lists. Other readers can skip to the next section with impunity.

The addresses within CONS cells can point to different types of objects, including symbols, numbers, and other lists. Table 3.2 contains a list of hypothetical memory addresses together with their types and contents — both as they might appear in the computer and as LISP would print out the contents. These addresses

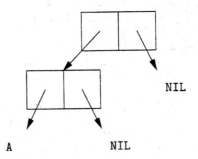

Figure 3.3: The List ((A))

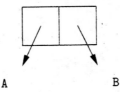

Figure 3.4: The List (A . B)

represent the objects depicted in figures 3.2, 3.3, and 3.4. In this example, we show sequential memory locations, with one CONS cell per memory location. In an actual LISP implementation, it is more likely that the addresses would be distributed throughout memory. Also, most implementations require more than one memory location for a single CONS cell.

Address 1000 contains a CONS cell, the head of which points to 1001, which contains the symbol A, and the tail of which points to 1002, which is another list. Address 1002 has a head that points to the symbol B in address 1003, and a tail that points to NIL, which lives in address 1004. Note that the car and cdr of NIL are both NIL.

A second list begins at address 1005. The head of this list points back to address 1001, which is the symbol A, and the tail points to the symbol B at 1003. This is a dotted pair, or improper list.

The final list at address 1006 has a car which points to the list (A) at 1007.

This example should give the reader some appreciation for how LISP's list structures can be implemented in a computer. Figure 3.5, page 87, is a partial diagram of the example given above, with the memory address noted at the side of each CONS cell or symbol.

The reader should now have a better understanding of the eq equality predicate. Two objects are eq if they are represented by the same memory location.

```
> (eq 'a 'a)                ;  Same memory locations for a.
T
```

Address	Type	Contents	Printed Version
1000	list	1001,1002	(A B)
1001	symbol	A	A
1002	list	1003,1004	(B)
1003	symbol	B	B
1004	null	1004,1004	NIL
1005	list	1001,1003	(A . B)
1006	list	1007,1004	((A))
1007	list	1001,1004	(A)

Table 3.2: Hypothetical Memory Contents

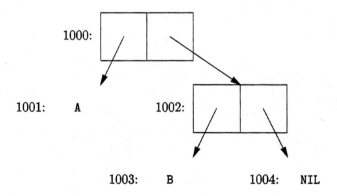

Figure 3.5: Diagram of Memory Addresses 1000-1004

```
> (eq nil nil)            ; Same memory locations for nil.
T

> (eq '(a) '(a))          ; Different memory locations for (a).
NIL
```

3.8   Keyword and Optional Arguments

In the previous chapter, we discussed the use of **&rest** to define functions that can be called with any number of arguments.

```
(defun test-rest (a &rest b) (list a b))
```

```
> (test-rest 1)       ; The argument 1 is bound to the parameter a.
(1 NIL)
```

```
> (test-rest 1 2)
(1 (2))
```

```
> (test-rest 1 2 3 4 5 6)
(1 (2 3 4 5 6))
```

The list (a &rest b), which specifies the parameters to the function, is called a *lambda list*. The term *lambda* comes from a computational notation developed by Alonzo Church, called the *lambda calculus*, [Church, 1941], which inspired John McCarthy at the inception of LISP [McCarthy, 1981]. The symbol lambda can be used to specify a local function definition, as described in chapter 8.

The components of the lambda list are either *parameter specifiers* or *keywords*. Lambda list keywords begin with an ampersand (&). For example, the list (a &rest b) contains two parameter specifiers a (a required argument) and b (a list of additional arguments) and the keyword **&rest**.

Two other useful lambda list keywords are **&optional** and **&key**, for specifying optional and keyword parameters, respectively.

Optional parameters follow the required parameters in the lambda list. There are three ways of specifying optional parameters:

- parameter – A single symbol. If no optional argument is given, the value is NIL.

- (parameter default-value) – A list of a symbol and a value. If no optional argument is given, the default-value is used.

- (parameter default-value supplied-p-flag) – A list of a symbol, a value, and a symbol. If no optional argument is given, the default-value is used, and the `supplied-p-flag` is set to NIL. If an optional argument is provided, then the `supplied-p-flag` is T.

Here are examples of all possibilities. In the function `test-optional`, a is a required parameter, b, c, and d are optional parameters, and e is a `supplied-p-flag`.

```
(defun test-optional (a &optional b (c 3) (d 4 e))
  (list a b c d e))

> (test-optional 10)
(10 NIL 3 4 NIL)

> (test-optional 10 11)
(10 11 3 4 NIL)

> (test-optional 10 11 12)
(10 11 12 4 NIL)

> (test-optional 10 11 12 13)
(10 11 12 13 T)
```

Notice that in `test-optional`, it is not possible to provide an argument for c or d unless you also specify an argument for the optional b parameter. Keyword parameters provide a solution to this problem.

The terminology is fraught with confusion. Lambda list keywords are a different species from argument keywords. First, we note that while lambda list keywords have an ampersand (`&`) prefix, argument keywords have a colon (`:`) prefix. Second, argument keywords are treated differently in LISP than symbols or functions.

```
> :c-double-sharp
Unknown top-level command: "c-double-sharp"                    ⇐ ∞

> (list :c-double-sharp)
(:C-DOUBLE-SHARP)

> (setf :c-double-sharp 0)
Error: Cannot setq :C-DOUBLE-SHARP — it is a keyword.
  [condition type: PROGRAM-ERROR]
```

A keyword is a symbol whose first character is a colon, whose value is always itself. You cannot reset the value of a keyword. In this dialect, keywords are interpreted at the top level as commands, such as `:res` to reset from a break loop.

The predicate for keywords is `keywordp`, illustrated below.

```
> (keywordp :test)
T
```

```
> (keywordp :c-double-sharp)
T

> (keywordp 'test)
NIL

> (keywordp ':test)
T
```

Keywords are special symbols consigned to the *keyword package*. In chapter 15, we discuss packages as a way to control LISP's name space. Keywords have their own package, keyword. The colon is a package syntax character. The keyword package commonly has a nickname of the empty string.

```
> (eq keyword:test :test)
T
```

Keyword parameters are specified in a manner similar to optional parameters, with a few additions.

- parameter — A single symbol. The respective keyword is the given symbol with a colon prefix. If no keyword argument is given, then the value is NIL.

- (parameter default-value) — A list of a symbol and a value. The keyword is the symbol prefixed with a colon. If no keyword argument is given, then the default-value is used.

- (parameter default-value supplied-p-flag) — A list of a symbol, a value, and a symbol. The keyword is the symbol with a colon prefix. If no optional argument is given, then the default-value is used and the supplied-p-flag is set to NIL. If an optional argument is provided, the supplied-p-flag is T.

However, if the programmer wishes to specify a keyword name different from the parameter name, she can replace the parameter in any of the above three expressions with the list (keyword parameter), in which case the given keyword will be used. Here are some examples.

```
(defun test-key (a &key b (c 3) (d 4 e) ((:omega f) 5))
  (list a b c d e f))

> (test-key 10)              ; Only the required parameter.
(10 NIL 3 4 NIL 5)

> (test-key 10 11)          ; No optional or rest parameters.
Error: Unpaired keyword argument passed to TEST-KEY
    [condition type: PROGRAM-ERROR]
∞ ⇒  > :res
```

```
> (test-key 10 :b 11)    ;  Uses keyword :b.
(10 11 3 4 NIL 5)

> (test-key 10 :c 12)    ;  Can skip over parameter b.
(10 NIL 12 4 NIL 5)

> (test-key 10 :d 13)
(10 NIL 3 13 T 5)

> (test-key 10 :omega 14)
(10 NIL 3 4 NIL 14)

> (test-key 10 :omega 14 :d 13 :c 12 :b 11)
(10 11 12 13 T 14)

> (test-key 10 :f 14)    ;  Keyword different from parameter name.
Error: TEST-KEY does not recognize :F as keyword.
  [condition type: PROGRAM-ERROR]
> :res                                                          ⇐ ∞

> (test-key 10 :allow-other-keys t :f 14)
(10 NIL 3 4 NIL 5)
```

Even though f is a parameter name, it is not a legal keyword because :omega has
been specified instead. However, LISP allows the programmer to use the special
keyword :allow-other-keys followed by a non-NIL value to indicate that non-
matching keys should not trigger errors. There is also a corresponding lambda list
keyword &allow-other-keys.

Moreover, the keyword does not have to be a keyword. LISP permits the
programmer to specify a symbol instead, as demonstrated below.

```
(defun test-key2 (a &key ((omega f) 5 g) &allow-other-keys)
  (list a f g))

> (test-key2 10 :f 9)         ;  :f is not an error.
(10 5 NIL)

> (test-key2 10 :omega 11)    ;  Neither is :omega.
(10 5 NIL)

> (test-key2 10 'omega 11)    ;  The symbol omega is the real keyword.
(10 11 T)
```

When combining various lambda list keywords, the programmer should remember the following two rules.

- Required parameters are given first.

- &optional parameters must precede &rest parameters.

```
(defun test-optional-rest-key (a &optional b (c 3) &rest d &key e)
    (list a b c d e))
```

```
> (test-optional-rest-key 10)                    ; Only required argument.
(10 NIL 3 NIL NIL)
```

```
> (test-optional-rest-key 10 11)                 ; One optional argument.
(10 11 3 NIL NIL)
```

```
> (test-optional-rest-key 10 11 12)              ; Two optional arguments.
(10 11 12 NIL NIL)
```

```
> (test-optional-rest-key 10 :e 13)              ; Keywords treated as optional.
(10 :E 13 NIL NIL)
```

```
> (test-optional-rest-key 10 11 12 :e 13)        ; One keyword argument.
(10 11 12 (:E 13) 13)
```

```
> (test-optional-rest-key 10 :e 13 :e 14)        ; Confusing? Yes!
(10 :E 13 (:E 14) 14)
```

```
> (test-optional-rest-key 10 11 12 :e 13 :e 14)
(10 11 12 (:E 13 :E 14) 13)
```

We note that combinations of optional, rest, and keyword arguments invite problems in binding the arguments. We suggest that the programmer be wary when using more than one of these critters.

There are limits both to the number of parameters in a given lambda list as well as to the number of arguments passed to a function. These limits are implementation dependent and specified by the constants lambda-parameters-limit and call-arguments-limit, respectively. They each must be at least 50. (Using &rest arguments, a function could have more arguments than parameters.)

∞ ⇒   > lambda-parameters-limit
        16384

∞ ⇒   > call-arguments-limit
        16384

We assume most programmers can stay within these constraints without breaking into a sweat.

3.9 Association Lists

We have seen how lists can be used to implement a stack structure. Another useful structure is the *association list*, or simply, *a-list*. Association lists are often used as tables for maintaining a correspondence between one piece of information and another. Thus, you might have a list of people's names with their respective ages and want to retrieve an age, given the name.

```
> (defvar name-age-list '((joe 22) (jane 21) (john 12)))
NAME-AGE-LIST

> name-age-list
((JOE 22) (JANE 21) (JOHN 12))

> (assoc 'john name-age-list) ;  (assoc object a-list) returns the first
(JOHN 12)                     ;  top-level list whose car is eq to object.

> (assoc 'jim name-age-list)  ;  Returns NIL if no match.
NIL
```

Below we have an association list to provide the English words for a few small integers.

```
> (assoc 3.0 '((1 one) (2 two) (3 three)))
NIL

> (assoc 3.0 '((1 one) (2 two) (3 three)) :test #'=)
(3 THREE)

> (assoc 3.0 '((1 one) (2 two) (3 three)) :key #'float)
(3 THREE)
```

The two last versions of the `assoc` function require some additional explanation. First, we introduce the keyword `:test`, which is followed by an explicit predicate argument in addition to the object key and the association list. We can override the default predicate of `eq` by using the `:test` keyword.

Second, we use the keyword argument `:key` to specify a function that is applied to each association list key prior to the test. Here, we convert each key to a floating point number before testing for equality.

We will see many other functions that have this same set of keyword options. The comparison predicate `tree-equal` has the optional `:test` and `:test-not` keyword arguments.

```
> (tree-equal '(1) '(1.0))
NIL

> (tree-equal '(1) '(1.0) :test #'equalp)
T

> (tree-equal '(1 2 3) '(2 3 4) :test #'<)
T

> (tree-equal '(1 2 3) '(2 3 4) :test-not #'>)
T
```

An association list is a list of lists. The key is the car of each given sublist. Here is an example with a price list for a grocery store. We first define an association list food-price-list that contains prices for various foods. Then, we define a function get-price for retrieving a price, given the food. This is an elementary table look-up scheme.

```
(defvar food-price-list
    '((apples 60) (bananas 70) (cabbages 55) (dates 89)
      (eggplants 79) (figs 75) (garlic 33)))
FOOD-PRICE-LIST

> food-price-list
((APPLES 60) (BANANAS 70) (CABBAGES 55) (DATES 89) (EGGPLANTS 79)
(FIGS 75) (GARLIC 33))

> (defun get-price (food)
    (cadr (assoc food food-price-list)))
GET-PRICE

> (get-price 'apples)
60

> (get-price 'figs)
75

> (get-price 'oranges)           ; Oranges were not in the list.
NIL
```

The association lists name-age-list and food-price-list given above are examples of *global variables*. In chapter 5, we discuss the dangers of global objects as well as the alternatives.

LISP provides three convenient functions specifically for building association lists: pairlis, copy-alist, and acons.

```
> (setf distance (pairlis '(atlanta chicago detroit seattle)
                          '(1000 500 600 2500)))
((SEATTLE . 2500) (DETROIT . 600) (CHICAGO . 500) (ATLANTA . 1000))

> (assoc 'detroit distance)
(DETROIT . 600)

> (pairlis '(la) '(3000) distance)
((LA . 3000) (SEATTLE . 2500) (DETROIT . 600)
(CHICAGO . 500) (ATLANTA . 1000))

> (setf new-distance (copy-alist distance))
((SEATTLE . 2500) (DETROIT . 600) (CHICAGO . 500) (ATLANTA . 1000))

> (setf new-distance (acons 'la 3000 new-distance))
((LA . 3000) (SEATTLE . 2500) (DETROIT . 600)
(CHICAGO . 500) (ATLANTA . 1000))
```

The pairlis function takes two or three arguments: a list of keys, a list of values, and an optional association list. The result is a new association list pairing the respective keys and values, prefixed to the optional a-list argument. copy-alist returns a new association list that is a copy of the given a-list. The acons function takes three arguments: a key, a value, and another association list. It returns a new association list with the given key and value added to the front.

One final association list function is rassoc, or *reverse association*, which retrieves information from an association list based on the value, rather than the key. rassoc makes an a-list *content addressable*.

```
> (rassoc 1000 new-distance)
(ATLANTA . 1000)

> (rassoc 2000 new-distance :test #'<)
(SEATTLE . 2500)

> (rassoc 2000 new-distance :test-not #'<)
(DETROIT . 600)

> (rassoc 1001 new-distance)
NIL

> (rassoc 1001 new-distance :key #'1+)
(ATLANTA . 1000)
```

Thus, rassoc returns entries based on the values, rather than the keys. Note that rassoc, like assoc, has optional keyword arguments, :test and :test-not, to specify comparison predicates, and the keyword :key, which provides a function of one argument to be applied to the a-list data before the test is run.

Another use of association lists is as a substitution table for the function sublis. The subst function is generally sufficient for making substitutions of list elements.

```
> (setf x '(john loves mary))        ; Creates a list.
(JOHN LOVES MARY)

> (subst 'joe 'john x)               ; No problem here.
(JOE LOVES MARY)
```

However, sometimes there can be problems. What if we wish to replace every occurrence of JOHN with MARY, and vice versa?

```
> (subst 'john 'mary (subst 'mary 'john x))
(JOHN LOVES JOHN)
```

While the result may be accurate, it does not reflect our original intent. The function sublis performs all the substitutions in one pass, using an association list to keep track of each substitution.

```
> (setf y (pairlis '(john mary) '(mary john)))
((MARY . JOHN) (JOHN . MARY))

> (sublis y x)
(MARY LOVES JOHN)

> (sublis y '(john (who is older than mary) loves mary
    (who is taller than john)))
(MARY (WHO IS OLDER THAN JOHN) LOVES JOHN (WHO IS TALLER THAN MARY))
```

We note that sublis, like subst, works on trees as well as lists. The keyword options :test, test-not, and :key also work with sublis.

3.10   Generalized Variables

A variable is an identifier with an associated value. For example, the symbol k, defined below, has a value.

```
> (defvar k '(1 2 3 4 5 6))          ; Creates a list: k.
K

> k
(1 2 3 4 5 6)
```

We can change a variable's value by using the `setf` macro. In addition, we can consider the use of accessor functions, such as `car`, as *generalized variables* which act as an identifier with an associated value. LISP permits the programmer to use `setf` to modify these generalized variables.

```
> (car k)
1

> (setf (car k) 0)              ; Changes the car of k with setf.
0

> k
(0 2 3 4 5 6)

> (nth 3 k)
4

> (setf (nth 3 k) 17)          ; Changes the nth element of k.
17

> k
(0 2 3 17 5 6)

> (cdr k)
(2 3 17 5 6)

> (setf (cdr k) '(the end))    ; Changes the cdr of k.
(THE END)

> k
(0 THE END)
```

With `setf`, we can modify a list, using the usual accessor functions to specify the location to be changed. The basic form of `setf` is

```
(setf place value)
```

where `place` is a variable or a generalized variable, which can be specified by most of the LISP accessor functions, and `value` is a LISP value. In general, `setf` can contain multiple `place value` pairs, as illustrated below.

```
> (setf (car k) 'hello (cdr k) '(brave new world))
(BRAVE NEW WORLD)

> k
(HELLO BRAVE NEW WORLD)
```

nth	car	cdadr	cdaaar
first	cdr	cddar	cdaadr
second	caar	cdddr	cdadar
third	cadr	caaaar	cdaddr
fourth	cdar	caaadr	cddaar
fifth	cddr	caadar	cddadr
sixth	caaar	caaddr	cdddar
seventh	caadr	cadaar	cddddr
eighth	cadar	cadadr	get
ninth	caddr	caddar	getf
tenth	cdaar	cadddr	rest

Table 3.3: Some Accessor Functions with `setf` Methods

Of the accessor functions which we initially encounter in Common LISP, table 3.3, page 98, lists the ones that are legimate for use with `setf`.

Note that `last` and `nthcdr` are not legal `setf` accessor functions. We will come across many other legitimate `setf` accessor functions, and in section 5.5, page 153, we shall see how to define our own `setf` functions. For reference, we have indicated `setf` accessor functions with the notation SETF in the index to this volume, starting on page 754.

By modifying a generalized variable, the programmer may also be changing other values indirectly. Below we create a three-element list.

```
> (setf x (make-list 3 :initial-element 'location))
(LOCATION LOCATION LOCATION)

> (setf y x)                      ; Assigns x to y.
(LOCATION LOCATION LOCATION)

> (setf (car x) 'price)           ; Modifies x.
PRICE

> x
(PRICE LOCATION LOCATION)

> y                               ; y has changed as well.
(PRICE LOCATION LOCATION)

> (setf z (copy-list x))          ; Assigns a copy of x to z.
(PRICE LOCATION LOCATION)
```

```
> z
(PRICE LOCATION LOCATION)

> (setf (second x) 'mortgage)    ; Modifies x.
MORTGAGE

> x
(PRICE MORTGAGE LOCATION)

> z                              ; z has not changed.
(PRICE LOCATION LOCATION)
```

We return to this topic in chapter 5.

3.11   Property Lists

Another method of data organization is afforded by *property lists*, which have long
been a part of LISP. In its basic incarnation, a property list is like an association list without the extra parentheses. The odd elements (1-based) are keys, and
the even elements are values. Such a list can be accessed by means of getf or
get-properties, and modified by means of setf or remf.

```
> (defvar name-age-list '(joe 22 jane 21 john 12))
NAME-AGE-LIST

> (getf name-age-list 'joe)             ; Gets Joe's age.
22

> (setf (getf name-age-list 'joe) 40)   ; Changes Joe's age.
40

> name-age-list
(JOE 40 JANE 21 JOHN 12)

> (get-properties name-age-list '(arthur mary))
NIL
NIL
NIL

> (get-properties name-age-list '(arthur jane))
JANE
21
(JANE 21 JOHN 12)
```

```
> (remf name-age-list 'joe)              ; Removes Joe from the list.
T
```

```
> name-age-list
(JANE 21 JOHN 12)
```

```
> (remf name-age-list 'arthur)           ; NIL value for missing item.
NIL
```

```
> (getf name-age-list 'arthur)           ; Arthur is not in the list.
NIL
```

```
> (getf name-age-list 'arthur 21)        ; Provides an optional value.
21
```

The function **get-properties** takes two arguments: a property list and a list of keys. It returns three values: the first matching key, the value associated with the first matching key, and the tail of the property list beginning with the first matching key. In section 9.9, page 312, we discuss how to handle functions which return extra values.

At this stage, property lists offer little improvement over association lists other than fewer parentheses. Association lists can be accessed based on their content, using **rassoc**. There is no comparable function for property lists, though it is not hard to define one, for example, **rgetf**.

```
> (defun rgetf (plist key) (getf (reverse plist) key))
RGETF
```

```
> (getf name-age-list 21)
NIL
```

```
> (rgetf name-age-list 21)
JANE
```

The main advantage of property lists derives from the fact that each symbol has its own property list. With property lists, one can associate arbitrary data with symbols and retrieve and modify that data. Property lists are global and, as such, form a database accessible from any level of LISP.

Property lists can easily be modified and accessed. Because of their convenience and simplicity, property lists often seduce programmers into sloppy and wasteful habits. Programmers may put arbitrary data on property lists in lieu of using more efficient and manageable data structures. Often, a programmer may use a property list in the initial design stage of a program when it is not yet clear what form the data will ultimately take. A good programmer should be prepared to go back later and review all uses of property lists to see if another data structure might be more appropriate.

Property list entries comprise a pair: the property name and its value, which are stored on a list associated with the given identifier. To retrieve or access information from a symbol's property list, we use the `get` function, which, like `getf`, can be used with `setf` for modifying a property list.

```
> (setf (get 'john 'age) 37)        ;  John is 37 years old.
37

> (setf (get 'john 'weight) 160)
160

> (get 'john 'age)                  ;  get retrieves the value.
37

> (setf (get 'john 'wife) 'mary)    ;  John's wife is Mary.
MARY

> (setf (get 'mary 'age) 35)        ;  Mary is 35 years old.
35

> (get (get 'john 'wife) 'age)      ;  How old is John's wife?
35
```

The object `nil` has a property list, but programmers are advised to avoid using it.

The property list of a symbol can be accessed directly, using the function `symbol-plist`, whose value can be manipulated with `getf` and `setf`.

```
> (symbol-plist 'john)
(WIFE MARY WEIGHT 160 AGE 37)

> (getf (symbol-plist 'john) 'age)
37

> (setf (getf (symbol-plist 'john) 'age) 40)
40

> (getf (symbol-plist 'john) 'age)
40

> (setf (symbol-plist 'john) '(wife louise age 20 weight 200))
(WIFE LOUISE AGE 20 WEIGHT 200)
```

```
> (symbol-plist 'john)
(WIFE LOUISE AGE 20 WEIGHT 200)

> (remf (symbol-plist 'john) 'age)
T

> (remprop 'john 'weight)        ;  (remprop symbol key).
T

> (symbol-plist 'john)
(WIFE LOUISE)
```

We note that the remprop function offers an alternative to using symbol-plist with remf.

As you might imagine, property lists provide a flexible (and undisciplined) way to organize data. We can reimplement our grocery store price list with property lists. We assign a price property to each food and redefine the get-price function to retrieve this property's value.

Older LISPs had a function put, which was used to set the values of a property list. We can define put in terms of setf and get and then initialize our database of prices.

```
(defun put (object property value)
  (setf (get object property) value))

(put 'apples    'price 60)
(put 'bananas   'price 70)
(put 'cabbages  'price 55)
(put 'dates     'price 89)
(put 'eggplants 'price 79)
(put 'figs      'price 75)
(put 'garlic    'price 33)

> (defun get-price (food)
    (get food 'price))
GET-PRICE

> (get-price 'garlic)
33
```

3.12 Lists as Sets

A list is a flexible data structure. It can be used in many different ways. One common use of a list is to represent a *set*, where a set is a collection of unique

objects. That is, no object in the set appears more than once. LISP provides a set
of functions for using lists as sets.

```
> (setf s1 '(agassi lendl))        ; Creates a couple of sets.
(AGASSI LENDL)

> (setf s2 '(ashe evert lendl))
(ASHE EVERT LENDL)

> (adjoin 'agassi s1)              ; Adds an item if not already there.
(AGASSI LENDL)

> (adjoin 'connors s1)
(CONNORS AGASSI LENDL)

> s1                               ; s1 has not changed.
(AGASSI LENDL)

> (pushnew 'connors s1)            ; Destructive adjoin.
(CONNORS AGASSI LENDL)

> s1
(CONNORS AGASSI LENDL)

> (intersection s1 s2)             ; Finds the set intersection.
(LENDL)

> (union s1 s2)                    ; Finds the set union.
(AGASSI CONNORS ASHE EVERT LENDL)

> (set-exclusive-or s1 s2)         ; Union minus the intersection.
(EVERT ASHE AGASSI CONNORS)

> (set-difference s1 s2)           ; S1 minus S2.
(AGASSI CONNORS)

> (set-difference s2 s1)           ; S2 minus S1.
(EVERT ASHE)

> (subsetp s1 s2)                  ; Is S1 a subset of S2?
NIL

> (subsetp s1 s1)                  ; Is S1 a subset of itself?
T
```

```
> (subsetp s1 (reverse s1))          ;  Order of elements does not matter.
T
```

```
> (subsetp (intersection s1 s2) s1)  ;  This should always be true.
T
```

```
> (subsetp s1 (intersection s1 s2))  ;  Order of sets does matter.
NIL
```

```
> (subsetp nil s1)                   ;  This should always be true.
T
```

All seven of these functions[1] have the same optional keyword arguments that we saw with `assoc` and `rassoc`, namely, `:test`, `:test-not`, and `:key`.

```
> (setf s3 '(1 2 3 4 5))
(1 2 3 4 5)
```

```
> (setf s4 '(3 4 5 6 7))
(3 4 5 6 7)
```

```
> (intersection s3 s4 :test #'>)
(5 4)
```

```
> (intersection s4 s3 :test #'>)
(7 6 5 4 3)
```

```
> (intersection s3 s4 :test-not #'>)
(5 4 3 2 1)
```

```
> (intersection s4 s3 :test-not #'>)
(5 4 3)
```

```
> (intersection s3 s4 :key #'1+)
(5 4 3)
```

```
> (intersection s4 s3 :key #'1+)
(5 4 3)
```

The `:test` predicate is the comparison test for matching set elements. The `:key` function takes one argument and is applied to the elements of both sets before matching.

---

[1] Actually, `pushnew` is a macro.

Function	car/cdr	Results
mapcar	car	list
mapcan	car	concatenation
mapc	car	side effects
maplist	cdr	list
mapcon	cdr	concatenation
mapl	cdr	side effects

Table 3.4: Mapping Functions

3.13 Advanced Subjects

We have one advanced topic in this chapter: additional mapping functions.

3.13.1 Rare Maps

In addition to mapcar, several other functions map a function onto one or more lists.

They differ in two ways: whether the function is applied to the successive cars or cdrs of the list or lists, and what type of results are returned. There are three types of results: a list of the separate results, a destructive concatenation of results, or no results. In the last case, the function works through side effects. There are six different combinations, which are summarized in Table 3.4, page 105, and demonstrated below.

We first look at the functions that operate on successive list elements. To demonstrate side effects, we define a function save, which stores its arguments on the symbol save.

```
> (mapcar #'list '(1 2 3) '(4 5 6))
((1 4) (2 5) (3 6))

> (mapcan #'list '(1 2 3) '(4 5 6))
(1 4 2 5 3 6)

> (mapc #'list '(1 2 3) '(4 5 6))
(1 2 3)

> (defun save (x y) (push (list x y) save))
SAVE

> (setf save nil)
NIL
```

```
> (mapc #'save '(1 2 3) '(4 5 6))
(1 2 3)
```

```
> save
((3 6) (2 5) (1 4))
```

We now look at the mapping functions which operate on successive list tails.

```
> (maplist #'list '(1 2 3) '(4 5 6))
(((1 2 3) (4 5 6)) ((2 3) (5 6)) ((3) (6)))
```

```
> (mapcon #'list '(1 2 3) '(4 5 6))
((1 2 3) (4 5 6) (2 3) (5 6) (3) (6))
```

```
> (mapl #'list '(1 2 3) '(4 5 6))
(1 2 3)
```

```
> (mapl #'save '(1 2 3) '(4 5 6))
(1 2 3)
```

```
> save
(((3) (6)) ((2 3) (5 6)) ((1 2 3) (4 5 6)) (3 6) (2 5) (1 4))
```

The most useful mapping functions are `mapcar` and `mapc`, which we will see again in chapter 8. LISP has additional mapping functions for other data structures.

3.14 Exercises

3.14.1 Name That Tune [2*]

What does the song *The Yellow Rose of Texas* have to do with one of this chapter's epigraphs?

3.14.2 Expression Drill, Part 1 [3]

Evaluate the following LISP expressions by hand. Check your answers with the help of your LISP interpreter. (From sections 3.1 through 3.2.)

```
(cons 3 4)
(cons 3 '(4))
(defvar x (cons 'a (cons 'b (cons 'c '() ))))
(defvar y (cons 'a (cons 'b (cons 'c 'd)))) (car (cdr x))
(car (cdr (cdr x)))
(car (cdr (cdr (cdr x))))
```

```
(cons x y)
(defvar z (cons y x)) (cdr (car z))
(symbolp (car x))
(symbolp (car z))
(atom (car x))
(consp x)
(listp y)
(listp (car (cdr z)))
(defvar w '(cons z (cons x y))) (car (cdr w))
(eq (car w) 'cons)
(eq w (cons (car w) (cdr w)))
(equalp w (cons (car w) (cdr w)))
(equalp (+ 4 3) (- 9 2))
(eq (+ 4 3) (- 9 2))
(equalp '(+ 4 3) '(- 9 2))
(eq '(+ 4 3) '(- 9 2))
```

3.14.3   Expression Drill, Part 2 [3]

Evaluate the following LISP expressions by hand. Check your answers with the help of your LISP interpreter. (From sections 3.3 through 3.6.)

```
(defvar x '(a b c d e))
(cadr x)
(caddr x)
(cadddr x)
(cddddr x)
(nth 4 x)
(nth 2 (cdr x))
(nthcdr 2 (cdr x))
(last (butlast x))
(last (butlast x 2))
(list 1 2 3 '(+ 2 2))
(list 1 2 3 (+ 2 2))
(list (cons x '()))
(defvar y (reverse x))
(append x y)
(append y x)
(reverse (append x x))
(length (append x (nthcdr 2 x)))
(defvar z '(-2 -1 0 1 2))
(some #'plusp z)
(every #'numberp z)
(every #'plusp z)
```

```
(member 0 z)
(member 3 z :test #'<)
(delete 'a x)
(delete  1 z)
(remove 1 z)
(mapcar #'+ z z)
(mapcar #'* z z)
(mapcar #'cons x y)
(mapcar #'list x y)
(subst 3 1 (mapcar #'abs z))
(+ (pop z) (pop z))
(cadr (push 7 z))
```

3.14.4   New List Functions [4*]

Define the functions no-zeros, collect-numbers, and verb-find, which are described below.

```
> (no-zeros '(1 0 2 0 3))            ; Removes all top-level zeros.
(1 2 3)

> (no-zeros '(a b c d e))
(A B C D E)

> (collect-numbers 1 '(2 3 4 5))     ; Puts numbers on the front of list,
(1 2 3 4 5)                          ; but not other data types.

> (collect-numbers 'a '(2 3 4 5))
(2 3 4 5)
```

verb-find returns a list of the verbs contained in the given sentence. You may need to define a secondary function. Also, you will find it convenient to use a defined list of verbs, such as verb-list.

```
> (defvar verb-list  '(is am are have has go went gone))
(IS AM ARE HAVE HAS GO WENT GONE)

> (verb-find '(tom went to the store))
(WENT)

> (verb-find '(tom went to the store and mary went to town))
(WENT WENT)

> (verb-find '(have you gone to the store))
(HAVE GONE)
```

3.14.5 Proper List [3*]

Write a predicate, `proper-listp`, that answers the question: Is my argument a
proper list? That is, does the list end in an empty list?

```
> (proper-listp 'x)          ;  A proper list must be a list.
NIL

> (proper-listp 9)
NIL

> (proper-listp '(a b c))    ;  The last cdr of a proper list is NIL.
T

> (proper-listp '(a b . c))
NIL
```

3.14.6 Last Atom [3*]

The `last` function returns the last cons or pair of a list. Write a function `last-atom`
that returns the last atom in a list.

```
> (last '(a b c))
(C)

> (last-atom '(a b c))
C

> (last '(d e . f))
(E . F)

> (last-atom '(d e . f))
F
```

3.14.7 Define pairlis [3*]

Use `mapcar` to define the `pairlis` function.

```
> (my-pairlis '(a b c) '(1 2 3))
((A . 1) (B . 2) (C . 3))
```

3.14.8 Association List Personnel File [4*]

Define a function called `make-person` that takes six arguments: name, age, weight,
sex, astrological sign, and a list of children's names. This function will return an
association list with the respective pairings of keywords with data elements, as

shown below. Then, define six accessor functions, one for each keyword: `get-name`, `get-age`, `get-weight`, `get-sex`, `get-sign`, and `get-children`.

Note that the elements of the a-list are dotted pairs.

```
> (setf joe (make-person 'joe 35 150 'male 'taurus '(irving mabel)))
((NAME . JOE) (AGE . 35) (WEIGHT . 150) (SEX . MALE)
 (SIGN . TAURUS) (CHILDREN IRVING MABEL)))


> (get-age joe)
35


> (get-children joe)
(IRVING MABEL)


> (get-sign joe)
TAURUS
```

3.14.9   Property List Personnel File [4*]

Define a function called `make-person2` that takes six arguments: name, age, weight, sex, astrological sign, and a list of children's names. This function will add the last five items to the property list of the given name. Then, define five accessor functions, one for each keyword: `get-age2`, `get-weight2`, `get-sex2`, `get-sign2`, and `get-children2`. Each of these functions takes the name as the only argument.

```
> (make-person2 'beth 23 110 'female 'cancer '())
BETH


> (get-age2 'beth)
23


> (get-children2 'beth)
NIL


> (get-sign2 'beth)
CANCER
```

3.14.10   More List People [4*]

Define two more functions for retrieving information about people, using either the association list or property list representation in the two preceding exercises. First, define a function called `get-name+age` that returns the obvious information as a list.

```
> (get-name+age 'beth)
(BETH 23)
```

Then, use the `get-name+age` function to define a second function called `age-of-children` that returns a list of name-age pairs of the children of the person given. You will first need to enter additional information about the children via the regular `make-person` function. Thus, suppose you had entered information about Joe's two children, Irving and Mabel, who are 12 and 10 years old, respectively. You could then make the following query.

```
> (age-of-children joe)
((IRVING 12) (MABEL 10))
```

The function `age-of-children` should not depend directly on whether the data is represented as an association list or in property lists. The accessor functions should take care of those details.

3.14.11   Daughter of Zeller [4*]

Building on your previous work at converting dates into days of the week, write a function `daughter-of-zeller` that is given the date with a quoted month name and returns the text for the day of the week. For example,

```
> (daughter-of-zeller 'september 1 1996)
SUNDAY
```

3.15   Chapter Summary

- The following LISP object types are introduced in this chapter. Indentation indicates subtypes.

  ```
  list
       cons
  ```

- The pervasive data structure of LISP is the list.

- List accessors and constructors:

  ```
  (car list)        ; Accesses the first element of a list.
  (cdr list)        ; Accesses the tail of a list.
  (cons obj1 obj2)  ; Constructs a list from two objects.
  ```

- The special form `quote` returns its argument without evaluating it. `quote` can be abbreviated with the single quote mark prefix: '

- The `symbol-value` function returns the value associated with a given symbol. This function is usually implicit in most contexts.

- The special form `function` returns the function associated with its argument. `function` can be abbreviated with the hash quote prefix: `#'`

- LISP type and comparison predicates:

```
(endp list)
(symbolp object)
(numberp object)
(consp object)
(atom object)
(listp object)
(null object)
(eq object1 object2)
(tree-equal object1 object2 [:test | :test-not])
(equal object1 object2)
(equalp object1 object2)
(eql object1 object2)
(tailp sublist list)
```

- More list accessors and constructors:

```
(caar list)
(cadr list)
(cdar list)
(cddr list)
(caaar list)
  ...
(cdddr list)
(caaaar list)
  ...
(cddddr list)
(rest list)
(first list)
(second list)
  ...
(ninth list)
(tenth list)
(nth integer list)
(ldiff list sublist)
(nthcdr integer list)
(last list)
(butlast list [n])
(lastcdr list)
```

```
(list {object}*)
(append {list}*)
(list* object {object}())
(revappend list list)
(make-list length [:initial-element])
(copy-list list)
```

- More operations and predicates:

```
(length list)
(reverse list)
(some #'predicate list {list}*)
(every #'predicate list {list}*)
(notany #'predicate list {list}*)
(notevery #'predicate list {list}*)
(member object list)
(remove object list)
(mapcar #'function {list}*)
(subst new old tree)
(nsubst new old tree)
```

- Lists can be used as stacks with the special forms push and pop.

- List structure can be diagrammed by using paired boxes and pointers.

- One way to represent list structure in a computer memory uses pairs of addresses pointing to other parts of memory.

- Optional and keyword parameters to functions are specified with the lambda list keywords &optional and &key, respectively. The programmer can also specify default values.

- LISP argument keywords are symbols with a colon (:) prefix. The function keywordp is the predicate for keywords.

- Association lists and property lists are useful data structures, especially for certain kinds of table look-up.

- Functions for association lists:

```
(assoc object a-list [options])
(pairlis keys data [a-list])
(copy-alist a-list)
(acons key datum a-list)
(rassoc object a-list [options])
(sublis alist tree [options])
```

where [options] comprise the keyword arguments: :test, :test-not, and
:key.

- Functions for property lists:

```
(getf plist key [default])
(setf (getf plist key) value)
(get-propertites plist keylist)
(remf plist key)
(setf (get symbol indicator) value)
(get symbol indicator [default])
(symbol-plist symbol)
(remprop symbol key)
```

- Lists can represent sets, using the following functions.

```
(adjoin item list [options])
(pushnew item list [options])
(intersection list list [options])
(union list list [options])
(set-exclusive-or list list [options])
(set-difference list list [options])
(subsetp list list [options])
```

where [options] comprise the keyword arguments: :test, :test-not, and
:key.

*A language that doesn't affect the way you think about
programming, is not worth knowing.*

◇ ALAN PERLIS, *Epigrams in Programming (1982)*

Chapter 4

Recursion

> *100 bottles of beer on the wall,*
> *100 bottles of beer,*
> *Take one down, pass it around,*
> *99 bottles of beer on the wall ...*
>
> ⋄ ANON., *Traditional*

> *Recursion entails self-reference.*
>
> ⋄ STEPHEN SLADE, *Object-Oriented Common LISP (1997)*

Just as the list is the aboriginal LISP data structure, so *recursion* is the typical LISP programming style. The verb from which the word *recursion* is derived is *recur: to happen again or repeatedly.* The programmer may at times suspect the spurious derivation from *recurse: to curse again or repeatedly.* Before we look at recursion in programming, it may be helpful first to explore the concept in general.

Recursion entails self-reference. A definition or a pattern that includes itself as a part is recursive. This may initially seem implausible. How can something include itself?

If you place two mirrors opposite one another, they will each reflect the other. Furthermore, they will reflect the reflections of themselves as seen in the opposing mirror. In fact, the images of mirrors within mirrors can seem to be infinite. Each mirror's image contains an image of itself. It is a recursive image.

Writers and artists have used recursive structures in works of art. An example is Shakespeare's play-within-a-play in *Hamlet.* The Luis Buñuel movie *The Discrete Charm of the Bourgeoisie* contains numerous dream sequences in which the dreamer wakes up from a dream to continue as a part of someone else's dream. These dreams within dreams imbue the film with a recursive absurdity. Douglas Hofstadter discusses the role of recursion and self-reference in art, music, mathematics, and computer science at great length in *Gödel, Escher, Bach: An Eternal Golden Braid* [Hofstadter, 1979].

A more formal example of recursion can be found in a definition of the list data structure:

1. A list is composed of a left parenthesis, zero or more objects, and a right parenthesis.

2. An object is either an atomic value or a *list*.

The second part of the definition of a list itself refers to the concept of list. This is a recursive definition. One might argue that it is a circular definition, like saying *A list is a list*. That is not the case, though. The first part of the definition serves to limit and focus the applicability of the second. The important fact about lists which this definition imparts is that *lists may contain lists*. The list is a recursive data structure.

We may similarly provide a recursive definition of positive integers.

1. A positive integer is any single digit from the set $\{1, 2, 3, 4, 5, 6, 7, 8, 9\}$.

2. A positive integer is any positive integer followed by any single digit from the set $\{0, 1, 2, 3, 4, 5, 6, 7, 8, 9\}$.

Recursion provides an elegant and concise method for creating definitions. Recursion is also a powerful programming technique.

4.1   Recursive Programs

In computer programming, recursion is the ability for a function to call itself — either directly or indirectly. Recursion offers an elegant way of solving a problem by progressively reducing it to a simpler form.

A recursive function generally reflects some inductive aspect of the problem.

1. There is a test for a boundary condition.

2. There is a method for reducing the problem in such a way that it converges to the boundary condition.

We can use the recursive definition of *list* to define a recursive function for building a list. The replicate function, which we define below, takes two arguments: an expression and a non-negative integer. It returns a list containing the expression copied the given number of times. For example,

```
> (replicate 'a 3)
(A A A)

> (replicate '(1 2) 5)
((1 2) (1 2) (1 2) (1 2) (1 2))
```

```
> (replicate '(as if by magic) 0)
NIL
```

The boundary condition for `replicate` is illustrated in the last example: if the number is 0, the function returns the empty list. Otherwise, `replicate` will `cons` the given expression to the result of `replicate` called with the same expression and one less than the given number. Here is a detailed expansion of the first example.

```
(replicate 'a 3)
   = (cons 'A (replicate 'a 2))
   = (cons 'A (cons 'A (replicate 'a 1)))
   = (cons 'A (cons 'A (cons 'A (replicate 'a 0))))
   = (cons 'A (cons 'A (cons 'A nil)))
   = (cons 'A (cons 'A '(A)))
   = (cons 'A '(A A))
   = (A A A)
```

Here is a recursive definition of `replicate`.

```
(defun replicate (expr num)
  (cond ((zerop num) nil)
        (T (cons expr (replicate expr (- num 1))))))
```

The `replicate` function exemplifies the use of recursion in processing lists. We also encounter recursion in processing numbers.

The epitome of mathematical recursive functions is factorial, which is the product of a positive integer with all smaller positive integers. The factorial of 4, notated as 4!, is $4 * 3 * 2 * 1$ or 24. $3! = 3 * 2 * 1$ or 6.[1]

We can give a recursive definition of factorial: the factorial of a positive integer is the product of that number and the factorial of one less than that number. The boundary condition is that the factorial of 0 is equal to 1.

This recursive definition can be applied to 4! as follows:

---

[1] We observe that computer scientists commonly pronounce the exclamation mark as "bang." (The origin of this practice is obscure.) Thus, 4! is pronounced "four bang." The *LISP ("starlisp") dialect of LISP for the massively parallel Connection Machine provides parallel versions of regular LISP functions that can execute simultaneously on thousands of processors. These functions are notated with the suffix !!, which suggests parallel lines. For example, the parallel version of the addition function is +!!, which is pronounced "plus bang bang."

```
  4! = 4*3!
   3! = 3*2!
    2! = 2*1!
     1! = 1*0!
      0! = 1
     1! = 1*1 = 1
    2! = 2*1 = 2
   3! = 3*2 = 6
  4! = 4*6 = 24
```

Here is a recursive LISP function `fact` to calculate the factorial of a given positive integer.

```
(defun fact (n)
  (cond ((zerop n) 1)
        (T (* n (fact (- n 1))))))
```

```
> (fact 4)
24
```

```
> (fact 5)
120
```

We use the `trace` macro below to print out the intermediate results, showing multiple calls to the factorial function, with the respective returned values of the embedded calls. Note that `trace` indents at each level of recursion. A counter at the left also indicates the depth of the current level.

```
> (trace fact)                    ;  trace is useful for debugging functions.
(FACT)
```

```
> (fact 4)                        ;  The following 10 lines are trace output.
  0: (FACT 4)
    1: (FACT 3)
      2: (FACT 2)
        3: (FACT 1)
          4: (FACT 0)
          4: returned 1
        3: returned 1
      2: returned 2
    1: returned 6
  0: returned 24
24
```

```
> (untrace fact)                  ;  untrace turns off trace.
(FACT)
```

```
> (fact 3)
6
```

Without any arguments, trace will return a list of all functions that currently are to be traced, and untrace without arguments will turn off all tracing.

The factorial function has little intrinsic interest, but it is illustrative of the process of recursion. The function keeps on calling itself until it reaches the boundary condition. At that point, it starts returning values and pops back up to the top again. (Note: Recursion is often implemented with a stack, as was discussed in section 3.6, page 83. Pending computations are pushed on the stack until results start being returned, at which point the stack is popped.)

What would happen if we tried to execute (fact -1) or (fact 1.5)? The argument to fact is supposed to be a positive integer, but that supposition does not guarantee that the argument will, in fact, be a positive integer. Thus, the programmer should be on guard for such errors. We discuss error checking and debugging in chapter 10. Also see exercise 4.7.1.

4.2 Recursive Money Changing

You can view the process of making change as recursive. You first see if any dollars are required, subtract them from the total, and then make change for what remains. The following function implements such a recursive approach to making change. The function make-change converts a given number of cents into dollars, half-dollars, quarters, and so forth.

```
(defun make-change (money)
  (cond ((>= money 100)
         (cons (list (truncate money 100) 'dollars)
               (make-change (rem money 100))))
        ((>= money 50)
         (cons (list (truncate money 50) 'half-dollar)
               (make-change (rem money 50))))
        ((>= money 25)
         (cons (list (truncate money 25) 'quarter)
               (make-change (rem money 25))))
        ((>= money 10)
         (cons (list (truncate money 10) 'dimes)
               (make-change (rem money 10))))
        ((>= money 5)
         (cons (list (truncate money 5) 'nickel)
               (make-change (rem money 5))))
```

```
      ((> money 0)
       (cons (list money 'pennies)
             '()))
      (t '()))))
```

```
> (make-change 123)
((1 DOLLARS) (2 DIMES) (3 PENNIES))
```

```
> (make-change 125)
((1 DOLLARS) (1 QUARTER))
```

```
> (make-change 97)
((1 HALF-DOLLAR) (1 QUARTER) (2 DIMES) (2 PENNIES))
```

```
> (make-change 292)
((2 DOLLARS) (1 HALF-DOLLAR) (1 QUARTER) (1 DIMES) (1 NICKEL)
(2 PENNIES))
```

The alert programmer will see that this is an inefficient algorithm, because the tests for higher denominations of coins and currency must be made repeatedly in most cases.

Note that there can never be more than one half-dollar, quarter, or nickel in a given set of change.

4.3   Recursive Roman Numerals

Another example of recursion converts Roman numerals into decimal notation. The two previous examples, fact and make-change, took a single number as an argument. This time, we shall take a list as an argument. The Roman numerals are represented as a list of letters. For example, the numeral XXIV would be represented as (X X I V). We shall use an association list to keep the correspondence between Roman numerals and decimal numbers. The function numeral-to-decimal, defined below, performs the table look-up.

The function roman-to-decimal takes the list of letters that represents a Roman numeral and produces the decimal equivalent. It first checks to see if the list is empty, in which case the function returns 0. This is the termination condition for the recursion.

If the list is not empty, the function calculates the value of the current Roman letter, which it adds to the remainder of the Roman letters through a recursive call to the roman-to-decimal function with the cdr of the input list.

The value of a Roman numeral depends very much on the order of the individual letters. The numeral XI is 11, but the numeral IX is 9. In the first case, the value of I is added to the value of X ($1 + 10 = 11$), and in the second case, the value of I is subtracted from the value of X ($-1 + 10 = 9$). In general, the value

of the current Roman letter is negative if its value is less than the next letter. In
that case, the current letter's value is subtracted from, rather than added to, the
total. The function does this first by checking to see if the cdr is not empty, that
is, if there are at least two letters. If there are, then it checks to see if the current
letter's absolute value is less than the absolute value of the next letter. If it is,
then the current letter's numerical value is negated. Otherwise, the positive value
is added to the result of converting the rest of the list. For example, (I V) would
yield $-1 + 5$, or 4, whereas (V I) would yield $5 + 1$, or 6.

```
(defvar roman-number-a-list
  '((I 1) (V 5) (X 10) (L 50) (C 100) (D 500) (M 1000)))

(defun numeral-to-decimal (numeral)
  (cadr (assoc numeral roman-number-a-list)))

(defun roman-to-decimal (num-list)
  (if (endp num-list)
      0
      (+ (or
           (and (cdr num-list)
                (< (numeral-to-decimal (car num-list))
                   (numeral-to-decimal (cadr num-list)))
                (- (numeral-to-decimal (car num-list))))
           (numeral-to-decimal (car num-list)))
         (roman-to-decimal (cdr num-list)))))

> (roman-to-decimal '(M C C C X X I I I))
1323

> (trace roman-to-decimal)
(ROMAN-to-DECIMAL)

> (roman-to-decimal '(M C M L X X X I V))
 0: (ROMAN-to-DECIMAL (M C M L X X X I V))
   1: (ROMAN-to-DECIMAL (C M L X X X I V))
     2: (ROMAN-to-DECIMAL (M L X X X I V))
       3: (ROMAN-to-DECIMAL (L X X X I V))
         4: (ROMAN-to-DECIMAL (X X X I V))
           5: (ROMAN-to-DECIMAL (X X I V))
             6: (ROMAN-to-DECIMAL (X I V))
               7: (ROMAN-to-DECIMAL (I V))
                 8: (ROMAN-to-DECIMAL (V))
                   9: (ROMAN-to-DECIMAL NIL)
```

```
                  9: returned 0
               8: returned 5
            7: returned 4
         6: returned 14
      5: returned 24
   4: returned 34
 3: returned 84
2: returned 1084
1: returned 984
0: returned 1984
1984
```

4.4 Recursive List Operations

The more common use of recursion in LISP is not for arithmetic functions like factorial or making change, but for list operations. The preceding Roman numeral example showed a way to traverse a list of items by using recursion. In fact, many of the list operations presented in the preceding chapter can be given recursive definitions. Here is a recursive definition of length.

```
(defun my-length (l)        ;  my-length traverses the top level of a list,
   (cond ((endp l) 0)       ;  assuming that the list ends in NIL.
         (t (+ 1 (my-length (cdr l)))))))

> (my-length '(a b c))
3


> (trace my-length)
(MY-LENGTH)


> (my-length '(a b))
  0: (MY-LENGTH (A B))
    1: (MY-LENGTH (B))
      2: (MY-LENGTH NIL)
      2: returned 0
    1: returned 1
  0: returned 2
2
```

Since the length function is already defined in LISP, we use the name my-length to avoid overwriting the existing definition with the above code. There are times when you may wish to change a system function, and your dialect of LISP may or may not let you do this easily. In any event, you should be careful not to destroy or redefine a system function by accident. LISP will likely print a warning message whenever you redefine any function — either a predefined system function or one originally defined by the programmer. The new definition will remain in effect until either the end of the session or when the function is defined yet again.

It should be obvious from the definition, but bears emphasizing, that the `my-length` function does not examine the elements of the list it is traversing. Hence, elements which are lists themselves are not thought of as longer than elements which are atoms. For example, the following three expressions yield the same result, namely, 4.

```
(my-length '(a b c d))
(my-length '(a (b) c d))
(my-length '(a (b e f g h) c d))
```

This type of recursion is often called *cdr recursion*, since the cdr selector function is used to traverse the top level of the list. The use of cdr recursion can also make your code more modular. The `make-change` function given in section 4.2 can be rewritten in a more flexible fashion, using cdr recursion.

```
(defun new-make-change (money currency-list)
  (cond ((endp currency-list) nil)
        ((zerop money) nil)
        ((>= money (caar currency-list))
         (cons (list (truncate money (caar currency-list))
                     (cadar currency-list))
               (new-make-change (rem money
                                      (caar currency-list))
                                (cdr currency-list))))
        (T
         (new-make-change money (cdr currency-list)))))
```

```
; Currencies are defined as lists in descending denominations,
; giving the value and name for each denomination.
(defvar *us-currency* '((100 dollar) (50 half-dollar)
  (25 quarter) (10 dime) (5 nickel) (1 penny)))
```

```
> (new-make-change 236 *us-currency*)
((2 DOLLAR) (1 QUARTER) (1 DIME) (1 PENNY))
```

One can easily introduce new currencies. For example, suppose that in the solar system of the binary star Algol, there is a currency that uses base 2, instead of base 10. We can use the same functions as before but simply change the currency list.

```
(defvar *algol-currency* '((64 grumpy) (32 dopey) (16 sneezy)
  (8 sleepy) (4 happy) (2 bashful) (1 doc)))
```

```
> (new-make-change 87 *algol-currency*)
((1 GRUMPY) (1 SNEEZY) (1 HAPPY) (1 BASHFUL) (1 DOC))
```

In this new version of `make-change`, we have separated the denomination data from the change calculations. The result is a function which is more versatile and more efficient.

4.5 Trees and car/cdr Recursion

Often, one would like to delve deeper into the structure of a list, going beyond the top level. A form of recursion called car/cdr recursion allows one to do just that. At each stage, one examines the `car` and the `cdr` of the list; if either is a list, then the function is applied recursively to the respective `car` or `cdr` or both. Treated this way, a list can be considered a *tree*, where the embedded lists are branches and the atoms are leaves.

The next example, `count-atoms`, is similar to `length` but tallies every atom in a list whether or not it is at the top level. Thus, `count-atoms` treats the list as a tree and counts all its leaves.

```
(defun count-atoms (l)
  (cond ((null l) 0)
        ((atom l) 1)
        (t
         (+ (count-atoms (car l))
            (count-atoms (cdr l)))))))

> (count-atoms '(a b c d))
4

> (count-atoms '(a (b e (f g) h) (c d)))
8
```

We note that we must use `null` to test for the end of the list instead of `endp` since the latter form does not allow atomic arguments.

Manipulating lists often requires taking them apart and putting them back together after making some changes. Here is an example of a function that takes the tree apart with car/cdr recursion to examine the branches and joins it back together again with `cons`. The function `subst` (which was described in section 3.5, page 82 above) travels down the various branches the tree. It replaces those nodes which are `eq` to `old` with the `new` value and returns the newly constituted tree as a result. `subst`, like `count-atoms`, traverses all branches of the tree, not just the top-level ones.

```
(defun my-subst (new old tree)
  (cond ((eq old tree) new)
        ((atom tree) tree)
        (t (cons (my-subst new old (car tree))
                 (my-subst new old (cdr tree))))))))
```

```
> (my-subst 3 1 '(1 2 (1 2 (1 2))))
(3 2 (3 2 (3 2)))
```

```
> (my-subst 'tulip 'rose '(a rose (is a (rose)) (is (a (rose)))))
(A TULIP (IS A (TULIP)) (IS (A (TULIP))))
```

Recursion is a very important and powerful programming technique. Most of the examples and exercises in the remainder of this book will further illustrate recursion. The reader should expect to be immersed in a flood of recursion.

4.6 Recursive Subfunctions

There are certain problems which cannot be solved with direct recursion. The function may need to keep more information or *state* around than is contained in the original arguments. In these cases, you can create a secondary function that is called by the primary function and then calls itself recursively.

Consider the common task of getting the average of a list of numbers. There is an easy way to do this in LISP.

```
(defun average (num-list)
  (/ (total num-list) (length num-list)))
```

```
(defun total (num-list)
  (cond ((endp num-list) 0)
        (t (+ (car num-list)
              (total (cdr num-list))))))
```

```
> (total '(1 2 3 4 5 6 7))
28
```

```
> (length '(1 2 3 4 5 6 7))
7
```

```
> (average '(1 2 3 4 5 6 7))
4
```

So far, there is nothing special about this example. The function **average** divides the sum of the numbers from **total** by the number of numbers from **length**. The **total** function uses cdr recursion, as does the **length** function as defined before.

Is there anything wrong with this approach? Yes. The `average` function requires that the number list be traversed *twice*: once for `total` and once for `length`. This is really not much of an issue for short lists such as the one given in the example, but it could be a significant efficiency problem for very long lists.

For example, consider a census taker who has to visit 10,000 homes and ask ten questions at each household. Which method is preferred?

1. Visit each household ten times, asking one question each time.

2. Visit each household once, asking ten questions each time.

Those readers who select the first method should do the taxpayers a favor and avoid careers in public administration.

What we would like to do is combine the `total` and `length` functions into one operation that keeps both a running count and a subtotal as it traverses the list. Here is one way to do that.

```
(defun above-average (num-list)
  (below-average num-list 0 0))

(defun below-average (num-list count total)
  (cond ((endp num-list) (/ total count))   ;  Done? Returns average.
        (T (below-average (cdr num-list)     ;  Goes to next number.
                          (+ count 1)        ;  Increments count.
                          (+ (car num-list)
                             total)))))       ;  Updates total.

> (above-average '(1 2 3 4 5 6 7))
4

> (trace below-average)
      3: (BELOW-AVERAGE (6 7 8 9) 3 12)
        4: (BELOW-AVERAGE (7 8 9) 4 18)
          5: (BELOW-AVERAGE (8 9) 5 25)
            6: (BELOW-AVERAGE (9) 6 33)
              7: (BELOW-AVERAGE NIL 7 42)
              7: returned 6
            6: returned 6
          5: returned 6
        4: returned 6
      3: returned 6
    2: returned 6
  1: returned 6
0: returned 6
6
```

The function `above-average` calls the secondary function `below-average` with the original list of numbers and zero values for the running count and total. Then, the function `below-average` uses cdr recursion to traverse the number list while doing the necessary bookkeeping for the running count and total. When it reaches the end of the list, the `below-average` function divides its running total by its running count and returns the result to the main function, `above-average`.

4.7 Exercises

You may find it helpful to use `trace` (and `untrace`) to help debug these functions.

4.7.1 Checking Facts [3]

The definitions of `replicate` and `fact` given above have a nasty problem when given improper arguments.

What is the result of (`replicate` 'A 1.5) or (`fact` -2)? Redefine both functions to check their arguments and catch these errors.

4.7.2 Legal Roman Numerals [5]

What happens if `roman-to-decimal` is given improper data, such as, '(C I I C)? Redefine `roman-to-decimal` to ensure that illegal Roman numerals are disallowed.

4.7.3 Making Changes [3*]

The `make-change` function defined above had a problem with number agreement. That is, it sometimes used a plural denomination for a singular instance. Modify the function so that it knows singular from plural.

```
> (make-change 123)
((1 DOLLAR) (2 DIMES) (3 PENNIES))

> (make-change 211)
((2 DOLLARS) (1 DIME) (1 PENNY))
```

4.7.4 Making More Changes [4]

Modify the `new-make-change` function to handle number agreement. The currency list should be changed to include irregular plural forms as a third element of the inner lists. For example:

```
(defvar *us-currency* '((100 dollar) (50 half-dollar)
   (25 quarter) (10 dime) (5 nickel) (1 penny pennies)))
```

Regular plurals can be formed by adding an S to the end of the singular form. To help you out, we provide a function `concatenate-symbol`, which creates a new symbol by combining two other symbols.

```
(defun concatenate-symbol (sym1 sym2)
  (values (read-from-string (format nil "~A~A" sym1 sym2))))
```

```
(defun mis (x)
  (concatenate-symbol 'mis x))
```

```
> (mis 'take)
MISTAKE
```

```
> (mis 'sissippi)
MISSISSIPPI
```

The function `mis` demonstrates the use of the `concatenate-symbol` function. We discuss the `values` function on page 211, the `read-from-string` function on page 175, and `format` on page 214.

4.7.5   Recursive reverse [4]

Write a recursive version of **reverse**.

4.7.6   Recursive append [4*]

Write a recursive version of **append**. Assume only two arguments.

4.7.7   Recursive nth [4]

Write a recursive version of **nth**.

4.7.8   Recursive last [4]

Write a recursive version of **last**.

4.7.9   Recursive remove-duplicates [4*]

LISP has a function `remove-duplicates`, which removes all the top-level duplicate symbols from a list, as shown below. Define `remove-duplicates`.

```
> (remove-duplicates '(a b c d a b f g))
(C D A B F G)
```

```
> (remove-duplicates '(a b c d (a b) f g))
(A B C D (A B) F G)
```

4.7.10 Recursive Check Balancing [5*]

Write a function check-book that takes two arguments: a balance and a list of transactions. The balance is a number. A transaction is either a credit (positive number), a debit (negative number), or an interest rate (a positive number enclosed in parentheses). The function returns the net balance by adding credits, subtracting debits, and compounding the interest. The interest is given as a multiplier; thus, a 10% interest rate would be given by (1.1). Interest is compounded by multiplying the current balance by the given interest rate. So, if the balance is $100 and the interest rate is 10% (or 1.1), the resulting balance would be $110. The function should also verify the form of its input, making sure that the balance is a number, the transactions are a list, and that the interest rate is a list of exactly one number.

```
> (check-book 100 '(100 50 -75))
175

> (check-book 100 '(-17.50 -1.73 -7.5))
73.27

> (check-book 100 '(100 50 -50 (1.1)))
220.0

> (check-book 100 '((1.1) 100 50 -50 (1.1)))
231.0

> (check-book 100 -17.50)
(ERROR--ATOM-INSTEAD-OF-LIST . -17.5)

> (check-book 'balance '(-17.50 -1.73 -7.5))
(ERROR--NON-NUMERIC-BALANCE . BALANCE)
```

4.7.11 Recursive NOW Account [5*]

Write a modified version of check-book called now-account to incorporate the following two rules:

1. If the balance drops below $500, then charge $0.10 for every check (debit) on the account.

2. Interest is compounded only if the balance is $500 or more.

```
> (now-account 100 '(100 50 -50 (1.1)))
199.9

> (now-account 500 '(100 50 -50 (1.1)))
660.0
```

4.7.12   Simple Pattern Matcher [6*]

One of the pervasive techniques in artificial intelligence is pattern matching. The
LISP predicate `equalp` might be thought of as a pattern matcher. Below we demonstrate a pattern matcher that allows wild cards in the pattern. The wild card patterns provide a way of making approximate matches based on the more important
aspects of the given pattern.

Write a predicate `matchp` that takes two arguments: a pattern and an input
list. The predicate returns true if the top-level items in the input list match the
corresponding items in the pattern according to the following rules.

1. All lists and patterns are flat. That is, there are no embedded lists.

2. A pattern symbol must match a respective symbol in the input list.

3. A pattern wild card, given by `*wild*`, may match any (possibly empty) set
   of adjacent symbols in the input list.

4. Every item in the input list must match either a literal or a wild card in the
   pattern.

As you might imagine, `matchp` should be written as a recursive function. Furthermore, since it has to deal just with flat lists and not trees, `matchp` will only require
cdr recursion — not car/cdr recursion.

Here are examples.

```
> (matchp '(a b c) '(a b c))
T

> (matchp '(a b c) '(a b c d))        ; Extra d on input list.
NIL

> (matchp '(a b c d) '(a b c))        ; Extra d on pattern list.
NIL

> (matchp '(a *wild*) '(a b c))       ; Matches any list starting with a.
T

> (matchp '(a *wild*) '(a))
T

> (matchp '(a *wild* b) '(a b c d b)) ; Must start with a
T                                     ; and end with b.

> (matchp '(a *wild* b) '(a b c d e)) ; Second list doesn't end in b.
NIL
```

```
> (matchp '(*wild* b *wild*) '(a b c d e))    ; Matches any list
T                                             ; containing b.

> (matchp '(*wild*) '(a b c))        ; (*wild*)  matches any list.
T
```

Hint on implementing *wild*: There are two cases for *wild*.

1. Empty match. Ignore the *wild* and match the rest of the pattern list with the current input list.

2. Match one (or more) input elements. Ignore the next input element and match the rest of the input list with the current pattern list.

4.7.13 Count Occurrences [4*]

Write a function count-occurrences that finds how many times something occurs in a tree. The function returns the number of times that the value of its first argument (an atom) occurs in the value of its second argument. This function, like count-atoms, uses car/cdr recursion.

```
> (count-occurrences 'a '(a ((a b)) d c (a)))
3

> (count-occurrences 'z '(a ((a b)) d c (a)))
0
```

4.7.14 Tree Addition [4*]

Write a function tree-addition that adds a given number to every number (or leaf) of a tree of numbers. Like the preceding problem, this function uses car/cdr recursion. However, in this case, you must return an entire tree, not just a number, as a value. Thus, it is more similar to subst than to count-atoms.

```
> (tree-addition 2 '(5 4 3 2 1))
(7 6 5 4 3)

> (tree-addition 3 '(1 2 (3 (4 (5) 6) (7)) 8 (9)))
(4 5 (6 (7 (8) 9) (10)) 11 (12))

> (tree-addition 5 '(((((1)))))))
(((((6)))))
```

4.7.15   Tree Average [5*]

Write a function `tree-average` that computes the average of a tree of numbers. *You should traverse the tree only once.* That is, you should create a secondary recursive function that both counts the number of leaves in the tree and adds up their values, similar to the `above-average` example before. This secondary function will return a pair of values as a list (the total and count) to `tree-average`, which will then calculate the average.

```
> (tree-average   '(1 2 (3 (4 (5)) 6) (7)) 8 (9)))
5

> (tree-average   '(((((((((1))))))))))
1
```

4.8   Chapter Summary

- Recursion is the typical LISP programming style.

- One can find examples of recursion and self-reference in art, literature, and especially mathematics.

- Recursion as used in programming helps to solve problems by progressively reducing the problem to a simpler form.

- The macros `trace` and `untrace` allow the programmer to monitor the run-time behavior of functions.

- Recursion provides a convenient way to traverse a list by examining the successive `cdrs`.

- Embedded lists, or trees, can be traversed by using car/cdr recursion.

- Sometimes it is useful to create a recursive subfunction, as in the averaging examples.

Recursion is the root of computation since it trades
description for time.

⋄ ALAN PERLIS, *Epigrams in Programming (1982)*

Chapter 5

Local vs. Global Reference

> *. . . as imagination bodies forth*
> *The forms of things unknown, the poet's pen*
> *Turns them to shapes, and gives to airy nothing*
> *A local habitation and name.*

◇ WILLIAM SHAKESPEARE, *A Midsummer-Night's Dream (1595-1596)*

> *Much of what Mr. Wallace calls his global thinking is,*
> *no matter how you slice it,*
> *still Globaloney.*

◇ CLARE BOOTH LUCE, *Speech, House of Representatives (February 9, 1943)*

From where do variables come? Where do they live? When do they die?

The alert and prescient reader may have noticed that we have been using variables in programs in two distinct ways:

- As an initial argument of a `defvar` (or `setf`) or `defun` expression.

  ```
  (defvar x 100)      ;  The symbol x is created and given
                      ;  the value of 100.

  (defun plus2 (y)    ;  The symbol plus2 is created and given
     (+ y 2))         ;  the value of a function that adds 2 to
                      ;  its argument.
  ```

- As a parameter in a lambda list in a `defun` expression. For example, in the above `plus2` definition, the symbol y is created but not given any value until the function is called.

133

The first type of variable is called *global*, and the second type is called *local*. Thus, in the examples above, x and plus2 are global, and y is local.

In the Roman numeral example in the preceding chapter (page 121), the defined function names, roman-to-decimal and numeral-to-decimal, are global, as is the name roman-number-a-list, the association list for converting Roman numerals. The variable names defined as parameters to the functions num-list and numeral are local.

What is the difference between global and local variables? The terms *global* and *local* are actually quite descriptive of the difference, which hinges on the range or scope of a variable's definition. Local variables are accessible only within the scope of their definition, such as within a particular function definition. A local variable resides in a contained neighborhood. A local variable lives its entire life in the same block.

Global variables are jet-setters. They are accessible from anywhere, at any time, *except when preempted by a local variable of the same name.*

For example, imagine you have a cat named George Washington. Your cat having the same name as the first president should not generally cause confusion. Usually, the context will provide sufficient means to resolve any ambiguity. The questions "Did you feed George Washington this morning?" and "Did George Washington sign the Declaration of Independence?" are not likely to be misinterpreted.

However, you might adopt another, more technical, method for resolving the reference. You could assume that whenever the words "George Washington" are said inside your house, they refer to your cat. If the words "George Washington" are said anywhere *except* inside your house, they refer to the president. In this sense, George Washington the cat is local to your house, and George Washington the president is global.

Here are some programming examples.

```
> (defvar x 25)          ;  x is a global variable.
X


> (defun plus2 (y)       ;  plus2 is global.
    (+ y 2))             ;  y is local to the function plus2.
PLUS2


> x
25


> (plus2 x)             ;  x's value of 25 is passed to the
27                      ;  local variable y.


> (defvar y 30)         ;  y is a global variable different from
Y                       ;  the local variable y in plus2.
```

```
> y
30

> (plus2 y)                ;  y's global value of 30 is passed to
32                          ;  the local variable y.

> y                        ;  y's global value is unchanged.
30
```

The y within the function plus2 was local; it was a parameter in the function definition. It is possible to have a global variable within a function, as we can see below.

```
> (defun plus-z (n)        ;  plus-z will add the global value of z       ⇐ Bad Idea
    (+ z n))               ;  to the local value of n.
PLUS-Z

> (defvar z 10)            ;  Creates and initializes the global z.
Z

> (plus-z 5)               ;  5 is passed to the local variable n,
15                         ;  which is added to the global value of z.

> (setf z 20)              ;  Gives a new value to z.
20

> (plus-z 5)              ;  Voilà.  A new result.
25
```

We thus created a function that depended on the value of a global variable, and the behavior of that function changed when that global variable was changed. There is an important moral lesson to be derived from this brief example.

- Refrain from using global variables within functions. The results can become unpredictable.

As an alternative to using global variables within functions, the programmer may choose to use global *constants*, using the defconstant macro.

```
> (defconstant w 100)      ;  Creates a constant w with value 100.
W

> (constantp w)            ;  constantp is the predicate for constants.
T
```

```
> (defun plus-w (n)          ; plus-w is like plus-z.
    (+ w n))
PLUS-W
```

```
> (plus-w 5)
105
```

```
> (setf w 200)               ; It is now an error to change w.
Error: Cannot change the value of W -- it is a constant.
   [condition type: PROGRAM-ERROR]
```

The lesson here is that certain global variables, such as `roman-number-a-list`, should really be global constants. There will be occasions, though, in which the programmer may want to use honest-to-goodness global variables, whose values will need to change. The preferred way to create these mutable variables is with the macro `defparameter`.

```
> (defparameter p 100)
P
```

```
> p
100
```

```
> (setf p 200)
200
```

Global parameters are intended to be set by the user at the top level and are used to control the execution of the program. We suggest that the programmer adopt the LISP notational convention of surrounding the names of global parameters with asterisks, for example, `*debug-switch*` or `*current-spouse*` or `*soup-of-the-day*`. This morphological practice has at least three advantages. First, it provides easy visual identification of global variables in code. Second, other LISP programmers are aware of this convention and will thus have little trouble interpreting your code. Third, by forcing the programmer to think about using global variables, this notation may remind the programmer to avoid them. A similar, though less common, naming convention is the use of the character + to surround constants, for example, `+avogadro+` or `+planck+`.

You can judge a generalization by the quality of the exceptions. One useful global constant is `else`, as demonstrated here.

```
> (defconstant else t)
ELSE
```

```
> (cond ((evenp 3) 'bad)
        (else 'good))
GOOD
```

We can now use the constant `else` instead of `T` as the default clause in a `cond` statement. This use of `else` is purely a matter of taste. It does not affect the performance of underlying code. Some may find that `else` more clearly conveys the logic of the default `cond` clause to the human reader of the program. Another reasonable constant serving the same purpose would be `otherwise`.

5.1 Modifying Values of Objects: setf

Consider the following interaction.

```
> (defvar mm 9)
MM

> mm
9

> (defvar mm 10)
MM

> mm
9
```

What is going on? We created a variable `mm` with a value of 9, then tried to create it again, but with a value of 10. However, the second time did not seem to take. We did not even get an error message.

All we really want to do is change the value of `mm`. As demonstrated before, the LISP macro `setf` is best used for modifying the values of objects, both local and global.

```
> (setf mm 10)
10

> mm
10

> (setf new-mm 11)
11

> new-mm
11
```

As the `new-mm` example shows, you can also use `setf` to create and initialize objects. The preferred usage is `defvar` for object creation and `setf` for object modification.

The programmer can use `setf` within function definitions as well. For example, the recursive subfunction `below-average` given in the preceding chapter was presented in typical LISP programming style, with function calls nested as arguments to other functions.

```
(defun below-average (num-list count total)
   (cond ((null num-list) (/ total count))   ; Done? Returns average.
          (t (below-average (cdr num-list)    ; Goes to next number.
                  (+ count 1)                  ; Increments the count.
                  (+ (car num-list) ; Adds current number
                      total)))))               ; to total
```

Everything is happening in the recursive call at one time. In other languages, programmers often change the values of local variables before passing them as arguments. Using `setf`, we could adopt this style.

Bad Idea ⇒
```
(defun below-average (num-list count total)
   (cond ((null num-list) (/ total count))   ; Done? Returns average.
          (t (setf count (+ count 1))          ; Increments the count.
          (setf total (+ (car num-list)
                      total))                  ; Updates total.
          (setf num-list (cdr num-list))       ; Gets remainder of list.
          ; Makes the next recursive call.
          (below-average num-list count total))))
```

This second version of `below-average` is less efficient than the first and does not represent accepted LISP idiomatic style. Notice that here `setf` is used to assign new values to the *local* variables `count`, `num-list`, and `total`.

For further contrast, we can see how we might have solved the average problem by using global variables instead of local variables.

Bad Idea ⇒
```
(defun above-average (num-list)
   (setf count 0)                ; Creates and initializes count.
   (setf total 0)                ; Creates and initializes total.
   (below-average num-list))
```

```
(defun below-average (num-list)
   (cond ((null num-list) (/ total count)) ; Done? Returns average.
          (t (setf count (+ count 1))        ; Increments the count.
          (setf total (+ (car num-list)
                          total))            ; Updates total.
          (setf num-list (cdr num-list)) ; Gets remainder of list.
          (below-average num-list))))        ; Makes the next recursive call.
```

This global-variable version of above-average and below-average will work pretty much the same as the local-variable version. Why choose one over the other? The reason is simple: safety. When you use a local variable, you can be certain that no other outside function will corrupt its value. With a global variable, there is no such assurance. If you get into the habit of using global variables, you very quickly have a bookkeeping problem to make sure that no function accidentally clobbers the value of a global variable. For example, if we implement above-average by using the global variables count and total, we have to make sure that no other function will have conflicting uses of these global variables. There is no such concern for the local-variable version of above-average. Two local variables of the same name will not conflict the way two identical global variables will.

One further aspect of the global versus local conflict stems from the precedence of local variables over global variables in the event of name conflicts. That is, if you have a global variable and a local variable with the same name, the local variable will win out within its own context. LISP compounds the possible confusion by allowing symbols not only to have local and global values but also to have functional and property list values. Here are some examples.

```
> (defvar x 10)
X

> (defun plus3 (x) (+ x 3))
PLUS3

> (plus3 11)                ;  The local value of x is
14                          ;  bound to 11, not 10.

> (defun double (l)         ;  The local variable l does
    (list l l))             ;  not conflict with any global value.
DOUBLE

> (double '(7 8))
((7 8) (7 8))

> (defun triple (list)      ;  The local variable list
    (list list list list))  ;  has an obvious conflict.
TRIPLE

> (triple '(7 8))
((7 8) (7 8) (7 8))
```

In the triple example, the local variable list would appear to be in conflict with the global function name list. However, an error does not occur. The LISP interpreter finds no ambiguity in the name list. One is a variable name and the other is a function name.

LISP permits a symbol to serve several purposes:

- A variable name, which may have a value

- A function name, which may be executed

- A symbol name, which may have an associated property list

```
> (defvar eve 21)                    ; The variable eve is 21.
EVE
```

```
> (setf (get 'eve 'age) 31)          ; eve's age property is 31.
31
```

```
> (defun eve ()
       (+ eve (get 'eve 'age)))      ; The function eve sums the other values.
EVE
```

```
> (eve)
52
```

```
> (symbol-value 'eve)                ; Retrieves the symbol's value.
21
```

```
> (symbol-function 'eve)             ; Retrieves the symbol's function.
#<Interpreted Function EVE @ #x10891a6>
```

```
> (fdefinition 'eve)                 ; More general than symbol-function.
#<Interpreted Function EVE @ #x10891a6>
```

```
> (symbol-plist 'eve)                ; Retrieves the symbol's property list.
(AGE 31)
```

Thus, one symbol can have at least three faces: a value, a function, and a property list.

5.2 Creating Local Variables: let

We have been trying to convey the virtue of local variables. So far, we have only seen one way to create local variables, namely, as parameters in function definitions. There is another useful method: the special form let.

Like defvar and setf, let assigns values to objects. However, since let is for defining local variables, there must be a means for specifying the range or scope of the variables' definitions. This specification is accomplished by the special syntax of let.

```
(let ((variable-1 value-1)
      (variable-2 value-2)
      ...
      (variable-n value-n))
   body)
```

The let clause works as follows: Each variable is created as a local variable with its respective initial value. The body, which may consist of any number of forms, is then executed within the scope of all the local variables. That is, each form within body may refer to and access the value of any of the local variables just instantiated. When the last form is completed, the let clause is exited and the local variables are no longer accessible.

Instead of the list (variable value), let also permits the programmer to provide just the variable, which gets an initial value of nil.

Here is our function profit from chapter 2, which shows how let can simplify a calculation. First, we give the original function.

```
(defun profit (volume unit-price unit-cost tax-rate)
  (- (* volume unit-price)
     (+ (* volume unit-cost)
        (* tax-rate
           (* volume unit-price)))))
```

Next, we use let to introduce some meaningful temporary variables.

```
(defun let-profit (volume unit-price unit-cost tax-rate)
  (let ((revenue (* volume unit-price))
        (overhead (* volume unit-cost)))
    (- revenue
       (+ overhead
          (* tax-rate revenue)))))
```

This function demonstrates a way in which local variables can be used to avoid repeated calculations and to introduce meaningful variable names. In the original profit function, the revenues were calculated twice. In let-profit, to avoid recalculating revenues, we use let to create a revenue local variable which can then be accessed directly. We also introduce a local variable overhead, not to avoid extra calculations but to add clarity for the human reader.

Admittedly, the cost of a couple of multiplications may not seem sufficiently expensive. However, in a typical client-server application, the profit function might call the main corporate database to get its data. Local variables are an inexpensive way to cache such data.

5.3 Closures

We have strongly advised against using global variables. The main problem is that the inadvertent behavior of one function can adversely affect another function.

LISP does provide a method of maintaining *global state* without the use of global variables. If a function is defined within the scope of a local variable, then that function may access that variable, and functions defined outside the local scope may not access the local variable. This marriage of local variables and functions is termed a *closure*.

In the following example, we create a local variable n within a `let` form and then define two functions, `next-n` and `set-n`, both of which access the local value of n.

```
(let ((n 0))
  (defun next-n ()
    (setf n (+ n 1))
    n)
  (defun set-n (val)
    (setf n val)))
```

```
> (next-n)                ; Gets the next value.
1

> (next-n)                ; It keeps changing.
2

> (setf n 100)            ; Changes the global value of n.
100

> (next-n)                ; The closure's local value is unaffected.
3

> (set-n 100)             ; Uses the closure's set-n function.
100

> (next-n)                ; The closure's value of n has changed.
101
```

Closures combine the best of both worlds: the safety of local reference with the universal access of global reference.

5.4 More Uses for Generalized Variables

As discussed in section 3.10, `setf` can be used to modify the value of any specified location, with a symbol being merely one way to indicate a location. Generalized variables are accessor or selector functions that can be used to specify a location.

```
> (defvar x 1)              ;  The symbol x is created and initialized.
X

> (setf x '(a b c d))       ;  A new value is assigned to x.
(A B C D)

> x
(A B C D)

> (setf (car x) '(1 2 3))   ;  A new value is assigned to (car x).
(1 2 3)

> x                         ;  x's value has been modified.
((1 2 3) B C D)

> (setf (cdr x) '(4 5 6 7))  ;  A new value is assigned to (cdr x).
(4 5 6 7)

> x                         ;  x's value has been modified again.
((1 2 3) 4 5 6 7)

> (setf (nth 4 x) '())      ;  A new value is assigned to (nth 4 x).
NIL

> x                         ;  x's value has been modified again.
((1 2 3) 4 5 6 NIL)
```

Early versions of LISP did not include setf. Some of the same power was provided by the functions rplaca (pronounced *re-PLACK-uh*) and rplacd (pronounced *re-plack-DEE*), which destructively replace the contents of a list's car and cdr, respectively. These functions persist in Common LISP, even though their use is obviated by the more general setf.

```
> (rplaca x 4)             ;  Replaces the car of x.
(4 4 5 6 NIL)

> (rplacd x '(5 6))        ;  Replaces the cdr of x.
(4 5 6)

> x
(4 5 6)
```

In addition to setf, generalized variables work with other macros that we have already encountered, including push, pop, pushnew, getf, and remf, demonstrated below.

```
> (setf z '((a) (b) (c)))
((A) (B) (C))

> (push 'd (car z))          ; Modifies the car of z.
(D A)

> z
((D A) (B) (C))

> (pop (cadr z))             ; Modifies the cadr of z.
B

> z
((D A) NIL (C))

> (pushnew 'd (third z))     ; Modifies the third of z.
(D C)

> (pushnew 'c (third z))     ; No change.
(D C)

> z
((D A) NIL (D C))

> (getf (first z) 'd)        ; Accesses a property list.
A

> (remf (third z) 'd)        ; Modifies a property list.
T

> z                          ; The final results.
((D A) NIL NIL)
```

Here are four more macros that modify generalized variables. They are all destructive.

- (incf place [increment]) increments its argument. An optional second argument specifies the increment.

- (decf place [decrement] decrements its argument. An optional second argument specifies the decrement.

- (rotatef {place}*) exchanges the values in sequence, with the last place getting the starting value of the first. Note: {place}* signifies zero or more place arguments.

- (shiftf {place}+ newval) exchanges the values in sequence, with the last place getting the specified newval. Note: {place}+ signifies one or more place arguments.

The shiftf function is a minor variant of rotatef.

```
> (setf y '(1 2 3))
(1 2 3)

> (incf (car y))          ;  incf increments the specified number.
2

> y
(2 2 3)

> (decf (cadr y))         ;  decf decrements the specified number.
1

> y
(2 1 3)

> (incf (first y) 10)     ;  Specifies an increment of 10.
12

> y
(12 1 3)

> (rotatef (first y) (second y) (third y))
NIL

> y
(1 3 12)

> (rotatef (second y) (third y))
NIL

> y
(1 12 3)

> (shiftf (second y) (third y) 100)
12
```

```
> y
(1 3 100)

> (shiftf (second y) (third y) (first y))
3

> y
(1 100 1)
```

We observe that that following two forms are equivalent.

```
    (rotate p1 p2 ... pn)
    (shift p1 p2 ... pn p1)
```

In the above examples, only the variable y was modified. However, the rotate and shift forms may work on more than one variable at once.

```
> (setf y '(1 2 3))
(1 2 3)

> (setf z '(4 5 6))
(4 5 6)

> (rotatef (first y) (second z))
NIL

> y
(5 2 3)

> z
(4 1 6)

> (rotatef y z)
NIL

> y
(4 1 6)

> z
(5 2 3)
```

Thus, rotatef is a more general version of a swap function.

These examples demonstrate the great versatility of generalized variables and their related modifier macros. The programmer should be aware that these macros *destructively* modify the object. That is, the object's previous value cannot be retrieved. Normally this is not a concern because the intended effect is to change the value of the object. However, when you have one object that points to the value of another object and you indirectly change the value of the second object, you have also changed the value of the first object. Here are some examples.

```
> (defvar x '(1 2 3 4))      ;  x is created and given an initial value.
X

> (defvar y x)               ;  y is created and given x's value.
Y

> x
(1 2 3 4)

> y
(1 2 3 4)

> (setf x '(2 2))            ;  x's value is changed.
(2 2)

> y                          ;  y still points to the old value of x.
(1 2 3 4)

> (setf y x)                 ;  Now set y to the new value of x.
(2 2)                        ;  (See figure 5.1.)

> (setf (car x) 5)           ;  x's value is modified indirectly.
5

> x                          ;  x has a new value,
(5 2)

> y                          ;  and so does y.
(5 2)

> (setf (first y) 7)         ;  By modifying y now, we also change x.
7

> y                          ;  y has a new value,
(7 2)

> x                          ;  and so does x.
(7 2)                        ;  (See figure 5.2.)
```

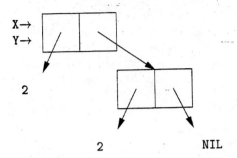

Figure 5.1: Shared List Structure

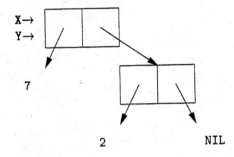

Figure 5.2: Shared List Structure, After Indirect Changes

From these examples, the programmer should see that one should be especially wary when dealing with shared structures to avoid unintended results. To appreciate how disastrous shared structure can be, consider the following example.

```
> (defvar x '(1 2))
(1 2)
```

Bad Idea ⇒
```
> (setf (car x) x)                    ;  Do not do this!
(((((# 2) 2) 2) 2) 2)
```

The last statement resulted in a *circular list*, which causes a problem for the print routine as it tries to print something infinitely long. In this case, the print routine inserts a # to indicate that it is not printing the entire object. Figure 5.3 depicts the result of the expression (setf (car x) x).

It is very easy to create circular lists.[1] The hard part is to print them.[2] In this example, the car of x is x itself.

---

[1]Circular lists embody the more general phenomenon of circular reference. (See next footnote.)

[2]Circular reference is exemplified by circular lists. (See preceding footnote.)

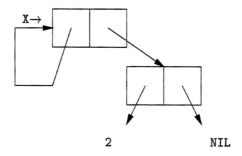

Figure 5.3: Circular List Example

It should be clear that one should avoid circular lists. It is important, however, that the programmer be aware of their existence, just as the prudent person can recognize poison ivy and rattlesnakes.[3]

One safety measure to employ in the case of circular lists is the `list-length` function, instead of the normal `length` function. `list-length` can detect circular lists, whereas `length` will shoot into hyperspace.

```
> (setf x '(1 2))            ;  Creates a normal list.
(1 2)

> (length x)                 ;  length works fine.
2

> (setf (cdr x) x)           ;  Creates a circular list.
(1 1 1 1 1 1 1 1 1 1 ...)

> (list-length x)            ;  list-length smells a problem,
NIL

> (length x)                 ;  whereas, length never returns.
...
```

We can avoid these unwanted interactions by using copies of lists instead of shared structure.

```
> (setf x '(2 3 4))
(2 3 4)

> (setf y x)
(2 3 4)
```

---

[3]Actually, there are occasions when circular lists are very useful, e.g., implementing a cyclical data structure.

```
> (eq x y)                    ;  x and y are the same object.
T

> (setf y (copy-tree x))      ;  y is now a copy of x.
(2 3 4)

> (eq x y)
NIL

> (setf (car x) 5)            ;  If we now modify x,
5

> x
(5 3 4)

> y                           ;  we no longer will affect y.
(2 3 4)
```

The function copy-tree recursively makes a copy of its argument. By contrast, copy-list copies only the top-level elements.

```
> (setf x '((i love paris)))
((I LOVE PARIS))

> (setf y (copy-list x))
((I LOVE PARIS))

> (setf z (copy-tree x))
((I LOVE PARIS))

> (setf (caar x) 'you)
YOU

> x
((YOU LOVE PARIS))

> y
((YOU LOVE PARIS))

> z
((I LOVE PARIS))
```

5.5 Defining setf Functions

Let us create a list data structure for dates. A date will be represented as a three-element list: (month day year). For example, the date for the signing of the Declaration of Independence would be given as (7 4 1776). We define some functions for handling this type of date.

```
(defun make-date (month day year)
  (list month day year))

(defun date-month (date) (first date))

(defun date-day   (date) (second date))

(defun date-year  (date) (third date))
```

Here is how a programmer might use these functions.

```
> (defvar independence-day (make-date 7 4 1776))
INDEPENDENCE-DAY

> independence-day
(7 4 1776)

> (date-month independence-day)
7

> (date-day independence-day)
4

> (date-year independence-day)
1776
```

Why go to the trouble? Why not use first instead of date-month? Good question. By defining the date- access functions, we provide a better interface: a meaningful *abstraction* of the underlying data.

Compare the following two functions, which check to ensure that a given date conforms to the numerical limits for months and days. The first one avoids the use of abstractions.

```
(defun legal-datep (date)
```
⇐ Bad Idea

```
(cond ((or (> (first date) 12)
           (< (first date) 1))
       'illegal-month)
      ((or (> (second date) 31)
           (< (second date) 1)
           (and (= (first date) 2)
                (not (leap-yearp (third date)))
                (> (second date 28)))
           (and (= (first date) 2)
                (leap-yearp (third date))
                (> (second date 29)))
           (and (member (first date) '(4 6 9 11))
                (> (second date 30))))
       'illegal-day)
      (t
       'ok-i-guess)))
```

The second function is equivalent to the preceding one but uses the `date-` abstractions.

```
(defun legal-datep (date)
  (cond ((or (> (date-month date) 12)
             (< (date-month date) 1))
         'illegal-month)
        ((or (> (date-day date) 31)
             (< (date-day date) 1)
             (and (= (date-month date) 2)
                  (not (leap-yearp (date-year date)))
                  (> (date-day date 28)))
             (and (= (date-month date) 2)
                  (leap-yearp (date-year date))
                  (> (date-day date 29)))
             (and (member (date-month date) '(4 6 9 11))
                  (> (date-day date 30))))
         'illegal-day)
        (t
         'ok-i-guess)))
```

The second `legal-datep` function might actually be slightly less efficient than the first, depending on the implementation. However, we suggest, and in fact insist, that the second version is better since it is easier for the *programmer* to read and comprehend.

Given our newly avowed love of abstractions, how can we use `setf` with them? That is, suppose we want to change the year of a date.

```
> (setf (third independence-day) 2000)        ; This works.
2000
```

```
> independence-day
(7 4 2000)
```

```
> (setf (date-year independence-day) 2000)   ; This does not work.
Error: No methods applicable for generic function
       #<STANDARD-GENERIC-FUNCTION (SETF DATE-YEAR) @ #x116f7ce>
       with args (2000 (7 4 2000)) of classes (INTEGER CONS)
  [condition type: PROGRAM-ERROR]
```

We need to define a setf function for each of our date- accessor functions. Here
is how.

```
(defun (setf date-month) (month date)
  (setf (first date) month))
```

```
(defun (setf date-day) (day date)
  (setf (second date) day))
```

```
(defun (setf date-year) (year date)
  (setf (third date) year))
```

It is important to note the order of parameters in the setf definition. The first
parameter, for example, month, is the new value to be assigned. The second parameter, for example, date, is the object being modified. The programmer must
adhere to this order.

These setf functions are unusual in that their names are not symbols, but
lists. As such, you cannot use symbol-function to access a setf function, but you
can use fdefinition.

```
> (fdefinition '(setf date-month))
#<Interpreted Function (SETF DATE-MONTH) @ #x108a37e>
```

We now can use setf with our date- functions.

```
> (setf (date-year independence-day) 2001)
2001
```

```
> independence-day
(7 4 2001)
```

We hold these truths to be self-evident.

5.6   Advanced Subjects

There are three advanced topics in this chapter.

- Additional Assignments

- More setf Definitions

- Creating Modifying Macros

5.6.1   Additional Assignments

In this text, we promote `setf` as the preferred method of assignment. However, LISP provides several other assignment forms. In particular, the `setq` special form has been around longer than `setf` and is present in almost any piece of legacy LISP code.

We can describe `setq`'s behavior as a subset, so to speak, of `setf`; it takes a series of variable-value pairs, assigning the value to its respective variable.

```
> (setq a 1 b 2 c 3)
3

> a
1

> (setq d '(a b c))
(A B C)

> d
(A B C)

> (setq (car d) 'x)
Error: Cannot setq (CAR D) -- not a symbol.
  [condition type: PROGRAM-ERROR]
[1]
```

You can always use `setf` instead of `setq`, but the reverse is not true, as the last example demonstrates.

Another assignment method is the `set` function. Unlike `setf` or `setq`, `set` evaluates all of its arguments.

```
> (set 'x 'y)              ;  The quoted value of x gets 'y.
Y

> x
Y
```

```
> (set x 5)          ;   The value of x gets 5.
5

> x
Y

> y                  ;   Y now has the value 5.
5

> (set 'z '(x y))
(X Y)

> (set (car z) 0)    ;   (car z) gets the value 0.
0

> z                  ;   x now has the value 0.
(X Y)

> x
0
```

Common LISP also provides *parallel* versions of setf and setq, namely, psetf and psetq. When multiple assignments are made, the parallel versions do not act in left-to-right order but rather in a simultaneous fashion.

```
> (setf a 3 b 4)     ;   Assigns initial values to ba and b.
4

> (setf a b b a)     ;   Attempts to swap values.
4

> a                  ;   a got the value of b.
4

> b                  ;   However, b got a's new value.
4

> (setf a 3 b 4)     ;   Try again.
4

> (psetf a b b a)    ;   This time we use parallel assignment.
NIL
```

```
> a
4

> b                          ;   It works.
3

> (setq x '(1 2 3))      ;   An example with lists.
(1 2 3)

> (setf (car x) (cadr x) (cadr x) (car x))
2

> x
(2 2 3)

> (psetf (first x) (third x) (third x) (first x))
NIL

> x                          ;   psetf works with generalized variables.
(3 2 2)
```

The psetq macro is analogous to psetf but applies only to variable assignment.

5.6.2   More setf Definitions

LISP provides other ways of defining setf functions. The macro defsetf permits the programmer to associate an accessor function with a given setf update function. The update function must take two arguments: the object and the new value. Here is an example using our earlier date functions.

```
> (setf x (make-date 7 4 1776))
(7 4 1776)

> (defun set-day (d m) (rplaca (cdr d) m) d)
SET-DAY

> (defsetf date-day set-day)
DATE-DAY

> (setf (date-day x) 25)
(7 25 1776)
```

The defsetf macro has an alternative syntax, which allows the programmer to define the update function within the defsetf expression. The arguments to this version of `defsetf` are the name of the access function, the lambda parameter list, a list containing the parameter name for the new value, and an expression that evaluates to the update function. Here is an example.

```
(defsetf date-month (date) (new-month)
  (list 'rplaca date new-month))

> (setf new-years (make-date 12 31 1999))
(12 31 1999)

> (setf (date-month new-years) 11)
(11 31 1999)

> new-years
(11 31 1999)
```

The programmer interested in examining the raw underbelly of `setf` updating functions can use the function `get-setf-method`, which returns five values.

```
> (get-setf-method '(date-day x))
(#:G607)
(X)
(#:G606)
(SET-DAY #:G607 #:G606)
(DATE-DAY #:G607)

> (get-setf-method '(date-month x))
(#:G609)
(X)
(#:G608)
(RPLACA #:G609 #:G608)
(DATE-MONTH #:G609)
```

These five values are, in order of appearance:

- A list of temporary variables

- A list of forms to which the values of the variables are bound

- A list containing a temporary variable into which the generalized variable will be stored

- The *storing form*, which is the code used for assigning the new value to the generalized variable

- The *accessing form*, which is the code used to retrieve the value of the generalized variable

For the sake of comparison, here are the results of `get-setf-method` for `car` and
`first`. Implementations may differ in appearance.

```
> (get-setf-method '(car x))
(#:G611)
(X)
(#:G610)
(EXCL::.INV-CAR #:G611 #:G610)
(CAR #:G611)

> (get-setf-method '(first x))
(#:G613)
(X)
(#:G612)
(EXCL::.INV-CAR #:G613 #:G612)
(FIRST #:G613)
```

The intrepid programmer can specify these five components directly herself, using
the macro `define-setf-method`, demonstrated below. The five forms specified
as arguments to `values` correspond to the five values returned by the function
`get-setf-method`. We note that the gensym function creates unique identifiers.

```
(define-setf-method date-month (date)
  (let ((temp-var (gensym))
        (store-form (gensym)))
    (values
      (list temp-var)
      (list date)
      (list store-form)
      (list 'rplaca temp-var store-form)
      (list 'car temp-var))))
```

```
> (get-setf-method '(date-month x))
(#:G616)
(X)
(#:G617)
(RPLACA #:G616 #:G617)
(CAR #:G616)

> x
(7 25 1776)

> (setf (date-month x) 1)
(1 25 1776)
```

In spite of these `setf` definition alternatives, we advocate the use of the `setf` definition syntax first presented in section 5.5.

5.6.3 Creating Modifying Macros

We have seen several ways to create new generalized variables. The programmer can also define her own macros, like `incf` or `decf`, which modify generalized variables. The programmer uses the macro `define-modify-macro`, which takes three arguments.

- The name of the new macro

- The lambda list for the new macro

- The function that is applied to the generalized variable and the lambda list arguments; the value returned by the function is the new value stored in the generalized variable

Below we define the following four new modifying macros.

- (timesf place multiple) resets place to its product with multiple.

- (modf place divisor) resets place with its remainder after division by divisor.

- (addf place {numbers}*) resets place to its sum with numbers.

- (reversef place) resets place with its top-level elements reversed.

```
> (define-modify-macro timesf (multiple) *)
TIMESF

> x
(1 4 1776)

> (timesf (car x) 23)
23

> x
(23 4 1776)

> (timesf (date-month x) 10)
(230 4 1776)

> (define-modify-macro modf (divisor) mod)
MODF
```

```
> (modf (date-month x) 10)
(0 4 1776)

> (modf (caddr x) 17)
8

> x
(0 4 8)

> (define-modify-macro addf (&rest numbers) +)
ADDF

> (addf (car x) 1 2 3)
6

> x
(6 4 8)

> (addf (car x))
6

> x
(6 4 8)

> (define-modify-macro reversef () reverse)
REVERSEF

> (reversef x)
(8 4 6)

> x
(8 4 6)
```

5.7   Exercises

5.7.1   Expression Drill [3]

Evaluate all of the following expressions by hand in order. Calculate the value of x
after each expression is evaluated. Then, check your answers with the help of your
LISP interpreter.

```
(defvar x '(1 2 3))
(setf (car x) '3)
(setf (cdr x) '(2 3))
(defun add-to-x (n) (setf (car x) (+ n (cadr x))))
(add-to-x 5)
(add-to-x 3)
(defun add-to-x (n) (setf (car x) (+ n (car x))))
(add-to-x 5)
(add-to-x 5)                  ; Yes. Do it twice.
(setf y x)
(setf (car y) 0)
```

5.7.2 Identifying Local and Global Variables [3*]

In the preceding exercise, identify all occurrences of global and local variables, specifying which is which.

5.7.3 defvar versus setf [4*]

The definition of above-average on page 138 used setf to create and initialize the global variables count and total. Suppose that we used defvar instead of setf, as shown below. Why would this version not work?

```
(defun above-average (num-list)                              ⇐ Bad Idea
  (defvar count 0)
  (defvar total 0)
  (below-average num-list))
```

5.7.4 Not For Profit [4*]

In section 5.2, we defined the function let-profit, which used let to avoid repeated calculations and add clarity to the definition of the profit function. Below we define let-profit2 which introduces another meaningful local variable taxes. However, there is a problem. What is wrong with this definition and what is the remedy?

```
(defun let-profit2 (volume unit-price unit-cost tax-rate)    ⇐ Bad Idea
  (let ((revenue (* volume unit-price))
        (overhead (* volume unit-cost))
        (taxes (* tax-rate revenue)))
    (- revenue
       (+ overhead taxes)))))
```

5.7.5 Local Variables and Making Change [4*]

The make-change function defined in the preceding chapter (page 119) was inefficient. With each recursive call, it would repeat checks for the higher denomination currency.

Rewrite make-change, using local variables, so that no test is performed more than once. You should find that you no longer need to use recursion.

5.7.6 Niece of Zeller [4*]

The answer to exercise 3.14.11 could have been written more clearly, using local variables for both the list of days of the week and the association list for the months of the year. Rewrite daughter-of-zeller, using these local variables.

5.7.7 Closure Audit Trail [3*]

Write a function a+ which adds two numbers and also keeps track of how many times it was called, and with what arguments. The functions count+ and args+ return the count and arguments, respectively, and reset them, as demonstrated below.

```
> (a+ 9 5)
14

> (a+ 2 3)
5

> (count+)
2

> (args+)
((2 3) (9 5))

> (a+ 1 2)
3

> (count+)
1

> (args+)
((1 2))
```

5.7.8 Rain Date [3*]

In section 5.5, we presented a date constructor and abstract accessors for the month, day, and year of a date.

Assume for the moment that the functions `list`, `first`, `second`, and `third`, which we used in our definitions, are not available. Define `make-date` and write definitions and `setf` definitions for `date-month`, `date-day`, and `date-year`, using other LISP functions.

5.7.9 Last Chance [4*]

For some reason, there is no `setf` form for the `last` function.

```
> (setf (last independence-day) '(2003))
Error: (SETF LAST) does not have a function definition
```

Write a `setf` definition for `last`, such that you get the following behavior.

```
> (last independence-day)
(2002)

> (setf (last independence-day) '(2003))
(2003)

> independence-day
(7 4 2003)
```

You may have to override your system's warnings about redefining native LISP functions.

5.8 Chapter Summary

- *Global* variables are accessible from all functions. *Local* variables are accessible only within the context in which they appear.

- Use `defvar` to create and initialize global variables.

- Use `let` to create and initialize local objects.

- Use `setf` to modify objects, globally or locally.

- The following functions access values of symbols and functions.

```
(symbol-value symbol)
(symbol-function symbol)
(symbol-plist symbol)
(fdefinition function-name)
```

- By defining a function within the local scope of a `let`, the programmer creates a *closure.*

- Accessor or selector functions can be used to specify generalized variables to be changed by `setf` and other macros.

- The functions `rplaca` and `rplacd` replace a list's `car` and `cdr`, respectively.

- The `incf` and `decf` macros destructively increment and decrement generalized variables, respectively. The macros `rotatef` and `shiftf` exchange values among generalized variables.

- Indirect structure modification can cause problems in shared structures, especially with circular lists. The `copy-tree` function provides a way to avoid shared structures.

- The use of abstraction in programming is a cardinal virtue.

- LISP provides a means for programmers to define their own `setf` functions.

*As Will Rogers would have said, "There is no such thing
as a free variable."*

◇ ALAN PERLIS, *Epigrams in Programming (1982)*

Chapter 6

Characters and Strings

The hell to be endured hereafter, of which theology tells,
is no worse than the hell we make for ourselves in this world
by habitually fashioning our characters in the wrong way.

◇ WILLIAM JAMES, *The Principles of Psychology (1890)*

Harp not on that string.

◇ WILLIAM SHAKESPEARE, *King Richard III (1592 - 1593)*

The chief defect of Henry King
Was chewing little bits of string.

◇ HILAIRE BELLOC, *Cautionary Tales (1907)*

Thus far, we have dealt primarily with numbers and symbols, which in turn were used to compose lists. We now look at more building blocks: characters and strings.

Strings are composed of characters linked together, just as a string of beads is composed of single beads threaded together. Characters are to strings what symbols and numbers are to lists — at least the lists we have seen so far. A string is merely a sequential set of characters, just as a list is a sequential set of objects. However, lists can also include other lists through embedding. Strings cannot be embedded.

In LISP, strings are denoted by characters surrounded by — no, not parentheses — double quotes. The string: `"a string"` is the sequence of characters a, *space*, s, t, r, i, n, and g. Note that the space between `a` and `s` is explicitly represented as a character.

Characters in LISP are a data type in their own right. They are denoted by the character itself, in the case of graphical characters, preceded by # and \, such as #\A, #\a, #\3, and #*. Note that upper- and lowercase characters are distinct.

Whitespace characters, such as tab, space, and newline (which moves to the beginning of the next output line), and nonprinting characters, such as null or bell, have symbolic names preceded by #\ as in #\tab, #\space, #\newline, #\null, and #\bel.

Characters and strings are self-evaluating in LISP, just like numbers. They need not be quoted. Here are some examples.

```
> "a string"                    ; Strings are self-evaluating.
"a string"

> ""                            ; This is the empty string.
""

> (defvar x "This is a string."); Strings can be bound to variables.
X

> x
"This is a string."

> (cons "hello" "there")        ; Strings can be used in lists.
("hello" . "there")

> #\A                           ; Characters are self-evaluating.
#\A

> (defvar y #\t)                ; Characters can be bound to variables.
Y

> y
#\t

> (defvar z #\tab)
Z

> z
#\tab

> (cons #\A #\Z)                ; Characters can be used in lists.
(#\A . #\Z)

> (list #\A "mixed" 'list)      ; You can mix data types in lists.
(#\A "mixed" LIST)
```

Note that #\a, #\A, and 'A are three different things, namely, the character a, the character A, and the symbol A.

We can also construct a string explicitly with the function `make-string`.

```
> (setf s1 (make-string 10 :initial-element #\0))
"0000000000"
```

The initial argument to `make-string` specifies the size of the string, and the keyword `:initial-element` provides the character to replicate in the string. Here we create a string of zeros. Omitting the `:initial-element` results in a string with a default value that is implementation dependent.   ⇐ ∞

6.1 String and Character Predicates

Characters and strings are important when writing programs that deal with text, such as formatters, editors, or natural language processing programs. Just as we had a wide variety of functions for dealing with lists and symbols, there is an abundance of string and character manipulation functions.

We shall first look at the predicates that deal with strings and characters.

```
> (characterp 3)          ; True if argument is of type character.
NIL

> (characterp #\3)
T

> (characterp #\tab)
T

> (stringp #\3)           ; True if argument is of type string.
NIL

> (stringp "3")
T

> (alpha-char-p #\a)      ; True if argument is an alphabetic character,
T                         ; that is, an uppercase letter A-Z or a
                          ; lowercase letter a-z.

> (alpha-char-p #\A)
T

> (alpha-char-p #\1)
NIL

> (alpha-char-p #\space)
NIL
```

```
> (digit-char-p #\3 10)  ;   True if first argument is a digit character
3                        ;   under the radix, or base, specified by the
                         ;   second argument.

> (digit-char-p #\3 2)   ;   3 is not a digit in base 2.
NIL

> (digit-char-p #\A 16)  ;   A is a digit (10) in hexadecimal (base 16).
10

> (alphanumericp #\A)    ;   True if character is a letter or digit.
T

> (alphanumericp #\3)
T

> (upper-case-p #\A)     ;   True if character is an uppercase letter.
T

> (lower-case-p #\A)     ;   True if character is a lowercase letter.
NIL

> (both-case-p #\a)      ;   True if character can be upper or lower case.
T

> (both-case-p #\1)
NIL

> (graphic-char-p #\a)   ;   True if character is a printing character.
T

> (graphic-char-p #\space)
T

> (graphic-char-p #\null)
NIL

> (standard-char-p #\a)  ;   True if character is a standard character.
T

> (standard-char-p #\null)
NIL
```

There are different types of characters. All characters are of type `character`. There is also a type `standard-char`, which is the subset of characters required of any LISP implementation.

In addition to the type predicates given above, there are a large number of comparison predicates. These correspond to the arithmetic comparison predicates such as greater than, or not equal to. The basis for comparing characters is their numeric representation, which is commonly implemented in LISP with the ASCII[1] ⇐ ∞ code. (We note that the language definition does not require the use of ASCII and leaves this choice up to the implementors.) Each character, both graphical and nonprinting, has a unique numeric code that supports a method for sorting characters. This collating sequence corresponds in large part to normal alphabetical order. Appendix D presents a LISP function that produces a listing of ASCII characters, together with its output.

Here are the case-sensitive character comparison predicates.

```
> (char= #\a #\A)          ;  True if characters are the same.
NIL

> (char= #\a #\a)
T

> (char< #\a #\b)          ;  True if first is alphabetically less than the
T                          ;  second.

> (char> #\a #\b)          ;  True if first is alphabetically greater than
NIL                        ;  the second.

> (char/= #\a #\b)         ;  True if characters are different.
T

> (char>= #\a #\b)         ;  Greater than or equal.
NIL

> (char<= #\a #\b)         ;  Less than or equal.
T
```

The case-sensitive predicates for strings are analogous.

```
> (string= "NO" "no")      ;  string= is case sensitive.
NIL

> (string= "s1" "s2")      ;  True if the strings are congruent,
NIL                        ;  that is, they correspond exactly.
```

---

[1]American Standard Code for Information Interchange. Pronounced *ASK-ey.*

```
> (string= "s1" "s1")
T

> (setf x "string")
X

> (setf y "string")
Y

> (string= x y)                 ; The strings are congruent.
T

> (eq x y)                      ; They do not have the identical memory
NIL                             ; locations.

> (equal x y)                   ; equal uses string=;
T                               ; thus, it returns true for congruent strings.

> (equal "s1" "S1")             ; equal is case sensitive.
NIL

> (equalp "s1" "S1")            ; equalp is case insensitive.
T

> (setf x #\a)                  ; We try the same comparisons
#\a                             ; with characters instead of strings.

> (setf y #\a)
#\a

> (eq x y)                      ; Characters, like symbols but unlike strings,
T                               ; are uniquely instantiated in this dialect.

> (eq #\space #\space)
T

> (eq "" "")                    ; There is no unique empty string.
NIL
```

The use of eq with characters is not recommended. In some dialects, characters
∞ ⇒ may not be eq. The programmer is urged to use eql instead.

Table 6.1 illustrates the differences among the Common LISP equality predicates when applied to characters and strings.

Arg1	Arg2	eq	eql	tree-equal	equal	=	equalp
A	A	T	T	T	T	NA	T
#\a	#\a	T	T	T	T	NA	T
#\a	#\b	NIL	NIL	NIL	NIL	NA	NIL
#\a	#\A	NIL	NIL	NIL	NIL	NA	T
"alpha"	"alpha"	NIL	NIL	NIL	T	NA	T
"alpha"	"ALPHA"	NIL	NIL	NIL	NIL	NA	T
""	""	NIL	NIL	NIL	T	NA	T

Table 6.1: Equality Predicates for Characters and Strings

6.2 Character Functions

There are few functions one uses with characters. The character functions either convert lowercase characters to upper case, or vice versa, or convert characters to their ASCII code value, or vice versa.

```
> (char-downcase #\M)        ;  Returns lowercase character.
#\m

> (char-upcase #\m)          ;  Returns uppercase character.
#\M

> (char-upcase #\4)          ;  Returns its argument if can't shift case.
#\4

> (char-upcase (char-downcase #\M))
#\M

> (char-code #\A)            ;  Returns the ASCII code for the character.     ⇐ ∞
65

> (code-char 66)             ;  Returns the character for the ASCII code.
#\B                          ;  Note: The 66 used here is decimal.
```

The function character converts its argument to type character.

```
> (character "A")            ;  Converts a string.
#\A

> (character 'a)             ;  Converts a symbol.
#\A
```

```
> (character 65)                ;  Converts an integer.
#\A
```

Functions that convert their input argument to some other data type are called *coercion functions*. We have already seen some numerical coercion functions, such as float, rational, and truncate. LISP provides a general coercion function, coerce, which takes two arguments: the object to be changed and the target type.

```
> (coerce "a" 'character)
#\a
```

```
> (coerce 66 'character)
#\B
```

```
> (coerce 66 'float)
66.0
```

```
> (coerce 66 'double-float)
66.0d0
```

```
> (coerce 66 'ratio)
Error: Can't coerce 66 to type RATIO.
[1]
> (coerce #\A 'string)
Error: Can't coerce #\A to type STRING.
[2]
> (coerce #\A 'integer)
Error: Can't coerce #\A to type INTEGER.
```

In LISP, as in life, coercion does not always work.

6.3 String Functions

Many string functions are analogous to list functions.

```
> (length "short")              ;  Number of characters in given string.
5
```

```
> (length "a very long string with lots of characters")
42
```

```
> (char "a string" 0)          ;  Returns the nth character (0-based) of given string.
#\a
```

```
> (concatenate 'string "a " "string")  ;  Joins copies of the given strings
"a string"                             ;  together; analogous to append for lists.
                                       ;  Note the space after #\a in "a string".

> (concatenate 'string "a " "big " "string")  ;  concatenate takes
"a big string"                         ;  any number of arguments.

> (elt "J. S. Bach" 3)                 ;  (elt string n), like char, returns the
#\S                                    ;  nth character (starting at 0) in string.

> (subseq "a string" 1)               ;  Returns the tail of given string.
" string"

> (subseq "J. S. Bach" 6 8)           ;  subseq has an optional argument
"Ba"                                   ;  to specify the end of the sequence.
```

- (position character string) returns the index of the first occurrence of character in string. If character does not appear in string, then (position character string) returns NIL.

```
> (position #\M "W. A. Mozart")
6

> (position #\space "W. A. Mozart")
2

> (position #\Z "W. A. Mozart")
NIL

> (find #\M "W. A. Mozart")            ;  find is like position
#\M                                    ;  except it returns the character itself.

> (find #\space "W. A. Mozart")
#\space

> (find #\Z "W. A. Mozart")
NIL

> (string-upcase "united states")     ;  Converts a copy of a string to
"UNITED STATES"                        ;  capital letters.

> (string-downcase "Little MARGIE")   ;  Converts a copy of the given
"little margie"                        ;  string to lowercase letters.
```

```
> (string-capitalize "america")      ; Uppercases initial letter of string.
"America"
```

```
> (string-capitalize " america")     ; Ignores leading whitespace.
" America"
```

- (map 'string function string) applies function to each successive character in string and copies the results together as a string.

```
> (map 'string #'char-upcase "lisp")
"LISP"
```

The last example using map suggest how one could define functions such as string-upcase. Here are some sample definitions of existing string functions.

```
(defun my-string-downcase (string)
  (map 'string #'char-downcase string))
```

```
(defun string-length (string) ;  Using string tail recursion.
  (cond ((string= "" string) 0)
        (t (1+ (string-length (subseq string 1)))))))
```

It is often useful to change other data types into strings, and vice versa. There are several coercion functions to facilitate such changes.

```
> (coerce '(#\h #\e #\l #\l #\o) 'string)   ; Converts a list of
"hello"                                      ; characters into a string.
```

```
> (coerce "hello" 'list)                     ; Converts a string into a
(#\h #\e #\l #\l #\o)                         ; list of characters.
```

```
> (string 'rubbish)                          ; Converts a symbol into
"RUBBISH"                                     ; a string.
```

```
> (intern "GARBAGE")                         ; Converts a string into
GARBAGE                                       ; a symbol.
```

It is also possible to use strings as simulated input to the LISP reader. The function read-from-string takes a string as argument and returns two values: the first object read and the string index where it stopped reading.

```
> (read-from-string "a")                     ; A string becomes a sym-
                                             bol.
A
1
```

```
> (read-from-string "a b")              ;  Only the first object is read.
A
2

> (read-from-string "(setf a 8)")       ;  A string becomes a list.
(SETF A 8)
10
```

6.4 Sequences

The alert reader may have noticed that some of the functions used on strings are similar, if not identical, to certain list functions.

```
> (length '(a b c))
3

> (length "abc")
3
```

This similarity is not a coincidence. Both lists and strings are *sequences* of objects. As such, there are many functions that are common to both. The Common LISP language designers have defined a collection of functions that work more or less the same on both lists and strings.

This approach is analogous to having arithmetic functions that work the same for both floating point numbers and integers.

Some of the string functions introduced earlier in this chapter are actually generic sequence functions that can also be used with lists.

```
> (concatenate 'list '(a) '(b) '(c))
(A B C)

> (elt '(1 2 3) 0)
1

> (subseq '(0 1 2 3 4 5 6) 3)
(3 4 5 6)

> (subseq '(0 1 2 3 4 5 6) 3 5)
(3 4)

> (position 'x '(w x y z))
1
```

```
> (find 'x '(w x y z))
X
```

```
> (map 'list #'1+ '(0 1 2 3 4))
(1 2 3 4 5)
```

Similarly, some of the list functions given in chapter 3 are general sequence functions that can also be used with strings.

```
> (reverse "abc")
"cba"
```

```
> (some #'upper-case-p "hello")      ; Is there an uppercase letter?
NIL
```

```
> (some #'lower-case-p "hello")     ; Is there a lowercase letter?
T
```

```
> (every #'lower-case-p "hello")     ; Are all characters lower case?
T
```

```
> (notany #'upper-case-p "hello")    ; Are no characters upper case?
T
```

```
> (notevery #'upper-case-p "hello") ; Is some character not upper case?
T
```

```
> (defvar s "hello")
S
```

```
> s
"hello"
```

```
> (remove #\o s)                     ; remove returns a copy.
"hell"
```

```
> s
"hello"
```

```
> (delete #\o s)                     ; delete is destructive.
"hell"
```

```
> s
"hell"
```

Both `elt` and `subseq` can be used with `setf`.

```
> (setf x "abcdefg")                    ;  First we try strings.
X

> (elt x 3)
#\d

> (setf (elt x 3) #\q)
#\q

> x
"abcqefg"

> (subseq x 3)
"qefg"

> (setf (subseq x 3) "xyz")
"xyz"

> x
"abcxyzg"

> (setf y '(a b c d e f g))             ;  Now do the same with lists.
Y

> y
(A B C D E F G)

> (elt y 3)
D

> (setf (elt y 3) 'q)
Q

> y
(A B C Q E F G)

> (subseq y 3)
(Q E F G)

> (setf (subseq y 3) '(x y z))
(X Y Z)
```

```
> y
(A B C X Y Z G)
```

We now lift the curtain to reveal an additional set of functions for sequences, that is, for both lists and strings. Some of these functions make a copy of a sequence; others destructively alter the given sequence. Generally, but not always, the destructive functions begin with the letter **n**.

```
> x                          ; This is our old value of x.
"abcxyzg"


> (setf x2 (copy-seq x))     ; x2 is a copy of x.
X2


> x2
"abcxyzg"


> (nreverse x2)              ; nreverse is a destructive version of reverse.
"gzyxcba"                    ; It does not make a copy.


> x                          ; x has not been changed.
"abcxyzg"


> x2                         ; x2 has.
"gzyxcba"


> (fill x2 #\z)              ; fill replaces every element of x2 with #\z.
"zzzzzzz"


> x2                         ; fill is destructive.
"zzzzzzz"
```

- (make-sequence type size) creates a new sequence of length size and optionally fills it with the item following the keyword :initial-element.

```
> (setf l1 (make-sequence 'list 10 :initial-element nil))
L1


> l1                         ; l1 is a 10-element list of NILs.
(NIL NIL NIL NIL NIL NIL NIL NIL NIL NIL)


> (replace x2 "123")         ; replace destructively writes the second sequence
"123zzzz"                    ; over the first sequence.
```

```
> (remove #\z x2)            ;  remove works on a copy.
"123"

> x2
"123zzzz"

> (delete #\z x2)            ;  delete is destructive.
"123"

> x2
"123"

> x
"abcxyzg"

> (replace x "ggg")
"gggxyzg"

> x
"gggxyzg"

> (remove-duplicates x)      ;  remove-duplicates works on a copy.
"xyzg"

> x
"gggxyzg"

> (delete-duplicates x)      ;  delete-duplicates is destructive.
"xyzg"

> x
"xyzg"

> l1                         ;  Now we try some lists.
(NIL NIL NIL NIL NIL NIL NIL NIL NIL NIL)

> (replace l1 '(1 2 3 4))
(1 2 3 4 NIL NIL NIL NIL NIL NIL)

> (delete-duplicates l1)
(1 2 3 4 NIL)
```

```
> 11
(1 2 3 4 NIL)
```

- (substitute old new sequence) replaces occurrences of old with new in
  the given sequence.

```
> (substitute 0 2 11)
(1 0 3 4 NIL)

> 11
(1 2 3 4 NIL)

> (nsubstitute 0 2 11)        ;  nsubstitute is destructive.
(1 0 3 4 NIL)

> 11
(1 0 3 4 NIL)

> x
"xyzg"

> (substitute #\a #\x x)       ;  They also work on strings.
"ayzg"

> x
"xyzg"

> (nsubstitute #\a #\x x)
"ayzg"

> x
"ayzg"
```

Those were functions for modifying sequences. We now look at functions for examining sequences.

```
> x
"ayzg"
```

- (count item sequence) returns a non-negative integer indicating the number of times item occurs in the given sequence.

```
> (count #\a x)
1
```

```
> (count #\space x)
0

> (count 1 '(1 1 2 2 3 3))
2
```

- (mismatch sequence1 sequence2) returns NIL if the sequences match; else, the position at which they first do not match.

```
> (mismatch x2 "123")
NIL

> (mismatch x2 "1234")
3

> (mismatch x2 "abc")
0

> (mismatch '(1 2 3) '(1 b c))
1
```

- (search sequence1 sequence2) is sort of the opposite of mismatch. If sequence1 matches some part of sequence2, then search returns the position at which the match begins. Otherwise, search returns NIL.

```
> (search x2 "123")
0

> (search x2 "1234")
0

> (search x2 "abc")
NIL

> (search '(1 2 3) '(1 b c))
NIL
```

One of the most common duties of a computer is sorting. LISP provides a convenient sort function for sequences.

- (sort sequence predicate) returns an ordered version of sequence, using predicate as the comparison predicate.

```
> x2
"123"
```

```
> (sort x2 #'char>)
"321"

> x2                              ; sort is destructive.
"321"

> (sort x2 #'char<)
"123"

> x2
"123"

> (setf l2 '(2 5 3 6 7 1 3 7))   ; Now we shall try to sort a list.
L2

> (sort l2 #'<)
(1 2 3 3 5 6 7 7)

> l2                              ; Something isn't quite right here.
(2 3 3 5 6 7 7)

> (sort l2 #'>)
(7 7 6 5 3 3 2)

> l2                              ; Mother of pearl! What's going on?
(2)
```

The problem is that **sort** is destructive in the worst way for lists. In the example above, the list L2 started with an initial cons cell whose **car** was 2. The value of the symbol L2 was a pointer to that cons cell. After each sort, the symbol L2 continued to point to that cons cell; however, that cell no longer remained at the front of the list.

The lesson is: When sorting lists, use a copy of the list.

There are two final sequence functions: **merge** and **reduce**.

```
;  (merge result-type seq1 seq2 predicate) interleaves two sequences.
> (merge 'list '(1 3 5 7 9) '(2 4 6 8 10) #'<)
(1 2 3 4 5 6 7 8 9 10)

> (merge 'list '(4 3 2 1) '(1 2 3 4) #'<)
(1 2 3 4 3 2 1 4)

> (merge 'string "aceh" "bdfg" #'char<)
"abcdefgh"
```

The `reduce` function takes two arguments: a function and a sequence. The functional argument must be a binary function, that is, a function of two arguments. `reduce` combines all the elements of the sequence by successive applications of the function.

```
> (reduce #'+ '(1 2 3 4 5))       ; Like (+ 1 2 3 4 5).
15

> (reduce #'min '(1 2 3 4 5))     ; Like (min 1 2 3 4 5).
1

> (reduce #'max '(1 2 3 4 5))     ; Like (max 1 2 3 4 5).
5

> (reduce #'list '(1 2 3 4 5))
((((1 2) 3) 4) 5)
```

This concludes the sequence functions. However, we are not finished with sequences. We shall later see that the LISP `vector` and `bit-vector` types are sequences as well.

6.5 Example: String Searching

One common task in word processing is searching for an occurrence of a specific string in a lengthy text. For example, you may have several files in a directory and one of them contains the phrase "list processing". To find the file which contains that phrase, you can use a string searching routine such as the following.

LISP has a built-in `search` function for sequences described above. However, for demonstration, we shall now define a specific search predicate for strings.

```
> (string-searchp "the" "now is the winter of our discontent")
T

> (string-searchp "The" "now is the winter of our discontent")
NIL                             ; Capital The is not in the string.
```

`string-searchp` behaves as follows.

- First, it makes sure the input arguments are strings. If not, it signals an error.

- If both strings are empty, they match.

- If only one string is empty, they do not match.

- If the first character of the pattern is not found in the text, there is no match.

- If the first character matches, see if the remainder matches at that position.

- Otherwise, start search again at new position.

```
(defun string-searchp (pattern text)
  (cond ((null (and (stringp pattern)
                    (stringp text)))
         (list 'error-non-strings pattern text))
        ((and (string= "" pattern)
              (string= "" text))
         t)
        ((or  (string= "" pattern)
              (string= "" text))
         nil)
        (t
         (let ((index (position (char pattern 0) text)))
           (cond ((null index) nil)
                 ((string= pattern
                           (subseq text
                                   index (+ index (length pattern))))
                  t)
                 (t (string-searchp pattern
                                    (subseq text (1+ index)))))))))
```

6.6   Example: Spelling Correction

We now present a program that is more complicated than anything given so far. Even though this program is larger, it has a clear and coherent structure which helps in understanding how the code works and simplifies the testing of the program by providing discrete modules to test separately. It illustrates how large LISP programs are put together.

Many programs, now available as part of word processing packages and related desktop applications, check and correct spelling. These programs usually consist of a large dictionary of common English words and a program to match words in the text with words in the dictionary. If a word in the text does not match a dictionary entry, then the word is probably misspelled.

Once you know that a word is misspelled, you need to find the *correct* spelling. Here is a method for proposing possible correct spellings by looking at minor variations of the misspelled word.

The function spell-match tries to correct the spelling of a word so that it matches one of the words from the dictionary. The function uses four methods for respelling a word:

1. *Letter deletion.* The function will sequentially delete each letter of the word and try to match the resulting word (which is one letter shorter) against the

dictionary. For example, commputer would become ommputer, then cmmputer, and finally, computer, which would presumably match.

2. *Letter transposition.* Typists commonly transpose adjacent letters. The spell-match function should check for this condition by swapping each adjacent pair of letters in the word in sequence. For example, copmuter would become ocpmuter, then cpomuter, and finally, computer.

3. *Letter duplication.* The function doubles each letter in sequence to see if that results in a correct spelling. This is a special case of the next method.

4. *Letter insertion.* Often a single letter is left out. The spell-match function will go through the word sequentially and insert all possible letters at each position of the word. Note that there are many more combinations using this technique (* 26 (+ 1 (string-length word))) than the previous three techniques combined. Therefore, for efficiency, this method should be the last resort — used only if the other three fail.

Here is how it works.

```
> (defun tag-word (word)          ; Function to mark dictionary
    (setf (get word 'ISA-WORD) T) ; words as correctly spelled.
    word)
TAG-WORD

;   Our demonstration dictionary will be quite small, just these six words.
> (mapcar #'tag-word
'(commuter computer computation computing compute computers))
(COMMUTER COMPUTER COMPUTATION COMPUTING COMPUTE COMPUTERS)

> (spell-match 'computter)        ; Using letter deletion.
COMPUTER

> (spell-match 'computtaion)      ; Using letter transposition.
COMPUTATION

> (spell-match 'comuter)          ; Using letter duplication.
COMMUTER

> (spell-match 'computin)         ; Using letter insertion.
COMPUTING
```

Now we present the code for spell-match, except for two functions, string-insert and string-swap, which you should define yourself (see exercise 6.8.6). In these functions, we assume that the words have all uppercase letters.

```
;;  spell-match is the main function.  It first checks to see if its
;;  argument is a symbol, in which case it is converted to a string.
;;  It then checks for an empty string and a correctly spelled word.
;;  If those tests both fail, it then tries its spelling correction
;;  techniques.

(defun spell-match (word)
  (cond ((symbolp word) (setf word (string word))))
  (let ((word-length (length word)))
    (cond ((string= "" word) nil)
          ((sm-check word))
          ((sm-deletion word word-length))
          ((sm-transposition word (- word-length 1)))
          ((sm-double word (- word-length 1)))
          ((sm-insertion word word-length))
          (t nil))))


;;  Membership check.
;;  Checks for the ISA-WORD property for the given word.
(defun sm-check (word)
  (cond ((stringp word) (setf word (intern word))))
  (cond ((get word 'ISA-WORD) word)
        (t nil)))


;;  Case 1: Deletes letters.
(defun sm-deletion (word-string index)
  (cond ((zerop index) nil)
        ((let ((new-word
                 (concatenate 'string
                   (subseq word-string 0 (- index 1))
                   (subseq word-string index))))
           (sm-check new-word)))
        (t (sm-deletion word-string (- index 1)))))

;;  Case 2: Transposes letters using the string-swap function.
(defun sm-transposition (word-string index)
  (cond ((zerop index) nil)
        ((sm-check (string-swap word-string index (- index 1))))
        (t (sm-transposition word-string (- index 1)))))
```

```
;;  Case 3: Doubles letters using the string-insert function.
(defun sm-double (word-string index)
  (cond ((minusp index) nil)
        ((sm-check (string-insert word-string
                                  (elt word-string index)
                                  index)))
        (t (sm-double word-string (- index 1)))))
```

```
;;  Case 4: Inserts letters using the string-insert function.
(defun sm-insertion (word-string index)
  (cond ((minusp index) nil)
        ((sm-insertion-check word-string index #\A))
        (t (sm-insertion word-string (- index 1)))))
```

```
;;  Recursively goes through entire alphabet inserting characters at
;;  index position; checks each resulting word.
(defun sm-insertion-check (word-string index new-char)
  (cond ((char> new-char #\Z) nil)
        ((sm-check (string-insert word-string new-char index) ))
        (t (sm-insertion-check word-string index
                               (incr-char new-char)))))
```

```
;;  Gets the next character, according to the ASCII code.
(defun incr-char (character)
  (code-char (1+ (char-code character))))
```

6.7 Advanced Subjects

This chapter has the following advanced topics.

- Bits Supporting Characters

- More Comparison Predicates

- String Trimming

- if and if-not Functions

- More Sorting

6.7.1 Bits Supporting Characters

Designers of computer keyboards have pushed the envelope of the ASCII character set. In addition to shift and control keys, PCs have ALT keys, and Macintosh

Key	Keyword	Constant	Decimal	Binary
Control	:control	char-control-bit	1	1
Meta	:meta	char-meta-bit	2	10
Super	:super	char-super-bit	4	100
Hyper	:hyper	char-hyper-bit	8	1000
Limit		char-bits-limit	16	10000

Table 6.2: Character Bits Attribute Weights

computers have command and option keys. LISP Machines have hyper, meta, and super keys. This latter terminology is adopted in Common LISP in extending its character set.

These keys are shift keys. That is, the programmer uses them in combinations with existing keys. Each new shift key does not add one more character, but it *doubles* the number of characters.

These shift keys can be used in combinations. Thus, all of the following are legitimate LISP character extensions of lowercase a. Many other combinations are possible.

```
#\Meta-a
#\Hyper-a
#\Super-a
#\Meta-Control-a
#\Meta-Hyper-a
#\Meta-Super-a
#\Control-Meta-Hyper-a
#\Control-Meta-Super-a
```

These extended characters are implemented with extra bits. That is, characters beyond the normal ASCII set have a *bits attribute* that encodes which of these other keys are active. Table 6.2 lists the keys and constants associated with the bits attribute.

The Common LISP committee voted not to require implementations to include bits attribute functions and constants. However, the programmer is likely to ∞ ⇒ find these features in her own LISP.

Below we explore the bits attribute of a character with four functions:

- (make-char character [bits]) creates a character with the given bits set, if present.

- (char-bits character) returns the bits attribute of the given character.

- (char-bit character bit) is a predicate that tests whether the given bit is set for the character.

- (set-char-bit character bit value) returns a copy of the character with
  the given bit set to the value. In some implementations, the character may   ⇐ ∞
  be directly modified, or the programmer may use `setf` with the `char-bit`
  function.

```
> (setf x (make-char #\a 7))    ; Creates a character.
#\CONTROL-META-SUPER-a


> (char-bits x)                 ; Examines the bits attribute.
7


> (char-bit x :control)         ; Is the control bit set?
T


> (char-bit x :meta)            ; Is the meta bit set?
T


> (setf y (set-char-bit x :meta nil))
#\CONTROL-SUPER-a


> y                             ; y has no meta bit set.
#\CONTROL-SUPER-a


> (char-bits y)
5


> x                             ; x is unchanged.
#\CONTROL-META-SUPER-a
```

As stated above, these new characters are extensions of the regular ASCII set. The
constant `char-code-limit` indicates how many distinct characters are provided
by the implementation's encoding. The `char-int` function will return the full   ⇐ ∞
integer encoding for extended characters, and the `char-code` function will reveal the
root ASCII code. The `int-char` function will convert an integer into a character,
extended or otherwise. The `digit-char` function converts digits into characters
with the default radix of 10.

```
> char-code-limit
256


> (char-int x)                  ; The decimal encoding of x.
1889


> (char-int y)
1377
```

```
> (char-int #\a)              ; ASCII a.
97

> (char-code x)               ; x is an extension of a.
97

> (char-code y)               ; So is y.
97

> (int-char 98)               ; Adds one to a.
#\b

> (int-char 1890)             ; Adds one to x.
#\CONTROL-META-SUPER-b

> (int-char 1378)             ; Adds one to y.
#\CONTROL-SUPER-b

> (digit-char 8)              ; There is a character for decimal 8.
#\8

> (digit-char 10)             ; There is no single character for 10,
NIL

> (digit-char 10 16)          ; unless you are in hexadecimal.
#\A
```

As in a Damon Runyon story, some characters have names. The functions char-name and name-char convert characters to their names, and vice versa.

```
> (char-name x)               ; There is no name for our new character.
NIL

> (char-name #\space)
"space"

> (char-name (int-char 10))
"newline"

> (name-char 'newline)        ; Argument is a symbol or string.
#\newline

> (name-char "space")
#\space
```

(predicate #\B arg2)	arg2					
	#\a	#\A	#\b	#\B	#\c	#\C
char=	NIL	NIL	NIL	T	NIL	NIL
char-equal	NIL	NIL	T	T	NIL	NIL
char<	T	NIL	T	NIL	T	T
char-lessp	NIL	NIL	NIL	NIL	T	T
char<	T	NIL	T	NIL	T	T
char-greaterp	T	T	NIL	NIL	NIL	NIL
char/=	T	T	T	NIL	T	T
char-not-equal	T	T	NIL	NIL	T	T
char>=	NIL	T	NIL	T	NIL	NIL
char-not-lessp	T	T	T	T	NIL	NIL
char<=	T	NIL	T	T	T	T
char-not-greaterp	NIL	NIL	T	T	T	T

Table 6.3: Character Comparison Predicates

```
> (name-char "a")
NIL
```

Just as modern personal computers have extra keys, they also have extra fonts. In the old days, computer screens were limited to a single, fixed-width font. Some screens did not support lowercase letters. Today, we have a vast selection of fonts. Most applications permit the user to change fonts with just the click of a mouse. Font attributes can include the font family (such as Courier or Times Roman), the size (such as 10 point or 12 point), the style (such as italic, bold, or underlined), and the color.

The initial version of Common LISP adopted a numeric coding scheme for fonts. However, the Common LISP committee has voted to eliminate this requirement and leave it up to implementors to decide how to encode fonts. The programmer is likely to find a more sensible method of specifying fonts.

6.7.2 More Comparison Predicates

When comparing characters and strings, the programmer has a number of additional comparison predicates at her disposal. In the case of both characters and strings, there are two sets of predicates. One is case-sensitive and the other is not. The case sensitive predicates use the symbolic suffixes, for example, = and <, and the case insensitive predicates use words, for example, equal and lessp.

Table 6.3 illustrates both sets of character comparison predicates, and table 6.4 demonstrates the similar set of string comparison predicates.

(predicate "BETA" arg2)	arg2				
	"ALPHA"	"beta"	"Beta"	"BETA"	"GAMMA"
string=	NIL	NIL	NIL	T	NIL
string-equal	NIL	T	T	T	NIL
string<	NIL	0	1	NIL	0
string-lessp	NIL	NIL	NIL	NIL	0
string<	NIL	0	1	NIL	0
string-greaterp	0	NIL	NIL	NIL	NIL
string/=	0	0	1	NIL	0
string-not-equal	0	NIL	NIL	NIL	0
string>=	0	NIL	NIL	4	NIL
string-not-lessp	0	4	4	4	NIL
string<=	NIL	0	1	4	0
string-not-greaterp	NIL	4	4	4	0

Table 6.4: String Comparison Predicates

We note that the character predicates take a variable number of arguments.

```
> (char= #\a)              ; Not too interesting.
T
```

```
> (char< #\a #\b #\c #\d)  ; All characters are in increasing order.
T
```

```
> (char< #\a #\b #\b #\d)
NIL
```

```
> (char<= #\a #\b #\b #\d)  ; All characters are in nondecreasing order.
T
```

```
> (char<= #\a #\b #\B #\d)  ; This comparison is case sensitive.
NIL
```

```
> (char-not-greaterp #\a #\b #\B #\d)  ; This comparison is not.
T
```

The string predicates exhibit another contrast. For string= and string-equal, the result is just T or NIL. However, for the remaining predicates, the result is either NIL when the comparison fails or an integer index indicating the position at which the strings differ. Note that this index is zero-based.

Furthermore, all of the string comparison predicates have keyword arguments specifying optional beginning and end positions for the comparison in the first and second strings. These keywords are `:start1`, `:end1`, `:start2`, and `:end2`. We provide examples of the use of some of these keywords.

```
> (setf u "UNITED" s "STATES" us "United States")
"United States"

> (string-equal s us)
NIL

> (string-equal s us :start2 7)       ; Case-insensitive comparison.
T

> (string= s us :start2 7)            ; Case-sensitive comparison.
NIL

> (string= (string-capitalize s) us :start2 7)
T

> (string-equal u us)
NIL

> (string-equal u us :end2 6)         ; OK if us ends at position 6.
T

> (string-equal u us :end2 7)
NIL
```

6.7.3 String Trimming

LISP provides three related functions for filtering the ends of strings: `string-trim`, `string-left-trim`, and `string-right-trim`. They each take two arguments: a sequence of characters and the string from which the characters are to be removed. Here are examples.

```
> (setf x "  LISP is a *!?* fine language.!!! * ")
"  LISP is a *!?* fine language.!!! * "

> (string-left-trim '(#\space) x) ; Removes spaces from the left.
"LISP is a *!?* fine language.!!! * "

> (string-right-trim " *!" x)         ; Trims space, *, and ! from the right.
"  LISP is a *!?* fine language."

> (string-trim " *!?" x)              ; Trims space, *, !, and ? from both ends.
"LISP is a *!?* fine language."
```

```
> (string-trim "*!?" x)             ; Trims *, !, and ? from both ends.
"  LISP is a *!?* fine language.!!! * "
```

In the last example, nothing gets trimmed because we omitted space from our bag of characters to be trimmed and the string had spaces at both ends. We can use either a list or a string here to specify the characters to be trimmed.

6.7.4   if and if-not Functions

Many of the functions that operate specifically on lists or generally on sequences have functional arguments. Typically, these functions are predicates that select or exclude elements from the list or sequence.

For example, we can use the regular `count` to find the number of elements in a list which a given number is less than or not less than.

```
> (setf l '(1 2 3 4 5 6 7))
(1 2 3 4 5 6 7)

> (count 3 l :test #'<)
4

> (count 3 l :test-not #'<)
3
```

LISP provides the programmer with an alternative construction for `count` and other functions. The functions `count-if` and `count-if-not` take two arguments: a predicate and a sequence.

```
> (count-if #'oddp l)       ; How many elements are odd?
4

> (count-if-not #'oddp l)   ; How many elements are not odd?
3
```

LISP has a dozen functions which have both `-if` and `-if-not` forms. These are listed in table 6.5 with their arguments. We note that many of these functions have optional arguments as well.

The options are specified by keywords, as follows:

- `:start` is a positive integer indicating the first element of the subsequence. It defaults to zero.

- `:end` is a non-negative integer indicating the last element of the subsequence to examine, where the first element is zero. The default is NIL, indicating that the entire sequence should be included.

Function	if	if-not	Arguments
assoc	assoc-if	assoc-if-not	pred a-list
count	count-if	count-if-not	test seq [options]
delete	delete-if	delete-if-not	test seq [options+]
find	find-if	find-if-not	test seq [options]
member	member-if	member-if-not	pred list [key]
nsubst	nsubst-if	nsubst-if-not	newitem pred tree [key]
nsubstitute	nsubstitute-if	nsubstitute-if-not	newitem pred tree [options+]
position	position-if	position-if-not	test seq [options]
rassoc	rassoc-if	rassoc-if-not	pred a-list
remove	remove-if	remove-if-not	test seq [options+]
subst	subst-if	subst-if-not	newitem pred tree [key]
substitute	substitute-if	substitute-if-not	newitem pred tree [options+]

Table 6.5: if and if-not Functions

- :key is a function to be applied to each element prior to testing. It defaults to the identity function. Some functions in table 6.5 have only this option, as indicated by the argument labeled "[key]".

- :from-end is a boolean value which, if non-NIL, specifies that the function should begin at the end. The default is NIL. We note that :from-end can have no effect with the function count but matters in other cases.

- :count is a positive integer providing a ceiling on the number of elements affected. This option is available only for those functions in table 6.5 indicated by the argument labeled "[options+]".

Here are examples that illustrate various function and keyword combinations.

```
> (count-if #'oddp 1 :start 2)      ; Starts at the second element.
3

> (count-if-not #'oddp 1 :start 2)
2

> (count-if-not #'oddp 1 :end 2)    ; Ends at the second element.
1

> (member-if #'oddp 1)              ; Is there any odd element?
(1 2 3 4 5 6 7)

> (member-if-not #'oddp 1)          ; Is there any element not odd?
(2 3 4 5 6 7)
```

```
> (member-if #'oddp l :key #'1+)      ;  Adds 1 to each element, then checks.
(2 3 4 5 6 7)

> (setf s "abcdefg123")
"abcdefg123"

> (count-if #'upper-case-p s)         ;  How many uppercase letters in s?
0

> (count-if #'upper-case-p s :key #'char-upcase)
7

> (position-if #'digit-char-p s)      ;  Where is the first digit?
7

> (position-if #'digit-char-p s :from-end t)
9

> (remove-if #'digit-char-p s)        ;  Removes the digits from s.
"abcdefg"

> s                                   ;  They are still there.
"abcdefg123"

> (delete-if #'digit-char-p s)        ;  Removes digits with extreme prejudice.
"abcdefg"

> s
"abcdefg"

> (delete-if #'characterp s :count 2) ;  Removes up to two characters.
"cdefg"

> (delete-if #'characterp s :count 2 :from-end t)
"cde"
```

We use association lists instead of sequences with the assoc and rassoc. They have no keyword options.

```
> (setf alist (pairlis '(john mary joe jane) '(19 20 21 22)))
((JANE . 22) (JOE . 21) (MARY . 20) (JOHN . 19))

> (assoc-if #'symbolp alist)
(JANE . 22)
```

```
> (rassoc-if #'oddp alist)
(JOE . 21)

> (rassoc-if-not #'oddp alist)
(JANE . 22)
```

6.7.5 More Sorting

We have discussed the problem associated with the destructive `sort` function. There other aspects of `sort`: a feature and a potential problem.

First, the feature. If we wish to sort a sequence of items but compare only parts of the items, we can use the `:key` keyword argument to specify a selection function. For example, here we have a list comprising pairs of names and ages. We can sort by name, using the `car` selector, or by age, using the `cadr` selector, together with the appropriate comparison predicate.

```
> (setf pals '(("John" 23) ("Mary" 22) ("Jane" 22) ("John" 21)
("Mary" 20)))
(("John" 23) ("Mary" 22) ("Jane" 22) ("John" 21) ("Mary" 20))

> (sort (copy-list pals) #'string-lessp :key #'car)
(("Jane" 22) ("John" 23) ("John" 21) ("Mary" 22) ("Mary" 20))

> (sort (copy-list pals) #'< :key #'cadr)
(("Mary" 20) ("John" 21) ("Mary" 22) ("Jane" 22) ("John" 23))
```

Second, we note that our list of `pals` contains two Johns, two Marys, and two persons aged 22. The Johns and Marys get sorted together with the name sort, and the 22 year olds get sorted together in the age sort. However, the `sort` function does not guarantee that the order of matching items in the sorted list will be the same as their order in the original list.

In these examples, the order is preserved, but in general, the programmer cannot depend on this property unless she uses the `stable-sort` function. `stable-sort` is identical to `sort` in every way except that it guarantees to maintain the order of matching items from the original input.

```
> (stable-sort (copy-list pals) #'string-lessp :key #'car)
(("Jane" 22) ("John" 23) ("John" 21) ("Mary" 22) ("Mary" 20))

> (stable-sort (copy-list pals) #'< :key #'cadr)
(("Mary" 20) ("John" 21) ("Mary" 22) ("Jane" 22) ("John" 23))
```

In some implementations, `stable-sort` may be slightly less efficient than `sort`, albeit more reliable.

6.8   Exercises

6.8.1   String Drill [3]

Evaluate the following expressions, first by hand, then with the help of the LISP interpreter.

```
(defvar x "the rain in Spain")
(defvar y "falls mainly on the plain.")
(stringp x)
(alpha-char-p (char y 0))
(upper-case-p (elt x 13))
(char< (elt x 7) (elt y 7))
(string= x x)
(string= x y)
(string= x "x")
(char-downcase #\T)
(char-upcase #\T)
(char-code #\newline)
(char-code #\space)
(coerce '(#\A #\space #\l #\i #\s #\t #\newline) 'string)
(coerce "No Exit." 'list)
(intern (string-upcase "Hello"))
(string (car '(concatenate 'string "this" " and " "that")))
```

6.8.2   String Functions [4*]

Write definitions for the following four string functions: `lastchar`, `capitalize`, `string-equalp`, and `string-lessp`.

```
> (lastchar "a string")        ; Returns the last character in a string.
#\g
```

```
> (capitalize "lisp")          ; Converts the first character in a string
"Lisp"                         ; to a capital.
```

```
> (string-equalp "LISP" "lisp") ; Compares two strings without regard to
T                               ; to upper- or lowercase (already exists).
```

```
> (string-equalp "LISP" "LISS")
NIL
```

```
> (string-lessp "alpha" "beta") ; True if two strings are in
T                               ; alphabetic order (already exists).
```

```
> (string-lessp "beta" "alpha")
NIL

> (string-lessp "alphabet" "alphabetize")
T

> (string-lessp "alphabetize" "alphabet" )
NIL
```

6.8.3   Sorting Lists [6*]

One very common and important computer application is sorting. The subject of sorting is a well-established discipline in itself, and the details are far beyond the scope of this book. The reader is referred to [Knuth, 1978] for a wealth of information.

There are many types of sorting routines. LISP has a built-in **sort** function, demonstrated earlier in the chapter.

In this exercise, we present a *merge sort* program for sorting lists of items. In our examples, we sort lists of either numbers or characters. This same method could be extended to sort other objects, such as symbols and strings. The idea behind this algorithm is to break up the list to be sorted into smaller lists that are sorted, and then merge the small lists back together again, maintaining the proper ordering.

Below, we present most of the functions required, except the central **lmerge** function. The reader must provide this function. *Do not use* **merge** *in defining* **lmerge**. *Write* **lmerge** *from scratch.*

The function should handle two data types: numbers and characters. We give examples of both **lmerge** and **msort**.

```
(defun msort (l)
  (sort2 l nil))

(defun sort2 (l tmplist)
  (cond ((null l) (sort3 tmplist nil))
        (t (sort2 (cdr l)
                  (sort-add (list (car l)) tmplist)))))

(defun sort3 (l tmplist)
  (cond ((null l) tmplist)
        (t (sort3 (cdr l) (lmerge (car l) tmplist)))))
```

```
(defun sort-add (x tmplist)
  (cond ((null tmplist) (list x))
        ((null (car tmplist)) (cons x (cdr tmplist)))
        (t
         (cons nil (sort-add (lmerge x (car tmplist))
                             (cdr tmplist))))))
```

```
> (lmerge '(2 7 9) '(1 8))
(1 2 7 8 9)
```

```
> (lmerge '(2 7 9) '())
(2 7 9)
```

```
> (lmerge '(9) '(5))
(5 9)
```

```
> (lmerge '(#\a #\c) '(#\b #\d))
(#\a #\b #\c #\d)
```

```
> (msort '(3 2 5 1))
(1 2 3 5)
```

```
> (msort '(#\x #\a #\d))
(#\a #\d #\x)
```

6.8.4 Roman Numeral Characters [4*]

Building on the roman-to-decimal function in section 4.3, write a function that converts a Roman numeral string into a decimal number.

```
> (roman-char-to-decimal "MCXX")
1120
```

```
> (roman-char-to-decimal "mlxvi")
1066
```

6.8.5 string-reverse [3*]

Write a function string-reverse that returns a backwards version of a given string. (Do not use reverse or nreverse.)

```
> (string-reverse "hello")
"olleh"
```

```
> (string-reverse "a man a plan a canal panama")
"amanap lanac a nalp a nam a"

> (string-reverse "a fool a tool a pool loop a loot a loof a")
"a fool a tool a pool loop a loot a loof a"
```

6.8.6 Spelling Correction [4*]

Define string-insert and string-swap, which are used in the spell-match program defined above. Note that string-insert should be able to insert a character in a string at any point, including the front and end of a string. If an index is out of bounds, then string-insert should return an error.

```
> (string-insert "hello" #\X 0)
"Xhello"

> (string-insert "hello" #\X 1)
"hXello"

> (string-insert "hello" #\X 4)
"hellXo"

> (string-insert "hello" #\X 5)
"helloX"

> (string-insert "hello" #\X 6)
ERROR-IN-STRING-INSERT

> (string-insert "hello" #\X -1)
ERROR-IN-STRING-INSERT

> (string-swap "hello there" 3 5)
"hel olthere"

> (string-swap "hello there" 5 3)
"hel olthere"

> (string-swap "hello there" 5 9)
"hellorthe e"

> (string-swap "hello there" 5 19)
ERROR-IN-STRING-SWAP
```

6.8.7   Expletive Not Deleted [4*]

Consider the following.

```
> (defvar q '(1 2 3 4 5))
Q

> (remove 1 q)            ; remove is not destructive.
(2 3 4 5)

> q                       ; So far, so good.
(1 2 3 4 5)

> (delete 1 q)            ; delete is destructive.
(2 3 4 5)

> q
(1 2 3 4 5)               ; !#@?*#  not deleted!
```

What is going on? Is delete destructive or not? Shouldn't q now have the value (2 3 4 5) ?

6.9   Chapter Summary

- The following LISP object types are introduced in this chapter. Indentation indicates subtypes.

```
character
    standard-char
sequence
    string
```

- Strings are composed of characters linked together, just as lists may be composed of objects linked together.

- Strings in LISP are delimited by double quotes, for example, "a string".

- Characters in LISP are denoted by the character itself preceded by # and \, for example, #\A.

- The function (make-string size :initial-element) creates a string of given size.

- String and character predicates:

```
(characterp object)
(stringp  object)
(alpha-char-p character)
(digit-char-p character radix)
(alphanumericp character)
(upper-case-p character)
(lower-case-p character)
(both-case-p character)
(graphic-char-p character)
(standard-char-p character)
(char= {character}+)
(char< {character}+)
(char> {character}+)
(char/= {character}+)
(char>= {character}+)
(char<= {character}+)
(string= string1 string2)
```

- String, character, and sequence operations:

```
(char-downcase character)
(char-upcase character)
(length sequence)
(char string index)
(concatenate 'string {sequence}*)
(elt sequence integer)
(subseq sequence start [end])
(position item sequence)
(string-upcase string)
(string-downcase string)
(string-capitalize string)
(map result-type function {sequence}+)
```

- Conversion functions:

```
(char-code character)
(code-char integer)
(coerce object type)
(string symbol)
(string character)
(intern string)
(read-from-string string)
```

- The following sequence functions can be used on either strings or lists.

```
(copy-seq sequence)
(length sequence)
(reverse sequence)
(nreverse sequence)                           ;  Destructive.
(make-sequence type size :initial-element)
(some predicate {sequence}+)
(every predicate {sequence}+)
(notany predicate {sequence}+)
(notevery predicate {sequence}+)
(reduce function {sequence}+))
(fill sequence item)                          ;  Destructive.
(replace sequence1 sequence2)                 ;  Destructive.
(remove item sequence)
(delete item sequence)                        ;  Destructive.
(remove-duplicates sequence)
(delete-duplicates sequence)                  ;  Destructive.
(substitute newitem olditem sequence)
(nsubstitute newitem olditem sequence)  ;  Destructive.
(find item sequence)
(position item sequence)
(count item sequence)
(mismatch sequence1 sequence2)
(search sequence1 sequence2)
(sort sequence predicate)                         ;  Destructive.
(merge result-type seq1 seq2 predicate)           ;  Destructive.
```

- LISP provides character comparison predicates that are case insensitive.

```
(char-equal {character}+)
(char-lessp {character}+)
(char-greaterp {character}+)
(char-not-equal {character}+)
(char-not-lessp {character}+)
(char-not-greaterp {character}+)
```

- LISP provides string comparison predicates that are case sensitive.

```
(string= str1 str2 &key :start1 :end1 :start2 :end2)
(string< str1 str2 &key :start1 :end1 :start2 :end2)
(string> str1 str2 &key :start1 :end1 :start2 :end2)
(string⁻ str1 str2 &key :start1 :end1 :start2 :end2)
(string>= str1 str2 &key :start1 :end1 :start2 :end2)
(string<= str1 str2 &key :start1 :end1 :start2 :end2)
```

- LISP provides string comparison predicates that are case insensitive.

```
(string-equal str1 str2 &key :start1 :end1 :start2 :end2)
(string-lessp str1 str2 &key :start1 :end1 :start2 :end2)
(string-greaterp str1 str2 &key :start1 :end1 :start2 :end2)
(string-not-equal str1 str2 &key :start1 :end1 :start2 :end2)
(string-not-lessp str1 str2 &key :start1 :end1 :start2 :end2)
(string-not-greaterp str1 str2 &key :start1 :end1 :start2 :end2)
```

- There are three functions for filtering characters from strings.

```
(string-trim character-bag string)
(string-left-trim character-bag string)
(string-right-trim character-bag string)
```

> *The string is a stark data structure and everywhere it*
> *is passed there is much duplication of process. It is a*
> *perfect vehicle for hiding information.*
>
> ◊ ALAN PERLIS, *Epigrams in Programming (1982)*

Chapter 7

Streams: Output and Input

The soul aspiring pants its source to mount,
As streams meander level with their fount.

◊ ROBERT MONTGOMERY, *The Omnipresence of the Deity (1828)*

We take this to be, on the whole, the worst similitude in the world.
In the first place, no stream meanders or can possibly
meander level with the fount. In the next place, if streams
did meander level with their founts, no two motions can be less like each
other than that of meandering level and that of mounting upwards.

◊ THOMAS BABINGTON, LORD MACAULAY, *Review of Montgomery's Poems*
(1830)

If you would not be forgotten,
as soon as you are dead and rotten,
either write things worth reading, or do things worth writing.

◊ BENJAMIN FRANKLIN, *Poor Richard's Almanac (1738)*

LISP is very helpful. It always prints out the value of the last expression that it has evaluated. For example, when you type (+ 3 4), LISP will not only evaluate the expression but will also print the resulting value 7.

Often, though, you are interested in seeing some intermediate values or messages from your programs. You may also want to have some results printed to a file instead of to the screen of your terminal or personal computer. Or, you may like your program to read in data that is stored in a file. LISP supports these types of *input* and *output* operations, both with your screen and with files.

Files and screens constitute the outside world for LISP, and there is a very basic way of viewing this input and output relationship. To LISP, input, from either a file or a screen's keyboard, is a source of data. Output, to either a file or a screen, is a receptacle for data. This source/receptacle idea is captured in the term *stream*, which is the abstraction LISP uses for its input and output.

A stream is something from which data can be read (input) and to which data can be written (output). You can take things out of a stream. You can put things into a stream. A stream is both a source and a receptacle; a faucet and a drain. At the lowest level, a program's input and output generally come one character at a time. An input stream is from where the program gets characters, and an output stream is to where the program sends characters.

7.1 The Screen Is a Stream

When you perform an input or output operation, LISP has to know to which stream you are referring. There are default streams which LISP uses for many operations. The primary ones are for screen input and output. They are called standard input and standard output.

```
> *standard-input*              ;  Default stream for input.
#<EXCL::BIDIRECTIONAL-TERMINAL-STREAM @ #x7c9bd6>                              ⇐ ∞


> *standard-output*             ;  Default stream for output.
#<EXCL::BIDIRECTIONAL-TERMINAL-STREAM @ #x7c9bd6>                              ⇐ ∞


> (streamp *standard-input*)    ;  streamp is the predicate for streams.
T


> (streamp 'standard-input)
NIL
```

These are LISP's generic streams. In addition, LISP provides five additional streams, all of which seem to be clones in this implementation.   ⇐ ∞

```
> *terminal-io*      ;  The user's keyboard and screen.
#<EXCL::BIDIRECTIONAL-TERMINAL-STREAM @ #x7c9bd6>


> *query-io*         ;  Preferred stream for user interaction.
#<EXCL::BIDIRECTIONAL-TERMINAL-STREAM @ #x7c9bd6>


> *debug-io*         ;  Stream for interactive debugging interaction.
#<EXCL::BIDIRECTIONAL-TERMINAL-STREAM @ #x7c9bd6>


> *trace-output*     ;  Stream for output from trace macro.
#<EXCL::BIDIRECTIONAL-TERMINAL-STREAM @ #x7c9bd6>
```

```
> *error-output*     ;  Stream for error messages.
#<EXCL::BIDIRECTIONAL-TERMINAL-STREAM @ #x7c9bd6>

> (eq *debug-io* *query-io*)
T

> (eq *trace-output* *terminal-io*)
T
```

We note that, initially, these streams are equivalent. However, during the course
of a program, the standard input and output streams can be redirected and other
special purpose streams will still function properly.

7.2 Output: Writing to Streams

We can print to the screen, using a set of basic output commands. Here we define
a function that prints a string on the screen, using several methods.

```
(defun name-output (name)
  (let ((screen *standard-output*))
    (print name screen)
    (write-char #\newline screen)
    (write-string name screen)
    (write-char #\I screen)
    (terpri screen)
    (write-line name screen)
    (write-char #\I screen)
    nil))

> (name-output "Richard II")

"Richard II"
Richard III
Richard II
I
NIL
```

Here is what happened in name-output:

1. screen is the local name given to the standard output stream.

2. (print object [stream]) prints out the given object on the given stream.
    Note that the output begins on a new line and double quotes are included in
    the result.

3. (write-char character [stream]) prints the character on the given stream.

4. (write-string string [stream]) prints the given string to the given stream but without the delimiting double quotes.

5. (terpri [stream]) goes to the beginning of the next line of the output stream.

6. (write-line string [stream]) prints the given string to the given stream, followed by a new line.

7. NIL is the value printed as the result of evaluating the function.

The stream argument is optional for print, write-char, write-string, terpri, and write-line.

If stream is not specified or nil, output goes to *standard-output*. If stream is T, output goes to *terminal-io*, which, as noted earlier, is usually, but not always, the same as *standard-input* and *standard-output*.

We demonstrate additional output functions below.

```
(defun more-output (char)
  (print char)
  (print char) (prin1 char) (prin1 char)
  (pprint char) (prin1 char)
  (fresh-line) (princ char) (princ char)
  (fresh-line) (write char) (write char)
  (fresh-line) (fresh-line) (write char)
  (terpri)
  (terpri) (write char)
  (values))

> (more-output #\x)

#\x                     ; print
#\x #\x#\x              ; print, prin1, prin1
#\x#\x                  ; pprint, prin1
xx                      ; fresh-line, princ, princ
#\x#\x                  ; fresh-line, write, write
#\x                     ; fresh-line, fresh-line, write
                        ; terpri
#\x                     ; terpri, write
```

The differences are subtle:

• (print object [stream]) outputs a newline, the object representation such that it can be read back in, followed by a space.

- (prin1 object [stream]) outputs the object such that it can be read back in, but no newline or space.

- (pprint object [stream]), like print, outputs a newline, the object representation such that it can be read back in, but no following space. pprint ("pretty print") may also add extra indentation to make the output easier for humans to read. Some implementations have elaborate pretty printers.

∞ ⇒

- (fresh-line [stream]) goes to the beginning of the next line of the output stream, unless the stream is already at the beginning of the line, in which case, it does nothing. By contrast, terpri will always produce a newline.

- (princ object [stream]) outputs the object without any escape characters and with no newline or space.

- (write object [options]) outputs the printed representation of the object, subject to a number of keyword options. We discuss these options in section 7.8.3.

There are also versions of prin1, princ, and write which send their output to a string instead of a stream.

```
> (prin1-to-string #\x)
"#\\x"

> (princ-to-string #\x)
"x"

> (write-to-string #\x)
"#\\x"
```

You can also have all output go to a string by using the with-output-to-string macro, which has the following syntax.

```
(with-output-to-string (var [string]) {form}*)
```

Here we specify s as the internal name of the output stream.

```
> (with-output-to-string (s)
    (write-string "once " s) (princ "upon" s) (write-char #\space s)
    (write-string "a time..." s))
"once upon a time..."
```

We shall now explore some examples from the world of text formatting. One of the most widespread uses of computers today is word processing, that is, editing and formatting text. This book has been prepared with computerized word-processing tools that make it very easy to specify where the text should appear on the page. For example,

text can be flush to the left margin,

or centered between the left and right margins,

or flush to the right margin.

We can write some LISP functions to produce these results.

The first function is `indent`, which prints a text string a given number of spaces from the left margin of the specified output stream, which defaults to the standard output.

```
(defun indent (text indentation &optional (stream *standard-output*))
  (terpri stream)
  (write-spaces indentation stream)
  (write-string text stream)
  (values))
```

```
; (write-spaces count stream)  prints count spaces on given stream.
(defun write-spaces (count &optional (stream *standard-output*))
  (cond ((zerop count) nil)
        (t
         (write-char #\space stream)
         (write-spaces (1- count) stream)))))
```

```
> (indent "hollow or depression" 10)

          hollow or depression
```

The reader should note the use of the new function (`values`) as the result returned by `indent`. Normally, a LISP function returns one and only one result. With `values`, a programmer can specify any number of values to be returned. The `values` function takes zero or more arguments, which it then returns as separate results.[1] In section 9.9, we discuss how to write functions that receive multiple values from other functions.

```
> (values)             ;  No results.

> (values 1 2 3 4)     ;  Four results.
1
2
3
4
```

---

[1] It may seem odd that the form (`values`) means "return no values." We note that the DEC® PDP-10™ assembly language command JUMP meant "do not jump."

```
> (values nil)              ;  The standard single value.
NIL
```

As in the case of `indent`, `(values)` is useful for those occasions when the programmer does not want the output cluttered with miscellaneous results such as T or NIL.

Given the indent function, it is trivial to define the `flushleft` function.

```
(defun flushleft (text &optional (stream *standard-output*))
   (indent text 0 stream))
```

```
> (flushleft "Rive gauche")
```

```
Rive gauche
```

Printing text flush to the right margin requires knowing where the right margin is or, at least, the maximum width of an output line. There is an appropriate global variable, `*print-right-margin*`, but it is not used in some implementations. We have defined a function `line-length` that returns the width (in characters) of the given output stream. See the online version of appendix A for equivalent definitions in other dialects.

```
(defun line-length (&optional (stream *standard-output*))
   (or lisp:*print-right-margin*
       (stream:stream-output-width stream)
       excl::*default-right-margin*
       79))
```

The prefixes `lisp:`, `stream:`, and `excl::` refer to *packages*, discussed in chapter 15.

```
(defun flushright (text &optional (stream *standard-output*))
   (let ((indentation (- (line-length stream)
                         (length text))))
     (indent text indentation stream)))
```

```
> (line-length *standard-output*)
79
```

```
> (flushright "right makes might" *standard-output*)
```

```
                                               right makes might
```

The `center` function is similar to `flushright`.

```
(defun center (text &optional (stream *standard-output*))
  (let ((indentation (truncate (- (line-length stream)
                                  (length text))
                               2)))
    (indent text indentation stream)))
```

> (center "of gravity, town, attention" *standard-output*)

of gravity, town, attention

Now we can put them all together.

```
(defun try-it ()
  (flushleft "This is flushleft")
  (center "This Is Centered")
  (flushright "and this is flushright")
  (indent "Indented 5" 5)
  (indent "Indented 10" 10))
```

> (try-it)

This is flushleft
                            This Is Centered
                                              and this is flushright

        Indented 5
             Indented 10

Another text formatting example is the split function, which prints its first argument flush to the left margin, and the second argument flush to the right margin on the same line to the given output stream — the third argument.

```
(defun split (left-text right-text
              &optional (stream *standard-output*))
  (flushleft left-text stream)
  (write-spaces (- (line-length stream)
                   (+ (hpos stream)
                      (length right-text)))
                stream)
  (write-string right-text stream)
  (values))
```

> (split "From here, ..." "... to eternity" *standard-output*)

From here, ... to eternity

The `split` function determines the number of spaces separating the left and right texts, which is the line width minus the sum of the right text length and the column position after printing the left text. This column position is given by the `hpos` function (horizontal position). `hpos`, like `line-length`, is not part of Common LISP. Here is the definition for one dialect. See the online version of appendix A for others.

```
(defun hpos (&optional (stream *standard-output*))
  (stream:stream-line-column stream))
```

∞ ⇒

7.3   format

A handful of output commands can be combined to format text in a variety of ways. Achieving these results can require a concerted programming effort. However, LISP provides a special function for formatting output: `format`. It is analogous to the `printf` and `fprintf` functions found in the C programming language's standard I/O library. Here are some examples.

```
> (format *standard-output* "Hello, my name is ~s.~%" 'Joey)
Hello, my name is JOEY.
NIL


> (format T "How old are you, ~A?~%" "Joey")
How old are you, Joey?
NIL


> (defvar joey-age 12)
JOEY-AGE


> (format nil "I am ~D year~P old." joey-age joey-age)
"I am 12 years old."


> (format T "My brothers are:
~5t~A: ~D year~P old and ~%~5t~A: ~D year~P old.~%"
"Paul" 5 5 "John" 1 1)
My brothers are:
     Paul: 5 years old and
     John: 1 year old.
NIL
```

The first argument to `format` is the destination of the output. The destination can be given as:

- A specific output stream, such as `*standard-output*`. The value returned by `format` is NIL.

- True (given as T). In this case, output is directed to *standard-output*. The value returned by format again is NIL.

- False (given as nil). Output is returned as a string as the value of format.

Thus, the output to format is NIL unless the destination is given as NIL.

The second argument to format is a control string, which comprises both characters to be printed and control codes, called *format directives*, to give spacing information and the printing specifications for the remaining arguments, which may include numbers, strings, and symbols. The format directives each begin with a *tilde* character (~). Format directives, like regular expression patterns found in languages such as awk or perl, make liberal and nontraditional use of punctuation characters, such that most expressive and powerful format control strings resemble random line noise.

The format directives that do not match parameters include:

~nT (tabulate) — Tabs to column number n

~nI (indent) — Indents to column number n; if n is omitted, defaults to zero

~n% (newline) — Prints n newlines; if no n is given, prints one newline

~n& (fresh-line) — If the output stream is not already at the beginning of a line, prints a newline; then prints $n - 1$ newlines

~n~ — Prints n tildes ("~"), if no n is given, prints one tilde

~n| — Prints n page separators; if no n is given, prints one page separator
Note that "|" is the vertical bar character.

~<newline> (ignore newline) — Ignores the newline character and any following whitespace characters
This formatting directive is sometimes useful in making the code itself easier to read.

~n* (ignore parameters) — Ignores the next n parameters; if n is absent, skips the next parameter

~n:* (backup parameters) — Backs up to the previous n parameters; if n is absent, reprocesses the previous parameter

The control codes that sequentially match the remaining parameters include:

~A (ASCII) — Prints the next argument without escape characters, in the manner of princ

~S (symbolic expression) — Prints the next argument, including escape characters, in the manner of prin1

~D (decimal) — Prints the next argument as a decimal number (base 10)

~B (binary) — Prints the next argument as a binary number (base 2)

~O (octal) — Prints the next argument as an octal number (base 8)

~X (hexadecimal) — Prints the next argument as a hexadecimal number (base 16)

~nR (radix) — Prints the next argument as a number with radix n, where n is a number specified between the tilde and the R, for example, ~5R for base 5

~R (english) — Prints the next argument as a number using English words, for example, "ten"

~:R (english ordinal) — Prints the next argument as an ordinal number using English words, for example, "tenth"

~@R (roman) — Prints the next argument (a number) as a Roman numeral

~P (plural) — Writes an "s" if the next argument is greater than 1; else, writes nothing
This code can be used to control for simple plurals.

~@P (special plural) — Writes "ies" if the next argument is greater than 1; else, writes "y"

~C (character) — Prints the next argument as a character, as with `write-char`

~F (floating point) — Prints the next argument as a fixed-format, floating point number, for example, 3.14159

~E (exponential floating point) — Prints the next argument as an exponential-format floating-point number, for example, $3.14E + 0$

~G (general floating point) — Prints the next argument as a floating point number in either fixed format or exponential format, as appropriate

~$ (dollars floating point) — Prints the next argument as a fixed format, floating point number which conforms to normal currency conventions
For example, .14159 would be printed as 0.14.

~? (indirection) — Directs that the next arguments must be a string followed by a list
The string is interpreted as formatting directives with arguments taken from the list.

~W (write) — Prints the next argument using `write`

Here are more examples of format. We first demonstrate the many ways in which numbers can be printed. Next, we use the control codes for skipping back and forth over the parameters and for using one format string as an argument to another format string.

```
(defun ascii-print (character)
  (let ((code (char-code character)))
    (format t "The ASCII code for ~A (~S) is:"
               character character)
    (format t "~%~5tBinary: ~35t~b" code)
    (format t "~%~5tOctal: ~35t~o" code)
    (format t "~%~5tDecimal: ~35t~d" code)
    (format t "~%~5tHexadecimal: ~35t~x" code)
    (format t "~%~5tBase 12: ~35t~12r" code)
    (format t "~%~5tEnglish: ~35t~r" code)
    (format t "~%~5tEnglish ordinal: ~35t~:r" code)
    (format t "~%~5tRoman numeral:~35t~@r" code)
    (format t "~%~5tCharacter:~35t~c" character)
    (format t "~%~5tFloating-point:~35t~f" code)
    (format t "~%~5tExponential floating-point:~35t~e" code)
    (format t "~%~5tGeneral floating-point:~35t~g" code)
    (format t "~%~5tDollars floating-point:~35t~$" code)
    (values)))

> (ascii-print #\A)
The ASCII code for A (#\A) is:
        Binary:                 1000001
        Octal:                  101
        Decimal:                65
        Hexadecimal:            41
        Base 12:                55
        English:                sixty-five
        English ordinal:        sixty-fifth
        Roman numeral:          LXV
        Character:              A
        Floating-point:         65.0
        Exponential floating-point:  6.5e+1
        General floating-point: 65.
        Dollars floating-point: 65.00

> (format t "Three parameters, two formats: ~D ~* ~r" 1 2 3)
Three parameters, two formats: 1  three
NIL
```

```
> (format t "One parameter, many formats: ~D ~:* ~x ~:* ~r" 45)
One parameter, many formats: 45  2d  forty-five
NIL

> (setf template "~%Dec: ~d Oct: ~o Hex: ~x")
"~%Dec: ~d Oct: ~o Hex: ~x"

> (format t "~?" template '(10 10 10))   ; We use the indirection code.

Dec: 10 Oct: 12 Hex: a
NIL
```

The indirection format code can be particularly useful if the programmer has lots of output requiring custom formatting.

Many format directives take arguments, inserted between the tilde and the directive. Usually, those arguments are given in the format control string when it is defined, but it is also possible to provide a value at run-time, using the V prefix instead of the parameter.

Below we define the function pbase, which prints a given number in the base specified.

```
(defun pbase (number base &optional (stream *standard-output*))
  (format stream "~VR" base number)
  (values))

> (pbase 100 2)
1100100

> (pbase 100 8)
144

> (pbase 100 16)
64
```

7.4   Input: Reading from Streams

It is possible to use strings as input and output streams. Here is an example of a string as an input stream. The function make-string-input-stream converts a given string into an input stream.

```
> (defvar x (make-string-input-stream "one two three"))
X
```

```
> x                        ;  The type is string-input-stream.
#<EXCL::STRING-INPUT-STREAM @ #x10d99be>

> (streamp x)              ;  x is a stream.
T

> (input-stream-p x)       ;  x is an input stream.
T

> (output-stream-p x)      ;  x is not an output stream.
NIL

> (read-char x)            ;  Reads a single character from given stream.
#\o

> (read-char x)            ;  Note that it now returns the second character.
#\n

> (unread-char #\n x)      ;  This reverses the previous read-char.
NIL

> (read-char x)            ;  read-char now reads the previous character.
#\n

> (read-char x)            ;  The third character is now read.
#\e

; (peek-char type stream) reads next character but does not advance the stream.
> (peek-char nil x)        ;  type nil indicates show the next character.b
#\space

> (peek-char t x)          ;  type t to show the next non-whitespace character.
#\t

> (listen x)               ;  Indicates whether there is an available character.
T

> (read-line x)            ;  Reads an entire line from the given stream.
"two three"
T                          ;  T indicates that read-line read the end of file.

> (listen x)               ;  listen shows nothing to read now.
NIL
```

```
> (defvar y (make-string-input-stream "three two one"))
Y

> y
#<EXCL::STRING-INPUT-STREAM @ #x11b55b6>

> (listen y)              ;  y has something to read.
T

> (clear-input y)         ;  clear-input flushes the contents of the stream.
NIL

> (listen y)              ;  y is now empty.
NIL

> (open-stream-p y)       ;  y is still open.
T

> (close y)               ;  (close stream) turns off the stream.
T

> (open-stream-p y)       ;  y is now closed.
NIL
```

This example demonstrates the basic properties of input streams.

- The streams are a source of characters (in this case, from a string).

- The streams are often given names (that is, bound to variables, like x and y here).

- The predicates streamp and input-stream-p will return true for input streams.

- Streams can be created (opened) and destroyed (closed).

- The predicate open-stream-p indicates the status of a stream.

- The listen function indicates whether a stream is empty.

- A one-character, look-ahead scheme is afforded by the peek-char function.

- In addition to character-by-character input, one can read entire lines as strings by using the read-line function.

- An input stream can be emptied with clear-input.

It is also possible to read whole LISP objects from streams. The load function for reading LISP expressions from files relies on this facility. When you load a file, LISP performs the following actions:

1. Opens a stream that reads characters from the given file.

2. Reads in the next LISP expression.

3. If end-of-file is encountered, then closes the stream and quits.

4. Evaluates the current LISP expression and returns to step 2.

The read operation from step 2 is demonstrated below.

```
> (defvar s (make-string-input-stream "1 23 456 7890"))
S

> (read s)              ;  Note that read returns a LISP number,
1                       ;  not the character #\1  or the string "1".

> (read s)              ;  The next number is now returned.
23

> (+ (read s) (read s)) ;  The values of read can be used as arguments
8346                    ;  for other functions.

> (listen s)            ;  The stream s is now empty.
NIL

> (defvar q (make-string-input-stream "a bb (* 3 4)"))
Q

> (read q)              ;  read returns the LISP symbol, not the
A                       ;  character #\A.

> (read q)
BB

> (read q)              ;  read returns a list expression.
(* 3 4)
```

Note that read did not evaluate the expressions.

The macro with-input-from-string allows the programmer to encapsulate the read operations from a string, creating a stream from a string, evaluating forms that reference the stream, and then closing the stream.

```
> (with-input-from-string (in "1 2 3 4 5 6")
    (+ (read in) (read in) (read in)))
6


> (with-input-from-string (in "1 2 3 4 5 6" :start 4)
    (+ (read in) (read in) (read in)))
12


> (with-input-from-string (in "1 2 3 4 5 6" :start 6)
    (+ (read in) (read in) (read in)))
15
```

The :start keyword specifies the *character* of the string (including whitespace) at which to begin reading, where the first character is 0. The :end keyword specifies where to stop reading (and when to close the stream).

```
> (with-input-from-string (in "1 2 3 4 5 6")
    (values (+ (read in) (read in)) (listen in)))
3
T


> (with-input-from-string (in "1 2 3 4 5 6" :end 3)
    (values (+ (read in) (read in)) (listen in)))
3
NIL
```

Finally, the :index keyword can be used to specify the name of a variable that contains the index of the next unread character in the string after the stream is closed.

```
> (with-input-from-string (in "1 2 3 4 5 6" :index next)
    (+ (read in) (read in)))
3


> next
4


> (with-input-from-string (in "1 2 3 4 5 6" :start next)
    (+ (read in) (read in)))
7
```

7.5   Files as Streams

The basic properties of string streams also apply to file input and file output.

The first step in reading or writing a file is to create a stream by opening the file. The **open** command takes several arguments: the name of the file and a number of keyword specifications. We shall focus on the **:direction** keyword, which specifies the type of access required. A file stream can be opened for input (using the **:input** keyword), or output (using the keyword **:output**), or for both input and output (using the **:io** keyword). The **:probe** keyword for **:direction** returns the file's status. Here is an example of an output file and associated common output operations.

```
> (probe-file "myfile.data")   ;  Predicate to tell if a file has been created.
NIL

> (defvar s1 (open "myfile.data" :direction :output))
S1                            ;  Output stream is bound to s1.

> (probe-file "myfile.data")   ;  The file now exists, returning a pathname.[2]
#p"/server/u18/homes.ai/slade/a/mss/l/myfile.data"

> (write-char #\A s1)          ;  Writes the given character on the stream.
#\A

> (terpri s1)                  ;  Begins a new line on output stream.
#\newline

> (write-spaces 1 s1)          ;  Writes a blank character to output stream.
NIL

> (write-string "This is a test" s1) ;  Prints given object to stream.
"This is a test"

> (defvar fact '(defun fact (n) (cond ((zerop n) 1)
(t (* n (fact (1- n)))))))
FACT

> (print fact s1)              ;  A simple function.
(DEFUN FACT (N) (COND ((ZEROP N) 1) (T (* N (FACT (1- N))))))

> (terpri s1)                  ;  Another new line on output stream.
#\newline

> (close s1)                   ;  End of output to stream s1.
T
```

---

[2]We discuss pathnames in section 7.7.

```
> (open "myfile.data" :direction :probe)
#<EXCL::CHARACTER-INPUT-FILE-STREAM
"/server/u18/homes.ai/slade/a/mss/l/myfile.data" closed @ #x1187276>
```

Now, let's look at the content of the file myfile.data to which we just wrote.

```
A
 This is a test
(DEFUN FACT (N) (COND ((ZEROP N) 1) (T (* N (FACT (1- N)))))))
```

Here is a breakdown of from where the characters came.

1. The A in line 1 came from the **write-char** command.

2. The blank at the beginning of line 2 came from the **terpri** function followed by the **write-spaces** function.

3. The string This is a test in line 2 is from the **write-string** function.

4. The list expression which starts on line 3 is from the **print** function.

We can now turn around and use that file for input. First, we open the file as an input file.

```
> (defvar s2 (open "myfile.data" :direction :input))
S2

> (list (read s2) (read s2) (read s2))   ;  Reads the first three objects.
(A THIS IS)

> (list (read s2) (read s2) (read s2))   ;  Reads the next three objects.
(A TEST (DEFUN FACT (N) (COND ((ZEROP N) 1) (T (* N #)))))

> (close s2)
T
```

7.6 Stream Examples

We shall now define several functions that do useful tasks with streams. The first one will copy one stream (the input) to another (the output).

```
(defun stream-copy (s-input s-output)
   (cond ((or (not (input-stream-p s-input)) ; Error checking.
              (not (output-stream-p s-output)))
          (write-string "Foul stream in STREAM-COPY." *error-output*))
         ((not (listen s-input))                    ; Checks for end of file.
          '*END-OF-STREAM-COPY*)
```

```
      (t                                        ;  Copies input to output.
      (write-string  (read-line s-input) s-output)
      (terpri s-output)
      (stream-copy s-input s-output))))   ;  Recursive call.
```

The stream-copy function does some error checking at first. If an error is found, a message is printed to the stream given by *error-output*. As noted earlier, this stream is usually defined to be the same as *standard-output*, that is, errors normally are printed to the screen.

The function is recursive. The termination condition is met when listen reports nothing in the input stream.

The following is a function that uses the stream-copy function. The type function takes a file name (given as a string) and prints the contents of the file on the standard output.

```
(defun type (file-name)
  (let ((file-stream (open file-name :direction :input)))
    (stream-copy file-stream *standard-output*)
    (close file-stream)
    (values)))
```

```
;  Here is how it works.
> (type "myfile.data")
A
 This is a test
(DEFUN FACT (N) (COND ((ZEROP N) 1) (T (* N (FACT (1- N)))))))
```

The next example is a *filter*, that is, a program that reads an input and prints selected (and possibly changed) parts to its output. For example, you may wish to find all the three-letter words contained in a file.

```
(defun filter-file (filter input-file output-file)
  (let ((in-stream (open input-file :direction :input))
        (out-stream (open output-file :direction :output)))
    (filter-stream filter in-stream out-stream)
    (close in-stream)
    (close out-stream)
    (values)))
```

```
(defun filter-stream (filter in-stream out-stream)
  (cond ((null (listen in-stream)) 'end-of-file)
        (t
         (let ((tmp (funcall filter (read in-stream))))
           (cond (tmp
                  (format out-stream "~A~%" tmp)))
           (filter-stream filter in-stream out-stream)))))
```

```
(defun 3-letter-word-p (word)
  (if (= (length (string word)) 3)
      word))
```

The first function, `filter-file`, opens the files to create the streams, calls the `filter-stream` function, and finally closes the streams, forcing any pending output to be printed to the output stream as it is closed.

There is a potential problem in `filter-file`: if the call to `filter-stream` results in an error, then the streams will never get closed properly. The preferred solution to this problem is the special form `unwind-protect`, which we discuss in section 9.11.

The second function, `filter-stream`, checks for the termination condition and then applies the filter function to the next object read from the input stream. If the object passes through the filter, it is printed on the output stream. The process continues with a recursive call to `filter-stream`.

The third function, `3-letter-word-p`, checks to see if its argument has three and only three letters.

Suppose that a file called `sample.in` contains a list of words: one two three four five six seven eight nine ten. We can use our filter program to extract the three-letter words.

```
> (type "sample.in")
one two three four five six seven eight nine ten

> (filter-file #'3-letter-word-p "sample.in" "sample.out")

> (type "sample.out")
ONE
TWO
SIX
TEN
```

The author actually had occasion to produce an exhaustive list of English three-letter words for use in a computer program to teach children how to read. The filter program given here, combined with an online English dictionary, provided such a list. Spelling correction is a possible filtering application. Using a predicate which checks for misspelled words, the user can filter a text file, sending the exceptions to an output file.

Filter programs, or file transducers, are very adaptable and useful *software tools*. They are discussed in Kernighan and Plauger's classic book [Kernighan and Plauger, 1976] of the same name.

The experienced programmer will realize that writing characters to a file does not always mean that she has written any characters to a file. That is, most file systems *buffer* output operations so that several write operations might be issued before anything is written to the actual disk. Normally, the use of buffers improves efficiency.

By comparison, as your household runs out of various groceries, you may compile a list for a weekly trip to the store instead of going to the supermarket once or more each day. Just as shopping takes time, so do output operations. The file system uses buffers to keep track of what it needs to write out to disk and, periodically, it writes out the buffers.

Sometimes, the programmer may want to override the file system's output buffers. LISP offers three ways to do this.

- (finish-output [stream]) writes the buffer and then returns nil.

- (force-output [stream]) returns nil immediately but also initiates the writing of the buffer.

- (clear-output [stream]) terminates any output operations on the stream, returning nil.

For each function, the optional stream argument can be nil (the default) to indicate *standard-output*, T to indicate *terminal-io*, or an explicit stream. Each of these functions returns nil. They are used solely for their side effects.

7.7 Pathnames

Common LISP is designed to support portability. That is, you should be able to run your LISP code on any machine, including machines that have different file systems. Filenames differ across operating systems, such as UNIX®, VMS®, DOS®, or Macintosh®. In an effort to capture the similarity among the different file systems, Common LISP provides the type pathname, which comprises the following components.

- *host* is the name of the file system.

- *device* names the logical or physical device containing the file.

- *directory* is the name of the group of files having the same parent.

- *name* is the base filename.

- *type* is the extension or type for the file.

- *version* is the incremental version number associated with each generation of the file.

Not all of these components are present in all implementations. Here is a sample ⇐ ∞ pathname for a file test.lisp which resides on a UNIX file system.

```
> (pathname "test.lisp")            ;  pathname creates a pathname.
#p"test.lisp"                        ;  Note the #p prefix.

> (setf p (pathname "test.lisp"))    ;  Assigns the pathname to p.
#p"test.lisp"

> (type-of p)                        ;  pathname is a LISP type.
PATHNAME

> (pathnamep p)                      ;  pathnamep is a predicate.
T

> (pathnamep "test.lisp")
NIL

> (truename p)                       ;  What is the full pathname?
#p"/server/u18/homes.ai/slade/a/mss/l/test.lisp"
```

We have created a pathname with the pathname function and have demonstrated the pathnamep predicate. The truename function finds the actual file associated with the pathname and fills in the other components, as best as it is able. There are accessor functions for the pathname components. Unknown component values return NIL.

```
> (pathname-host p)                  ;  What is the host?
NIL

> (pathname-device p)                ;  What is the device?
NIL

> (pathname-directory p)             ;  What is the directory?
NIL

> (pathname-directory (truename p))  ;  What is the true directory?
(:ABSOLUTE "server" "u18" "homes.ai" "slade" "a" "mss" "l")

> (pathname-device (truename p))     ;  What is the true device?
NIL

> (pathname-name p)                  ;  What is the name?
"test"

> (pathname-type p)                  ;  What is the type?
"lisp"
```

```
> (pathname-version p)              ;  What is the version?
NIL
```

In some implementations, instead of the value NIL, a missing component is given with the keyword :unspecific.   ⇐ ∞

There are also a series of functions which convert the parts of a pathname into strings.

```
> (namestring p)                    ;  Converts the name to a string.
"test.lisp"
```

```
> (namestring (truename p))         ;  Converts the true name to a string.
"/server/u18/homes.ai/slade/a/mss/l/test.lisp"
```

```
> (file-namestring (truename p))    ;  Returns a string for the true file name.
"test.lisp"
```

```
> (directory-namestring (truename p))   ;  Returns a string for the directory.
"/server/u18/homes.ai/slade/a/mss/l/"
```

```
> (host-namestring (truename p))    ;  Returns a string for the true host.
NIL
```

```
> (enough-namestring (truename p))  ;  Returns enough of the pathname.
"test.lisp"
```

The sense of *enough* in enough-namestring is to provide sufficient information to identify the given file, using default values for the other components, such as the default directory.

LISP is aware of two standard directories: the default directory and the user's home directory. The global variable *default-pathname-defaults* describes the former, and the latter is returned by the function (user-homedir-pathname).

```
> *default-pathname-defaults*
#p"/server/u18/homes.ai/slade/a/mss/l/"
```

```
> (user-homedir-pathname)
#p"/homes/ai/slade/"
```

There are several ways to create a new pathname. One is to specify a string as the argument to the pathname function. Another method is to use the constructor function make-pathname, which builds a pathname component by component, using keyword arguments.

```
> (setf np (make-pathname :name "test" :type "lisp"))
#p"test.lisp"

> (pathname-name np)
"test"

> (pathname-type np)
"lisp"

> (setf np (make-pathname :name "test" :type "lisp"
        :defaults *default-pathname-defaults*))
#p"/server/u18/homes.ai/slade/a/mss/l/test.lisp"
```

The :defaults keyword specifies a pathname to use for any unspecified components. If the :defaults keyword is not given, then just the unspecified host component is taken from *default-pathname-defaults*.

The programmer can also use keywords to specify :host, :device, :directory, :version, and :case.

One problem with portable pathnames is the fact that different file systems have different case conventions. For example, UNIX is case sensitive, meaning that LISP, lisp, and Lisp would be three different names, whereas in DOS, they would all end up as LISP. The :case option to make-pathname, which may also be used with the pathname component access functions, such as pathname-host and pathname-device, can be either :local or :common.

- :local adheres to the local file system's case convention.

- :common adopts one of three possible case conventions, relative to the file system's convention:

  - If a string is all upper case, use the file system's case convention.
  - If a string is all lower case, use the *opposite* of the file system's case convention.
  - If a string is in mixed case, leave it alone.

∞ ⇒ Not all dialects have implemented the :case option.

Another way to create a new pathname is with the function merge-pathnames, which combines its first pathname argument with the default components provided in the second pathname argument.

```
> (truename ".")
#p"/server/u18/homes.ai/slade/a/mss/l/"

> (setf mp (merge-pathnames "test.lisp" (truename ".")))
#p"/server/u18/homes.ai/slade/a/mss/l/test.lisp"
```

```
> (merge-pathnames "new" mp)
#p"/server/u18/homes.ai/slade/a/mss/l/new.lisp"

> (merge-pathnames "/" mp)
#p"/test.lisp"
```

It looks like **merge-pathnames** works fairly well for creating pathnames with new names or directories. However, we find that there is a problem with new file types.

```
> (merge-pathnames ".old" mp)
#p"/server/u18/homes.ai/slade/a/mss/l/.old.lisp"

> (setf (pathname-type mp) "old")
Error: (SETF PATHNAME-TYPE) does not have a function definition
[1]
> :res

> (make-pathname :type "old" :defaults mp)
#p"/server/u18/homes.ai/slade/a/mss/l/test.old"
```

We observe that the pathname functions do not work with **setf**. However, we can use **make-pathname** with the :type and :defaults keywords to get the desired effect.

One more way to create a pathname is with the **parse-namestring** function, which returns two values: the resulting pathname and an integer that is an index to the end of the pathname in the input string.

```
> (parse-namestring "/a/b/c/d/e.f")
#p"/a/b/c/d/e.f"
12

> (setf np (parse-namestring "/a/b/c/d/e.f"))
#p"/a/b/c/d/e.f"

> (pathname-directory np)
(:ABSOLUTE "a" "b" "c" "d")

> (pathname-name np)
"e"

> (pathname-type np)
"f"
```

The first argument to **parse-namestring** is a string, pathname, stream, or symbol which gets converted to a pathname. **parse-namestring** has additional optional arguments for specifying a host, a defaults pathname, the `:start` and `:end` positions for reading the input string, and a keyword, `:junk-allowed`, which can signal an error when set to `NIL` when the pathname does not conform to the native file system requirements.

7.8   Advanced Subjects

This chapter has the following advanced topics:

- Input Options

- Reader Syntax

- Output Options

- File Options

- Stream Options

- More Format Directives

7.8.1   Input Options

LISP provides a couple of convenient input functions for interrogating the user.

```
> (y-or-n-p "Are you sure you want to quit? ")
Are you sure you want to quit? yes
T


> (y-or-n-p "Are you sure you want to quit? ")
Are you sure you want to quit? maybe
Type "y" for yes or "n" for no.
Are you sure you want to quit? OK
Type "y" for yes or "n" for no.
Are you sure you want to quit? fine
Type "y" for yes or "n" for no.
Are you sure you want to quit? y
T


> (y-or-n-p "Are you over ~A year~P old? " 21 21)
Are you over 21 years old? no
NIL
```

```
> (yes-or-no-p "Are you sure you want to quit? ")
Are you sure you want to quit? n
Type "yes" for yes or "no" for no.
Are you sure you want to quit? no
NIL

> (yes-or-no-p "Are you over ~A year~P old? " 18 18)
Are you over 18 years old? sure thing
Type "yes" for yes or "no" for no.
Are you over 18 years old? yes
T
```

Both `y-or-n-p` and `yes-or-no-p` prompt the user with optional format string arguments. The latter function requires an explicit yes or no, not just y or n. They each return T or NIL, depending on the user input.

When reading numbers, LISP permits the programmer to specify the default radix and floating point type with the global parameters `*read-base*` and `*read-default-float-format*`, respectively.

```
> *read-base*                    ; The default is decimal.
10

> (setf *read-base* 8)           ; Changes to octal.
8

> 10
8

> 100
64

> (setf *read-base* 2)           ; Changes to binary.
2

> 10000
16

> (setf *read-base* 10)          ; Tries to return to base 10.
2                                ; Hmmm. Still in binary.

> (setf *read-base* 1010)        ; That's better.
10
```

```
> (setf *read-base* 16)          ; Tries hexadecimal.
16

> (list a bad babe faced a deaf ace)
(10 2989 47806 1027309 10 57007 2766)

> (list a faded bee effaced a dead decade)
(10 1027565 3054 251636973 10 57005 14600926)

> (setf *read-base* a)           ; Back to base 10.
10

> *read-default-float-format*    ; The default is single-float.
SINGLE-FLOAT

> 9.5d0                          ; A double.
9.5d0

> 9.5f0                          ; A single.
9.5

> (type-of 9.5)
SINGLE-FLOAT

> (setf *read-default-float-format* 'double-float)
DOUBLE-FLOAT

> (type-of 9.5)
DOUBLE-FLOAT

> 9.5d0                          ; A double.
9.5

> 9.5f0                          ; A single.
9.5f0
```

The basic read function described earlier had an optional argument that specified
an input stream. read has three other optional arguments.

- eof-error-p — A flag indicating whether it is an error to read the end of
  file (or the end of stream). The default, T, signals an error. A value of nil
  indicates that no error is triggered.

- eof-value — If eof-error-p is nil, then eof-value is returned when read encounters an end of file. The default eof-value is nil.

- recursive-p — A flag indicating a recursive call to read. The default value is nil. We will find this useful in defining macro characters, discussed in section 11.8.

Below, we demonstrate the use of the eof-error-p and eof-value parameters.

```
> (setf is (make-string-input-stream "1 2 3"))
#<EXCL::STRING-INPUT-STREAM @ #x10a0bae>

> (+ (read is) (read is))      ; Reads from the stream.
3

> (read is nil '*EOF*)         ; Reads until end of stream.
3

> (read is nil '*EOF*)         ; Reached the end of stream.
*EOF*

> (read is nil)                ; Still there.  No error, though.
NIL

> (read is)                    ; Now we signal an error.
Error: eof encountered on stream
  #<EXCL::STRING-INPUT-STREAM @ #x10a0bae>
  [condition type: END-OF-FILE]
```

These options are also available with read-char, read-char-no-hang, and read-preserving-whitespace. The read-char-no-hang function is analogous to read-char, but it does not wait when there is no character to be read. Below, read-char waits until the user types something, whereas read-char-no-hang returns immediately.

```
> (read-char *terminal-io*)
x

#\x

> (read-char-no-hang *terminal-io*)
NIL
```

The read-preserving-whitespace function is like read but does not discard whitespace characters, such as space or newline.

```
> (setf is (make-string-input-stream "1 2 3 4 5"))
#<EXCL::STRING-INPUT-STREAM @ #x10afcee>
```

```
> (read is)                          ; Reads an expression.
1
```

```
> (read-char is)                     ; The first space is gone.
#\2
```

```
> (read-preserving-whitespace is)    ; Reads an expression.
3
```

```
> (read-char is)                     ; The next space remains.
#\space
```

```
> (+ (read is) (read is) (read is nil 0))
9
```

```
> (read-preserving-whitespace is nil 'thats-all-folks)
THATS-ALL-FOLKS
```

The function `read-from-string` has a required string argument and the optional
`eof-error-p` and `eof-value` arguments, as well as keyword arguments `:start`,
`:end`, and `:preserve-whitespace`. `read-from-string` returns two values: the
LISP object that it read and the index to the next unread character in the given
string.

```
> (read-from-string "(a list) (another list)")
(A LIST)
9
```

```
> (read-from-string "(a list) (another list)" :start 9)
(A LIST)
9
```

```
> (read-from-string "(a list) (another list)" nil 'eof :start 9)
(ANOTHER LIST)
23
```

```
> (read-from-string "(a list) (another list)" nil 'eof :start 23)
EOF
23
```

```
> (read-from-string "(a list) (another list)" nil
    'eof :preserve-whitespace t)
(A LIST)
8
```

```
> (read-from-string "(a list) (another list)" nil
    'eof :start 10 :end 15)
ANOTH
15
```

In the second example above, :start and 9 are interpreted as optional arguments, not as keyword arguments.

A related function is parse-integer, which converts a string into an integer. As a second value, it returns the index to the next character to be read. In addition to the keywords :start and :end, parse-integer supports the additional keyword arguments :radix, which specifies the base of the integer, and :junk-allowed, which indicates that non-numeric characters should not signal an error.

```
> (parse-integer "12345")
12345
5
```

```
> (parse-integer "12345" :start 3)
45
5
```

```
> (parse-integer "12345" :end 3)
123
3
```

```
> (parse-integer "100" :radix 8)
64
3
```

```
> (parse-integer "100" :radix 2)
4
3
```

```
> (parse-integer "100 :radix" :junk-allowed t)
100
3
```

```
> (parse-integer "100 :radix")
Error: There's junk in this string: "100 :radix".
```

One final variation on the read function is `read-delimited-list`, which has a required argument of a character delimiter and optional arguments specifying the input stream and the `recursive-p` flag.

```
> (setf is (make-string-input-stream "1 2 3 4 5"))
#<EXCL::STRING-INPUT-STREAM @ #x10bfcfe>

> (read-delimited-list #\2 is)
(1)

> (read-delimited-list #\4 is)
(3)

> (read-delimited-list #\5 is)
NIL
```

7.8.2 Reader Syntax

We refer to the part of LISP that reads the incoming stream of data as the *reader*, not to be confused with the person reading this book. The LISP reader must handle a variety of objects, including numbers, symbols, lists, characters, and strings. The language supports syntactic conventions to help the reader decide at what kind of object it is looking.

Since the LISP reader processes the input from left to right, the syntactic clues tend to be prefixes that tell the reader what to expect. Table 7.1 provides a summary of the syntactic prefixes. Some of them we have already encountered, and others we will see in future chapters. The remainder we demonstrate below.

```
> (read-from-string "#3r100")    ;  Reads a number in base 3.
9
6

> (read-from-string "#20r100")   ;  Reads a number in base 20.
400
7

> (read-from-string "(george #|the first president|# washington)")
(GEORGE WASHINGTON)
43

> (read-from-string "(mac#|the|# knife)")
(|MAC#the#| KNIFE)
18
```

Prefix	Object or Effect	Reference
;	comment	chapter 2
'	symbol	chapter 2
`	backquote	chapter 11
(	cons or list	chapter 3
"	string	chapter 6
\	quote next character	chapter 2
|	delimit quoted characters	chapter 2
#	macro dispatch character	chapter 11
#a	array	chapter 14
#b	binary rational	chapter 7
#c	complex number	chapter 2
#o	octal rational	chapter 7
#p	pathname	chapter 7
#nr	rational of radix n	
#s	structure	chapter 12
#x	hexadecimal rational	chapter 7
#|	nested comment	
#`	function	chapter 3
#(	vector	chapter 14
#*	bit vector	chapter 14
#:	uninterned symbol	
#\	character	chapter 6
#+	conditional read	
#-	conditional read	
#.	read-time evaluation	
#,	load-time evaluation	
#=	unique labeled object	
##	previously labeled object	
#<	error during read	

Table 7.1: Reader Syntax Prefixes

The nested comment examples illustrate the point that the reader prefixes must occur at the beginning of the word. Otherwise, the reader treats them as regular characters.

```
> (gensym)                          ;  Temporary symbols are not interned.
#:G553
```

```
> (intern (gensym))
G554
NIL
```

The function `intern` adds a symbol to a package's table of symbols. We discuss packages in chapter 15.

Using the `#+` and `#-` prefixes, we can conditionally read objects if a given keyword is a member of the `*features*` list or not. These reader prefixes allow the programmer to make the definition or execution of code conditional on the presence or absence of a given feature. Most implementations populate the `*features*` list with keywords, though some may use symbols.

```
> *features*
(:COMPOSER-V2.0 :COMPOSER :CW-MOTIF :CW-X-V2 :CW-X :CLX-MIT-R5
:CLX-MIT-R4 :XLIB :CLX :HAS-RCSNOTE ...)
```

```
> (member :test *features*)
NIL
```

```
> (list #+:test 'yes #-:test 'no)
(NO)
```

```
> (pushnew :test *features*)
(:TEST :COMPOSER-V2.0 :COMPOSER :CW-MOTIF :CW-X-V2 :CW-X :CLX-MIT-R5
:CLX-MIT-R4 :XLIB :CLX ...)
```

```
> (list #+:test 'yes #-:test 'no)
(YES)
```

Sometimes, we want to evaluate an expression at the time it is read. The `#.` and `#,` prefixes provide this functionality.

```
> (setf *switch* nil)
NIL
```

```
> (read-from-string "(+ 1 2 *switch*)")
(+ 1 2 *SWITCH*)
16
```

```
> (read-from-string "(+ 1 2 #.*switch*)")
(+ 1 2 NIL)
18

> (read-from-string "(+ 1 2 #,*switch*)")
(+ 1 2 NIL)
18

> (read-from-string "#.(make-list 3 :initial-element 10)")
(10 10 10)
35

> (read-from-string "(make-list 3 :initial-element 10)")
(MAKE-LIST 3 :INITIAL-ELEMENT 10)
33
```

In these examples, there is no apparent difference between #. and #,. However, the latter prefix is useful when you are compiling code and want the resulting expression to be evaluated at the time it is loaded, but not when it is read by the compiler.

The next two prefixes are useful for printing circular lists and other unusual expressions.

```
> *print-circle*              ; Discussed in section 7.8.3.
NIL

> (setf x '(1 2 3 4))
(1 2 3 4)

> (setf (car x) x)
(((((# 2 3 4) 2 3 4) 2 3 4) 2 3 4) 2 3 4)

> (setf *print-circle* t)     ; Turns on circular printing.
T

> x
#1=(#1# 2 3 4)

> (setf (car (cdr x)) x)
#1=(#1# #1# 3 4)

> (setf (car (cdr x)) (cddr x))
(3 4)
```

```
> x
#1=(#1# #2=(3 4) . #2#)

> (setf y (gensym))
#:G555

> (list y y y)
(#1=#:G555 #1# #1#)
```

The #= and ## prefixes permit the concise notation of objects that might otherwise have no finite representation.

The final reader prefix is #<, which is used to identify objects that have no readable printed representation. If the reader encounters such a beast, it signals an error.

```
> (read-from-string "(standard-input is *standard-input*)")
(STANDARD-INPUT IS *STANDARD-INPUT*)
36

> (read-from-string "(standard-input is #.*standard-input*)")
(STANDARD-INPUT IS #<EXCL::BIDIRECTIONAL-TERMINAL-STREAM @ #x7c9bd6>)
38

> (read-from-string
"(STANDARD-INPUT IS #<EXCL::BIDIRECTIONAL-TERMINAL-STREAM @ #x7c9bd6>)")
Error: Illegal sharp character #\< [file position = 21]
   [condition type: READER-ERROR]
```

LISP provides the global variable *read-suppress* to support implementation of the #+ and #- prefixes. If *read-suppress* is non-NIL, the LISP reader ignores most tokens and reader macros. Exceptions include lists, vectors, and strings.

```
(defun suppress-read (string)
  (let ((*read-suppress* t))
    (read-from-string string)))

> (suppress-read "hello")
NIL
5

> (suppress-read "\"hello\"")
"hello"
7
```

Variable	Controls	Values	Initially
`*print-array*`	array printing	T/NIL	
`*print-base*`	radix for rationals	integer between 2 and 36	10
`*print-case*`	symbol case	`:upcase` `:downcase` `:capitalize`	`:upcase`
`*print-circle*`	circular structures	T/NIL	NIL
`*print-escape*`	readable escape character	T/NIL	T
`*print-gensym*`	prefix for gensyms	T/NIL	T
`*print-length*`	number of elements	NIL or integer	NIL
`*print-level*`	number of nested levels	NIL or integer	NIL
`*print-pretty*`	formatted indentation	T/NIL	
`*print-radix*`	radix prefix	T/NIL	NIL

Table 7.2: Output Option Variables

```
> (suppress-read "(1 2 3)")
(NIL NIL NIL)
7
```

The programmer will seldom find it necessary, useful, or prudent to change the value of *read-suppress*.

7.8.3 Output Options

Often, a programmer will want to produce output that can be used as input to another LISP program. Most, but not all, LISP objects can produce *readable* output. Objects of type character, cons, number, string, and symbol can all be printed such that LISP can read them back accurately.

Other objects can be printed in a readable fashion under certain circumstances. LISP provides a number of global variables that can be set to control the appearance of your output. These variables are given in table 7.2 and demonstrated below. The various possible settings of these variables can affect the ease with which either you or LISP may be able to read the results.

```
> *print-array*            ; Default displays array values.
T

> (setf a (make-array '(2 2)
    :initial-contents '((one two) (three four))))
#2A((ONE TWO) (THREE FOUR))
```

```
> (setf *print-array* nil)
NIL

> a
#<Array of rank 2 @ #x106ca6e>
```

We discuss arrays in chapter 14. For now, we observe that there are two ways of printing arrays. If *print-array* is T, then arrays are printed in a manner readable by LISP.

```
> *print-base*              ; Default base is 10 (decimal).
10

> (setf *print-base* 2)     ; Changes to base 2 (binary).
10

> 2
10

> 8
1000

> (setf *print-base* 16)    ; Changes to base 16 (hexadecimal).
10

> 10
a

> *print-case*              ; Default case is UPPER CASE.
:UPCASE

> 'foo
FOO

> (setf *print-case* :downcase)
:downcase

> 'FOO
foo

> 'Foo
foo
```

```
> (setf *print-case* :capitalize)
:Capitalize

> 'foo
Foo

> *print-circle*              ;  Default for circular structures.
Nil

> (setf x '(forever and ever))
(Forever And Ever)

> (setf (cddr x) x)           ;  Creates a circular list.
(Forever And Forever And Forever And Forever And Forever And ...)

> (setf *print-circle* t)
T

> x
#1=(Forever And . #1#)
```

When *print-circle* is NIL, the number of elements printed is controlled by
print-length, described below.

```
> *print-escape*             ;  Default for control characters.
T

> (write #\newline)
#\newline
#\newline

> (setf *print-escape* nil)
Nil

> (write #\newline)

#\newline

> *print-gensym*             ;  Default for printing gensyms.
T

> (gensym)
#:G22\c
```

```
> (setf *print-gensym* nil)
Nil

> (gensym)
G22\d
```

The gensym function creates new, unique symbols.

```
> *print-length*              ;  Current maximum print length.
a                             ;  (We are still in hexadecimal.)

> (setf y '(1 2 3 4 5 6 7 8 9 10 11 12 13 14 15 16 17 18 19 20))
(1 2 3 4 5 6 7 8 9 a ...)

> (setf *print-length* 16)    ;  Increases the print length.
10

> y
(1 2 3 4 5 6 7 8 9 a b c d e f 10 ...)

> (setf *print-length* nil)   ;  Prints everything.
Nil

> y
(1 2 3 4 5 6 7 8 9 a b c d e f 10 11 12 13 14)

> *print-level*               ;  Current maximum print depth.
5

> (setf z '(1 (2 (3 (4 (5 (6 (7 (8 (9 (10 (11 (12))))))))))))
(1 (2 (3 (4 (5 #)))))

> (setf *print-level* 10)     ;  Increases the print level.
a

> z
(1 (2 (3 (4 (5 (6 (7 (8 (9 (a #))))))))))

> (setf *print-level* nil)    ;  Prints everything.
Nil

> z                                     ;  Hexadecimal, remember?
(1 (2 (3 (4 (5 (6 (7 (8 (9 (a (b (c)))))))))))
```

```
> *print-pretty*              ;  By default, pretty print is on.
T

> (setf w '(defun fact (n)
"This is a documentation string for factorial."
(cond ((zerop n) 1) (t (* n (fact (- n 1))))))))
(Defun Fact (N)
  "This is a documentation string for factorial."
  (Cond ((Zerop N) 1) (T (* N (Fact #)))))
```

We discuss documentation strings in chapter 10.

```
> w
(Defun Fact (N)
  "This is a documentation string for factorial."
  (Cond ((Zerop N) 1) (T (* N (Fact #)))))

> (setf *print-pretty* nil)
Nil

> w                         ;  Pretty print is turned off.
(Defun Fact (N) "This is a documentation string for factorial."
(Cond ((Zerop N) 1) (T (* N (Fact #)))))

> (print w)                 ;  print uses the current setting.

(Defun Fact (N) "This is a documentation string for factorial."
(Cond ((Zerop N) 1) (T (* N (Fact #)))))
(Defun Fact (N) "This is a documentation string for factorial."
(Cond ((Zerop N) 1) (T (* N (Fact #)))))

> (pprint w)                ;  pprint always prints pretty.

(Defun Fact (N)
  "This is a documentation string for factorial."
  (Cond ((Zerop N) 1) (T (* N (Fact (- N 1)))))))

> *print-radix*             ;  Default is no radix prefix.
Nil

> (setf *print-radix* t)
T
```

Variable	Keyword
output stream	:stream
print-array	:array
print-base	:base
print-case	:case
print-circle	:circle
print-escape	:escape
print-gensym	:gensym
print-length	:length
print-level	:level
print-pretty	:pretty
print-radix	:radix

Table 7.3: write Keywords

```
> 10                        ; Hexadecimal: #x.
#xa


> 16
#x10


> (setf *print-base* 2)     ; Binary: #b.
#b10


> (setf *print-base* 8)     ; Octal: #o.
#o10


> (setf *print-base* 10)    ; Decimal: point.
10.


> (setf *print-base* 27)    ; Other base: # + number + r.
#27r10
```

In addition to using these global variables to control output, LISP allows the programmer to specify comparable keyword arguments for the functions write and write-to-string, as given in table 7.3 and demonstrated below.

```
> (write-to-string 10 :base 16)
"a"


> (write-to-string 10 :base 16 :radix t)
"#xa"
```

```
> (setf a (make-array '(2 3) :initial-element 1))
#2A((1 1 1) (1 1 1))

> (write a :array nil)
#<Array of rank 2 @ #x106da96>
#2A((1 1 1) (1 1 1))

> (write a :length 2)
#2A((1 1 ...) (1 1 ...))
#2A((1 1 1) (1 1 1))

> (write a :level 1)
#2A(# #)
#2A((1 1 1) (1 1 1))

> (write a :radix t)
#2A((1. 1. 1.) (1. 1. 1.))
#2A((1 1 1) (1 1 1))
```

7.8.4   File Options

In describing the open function above, we mentioned that there were other keyword options in addition to :direction. Here they are.

- :if-does-not-exist specifies what action to take in the event that the given file does not already exist.

- :if-exists specifies what action to take in the event that the given file *does* already exist.

- :element-type specifies data type to be read on the given stream.

- :external-format specifies the file's format. A value other than :default is implementation specific.

The options for :if-does-not-exist are as follows:

- :error signals an error if the file is not there. This is the default for reading a file.

- :create makes a new file with the given name. This is the default for writing to a file.

- nil means no action, and returns nil. This is the default for probing a file.

Here we try to read from a file that is not there. The default action is to signal an error.

```
> (setf s (open "test" :direction :input))
Error: File "/server/u18/homes.ai/slade/a/mss/1/test" does not exist.
  [condition type: FILE-ERROR]
[1]
> :res

> (setf s (open "test" :direction :input :if-does-not-exist nil))
NIL

> (setf s (open "test" :direction :input
                       :if-does-not-exist :create))
#<EXCL::CHARACTER-INPUT-FILE-STREAM
"/server/u18/homes.ai/slade/a/mss/1/test" pos 0 @ #x118c2f6>

> (setf s (open "test" :direction :input))
#<EXCL::CHARACTER-INPUT-FILE-STREAM
"/server/u18/homes.ai/slade/a/mss/1/test" pos 0 @ #x118cd3e>

> (close s)
T
```

The options for :if-exists are similar, but more numerous.

$\infty \Rightarrow$

- :error signals an error.

- :new-version creates a new file with the same name but a new version number. Some implementations will not support this feature.

- :rename changes the name of the existing file, and creates a new file with the old name.

- :rename-and-delete changes the name of the existing file, deletes it, and creates a new file with the old name.

- :overwrite leaves the old file but starts writing over it from the beginning.

- :append leaves the old file but starts writing at the end of it.

- :supersede replaces the old file with a new one.

- nil means not to create a file or a stream, and to return nil.

Now we try writing to the file and signal an error if it exists.

```
> (setf s (open "test" :direction :output :if-exists :error))
Error: File "/server/u18/homes.ai/slade/a/mss/1/test" already exists.
  [condition type: FILE-ERROR]
[1]
> :res
```

```
> (setf s (open "test" :direction :output :if-exists :new-version))
#<EXCL::CHARACTER-OUTPUT-FILE-STREAM
"/server/u18/homes.ai/slade/a/mss/l/test" pos 0 @ #x118ef66>

> (close s)
T
```

The :new-version option did nothing in this implementation. The :rename option below named the old file test-old.

```
> (setf s (open "test" :direction :output :if-exists :rename))
#<EXCL::CHARACTER-OUTPUT-FILE-STREAM
"/server/u18/homes.ai/slade/a/mss/l/test" pos 0 @ #x1192336>

> (close s)
T

> (setf s (open "test" :direction :output :if-exists nil))
NIL
```

The :element-type options are stream element data types which must be subtypes of character or integer or the keyword :default. In any case, the true element type of a stream can be determined with the function stream-element-type. Here are some examples.

First, assume we have a file test that contains the following.

```
12 23 34 45 56 67
```

We open this file for input, specifying the default element type of character.

```
> (setf s1 (open "test" :direction :input :element-type 'character))
#<EXCL::CHARACTER-INPUT-FILE-STREAM
"/server/u18/homes.ai/slade/a/mss/l/test" pos 0 @ #x108f2ce>

> (stream-element-type s1)
CHARACTER

> (read s1)                    ; Reads an expression.
12

> (file-position s1)          ; How many characters have we read?
3

> (file-length s1)            ; How long is the file?
18
```

```
> (file-string-length s1 "Hi")   ;  How much space is needed for "Hi"?
2
```

```
> (file-string-length s1 #\A)
1
```

```
> (read s1)                        ;  Reads the next expression.
23
```

```
> (read-char s1)                   ;  Reads one character.
#\3
```

```
> (read s1)                        ;  Reads the next expression.
4
```

```
> (close s1)
T
```

With the default character elements, LISP can read more than one character at a time. Below, we specify stream elements to be unsigned bytes instead of characters. Now we can read only one byte at a time.

The function `read-byte` has a required input stream argument and the optional `eof-error-p` and `eof-value` arguments. `read-byte` returns the integer value of the byte that it reads.

```
> (setf s1
    (open "test" :direction :input :element-type 'unsigned-byte))
#<EXCL::BINARY-INPUT-FILE-STREAM
"/server/u18/homes.ai/slade/a/mss/l/test" pos 0 @ #x1091906>
```

```
> (read-byte s1)
49
```

```
> (read-byte s1)
50
```

```
> (file-position s1)
2
```

```
> (file-length s1)
18
```

```
> (read-byte s1)
32
```

```
> (read-byte s1)
50

> (stream-element-type s1)
(UNSIGNED-BYTE 8)

> (close s1)
T
```

The companion function to `read-byte` is `write-byte`, which takes two arguments: an integer representing a byte, and an output stream.

```
> (setf s1
    (open "test2" :direction :output :element-type 'unsigned-byte))
#<EXCL::BINARY-OUTPUT-FILE-STREAM
"/server/u18/homes.ai/slade/a/mss/l/test2" pos 0 @ #x106cc46>

> (write-byte 49 s1)
49

> (write-byte 50 s1)
50

> (close s1)
T

> (with-open-file (is "test2" :direction :input)
    (read is))
12
```

The macro `with-open-file` provides an easy way to read and write files within a local context. Just as `let` creates local variable bindings to values, `with-open-file` creates a local stream binding to a file. In the last example, the variable in was given the value of an input stream bound to the file `test2`. When `with-open-file` concludes, it closes the file and its stream. Here is another example.

```
> (with-open-file (os "test3" :direction :output)
    (format os "1 2 3 4"))
NIL

> (with-open-file (is "test3" :direction :input)
    (+ (read is) (read is) (read is) (read is)))
10
```

Or, more compactly:

```
> (with-open-file
    (os "test3" :direction :output :if-exists :supersede)
    (with-open-file
      (is "test3" :direction :input)
      (format os "1 2 3 4")
      (finish-output os)
      (+ (read is) (read is) (read is) (read is))))
10
```

A related macro, with-open-stream, is a more general form of with-open-file.

```
> (with-open-stream (is (make-string-input-stream "1 2 3 4"))
    (+ (read is) (read is) (read is) (read is)))
10
```

7.8.5 Stream Options

Streams are a source of input and a direction for output. LISP provides several stream variations.

- synonym-stream is a stream that provides another name for a given stream.

- broadcast-stream is an output stream that writes to zero or more output streams simultaneously.

- concatenated-stream is an input stream that reads from zero or more input streams in sequence.

- two-way-stream is a bidirectional stream that reads from a specified input stream and writes to a specified output stream.

- echo-stream is a two-way-stream that additionally echos its input to its output.

The constructors for these streams have the standard prefix make-, as demonstrated below.

We first create a stream s with a synonym stream ss. We also assign s2 the value of s. Note that when we later assign s to a new stream, the synonym stream ss uses the new value, and s2 retains the old value.

```
> (setf s (make-string-input-stream "1 23 456"))
#<EXCL::STRING-INPUT-STREAM @ #x109f486>

> (setf ss (make-synonym-stream 's))
#<SYNONYM-STREAM @ #x109fe7e>
```

```
> (setf s2 s)
#<EXCL::STRING-INPUT-STREAM @ #x109f486>

> (+ (read s2) (read ss))
24

> (setf s (make-string-input-stream "1 23 456"))
#<EXCL::STRING-INPUT-STREAM @ #x10a0cc6>

> (read s2)
456

> (read ss)
1

> (synonym-stream-symbol ss)
S
```

We next create two string output streams, using `make-string-output-stream`, from which we build a single broadcast stream. The `get-output-stream-string` function returns the value of a string output stream as a string and resets the stream.

```
> (setf os (make-string-output-stream))
#<EXCL::STRING-OUTPUT-STREAM @ #x108f8fe>

> (setf os2 (make-string-output-stream))
#<EXCL::STRING-OUTPUT-STREAM @ #x10a1e66>

> (setf bs (make-broadcast-stream os os2))
#<BROADCAST-STREAM @ #x10a2bae>

> (format bs "Hello world")        ;  Writes to both streams.
NIL

> (get-output-stream-string os)
"Hello world"

> (get-output-stream-string os2)
"Hello world"

> (format os "Hello Again")        ;  Writes to just one stream.
NIL
```

```
> (format bs "What is new?")          ;  Writes to both.
NIL

> (get-output-stream-string os)
"Hello AgainWhat is new?"

> (get-output-stream-string os2)
"What is new?"

> (get-output-stream-string os)       ;  The stream is now empty.
""

> (broadcast-stream-streams bs)
(#<EXCL::STRING-OUTPUT-STREAM @ #x108f8fe>
#<EXCL::STRING-OUTPUT-STREAM @ #x10a1e66>)
```

The last function, broadcast-stream-streams, returns a list of the streams associated with the given broadcast stream. The next example is a concatenated stream.

```
> (setf s (make-string-input-stream "1 23 456"))
#<EXCL::STRING-INPUT-STREAM @ #x10a546e>

> (setf s2 (make-string-input-stream "1 23 456"))
#<EXCL::STRING-INPUT-STREAM @ #x10a5a5e>

> (setf cs (make-concatenated-stream s s2))
#<CONCATENATED-STREAM @ #x10a60a6>

> (+ (read cs) (read cs))             ;  1 + 23
24

> (+ (read cs) (read cs))             ;  4561 + 23
4584

> (read cs)
456

> (concatenated-stream-streams cs)
(#<EXCL::STRING-INPUT-STREAM @ #x10a546e>
#<EXCL::STRING-INPUT-STREAM @ #x10a5a5e>)
```

In the above example, we note that the third number read from the stream is not 456, but 4561, which results from concatenating 456 from the end of stream s and 1 from the start of stream s2.

Moreover, our default LISP implementation did not include a definition of ⇐ ∞
concatenated-stream-streams, so the result is based on other implementations.

We next create a two-way stream — a bidirectional stream. We make an input stream and an output stream and then join them as a two-way stream.

```
> (setf is (make-string-input-stream "1 2 3 4 5 6"))
#<EXCL::STRING-INPUT-STREAM @ #x1079aee>

> (setf os (make-string-output-stream))
#<EXCL::STRING-OUTPUT-STREAM @ #x105e79e>

> (setf tws (make-two-way-stream is os))
#<TWO-WAY-STREAM @ #x107bbe6>

> (two-way-stream-input-stream tws)
#<EXCL::STRING-INPUT-STREAM @ #x1079aee>

> (two-way-stream-output-stream tws)
#<EXCL::STRING-OUTPUT-STREAM @ #x105e79e>

> (print (+ (read tws) (read tws)) tws)
3

> (print (+ (read tws) (read tws)) tws)
7

> (print (+ (read tws) (read tws)) tws)
11

> (get-output-stream-string os)
"
3
7
11 "
```

The next hybrid stream is an echo stream. We again create an input stream and an output stream and then join them as an echo stream.

```
> (setf is (make-string-input-stream "1 2 3 4 5 6"))
#<EXCL::STRING-INPUT-STREAM @ #x1068e46>
```

```
> (setf os (make-string-output-stream))
#<EXCL::STRING-OUTPUT-STREAM @ #x105d24e>

> (setf es (make-echo-stream is os))
#<ECHO-STREAM @ #x106bade>
```

∞ ⇒
```
> (echo-stream-input-stream es)        ; Not actually implemented.
#<EXCL::STRING-INPUT-STREAM @ #x1068e46>
```

∞ ⇒
```
> (echo-stream-output-stream es)        ; Not actually implemented.
#<EXCL::STRING-OUTPUT-STREAM @ #x105d24e>
```

```
> (read es)
1

> (format es "Hello There")
NIL

> (+ (read es) (read es) (read es))
9

> (format es "good bye")
NIL

> (get-output-stream-string os)
"1 Hello There2 3 4 good bye"
```

Both the input and output values appear in the echo stream.
    There are three additional functions for streams.

- interactive-p is a predicate that indicates if the given stream is interactive.

∞ ⇒
- stream-external-format returns the value of the external file format for the stream. Values other than :default are implementation dependent.

- stream-element-type returns the type of element associated with the stream.

```
> (interactive-stream-p tws)
NIL

> (interactive-stream-p *terminal-io*)
T

> (stream-external-format tws)
:DEFAULT
```

```
> (stream-external-format *terminal-io*)
:DEFAULT

> (stream-external-format os)
:DEFAULT

> (stream-element-type tws)
STRING-CHAR

> (stream-element-type *terminal-io*)
STRING-CHAR
```

7.8.6   More Format Directives

The format function has additional control codes that provide such features as case conversion, conditional selection, iteration, and justification. Here are the directives, followed by examples.

The first set of format directives converts the case of strings.

~(str~) (case conversion) — The control string str is processed and printed in either all lower case [~(], initial capital for each word [~:(], all lowercase except initial capital [~@(], or all uppercase [~:@(]

~) (delimiter) — Terminates a case conversion control expression

```
> (format nil "~R" 2001)
"two thousand one"

> (format nil "~(~R~)" 2001)
"two thousand one"

> (format nil "~:(~R~)" 2001)
"Two Thousand One"

> (format nil "~@(~R~)" 2001)
"Two thousand one"

> (format nil "~:@(~R~)" 2001)
"TWO THOUSAND ONE"
```

The next set of format directives controls conditional alternatives.

~[s0~;s1~;...~;sn~] (conditional expression) – One of the control strings (or clauses) $s0, s1, \ldots, sn$ is selected by the corresponding argument, where the first clause is number 0.

~[s0~;s1~;...~;:default~] (conditional expression with default) – If none of the other clauses are selected, uses the last **default** clause (preceded by ~:;)

~:[false~;true~] (true or false conditional expression) – If the argument is NIL, uses the **false** string; otherwise, uses the **true** string

~] (delimiter) – Terminates a conditional expression

~; (separator) – Separates clauses in conditional and justification format control codes

~:; (default separator) – Indicates the default clause in a conditional expression

```
> (format nil "~[Gold~;Silver~;Bronze~] Medal" 0)
"Gold Medal"

> (format nil "~[Gold~;Silver~;Bronze~] Medal" 1)
"Silver Medal"

> (format nil "~[Gold~;Silver~;Bronze~;No~] Medal" 4)  ;  Out of range.
" Medal"

> (format nil "~[Gold~;Silver~;Bronze~:;No~] Medal" 4);  Default specified.
"No Medal"

> (format nil "~[empty handed~;medal winner~]" nil)    ;  Needs a number.
""

> (format nil "~:[empty handed~;medal winner~]" nil)   ;  True/false case.
"empty handed"

> (format nil "~:[empty handed~;medal winner~]" T)
"medal winner"
```

Our third set of format directives supports iterative execution.

~{str~} (iteration) – The argument is a list whose elements are used recursively as the arguments to the given control string **str**.

~:{str~} (iteration) – The argument is a list of lists whose sublists are used recursively as the arguments to the given control string **str**.

~@{str~} (iteration) – The remaining arguments in the **format** expression are used recursively as the arguments to the given control string **str**.

~:@{str~} (iteration) – The remaining arguments in the `format` expression are lists that are used recursively as the arguments to the given control string `str`.

~} (delimiter) – Terminates an iteration expression.

```
> (format nil "Stooges:~{ ~A~}" '(moe larry curly))
"Stooges: MOE LARRY CURLY"

> (format nil "Stooges:~:{ ~A (~A)~}" '((moe 1) (larry 2) (curly 3)))
"Stooges: MOE (1) LARRY (2) CURLY (3)"

> (format nil "Stooges:~@{ ~@(~A~)~}" 'moe 'larry 'curly)
"Stooges: Moe Larry Curly"

> (format nil "Stooges:~@{ ~@(~A~) (~:R)~}" 'moe 1 'larry 2 'curly 3)
"Stooges: Moe (first) Larry (second) Curly (third)"
```

We earlier noted that V can be used to replace a `format` prefix parameter, getting its value from a argument. The programmer can also use the # character instead of a prefix parameter. Its value is the number of arguments remaining to be processed, as demonstrated below.

```
> (format t "~@~%~#T~A~" 1 2 3 4 5)

    1
   2
  3
 4
5
NIL
```

In this example, the number of remaining arguments determines the tab column.

The final set of format directives specifies text justification.

~mincol,colinc,minpad,padchar<str~> (justification) – justifies the given string `str` within a field at least `mincol` wide (minimum column). The string may be segmented, using the ~; directive, in which case the space is equally divided among the segments. If there are only two segments, the first one is left justified and the second is right justified.

The optional `colinc` parameter (column increment) specifies the increment by which to increase the field if `mincol` is not wide enough. When `colinc` is not specified, the default value is 1.

The optional `minpad` parameter specifies the minimum number of characters to separate the segments. It defaults to 0.

The optional padchar parameter gives the character used to separate the segments. The default character is a space. Use a single quote as a prefix for the character.

The modifier : (as in ~10:<str~>) allows space to appear before the first segment.

The modifier @ (as in ~10@<str~>) allows space to appear after the last segment.

Using both modifiers, : and @ (as in ~10@:<str~>), allows space to appear at both the beginning and the end of the segments.

~> (delimiter) – Terminates a justification expression.

~^ (up and out) – Escapes from a formatting operation, such as stopping an iteration or justification expression.

```
> (format nil "~20<~A~;~A~>" "alpha" "omega")
"alpha          omega"

> (format nil "~20<~A~;~A~;~A~>" "alpha" "beta" "omega")
"alpha    beta    omega"

> (format nil "~20:<~A~;~A~;~A~>" "alpha" "beta" "omega")
"  alpha  beta  omega"

> (format nil "~20@<~A~;~A~;~A~>" "alpha" "beta" "omega")
"alpha  beta   omega  "

> (format nil "~20:@<~A~;~A~;~A~>" "alpha" "beta" "omega")
"  alpha  beta omega "

> (format nil "~20,1,1,'.<~A~;~A~>" "alpha" "omega")
"alpha..........omega"

> (format nil "~20,1,1,'.<~A~;~A~;~A~>" "alpha" "beta" "omega")
"alpha...beta...omega"

> (format nil "~20,1,1,'.<~A~;~A~;~A~>")
Error: Insufficient format args
   [condition type: PROGRAM-ERROR]
[1]

> (format nil "~20,1,1,'.<~^~A~;~A~;~A~>")   ; No error using ~^
""
```

We close with an example that borders on the useful: a format string for printing ordinal numbers. First, it prints the decimal number. Then, it selects a suffix based on the rightmost digit, providing the default "th" for 0 and 4 through 9.

```
(defun ordinal (n)
  (format nil "~d~[th~;st~;nd~;rd~:;th~]" n (mod n 10)))

> (ordinal 1)
"1st"

> (ordinal 2)
"2nd"

> (ordinal 23)
"23rd"

> (ordinal 144)
"144th"

> (ordinal 1000)
"1000th"
```

7.9 Exercises

7.9.1 column-print [4*]

Write a function column-print that uses cdr recursion to print out string elements of a list indented in a column to the given output stream.

```
> (column-print '("Go ahead" "make" "my" "  day") 5
    *standard-output*)

    Go ahead
    make
    my
      day
```

7.9.2 multi-column-print [5*]

Write a function multi-column-print that uses cdr recursion to print out elements of a list in a given number of columns of a given width to the given output stream. If there are C columns and N items, the first N/C items should print to the first column, then the next N/C items to the second column, and so forth. Each column should be of the same length, plus or minus 1.

The function takes the keyword arguments: :columns, :width, :stream, and :indent. The default number of columns is 1. The default width is 80 divided by the number of columns. The default output stream is *standard-output*, and the default indentation is 0. You might find it useful to define a function split-list, which is demonstrated below.

```
> (setf x '(1 2 3 4 5 6 7 8 9 10 11 12))
(1 2 3 4 5 6 7 8 9 10 ...)

> (split-list x 6)
((1 7) (2 8) (3 9) (4 10) (5 11) (6 12))

> (multi-column-print x :columns 2)
```

```
1                           7
2                           8
3                           9
4                           10
5                           11
6                           12
```

```
> (split-list x 3)
((1 4 7 10) (2 5 8 11) (3 6 9 12))

> (multi-column-print x :columns 4 :width 5)
```

```
1    4    7    10
2    5    8    11
3    6    9    12
```

```
> (split-list x 2)
((1 3 5 7 9 11) (2 4 6 8 10 12))

> (multi-column-print x :columns 6 :width 5 :indent 5)
```

```
     1    3    5    7    9    11
     2    4    6    8    10   12
```

7.9.3   split Command [4*]

This is a two-part question concerning the function split, which was given on page 213. First, what's wrong with defining split as follows?

```
(defun split (left-text right-text stream)
  (flushleft left-text stream)
  (flushright right-text stream))
```

Second, redefine `split` without using the hpos function.

7.9.4 tab Command [4*]

Write a `tab` function that moves to a specified column in the given output stream.
If necessary, `tab` will move to the next line to arrive at the proper column. Here is
a sample program that shows how `tab` works.

```
(defun sample-tab ()
  (let ((s *standard-output*))
    (write-string "This" s)
    (tab 10 s)
    (write-string "is" s)
    (tab 30 s)
    (write-string "a sample" s)
    (tab 5 s)
    (write-string "of tab..." s)
    (values)))

> (sample-tab)
This      is                    a sample
      of tab...
```

7.9.5 Two-Digit Romans [4*]

In chapter 1, we belittle the concept of a 2-digit Roman numeral. Write a function
`romans` that generates a list of all $N - digit$ Roman numerals less than or equal a
given limit. Below, we produce all 2-digit numerals below 1000 and 4-digit numerals
less than 40.

```
> (romans 1000 2)
("CM" "DC" "DL" "DX" "DV" "DI" "CD" "CC" "CL" "CX" "CV" "CI"
 "XC" "LX" "LV" "LI" "XL" "XX" "XV" "XI" "IX" "VI" "IV" "II")

> (romans 40 4)
("XXXV" "XXXI" "XXIX" "XXVI" "XXIV" "XXII" "XVII" "XIII" "VIII")
```

7.9.6 peek-char Problem [3*]

What is wrong with this definition of `peek-char`?

```
(defun bad-peek-char (type stream)
  (let ((char (read-char stream)))
    (unread-char char stream)))
```

7.9.7   split-fill [4*]

Write a function `split-fill` that is similar to the `split` function defined in section 7.2, except that the new function will print a specified character repeatedly in the space between the left and right texts.

```
(split-fill "Birds, for the " #\. " pages 1-217" *standard-output*)
Birds, for the ...................................... pages 1-217
```

7.9.8   Defining format [6]

Write a simple version of the `format` function that takes exactly three arguments: an output stream, a control string, and a single output argument.

The control string can include any of the control codes of the real `format`, but a given control string can have only one occurrence of a control code which requires an argument. Thus, "~A loves Mary." is OK, but "~A loves ~A" is not. One exception is numeric control codes, such as "~D" and "~P". A control string can have multiple numeric control codes, but they all match the same third argument, as in the following:

```
> (my-format *standard-output* "John ate ~D pizza~P.~%" 3)
John ate 3 pizzas.
NIL

> (my-format *standard-output* "Mary ate ~D pizza~P.~%" 1)
Mary ate 1 pizza.
NIL
```

7.9.9   Error in 3-letter-word-p [3*]

The predicate `3-letter-word-p` fails to detect an important case. Which one?

7.9.10   File Revision [6]

One useful type of file filter is one that can change or correct parts of the file. For example, suppose you have a file containing a boilerplate paragraph with places for a name to be substituted. Here are the contents of "gift.file", an example of a boilerplate text.

```
Thank you so much for the *GIFT*.
How did you know that Pat and I needed a
*GIFT*? Every time we look at the *GIFT*
we think of you.
```

Write a function `revise-file` that takes four arguments: an input file, an output file, a search pattern, and a replacement pattern. Here is a sample run on the above text.

```
> (revise-file "gift.file" "gift.out" "*GIFT*" "keyboard duster")

old: "Thank you so much for the *GIFT*."
new: "Thank you so much for the keyboard duster."

old: "*GIFT*? Every time we look at the *GIFT*"
new: "keyboard duster? Every time we look at the keyboard duster"
*END-OF-FILE-REVISION*
```

Note that the program prints out intermediate results when it makes a change and that the program can handle multiple changes on one line. Here are the resulting contents of the output file.

```
Thank you so much for the keyboard duster.
How did you know that Pat and I needed a
keyboard duster? Every time we look at the keyboard duster
we think of you.
```

7.9.11   File Comparison [5*]

Another useful software tool is a utility which compares files. That is, if you have two versions of a file, you can compare the two files to identify the precise ways in which they differ.

Write a function `compare-file` that takes two filenames as arguments and prints out lines that are different. Assume that both files are the same length — no deleted or inserted lines.

Here is an example, using the sample files from the preceding exercise.

```
> (compare-file "gift.file" "gift.out")

1: "Thank you so much for the *GIFT*."
2: "Thank you so much for the keyboard duster."

1: "*GIFT*? Every time we look at the *GIFT*"
2: "keyboard duster? Every time we look at the keyboard duster"
*END-OF-FILE-COMPARE*

> (compare-file "gift.file" "gift.file")
*END-OF-FILE-COMPARE*
```

In the second example, the files are identical, so no differences were found. You may choose to handle the case in which one file is longer than the other.

7.9.12   File Sorting [7]

Yet another common type of file transducer is a sort utility. We briefly looked at sorting in exercise 6.8.3.

In this exercise, we invite the reader to create a sort utility that will read in a file, sort each line of the file based a given set of key fields, lengths, and comparison predicates, and write the results to a given output file. Here is an example.

```
;; Contents of file: names.txt
Mary        Jones        345-9090    123 Pine Street
Deborah     Smith        782-1245    456 Elm Street, 12-B
Susan       Brown        889-4321    789 Maple Street
Jane        Smith        345-7766    1212 Grove Terrace
Mary        White        889-3758    321 Avenue of Trees
Louise      Brown        782-3299    43 Oak Drive
```

```
;; filesort takes three arguments:
;        input-file
;        output-file
;        list of key fields and comparison predicates
> (filesort "names.txt" "names.out" '((13 12 #'string-lessp)
          (1 12 #'string-lessp)))
*END-OF-FILESORT*
```

```
;; Resulting contents of file: names.out
Louise      Brown        782-3299    43 Oak Drive
Susan       Brown        889-4321    789 Maple Street
Mary        Jones        345-9090    123 Pine Street
Deborah     Smith        782-1245    456 Elm Street, 12-B
Jane        Smith        345-7766    1212 Grove Terrace
Mary        White        889-3758    321 Avenue of Trees
```

The primary sort key is given first; in this case, it is the last names, which start at the 13th character in each line and extend for 12 characters. The second sort key is the first names, which begin at the first position and extend for 12 characters.

7.9.13   Eliza [3]

The pattern matcher from exercise 4.7.12 can be used to implement a simple conversation program, modeled after ELIZA [Weizenbaum, 1966].

ELIZA is a parlor trick. The original version of ELIZA simulated a Rogerian psychotherapist. In order for someone to believe that ELIZA is actually coherent, the domain of discourse must be constrained. The example domain below is a disoriented college roommate. User input here is <u>underlined</u>.

```
> (eliza)
Hi.

--> (my name is john)
(GLAD TO MEET YOU. MY FRIENDS CALL ME DR. DEATH.)

--> (I am a chemistry major)
(DO YOU THINK I CARE ABOUT THAT)

--> (what year are you)
(IF I 'M LUCKY I 'LL GRADUATE BEFORE THE TURN OF THE CENTURY.)

--> (I need to check with the housing office)
(REALLY.)

--> quit
End of ELIZA.
```

Here is the code for this simple version of Eliza.

```
;;  This is the master function.
(defun eliza ()
  (format t "~%Hi.")
  (process-reply)
  (format t "End of ELIZA.~%~%")
  (values))

;; This function reads the input from the user, checks for
;; termination and errors, then sends the input to the matcher,
;; and repeats recursively.
(defun process-reply ()
  (format t "--> ")
  (let ((reply (read *standard-input*)))
    (cond
      ((member reply '(nil q quit)) nil)
      ((not (listp reply))
       (format
        t "~%*** Give input as a ( list ). Type Q to quit. ***~%")
       (process-reply))
      ((script-match reply *master-script*)
       (process-reply))
      (t nil))))
```

```
;; script-match uses cdr recursion to try each script pattern,
;; using the matchp predicate from exercise 4.7.12.
(defun script-match (reply script)
  (cond ((null script) nil)
        ((let ((match (matchp (caar script) reply)))
           (cond (match (fix-reply match (cadar script)))
                 (t (script-match reply (cdr script)))))))))
```

```
;; fix-reply prints out the response.
(defun fix-reply (match response)
  (format t "~A~%" response)
  t)
```

```
;; The script for the crazy roommate.
;; Note that the default reply "Really" is triggered by the pattern: *wild*
(defvar *master-script*
  '(((*wild* laundry *wild*)
     (When my clothes get too dirty I just burn them.))
    ((i am *wild*)
     (do you think I care about that))
    ((i want you *wild*)
     (why do you want me *wild*))
    ((do you *wild*)
     (why should you care about me))
    ((*wild* year *wild*)
     (If I'm lucky I'll graduate before the turn of the century.))
    ((*wild* mother *wild*)
     (Don't make any cracks about my mother.  She's a saint.))
    ((My name *wild*)
     (Glad to meet you.   My friends call me Dr. Death.))
    ((No *wild*)
     (Well pardon me for living.))
    ((*wild* sick)
     (I think this room has lead paint.  It makes you crazy.))
    ((*wild*) (Really.))))
```

In this exercise, you are asked to create a script for a new domain in which the trick might reasonably work. Sample domains might be a parent addressing a child, a child addressing a parent, a senile professor, an incompetent psychotherapist, a bad (?good) politician at a press conference, or a valley-speak computer nerd (gag me with a mouse). To be at all robust, your script should have 20 or more separate pattern/response clauses.

7.9.14   More Eliza [5*]

You can make Eliza more convincing with a minor addition. Modify the program to echo part of the input in the response and, in the process, handle pronoun agreement.

For example, if the input is I DON'T LIKE MY COACH and the phrase I DON'T LIKE matches a pattern, the program should be able to respond with something like WHY DON'T YOU LIKE YOUR COACH. So, it should convert MY to YOUR, and vice versa, I to YOU, and vice versa (actually this is ambiguous, since YOU could become either I or ME). This requires that you alter the matchp predicate so that it returns the portion of the input that matched *wild*. For example,

```
> (matchp '(I DON'T LIKE *WILD*) '(I DON'T LIKE MY CRAZY COACH))
(MY CRAZY COACH)
```

The response, *mutatis mutandis*, could then be (WHY DON'T YOU LIKE YOUR CRAZY COACH).

The pattern/response pair for this example would be

```
((I DON'T LIKE *WILD*) (WHY DON'T YOU LIKE *WILD*))
```

where the *WILD* in the response is replaced with the value returned by matchp with appropriate pronoun changes.

Note that if you simply make successive global pronoun changes in a pattern, you may end up with a problem. For example:

Initial input: (I DON'T LIKE THE WAY YOU TALK TO ME.)

matchp result: (THE WAY YOU TALK TO ME.)

Change ME to YOU: (THE WAY YOU TALK TO YOU.)

Change YOU to I: (THE WAY I TALK TO I.)

Final response: (WHY DON'T YOU LIKE THE WAY I TALK TO I)

In addition to matchp, the only other changes needed are to fix-reply and the script itself. The fix-reply function will probably need to call a pronoun-shift function to fix the pronouns, as shown here.

```
> (pronoun-shift '(i am not your friend))
(YOU ARE NOT MY FRIEND)

> (pronoun-shift '(the way you talk to me))
(THE WAY I TALK TO YOU)
```

There is a standard LISP function well suited to this task.

7.9.15　Better type and filter [4*]

Rewrite the functions `type` and `filter-file` from section 7.6, using `with-open-file`.

7.9.16　Halloween = Christmas [3*]

Under what circumstances does the following relation hold?

```
31 OCT = 25 DEC
```

7.10　Chapter Summary

- The following LISP object types are introduced in this chapter.

  ```
  stream
  pathname
  ```

- In LISP, *streams* are used both for input (a source for reading data) and output (a receptacle for writing data).

- Files and screens are examples of streams. The predefined LISP streams are assigned to the following global variables.

  ```
  *standard-input*
  *standard-output*
  *query-io*
  *debug-io*
  *terminal-io*
  *error-output*
  *trace-output*
  ```

- LISP provides a variety of basic functions for writing data to stream:

  ```
  (pprint object [stream])
  (princ object [stream])
  (print object [stream])
  (prin1 object [stream])
  (terpri [stream])
  (fresh-line [stream])
  (write object [options])
  (write-char character [stream])
  (write-line string [stream])
  (write-string string [stream])
  ```

- There are two predicates for output streams.

```
(streamp stream)
(output-stream-p stream)
```

- The programmer can also write output to strings.

```
(princ-to-string object)
(prin1-to-string object)
(write-to-string object [[options]])
(with-output-to-string (var [string]) {form}*)
```

- For more complex output operations, the programmer can use `format`, which has a number of options.

- The function `values` is useful to return as a nonprinting result of output routines.

- Strings can be used as input streams, using either of the following:

```
(make-string-input-stream string)
(with-input-from-string (var string [:index place]
      [:start sn] [:end en]) {form}*)
```

- Files can be used for input and output. Useful predicates and operations include:

```
(probe-file filename)
(open filename [:direction in-out] [:element-type type]
      [:if-exists y-action] [:if-does-not-exist n-action])
(close stream)
```

- LISP provides a variety of basic functions for reading data:

```
(read-char stream)
(unread-char character stream)
(peek-char type stream)
(read-line stream)
(clear-input stream)
(read stream)
```

as well as functions for getting information about the input stream:

```
(input-stream-p stream)
(listen stream)
```

- LISP file system output operations are normally buffered. The programmer can change the default stream output behavior with the functions:

```
(finish-output [stream])
(force-output [stream])
(clear-output [stream])
```

- The LISP pathname provides a platform-independent way to refer to files. The components of a pathname include host, device, directory, name, type, and version. LISP supports the following pathname functions.

```
(pathname object)
(pathnamep object)
(truename object
(pathname-host pathname)
(pathname-device pathname)
(pathname-directory pathname)
(pathname-name pathname)
(pathname-type pathname)
(pathname-version pathname)
(namestring pathname)
(namestring pathname)
(file-namestring pathname)
(directory-namestring pathname)
(host-namestring pathname)
(enough-namestring pathname)
(user-homedir-pathname)
(make-pathname {:host h] [:device d] [:directory r] [:name n]
        [:type t] [:version v] [:defaults path])
(merge-pathnames pathname [pathname [version]])
(parse-namestring object [host [defaults]
        [:start s] [:end e] [:junk-allowed ja]])
```

The global variable *default-pathname-defaults* contains the default component values for pathname construction.

You think you know when you can learn, are more sure when you can write, even more when you can teach, but certain when you can program.

◇ ALAN PERLIS, *Epigrams in Programming (1982)*

Chapter 8

lambda and labels

Objects in LISP can be created and assigned as values of variables. Thus, numbers, lists, characters, strings, streams, and functions can be given names by binding them to symbols. If we define x to have the value of '(a-long-expression), we have in effect given '(a-long-expression) the name x. This technique provides a convenient shorthand or abbreviation, especially if we wish to refer to '(a-long-expression) more than once. For example, assume we have an ordered list of presidents of the United States.

```
(defvar *us-presidents* '(washington adams jefferson ...))

(defun presidentp (x)
  (member x *us-presidents*))

(defun first-presidentp (x)
  (eq x (car *us-presidents*)))
```

To use this list in different places, we need not duplicate the list. Instead, we just use its name. This use of names to refer to frequently used data objects is the preferred method. In the above example, one can easily add new presidents to the global variable without having to change the existing code that refers to *us-presidents*.

Often, however, the object is used in only one location, so there is no need to have a special name for it. We can use the explicit description of the object itself. For example, if we have a function that checks to see if its argument is the name of the first president of the United States, we can represent that name directly in the code.

```
(defun first-presidentp (x)
  (eq x 'washington))
```

We use the literal washington without recourse to a variable. When we use defun to create a function, we are likewise assigning a name to the function. As with other named objects, the function's name makes it easier for us to reuse that object. In our examples so far, all of our functions have been given names. We shall now see how to write nameless functions.

8.1   lambda

The LISP language was derived in part from a mathematical formalism, developed in the 1930s by Alonzo Church, called the *lambda*-calculus or λ-calculus. [Church, 1941] The use of the reserved word lambda is one vestige of that early history. In LISP, one uses lambda at the beginning of a list to indicate the description of a function. The list element immediately following the *lambda* is a list of the variable names local to the function. Here are some examples.

```
> #'(lambda (n) (+ n 2))        ; Adds 2 to its argument.
∞ ⇒ #<Interpreted Function (unnamed) @ #x109036e>

> ((lambda (n) (+ n 2)) 5)      ; We can use it as a function.
7

> #'(lambda (x) (* x 2))        ; Doubles its argument.
#<Interpreted Function (unnamed) @ #x1090d1e>

> ((lambda (x) (* x 2)) 5)      ; It works just fine.
10

> (functionp #'car)             ; functionp is a predicate for functions.
T
```

```
> (functionp 'car)            ;  The symbol car is not a function.
NIL

> (functionp #'(lambda (x) (* x 2)))
T
```

.2 Functional Arguments

In earlier chapters, we saw examples of functions which had other functions as arguments. For example, the LISP functions mapcar and some take functional arguments. Previously, we used named functions as the arguments, but it is also possible to use lambda expressions. Here are examples of the use of mapcar with named functions as well as lambda expressions.

```
> (mapcar #'1+ '(1 2 3 4))
(2 3 4 5)

> (mapcar #'(lambda (x) (+ x 2)) '(1 2 3 4))
(3 4 5 6)

> (mapcar #'+ '(1 2 3 4) '(5 6 7 8))
(6 8 10 12)

> (mapcar #'(lambda (x) (format t "~A~%" (+ x 1))) '(1 2 3 4))
2
3
4
5
(NIL NIL NIL NIL)

> (mapc #'(lambda (x) (format t "~A~%" (+ x 1))) '(1 2 3 4))
2
3
4
5
(1 2 3 4)

> (mapcar #'(lambda (x y) (+ x (* 2 y))) '(1 2 3 4) '(5 6 7 8))
(11 14 17 20)
```

We use the list function mapc, introduced in section 3.13.1, which is similar to mapcar, but only for performing side effects on lists. Unlike mapcar, mapc does not accumulate results.

It is important to recognize that lambda affords us a way to use functions without giving them explicit names. The last example could easily have been accomplished by defining another function that would add its first argument to twice the value of its second argument. However, lambda lets us avoid that intermediate step.

In fact, you can assign names to lambda expressions as an alternative way of defining functions, using the accessor function symbol-function, which can be used with setf.

```
> (setf (symbol-function 'triple) #'(lambda (n) (* n 3)))
#<Interpreted Function TRIPLE @ #x10a48b6>

> (triple 5)
15
```

Here is the method used in previous chapters:

```
> (defun triple (n) (* n 3))
TRIPLE

> (symbol-function 'triple)
#<Interpreted Function TRIPLE @ #x10a54fe>

> (triple 6)
18
```

Consider the following cryptography example. We define a function encode, which increments the ASCII value of a character by some given integer. The decode function reverses that operation. Then, we define two additional functions, string-encode and string-decode, to extend the operation to entire strings.

```
(defun encode (char n)
  (code-char (+ (char-code char) n)))

(setf (symbol-function 'decode)
      #'(lambda (char n) (code-char (- (char-code char) n))))

(defun string-encode (string n)
  (map 'string #'(lambda (char) (encode char n)) string))

(setf (symbol-function 'string-decode)
      #'(lambda (string n)
          (map 'string #'(lambda (char) (decode char n)) string)))

> (defvar x (string-encode "mary had a little lambda" 1))
"nbsz!ibe!b!mjuumf!mbnceb"
```

```
> (string-decode x 1)
"mary had a little lambda"
```

Note that we have used `lambda` expressions in two distinct fashions. First, we have defined the functions `decode` and `string-decode` with the explicit `lambda` syntax. Compare those definitions with the functions `encode` and `string-encode`. They are equally acceptable.

Second, within the functions `string-encode` and `string-decode`, we used `lambda` expressions as arguments to the function `mapc`. In each case, the `lambda` expression has one variable that gets bound to successive characters of the given string. Note that the increment variable, n, is embedded in the `lambda` expression, since it is the same for each character of the string.

8.3 apply

When we call a function, we have a number of ways in which we can specify the relationship between the function and its arguments. Here are four examples, which yield equivalent results.

```
> (+ 3 4)                    ;  Normal LISP function call.
7


> (funcall #'+ 3 4)          ;  funcall calls +.
7


> ((lambda (x y) (+ x y)) 3 4)  ;  A lambda expression is a function.
7


> (car (mapcar #'+ '(3) '(4)))  ;  mapcar returns a list of results.
7
```

The third example may seem contorted. In each case, LISP is following the same underlying process: interpret the leftmost item as a function and the remaining items as arguments; evaluate the arguments, then pass them as parameters to the function.

The LISP syntax provides this implicit interpretation. However, there is an explicit way of notating this process through the use of the function `apply`. Here are two examples of `apply`.

```
> (apply #'+ '(3 4))
7


> (apply #'(lambda (x y) (+ x y)) '(3 4))
7
```

The first argument to `apply` is the function that is being invoked. The remaining arguments constitute that function's arguments. Thus, in the first case, + is applied to the list (3 4).

Multiple arguments can be separated as long as the final argument given in `apply` is a proper list. The functional argument to `apply` will use all of the remaining arguments.

```
> (apply #'+ 3 '(4))
7


> (apply #'+ 3 4 '())
7


> (apply #'+ 3 4 5 6 7 NIL)        ;  NIL is the same as ().
25


> (apply #'append '(1 2) '(3 4) '(5 6) '())
(1 2 3 4 5 6)


> (apply #'append '((1 2) (3 4) (5 6)))
(1 2 3 4 5 6)
```

Thus, `apply` provides an explicit way of indicating the process of functional application. In LISP, the use of `apply` is particularly transparent because functions can be used freely as arguments themselves. Here are four examples of `apply` with equivalent expressions.

```
(apply #'car '((a b)))           ==>      (car '(a b))
(apply #'* '(7 5))               ==>      (* 7 5)
(apply #'list 1 2 3 '())         ==>      (list 1 2 3)
(apply #'apply #'+ 1 2 () ()) ==>         (apply #'+ 1 2 '())
```

The last example shows that `apply` can be given as a functional argument to itself.

As promised in section 3.4, we shall give a recursive definition of `append`, using `apply`. Note that this definition requires a second function, `append2`, which takes exactly two arguments. The regular append function takes any number of arguments.

```
(defun my-append (&rest lists)
  (cond ((endp lists) '())
        ((endp (cdr lists)) (car lists))
        ((endp (cddr lists)) (my-append2 (car lists) (cadr lists)))
        (t (my-append (car lists) (apply #'my-append (cdr lists))))))
```

```
(defun my-append2 (list1 list2)
  (cond ((endp list1) list2)
        (t (cons (car list1) (my-append2 (cdr list1) list2)))))
```

8.4   Naming Local Functions: flet and labels

We have seen how lambda expressions can be used anonymously within other functions. The cryptography function string-encode given on page 278 uses both a
lambda expression and a call to another named function: encode. If no other functions call encode, then it is not really useful or necessary to define it on its own. It
could be incorporated directly into the definition of string-encode.

```
(defun string-encode (string n)
  (map 'string
       #'(lambda (char)
           (code-char (+ (char-code char) n)))
       string))
```

Alternatively, we could actually give a *local* name to encode that could only be
referenced from within the string-encode function.

```
(defun string-encode2 (string n)
  (flet ((encode (ch num)
                 (code-char (+ (char-code ch) num))))
        (map 'string #'(lambda (char) (encode char n)) string)))
; or simply:
(defun string-encode3 (string n)
  (flet ((encode (ch)
                 (code-char (+ (char-code ch) n))))
        (map 'string #'encode string)))
```

We saw in chapter 5 how to use let to create variables that are local to a given
function. The flet form provides similar support for defining local functions.
The use of local variables is especially helpful in avoiding name conflicts when a
program is large and complex. By using local variables, a programmer generally
makes certain that the variable to which she is referring is in fact the one she
intended.

Similarly, naming conflicts can occur with function names as well as with
variable names. If a programmer is developing a very large program, possibly as
part of a group effort involving a team of programmers, it is extremely important
that the programmer avoid creating global objects — either variables or functions
— that might collide with other objects. The most general solution to this problem
uses *packages*, discussed in chapter 15.

In the present example, `encode` is local within `string-encode`. Thus, even if another `encode` function was defined elsewhere, the code for `string-encode` will still perform as expected.

Just as LISP provides a special syntax for defining global functions, `flet` provides a special form for defining local functions. The use of `flet` can be viewed as a cross between `defun` and `let`.

Common LISP provides another form for creating local function definitions: `labels`. The basic syntactic forms for `flet` and `labels` are quite similar.

```
(flet ({(name lambda-list {function-form}*)}*) {form}*)
```

```
(labels ({(name lambda-list {function-form}*)}*) {form}*)
```

Here is a definition of `string-encode` using `labels`.

```
(defun string-encode4 (string n)
  (labels
    ((encode (ch num)
            (code-char (+ (char-code ch) num))))
    (map 'string
         #'(lambda (char) (encode char n)) string)))
```

This example is virtually identical to the use of `flet` given above. It does not reveal the key difference between `flet` and `labels`: functions defined with `labels` can themselves refer to other functions defined in the same expression, including references to themselves. Thus, `labels` allows the programmer to create local recursive functions.

For example, here is a definition of the `length` function, which is implemented with a local recursive function.

```
(defun my-length (list)
  (labels
    ((count-length (list n)
                  (cond
                    ((null list) n)
                    (t (count-length (cdr list) (1+ n)))))))
    (count-length list 0)))
```

This definition would not work if `labels` is replaced by `flet` because `count-length` is a recursive local function. The `count-length` function keeps an accumulator variable, n, which it increments at each recursive call.

This use of an accumulator is similar to the `above-average` and `below-average` functions defined earlier (see page 126). Using `labels`, we can easily incorporate the recursive subfunction `below-average` as a local function.

```
(defun above-average (num-list)
  (labels
   ((below-average (num-list count total)
                   (cond
                    ((null num-list) (/ total count))
                    (t (below-average (cdr num-list)
                                      (+ count 1)
                                      (+ (car num-list)
                                         total))))))
   (below-average num-list 0 0)))
```

In addition to this facility of recursive reference, another feature that a programmer may sometimes wish to use is to cross-reference local variables — that is, have one local variable defined in terms of another. Here is a variation on the son-of-zeller exercise, which appeared on page 63, but with the argument given as a list of the form (day month year).

```
(defun bad-zeller (date)
  (let ((day    (car date))
        (month  (cadr date))
        (year   (caddr date))
        (century (truncate year 100))
        (decades (- year (* 100 century)))
        (leap   (cond ((leap-yearp year) 1)
                      (t 0))))
    (zeller day month century decades leap)))
```

In this example, several of the local variables are defined in terms of other local variables: century refers to year, decades refers to both year and century, and leap refers to year. As might be inferred from the function's name, this use of let does not work. This limitation of let becomes apparent when you understand that let can be described in terms of lambda in the following fashion.

```
(let ((variable-1 value-1)
      (variable-2 value-2)
        . . .
      (variable-n value-n))
   body-of-function )
```

is equivalent to

```
(funcall
 #'(lambda (variable-1 variable-2 ... variable-n)
     body-of-function)
   value-1 value-2 ... value-n)
```

Thus, our definition of bad-zeller is translated into the following.

```
(defun bad-zeller (date)
  (funcall
    #'(lambda (day month year century decades leap)
        (zeller day month century decades leap))
    (car date)
    (cadr date)
    (caddr date)
    (truncate year 100)        ;  year is undefined here and below.
    (- year (* 100 century)) ;  century is undefined here.
    (cond ((leap-yearp year) 1)
          (t 0))))
```

The problem arises when the value of the variable year is referred to by the other local variables, century, decades, and leap. Also, the value of the variable decades refers to the value of another local variable, century. One method to solve the problem would be to replace references to the variable year with its value (caddr date) and to define decades in another fashion, for example, as (remainder (caddr date) 100). A second way would be to use nested let expressions, as follows.

```
(defun good-zeller (date)
  (let ((day (car date))
        (month (cadr date))
        (year (caddr date)))
    (let ((century (truncate year 100))
          (leap  (cond ((leap-yearp year) 1)
                       (t 0))))
      (let ((decades (- year (* 100 century))))
        (zeller day month century decades leap)))))
```

which is equivalent to

```
(defun good-zeller (date)
  (funcall
   #'(lambda (day month year)
       (funcall
        #'(lambda (century leap)
            (funcall #'(lambda (decades)
                         (zeller day month century decades leap))
                     (- year (* 100 century)))))
           (truncate year 100)
           (cond ((leap-yearp year) 1)
                 (t 0)))))
    (car date)
    (cadr date)
    (caddr date)))
```

The good-zeller function solves the problem of cross-reference by defining the local variables century and leap nested within the scope of the year variable, and by defining decades nested within the scope of the century variable. This nesting method is effective in these cases, but there is a third alternative which is cleaner and clearer: let*, which behaves like let except it allows local variables to refer to earlier local variables. Here is an example.

```
> (defvar a 5)
5

> (let ((a 10) (b a)) b)
5

> (let* ((a 10) (b a)) b)
10
```

In the let expression, the variable b gets its value from the global value of a, which is 5. In the let* expression, b gets its value from the local value of a, which is 10.

We can apply let* to our zeller problem.

```
(defun better-zeller (date)
  (let* ((day    (car date))
         (month  (cadr date))
         (year   (caddr date))
         (century (truncate year 100))
         (decades (- year (* 100 century)))
         (leap   (cond ((leap-yearp year) 1)
                       (t 0))))
    (zeller day month century decades leap)))
```

```
> (better-zeller '(1 7 1996))     ;     1 September 1996
0                                  ;     was a Sunday.
```

This definition works because `let*` provides sequential binding of variables. Thus, `better-zeller` is equivalent to the following definition using `let`.

```
(defun better-zeller (date)
  (let ((day   (car date)))
    (let ((month (cadr date)))
      (let ((year  (caddr date)))
        (let ((century (truncate year 100)))
          (let ((decades (- year (* 100 century))))
            (let ((leap  (cond ((leap-yearp year) 1)
                               (t 0))))
              (zeller day month century decades leap)))))))))
```

Similarly, `labels` appears to do the right thing as well.

8.5 Mutually Recursive Functions

In the preceding section, we argued for the use of `labels` on grounds of clarity and conciseness. These are important criteria. However, there are situations that require `labels` out of necessity — cases which `flet` cannot handle directly. These cases involve recursion. The locally recursive definition of `length` given on page 282 would be much trickier with `flet`. (See exercise 8.7.7.)

An extension of recursion is *mutual recursion*, that is, multiple functions that are each defined in terms of the other.

In the answer to exercise 7.9.7, we defined a function `repeat-char` that repeatedly prints a given character to a stream.

```
(defun repeat-char (stream char count)
  (cond ((zerop count) (values))
        (t (write-char char stream)
           (repeat-char stream char (1- count)))))
```

```
> (repeat-char *standard-output* #\* 10)
**********
```

Consider an extended version of `repeat-char` that prints a series of three characters, instead of just one. However, the number of characters in the resulting string might not be an even multiple of three. One way to handle this is with three subfunctions, which call each other in sequence. These functions can be created by using `labels`.

```
(defun repeat-trio (stream ch1 ch2 ch3 count)
  (labels ((pr-ch1 (count)
                  (cond ((zerop count) (values))
                        (t (write-char ch1 stream)
                           (pr-ch2 (1- count)))))
           (pr-ch2 (count)
                  (cond ((zerop count) (values))
                        (t (write-char ch2 stream)
                           (pr-ch3 (1- count)))))
           (pr-ch3 (count)
                  (cond ((zerop count) (values))
                        (t (write-char ch3 stream)
                           (pr-ch1 (1- count))))))
    (pr-ch1 count)))

> (repeat-trio *standard-output* #\* #\. #\- 10)
*.-*.-*.-*
```

The function `repeat-trio` comprises three subfunctions, `pr-ch1`, `pr-ch2`, and `pr-ch3`, each of which checks for the termination condition (if `count` is zero), then writes its respective character to the stream and calls the next subfunction. Following these three definitions, the body of the `labels` is a call to the first function, `pr-ch1`, which starts the ball rolling.

The reader might have noticed that the three subfunctions in `repeat-trio` have virtually identical definitions. It is possible to take advantage of this similarity and define all three functions in terms of the underlying operations. Here is another definition of `repeat-trio`.

```
(defun repeat-trio (stream ch1 ch2 ch3 count)
  (labels ((pr-char (char count next)
                  (cond ((zerop count) (values))
                        (t (write-char char stream)
                           (funcall next (- count 1)))))
           (pr-ch1 (count) (pr-char ch1 count #'pr-ch2))
           (pr-ch2 (count) (pr-char ch2 count #'pr-ch3))
           (pr-ch3 (count) (pr-char ch3 count #'pr-ch1)))
    (pr-ch1 count)))
```

In this example, the function `pr-char` is used to define each of the other subfunctions. Note that the arguments to `pr-char` include not only the specific character to be printed and the number of characters left to be printed but also the name of the next function to be called. That is, the functions themselves are used as arguments to `pr-char`.

8.6   Advanced Subjects

This chapter has the following advanced topic:

- Aux Arguments

8.6.1   Aux Arguments

In section 3.8, we discussed the use of optional and keyword arguments, noted by
the lambda-list keywords &optional and &key, respectively.

The keyword &aux can be used following other lambda-list keywords to introduce additional local variables. These variables can derive their values from
lambda-list parameters at their left.

```
(defun test-aux (a &aux b (c (cdr a)) (d (car c)))
   (list a b c d))
```

```
> (test-aux '(1 2 3))
((1 2 3) NIL (2 3) 2)
```

```
> (test-aux '(1 2 3) '(4 5 6))
Error: TEST-AUX got 2 args, wanted at most 1.
   [condition type: PROGRAM-ERROR]
```

In this example, a is a required parameter. The aux variable b gets a default value
of NIL, c gets the cdr of a, and d gets the car of c. Note that it is an error to call
test-aux with more than one argument.

The &aux construct is a notational variant of let*. That is, we can rewrite
test-aux by using let* instead of &aux.

```
(defun test-let* (a)
   (let* ((b)
          (c (cdr a))
          (d (car c)))
      (list a b c d)))
```

```
> (test-let* '(1 2 3))
((1 2 3) NIL (2 3) 2)
```

The programmer can even use both.

```
(defun test-aux+let* (a &aux b (c (cdr a)))
   (let* ((d (car c)))
      (list a b c d)))
```

```
> (test-aux+let* '(1 2 3))
((1 2 3) NIL (2 3) 2)
```

De gustibus non disputandum est.

8.7 Exercises

8.7.1 Expression Drill [4]

Evaluate the following expressions, first by hand, then with the help of the LISP interpreter.

```
#'(lambda (y z) (+ y z 3))
(funcall #'(lambda (y z) (+ y z 3)) 4 5)
(setf (symbol-function 'x) #'(lambda (y z) (+ y z 3)))
(x 6 7)
(mapcar #'x '(1 2 3 4) '(5 6 7 8))
(setf (symbol-function 'y) #'(lambda (n m) (funcall n 3 m)))
(y #'x 5)
(apply #'y #'x 5 '())
(apply #'apply #'y #'x 5 '() '())
(apply #'list (list '(y #'x 7) '(y #'x 8)))
(apply #'list (list (y #'x 7) (y #'x 8)))
(apply #'x (list (y #'x 7) (y #'x 8)))
(apply #'x (apply #'list (list (y #'x 7) (y #'x 8))))
(apply #'append (apply #'list (list '(y #'x 7) '(y #'x 8))))
(defvar x 0)
(let ((x 5) (y x)) y)
(let* ((x 5) (y x)) y)
```

8.7.2 Mystery Expressions [4*]

What do the following five Common LISP expressions have in common?

```
3.14159
```

```
"pi"
```

```
T
```

```
NIL
```

```
((LAMBDA (X) (LIST X (LIST 'QUOTE X)))
  '(LAMBDA (X) (LIST X (LIST 'QUOTE X))))
```

8.7.3 More Cryptography [6*]

The simple cryptography system given in this chapter is fairly easy to crack. One way of making it more difficult is to use a more complex key. That is, instead of incrementing each letter the same amount, change the increment amount for every letter, using a prearranged key text.

Write two functions, `new-string-encode` and `new-string-decode`, that each take three arguments: the text to be encoded (or decoded), a key text, and an integer. Each character of the key text is converted to its ASCII code and then divided by the integer. The resulting remainder is added to the respective character in the target text. If the key text is longer than the target text, then it is appropriately truncated. If the key text is shorter, then it is repeated as necessary.

Here is an example.

```
(defvar *key-text* "He who hesitates is last.")

> (defvar x
        (new-string-encode "Mary had a little lambda" *key-text* 7))
X


> x
"Odvy&nej#d poxwoi oephge"

> (new-string-decode x *key-text* 7)
"Mary had a little lambda"
```

The programmer should note that map can have multiple sequence arguments.

8.7.4   Deck of Cards [5*]

Write a function `make-deck` that takes two arguments, a list of ranks and a list of suits, and produces a list of individual pairs.

```
> (defvar *suits* '(clubs diamonds hearts spades))
*SUITS*

> (defvar *ranks* '(ten jack queen king ace))
*RANKS*

> (make-deck *ranks* *suits*)
((TEN . CLUBS) (JACK . CLUBS) (QUEEN . CLUBS) (KING . CLUBS)
(ACE . CLUBS) (TEN . DIAMONDS) (JACK . DIAMONDS) (QUEEN . DIAMONDS)
(KING . DIAMONDS) (ACE . DIAMONDS) (TEN . HEARTS) (JACK . HEARTS)
(QUEEN . HEARTS) (KING . HEARTS) (ACE . HEARTS) (TEN . SPADES)
(JACK . SPADES) (QUEEN . SPADES) (KING . SPADES) (ACE . SPADES))
```

This function can be written using map twice with lambda expressions, as well as apply. Exercise 14.8.13 discusses how to shuffle the cards.

8.7.5 reverse with labels [5*]

Rewrite the function `reverse` using `labels` to create a local recursive function.

8.7.6 Power Set [5*]

The power set is all possible combinations of the elements of a set. If we represent a set as a simple list, the power set would be a list of all possible sublists of the top-level elements, as produced by the `power` function below.

```
> (power '(a))
((A) NIL)              ; NIL denotes the empty set.

> (power '(a b))
((A B) (A) (B) NIL)

> (power '(a b c))
((A B C) (A B) (A C) (A) (B C) (B) (C) NIL)
```

Write a definition of `power`.

8.7.7 Length Problems [6*]

There are two problems with the following definition of `length`. The first is its name. The second is that it does not work.

```
(defun bad-length (l)
  (flet
    ((count-length (l n)
                  (cond ((null l) n)
                        (t (count-length (cdr l) (+ 1 n)))))))
  (count-length l 0)))
```

The local function `count-length` is defined with `flet`, which does not permit recursive reference. Thus, when the code is executed, LISP will complain that `count-length` is unbound.

Rewrite this function, using `flet` in a way that overcomes this limitation. (Hint: you need to add a third argument to `count-length`.)

8.8 Chapter Summary

- `lambda` expressions provide a means of creating unnamed functions.

- `functionp` is a predicate for functions.

- The function `mapc` is similar to `mapcar` but does not accumulate its results. `mapc` is used for performing side effects.

- A `lambda` expression can be used as a functional argument in LISP expressions, such as `mapcar` and `mapc`.

- `lambda` expressions can be given names through assignment to variables via `setf` and `symbol-function`.

- `apply` is a function that invokes a given function explicitly on a list of objects.

- LISP allows the creation of local functions with either `flet` or `labels`.

- Local variables created with `let*` can refer to earlier local variables within the `let*` scope.

- `labels` provides a convenient way to create mutually recursive functions.

A LISP programmer knows the value of everything, but the
cost of nothing.

◇ ALAN PERLIS, *Epigrams in Programming (1982)*

Chapter 9

Control

100 bottles of beer on the wall,
100 bottles of beer,
Take one down, pass it around,
99 bottles of beer on the wall ...

⋄ ANON., *Traditional*

You blocks, you stones, you
worse than senseless things!

⋄ WILLIAM SHAKESPEARE, *Julius Caesar, I.i.*

O! thou hast damnable iteration,
and art, indeed, able to corrupt a saint!

⋄ WILLIAM SHAKESPEARE, *Henry IV, Part 1, I.ii*

Wet hair. Apply shampoo. Lather.
Rinse. Repeat.

⋄ ANON., *Shampoo Instructions*

In our apprenticeship in the LISP program building trade, we have encountered a variety of building materials and techniques. We have seen many kinds of objects, including numbers, symbols, lists, functions, characters, strings, and streams. We have learned a number of ways of writing programs to manipulate those objects, primarily through conditional evaluation, function calls, and particularly recursion.

In this chapter, we examine a variety of control techniques – methods for specifying the order of evaluation within a program.

9.1   prog1, prog2, and progn

The order of evaluation of *arguments* to a function is undefined in LISP. That is, if you have an expression (f (g x) (h y)), the arguments to f may or may not be evaluated in left-to-right order. Thus, h might be evaluated before g, due to efficiency considerations decided by the compiler. Usually, this undefined order of evaluation is not a problem. However, if the evaluation of arguments results in side effects, then incorrect code could result. Consider the following expression.

```
    (put (pop lst) (pop lst) (pop lst))
;   Where lst is (john father-of jack)
;   and (put x y z) is (setf (get x y) z).
```

Depending on the order of evaluation of arguments, any of the following expressions could result:

```
    (put john father-of jack)    ;  The intended result.
    (put john jack father-of)
    (put father-of john jack)
    (put father-of jack john)
    (put jack father-of john)
    (put jack john father-of)
```

Programmers should be aware of this hazard and plan accordingly.

Fortunately, the order of evaluation of *expressions* within a lambda body is predictable. Given a LISP function with a list of expressions to be evaluated, there is an implicit order of evaluation, namely, left to right, and top to bottom. Furthermore, the value returned by the function is the value of the last expression evaluated. Here is a modest example.

```
> ((lambda () 1 2 3 4 5))
5
```

In this case, the integers — themselves LISP expressions — are evaluated from left to right, and the value of the final expression, 5, is returned as the result. Thus, the fact that the last value is returned is a consequence of the order of evaluation.

There are times when the programmer may prefer to return some value other than the value of the last expression. For example, the programmer may wish to calculate some value, perform some operation (usually one with side effects), and then return the value calculated.

It should be apparent how to accomplish this with local variables, but LISP provides a sequencing mechanism, the prog1 form, (pronounced *progue-one*), which evaluates a sequence of one or more expressions and returns the value of the *first*, not the last. The opposite effect is achieved with progn, (pronounced *progue-enn*), which is equivalent to LISP's normal actions. LISP also provides a prog2 form, which returns the value of the second form. Here are examples.

```
> (progn 1 2 3 4)
4

> (prog1 1 2 3 4)
1

> (prog2 1 2 3 4)
2

> (progn (setf x '(a b c d)) 'x)
X

> (prog1 (setf x '(a b c d)) 'x)
(A B C D)

> (progn (prog1 1 2) (progn 3 4) (prog1 5 6))
5

> (prog1 (setf age 30) (setf age (1+ age)))
30

> age
31
```

This last example demonstrates the utility of **prog1**. The C postfix operator **++** is analogous. The expression i++ increments i but returns the previous value of i.

The programmer will find less need to use **progn**, since it mirrors LISP's default sequencing behavior. However, in contexts that expect a single argument, **progn** can provide a convenient way to package multiple expressions into one form.

9.2 case and typecase

In sections 3.9 and 3.11, we saw how to use a key to retrieve data from a table, represented either as an association list or as a property list. It is also possible for a key to control the execution of a program, using LISP's **case** and **typecase** forms, which have the following syntax.

```
(case keyform {(({({key}*) | key } {form}*)}*)
(typecase keyform {(type {form}*)}*)
```

The **case** form can be viewed as a hybrid between association lists and cond. Here is an example.

```lisp
(defun classify (x)
  (case x
        ((whale bear cat dog horse) 'mammal)
        ((penguin sparrow eagle ostrich) 'bird)
        ((lawyer accountant stock-broker) 'yuppie)
        ((trout bass catfish cod) 'fish)
        (programmer 'servant-to-mankind)
        (otherwise 'plant)))
```

```lisp
> (classify 'cat)
MAMMAL
```

```lisp
> (classify 'programmer)
SERVANT-TO-MANKIND
```

```lisp
> (classify 'lawyer)
YUPPIE
```

```lisp
> (classify 'tulip)
PLANT
```

The structure of case should be apparent. There are two arguments: a key and
a set of clauses. The car of each clause is a list of keys or a single key (like
programmer above), and the cdr is a set of expressions. The last clause may have
otherwise as its car. If the key matches one of keys in a given clause (using eql),
then, as in cond, the cdr of that clause is evaluated and the rest of the case clauses
are skipped. If none of the keys of the clauses match the given key and the last
clause contains otherwise as its car, then the cdr of the last clause is evaluated.
Note that the keys in the case clauses are not evaluated; they are constants. They
should not be quoted.

The typecase form is similar to case, except its keys are Common LISP
types.

```lisp
(defun check-arg-type (arg)
  (typecase arg
           ((or fixnum bignum) 'integer)
           ((or string character symbol) 'text)
           ((or complex float rational) 'funny-number)
           (function 'code)
           (sequence 'like-a-list)
           ((or list cons) 'like-a-list)
           (otherwise 'who-knows)))
```

```lisp
> (check-arg-type 0)
INTEGER
```

```
> (check-arg-type 0.0)
FUNNY-NUMBER

> (check-arg-type #'check-arg-type)
CODE

> (check-arg-type 'check-arg-type)
TEXT
```

Note also that we have to use or to indicate a disjunction of types, which was implicit in the case form. Type specifications, per se, are discussed in the next chapter.

9.3 Iteration and do

In most programming languages, the usual method for performing some repetitive process is a loop. Looping constructs in programming languages take various forms, including do/while, do/until, repeat loops, for loops, and the notorious goto. A loop, be it in C, FORTRAN, BASIC, or Pascal, has several components.

- Initial conditions – The state of the variables when beginning the loop

- Termination condition – The state required for ending the loop

- Termination result – The value returned upon exiting the loop

- Transition specifications – How the state changes from one cycle to the next

- Body – Code to be executed each cycle through the loop

The looping control method is also called *iteration*. Up until now, we have not used iteration in LISP. We have used recursion. The same basic phenomena underlie both. In principle, anything you can do with recursion, you can accomplish with iteration, and vice versa.

LISP provides several iterative constructs: do, do*, dolist, and dotimes. We shall first examine do, which has the following syntax. (We discuss tags later in this chapter.)

```
(do ({(var [init [step]])}*)
    (exit-test {result}*)
    {tag | statement}*)
```

Here is an iterative function to find the average of a list of numbers by means of do. The comments on each line indicate the components.

```
(defun i-average (lst)
   (do ((nlist lst (cdr nlist))          ; (var init step).
        (count 0 (1+ count))             ; (var init step).
        (total 0 (+ (car nlist) total))) ; (var init step).
       ((null nlist) (/ total count))))) ; (exit-test result).

> (i-average '(1 2 3 4 5 6 7))
4
```

The function i-average demonstrates the basic structure of do. The first argument to do is a list of three-part variable specifications. The do local variables in i-average are nlist, count, and total.

The first part of each specification is the name of the local variable, for example, nlist. The second part is that variable's initial value, for example, lst, and the third part is the transition specification for that variable, for example, (cdr nlist). During each iteration, the variables are given new values according to these transition functions. For example, the count variable is given an initial value of 0, and each time through the loop, the value of count is incremented by 1.

The second argument to do is the termination clause. The do termination clause in i-average is ((null nlist) (/ total count)). The car of the clause is the exit test, and the cdr contains expressions which are evaluated upon termination. The value returned by do is the value of the last of these expressions — or NIL if there are no result expressions. So, i-average stops when nlist becomes empty and then returns the final total divided by the final count as the value of i-average.

Here is a step-by-step account of i-average.

```
1.   (setf nlist nlist)         ; Initializes variables.
     (setf count 0)
     (setf total 0)


2.   (null nlist)               ; Termination test.
     if true, goto step 5
     else, continue to next step.


3.   (setf nlist (cdr nlist))   ; Updates values of variables.
     (setf count (+ 1 count))
     (setf total (+ total (car nlist)))


4.   goto step 2                ; Resumes loop.


5.   Terminate loop.            ; End of loop.
     Return value: (/ total count)
```

Actually, LISP is smarter than the above detail would suggest. In particular, there is a problem with the order of assignment statements in step 3. As shown here, the algorithm would not add the first element into the total.

Note that `trace` will be of little value in debugging a faulty `do` expression. There are no recursive calls to trace. Instead, the programmer can take advantage of the optional third argument to `do`, which allows zero or more arbitrary LISP expressions. These expressions are evaluated if the exit test fails. They would appear between steps 2 and 3 in our description above. Thus, `i-average` could be rewritten to produce intermediate output.

```lisp
(defun i-average (nlist)
  (do ((nlist nlist (cdr nlist))
       (count 0 (+ 1 count))
       (total 0 (+ (car nlist) total)))
      ((null nlist) (/ total count))
    (format t "count: ~d" count)
    (format t "~15T total: ~d ~%" total)))
```

```
> (i-average '(1 2 3 4 5))
count: 0        total: 0
count: 1        total: 1
count: 2        total: 3
count: 3        total: 6
count: 4        total: 10
3
```

Note that the final case, where `count` becomes 5, is not printed. The `format` statements are not evaluated on the last element of the list, because the termination test has been triggered.

9.4 Iteration versus Recursion

To give the reader a feel for the differences between iteration and recursion, we now present examples of problems treated both ways. First, the reader might review the recursive definitions for average given earlier. (See page 125 and following.)

Next, we provide two definitions of `length`. The first is recursive, and the second is iterative.

```lisp
;  Recursive implementation of length.
(defun r-length (lst)
  (cond ((null lst) 0)
        (t (1+ (r-length (cdr lst))))))
```

```
;  Iterative implementation of length.
(defun i-length (lst)
  (do ((l lst (cdr l))
       (result 0 (1+ result)))
      ((null l) result)))
```

Which is better? Which is clearer? It is largely a matter of taste. There can also be differences in efficiency. These are discussed in chapter 16.

We give one more set of examples for comparison, slightly more involved. The task of remove-pairs is to reduce all adjacent duplicate items in a list to a single item. For example, (a b b c) becomes (a b c); (b a a a) becomes (b a). The first implementation is recursive, and the next is iterative.

```
(defun r-remove-pairs (list)
  (cond ((null list) list)
        ((null (cdr list)) list)
        ((eql (car list) (cadr list))
         (r-remove-pairs (cdr list)))
        (t
         (cons (car list)
               (r-remove-pairs (cdr list))))))

(defun i-remove-pairs (list)
  (do ((list list (cdr list))
       (result () (cond ((eql (car list) (cadr list))
                         result)
                        (t
                         (append result (cons (car list) nil))))))
      ((or (null list))
       (and (null (cdr list))
            (setf result (append result list)))
       result)))
```

There is another version of do, called do*, which, like let*, provides sequential bindings of the local variables. The do* macro has the same syntax as do. We can compare the actions of do and do* with a test.

```
(defun test-do ()
  (do ((x 1 (1+ x))
       (y 2 (* x y)))
      ((= x 4) (list x y))
      (format t "~%x: ~A~15Ty: ~A" x y)))
```

```
(defun test-do* ()
  (do* ((x 1 (1+ x))
        (y 2 (* x y)))
       ((= x 4) (list x y))
       (format t "~%x: ~A~15Ty: ~A" x y)))
```

```
> (test-do)
```

```
x: 1          y: 2
x: 2          y: 2
x: 3          y: 4
(4 12)
```

```
> (test-do*)
```

```
x: 1          y: 2
x: 2          y: 4
x: 3          y: 12
(4 48)
```

The difference creeps in during the evaluation of the step form for y, namely, (* x
y). With do, the step form takes the old value of x, whereas the do* version takes
the new value of x, which has already been set at this point. The programmer is
urged to distinguish carefully between these two cases in her own code.

The reader who is not yet convinced that recursion and iteration can achieve
the same results should review the examples in this section. The obdurately in-
credulous reader may still proceed to the next sections for further evidence.

9.5 dolist and dotimes

The iteration forms do and do* are general. LISP offers two specialized control
forms: dolist and dotimes, with the following syntax.

```
(dolist  (var listform [result]) {tag | statement}*)
(dotimes (var countform [result]) {tag | statement}*)
```

Here are two examples.

```
(defun dl-average (list)
  (let ((total 0)
        (count 0))
    (dolist (item list (/ total count))
            (setf total (+ total item))
            (setf count (1+ count)))))
```

```
> (dl-average '(1 2 3 4 5))
3


(defun dt-average (list)
  (let ((total 0)
        (count (length list)))
    (dotimes (count (1- count) (/ total count))
             (setf total (+ total (pop list))))))


> (dt-average '(2 3 4 5 6 7))
4
```

The first argument to dolist is a list comprising a variable name, for example, item, a list, and an optional result form. The variable is assigned to the successive items in the list on each iteration. The remaining arguments to dolist are the expressions to be evaluated each time through the loop. When the end of the list is reached, the iteration terminates and the result form is returned. If there is no result form, dolist returns NIL.

Similarly, the first argument to dotimes is a list comprising a variable name, for example, count, an expression that evaluates to a number, and an optional result form. The variable is assigned to the successive values of the numeric expression on each iteration. The remaining expressions to dotimes constitute the body of the loop executed on each cycle. When the numeric form has a zero or negative value, the result form is returned. If there is no result form, dotimes returns NIL.

```
(dolist (var listform resultform)
    expressions)
;  is roughly equivalent to
(do* ((list listform (cdr listform))
      (var  (car list) (car list)))
     ((null listform) resultform)
     expressions)
;  and
(dotimes (var countform resultform)
    expressions)
;  is roughly equivalent to
(do* ((var countform countform))
     ((not (plusp var)) resultform)
     expressions)
```

9.6   when and unless

The termination condition for an iteration or recursion requires a test. LISP provides the two macros, `when` and `unless`, as alternatives to the conditional forms `if` and `cond`. Their names are suggestive of their function. Here are their syntax and examples of their use.

```
(when   test {form}*)
(unless test {form}*)
```

```
> (setf x 1)
1
```

```
> (when x 1 2 3 4)
4
```

```
> (unless x 1 2 3 4)
NIL
```

```
> (when (evenp x) 1 2 3 4)
NIL
```

```
> (unless (evenp x) 1 2 3 4)
4
```

```
> (when t)
T
```

```
> (unless nil)
T
```

```
> (when nil)
NIL
```

```
> (unless t)
NIL
```

In each case, the first argument is a test, and the remaining arguments are evaluated left to right, depending on the result of the test. For `when`, the rest of the arguments are evaluated when the test is true. For `unless`, the arguments are evaluated unless the test is true, that is, when the test is false.

Thus, the following expressions are equivalent.

```
(when x y)
(unless (not x) y)
(if x y)
(cond (x y))
(and x y)
(or (not x) y)
```

9.7   loop and block

Another set of control structures uses `return` to exit from iterative blocks of code.
There are several such iterative constructs. The first one has the straightforward
name: loop. The loop form executes its argument expressions repeatedly until the
flow of control is explicitly changed, such as with a `return` form. The syntax of
loop is trivial.

```
(loop {form}*)
```

Here are some examples. The first, `repeat-char`, is taken from the answer
to exercise 7.9.7.

```
(defun repeat-char (ch count stream)
  (loop
    (cond ((zerop count) (return (values)))
          (t (write-char ch stream)
             (decf count)))))
```

```
> (repeat-char #\+ 9 *standard-output*)
+++++++++
```

The loop body is executed repeatedly until the `return` statement is encountered,
which terminates the iteration. The argument to `return` is optional. The default
value is NIL. count is the single iteration argument in this example. The iteration
body in `repeat-char` is a cond clause. The execution terminates when the count
reaches zero.

We can implement the familiar `length` function by using loop.

```
(defun it-length (lst)
  (let ((result 0))
    (loop
      (unless lst (return result))
      (setf lst (cdr lst))
      (incf result))))
```

```
> (it-length '(a b c d e))
5
```

In it-length, we use a local variable result to keep track of the length of the list. The body of the loop uses an unless clause instead of the cond clause in repeat-char.

Another control structure form, albeit not an iterative one, is block, which has the following syntax.

```
(block name {form}*)
```

block is similar to progn, but with an escape hatch.

```
> (block exit 1 2 3 4 5)
5

> (block exit 1 2 (return-from exit 17) 4 5)
17

> (block nil 1 2 (return 17) 4 5)
17

> (block a
    (+ (block b 1 2 (return-from b 3) 4)
       (block c 5 6 (return-from a 7) 8)))
7
```

The first argument to block is a name which may be used as the first argument to the return-from form. return-from provides the escape route from the body of the block. If the name given to the block is NIL, then the programmer can use the return form, which defaults to a block name of NIL.

The expression (return x) is the same as (return-from nil x). The last example above illustrates the nesting of blocks, in which an inner block terminates an outer block.

9.8 go

LISP has been around since the 1950s. In those days, the primary control statement for all higher-level languages was goto. That is, the programmer would insert labels at various points in the code and conditionally (or unconditionally) transfer execution control to those locations by using a goto statement. The following pseudo-code example illustrates this programming style.

```
label1:
    statement
    if x<y, goto label1
    if x>y, goto label2
    statement
label2:
    statement
```

In the 1970s, programmers discovered the revealed truth about goto statments, namely, that they were bad (the goto statements, not the programmers.) The problem was that gotos allowed the programmer too much freedom. The code could jump all over the place in a confusing and unstructured manner.

The solution was termed *structured programming*. This technique involved two main tenets.

1. Do not use goto statements.

2. Use some other kind of statement.

The other kind of statement included control structures, such as do and while loops, in which the scope of control was narrowed to the scope of the structure. That is, nothing would happen outside the do loop. The programmer was therefore able more easily to write, debug, document, maintain, and even comprehend the resulting code.

LISP, being a child of the 1950s, was born with gotos in its blood. It is with no little sorrow that the author reports that Common LISP retains these seductive devils. (We note that C and C++ also have "infinitely abusable" goto's [Kernighan and Ritchie, 1988, page 65], so there.)

In C, the programmer can introduce goto statements almost anywhere. In LISP, the programmer is restricted to a few contexts, the first being tagbody, illustrated below.

```
; tagbody syntax:
    (tagbody {tag | statement}*)

; tagbody example:
(defun tagbody-length (l)
   (let ((length 0))
     (tagbody
      top
      (cond (l
             (incf length)
             (setf l (cdr l))
             (go top))))
       length))
```

```
> (tagbody-length '(a b c))
3

> (tagbody 1 2 3 4)      ;  The result of tagbody is always NIL.
NIL

> (tagbody)
NIL
```

The body of a `tagbody` form comprises zero or more tags alternating with zero or more statements. A tag is either a symbol or an integer, like `top` in the above example. The statements may include a `go` form, which is LISP's version of `goto`.

The body of the a `do`, `do*`, `dolist`, or `dotimes` is an implicit block named NIL and thus may contain a `return`. Moreover, the body of the forms in `do`, `do*`, `dolist`, or `dotimes` is an implicit `tagbody` and thus may contain tags and `go` forms.

Below we present a `tagbody` version of the `check-arg-type` function we defined earlier in this chapter using `typecase`. The structured programming priesthood would label the following bit of code as heretical. We hope you agree.

```
(defun tagbody-check-arg-type (x)                               ⇐ Ugly Code
  (let ((result 'who-knows)
        (xtype (type-of x)))
    (tagbody
     (cond ((eq xtype 'fixnum) (go fixnum))
           ((eq xtype 'bignum) (go bignum))
           ((eq xtype 'string) (go string))
           ((eq xtype 'character) (go character))
           ((eq xtype 'symbol) (go symbol))
           ((eq xtype 'complex) (go complex))
           ((eq xtype 'float) (go float))
           ((eq xtype 'single-float) (go single-float))
           ((eq xtype 'rational) (go rational))
           ((eq xtype 'function) (go function))
           ((eq xtype 'sequence) (go sequence))
           ((eq xtype 'list) (go list))
           ((eq xtype 'cons) (go cons)))
     fixnum bignum
     (setf result 'integer)
     (go finish)
     string character symbol
     (setf result 'text)
     (go finish)
```

```
        complex float single-float rational
        (setf result 'funny-number)
        (go finish)
        function
        (setf result 'code)
        (go finish)
        sequence list cons
        (setf result 'like-a-list)
        finish)
      result))
```

```
> (tagbody-check-arg-type 0)
INTEGER
```

```
> (tagbody-check-arg-type 0.0)
FUNNY-NUMBER
```

```
> (tagbody-check-arg-type #'tagbody-check-arg-type)
CODE
```

```
> (tagbody-check-arg-type 'tagbody-check-arg-type)
TEXT
```

It behaves just the same as the earlier version, check-arg-type. In fact, it would be improved somewhat if the go form could evaluate its argument. Then, we could replace the ridiculous cond statement with the expression (go (type-of x)).

The remainder of the code would still be hideous. The replacement of cond would be like giving a manicure to a rhinoceros. The benefit of such grooming is minimal.

We hope we have persuaded the reader to steer clear of go and its profligate ways. However, in the interest of completeness and accuracy, we present two other control forms in which go is allowed: prog and prog*, which have the following syntax.

```
(prog  ({var | (var [init])}*) {tag | statement}*)
(prog* ({var | (var [init])}*) {tag | statement}*)
```

The prog macro acts like a combination of let, tagbody, and block. That is, the programmer can bind initial variable values, use go within the body, and specify a result using return. Here is an example, once with cond and once with unless.

Ugly Code ⇒ (defun prog-length-cond (l)

```
(prog
 ((length 0))
 top
 (cond (l
        (incf length)
        (setf l (cdr l))
        (go top)))
 (return length)))
```

```
(defun prog-length-unless (l)                          ⇐ Ugly Code
  (prog
   ((length 0))
   top
   (unless l (return length))
   (incf length)
   (setf l (cdr l))
   (go top)))
```

```
> (prog-length-cond '(a b c d))
4
```

```
> (prog-length-unless '(a b c d))
4
```

We note that prog is a marginal improvement on tagbody because it permits the
use of return. We could simplify tagbody-check-arg-list with prog.

```
(defun prog-check-arg-type (x)                         ⇐ Ugly Code
  (prog
   ((xtype (type-of x)))
   (cond ((eq xtype 'fixnum) (go fixnum))
         ((eq xtype 'bignum) (go bignum))
         ((eq xtype 'string) (go string))
         ((eq xtype 'character) (go character))
         ((eq xtype 'symbol) (go symbol))
         ((eq xtype 'complex) (go complex))
         ((eq xtype 'float) (go float))
         ((eq xtype 'single-float) (go single-float))
         ((eq xtype 'rational) (go rational))
         ((eq xtype 'function) (go function))
         ((eq xtype 'sequence) (go sequence))
         ((eq xtype 'list) (go list))
         ((eq xtype 'cons) (go cons)))
   (return 'who-knows)
```

```
        fixnum bignum
        (return 'integer)
        string character symbol
        (return 'text)
        complex float single-float rational
        (return 'funny-number)
        function
        (return 'code)
        sequence list cons
        (return 'like-a-list)))
```

```
> (prog-check-arg-type 0)
INTEGER
```

```
> (prog-check-arg-type 0.0)
FUNNY-NUMBER
```

```
> (prog-check-arg-type #'prog-check-arg-type)
CODE
```

```
> (prog-check-arg-type 'prog-check-arg-type)
TEXT
```

However, the function would be simpler if we eliminated the gos and put the return statements within the cond form.

Ugly Code ⇒
```
(defun prog-check-arg-type2 (x)
  (prog
    ((xtype (type-of x)))
    (cond ((eq xtype 'fixnum) (return 'integer))
          ((eq xtype 'bignum) (return 'integer))
          ((eq xtype 'string) (return 'text))
          ((eq xtype 'character) (return 'text))
          ((eq xtype 'symbol) (return 'text))
          ((eq xtype 'complex) (return 'funny-number))
          ((eq xtype 'float) (return 'funny-number))
          ((eq xtype 'single-float) (return 'funny-number))
          ((eq xtype 'rational) (return 'funny-number))
          ((eq xtype 'function) (return 'code))
          ((eq xtype 'sequence) (return 'like-a-list))
          ((eq xtype 'list) (return 'like-a-list))
          ((eq xtype 'cons) (return 'like-a-list)))
    (return 'who-knows)))
```

For that matter, if we are not using go and only want `return`, we can use `block` with `let` for the local variable.

```
(defun block-check-arg-type (x)                          ⇐ Ugly Code
  (let ((xtype (type-of x)))
    (block
     nil
     (cond ((eq xtype 'fixnum) (return 'integer))
           ((eq xtype 'bignum) (return 'integer))
           ((eq xtype 'string) (return 'text))
           ((eq xtype 'character) (return 'text))
           ((eq xtype 'symbol) (return 'text))
           ((eq xtype 'complex) (return 'funny-number))
           ((eq xtype 'float) (return 'funny-number))
           ((eq xtype 'single-float) (return 'funny-number))
           ((eq xtype 'rational) (return 'funny-number))
           ((eq xtype 'function) (return 'code))
           ((eq xtype 'sequence) (return 'like-a-list))
           ((eq xtype 'list) (return 'like-a-list))
           ((eq xtype 'cons) (return 'like-a-list)))
     (return 'who-knows))))
```

Or, we can dispense with `block` and `return` entirely and use `cond` by itself.

```
(defun cond-check-arg-type (x)                           ⇐ Ugly Code
  (let ((xtype (type-of x)))
    (cond ((eq xtype 'fixnum) 'integer)
          ((eq xtype 'bignum) 'integer)
          ((eq xtype 'string) 'text)
          ((eq xtype 'character) 'text)
          ((eq xtype 'symbol) 'text)
          ((eq xtype 'complex) 'funny-number)
          ((eq xtype 'float) 'funny-number)
          ((eq xtype 'single-float) 'funny-number)
          ((eq xtype 'rational) 'funny-number)
          ((eq xtype 'function) 'code)
          ((eq xtype 'sequence) 'like-a-list)
          ((eq xtype 'list) 'like-a-list)
          ((eq xtype 'cons) 'like-a-list)
          (t 'who-knows))))
```

In case you have forgotten, the original function used `typecase` and is still the preferred approach for this particular task.

```
(defun check-arg-type (arg)
  (typecase arg
            ((or fixnum bignum) 'integer)
            ((or string character symbol) 'text)
            ((or complex float rational) 'funny-number)
            (function 'code)
            (sequence 'like-a-list)
            ((or list cons) 'like-a-list)
            (otherwise 'who-knows)))
```

The prog* macro is to prog as let* is to let, and as do* is to do. That is, it provides sequential bindings for its local variables, as illustrated below.

Ugly Code ⇒
```
(defun prog*-average (l)
  (prog*
    ((len (length l))
     (sum 0)
     (average (/ sum len)))
    start
    (format t "Average so far: ~a~%" average)
    (unless l (return average))
    (setf sum (+ sum (car l)))
    (setf average (/ sum len))
    (setf l (cdr l))
    (go start)))
```

```
> (prog*-average '(1 2 3 4 5))
Average so far: 0
Average so far: 1/5
Average so far: 3/5
Average so far: 6/5
Average so far: 2
Average so far: 3
3
```

Readers who find this sort of program appealing should abandon LISP and try FORTRAN.

9.9 Multiple Values

A LISP function can take zero or more arguments and return zero or more values. Typical functions return a single value. Using the values or values-list functions, the programmer can define functions which return fewer or more than one value.

```
> (values 1 2 3)
1
2
3

> (values-list '(1 2 3))     ;  Like (apply #'values list).
1
2
3

> (values)

> (values-list ())
```

Certain native LISP functions, such as `truncate`, normally return more than one value. However, most functions ignore the extra values.

```
> (truncate 1.5)
1
0.5

> (+ (truncate 1.5))
1
```

How can the programmer do something useful with those extra values besides printing them to the screen? LISP provides a handful of macros for managing multiple values, with the following syntax.

```
(multiple-value-setq varlist values-form)
(multiple-value-bind ({var}*) values-form {form}*)
(multiple-value-call function {form}*)
(multiple-value-list form)
(multiple-value-prog1 {form}+)
```

First, there is an implementation limit on the number of possible multiple values, as specified with the constant, `multiple-values-limit`.

```
> multiple-values-limit                                        ⇐ ∞
500
```

We can explicitly set variables by using `multiple-value-setq`, which takes a variable list and a form whose values are assigned to the respective variables in the global context.

```
> (multiple-value-setq (x y) (values 1 2))
1
```

```
> x
1

> y
2

> (multiple-value-setq (x y) (values))
NIL

> y
NIL
```

Extra values are ignored. Missing values default to NIL.

If we want to bind the variables in a local environment, we can wrap a let statement around `multiple-value-setq` or we can use `multiple-value-bind`, which has a similar effect.

```
> (let ((a) (b))
    (multiple-value-setq (a b) (values 1 2))
    (+ a b))
3
> (multiple-value-bind (a b) (values 1 2)
    (+ a b))
3
```

The macro `multiple-value-list` collects the values returned by a form into a list.

```
> (multiple-value-list (truncate 1.5))
(1 0.5)

> (multiple-value-list (values 1 2 3 4))
(1 2 3 4)

> (multiple-value-list (values))
NIL
```

The macro `multiple-value-call` applies a given function to the values returned by any number of other forms.

```
> (multiple-value-call #'list (truncate 1.5) (truncate 3.5) 7)
(1 0.5 3 0.5 7)

> (multiple-value-call #'+ (truncate 1.5) (truncate 3.5) 7)
12.0
```

Finally, prog1 permits only a single value to be returned. The multiple-value-prog1 macro provides an alternative.

```
> (prog1 (values 1 2 3) 4 5 6)
1

> (multiple-value-prog1 (values 1 2 3) 4 5 6)
1
2
3
```

9.10   catch and throw

Another type of control structure is afforded by the catch and throw forms, which provide a very general mechanism for returning values from computations. The structure of catch comprises two parts: an identifier and a body of expressions to be evaluated. The identifier becomes the argument to throw, an exit function from the body of expressions which returns its own second argument as its value. The throw cannot be invoked outside the scope of the originating expression, that is, outside the catch.

Here is an example in which the identifier finish becomes the argument tag for the escape function, also called a *throw*, which terminates the catch expression. The throw function has a second argument, result, which is returned as the value of catch.

```
(defun fact (n)
  (catch 'finish
    (labels
      ((sub-fact (n result)
                 (cond ((zerop n) (throw 'finish result))
                       (t (sub-fact (1- n)
                                    (* n result))))))
      (sub-fact n 1))))

;    Another definition of fact.
(defun fact (n)
  (catch 'finish
(sub-fact n 1 'finish)))

(defun sub-fact (n result catch)
  (cond ((zerop n) (throw catch result))
(t (sub-fact (1- n) (* n result) catch))))
```

```
;     One more definition of sub-fact.
(defun sub-fact (n result catch)
  (cond ((zerop n) result)
(t (sub-fact (1- n) (* n result) catch))))
```

The last definition above of sub-fact also uses catch, but the escape function throw is never invoked. In this case, the value returned by catch is the value returned by the sub-fact function. This shows that catch does not have to exit with throw.

Here is a more compelling example of catch, using an iterative version of member-if.

```
(defun it-member-if (predicate lst)
  (catch 'out
    (do ((lst lst (cdr lst)))
        ((null lst) nil)
        (if (funcall predicate (car lst)) (throw 'out lst)))))
```

```
> (it-member-if #'numberp '(a b c d))
NIL
```

```
> (it-member-if #'numberp '(a b 1 2 3))
(1 2 3)
```

Here are some trivial examples in which the use of the escape function makes a difference in the value of the catch expression.

```
> (catch 'f (reverse (append (cons 1 '(2)) (cons 3 '(4)))))
(4 3 2 1)
```

```
> (catch 'f
(reverse (append (cons (throw 'f 1) '(2)) (cons 3 '(4)))))
1
```

The latter example shows how the programmer can use catch precipitously to interrupt the normal execution of an expression.

The short examples of catch given in this section illustrate how it works. However, in each case, it would be very easy to get rid of catch and achieve the same results. In fact, it would preferable. In short code segments, catch is rarely needed. The utility of catch becomes apparent in larger code segments in which the flow of control can be complex, and catch provides a convenient escape mechanism.

9.11   Example: Binary Guessing Game

A common computer game is one that attempts to guess an animal of which the
player has thought. The program asks a number of yes or no questions and finally
makes a guess, based on the player's responses to the questions. If the computer
guesses incorrectly, the program asks the player to tell it the name of the animal
and a yes/no question that can be used to differentiate between the new animal
and the program's previous guess. This new information then becomes part of the
program's knowledge base.

. Here is output from a sample session for the animal guessing game. User
input is <u>underlined</u>.

```
> (binary)

Think of an animal.         ;  The player responds to
Have you got one yet? y     ;  the program's questions.

Does it purr? n

Is it gray? n

Is it bigger than a person? y

Does it have stripes? n

Are you thinking of a GORILLA? n

What animal were you thinking of? horse

Type a yes/no question that can distinguish
between a GORILLA and a HORSE.
=> Is it a domestic animal?      ;  The player types this question.

And how would you answer that question for a HORSE? y

Do you want to play again? y

Think of an animal.
Have you got one yet? y

Does it purr? n

Is it gray? y
```

Are you thinking of an ELEPHANT? <u>y</u>

Hot tomatoes! I guessed it!

Do you want to play again? <u>n</u>

Do you wish to save the current animal database? <u>y</u>
Backing up data to file: binary.animal

Backup complete.
To restore data, type (load "binary.animal")

So long, animal lover.

As the final lines show, the program allows the player to save the current information
in a file. If the player subsequently loads the file and invokes (binary), the program
will start again, including the new information about horses.

The structure of the program itself is actually independent of any knowledge
about animals. In fact, the program can be used for virtually any domain of knowledge, including one close to the author's heart, as shown below. The binary-init
function sets up the program for a new session.

> <u>(binary-init 'reverse "LISP function" nil)</u>
NIL

> <u>(binary)</u>

Think of a LISP function.
Have you got one yet? <u>y</u>

Are you thinking of REVERSE? <u>n</u>

What LISP function were you thinking of? <u>length</u>

Type a yes/no question that can distinguish
between REVERSE and LENGTH.
=> <u>Does this function return a list?</u>

And how would you answer that question for LENGTH? <u>n</u>

Do you want to play again? <u>y</u>

Think of a LISP function.
Have you got one yet? <u>y</u>

```
Does this function return a list? n

Are you thinking of LENGTH? n

What LISP function were you thinking of? string-upcase

Type a yes/no question that can distinguish
between LENGTH and STRING-UPCASE.
=> Does this function take a string as its only argument?

And how would you answer that question for STRING-UPCASE? y

Do you want to play again? y

Think of a LISP function.
Have you got one yet? ?        ;  The player types a ?

Type Yes, No, or Quit.         ;  The program gives directions.

Think of a LISP function.
Have you got one yet? quit
*END-OF-BINARY*
```

As this session demonstrates, the program can operate in diverse domains.

The reader should notice that this second session ended abruptly, at the request of the player, who typed quit in response to a yes/no question. The program allows the player to end a session at any time through this means. This facility is implemented with catch.

We shall now look at the code itself. There are only two functions: binary-init and binary. The former is far shorter. It initializes the global variables used by binary.

```
(defun binary-init (item category flag)
  (setf *category* category
*determiner-flag* flag
(get '*binary-tree* 'answer)  item
(get '*binary-tree* 'question) nil
(get '*binary-tree* 'yes)     nil
(get '*binary-tree* 'no)      nil))
```

The variable *category* contains a string, such as "animal", and is used in several messages to the player. The variable *determiner-flag* is set to true to indicate that items should be preceded by a determiner ("a" or "an") when printed; otherwise, false.

The information about the items themselves, be they animals or LISP functions or plays by Shakespeare, is kept on a network of property lists. There are four possible data elements for each node.

1. answer is the value of a terminal node. For example, ELEPHANT or REVERSE.

2. question is a yes/no question represented as a string. For example, "Does this animal have webbed feet?"

3. yes is the name of another node in the network, in this case, the one to visit if the answer to question is yes.

4. no is the name of another node in the network, in this case, the one to visit if the answer to question is no.

Using binary-init, the player sets up a root node to the question tree with an answer item, and empty values for question, yes, and no.

We now turn our attention to the program itself. However, even though binary is only one function, it is made up of several secondary functions that are defined with labels. We shall therefore look at binary in stages, rather than present it in one whole piece.

```
(defun binary ()
  (catch 'quit-action
    (let ((back-up-flag nil))
      (labels
        ((query
           (yes-action no-action else-action)
           (case (read *standard-input*)
                 ((y yes t)    (funcall yes-action))
                 ((n no nil)   (funcall no-action))
                 ((q quit)     (throw 'quit-action '*end-of-binary*))
                 (otherwise
                  (format t "~%Type Yes, No, or Quit.~%")
                  (funcall else-action)))))

        (start
         ()
         (format t "~%Think of ~A~A."
                 (sub-determ *category*) *category*)
         (format t "~%Have you got one yet? ")
         (query
          #'(lambda () (process-node '*binary-tree*))
          #'start
          #'start))
```

The first element of the function definition is the `catch` form. The rest of the function is contained as the body of the `catch`.

The `let` form is used to create a local variable `back-up-flag`, which will be set when any changes are made that have not been saved to disk.

The `labels` form opens the body of the `catch` clause, and we then begin to define local functions. In this code segment we get `query` and `start`. We shall use the `query` function throughout the program to prompt the user for yes/no responses. The three arguments to `query` are the functions to invoke based on the player's input: yes, no, or other. The fourth alternative, quit, is handled directly within `query` as a call, or throw, to the `catch` identifier `quit-action`.

The second local function, `start`, will be the first to get called. It prompts the player to select an item of the given category. If the player is not ready, the `start` function is called again. Otherwise, the first `query` argument is invoked.

The output routines often check to see what kind of determiner is appropriate, using the following two functions.

```
(determiner (word)
   (cond ((null *determiner-flag*) "")
         (t (sub-determ word))))

(sub-determ (word)
   (let ((str (cond ((stringp word) word)
                    (t (string word)))))
     (case (char str 0)
        ((#\a #\e #\i #\o #\u #\y
          #\A #\E #\I #\O #\U #\Y)  "an ")
        (otherwise               "a ")))))
```

If the next word starts with a vowel, use `"an"`; otherwise, use `"a"`.

The `start` function begins the traversal of the question tree with the call `(process-node '*binary-tree*)`, which invokes the following function.

```
(process-node (tree-node)
   (cond ((get tree-node 'question)
          (process-question (get tree-node 'question) tree-node))
         ((get tree-node 'answer)
          (process-answer (get tree-node 'answer) tree-node))
         (t 'error-in-process-node)))
```

If the current node has a question, then the program processes that question. If there is no question, then the current node is a terminal node, so there must be an answer to process.

```
(process-question (ques node)
  (format t "~%~A " ques)
  (query
    #'(lambda () (process-node (get node 'yes)))
    #'(lambda () (process-node (get node 'no)))
    #'(lambda () (process-question ques node))))

(process-answer (ans node)
  (format t "~%Are you thinking of ~A~S? "
          (determiner ans) ans)
  (query
    #'(lambda () (format t "~%Hot tomatoes!  I guessed it!~%")
        (play-again?))
    #'(lambda () (add-item node ans)
        (play-again?))
    #'(lambda () (process-answer ans node))))
```

To process a question, the program asks the question and prompts for a response. The program then either processes the appropriate yes or no node or it asks the question again.

When there are no questions to ask at the current node, the process-answer function makes a guess. If it is correct, the program displays unbounded excitement. In the event of failure, the program resolutely tries to learn from its mistakes and become a better program.

```
(add-item (old-node old-item)
  (let ((yes-node (gensym "NODE"))
        (no-node  (gensym "NODE"))
        (new-item nil)
        (new-question nil))
    (format t "~%What ~A were you thinking of? " *category*)
    (setf new-item (read *standard-input*))
    (format t "~%Type a yes/no question that can distinguish")
    (format t "~%between ~A~S and ~A~S.~%=> "
            (determiner old-item) old-item
            (determiner new-item) new-item)
    (clear-input *standard-input*)
    (setf new-question (read-line *standard-input*))
    (set-up-old-node old-node new-question yes-node no-node)
    (setf back-up-flag t)
    (format t
            "~%And how would you answer that question for ~A~S? "
            (determiner new-item) new-item)
```

```
(tagbody again
        (query
          #'(lambda ()
              (set-up-new-node yes-node new-item)
              (set-up-new-node no-node  old-item))
          #'(lambda ()
              (set-up-new-node no-node  new-item)
              (set-up-new-node yes-node old-item))
          #'(lambda () (go again))))))
```

The **gensym** function creates unique identifiers, such as **#:NODE55**, for naming new nodes.

Note the use of **tagbody** at the end of **add-item** to provide explicit repetition if the player types an inappropriate response. The **add-item** function does some bookkeeping with the old and new nodes, setting and resetting property list values.

```
(set-up-old-node (old-node new-question yes-node no-node)
    (setf (get old-node 'question) new-question
  (get old-node 'answer) nil
  (get old-node 'yes) yes-node
  (get old-node 'no)  no-node))

(set-up-new-node (node item)
  (setf (get node 'answer) item))
```

That completes the main portion of the program. The remainder of the code is concerned with replaying the game and saving the new information in a file.

```
(play-again? ()
    (format t "~%Do you want to play again? ")
    (query
      #'start
      #'(lambda ()
          (save-data?)
          (format t "~%So long, ~A lover.~%~%" *category*)
          (values))
      #'play-again?))
```

Once again, the **query** function appears as the backbone of this program.

```
(save-data? ()
   (cond ((null back-up-flag) nil)
         (t
          (format t
                  "~%Do you wish to save the current ~A data base? "
                  *category*)
          (query
           #'back-up-data
           #'(lambda () nil)
           #'save-data?))))
```

The function add-item, which adds information, sets back-up-flag to true. So, if the player tries to exit the program after changes have been made, the program gives the player the opportunity to save the changes.

```
(back-up-data ()
   (let ((filename (concatenate 'string "binary." *category* ))
         (stream nil))
     (format t "Backing up data to file: ~A~%" filename)
     (setf stream (open filename :direction :output))
     (format stream "(setf *category* ~S)~%" *category*)
     (format stream "(setf *determiner-flag* ~A)~%"
             *determiner-flag*)
     (back-up-node '*binary-tree* stream)
     (close stream)
     (format t "~%Backup complete.")
     (format t "~%To restore data, type (load ~S)~%"
             filename)))
```

The program saves the data in a file, in a way that can be reloaded conveniently. The function back-up-data first opens the file and writes out the global variable information, then it calls the function back-up-node, which recursively traverses the question tree, writing out the information at each node.

```
(back-up-node (node stream)
   (let ((question (get node 'question))
         (answer   (get node 'answer)))
     (cond ((and (null question)
                 (null answer))
            nil)
```

```
                (question
                 (format stream "(setf (get '~A 'question) ~S)~%"
                         node question)
                 (let ((yes-node  (get node 'yes))
                       (no-node   (get node 'no)))
                   (format stream "(setf (get '~A 'yes) '~A)~%"
                           node yes-node)
                   (back-up-node yes-node stream)
                   (format stream "(setf (get '~A 'no) '~A)~%"
                           node no-node)
                   (back-up-node no-node stream)))
                (answer
                 (format stream
                         "(setf (get '~A 'answer) '~A)~%" node answer))
                (t nil)))))
;;  -----   ** end of labels definitions ** -----
      (start)))))
```

As the comment indicates, back-up-node is the last local function definition. It is followed by the body of the labels expression, which is a call to start.

Here are the contents of the file "binary.animal" that resulted from the first example run above.

```
(setf *category* "animal")
(setf *determiner-flag* T)
(setf (get '*BINARY-TREE* 'question) "Does it purr?")
(setf (get '*BINARY-TREE* 'yes) 'NODE99)
(setf (get 'NODE99 'question) "Does it run on regular gas?")
(setf (get 'NODE99 'yes) 'NODE101)
(setf (get 'NODE101 'answer) 'FERRARI)
(setf (get 'NODE99 'no) 'NODE102)
(setf (get 'NODE102 'answer) 'CAT)
(setf (get '*BINARY-TREE* 'no) 'NODE100)
(setf (get 'NODE100 'question) "Is it gray?")
(setf (get 'NODE100 'yes) 'NODE103)
(setf (get 'NODE103 'answer) 'ELEPHANT)
(setf (get 'NODE100 'no) 'NODE104)
(setf (get 'NODE104 'question) "Is it bigger than a person?")
(setf (get 'NODE104 'yes) 'NODE107)
(setf (get 'NODE107 'question) "Does it have stripes?")
(setf (get 'NODE107 'yes) 'NODE109)
(setf (get 'NODE109 'answer) 'TIGER)
(setf (get 'NODE107 'no) 'NODE110)
(setf (get 'NODE110 'question) "Is it a domestic animal?")
```

```
(setf (get 'NODE110 'yes) 'NODE105)
(setf (get 'NODE105 'answer) 'HORSE)
(setf (get 'NODE110 'no) 'NODE106)
(setf (get 'NODE106 'answer) 'GORILLA)
(setf (get 'NODE104 'no) 'NODE108)
(setf (get 'NODE108 'answer) 'MONKEY)
```

This program was intended to demonstrate the utility of catch in the context of a complex control setting. (See exercise 9.12.6.)

Useful though catch may be in these circumstances, it may also introduce a new of source of problems. Consider the following code segment for a program that interactively interrogates the user, based on questions it reads from a file.

```
(catch 'finish
    (open-a-file-and-ask-questions-of-user 'finish)
    (close-file))
```

If the (open-a-file-and-ask-questions-of-user) segment ends with a throw to the catch via finish, then the (close-file) code is never executed. Chances are, this is not the effect intended by the programmer.

What the programmer most likely wanted was to provide a way to end the session early, but still wanted to close the file. LISP permits the programmer to have her cake and eat it too with unwind-protect.

```
(catch 'finish
    (unwind-protect
        (open-a-file-and-ask-questions-of-user 'finish)
        (close-file)))
```

Here, unwind-protect acts as a barrier, of sorts, between the catch and the expressions. If any throw occurs inside (open-a-file-and-ask-questions-of-user), the unwind-protect intervenes and does not let control pass back to the respective catch until the (close-file) has been evaluated. unwind-protect is triggered only by a throw from its first argument, in which case the remaining zero or more arguments are evaluated.

The situation of recovering from errors with an open stream is so common that LISP has a macro just for the occasion: with-open-stream, introduced in the advanced topics section 7.8.4.

```
(with-open-stream (identifier stream-expression) &rest body)
```

The stream-expression is normally a call to open, which then returns a stream bound to its respective identifier. After the body is evaluated, the local stream is closed — even if there was a nonstandard exit from body, as with throw. Thus, unwind-protect is built into with-open-stream.

Here is our earlier example, now using with-open-stream.

```
(catch 'finish
  (with-open-stream
    (stream-id (open-a-file))
    (ask-questions-of-user 'finish)))
```

Another example of unwind-protect is found in section 15.5.

9.12   Exercises

9.12.1   Bottles of Beer [2*]

Why does this chapter have one of the same epigraphs as the recursion chapter?

9.12.2   loop Average [5*]

Rewrite the i-average function, using the loop form instead of do.

9.12.3   Remove String Pairs [3*]

Define remove-pairs to work with strings. For example:

```
> (remove-pairs "aaabbb")
"ab"

> (remove-pairs "bookkeeper")
"bokeper"
```

Your function can call r-remove-pairs or i-remove-pairs.

9.12.4   More Spelling Correction: Soundex [7*]

In section 6.6, we developed one way to detect and correct spelling errors. Another method, which depends on detecting words spelled the way they sound, is the Soundex algorithm, which is described in [Knuth, 1978].

The idea behind Soundex is psychologically appealing, namely, that people can detect misspelled words that *sound* like actual words. Thus, a person would not be at a loss when confronted with *Misisipy*, or *Road Island*, or *Dellawear*. Note that the spelling corrector in section 6.6 would not have corrected any of those errors. Soundex could fix them all.

Here is how it works. To see how a word should be spelled, Soundex first creates a phonetic code for that word, consisting of a letter followed by one to three digits. It then retrieves the correctly spelled word corresponding to that code. If there is more than one correct word for that code, or there are no correct words, then Soundex fails.

The codes themselves are based on the sounds of the words, according to the following method.

1. All double letters are removed from the word (as with our `remove-pairs` function in the previous exercise.)

2. The first letter of the word is used as the first letter of the code.

3. Each subsequent letter of the word is examined, until either the end of the word is reached or the code length is four characters.

4. The digit corresponding to the given letter is added to the code. The following table gives the digit-letter groupings. Note that vowels are not coded.

```
1:    B F P V
2:    C G J K Q X
3:    D T
4:    L
5:    M N
6:    R
7:    S Z
```

The algorithm presented in Knuth does not have a category 7; "S" and "Z" had been included in category 2. However, that resulted in a duplicate Soundex code (A625) for "Arizona" and "Arkansas." Under the revised scheme, "Arizona" becomes A675.

Here are examples of Soundex at work.

```
> (soundex 'harry)
H6

> (soundex 'hairy)
H6

> (soundex 'Missouri)
M76

> (soundex 'misery)
M76

> (soundex 'Arizona)
A675

> (soundex 'Arkansas)
A625
```

Simply generating a code for a word is not intrinsically useful. However, the code can be used as an index to the correct spelling of the word. In the example below, the `tag-word` function enters the code-word pair in a table (such as a property list or association list). The `isa-word` function retrieves the correctly spelled word and compares it with the given word.

```
> (mapcar #'tag-word
      '("Georgia" "Mississippi" "Delaware" "Rhode Island"))
("GEORGIA" "MISSISSIPPI" "DELAWARE" "RHODE ISLAND")

> (isa-word "Road Island")
"No. How about RHODE ISLAND ?"

> (isa-word 'misisipy)
"No. How about MISSISSIPPI ?"

> (isa-word "dellawear")
"No. How about DELAWARE ?"

> (isa-word 'georgia)
T

> (isa-word 'quebec)
"No match at all."
```

Write the three functions `soundex`, `tag-word`, and `isa-word`. Then, load all 50 states and try it out.

9.12.5   Unwind Protection [4*]

`unwind-protect` protects only its first argument. Suppose you have the following code.

```
(catch 'finish
  (unwind-protect
      (step-one 'finish)
      (step-two 'finish)
      (step-three)))
```

As it stands, if a throw occurs in (step-one), then `unwind-protect` will ensure that (step-two) and (step-three) will be executed. However, if the throw occurs in (step-two), `unwind-protect` will not guarantee execution of (step-three). In fact, it will generate an error.

How could you rewrite the code so that both (step-one) and (step-two) will be protected, and guarantee execution of (step-three) if there is a throw in the two earlier steps?

9.12.6   Binary Game Catch [5*]

What would happen if within the `query` local function given on page 320 the line
of code is altered as follows?

```
        ((q quit)      (throw 'quit-action '*end-of-binary*))
;   is changed to:
        ((q quit)      '*end-of-binary*)
```

9.13   Chapter Summary

- The order of evaluation of arguments to a function is undefined in LISP.

- The `progn`, `prog1`, and `prog2` forms are sequencing constructs. `progn` returns
  the value of the last expression, mirroring LISP's normal evaluation. `prog1`
  returns the value of its first expression, and `prog2` returns the value of its
  second expression.

```
(progn {form}*)
(prog1 form1 {form}*)
(prog2 form1 form2 {form}*)
```

- `case` and `typecase` allow a programmer to use key values to control program
  execution.

```
(case keyform {(({({key}*) | key } {form}*)}*)
(typecase keyform {(type {form}*)}*)
```

- Iteration and recursion are the two fundamental control techniques.

- LISP provides several iterative control forms, including the following:

```
(do  ({(var [init [step]])}*) (exit-test {result}*)
         {tag | statement}*)
(do* ({(var [init [step]])}*) (exit-test {result}*)
         {tag | statement}*)
(dolist  (var listform [result]) {tag | statement}*)
(dotimes (var countform [result]) {tag | statement}*)
```

- As alternatives to `if` or `cond`, LISP provides the additional conditional forms.

```
(when    test {form}*)
(unless test {form}*)
```

- The `loop` macro executes its body of expressions repeatedly until it encounters
  a `return` form.

```
(loop {form}*)
```

- The special form (`block name {form}*`) executes the forms from left to right and returns the value of the last one. However, either (`return value`) or (`return-from name value`) will terminate the execution of forms and return the given `value`.

- LISP permits go statements within a number of control forms, including the following.

```
(tagbody {tag | statement}*)
(prog  ({var | (var [init])}*) {tag | statement}*)
(prog* ({var | (var [init])}*) {tag | statement}*)
```

Both `prog` and `prog*` can also contain `return` statements.

- Functions can return multiple values, using the `values` or `values-list` functions. The constant `multiple-values-limit` indicates the maximum number of values that can be returned. LISP provides the following macros for using multiple values.

```
(multiple-value-setq varlist values-form)
(multiple-value-bind ({var}*) values-form {form}*)
(multiple-value-call function {form}*)
(multiple-value-list form)
(multiple-value-prog1 {form}+)
```

- `catch` and `throw` provide a means for nonlocal control flow.

- `catch` is best used in programs with large, complex flow of control.

- `unwind-protect` can guard against dangerous `catch` side effects. The macro `with-open-stream` uses `unwind-protect` to ensure that streams get closed in the event of nonstandard exits.

A program without a loop and a structured variable isn't
worth writing.

◇ ALAN PERLIS, *Epigrams in Programming (1982)*

Chapter 10

Debugging and Style

> *A man of genius makes no mistakes.*
> *His errors are volitional and are the portals of discovery.*
>
> ◊ JAMES JOYCE, *Ulysses (1922)*

> *And yes I said yes I will Yes.*
>
> ◊ JAMES JOYCE, *Ibid.*

> *Let these describe the undescribable.*
>
> ◊ GEORGE NOEL GORDON, LORD BYRON, *Childe Harold's Pilgrimage (1821)*

> *A survey was made of several programmers who use DDT*
> *frequently, and it was learned that most debugging is done*
> *with a limited set of commands.*
>
> ◊ DIGITAL EQUIPMENT CORPORATION, *DECSystem10 Assembly Language*
> *Handbook, Second Edition (1972)*

Programmers make errors. Ineluctably, computers make errors. It is the job of the programmer to

- Prevent errors
- Detect errors
- Elucidate errors
- Recover from errors

These activities are aspects of the debugging enterprise. The term *debugging*, with its underlying connotations of pestilence and epidemics, is most apt. Programmers soon realize that the most benign error — a typing mistake or a faulty assumption — can result in a computer wreaking havoc at the speed of light.

Continuing the health/disease metaphor, the four aspects of debugging can be viewed as immunization, presentation of symptoms, diagnosis of the disease, and finally, treatment and cure.

10.1 Preventing Errors

An ounce of prevention is worth a pound of cure. Preventing computer errors can be much more important than recognizing and correcting them when the damage is already done. Knowing after the fact how to repair the tiny bug in your electronic funds transfer program is of little solace once the error has resulted in wiring all the bank's assets to the mob's offshore bank account.

Clearly, the best way to handle errors is not to create them in the first place. One of the common sources of errors in LISP programs is improper or unbalanced parentheses. The best solution for this problem is a good text editor that can automatically balance parentheses.

However, even if a definition has the right number of parentheses, they may not always be in the right places. Here is an example in which LISP does not complain when the function is defined, just when it is called.

```
(defun fact (n ;  Fatal missing right paren.
   (cond ((zerop n) 1)
         (t
          (fact (* n (fact (- n 1)))))))))
```

```
> (fact 4)
Error: Non-symbol used as a lambda argument name in function FACT.
  [condition type: PROGRAM-ERROR]
[1]
> (describe 'fact)
FACT is a SYMBOL
  It is unbound.
  It is INTERNAL in the COMMON-LISP-USER package.
  Its function binding is #<Interpreted Function FACT @ #x119f606>
    The function takes arguments
        (N (COND ((ZEROP N) 1) (T (FACT (* N (FACT (- N 1)))))))
```

The problem is that the initial argument list did not get closed. The programmer indented the code properly and added enough parentheses at the end to allow the function to be defined, but the definition is faulty. The call to `describe` indicates that `fact` expects multiple arguments, not one. Thus, we got an error because

LISP wanted another argument. LISP could not figure out what we really meant to do. All LISP knew was that we had promised to deliver two arguments every time we called fact.

Once the error in fact has been identified, the programmer will want to correct it. Usually, this means invoking an editor on the file in which fact was ∞ ⇒ defined. Some implementations have a resident editor which can be called directly within LISP with the ed function.

```
(ed)              ; Invokes the editor.
(ed nil)          ; Invokes the editor.
(ed pathname)     ; Edits the given file.
(ed symbol)       ; Edits the function with the given name.
```

The describe function used above can help the programmer find out how many arguments a function requires. The exact output of describe may vary with different ∞ ⇒ implementations. We next ask describe about subst.

```
> (describe 'subst)
SUBST is a SYMBOL
  It is unbound.
  It is EXTERNAL in the COMMON-LISP package and accessible in the
ANTCW, CLIM, CLIM-DEMO, CLIM-LISP, CLIM-USER, CLIM-UTILS, CLOS,
CLOS-X-RESOURCES, CLTL1, COMMON-LISP-USER, COMMON-WINDOWS, COMPILER,
COMPOSER, CROSS-REFERENCE, DEBUGGER, DEFSYSTEM, EXCL, EXTENDED-IO,
FLAVORS, FOREIGN-FUNCTIONS, FRANZ, GPROFILER, GRAPHER, HYPERION,
INSPECT, IPC, LEP, MULTIPROCESSING, PATCH, PROFILER, QUAD-LINE, SCM,
STREAM, SYSTEM, TOP-LEVEL, WINX, XLIB, and XTK packages.
  Its function binding is #<Function SUBST @ #x71fafe>
    The function takes arguments
        (NEW OLD TREE &KEY KEY TEST TEST-NOT)
  Its property list has these indicator/value pairs:
EXCL::%FUN-DOCUMENTATION
        "Substitutes new for subtrees matching old."
```

In this implementation, describe provides the following information.

- The type of the object, for example, a symbol

- The value binding of the object, for example, the symbol's value

- The packages from which it is accessible (see chapter 15)

- The function binding of the object, that is, what function is associated with the object

- The argument list for that function

• The property list for the object; in this case, the documentation string

We now ask about the addition function.

```
> (describe '+)
+ is a SYMBOL
  Its value is (DESCRIBE 'SUBST)
  It is EXTERNAL in the COMMON-LISP package and accessible in the
ANTCW, CLIM, CLIM-DEMO, CLIM-LISP, CLIM-USER, CLIM-UTILS, CLOS,
CLOS-X-RESOURCES, CLTL1, COMMON-LISP-USER, COMMON-WINDOWS, COMPILER,
COMPOSER, CROSS-REFERENCE, DEBUGGER, DEFSYSTEM, EXCL, EXTENDED-IO,
FLAVORS, FOREIGN-FUNCTIONS, FRANZ, GPROFILER, GRAPHER, HYPERION,
INSPECT, IPC, LEP, MULTIPROCESSING, PATCH, PROFILER, QUAD-LINE, SCM,
STREAM, SYSTEM, TOP-LEVEL, WINX, XLIB, and XTK packages.
  Its function binding is #<Function + @ #x72c776>
    The function takes arguments (&REST ARGS)
  Its property list has these indicator/value pairs:
COMPILER::.NL-TRANSFORM.    #<Function TR-+ @ #x81e19e>
COMPILER::PT-CALL-HANDLER    COMPILER::PT-+
COMPILER::.CONSTANT-FOLDING.  T
COMPILER::A-PRIORI          12
EXCL::%VAR-DOCUMENTATION
        "Holds the value of the most recent top-level read."
EXCL::.GLOBALLY-SPECIAL.    T
```

What is this? It says that + is a symbol and its value is (DESCRIBE 'SUBST)? From where did that come?

It happens that + in Common LISP has two separate roles. As a function, + denotes addition. As a symbol, + is bound to the previous expression read by the read-eval-print loop. Thus, the symbol + above was bound to (describe 'subst) because that was what had been typed previously. Moreover, LISP defines the following read-eval-print loop variables.

• ++ contains the previous value of +, that is, two expressions back.

• +++ contains the previous value of ++, that is, three expressions back.

• - contains the *current* top-level expression being evaluated.

• * contains the result of the previous expression. If several results were returned, only the first is bound to *. If no results were returned, for example, with (values), then * is set to NIL.

• ** contains the previous value of *, that is, the result from two expressions back.

- *** contains the previous value of **, that is, the result from three expressions back.

- / contains a list of the results from the previous expression. The `car` of / should be the same as *.

- // contains the previous value of /, that is, the list of results from two expressions back.

- /// contains the previous value of //, that is, the list of results from three expressions back.

Here are some examples.

```
> (* 9 9)                 ;  Start with a normal expression.
81


> +                       ;  + is bound to the previous input form.
(* 9 9)


> **                      ;  ** is bound to the result from two back.
81


> ///                     ;  /// is the list of results from three back.
(81)


> (list - - -)            ;  - is the current input form.
((LIST - - -) (LIST - - -) (LIST - - -))


> (car -)                 ;  Pretty tricky, eh?
CAR


;  Now for trick city.
> (list '(a b c d e f) 'has 'length (length (cadadr -)))
((A B C D E F) HAS LENGTH 6)


;  Returns multiple values instead of a list.
> (values '(a b c d e f) 'has 'length (length (cadadr -)))
(A B C D E F)
HAS
LENGTH
6


> *                       ;  Returns the first value only.
(A B C D E F)
```

```
> //                        ;  Returns all values in a list.
((A B C D E F) HAS LENGTH 6)
```

This digression should serve to emphasize the pluralism of LISP symbols. They may have associated values, functions, and property lists. We now return to our informative friend describe.

```
> (describe 'map)
MAP is a SYMBOL
  It is unbound.
  It is EXTERNAL in the COMMON-LISP package and accessible in the
ANTCW, CLIM, CLIM-DEMO, CLIM-LISP, CLIM-USER, CLIM-UTILS, CLOS,
CLOS-X-RESOURCES, CLTL1, COMMON-LISP-USER, COMMON-WINDOWS, COMPILER,
COMPOSER, CROSS-REFERENCE, DEBUGGER, DEFSYSTEM, EXCL, EXTENDED-IO,
FLAVORS, FOREIGN-FUNCTIONS, FRANZ, GPROFILER, GRAPHER, HYPERION,
INSPECT, IPC, LEP, MULTIPROCESSING, PATCH, PROFILER, QUAD-LINE, SCM,
STREAM, SYSTEM, TOP-LEVEL, WINX, XLIB, and XTK packages.
  Its function binding is #<Function MAP @ #x729956>
    The function takes arguments
      (OUTPUT-TYPE-SPEC FUNCTION FIRST-SEQUENCE &REST MORE-SEQUENCES)
  Its property list has these indicator/value pairs:
COMPILER::.NL-TRANSFORM.    #<Function TR-MAP @ #x81cf46>
EXCL::%FUN-DOCUMENTATION "function must take as many arguments as
there are sequences provided.  The result is a sequence such that
element i is the result of applying function to element i of each of
the argument sequences."

> (describe 'describe)
DESCRIBE is a SYMBOL
  It is unbound.
  It is EXTERNAL in the COMMON-LISP package and accessible in the
ANTCW, CLIM, CLIM-DEMO, CLIM-LISP, CLIM-USER, CLIM-UTILS, CLOS,
CLOS-X-RESOURCES, CLTL1, COMMON-LISP-USER, COMMON-WINDOWS, COMPILER,
COMPOSER, CROSS-REFERENCE, DEBUGGER, DEFSYSTEM, EXCL, EXTENDED-IO,
FLAVORS, FOREIGN-FUNCTIONS, FRANZ, GPROFILER, GRAPHER, HYPERION,
INSPECT, IPC, LEP, MULTIPROCESSING, PATCH, PROFILER, QUAD-LINE, SCM,
STREAM, SYSTEM, TOP-LEVEL, WINX, XLIB, and XTK packages.
  Its function binding is #<Function DESCRIBE @ #x7e27ee>
    The function takes arguments (X &OPTIONAL STREAM)
```

The optional stream argument for describe specifies where the output should appear.

Two functions related to describe are apropos and apropos-list, which find all symbols containing the given string of characters. For example, if you

wanted to find all the mapping functions that contain the string MAPC, you could
do the following.

```
> (apropos 'mapc)
MAPCAR              [function]  (FUNCTION LIST &REST MORE-LISTS)
MAPCAN              [function]  (FUNCTION LIST &REST MORE-LISTS)
MAPCON              [function]  (FUNCTION LIST &REST MORE-LISTS)
MAPC                [function]  (FUNCTION LIST &REST MORE-LISTS)
COMP::TR-MAPCAR     [function]  (XFORM)
COMP::TR-MAPC       [function]  (XFORM)


> (apropos-list 'mapc)   ;  Returns a list of symbols.
(COMPILER::TR-MAPC COMPILER::TR-MAPCAR MAPCON MAPC MAPCAN MAPCAR)


> (apropos "apropos")    ;  Case-sensitive for strings.  No matches.


> (apropos "APROPOS")
EXCL::APROPOS-SEARCH [function] (SYMBOL FIXNUMS LENGTH)
EXCL::APROPOS-REGEXP [function]
                    (STRING &OPTIONAL PACKAGE EXTERNAL-ONLY)
EXCL::APROPOS-FIXNUMS [function] (STRING LENGTH)
APROPOS-LIST        [function]
                    (STRING &OPTIONAL PACKAGE EXTERNAL-ONLY)
APROPOS             [function]
                    (STRING &OPTIONAL PACKAGE EXTERNAL-ONLY)
LEP::APROPOS-SESSION
```

The prefixes followed by colons specify packages, which are discussed in chapter 15.

The basic advice for error prevention is probably as useful as it is profound:
be careful. Typing errors (typos) can be prevented by the attentive programmer.
Conceptual errors (thinkos) can be avoided by similar diligence and energy.

This book presents techniques for designing and developing programs. These
techniques — such as the use of local variables instead of global variables, modular
program design, and proper indentation and commenting styles — are meant to
make it easier for the programmer to write correct code. However, these techniques
do not make it impossible to write incorrect code.

The hope is that the suggestions presented in this chapter, and throughout
this text, will enable the programmer not only to make fewer errors but also to
limit the scope and damage of those errors that do occur.

In years of teaching programming, we have developed a rule for evaluating
computer programs. Students seem to find it easy to apprehend. We call it the
Clint Eastwood Programming Rule:

> A program is either good, bad, or ugly.

We define our terms.

- A program is *good* if it does what it is supposed to do efficiently and is written in a clean, well-documented style.

- A program is *bad* if it does not do what it is supposed to do. The program produces errors.

- A program is *ugly* even if it does what it is supposed to do but is either inefficient or is difficult to read or maintain.

Thus, a good program is one that is neither bad nor ugly. A bad program should be easy to label. Ugly programs can be ugly for many varied reasons. Programmers may be reluctant to identify a program as ugly. Remember, an ugly program actually works − otherwise, it would be bad. However, ugly programs are on the verge of being bad. Here are some symptoms of ugly code.

- *Inefficient.* The programmer may have used a poor algorithm or data structure when a more efficient alternative is available.

- *Poor indentation.* The computer does not care about indentation, but humans do. Poorly indented code is hard to read and may lead to errors in balancing parentheses.

- *Poor function or variable names.* LISP places very few restrictions on identifiers. Still, programmers continue to use names like `df` or `i` instead of `depth-first` or `interest-rates`. Meaningful identifiers are a blessing for all.

- *Poor style.* The code may be perfectly fine but written in a nonidiomatic style, likely to confuse the normal programmer. Code may be ugly simply if there is a prettier way to write it. Many of the ugly code examples in the previous chapter suffer on this account.

- *Poor comments.* Again, the computer ignores comments, but humans rely on them. Programmers should develop the habit of providing helpful comments.

- *Poor documentation.* Are we being redundant here? What is the difference between comments and documentation? In LISP, there is an important difference. Documentation strings, unlike comments, are *not* ignored by the computer.

What is documentation? Above, we showed the output from `describe` for `subst`. One of the items listed was the `DOCUMENTATION` property for `subst`. The documentation string was not a comment but rather became associated with the internal LISP representation.

The programmer can create her own documentation strings when defining variables or functions. With `defvar`, `defconstant`, and `defparameter`, the documentation string is an optional third argument.

```
> (defvar *guests* 28 "The number of guests who have RSVP'd")
*GUESTS*

> *guests*
28

> (describe '*guests*)

*GUESTS* is a SYMBOL
  Its value is 28
  It is INTERNAL in the COMMON-LISP-USER package.
  Its property list has these indicator/value pairs:
EXCL::%VAR-DOCUMENTATION    "The number of guests who have RSVP'd"
EXCL::.GLOBALLY-SPECIAL.     T


;  (documentation symbol doc-type) returns the documentation string for
;  the given symbol and the specified type, for example, variable or function.
> (documentation '*guests* 'variable)
"The number of guests who have RSVP'd"

> (defconstant *capacity* 100 "The number of seats in the hall.")
*CAPACITY*

> (describe '*capacity*)

*CAPACITY* is a SYMBOL
  Its value is 100
  It is INTERNAL in the COMMON-LISP-USER package.
  Its property list has these indicator/value pairs:
EXCL::%VAR-DOCUMENTATION    "The number of seats in the hall."
EXCL::.CONSTANT.             T
EXCL::.GLOBALLY-SPECIAL.     T
```

The defun form also allows documentation strings as a third argument after the lambda list and before the body of the definition.

```
> (defun fact (n)
    "The factorial function."
    (cond ((zerop n) 1)
          (t (* n (fact (1- n))))))
FACT

> (fact 4)
24
```

```
> (describe 'fact)

FACT is a SYMBOL
  It is unbound.
  It is INTERNAL in the COMMON-LISP-USER package.
  Its function binding is #<Interpreted Function FACT @ #x11cafb6>
    The function takes arguments (N)
  Its property list has these indicator/value pairs:
EXCL::%FUN-DOCUMENTATION    "The factorial function."


> (documentation 'fact 'function)
"The factorial function."

;  Here is a little trick — define a variable with a functional value.
> (defvar fact #'fact "The symbol fact is the function.")
FACT

> (describe 'fact)

FACT is a SYMBOL
  Its value is #<Interpreted Function FACT @ #x11cafb6>
  It is INTERNAL in the COMMON-LISP-USER package.
  Its function binding is #<Interpreted Function FACT @ #x11cafb6>
    The function takes arguments (N)
  Its property list has these indicator/value pairs:
EXCL::%VAR-DOCUMENTATION    "The symbol fact is the function."
EXCL::.GLOBALLY-SPECIAL.    T
EXCL::%FUN-DOCUMENTATION    "The factorial function."


> (mapcar fact '(3 4 5))    ;  Equivalent to (mapcar #'fact '(3 4 5)).
(6 24 120)
```

In this last example, we see that a symbol can have more than one associated documentation string.

10.2 Detecting Errors

Murphy's Law states that if anything can go wrong, it will. The programmer's corollary is: Murphy was an optimist.

Here is a partial list of the types of errors that LISP can detect and complain about.

- Wrong number of arguments to a function

- Unbound variable reference

- Calling a nonfunction

- Wrong object type as argument to a function

- Index out of range

Below, we provide examples of each of these errors. In our example, the programmer wishes to find the absolute value of 3.1.

```
> (abs 3. 1)                      ; Typed space before 1.
Error: ABS got 2 args, wanted at most 1.
   [condition type: PROGRAM-ERROR]
[1]
> (abbs 3.1)                      ; Spelling error.
Error: attempt to call 'ABBS' which is an undefined function.
   [condition type: UNDEFINED-FUNCTION]

Restart actions (select using :continue):
 0: Try calling ABBS again
 1: Return a value
 2: Try calling a different function
 3: Setf the symbol function of ABBS and call it again
[2]
> ('abs 3.1)                      ; Quoted abs by mistake.
Error: Illegal function object: 'ABS.
   [condition type: PROGRAM-ERROR]

Restart actions (select using :continue):
 0: Try calling ABBS again
 1: Return a value
 2: Try calling a different function
 3: Setf the symbol function of ABBS and call it again
[3]
> (abs "3.1")                     ; Should not use string.
Error: non-number to abs: "3.1"
   [condition type: TYPE-ERROR]

Restart actions (select using :continue):
 0: Try calling ABBS again
 1: Return a value
 2: Try calling a different function
 3: Setf the symbol function of ABBS and call it again
[4]
```

```
> (abs (nth 2 '(2.1 3.1)))        ;  nth is zero-based.
Error: non-number to abs: NIL
  [condition type: TYPE-ERROR]

Restart actions (select using :continue):
 0: Try calling ABBS again
 1: Return a value
 2: Try calling a different function
 3: Setf the symbol function of ABBS and call it again
[5]
```

In these examples, it is not too difficult to identify what is wrong and how to correct it. The error messages are fairly helpful, even though they do not precisely explain the underlying cause of the error. The messages reveal the symptoms, which usually lead to the diagnosis of the disease.

However, imagine that you have written a large program comprising dozens of files and thousands of lines of code. In the course of execution, the program hits one of these errors and LISP spits out one of these messages. These error messages are generated by calls to LISP's own functions. However, it is the functions that you defined that made the mistake of too many arguments or an unbound variable. How do you find the error in your code?

Furthermore, imagine that you execute your enormous program and it does not produce any error messages. However, it does not produce the expected answer either. How do you find the error in your code?

The answer is to do what LISP does. If LISP's functions can detect errors and signal them, so can your code. Here is an example of error checking.

```
(defun set-salary-of (person salary)
  (cond
   ((not (symbolp person))
    (error "SET-SALARY-OF. expected a symbol but got:~%~A [~A]"
           (type-of person) person))
   ((not (floatp salary))
    (error "SET-SALARY-OF. expected a float but got:~%~A [~A]"
           (type-of salary) salary)))
  (setf (get person 'salary) salary))

> (set-salary-of "Joe" 10000)
Error: SET-SALARY-OF. expected a symbol but got:
(SIMPLE-ARRAY CHARACTER (3)) [Joe]
```

One of the greatest sources of errors is bad data. Therefore, it is important to check any data to make sure that it is what you expect. The function `set-salary-of` is little more than a call to the `setf` function. However, it first checks its arguments to make sure that they are of proper types. When we call `set-salary-of` with a first argument of "Joe", which is not a symbol, we trigger the `error` clause.

The `error` function is very similar to `format`. It prints out its arguments in the same fashion as `format`, with several exceptions. First, the errors are always printed to the stream `*error-output*`, which is usually the same stream as `*standard-output*`. Second, `error` prepends the the string "Error: " to the format control string. Finally, `error` stops execution and places LISP at the next command level in another read-eval-print loop.

If the reader takes a moment to review LISP's regular error messages, it should be apparent that they, too, are based on the `error` function.

Many errors can be fixed on the spot at run-time. These are *continuable errors*. The function `cerror` allows the programmer to make changes on the fly. `cerror` has two format string arguments: a string for the continuation choice and a string for the error message. These are followed by the format arguments, shared by both strings. If the programmer chooses to continue, `cerror` returns NIL. Here is an example.

```
(defun safe-abs (n)
  (cond ((numberp n)
         (abs n))
        (t
         (cerror "Enter a number" "~s is not a number" n)
         (format t "Enter a number: ")
         (safe-abs (read)))))
```

```
> (safe-abs "3.1")
Error: "3.1" is not a number        ;  The error message string.

Restart actions (select using :continue):
 0: Enter a number                   ;  The continuation choice string.
[1c]
> :continue
Enter a number: '3.1
Error: '3.1 is not a number

Restart actions (select using :continue):
 0: Enter a number
[1c]
> :continue
Enter a number: 3.1
3.1
```

The use of `cerror` to check the type of arguments is so common or worthwhile, or both, that LISP provides a convenient macro, `check-type`, which directly implements the entire process, as shown here.

```
(defun safe-abs2 (n)
  (check-type n number)
  (abs n))

> (safe-abs2 "9")
Error: the value of N is "9", which is not of type NUMBER.
  [condition type: TYPE-ERROR]

Restart actions (select using :continue):
 0: supply a new value for N.
[1]
> :continue
Type a form to be evaluated: 9   ; We continue and supply a number.
9
```

The check-type macro takes three arguments: the object being checked, its type specification, and an optional string to be printed in the error message.

```
> (setf j "Joe")
"Joe"

> (check-type j symbol "an honest to God symbol")
Error: the value of J is "Joe", which is not an honest to God symbol.
  [condition type: TYPE-ERROR]

Restart actions (select using :continue):
 0: supply a new value for J.
[1]
> :continue 0
Type a form to be evaluated: 'joe
NIL

> j
JOE
```

The check-type macro does not return a useful value. It works through side effects. An alternative is the special form with the peculiar name the. That's right: the. The first argument to the is a type specification, and the second argument is a form to be evaluated. If the form is of the given type, the returns the value of the form; otherwise, it may trigger an error. We note that not all implementations trigger errors for the. Here is an example.   ⇐ ∞

```
> (the integer 23)
23
```

```
> (+ (the integer "9") (the integer 23))
Error: object ""9"" is not of type "INTEGER".
  [condition type: PROGRAM-ERROR]

Restart actions (select using :continue):
 0: prompt for a new object.
[1c]
> :cont

New object of type "INTEGER": 9
32
```

The form the provides a convenient way to perform type checking in function calls. Here is our **safe-abs** example using **the**.

```
(defun safe-abs3 (n)
  (abs (the number n)))

> (safe-abs3 "3.1")
Error: object ""3.1"" is not of type "NUMBER".
  [condition type: PROGRAM-ERROR]

Restart actions (select using :continue):
 0: prompt for a new object.
[1c]
> :cont

New object of type "NUMBER": 3.1
3.1
```

Table 10.1 provides a list of the standard LISP types. LISP does not restrict the risk-averse programmer to its built-in set of types. The programmer can build her own types. First, we note that the **typep** function allows the user to specify type predicates.

```
> (typep 1 'integer)
T

> (typep 1 'real)
T

> (typep 1 'symbol)
NIL
```

array	hash-table	sequence
atom	integer	short-float
base-character	keyword	signed-byte
bignum	list	simple-array
bit	long-float	simple-bit-vector
bit-vector	nil	simple-string
character	null	simple-vector
compiled-function	number	single-float
complex	package	standard-char
cons	pathname	stream
double-float	random-state	string
extended-character	ratio	symbol
fixnum	rational	t
float	readtable	unsigned-byte
function	real	vector

Table 10.1: Standard Type Specifiers

```
> (typep "1" 'string)
T
```

Second, there is a hierarchy of types. That is, some types are more general than others. The subtypep function tells us if one type is a subset of another.

```
> (subtypep 'integer 'number)
T
T
```

```
> (subtypep 'number 'integer)
NIL
T
```

```
> (subtypep 'integer 'real)
T
T
```

```
> (subtypep '(satisfies plusp) '(satisfies evenp))
NIL
NIL
```

subtypep returns two values: whether or not the first type is a subtype of the second, and if not, whether subtypep is certain about the answer. The last example,

which illustrates the next topic, provides an example in which `subtypep` is not
certain about the relationship.

LISP provides ways to combine and refine existing types. The programmer
can define other types by using the following type specifiers.

- (satisfies predicate) complies with given predicate (which must be specified as a symbol name, not a lambda expression).

- (member {object}*) is eq to one of the given elements.

- (eql object) is eql the given object.

- (not type) is not the given type.

- (and {type}*) satisfies all of the given types.

- (or {type}*) satisfies at least one of the given types.

Here are examples.

```
> (typep 3 '(satisfies oddp))     ;  3 is odd.
T

> (typep 4 '(satisfies oddp))     ;  4 is not odd.
NIL

> (typep 'x '(member a b c))      ;  x is not a member of (a b c).
NIL

> (typep 'a '(member a b c))
T

> (typep 1 '(eql 1.0))            ;  1 is not eql 1.0.
NIL

> (typep 1 '(eql 1))
T

> (typep 'x '(not string))        ;  x is not a string.
T

> (typep 'x '(not symbol))        ;  x is not, not a symbol.
NIL

> (typep 3 '(and integer (satisfies oddp)))
T
```

```
> (typep 4 '(and integer (satisfies minusp)))
NIL

> (typep 4 '(or (satisfies plusp) symbol))
T

> (typep 'x '(or integer symbol))
T
```

In addition, it is possible to specialize existing types, narrowing their scope, by using the following type specifiers.

- (integer low high) — An integer in the range of low to high. A limit is inclusive unless given in parentheses, in which case it is exclusive. Thus, the range of integers 1 through 10 could be given by any of the following:

```
(integer 1 10)
(integer (0) 10)
(integer 1 (11))
(integer (0) (11))
```

An indefinite limit (either negative or positive infinity) is given with an asterisk (*).

- (mod n) — The non-negative integers from 0 to $n - 1$. Equivalent to (integer 0 (n)).

- (rational low high) — The rational numbers between low and high.

- (float low high) — Floating point numbers between low and high.

- (real low high) — Real numbers between low and high.

- (string size) — Strings of length size.

Here are examples.

```
> (typep 5 '(integer 2 9))      ;  Integers between 2 and 9.
T

> (typep 50 '(integer 2 9))
NIL

> (typep 9 '(integer 2 9))
T
```

```
> (typep 100000 '(integer 1 *)) ;  The sky is the limit.
T

> (typep 9 '(integer 2 (9)))      ;  Integers between 2 and 8.
NIL

> (typep 9 '(mod 9))              ;  Integers between 0 and 8.
NIL

> (typep 8 '(mod 9))
T

> (typep 8/3 '(rational 1 4))     ;  Rationals between 1 and 4.
T

> (typep 8/3 '(rational 1 2))
NIL

> (typep 8.0 '(float 1 10))       ;  Floats between 1 and 10.
T

> (typep 8.0 '(float 1 8))
T

> (typep 8.0 '(float 1 (8)))
NIL

> (typep 4 '(real 1 5.0))         ;  Reals between 1 and 5.
T

> (typep "hello" '(string 10))    ;  Strings of length 10.
NIL

> (typep "hello" '(string 5))
T
```

LISP allows us to combine various type specifiers to describe complex types. Here we permit human temperatures to be entered as either floating point numbers or integers, with an appropriate range.

```
> (typep 98.6 '(or (float 90 107) (integer 90 107)))
T
```

```
> (typep 99 '(or (float 90 107) (integer 90 107)))
T

> (typep "99" '(or (float 90 107) (integer 90 107)))
NIL
```

In fact, we can define new data types with the `deftype` special form.

```
(deftype human-temp ()
  '(or (float 90 107) (integer 90 107)))

> (typep 99 'human-temp)
T

> (typep 1 'human-temp)
NIL
```

Using `deftype`, we define a new LISP type, `human-temp`, that we can use in any normal type context, including `check-type`.

```
> (setf x 99)
99

> (check-type x human-temp)
NIL

> (setf x 32)
32

> (check-type x human-temp)
Error: the value of X is 32, which is not of type HUMAN-TEMP.
  [condition type: TYPE-ERROR]
```

In the next chapter, we shall see how to specify arguments to `deftype` to create more general types.

As the programmer should be aware, error checking is not without cost. Most computers perform a single, defined sequence of actions. The time that the computer spends checking arguments is time *not* spent executing the other instructions. That is, error checking slows down the code. Also, adding special error checking routines to programs slows down the programmer. The assumption is that the time invested by both programmer and computer in checking for errors will be offset by the time not spent by both woman and machine later due to errors. The programmer will find it easier and quicker to fix mistakes, and the computer will devote its energies to productive execution, not infinite loops.

Moreover, we will see in chapter 16 that adding type information to your code can actually improve performance. That is, if the compiler knows ahead of time exactly what type of arguments are being used, the most specific and efficient code can be generated and executed.

Some programming languages, such as C++, enforce mandatory type checking. That is, the C++ programmer is stuck. The LISP programmer at least has a choice.

In detecting errors, we are identifying symptoms. We are looking for indications of trouble. The programmer should freely use `error`, `cerror`, and `check-type` to reveal the problem before it spreads.

Two other error detection options available to the LISP programmer are *warnings* and *assertions*.

The `warn` form is similar to `error` except that it prints the word `Warning:` instead of `Error:` and does not (usually) cause a break in the execution.

```
> (warn "It is getting hot!  The temperature is ~A!" 100)
Warning: It is getting hot!  The temperature is 100!
NIL

> (error "The room is on fire!  The temperature is ~A!" 300)
Error: The room is on fire!  The temperature is 300!
[1]
>
```

The programmer can make `warn` cause a break in execution by setting the global variable `*break-on-signals*` to true.

```
> *break-on-signals*
NIL

> (setf *break-on-signals* T)
T

> (warn "It is getting hot!  The temperature is ~A!" 100)
Break: It is getting hot!  The temperature is 100!
break entered because of *break-on-signals*.

Restart actions (select using :continue):
 0: return from break.
 1: skip warning.
[1c]
```

Finally, the programmer can sprinkle assertions throughout her code by using the `assert` macro. Consider the following safer version of `make-date` originally defined in section 5.5, on page 151.

```
(defun make-date (month day year)
  (check-type month fixnum)
  (check-type day fixnum)
  (check-type year fixnum)
  (list month day year))
```

This version of make-date ensures that the inputs are small integers. We can exert greater control by using type specifiers with ranges.

```
(defun make-date (month day year)
  (check-type month (integer 1 12))
  (check-type day (integer 1 31))
  (check-type year (integer 1900 2000))
  (list month day year))
```

We now catch more errors.

```
> (make-date 13 4 1994)
Error: the value of MONTH is 13, which is not of type (INTEGER 1 12).
  [condition type: TYPE-ERROR]

Restart actions (select using :continue):
 0: supply a new value for MONTH.
[1]
> (make-date 12 44 1994)
Error: the value of DAY is 44, which is not of type (INTEGER 1 31).
  [condition type: TYPE-ERROR]

Restart actions (select using :continue):
 0: supply a new value for DAY.
 1: supply a new value for MONTH.
[2]
> (make-date 12 4 0)
Error: the value of YEAR is 0, which is not of type (INTEGER 1900 2000).
  [condition type: TYPE-ERROR]

Restart actions (select using :continue):
 0: supply a new value for YEAR.
 1: supply a new value for DAY.
 2: supply a new value for MONTH.
```

We can achieve a similar result with assert.

```
(defun make-date (month day year)
  (check-type month fixnum)
  (check-type day fixnum)
  (check-type year fixnum)
  (assert (and (plusp month) (< month 13))
          (month)
          "month ~D is out of range (1-12)"
          month)
  (assert (and (plusp day) (<= day 31))
          (day))
  (assert (plusp year))
  (list month day year))
```

We have used assert in three different ways in this example. The first argument to
assert is a predicate, which is required. If this test evaluates to NIL, then assert
triggers an error. assert itself returns NIL.

The second argument to assert is a list of locations that can be altered.
These locations can be either symbol names or setf accessor specifications.

The third argument is a format string followed by its associated parameters.
Below, we demonstrate assert.

```
> (make-date 13 4 1994)
Error: month 13 is out of range (1-12)

Restart actions (select using :continue):
 0: retry assertion with new value for MONTH.
[1]
> (make-date 12 44 1994)
Error: the assertion (AND (PLUSP DAY) (<= DAY 31)) failed.
  [condition type: SIMPLE-ERROR]

Restart actions (select using :continue):
 0: retry assertion with new value for DAY.
 1: retry assertion with new value for MONTH.
[2]
> (make-date 12 4 0)
Error: the assertion (PLUSP YEAR) failed.
  [condition type: SIMPLE-ERROR]

Restart actions (select using :continue):
 0: retry assertion.
 1: retry assertion with new value for DAY.
 2: retry assertion with new value for MONTH.
[3]
>
```

We also could have defined `make-date` using only one `assert`.

```
(defun make-date (month day year)
  (check-type month fixnum)
  (check-type day fixnum)
  (check-type year fixnum)
  (assert (and (and (plusp month) (< month 13))
               (and (plusp day) (<= day 31))
               (plusp year))
          (month day year)
          "month (~D) is out of range (1-12)
or day (~D) is out of range (1-31)
or year (~D) is negative."
          month day year)
  (list month day year))
```

We observe the new behavior.

```
> (make-date 13 5 1994)
Error: month (13) is out of range (1-12)
or day (5) is out of range (1-31)
or year (1994) is negative.

Restart actions (select using :continue):
 0: retry assertion with new values for MONTH, DAY, YEAR.
[1]
> :continue 0
the old value of MONTH is 13.
do you want to supply a new value? y
Type a form to be evaluated: 12
the old value of DAY is 5.
do you want to supply a new value? n
the old value of YEAR is 1994.
do you want to supply a new value? n
(12 5 1994)
```

The standard C library [Plauger, 1992] used in both C and C++ contains an `assert` form. However, unlike LISP's `assert`, the use of `assert` in unforgiving compiled languages like C and C++ usually results in the program halting without the possibility of recovery. The merciful LISP interpreter grants the programmer parole, not the death penalty, from assertion failures.

10.3 Elucidating Errors

Even if we know we have an error, we still may not know what caused the error. A message like "wrong number of arguments to function" is about as helpful as telling the doctor that you have a stomach pain. Neither piece of information, by itself, provides a diagnosis. However, each may suggest alternatives to explore.

How can the LISP programmer clarify and explain errors? Several techniques are available. The first method is one introduced in section 4.1, trace. When the programmer traces a function, particularly a recursive function, LISP prints out helpful information indicating every time that function was called, the values of the arguments, and the values of the result.

Here is a definition of factorial with a subtle error.

```
(defun fact (n)
  (cond ((<= n 1) 1)
        (t (+ n (fact (- n 1)))))))

> (fact 0)
1

> (fact 1)
1

> (fact 3)
6                          ; No errors so far.  Must be correct.

> (fact 4)
10                         ; Hmmm.  Answer should be 24.

> (trace fact)
(FACT)

> (fact 4)
 0: (FACT 4)
   1: (FACT 3)
     2: (FACT 2)
       3: (FACT 1)
       3: returned 1
     2: returned 3        ; Expected result to be 2.
   1: returned 6
 0: returned 10
10
> (untrace)
NIL
```

This example demonstrates one of the most insidious and beguiling types of errors: a program that is sometimes correct. We almost cannot believe that the program is making a mistake. After all, it gave the right answer on three test cases in a row;

it must be correct. We become like a mother defending her child. "How can you accuse my son of stealing apples? Little Joey is an angel. He always helps me wash the dishes."

Yet, we know in our heart of hearts that a program that makes mistakes is a bad program. It must be repaired. The fact that it sometimes works properly may make it even harder to locate the error.

If tracing the function does not reveal the problem, the programmer can turn to the step macro, which provides even more information, as illustrated below.

```
> (step (fact 2))
 1: (FACT 2)
[step]
>                              ;  The user simply presses RETURN.
  2: 2 => 2
  2: (BLOCK FACT (COND ((<= N 1) 1) (T (+ N #))))
[step]
>
   3: (COND ((<= N 1) 1) (T (+ N (FACT #)))) 
[step]
>
    4: (<= N 1)
[step]
>
     5: N => 2
     5: 1 => 1
    result 4: NIL
    4: T => T
    4: (+ N (FACT (- N 1)))
[step]
>
     5: N => 2
     5: (FACT (- N 1))
[step]
>
      6: (- N 1)
[step]
>
       7: N => 2
       7: 1 => 1
      result 6: 1
      6: (BLOCK FACT (COND ((<= N 1) 1) (T (+ N #))))
[step]
>
       7: (COND ((<= N 1) 1) (T (+ N (FACT #))))
```

```
[step]
>
          8: (<= N 1)
[step]
>
           9: N => 1
           9: 1 => 1
         result 8: T
         8: 1 => 1
        result 7: 1
       result 6: 1
      result 5: 1
     result 4: 3
    result 3: 3
   result 2: 3
  result 1: 3
3
```

∞ ⇒   The exact behavior of **step** varies with implementations.

A practical problem with using **trace** and **step** can be that they may produce too much output to view on the screen. That is, some of the information printed may scroll off the top of the screen before everything is completed. Also, it is sometimes useful to be able to review an entire LISP session at the terminal, to track down where the programmer may have made a mistake.

LISP allows the programmer to copy the terminal session to an output file by using the unprepossessingly named **dribble** function. Given a pathname as its only argument, **dribble** writes everything that appears on the terminal — entered by either the programmer or LISP itself — to the specified file. A second call to the **dribble** function (with no arguments) terminates the copying and closes the file, which can then be viewed in an editor, printed, or whatever. Here is an expurgated example.

```
> (dribble "fact.output")
dribbling to file "/server/u18/homes.ai/slade/a/mss/1/fact.output"

NIL

> (trace fact)
(FACT)
```

```
> (fact 100)
 0: (FACT 100)

...      ;    Lots of output here...

 0: returned 5050
5050

> (dribble)
Dribble file /server/u18/homes.ai/slade/a/mss/l/fact.output closed
NIL
```

A copy of the terminal session now appears in the file fact.output, an edited copy of which is presented below.

```
dribbling to file "/server/u18/homes.ai/slade/a/mss/l/fact.output"

NIL

> (trace fact)
(FACT)

> (fact 100)
 0: (FACT 100)

...      ;    Lots of output here...

 0: returned 5050
5050

> (dribble)
```

On windowing systems, transcripts are provided automatically in LISP process windows, so there is no need for their explicit creation. However, with most terminals, transcript files can be quite useful.

While we are talking about files, it is common to encounter errors when loading function definitions in from a file. The LISP interpreter will display its error message, and the programmer has to go back to the file to find out where in the file the error occurred. One way to help identify the specific function responsible for the error is through the values printed by LISP when loading files.

The load keyword :print can be specified as true to indicate that these values should be printed. Here is an example.

```
> (load "foo.cl")
; Loading /server/u18/homes.ai/slade/a/mss/l/foo.cl.
Error: eof encountered on stream
        #<EXCL::CHARACTER-INPUT-FILE-STREAM
        "/server/u18/homes.ai/slade/a/mss/l/foo.cl" pos 100 @
          #x11dfd76>
  [condition type: END-OF-FILE]


Restart actions (select using :continue):
 0: retry the load of foo.cl
[1]
> :res

> (load "foo.cl" :print t)        ; The programmer turns on printing.
; Loading /server/u18/homes.ai/slade/a/mss/l/foo.cl.

CD
D
PWD
Error: eof encountered on stream
        #<EXCL::CHARACTER-INPUT-FILE-STREAM
        "/server/u18/homes.ai/slade/a/mss/l/foo.cl" pos 100 @
          #x11e203e>
  [condition type: END-OF-FILE]


Restart actions (select using :continue):
 0: retry the load of foo.cl
[1]
```

With :print option turned off, the programmer has little information to help her identify where in the file the error occurred. As usual, LISP's error message says a lot less than desired. However, when we turn :print on, LISP produces the names of the variables and functions that are defined in the file. Thus, when the error occurs this second time, it is after LISP has read and evaluated the definitions of cd, d, and pwd. Therefore, we know that the error appears in the function definition immediately following the pwd definition.

10.4   Error Recovery

As the reader must have noticed by now, when LISP signals an error or when the error, cerror, or check-type functions signal an error, LISP prints out a message, displays a slightly different prompt, and waits for input from the user. LISP is then at a nested command level, with a read-eval-print loop. These nested command levels are called *breakpoints* — they are points where there is a break in the execution of the program.

Until now, we have encountered breakpoints only when LISP detected errors or our own code signaled an error. It is also possible for the programmer to place an explicit breakpoint in her code, using the break function, shown here.

```
(defvar *name* 'joe)
(defun print-name ()
  (break "I assume your name is ~A (*name*)" *name*)
  (format t "~%Glad to meet you, ~A.~%" *name*)
  values)
```

```
> (print-name)
Break: I assume your name is JOE (*name*)

Restart actions (select using :continue):
 0: return from break.
[1c]
> (setf *name* 'mary)        ; Typed by the programmer.
MARY
[1c]
> :continue 0               ; Typed by the programmer.

Glad to meet you, MARY.
Error: Attempt to take the value of the unbound variable 'VALUES'.
  [condition type: UNBOUND-VARIABLE]
[1]
> :return                   ; Typed by the programmer.

>
```

There are several things to note, starting with the behavior of break. The argument to break is a message to be printed upon entering the breakpoint. Note that the message is prefixed by Break:.

At the breakpoint itself, the programmer uses the setf form to change the value of the variable *name*. The break function itself returns NIL as its value.

The function print-name continues, but there is trouble. This time, we have a typo — we left out the parentheses around (values) — so LISP complains. In our dialect, we use the :return keyword to resume the computation.   ⇐ ∞

This example shows that it is often possible to catch and patch errors on the fly. error, cerror, and check-type enter breakpoints.

We should emphasize that the breakpoint is a read-eval-print loop, and the programmer can use it in much the same way she would the normal, top-level command loop. The programmer can define, redefine, or invoke functions, or virtually anything else she chooses. Usually though, the programmer just wants to get back to the previous level.

Thus far, we have seen two ways to exit a breakpoint in this implementation. The first was with :reset, which returned us to the top command level. The second is :return, which returns us to the previous command level and allows us to pass a result back as well, continuing the previous computation. :return with no arguments is equivalent to :return nil.

We can also return to the previous level and cancel the current computation by typing the end-of-file character at the breakpoint prompt, as shown below.

```
> (print-name)
Break: I assume your name is MARY (*name*)

Restart actions (select using :continue):
 0: return from break.
[1c]
>> (+ 3 4)                ;  The break loop is still
7                         ;  a read-eval-print loop.
[1c]
> (car (cdr '(a b c d)))
B
[1c]
> (print-name)
Break: I assume your name is MARY (*name*)

Restart actions (select using :continue):
 0: return from break.
 1: return from break.
[2c]
> ^D                      ;  The programmer types the end-of-file
:pop                      ;  character, which LISP echoes as ^D
Previous error: I assume your name is MARY (*name*)
If continued, return from break.
[1c]
> [1c]
> ^D
:pop

> ^D                      ;  EOF does not work at the top command level.
EOF
Really exit lisp [n]?
>
```

∞ ⇒

We see here that the end-of-file character (Control-d (^D) in UNIX) pops the programmer back a level without trying to continue the previous computation at that

otherwise	error	cerror
case	ecase	ccase
typecase	etypecase	ctypecase

Table 10.2: case and typecase Error Statements

level. In our dialect, it is equivalent to :pop. See the online version of appendix A   ⇐ ∞
for a description of the different implementations.

In addition to calls to error and break, the programmer can usually cause
LISP to stop what it is doing and enter a breakpoint by typing the interrupt
character. The interrupt and end-of-file characters vary according to the machine's
operating system. In UNIX, ^C (control-C) is the interrupt character.

10.5   Advanced Subjects

This chapter has the following advanced topics.

- case and typecase Errors

- Inspecting the Stack

10.5.1   case and typecase Errors

In section 9.2, we introduced the case and typecase constructs. Each had an
otherwise condition to handle those cases not matching any of the explicit conditions.

Sometimes, a missing otherwise condition might trigger an error, that is, a
call to either error or cerror. LISP provides specific macros for these conditions,
as given in table 10.2.

We illustrate ccase and ecase below.

```
(defun day-check-c (n)
  (ccase n
        ((monday tuesday wednesday thursday friday) 'weekday)
        ((saturday sunday) 'weekend)))

(defun day-check-e (n)
  (ecase n
        ((monday tuesday wednesday thursday friday) 'weekday)
        ((saturday sunday) 'weekend)))

> (day-check-c 'monday)
WEEKDAY
```

```
> (day-check-c 'mon)
Error: MON fell through a CCASE form.
        The valid cases were MONDAY, TUESDAY, WEDNESDAY, THURSDAY,
        FRIDAY, SATURDAY, and SUNDAY.
   [condition type: CASE-FAILURE]

Restart actions (select using :continue):
 0: supply a new value for N.
[1]
> :cont
Type a form to be evaluated: 'monday
WEEKDAY

> (day-check-e 'sunday)
WEEKEND

> (day-check-e 'sun)
Error: SUN fell through a ECASE form.
        The valid cases were MONDAY, TUESDAY, WEDNESDAY, THURSDAY,
        FRIDAY, SATURDAY, and SUNDAY.
   [condition type: CASE-FAILURE]
[1]
```

We cannot continue from an ecase error. Here are examples of ctypecase and etypecase.

```
(defun type-check-c (obj)
   (ctypecase obj
            ((or integer float rational) 'numerical-data)
            ((or string symbol character) 'text-data)))

(defun type-check-e (obj)
   (etypecase obj
            ((or integer float rational) 'numerical-data)
            ((or string symbol character) 'text-data)))

> (type-check-c 9)
NUMERICAL-DATA

> (type-check-c "9")
TEXT-DATA
```

```
> (type-check-c (complex 9 9))
Error: #c(9 9) fell through a CTYPECASE form.
       The valid cases were (OR INTEGER FLOAT RATIONAL)
       and (OR STRING SYMBOL CHARACTER).
   [condition type: CASE-FAILURE]

Restart actions (select using :continue):
 0: supply a new value for OBJ.
[1]
> :cont
Type a form to be evaluated: 9
NUMERICAL-DATA

> (type-check-e 9)
NUMERICAL-DATA

> (type-check-e '(9))
Error: (9) fell through a ETYPECASE form.
       The valid cases were (OR INTEGER FLOAT RATIONAL) and
       (OR STRING SYMBOL CHARACTER).
   [condition type: CASE-FAILURE]
[1]
```

We cannot continue from an etypecase error.

10.5.2 Inspecting the Stack

If you are getting ready to drive to work in the morning and discover that your car has a flat tire, you have some options, including: replace the tire, repair the tire, take another car, walk, or have someone else drive you. However, if you are 1,000 miles from home and have a flat tire, your choices have narrowed. You are less likely to walk back home or have someone drive there to pick you up. Chances are, you will try to solve the problem and then continue.

LISP's flat tires are signalled by breakpoints. The programmer may choose to abandon the computation and start over. However, LISP also makes it possible to repair the program without losing the current state and to continue from the point of interruption.

When the programmer types end-of-file at a breakpoint, she is telling LISP to forget about continuing the original computation. Implicit in this action is the fact that LISP keeps track of *how* to continue the computation, should it be necessary. That is, when LISP hits a breakpoint, for whatever reason, it has to retain the state of the computation necessary for it to resume execution where it left off. It can sometimes be helpful for the programmer to examine the state information that

LISP retains. She may look under the hood to find out from where the smoke is coming.

For the programmer who wants to explore the control stack in greater detail, LISP implementations typically provide an interactive mechanism for climbing up and down the stack, examining its contents, and returning values to the previous computations. Here is a brief example.

```
> (print-name)
Break: I assume your name is MARY (*name*)

Restart actions (select using :continue):
 0: return from break.
[1c]
> :help                 ; Asks for a list of possible commands.
```

COMMAND	ABBR	DESCRIPTION
aliases	ali	print all command aliases
args	arg	save arguments before calls
arrest	arr	arrest a process for debugging
boe		mark frame to break when exited
bottom	bo	zoom at the oldest frame on the stack
bt		zoom in a very brief manner
cd		change into another directory
cf		compile a file
cload	cl	compile and load a file
continue	cont	continue from a continuable error
current	cur	return the expression given by the current stack frame
dirs	di	print the Allegro directory stack
dn		move down the stack 'n' frames, default 1
edit	ed	edit the source for the current stack frame
EOF		either :pop or :exit
error	err	print the last error message
evalmode	eval	examine or set evaluation mode
exit	ex	exit and return to the shell
find	fin	find the stack frame calling the function 'func'
focus	fo	focus the top level on a process
frame	fr	print info about current frame
function	fun	print and set * to the function object of this frame
help	he	print this text -- use ':help cmd-name' for more info
hide	hid	hide functions or types of stack frames
history	his	print the most recently typed user inputs
inspect	i	
kill	ki	kill a process
ld		load one or more files

```
local      loc  print the value of a local variable
macroexpand ma  call macroexpand on the argument, and pretty print it
optimize   opt  interactively set compiler optimizations
package    pa   go into a package
pop             pop up 'n' (default 1) break levels
popd            cd into the previous entry on directory stack
printer-variables pri  interactively set printer control variables
processes  pro  list all processes
prt             pop-and-retry the last expression which caused an error
pushd      pu   cd to a directory, pushing the directory on the stack
pwd        pw   print the process current working directory
reset      res  return to the top most break level
restart    rest restart the function in the current frame
return     ret  return values from the current frame
scont      sc   step 'n' forms before stopping
set-local  set-l set the value of a local variable
sover      so   eval the current step form, with stepping turned off
step       st   turn on or off stepping
top        to   zoom at the newest frame on the stack
trace      tr   trace the function arguments
unarrest   unar revoke the debugging arrest reason on a process
unhide     unh  unhide functions or types of stack frames
untrace    untr stop tracing some or all functions
up              move up 'n' (default 1) stack frames
wdebug     wd   create a window debugger for the given process
who-binds  who-b find bindings of a variable
who-calls  who-c find callers of a function
who-references who-r find references to a variable
who-sets   who-s find setters of a variable
who-uses   who-u find references, bindings, and settings of a variable
winspect   wi   window inspect a component or *
zoom       zo   print the runtime stack
[1c]
```

> :zoom   ; Let's see what is on the stack.

```
Evaluation stack:

   (BREAK "I assume your name is ~A (*name*)" MARY)
 ->(PRINT-NAME)
   (EVAL (PRINT-NAME))
   (TPL:TOP-LEVEL-READ-EVAL-PRINT-LOOP)
   (TPL:START-INTERACTIVE-TOP-LEVEL
       #<EXCL::BIDIRECTIONAL-TERMINAL-STREAM @ #x7c9bd6>
```

```
        #<Function TOP-LEVEL-READ-EVAL-PRINT-LOOP @ #x7d288e> ...)
[1c]
> :pop
```

In addition to the interactive breakpoint commands, LISP supports interactive examination of LISP objects with the inspect function. The exact behavior of $\infty \Rightarrow$ inspect is implementation dependent. The programmer can consider inspect to be an interactive version of describe.

Here is an example from Allegro Common LISP. Note that inspect has its own breakpoint and its associated commands start with the keyword :i.

```
> (inspect 'inspect)
The symbol INSPECT @ #x104d7fa
   which is an EXTERNAL symbol in the COMMON-LISP package
      0 value --------> ..unbound..
      1 package ------> The COMMON-LISP package
      2 function -----> #<Function INSPECT @ #x8d4a9e>
      3 name ---------> A simple-string (7) "INSPECT"
      4 plist --------> <...>, a proper list with 2 elements
      5 hash ---------> Bit field: #x2fdf
      6 flags --------> Bit field: #x2000
[1i]
> :i ?
Inspector commands are entered as :i, :i <x>, :i <x> <y>, or
:i <x> <y> <z>.  The options are:
   :i              redisplay the current object
   :i *            initialize inspector to display the value of *
   :i print <y>    set limit on number of components displayed to <y>
   :i skip <y>     redisplay the current object, skipping <y> elements
   :i <name>       descend to the named component of current object
   :i <integer>    descend to the indexed component of current object
   :i >            select the next indexed element of parent object
   :i <            select the previous indexed element of parent object
   :i -            ascend to the parent of current object
   :i tree         show the inspection stack
   :i set <y> <z>  put <z> (evaluated) in the component designated by <y>
   :i q            clear inspector stack - exit (inspect ...)
   :i ?            display this message
   :i form         when form is not a symbol or integer: eval form
                       and initialize inspector to display the value
   :i form x       when form is not a symbol or integer:
                       do (inspect (eval x))
[1i]
> :i tree
```

```
In first recursive call to inspect.
The current object is:
The symbol INSPECT, which was selected by "(inspect ...)"
[1i]
> :i 3
A simple-string (7) "INSPECT" @ #x71b0e6
   0-> The field #xI
   1-> The field #xN
   2-> The field #xS
   3-> The field #xP
   4-> The field #xE
   5-> The field #xC
   6-> The field #xT
[1i]
> :i
A simple-string (7) "INSPECT" @ #x71b0e6
   0-> The field #xI
   1-> The field #xN
   2-> The field #xS
   3-> The field #xP
   4-> The field #xE
   5-> The field #xC
   6-> The field #xT
[1i]
> :i <
#<Function INSPECT @ #x8d4a9e>
  lambda-list: (INSPECT::X)
   0 excl-type ----> Bit field: #x08
   1 start --------> Bit field: #x003b62f4
   2 flags/hash ---> Bit field: #x80004912
   3 closure ------> The symbol NIL
   4 symdef -------> The symbol INSPECT
   5 code ---------> Simple CODE vector (191) = #(3422633919 ...)
   6 formals ------> (INSPECT::X), a proper list with 1 element
   7 cframe-size --> fixnum 0 [#x00000000]
   8 call-count ---> fixnum 1 [#x00000008]
   9 locals -------> Simple T vector (13) = #(INSPECT::X ...)
   ...
  20 <constant> ---> The symbol EXCL::READ-EVAL-PRINT-LOOP
[1i]
> :i q
INSPECT
```

For most programmers, crawling up and down the control stack or inspecting LISP objects are techniques of last resort. Given the choice, most of us will call AAA or, better yet, get a new car, rather than fix a flat. Stack crawling, like spelunking or bungee jumping, is a sport for thrill-seekers.

10.6   Exercises

10.6.1   my-error [5*]

The `error` function is useful for signalling errors in a programmer's own code. Write a customized version called `my-error`, which performs the same tasks as `error` but prepends a slightly different message, as shown below.

```
> (my-error "~A is not a person" 'fido)

** My error: FIDO is not a person
Break:

Restart actions (select using :continue):
 0: return from break.
[1c]
> (my-error "I need a number less than 10. ~D is not." 99)

** My error: I need a number less than 10. 99 is not.
Break:

Restart actions (select using :continue):
 0: return from break.
 1: return from break.
[2c]
>
```

10.6.2   Buggy Fact [3*]

There was a problem with the `fact` function given on page 356. What was the bug?

10.6.3   bad-length Problem [4*]

The `bad-length` function described in this chapter results in an infinite loop. The text points out the misplaced parenthesis, which thus undermines the termination test and is therefore the fundamental cause of the error. However, that does not completely explain why `bad-length` never terminates. What exactly is `bad-length` trying to do as it burns up computer cycles from here to eternity?

10.6.4   Argument Checking [5]

Add argument error checking to each of the exercises listed below. Try to make the error detection code as specific as possible without undermining the purpose of the original program.

1. `leap-yearp` — Exercise 2.11.11, page 62.

2. `make-person` — Exercise 3.14.8, page 109.

3. `make-person2` — Exercise 3.14.9, page 110.

4. `daughter-of-zeller` — Exercise 3.14.11, page 111.

5. `make-change` — Exercise 4.7.3, page 127.

6. `check-book` — Exercise 4.7.10, page 129.

7. `now-account` — Exercise 4.7.11, page 129.

8. `make-change` — Exercise 5.7.5, page 162.

9. `case-string-equalp` — Exercise 6.8.2, page 198.

10. `roman-char-to-decimal` — Exercise 6.8.4, page 200.

11. `string-swap` — Exercise 6.8.6, page 201.

12. `string-insert` — Exercise 6.8.6, page 201.

13. `split` — Exercise 7.9.3, page 264.

14. `soundex` — Exercise 9.12.4, page 327.

10.7   Chapter Summary

- Errors are a fact of programming life. Programmers need techniques to prevent, detect, diagnose, and correct errors.

- LISP checks for and signals errors in most of its functions.

- The following symbols are bound to values associated with the read-eval-print loop (REPL).

```
+       ;  The previous expression read by REPL.
++      ;  The previous value of +.
+++     ;  The previous value of ++.
-       ;  The current expression being read by REPL.
*       ;  The first result of the previous expression read by REPL.
**      ;  The previous value of *.
***     ;  The previous value of **.
/       ;  The list of results of the previous expression read by REPL.
//      ;  The previous value of /.
///     ;  The previous value of //.
```

- LISP provides the programmer with a number of useful tools for debugging, including the following:

```
(describe object [stream])
(ed [object])
(warn format-string {args}*)
(trace function)
(untrace)
(step form)
(dribble pathname)
(dribble)
(load pathname :print t)
```

- The programmer can add documentation strings to symbols and functions which can then be accessed with the documentation function.

- Type predicates can be created using typep, and subtype relations can be checked with subtypep.

- Complex types can be formed, using the following type specifiers:

```
(satisfies predicate)
(member {object}*)
(eql object)
(not type)
(and {type}*)
(or {type}*)
```

- Type ranges can be specified, using the following constructs:

```
(integer low high)
(mod n)
(rational low high)
(float low high)
(real low high)
(string size)
```

- The programmer can define new types with `deftype`.

- Breakpoints are nested command levels that occur when the previous command level has been interrupted. Here are several ways to trigger a breakpoint:

```
(check-type object typespec [string])
(error format-string {args}*)
(cerror continue-format-string error-format-string {args}*)
(the typespec form)
(break [format-string {args}*])
(assert testform places assert-message)
interrupt character (^C in UNIX)
```

- A breakpoint is a read-eval-print loop, but the programmer can exit the breakpoint and return to a higher command level by using these methods, or their   ⇐ ∞
equivalent, in her implementation.

```
:return
:reset
end-of-file character (^D in UNIX)
```

- The `inspect` function provides a detailed, interactive version of `describe`.

It is easier to write an incorrect program than
understand a correct one.

◇ ALAN PERLIS, *Epigrams in Programming (1982)*

Chapter 11

Macros

LISP is extensible. It is possible for the programmer to redefine or expand the LISP programming language.

Clearly, one way to change LISP is through function definitions. When we create a new function, we have, in a sense, enlarged the language. We can also define synonyms for existing functions. For instance, we could create two new (and more perspicuous) names for LISP's basic accessor primitives.

```
(defun head (x) (car x))

(defun tail (x) (cdr x))

> (head (tail '(a b c d)))
B
```

There are two other ways to modify the LISP language: creating new *macros* and creating new interpretations for individual characters with *macro characters*. These methods affect the syntax of the language. In this chapter, we examine each method.

11.1 Defining Macros

We have seen a number of different control mechanisms in LISP, including recursion and iterative forms such as do and loop. However, readers familiar with other programming languages will realize that additional control structures are possible, including repeat loops, do/while loops, do/until loops, and for loops. Some programmers may prefer to use these control structures in LISP, especially when translating code to LISP from some language which uses these forms.

In the answer to exercise 7.9.7 on page 266, we defined a function repeat-char, which printed a given character a specified number of times. Here is a revised definition of repeat-char using the, as yet undefined, repeat loop.

```
(defun repeat-char (stream char count)
  (repeat count
        (write-char char stream)))
```

```
> (repeat-char *standard-output* #\x 5)
xxxxx
NIL
```

This definition of repeat-char is arguably cleaner than the previous recursive definition. The repeat macro consists of two arguments: the number of times to execute the given code and the body of the code. We might consider writing repeat as a function, f-repeat.

```
(defun f-repeat (n body)
  (do ((count n (- count 1)))
      ((<= count 0) nil)
    (funcall body)))
```

However, this does not behave exactly the way we intended.

```
> (f-repeat 5 (write-char #\x *standard-output*))
x
Error: Funcall of #\x which is a non-function.
   [condition type: SIMPLE-ERROR]
```

The problem is that the code gets evaluated too soon, printing the x. Then the f-repeat function ends up trying to evaluate #\x as a function, as #\x is the value returned by the initial call to write-char.

One way around this problem is to pass an actual function instead of the list expression. The easiest way to do this is with a lambda expression.

```
> (f-repeat 5 #'(lambda () (write-char #\x *standard-output*)))
xxxxx
NIL
```

This method works, but it does not really conform with our stated desire to create a new syntactic control structure. The underlying problem is the initial evaluation of the arguments. In functions, the order of evaluation is as follows:

1. Evaluate each of the function's arguments.

2. Evaluate the body of the function.

In macros, the order of evaluation is:

1. Evaluate the body of the macro.

2. Evaluate the resulting body of the expanded macro.

The evaluation of a function's arguments is occasionally delayed until step 2 by using the `quote` (') special form. Here is one way to define a synonym for `quote`.

```
(defmacro qu (x)
  (list (quote quote) x))
```

```
> (qu a)                    ; Expands into: (quote A).
A
```

The `qu` macro goes through two stages of evaluation. When it is called, as in `(qu a)`, the expression `(list (quote quote) x)`, with the parameter `x` bound to the argument `A`, is evaluated in the first stage, which results in `(quote A)`. Then, the latter expression is evaluated, resulting in `A`.

Thus, macros must build a list structure which can then be evaluated. Note that macros are created with the `defmacro` macro, which is quite similar in style to the `defun` macro used for creating functions. Here is the basic syntax for `defmacro`.

```
(defmacro name lambda-list {form}*)
```

We now return to our `repeat` form, which we can define as a macro.

```
(defmacro repeat (n &rest body)
  (append '(do)
          (list (list (list 'count n (list '- 'count 1))))
          (list (list (list '<= 'count 0) nil))
          body))
```

```
(repeat 5 (write-char #\x *standard-output*))
```

```
;  Expands into:
(do ((count 5 (- count 1)))
    ((<= count 0) nil)
    (write-char #\x *standard-output*))
```

; Which gives a final result of:

```
xxxxx
NIL
```

Note that the definition of **repeat** allows for multiple expressions in the body of the code. The **&rest** which separates the parameter names **n** and **body** indicates that more than one expression may appear following the repetition count. The resulting list of expressions are bound together to the **body** parameter. Here are examples showing this feature.

```
> (let ((x 0)
        (y 1))
    (repeat 4 (setf x (+ x 1))          ; Two expressions in body.
              (setf y (* x (* y y))))
    y)
576
```

```
> (repeat 4)                            ; Empty body.
NIL
```

As defined above, **repeat** always returns **NIL**. However, you might wish to define **repeat** to return a specific value. (See exercise 11.10.3.)

11.2 Backquote

As discussed in the chapter on debugging, parentheses are the cause of both joy and sorrow for the LISP programmer. Proper indentation, pretty printers, and clever text editors that know how to balance parentheses go a long way toward preventing problems caused by mismatched parentheses.

But just when we might think that the problem of balancing parentheses is under control, we encounter macros where the parentheses lay hidden until after the first-stage evaluation. The programmer may never see this level of parentheses at all but still have to specify it with complete accuracy in terms of **list**, **append**, **cons**, and friends.

It would be much easier if the programmer could merely describe how the first-stage result should appear, rather than having to give directions for how to build it.

A solution is at hand — the backquote. If you examine your computer's keyboard, you will observe three types of quoting punctuation: the double quote ("), the single quote ('), and the backquote (`). In LISP, the backquote character acts similarly to the regular single quote. They both inhibit evaluation.

```
> 'atom
ATOM

> `atom
ATOM

> '(a b c d)
(A B C D)

> `(a b c d)
(A B C D)

> '(setf x (* 3 7))
(SETF X (* 3 7))

> `(setf x (* 3 7))
(SETF X (* 3 7))
```

The difference is that backquote can be used to specify *partial evaluation* of its constituents, by use of a comma prefix.

```
> `(setf x ,(* 3 7))
(SETF X 21)

> `(setf x ,(car '((+ 3 4) (- 7 3) (* 2 6))))
(SETF X (+ 3 4))

> `(setf x ,(car `(,(+ 3 4) (- 7 3) (* 2 6))))
(SETF X 7)
```

The effect of the comma should be apparent (though maybe not immediately). It causes the expression following the comma to be evaluated. All other expressions within the backquoted expression are not initially evaluated.

One additional feature of the backquote facility is the ability to *splice* lists, that is, interpolate a list structure without its outside layer of parentheses. The splice operation is specified with a comma followed by an at-sign (,@). Here are examples.

```
> `(setf x (* ,(cdr '((+ 3 4) (- 7 3) (* 2 6)))))      ; Not quite right.
(SETF X (* ((- 7 3) (* 2 6))))

> `(setf x (* ,@(cdr '((+ 3 4) (- 7 3) (* 2 6)))))     ; ,@ works fine.
(SETF X (* (- 7 3) (* 2 6)))

> `(setf y (list ,@(cdr '('(j jones) '(m smith) '(d white)))))
(SETF Y (LIST (QUOTE (M SMITH)) (QUOTE (D WHITE))))
```

The most common use of backquote is in macro definitions. The backquote allows the programmer to specify the result of the first-stage evaluation. Here are our earlier definitions of qu and **repeat** rewritten using the backquote facility.

```
(defmacro qu (x)
  `(quote ,x))

;  Or even shorter!
(defmacro qu (x)
  `',x)

(defmacro repeat (n &rest body)
  `(do ((count ,n (- count 1)))
       ((<= count 0) nil)
       ,@body))
```

Backquote is also useful in defining new types with deftype. In section 10.2, we showed how the programmer could create new types, such as temperature ranges.

```
(deftype human-temp ()
  '(or (float 90 107) (integer 90 107)))

(deftype hawaii-temp ()
  '(or (float 55 85) (integer 55 85)))

(deftype new-york-city-temp ()
  '(or (float 0 110) (integer 0 110)))

(deftype hell-temp ()
  '(or (float 110 *) (integer 110 *)))
```

Using backquote, we can create a parameterized temperature type with which we can define these other types.

```
(deftype temperature (low high)
  `(or (float ,low ,high) (integer ,low ,high)))

> (deftype hawaii-temp () '(temperature 55 85))
HAWAII-TEMP

> (deftype new-york-city-temp () '(temperature 0 110))
NEW-YORK-CITY-TEMP

> (deftype hell-temp () '(temperature 110 *))
HELL-TEMP
```

```
> (typep 32 'hawaii-temp)
NIL

> (typep 32 'new-york-city-temp)
T

> (typep 32 'hell-temp)
NIL
```

The backquote greatly increases the ease of expression in LISP.

11.3   More lambda List Keywords

In defining macros with `defmacro`, we can include the same lambda list keywords available with `defun`, namely:

```
&rest
&key
&optional
&aux
&allow-other-keys
```

∞ ⇒   Three other lambda list keywords are generally used only with macros. Some LISP implementations permit other constructs to use these keywords as well.

- **&body** specifies a variable to which the remaining arguments (the body) of the macro expression are bound as a list. This is similar to **&rest**.

- **&whole** specifies a variable to which the entire macro form is bound. **&whole** must be the first element of the lambda list.

- **&environment** specifies a variable containing the lexical environment of the macro expansion. We will demonstrate this keyword in the advanced topics section at the end of the chapter.

Using **&body**, we can redefine our `repeat` macro.

```
(defmacro repeat (n &body body)
   `(do ((count ,n (- count 1)))
        ((<= count 0) nil)
      ,@body))

> (repeat 5 (write-char #\x *standard-output*))
xxxxx
NIL
```

```
(defmacro whole-demo (&whole a &body b)
  `(progn
     (format t "My name is: ~A~%" (car ',a))
     (format t "My argument~P ~[are~;is~:;are~]: ~A~%"
             ,(length (cdr a))
             ,(length b)
             ',(cdr a))
     (format t "(eq (cdr a) b)? ~A" ,(eq (cdr a) b))))

> (whole-demo 1 2 3)
My name is: WHOLE-DEMO
My arguments are: (1 2 3)
(eq (cdr a) b)? T
NIL

> (whole-demo x)
My name is: WHOLE-DEMO
My argument is: (X)
(eq (cdr a) b)? T
NIL

> (whole-demo)
My name is: WHOLE-DEMO
My arguments are: NIL
(eq (cdr a) b)? T
NIL
```

We note that in whole-demo, the cdr of the whole is not just equal to the body —
they are eq.

The lambda list keywords available in a given implementation are specified   ⇐ ∞
with the constant: lambda-list-keywords.

```
> lambda-list-keywords
(&OPTIONAL &REST &KEY &AUX &BODY &WHOLE
&ALLOW-OTHER-KEYS &ENVIRONMENT)
```

11.4   Protecting Macro Parameters

We observe that even though repeat seems to behave just the way we specified,
there is a problem with both of our definitions. Consider the following code.

```
> (let ((count 1)) (repeat 5 (format t "~A" count)))
54321
NIL
```

What happened? We expected this code to print five 1's. Here is the expanded version of that last expression.

```
(let ((count 1))
     (do ((count 5 (- count 1)))
         ((<= count 0) NIL)
       (format t "~A" count)))
```

We have a serious collision of identifiers. The count variable within the format statement was intended to refer to the let count, but it actually refers to the do count, which is the name of the variable within repeat.

There are several ways around this dilemma. One common way, which is not guaranteed, is to pick unusual names for macro variables. So instead of count, we might use %%??count??%% or some other ridiculous-looking name, on the assumption that no programmer would ever call our macro with an expression containing another variable of the same name.

A better way is to bind the arguments of the macro outside the scope of the local macro variables, using flet and let. Here is repeat with safety bindings.

```
(defmacro repeat (n &body body)
  `(flet
    ((code () ,@body))
    (let ((n ,n))
      (do ((count n (- count 1)))
          ((<= count 0) nil)
        (code)))))
```

```
> (let ((count 1)) (repeat 5 (format t "~A" count)))
11111
NIL
```

Now the code runs properly.

One of the widely held tenets of software engineering is that of "minimizing keystrokes" (or simply "mk"). The thought is that the less one has to type, the less the chance for error, and the less time required. (However, short identifiers can be harder for people to read and understand.)

In the spirit of this mk principle, the programmer can create a useful abbreviation for lambda, using the macro facility. We pick the infrequently used ASCII caret character: ^. Below, we give the macro definition and some examples of its use.

```
(defmacro ^ (&body body)
  `#'(lambda ,@body))
```

```
> (funcall (^ (x) (+ x 5)) 3)
8
```

```
> (mapcar (^ (y) (* y 2)) '(1 2 3 4))
(2 4 6 8)
```

Note that we do not need to quote the lambda expression, because the function quote prefix **#'** is part of the macro definition. Thus, we may write:

```
(mapcar (^ (n) (* n n)) '(1 2 3))
; Instead of
(mapcar #'(^ (n) (* n n)) '(1 2 3))
```

The use of this abbreviation can be made more meaningful and appealing when combined with a bit-mapped display screen that allows the programmer to control the display's fonts. Specifically, a programmer can redefine ^ to be the actual Greek character λ.

```
> (funcall (λ (z) (* z 9)) 7)
63

> (mapcar (λ (n) (- n 1)) '(10 11 12 13))
(9 10 11 12)
```

Some programmers find great psychic rewards in such symbolic achievements.

11.5   Macros versus Functions

Many of Common LISP's special forms are implemented as macros. Furthermore, LISP provides many predefined macros. Examples include **defun**, **setf**, **push**, and **pop**. Here are macro definitions of the last two. The actual definitions of **push** and **pop** may be more involved, to ensure that their arguments do not get evaluated twice.

```
(defmacro my-pop (stack)
  `(prog1
      (car ,stack)
      (setf ,stack (cdr ,stack))))

(defmacro my-push (obj stack)
  `(setf ,stack
        (cons ,obj ,stack)))

> (setf x '(coke beer bread butter))
(COKE BEER BREAD BUTTER)

> (my-pop x)
COKE
```

```
> (my-push 'detergent x)
(DETERGENT BEER BREAD BUTTER)


> x
(DETERGENT BEER BREAD BUTTER)


> (my-push 'apples (car (my-push '(bananas oranges) x)))
(APPLES BANANAS ORANGES)

;   The second my-push was evaluated twice by the first one.
;   This resulted in an extra push.
> x
((BANANAS ORANGES) (APPLES BANANAS ORANGES) DETERGENT BEER BREAD BUTTER)


> (setf y '(detergent beer bread butter))
(DETERGENT BEER BREAD BUTTER)


;   The real push works correctly, with no second evaluation.
> (push 'apples (car (push '(bananas oranges) y)))
(APPLES BANANAS ORANGES)


> y
((APPLES BANANAS ORANGES) DETERGENT BEER BREAD BUTTER)
```

The reader may wonder why push and pop were not defined as functions. Would
that not have been simpler?

     Let's try defining pop as a function.

Bad Idea ⇒
```
(defun bad-pop (stack)
   (prog1
      (car stack)
    (setf stack (cdr stack)))))


> (setf x '(1 2 3 4))
(1 2 3 4)


> (bad-pop x)
1                                  ;  So far, so good.


> x
(1 2 3 4)                          ;  Oops – something went wrong.


> (bad-pop x)
1
```

The problem with `bad-pop` is that the `setf` form does not evaluate its first argument. Thus, the expression (`setf stack (cdr stack)`) changes the value of the local variable `stack`, but not the global variable `x`. Macros provide a way to get at the difference between a variable's name and its value. Problems can sometimes arise, as discussed earlier with the variable `count` in the `repeat` macro and in exercise 11.10.7.

If macros provide such flexibility, why not use them exclusively, instead of functions? Good question. Let's try a simple case − a macro that increments its argument.

```
(defmacro madd1 (x)
  `(+ 1 ,x))

> (madd1 5)
6

> (madd1 (* 7 8))
57
```

Our `madd1` macro appears to work fine. However, there are other uses for functions.

```
> (mapcar #'1+ '(1 2 3 4 5))    ;  1+ is a function.
(2 3 4 5 6)

> (apply #'1+ '(8))
9

> (mapcar #'madd1 '(1 2 3 4 5))
Error: MADD1 names a macro -- bad arg for function.
  [condition type: PROGRAM-ERROR]
[1]
> (apply #'madd1 '(8))
Error: MADD1 names a macro -- bad arg for function.
  [condition type: PROGRAM-ERROR]
[2]
```

LISP seems to get mad when the programmer uses the `madd1` macro as a named argument.

Functions in LISP are data objects. They can be passed as arguments. Macros, on the other hand, are ephemeral. A macro is expanded and the resulting list structure is inserted directly into the given context. This means that macros cannot be passed as objects. The above example with `apply` would be like writing the following.

```
> (apply #'' (+ 1 x) '(8))
Error: '(+ 1 X) does not have a function definition
[1]
```

Another important difference between functions and macros is that functions can
be traced, whereas macros cannot. However, in section 11.9.4, we shall see how
we might create a mechanism for tracing macros.

11.6   Local and Global Macros

When we use defmacro to create a macro, we get a global definition. It is also
possible to create local macros by using the macrolet special form.

```
(defun local-test (n)
  (macrolet ((plus5 (x) `(+ 5 ,x)))
            (plus5 n)))
```

```
> (local-test 7)
12
```

The syntax of macrolet is similar to that of flet or labels. However, instead of
defining a local function, macrolet creates a local macro.

It is also possible to define a local variable that expands as a macro, using the
special form symbol-macrolet. The programmer can use symbol-macrolet in the
same contexts in which let would appear.

```
(defun symbol-macrolet-profit (volume unit-price unit-cost tax-rate)
  (symbol-macrolet
    ((revenue (* volume unit-price))
     (overhead (* volume unit-cost)))
    (- revenue
       (+ overhead
          (* tax-rate revenue)))))
```

```
> (symbol-macrolet-profit 100 2 1 .1)
80.0
```

In general, when LISP is evaluating a list whose car is a symbol, one of the following
three possibilities should hold.

1. If the symbol is a *special form*, that is, a reserved word in the language, then
   the list is evaluated using the appropriate code for the given special form.
   The symbols given in Table 11.1 are Common LISP special forms from the
   original language definition. They should each respond T to the predicate
   special-form-p.

block	labels	quote
catch	let	return-from
declare	let*	setq
eval-when	macrolet	tagbody
flet	multiple-value-call	the
function	multiple-value-prog1	throw
go	progn	unwind-protect
if	progv	

Table 11.1: Original Common LISP Special Forms

2. Otherwise, if the symbol has a macro function, expand the macro and reevaluate the resulting expression.

3. Otherwise, evaluate the symbol as a function.

A symbol cannot be used both as a macro and as a function. We also note that some LISP implementators may choose to define special forms as macros, and *vice* $\Leftarrow \infty$ *versa.*

    A macro can be viewed as a source-to-source transformation of code. For each LISP macro symbol, there is a corresponding transformation function. LISP indexes these associations between symbols and transformations through the predicate and access function: `macro-function`. In one implementation, we observe some overlap between special forms and macros.

```
> (special-form-p 'if)          ;  if is a special form,
#<function object IF (a special) @ #x72b06e>

> (macro-function 'if)          ;  but it is not a macro.
NIL

> (special-form-p 'cond)        ;  cond is both a special form,
#<function object COND (a special) @ #x729e5e>

> (macro-function 'cond)        ;  and a macro.
#<Function (:PROPERTY COND EXCL::.MACROEXPAND-MACRO.) @ #x731706>

> (special-form-p 'defmacro)    ;  defmacro is not a special form,
NIL

> (macro-function 'defmacro)    ;  but is a macro.
#<Function DEFMACRO @ #x76de86>
```

Furthermore, the `macro-function` function is a `setf` function. That is, we can define macros by using `macro-function`. Here, we create yet another quote macro.

```
> (setf (macro-function 'q) #'(lambda (call env) `',(cadr call)))
#<function object Q (a macro) @ #x11abcd6>
```

```
> (q (this is a list))
(THIS IS A LIST)
```

The `setf` value for `macro-function` must be a two-argument function: the first argument is the entire macro call, and the second argument is the *environment*. We discuss environments at the end of the chapter. In our quote example, the variable `call` is bound to `(Q (THIS IS A LIST))`, and thus we need to return the `cadr` to get the needed result.

You may not use `setf` or `macro-function` to change the definition of a special form that happens to be implemented as a macro.

In debugging macro definitions, it is often useful to examine their expansion. This can be done with the `macroexpand` function, which takes two arguments: the expression to be expanded and an optional environment. Note that the resulting expression is not actually evaluated.

`macroexpand` returns two values: the result of the macro expansion, and T or NIL, indicating if there was in fact a macro call. For predefined macros, the results

∞ ⇒ of the macro expansion can vary across implementations.

```
> (macroexpand '(q (this is a list)))
'(THIS IS A LIST)
T
```

```
> (macroexpand '(defvar x 789))
(PROGN (DECLAIM (SPECIAL X))
       (RECORD-SOURCE-FILE 'X :TYPE :VARIABLE)
       (OR (BOUNDP 'X) (SETQ X 789))
       'X)
T
```

```
> (macroexpand '(+ 3 4))          ; Tries to expand a function.
(+ 3 4)
NIL                               ; NIL indicates no macro call.
```

Some macros may expand into other macros. `macroexpand` will keep cycling until it runs out of macros to expand. We can use `macroexpand-1` to show incremental macro expansion.

```
(defmacro qq (x) `(q ,x))
```

```
> (qq ll)                        ;  The complete macro call.
LL

> (macroexpand '(qq ll))         ;  The complete macro expansion.
'LL
T

> (macroexpand-1 '(qq ll))       ;  The first macro expansion.
(Q LL)
T
```

We define two convenient functions, ma and ma1, which are synonyms for macroexpand and macroexpand-1, respectively.

```
(defun ma (exp)
  (macroexpand exp))

(defun ma1 (exp)
  (macroexpand-1 exp))

> (ma '(defun (fact x)
          (cond ((zerop x) 1)
                (t (* x (fact (- x 1)))))))
(PROGN (EVAL-WHEN (:COMPILE-TOPLEVEL)
         (EXCL::CHECK-LOCK-DEFINITIONS-COMPILE-TIME '(FACT X)
            'FUNCTION 'DEFUN (FBOUNDP '(FACT X))))
       (RECORD-SOURCE-FILE '(FACT X))
       (SETF (FDEFINITION '(FACT X))
            (LET ((EXCL::F #)) (EXCL::.INV-FN_SYMDEF EXCL::F
                  '(FACT X)) EXCL::F))
      NIL '(FACT X))
T

> (ma '(cond ((zerop x) 1) (t (* x (fact (- x 1))))))
(IF (ZEROP X) (PROGN 1) (COND (T (* X (FACT #)))))
T

> (ma '(repeat 5 (format t "a")))
(FLET ((CODE NIL (FORMAT T "a")))
    (DO ((COUNT 5 (- COUNT 1))) ((<= COUNT 0) NIL)  (CODE)))
T
```

```
> (ma1 '(pop x))
(PROG1 (CAR X) (SETQ X (CDR X)))
T


> (ma '(pop x))
(LET ((#:G570 (CAR X))) (SETQ X (CDR X)) #:G570)
T


> (ma '(defmacro qu (x) (list (quote quote) x)))
(PROGN (EVAL-WHEN (:COMPILE-TOPLEVEL)
         (EXCL::CHECK-LOCK-DEFINITIONS-COMPILE-TIME 'QU 'FUNCTION
           'DEFMACRO (FBOUNDP 'QU)))
       (RECORD-SOURCE-FILE 'QU)
       (EVAL-WHEN (:COMPILE-TOPLEVEL)
         (COMPILER::COMPILER-PUTPROP 'QU (NAMED-FUNCTION QU
           (LAMBDA # # # #))
           'COMPILER::.MACRO-IN-COMPILER.))
       (SETF (MACRO-FUNCTION 'QU)
             (NAMED-FUNCTION QU
                             (LAMBDA (EXCL::**MACROARG**
                                      EXCL::..ENVIRONMENT..)
                               (DECLARE #)
                               (EXCL::DT-MACRO-ARGUMENT-CHECK 1 1
                                 'QU EXCL::**MACROARG** :MACRO)
                               (BLOCK QU #))))
       (EXCL::.INV-FN_SYMDEF (MACRO-FUNCTION 'QU) 'QU)
       (EXCL::.INV-FN_FORMALS (FBOUNDP 'QU) '(X))
       'QU)
T
```

These examples begin to expose some of the internals of LISP. We shall not here endeavor to explain what all these creatures do but merely acknowledge their existence. We first expand a defun form, which becomes a progn. We then expand the cond form, which turns into an if. Our old friend repeat expands in the expected way. Finally, we expand the defmacro definition of qu given earlier. At the heart of the definition is a setf of macro-function.

The programmer will find macro expansion to be quite helpful when writing macros on her own. Macro expansion also provides an instructive means to explore the way in which LISP is implemented.

11.7 Destructuring

In a normal function or macro call, all of the arguments are top-level elements of the surrounding list. For example, suppose we have a function that takes a person's name and date of birth and then prints a message. We have several choices.

```
(defun message (name day month year)
  (format t "~A was born on ~A/~A/~A~%" name day month year)
  (values))

(defun message2 (name bday)
  (message name (car bday) (cadr bday) (caddr bday)))

(defun message3 (name-bday)
  (message (car name-bday)
           (cadr name-bday)
           (caddr name-bday)
           (cadddr name-bday)))

(defun message4 (name-bday)
  (message (car name-bday)
           (caadr name-bday)
           (cadadr name-bday)
           (caddar (cdr name-bday)))))
```

```
> (message 'alexandra 4 19 93)
ALEXANDRA was born on 4/19/93

> (message2 'alexandra '(4 19 93))
ALEXANDRA was born on 4/19/93

> (message3 '(alexandra 4 19 93))
ALEXANDRA was born on 4/19/93

> (message4 '(alexandra (4 19 93)))
ALEXANDRA was born on 4/19/93
```

The first function `message` may be the easiest to understand, but the last function `message4` has the advantage that its arguments are more meaningfully structured: a list comprising a name and a date. The problem is that the code is virtually impenetrable. The `cars` and `cdrs` are bewildering.

LISP provides an alternative means of handling structured arguments, namely, *destructuring*. We can use `defmacro`'s lambda list to mirror the structure of the arguments.

```
(defmacro macro-message (name day month year)
  `(progn
     (format t "~A was born on ~A/~A/~A~%"
             ,name ,day ,month ,year)
     (values)))

(defmacro macro-message2 (name (day month year))
  `(macro-message ,name ,day ,month ,year))

(defmacro macro-message3 ((name day month year))
  `(macro-message ,name ,day ,month ,year))

(defmacro macro-message4 ((name (day month year)))
  `(macro-message ,name ,day ,month ,year))
```

```
> (macro-message 'francesca 10 4 88)
FRANCESCA was born on 10/4/88

> (macro-message2 'francesca (10 4 88))
FRANCESCA was born on 10/4/88

> (macro-message3 ('francesca 10 4 88))
FRANCESCA was born on 10/4/88

> (macro-message4 ('francesca (10 4 88)))
FRANCESCA was born on 10/4/88
```

The destructuring capability of macros is useful. However, it would also be useful to have functions with the same destructuring facility. For example, we might want to map one of our message functions over a list of people. We cannot map a macro. Using the destructuring-bind macro, we can use destructuring within a function. We demonstrate by combining message4 with macro-message4.

```
(defun message4-db (name-bday)
  (destructuring-bind (name (day month year)) name-bday
                      (message name day month year)))
```

```
> (message4-db '(francesca (10 4 88)))
FRANCESCA was born on 10/4/88

> (mapc #'message4-db
        '((francesca (10 4 88)) (alexandra (4 19 93))))
FRANCESCA was born on 10/4/88
ALEXANDRA was born on 4/19/93
(NIL NIL)
```

11.8   Macro Characters

LISP's macro facility allows the programmer to tailor the language to her own requirements, extending the language with new constructs, and even altering the way in which old constructs are interpreted.

We discussed the standard syntax of LISP characters in section 7.8.2. LISP allows the programmer to change the way in which individual characters are interpreted. The programmer has no way of creating new characters – of enlarging the size of LISP's alphabet. However, the programmer can provide a new meaning for an old character by using *macro characters*.

LISP interprets the meaning of characters as it reads them from an input stream, usually the terminal or a file. Characters fall into several categories:

- *Whitespace.* This category includes characters like space, tab, or newline. LISP's reader ignores these.

- *Macro characters.* These are characters that have a mind of their own, as it were. These each invoke special reading routines, discussed below.

- *Escape.* The backslash character (\) or the vertical bar (|) is used to turn off any extra interpretation of the next character. For example, a\;b produces the symbol A;B, including the embedded semicolon. |a\;b| produces the symbol a\;b which also contains the semicolon as well as the backslash.

- *Others.* These characters, such as letters and digits, are read sequentially until some other category of character is encountered, for example, whitespace or macro characters. At that point, accumulated characters are converted into a symbol or number, as appropriate. Lowercase letters are converted to upper case.

Standard macro characters in LISP include the following:

;   Comment character – Ignores the remaining input on the current line

"   Doublequote character – Delimits a string

'   Quote character – Converts 'foo to (quote foo)

`   Backquote character – Inhibits evaluation. Discussed in section 11.2

,   Comma character – Used with backquote

(Left parenthesis – Begins a list

)   Right parenthesis – Ends a list

LISP uses tables to keep track of what characters are in which categories and which ones are exceptions. These tables are called *readtables*.

Just as LISP has standard streams for input and output, LISP has a default readtable, namely, *readtable*. It is possible to change this readtable directly, but it is safer and wiser to make changes to a copy rather than to *readtable* itself. Here is how to make your own readtable and associate it with an input stream.

```
> (defvar my-readtable
      (copy-readtable *readtable*))
MY-READTABLE

> (readtablep my-readtable)
T

> (readtablep *readtable*)
T
```

copy-readtable returns as its value a new readtable, which is a copy of its first argument. The readtablep predicate indicates whether an object is a readtable. We can use the following functions to change readtables in a fairly safe manner.

```
(defun new-readtable (new)
  (if (not (readtablep new))
      (error "new-readtable: Bad readtable: ~A" new))
  (setf *old-readtable* *readtable*)
  (setf *readtable* new))

(defun old-readtable ()
  (setf *readtable* *old-readtable*))

> (new-readtable my-readtable)
#<readtable @ #x1176026>

> (old-readtable)
#<readtable @ #x116ba76>
```

Now that we know how to tell LISP which readtable to use when, we can start examining and changing the contents of the table. We use the function get-macro-character, which takes two arguments: a character and an optional readtable.

```
> (get-macro-character #\space)      ; Ignores spaces.
NIL
```

```
> (get-macro-character #\1)              ; 1 can be part of a token.
#<Function READ-TOKEN @ #x73ed26>
T


> (get-macro-character #\M)              ; M can be part of a token.
#<Function READ-TOKEN @ #x73ed26>
T


> (get-macro-character #\%)              ; % can be part of a token.
#<Function READ-TOKEN @ #x73ed26>
T


> (get-macro-character #\()              ; Starts reading a list.
EXCL::READ-LIST
NIL


> (get-macro-character #\))              ; Matches a left parenthesis.
EXCL::READ-RIGHT-PAREN
NIL


> (get-macro-character #\;)              ; Begins a comment.
EXCL::READ-COMMENT
NIL


> (get-macro-character #\#)              ; Begins a special input form.
#<Function READ-DISPATCH-CHAR @ #x740fe6>
T
```

Now we shall switch the readtable definitions of #\% and #\;.

```
> (set-macro-character #\%
    (symbol-function (get-macro-character #\;)) nil my-readtable)
#<Function READ-COMMENT @ #x738cc6>


> (get-macro-character #\% my-readtable)
#<Function READ-COMMENT @ #x738cc6>
NIL


> (get-macro-character #\a)
#<Function READ-TOKEN @ #x73ed26>
T


> (set-macro-character #\; (get-macro-character #\a) t my-readtable)
#<Function READ-TOKEN @ #x73ed26>
```

```
> (get-macro-character #\; my-readtable)
#<Function READ-TOKEN @ #x73ed26>
NIL

> (new-readtable my-readtable)              ; Switches the readtables.
#<readtable @ #x1171df6>

> (defun x;2 (x) (* 2 x))  % This is a comment.
|X;2|

> (|X;2| 4)
8
```

In this implementation, whitespace characters have readtable entries of NIL. Regular graphics characters have entries of the function READ-TOKEN, and macro characters have entries that are functions to be executed. The standard entries for all the ASCII characters are given in appendix D.

In the above example, we made % a comment character, and ; a regular character, using set-macro-character. The arguments to set-macro-character are the character, the function, and two optional arguments: a flag indicating a nonterminating macro and the readtable, which defaults to *readtable*. The flag value is returned as the second value from get-macro-character.

The function set-syntax-from-char provides another way to clone a character's behavior, using the following syntax.

```
    (set-syntax-from-char to-char from-char
                          [to-readtable [from-readtable]]])
```

We could have switched #\% and #\; as follows.

```
> (set-syntax-from-char #\% #\; my-readtable)
T

> (set-syntax-from-char #\; #\a my-readtable)
T
```

We can also define new functions for macro characters. For example, in some artificial intelligence pattern matchers, such as described in [Charniak et al., 1987], a symbol preceded by a question mark, such as ?person, is a variable that can match any token in the input. So, the pattern "?person went to the store" would match the input sentence "John went to the store," and the variable ?person would be bound to John. We can define a macro character function for ? that will convert ?person into (*var* person) so that the pattern matcher will have an easier time recognizing variables in the pattern lists. Namely, a variable will be any list whose car is *var*.

Here is a macro character definition for ?.

```
(set-macro-character #\?
  #'(lambda (stream char)
      (declare (ignore char))
      (list '*var* (read stream t nil t)))
  t my-readtable)

> (new-readtable my-readtable)
#<readtable @ #x117217e>

> (setf x '?person)
(*VAR* PERSON)

> '?(one two three)
(*VAR* (ONE TWO THREE))
```

A macro character function takes two arguments, a stream and a character. In this case, the character argument, which is bound to the character being assigned, is not used, and the `ignore` declaration tells the compiler not to worry about that fact. The function then creates a list, with a `car` of `*var*` and a `cdr` comprising the next object read from the stream. Instead of `(read stream)`, macro character functions typically call `(read stream t nil t)`, which is a version of `read` which does not expect an end of file. The last three arguments are flags that specify:

- *eof-error-p*: If non-NIL and if `read` encounters an end-of-file, it signals an error, depending on the value of *recursive-p*.

- *eof-value*: The value returned by end-of-file.

- *recursive-p*: If non-NIL and if an end-of-file is detected, then `read` did not finish. If `nil` and an end-of-file is detected, assume that `read` is between objects.

We discussed these options to `read` in section 7.8.1 and suggested that macro character functions can make proper use of the `recursive-p` flag. Here is an example using `read-delimited-list`. We will create a macro character [, which reads numbers until it reaches a] and then returns the sum. The arguments to `read-delimited-list` are the character at which to stop reading, the optional input stream, and the optional `recursive-p` flag.

```
(set-macro-character #\[
  #'(lambda (stream char)
      (declare (ignore char))
      (apply #'+ (read-delimited-list #\] stream t)))
  t my-readtable)
```

```
> (new-readtable my-readtable)
#<readtable @ #x117b5c6>

> [1 2 3 ]
6

> [12 23 34 ]
69

> [1 2 [3 4 ] 5 6 ]              ;  It is recursive.
21

> (set-macro-character #\] (get-macro-character #\) nil))
EXCL::READ-RIGHT-PAREN

> [12 23 34]
69

> [1 2 [4 5]]
12
```

By redefining the macro for the character #\], we no longer had to use a space as a delimiter. Like the right parenthesis, the right square bracket became a terminating character instead of a constituent character.

11.9   Advanced Subjects

This chapter has the following advanced topics.

- Case-Sensitive Symbols

- Read-Modify-Write Macros

- Dispatch Macro Characters

- *macroexpand-hook* and Environments

11.9.1   Case-Sensitive Symbols

According to [Steele Jr., 1990, page 28], the programmer can specify the manner in which case conversion is performed on symbols by using the readtable-case function. As discussed above, LISP uses a readtable object to interpret the meaning of characters that it reads. Associated with this table is one of the following keywords, indicating how to perform case conversion.

- :UPCASE – This is the default. Lowercase characters are converted to upper case.

- :DOWNCASE – This is the opposite of :UPCASE. Uppercase characters are converted to lower case.

- :PRESERVE – No case conversion takes place.

- :INVERT – If a symbol is all one case, it is converted to the opposite case.

The author suggests that the programmer avoid experiments with altering the case conversion of her LISP. There are two reasons for this admonition. First, her version of LISP probably does not implement the readtable-case function. (Why? See reason number two.) Second, versions of Common LISP that do support readtable-case often fail to do it in a manner that prevents the programmer from causing all normal code to stop working normally.

```
> *readtable*
#<READTABLE >

> (readtable-case *readtable*)    ; Gets the default value.
:UPCASE

> (setf (readtable-case *readtable*) :downcase)
:DOWNCASE                          ; Now input will be in lower case.

> (defvar x 4)                     ; Try an example.

Error: the variable |x| is unbound.
  1 (continue) Try evaluating it again
  2 Return a value to use
  3 Return a value to set it to
  4 (abort) return to level 0.
  5 return to top loop level 0.

Type :c followed by a number to proceed

> :|C| 5                           ; By :c they mean :C

> (|DEFVAR| x 8)                   ; We need to use uppercase DEFVAR.
|x|

> x
8
```

```
> (|SETF| (|READTABLE-CASE| |*READTABLE*|) :|UPCASE|)
:UPCASE                          ;  End this madness.
```

The problem we experienced was that after we changed LISP's case conversion behavior, LISP could no longer locate its function or macro names. That is, inside LISP, defvar and DEFVAR are not the same.

11.9.2   Read-Modify-Write Macros

In section 5.6.3, we first discussed how to define modifying macros, such as incf and decf. Now that we know about macros, we can define our own version of incf as follows.

```
(defmacro my-incf (n &optional (delta 1))
  `(setf ,n (+ ,n ,delta)))
```

However, LISP provides a special way to define macros that have side effects modifying their referenced location. This type of macro is called a *read-modify-write macro*, and LISP provides a special way to define these creatures, namely, define-modify-macro. We can define my-incf directly.

```
(define-modify-macro my-incf2 (&optional (delta 1)) +)
```

```
> (setf x 1)
1
```

```
> (my-incf2 x)
2
```

```
> x
2
```

```
> (macroexpand '(my-incf2 x))
(LET* ((#:G605 (+ X 1))) (SETQ X #:G605))
T
```

We note that define-modify-macro has as arguments the name of the macro, the lambda list for arguments *other* than the initial reference, and the function used for modification.

The resulting macros are guaranteed not to evaluate the reference more than once. By convention, these macros are named with an f suffix, to suggest their similarity to setf. Here is another example, notf, which toggles a symbol's truth value.

```
(define-modify-macro notf () not)

> *print-pretty*
T

> (notf *print-pretty*)
NIL

> *print-pretty*
NIL

> (notf *print-pretty*)
T

> (macroexpand '(notf *print-pretty*))
(LET* ((#:G643 (NOT *PRINT-PRETTY*))) (SETQ *PRINT-PRETTY* #:G643))
T
```

11.9.3 Dispatch Macro Characters

Most programmers are familiar with the term *baud*, which refers to the standard data transmission rate of *bits per second* (or, more precisely, the maximum possible transmitted state changes per second). The dimensional name honors *J. M. E. Baudot*, the inventor of the paper tape code used for Teletypewriters. The Baudot code used only 5 bits to encode the character set.

Five bits results in only 32 possible characters (2^5). Even with just uppercase letters, that is not enough for the 26 letters of the alphabet and the 10 digits. In order to extend the character set, two codes were used as dispatch or shift codes, which changed the interpretation of the following characters. The codes were known as LTRS and FIGS, for *letters* and *figures*. The codes for the characters ABCD in LTRS mode would become -?:$ following the FIGS code.

The two dispatch codes plus the 30 remaining codes resulted in 60 possible characters ($2 * 30$). However, three other codes − carriage return, line feed, and error − were the same for both LTRS and FIGS, and one code was not assigned. Thus, sending a carriage return did not require shifting to LTRS or FIGS.

Similarly, programmers can extend the LISP character set through the use of dispatch codes. The standard macro character dispatch character is #. The programmer can define new macro characters triggered by # or even create her own additional dispatch characters.

First, we define a macro character function `read-total`, which reads a list of numbers until it encounters a right bracket (]) and returns the total.

```
(defun read-total (stream char arg)
  (declare (ignore char))
  (declare (ignore arg))
  (apply #'+ (read-delimited-list #\] stream t)))
```

A dispatch macro character function has three arguments.

- stream — The input stream.

- char — The character associated with this function. If the function is assigned to only one character, then this argument is not too useful. However, sometimes the programmer might write one function that is used by different characters.

- arg — The argument bound to nil or a number which is entered between the dispatch character and the macro character. For example, in #3r, arg is bound to 3, setting the radix to base 3.

We now assign the function read-total as the macro character function for the dispatch character sequence #[, and redefine] to act like the right parenthesis.

```
> (set-dispatch-macro-character #\# #\[ #'read-total my-readtable)
#<Interpreted Function READ-TOTAL @ #x106d44e>

> (new-readtable my-readtable)
#<readtable @ #x1068df6>

> (set-macro-character #\] (get-macro-character #\) nil))
EXCL::READ-RIGHT-PAREN

> #[1 2 3]
6

> #[12 23 34]
69

> #[1 2 #[3 4]]
10
```

This is fine. However, suppose we want to use another dispatch character instead of #? We will make % a dispatch character and then set the sequence %[to trigger the read-total macro.

```
> (get-macro-character #\%)
#<Function READ-TOKEN @ #x73ed26>
T
```

```
> (make-dispatch-macro-character #\%)
T

> (set-dispatch-macro-character #\% #\[ #'read-total my-readtable)
#<Interpreted Function READ-TOTAL @ #x106d44e>

> %[1 2 3]
6

> (get-dispatch-macro-character #\% #\[)
#<Interpreted Function READ-TOTAL @ #x106d44e>

> (get-dispatch-macro-character #\# #\[)
#<Interpreted Function READ-TOTAL @ #x106d44e>
```

We can extend our `read-total` function to multiply the result by the argument, if present.

```
(defun read-total (stream char arg)
  (declare (ignore char))
  (if (not arg) (setf arg 1))
  (* arg (apply #'+ (read-delimited-list #\] stream t))))

> (set-dispatch-macro-character #\% #\[ #'read-total my-readtable)
#<Interpreted Function READ-TOTAL @ #x107c646>

> %[1 2 3]
6

> %2[1 2 3]
12

> %43[1 2 3]
258
```

Using the `char` argument, we can define a macro character function that replicates the *read-base* reader syntax.

```
(defun read-base (stream char arg)
  (let ((*read-base*
         (case char
               ((#\d #\D) 10)
               ((#\o #\0) 8)
               ((#\b #\B) 2)
               ((#\x #\X) 16)
               ((#\r #\R) (if arg arg 10))
               (otherwise 10))))
    (read stream)))

(mapc
 #'(lambda (c)
     (set-dispatch-macro-character #\% c #'read-base))
 (list #\d #\D #\o #\0 #\x #\X #\b #\B #\r #\R))

> %o10
8

> %x10
16

> %b10
2

> %d10
10

> %5r10
5

> %5r100
25
```

Here is a macro character function for reading temperatures in either Celsius or Fahrenheit.

```
(defun read-temp (stream char arg)
  (let* ((degree-type (case char
                        ((#\c #\C) 'celsius)
                        ((#\f #\F) 'fahrenheit)))
         (temp (read stream))
         (c-temp (if (member char '(#\c #\C))
                     temp
                     (* 5/9 (- temp 32))))
         (f-temp (if (member char '(#\f #\F))
                     temp
                     (+ 32 (* temp 9/5)))))
    (format t "F: ~A C: ~A~%" f-temp c-temp)))

(mapc
 #'(lambda (c)
     (set-dispatch-macro-character #\% c #'read-temp))
 (list #\c #\C #\f #\F))

> %f32
F: 32 C: 0
NIL

> %C100
F: 212 C: 100
NIL

> %c20
F: 68 C: 20
NIL

> %f0
F: 0 C: -160/9
NIL
```

11.9.4   *macroexpand-hook* and Environments

Macro expansion is a standard component of the eval part of the read-eval-print loop. LISP permits the programmer to insinuate herself into this process through the variable *macroexpand-hook*.

```
> *macroexpand-hook*
FUNCALL
```

We see that the initial value is the symbol FUNCALL. However, the user can assign another value, provided it is a symbol with a function value that takes three argu-

ments: a macro-expansion function, a macro-call form, and an *environment*. Here
is an example.

```
(defun macroexpand-hook-test (fn call env)
   (format t "~%My macro expansion!")
   (funcall fn call env))

> (setf *macroexpand-hook* 'macroexpand-hook-test)
MACROEXPAND-HOOK-TEST

My macro expansion!
My macro expansion!
My macro expansion!
My macro expansion!
My macro expansion!
My macro expansion!
My macro expansion!
My macro expansion!
> (setf x 0)

My macro expansion!
0

My macro expansion!
My macro expansion!
My macro expansion!
My macro expansion!
My macro expansion!
My macro expansion!
My macro expansion!
My macro expansion!
```

Our `macroexpand-hook-test` function merely prints a message every time it is
called. It appears to be called eight times at the end of each read-eval-print loop!

We can modify our function to provide more useful information. We might
want to see the values of the function, call, or environment arguments, depending
on the value of another global variable.

```
(defvar *macroexpand-hook-test-debug* nil)
```

Bad Idea ⇒   `(defun macroexpand-hook-test (fn call env)`

```
(case *macroexpand-hook-test-debug*
  ((fn)   (format t "~%hook-test function:~%  ~A" fn))
  ((call) (format t "~%hook-test call:~%  ~A" call))
  ((env)  (format t "~%hook-test env:~%  ~A" env)))
(funcall fn call env))
```

This version of `macroexpand-hook-test` looks reasonable, except that it has a fatal flaw. Its definition contains the `case` macro, which means that it will trigger an infinite loop during macro expansion.

We need to make sure that our `*macroexpand-hook*` functions do not themselves use macros. Here we replace `case` with the `if` special form. Note that this version may not work on an implementation in which `if` is defined as a macro.   ⇐ ∞

```
(defun macroexpand-hook-test (fn call env)
  (if (eq *macroexpand-hook-test-debug* 'fn)
      (format t "~%hook-test function:~%  ~A" fn))
  (if (eq *macroexpand-hook-test-debug* 'call)
      (format t "~%hook-test call:~%  ~A" call))
  (if (eq *macroexpand-hook-test-debug* 'env)
      (format t "~%hook-test env:~%  ~A" env))
  (funcall fn call env))

> (setf *macroexpand-hook* 'macroexpand-hook-test)
MACROEXPAND-HOOK-TEST

> (setf x 9)                  ;  No printing is triggered yet.
9

> (setf *macroexpand-hook-test-debug* 'fn)
FN

hook-test function:
  #<Function WHEN>
hook-test function:
  #<Function (PROPERTY COND .MACROEXPAND-MACRO.)>
hook-test function:
  #<Function WHEN>
hook-test function:
  #<Function (PROPERTY COND .MACROEXPAND-MACRO.)>
hook-test function:
  #<Function IF*>
hook-test function:
  #<Function (PROPERTY COND .MACROEXPAND-MACRO.)>
hook-test function:
  #<Function WHEN>
```

```
hook-test function:
  #<Function (PROPERTY COND .MACROEXPAND-MACRO.)>

> (setf *macroexpand-hook-test-debug* 'call)

hook-test function:
  #<Function WHEN>
hook-test function:
  #<Function (PROPERTY COND .MACROEXPAND-MACRO.)>
hook-test function:
  #<Function WHEN>
hook-test function:
  #<Function (PROPERTY COND .MACROEXPAND-MACRO.)>
hook-test function:
  #<Function IF*>
hook-test function:
  #<Function (PROPERTY COND .MACROEXPAND-MACRO.)>
hook-test function:
  #<Function WHEN>
hook-test function:
  #<Function (PROPERTY COND .MACROEXPAND-MACRO.)>
hook-test function:
  #<Function SETF>
CALL

hook-test call:
  (WHEN PROCESS (FORMAT STREAM [Current process: ~a]~% PROCESS-NAME))
hook-test call:
  (COND (PROCESS (FORMAT STREAM [Current process: ~a]~% PROCESS-NAME)))
hook-test call:
  (WHEN FOCUS (FORMAT STREAM [Current process focus: ~a]~% FOCUS))
hook-test call:
  (COND (FOCUS (FORMAT STREAM [Current process focus: ~a]~% FOCUS)))
hook-test call:
  (IF* STEPPING
      THEN (FORMAT STREAM [step] )
      ELSE (WHEN BREAK-LEVEL
              (PRINC [ STREAM)
              (PRINC BREAK-LEVEL STREAM)
              (WHEN CONTINUABLE (PRINC c STREAM))
              (WHEN INSPECTING (PRINC i STREAM))
              (PRINC ]  STREAM)))
```

```
hook-test call:
  (COND (STEPPING (FORMAT STREAM [step] ))
        (T
         (WHEN BREAK-LEVEL
           (PRINC [ STREAM)
           (PRINC BREAK-LEVEL STREAM)
           (WHEN CONTINUABLE (PRINC c STREAM))
           (WHEN INSPECTING (PRINC i STREAM))
           (PRINC ]  STREAM)))))
hook-test call:
  (WHEN BREAK-LEVEL
    (PRINC [ STREAM)
    (PRINC BREAK-LEVEL STREAM)
    (WHEN CONTINUABLE (PRINC c STREAM))
    (WHEN INSPECTING (PRINC i STREAM))
    (PRINC ]  STREAM))
hook-test call:
  (COND (BREAK-LEVEL
          (PRINC [ STREAM)
          (PRINC BREAK-LEVEL STREAM)
          (WHEN CONTINUABLE (PRINC c STREAM))
          (WHEN INSPECTING (PRINC i STREAM))
          (PRINC ]  STREAM)))

> (setf *macroexpand-hook-test-debug* 'env)

hook-test call:
  (SETF *MACROEXPAND-HOOK-TEST-DEBUG* 'ENV)
ENV

hook-test env:
  (NIL (COMMAND-NUMBER . 9) (PACKAGE-NAME . USER)
   (INSPECTING) (CONTINUABLE)
   (BREAK-LEVEL) (STEPPING) (FOCUS) (PROCESS)
   (STREAM . #<BIDIRECTIONAL-TERMINAL-STREAM>))
hook-test env:
  (NIL (COMMAND-NUMBER . 9) (PACKAGE-NAME . USER)
   (INSPECTING) (CONTINUABLE)
   (BREAK-LEVEL) (STEPPING) (FOCUS) (PROCESS)
   (STREAM . #<BIDIRECTIONAL-TERMINAL-STREAM>))
```

```
hook-test env:
   (NIL (COMMAND-NUMBER . 9) (PACKAGE-NAME . USER)
   (INSPECTING) (CONTINUABLE)
   (BREAK-LEVEL) (STEPPING) (FOCUS) (PROCESS)
   (STREAM . #<BIDIRECTIONAL-TERMINAL-STREAM>))
hook-test env:
   (NIL (COMMAND-NUMBER . 9) (PACKAGE-NAME . USER)
   (INSPECTING) (CONTINUABLE)
   (BREAK-LEVEL) (STEPPING) (FOCUS) (PROCESS)
   (STREAM . #<BIDIRECTIONAL-TERMINAL-STREAM>))
hook-test env:
   (NIL (COMMAND-NUMBER . 9) (PACKAGE-NAME . USER)
   (INSPECTING) (CONTINUABLE)
   (BREAK-LEVEL) (STEPPING) (FOCUS) (PROCESS)
   (STREAM . #<BIDIRECTIONAL-TERMINAL-STREAM>))
hook-test env:
   (NIL (COMMAND-NUMBER . 9) (PACKAGE-NAME . USER)
   (INSPECTING) (CONTINUABLE)
   (BREAK-LEVEL) (STEPPING) (FOCUS) (PROCESS)
   (STREAM . #<BIDIRECTIONAL-TERMINAL-STREAM>))
hook-test env:
   (NIL (COMMAND-NUMBER . 9) (PACKAGE-NAME . USER)
   (INSPECTING) (CONTINUABLE)
   (BREAK-LEVEL) (STEPPING) (FOCUS) (PROCESS)
   (STREAM . #<BIDIRECTIONAL-TERMINAL-STREAM>))
hook-test env:
   (NIL (COMMAND-NUMBER . 9) (PACKAGE-NAME . USER)
   (INSPECTING) (CONTINUABLE)
   (BREAK-LEVEL) (STEPPING) (FOCUS) (PROCESS)
   (STREAM . #<BIDIRECTIONAL-TERMINAL-STREAM>))

> (setf *macroexpand-hook-test-debug* nil)

hook-test env:
   (NIL)
NIL
```

Instead of printing all this information, we might be satisfied with storing it somewhere. We could try the following.

```
(defvar *macroexpand-hook-test-archive* nil)
```

Bad Idea ⇒
```
(defun macroexpand-hook-test (fn call env)
   (push (list fn call env) *macroexpand-hook-test-archive*)
   (funcall fn call env))
```

However, we encounter the same problem as before: a `macroexpand-hook` function
cannot contain a macro. Here, `push` is no good. We cannot use `setf` either. In
our implementation, `setq` is not a macro, but we shall use `set`, which is a pure
function, and `quote`, which is a special form.

```
(defun macroexpand-hook-test (fn call env)
  (set '*macroexpand-hook-test-archive*
       (cons (list fn call env)
             *macroexpand-hook-test-archive*))
  (funcall fn call env))
```

```
> (setf *macroexpand-hook* 'MACROEXPAND-HOOK-TEST)
MACROEXPAND-HOOK-TEST
```

```
> (length *macroexpand-hook-test-archive*)
8
```

```
> (length *macroexpand-hook-test-archive*)
16
```

The macro expansion information is being saved.

We can use the `*macroexpand-hook*` to implement a tracing mechanism for
macros. The macros `macro-trace` and `macro-untrace` turn on and off the tracing
of macro calls by setting the value of the global variable `*macro-trace-list*`.
Below, we trace `setf` and `when`.

```
(defvar *macro-trace-list* nil)
```

```
(defmacro macro-trace (&optional (macro nil))
  (if macro
      `(pushnew ',macro *macro-trace-list*)
      '*macro-trace-list*))
```

```
(defmacro macro-untrace (&optional (macro nil))
  (if macro
      `(delete ',macro *macro-trace-list*)
      '(setf *macro-trace-list* nil)))
```

```
(defun macroexpand-hook-test (fn call env)
  (if (member (car call) '*macro-trace-list*)
      (format t "~%tracing call:~%  ~A" call))
  (funcall fn call env))
```

```
> (setf x 9)
9
```

```
> (macro-trace setf)
(SETF)

> (setf x 10)

tracing call:
  (SETF X 10)
10

> (macro-trace when)
(WHEN SETF)

tracing call:
  (WHEN PROCESS (FORMAT STREAM [Current process: ~a]~% PROCESS-NAME))
tracing call:
  (WHEN FOCUS (FORMAT STREAM [Current process focus: ~a]~% FOCUS))
tracing call:
  (WHEN BREAK-LEVEL
    (PRINC [ STREAM)
    (PRINC BREAK-LEVEL STREAM)
    (WHEN CONTINUABLE (PRINC c STREAM))
    (WHEN INSPECTING (PRINC i STREAM))
    (PRINC ]  STREAM))

> (macro-untrace)

tracing call:
  (SETF *MACRO-TRACE-LIST* NIL)
NIL
```

The third argument to the *macroexpand-hook* function was the *environment*. Here is the environment output from one of the earlier macro expansions.

```
(NIL (COMMAND-NUMBER . 8) (PACKAGE-NAME . USER) (INSPECTING)
     (CONTINUABLE) (BREAK-LEVEL) (STEPPING) (FOCUS) (PROCESS)
     (STREAM . #<BIDIRECTIONAL-TERMINAL-STREAM>))
```

The environment is a source of variable bindings during the evaluation process. We note that the environment here is represented as an association list. Many of items in the list, such as INSPECTING and FOCUS, have values of NIL.

Usually, LISP does all the bookkeeping associated with the environment, so that the programmer does not need to think about it. LISP, like the EPA, preserves and protects the environment.

However, in some circumstances, the programmer may wish to specify the environment in which a macro is expanded. LISP provides a special lambda list keyword &environment for defmacro, which may be used to specify a single variable whose value is bound to the environment in which to interpret the macro call.

This feature is of use primarily in macros that expand other macros. Below, we define three macros. The second and third explicitly expand the first.

```
(defmacro endangered () '(spotted owls))

(defmacro pc (x)
  `(list ,x (macroexpand '(endangered))))

(defmacro not-pc (x &environment env)
  `(list ,x (macroexpand '(endangered) ',env)))

> (pc 'endangered)
(ENDANGERED (SPOTTED OWLS))

> (not-pc 'endangered)
(ENDANGERED (SPOTTED OWLS))

> (macrolet ((endangered () '(loggers))) (pc 'endangered))
(ENDANGERED (SPOTTED OWLS))

> (macrolet ((endangered () '(loggers))) (not-pc 'endangered))
(ENDANGERED (LOGGERS))
```

In the last case, the macroexpansion in not-pc uses the local environment created by macrolet.

11.10   Exercises

11.10.1   Expression Drill [3]

Evaluate the following expressions, first by hand, then with the help of the LISP interpreter.

```
(setf x (* (+ 5 4) (+ 7 3)))
`(setf x (* (+ 5 4) (+ 7 3)))
`(setf x (* ,(+ 5 4) (+ 7 3)))
`(setf x (* ,(+ 5 4) ,(+ 7 3)))
`(setf x ,(* (+ 5 4) (+ 7 3)))
(car (cdr (cdr '(a (b c (d)) (e)))))
`(car (cdr (cdr '(a (b c (d)) (e)))))
`(car (cdr ,(cdr '(a (b c (d)) (e)))))
`(car (cdr ,@(cdr '(a (b c (d)) (e)))))
`(car ,(cdr (cdr '(a (b c (d)) (e)))))
`(car ,@(cdr (cdr '(a (b c (d)) (e)))))
```

11.10.2   swap Macro [5*]

Write a macro swap that exchanges the values of its two arguments.

```
> (setf a '(1 2 3) b '(4 5 6))
(4 5 6)

> (swap (car a) (car b))
1

> a
(4 2 3)

> b
(1 5 6)

> (swap a b)
(4 2 3)

> a
(1 5 6)

> b
(4 2 3)
```

11.10.3   repeat Macro with a Value [5*]

Redefine the repeat macro, but add an argument that will be returned as the value upon completion. For example,

```
(defun repeat-char (stream char count)
  (repeat count (values)
          (write-char char stream)))
```

```
(repeat-char *standard-output* #\! 10)
!!!!!!!!!!
```

Protect the arguments to the repeat macro from side effects.

11.10.4   repeat with loop [5*]

Rewrite repeat one more time, but use loop instead of do. Have this repeat take a result argument, as in the preceding exercise.

11.10.5   while Macro [5*]

Write a while macro that takes two or more arguments. The first argument is a test expression, and the second argument is the result to be returned. The remaining expressions are the body of the calculation. As long as the first expression is non-NIL, then the remaining expressions are repeatedly evaluated. Here is an example with repeat-char defined using while.

```
(defun repeat-char (stream char count)
  (while
      (> count 0)             ;  Test clause.
    (values)                  ;  Result clause.
    (write-char char stream)
    (decf count)))

> (repeat-char *standard-output* #\! 10)
!!!!!!!!!!
```

11.10.6   until Macro [5*]

Based on the previous exercise, write an until macro that takes two or more arguments. until has the same form as while, except the polarity of the test is reversed: as long as the test is false, the remaining expressions are repeatedly evaluated. Here is an example with repeat-char defined using until.

```
(defun repeat-char (stream char count)
  (until
    (= count 0)               ;  Test clause.
    (values)                  ;  Result clause.
    (write-char char stream)
    (decf count)))

(repeat-char *standard-output* #\^ 10)
^^^^^^^^^^
```

11.10.7   prog1 Macro [7*]

There is a problem with the following macro definition for prog1.

```
(defmacro bad-prog1 (first &body body)
  `((lambda (x) ,@body x) ,first))
```

There are certain cases in which it will not work properly.

The local variable x used in the definition of bad-prog1 may conflict with an occurrence of a variable in the body expressions, as below.

```
> (bad-prog1 1 (setf x 2) 3)
2
```

The solution given before to this problem was to bind the executable body as a local function outside the scope of the other local variables, as below.

```
(defmacro my-prog1 (first &body body)
  `(flet ((body () ,@body))
     ((lambda (x) (body) x) ,first)))
```

Other solutions are variations on this method. Rewrite prog1 in another way that eliminates the variable name conflict.

11.10.8   dpsq Macro [6*]

One common use of macros is for situations in which the programmer does not want the arguments evaluated. Here is such a case: the Define PropertieS-Quoted, or dpsq macro.

We shall first describe the function dps, which takes one or more arguments of the form: node-name property value property value, etc. It returns NIL and, as a side effect, puts the given values on the property list of the node. dpsq is a macro version of dps which does not evaluate its arguments. Here are examples of both.

```
> (dps 'john 'age 23 'mother 'mary 'father 'jack)
NIL

> (get 'john 'age)
23

> (get 'john 'father)
JACK

> (dpsq jack age 53 wife mary son john)
NIL

> (get 'jack 'son)
JOHN
```

Here is one definition of the `dps` function, albeit a faulty one.

```
(defun dps (&rest 1)
  (let ((node (pop 1)))
    (cond ((null 1) nil)
          (t
           (put node (pop 1) (pop 1))
           (apply #'dps (cons node 1))))))
```

Identify and correct the problem in this definition, and then define the `dpsq` macro in terms of `dps`.

We should state that by encouraging or promulgating the use of property lists, we may be considered guilty of contributing to the delinquency of programmers. In some circles, this is a felony offense, equivalent to the use of `gotos`. Just as structured programming in the 1970s led to the widespread use of clearer control structures, less dissolute data structures have largely replaced profligate property lists.

Our personal position is that object-oriented programming provides a principled method for improving both control and data structures. In a few more chapters, the reader will witness the revealed truth.

11.10.9   ISA Inheritance Hierarchy [4*]

In artificial intelligence programs, programmers often represent knowledge with inheritance hierarchies. That is, if an item is an instance of a particular class, then that item assumes the properties of that parent class unless otherwise indicated. One way of implementing property inheritance is with "ISA" links in a property list database. Here is an example.

```
(mapc #'(lambda (1) (apply #'dps 1))
      '((jane isa programmer sex female income sixty-k)
        (john isa programmer sex male ingests junk-food)
        (programmer isa person income fifty-k)
        (person isa mammal)
        (mammal isa organism)
        (organism ingests (food air))))

> (isa-get 'jane 'sex)
FEMALE

> (isa-get 'jane 'income)
SIXTY-K

> (isa-get 'john 'income)
FIFTY-K
```

```
> (isa-get 'jane 'ingests)
(FOOD AIR)

> (isa-get 'john 'ingests)
JUNK-FOOD
```

We created a class hierarchy of organisms, including two individuals, Jane and John. The function `isa-get` checks the local node for the given property. If it is not found, then `isa-get` recursively climbs the inheritance hierarchy.

Write the `isa-get` function.

11.10.10   Data-Driven dpsq Macro [8*]

Data has structure. Knowledge has content. We can begin to add content to our data structures by making them behave differently according to the content of the input. For example, we know that a person can have only one spouse at a time but can have several children and several siblings concurrently. We know that if X is the spouse of Y, then Y is the spouse of X. We know that if X is the sibling of Y, then Y is the sibling of X, and so forth.

Just as we used the `isa` property in the preceding exercise to model inheritance, we can create a data-driven version of put — ddput — which reacts in specific ways to other properties. We can then use ddput instead of put inside dps.

Here is an example of this revised version of dps and dpsq that is triggered by a set of special properties, marked with a + prefix.

```
(mapc #'(lambda (l) (apply #'dps l))
      '((isa +invert-onto instances)
        (instances +multiple-values t)
        (*relationship +multiple-values t)
        (relationship +save-property t)
        (children isa *relationship)
        (sibling isa *relationship +invert-value t)
        (father isa relationship)
        (spouse isa relationship +invert-value t)
        (joe-jr father joe-sr spouse mary children pat
                children sue)))

> (pppq joe-jr)

JOE-JR
      CHILDREN        (SUE PAT)
      SPOUSE          MARY
      FATHER          JOE-SR
```

```
> (pppq relationship)

RELATIONSHIP
    INSTANCES           (SPOUSE FATHER)
    +SAVE-PROPERTY      T

> (pppq *relationship)

*RELATIONSHIP
    INSTANCES           (SIBLING CHILDREN)
    +MULTIPLE-VALUES    T

> (dpsq mary sibling dorothy sibling arthur)
NIL

> (pppq mary)

MARY
    SIBLING             (ARTHUR DOROTHY)
    SPOUSE              JOE-JR

> (pppq arthur)

ARTHUR
    SIBLING             MARY
```

A lot is going on beneath the surface in this example. Here is a list of the properties with which ddput must deal.

- +invert-onto — When ddput encounters a property whose own property list contains the +invert-onto property, ddput calls itself recursively, reversing the current node and value on the property specified by the flag. In this example, the isa property automatically inverts its arguments via an instances property.

- +multiple-values — This property flag tells ddput that the value should be added to any existing values on this node's given property but without duplication. Here, the properties of instances and *relationship may have multiple values. Also, children and sibling properties may have multiple values, as inherited via the isa hierarchy from *relationship.

- +save-property — This flag is one alternative to the +multiple-values flag. If ddput encounters a property flagged as +save-property and there is an existing value, this old value is moved to a backup node, which is given as the value to a `save-node` property on the main node. We shall see an example below.

- `+invert-value` — Some properties, like spouse and sibling, are commutative. These values can be automatically inverted. In this example, entering the fact that Joe's spouse is Mary results in the automatic entry of Mary's spouse being Joe.

- `(pppq node)` — This is a macro that calls the function `(ppp node)`, just as `dpsq` calls `dps`. The function `ppp` prints out the properties and values associated with the node. This function requires that `ddput` keep a list of the properties assigned in the first place. The most convenient place for such a list is on the node itself under some special property, such as `+ddprops`.

- `+invert-property` — This property is similar to the `+invert-value`, with the value and property reversed. That is, the additional entry is made on the property list of the property itself. This feature is demonstrated below with the `job` property.

- `+lambda-property` — The idea here is to allow complete flexibility to the programmer. The value of a `+lambda-property` is a function that takes the three put variables: node, property, and value. This function is invoked when its property is asserted. We demonstrate this feature below.

Continuing this example, we have Joe remarry, have another child, and go to work at two jobs to support his growing family.

```
> (dpsq joe-jr spouse louise children jackie)
NIL

> (pppq joe-jr)

JOE-JR
    SAVE-NODE         SAVE577
    CHILDREN          (JACKIE SUE PAT)
    SPOUSE            LOUISE
    FATHER            JOE-SR

> (ppp (get 'joe-jr 'save-node))

SAVE577
    SPOUSE            MARY

> (dpsq job +invert-property t +multiple-values t)
NIL
```

```
> (dpsq plumber isa job)
NIL

> (dpsq carpenter isa job)
NIL

> (dpsq joe-jr job plumber job carpenter)
NIL

> (pppq joe-jr)

JOE-JR
    JOB                (CARPENTER PLUMBER)
    SAVE-NODE          SAVE577
    CHILDREN           (JACKIE SUE PAT)
    SPOUSE             LOUISE
    FATHER             JOE-SR

> (pppq job)

JOB
    CARPENTER          (JOE-JR)
    PLUMBER            (JOE-JR)
    INSTANCES          (CARPENTER PLUMBER)
    +MULTIPLE-VALUES   T
    +INVERT-PROPERTY   T
```

The +save-property flag under relationship resulted in saving Joe's previous spouse under a separate node. We then defined job to allow multiple values and to be inverted under the job node. Thus, we can keep track of all the plumbers and carpenters automatically.

We close with an example of the +lambda-property. We decide to treat sons as male children, with a specified father.

```
> (dps 'son '+lambda-property
    #'(lambda (node prop val)
        (ddput node 'children val)
        (ddput val 'sex 'male)
        (ddput val 'father node)))
NIL

> (dpsq joe-jr son lester)
NIL
```

```
> (pppq joe-jr)

JOE-JR
     JOB                 (CARPENTER PLUMBER)
     SAVE-NODE           SAVE577
     CHILDREN            (LESTER JACKIE SUE PAT)
     SPOUSE              LOUISE
     FATHER              JOE-SR

> (pppq lester)

LESTER
     FATHER              JOE-JR
     SEX                 MALE
```

Modify dps to use ddput, and write ddput, ppp, and pppq.

11.10.11 msg Macro [8*]

The format function in LISP is convenient and helpful. However, it is sometimes difficult to manage to get all the control string options associated with their respective arguments. It would be preferable to be able to give the formatting information side by side with the arguments. The msg macro, which is found in some older dialects of LISP, provides just this capability. msg is to format as C++'s cout is to C's printf.

Here is an example of msg at work.

```
> (msg "Hello" t)
Hello
**VALUE-OF-MSG**

> (msg t "Hello" t "there" t)

Hello
there
**VALUE-OF-MSG**

> (setf x 5)
5

> (msg "John is" 1 x 1 "year" (plur x) 1 "old" t)
John is 5 years old
**VALUE-OF-MSG**
```

```
> (msg (bin x) " + " (bin x) " = " (bin (+ x x)) t)
101 + 101 = 1010
```

`msg` takes a variable number of arguments, each of which may be one of over a dozen types listed below.

- *string* displays the string.

- *symbol* displays the value of the symbol.

- `t` starts a new line.

- *number* moves that number of spaces.

- *-number* skips that number of lines.

- `(TO stream)` redirects output to the given stream. The default output stream is `*standard-output*`.

- `(TAB number)` tabs to the specified column number.

- `(RIGHT string)` displays the given text flush right. Uses the current output line if possible. Otherwise, starts on the next line.

- `(CENTER string)` displays the given text centered on the line. Moves to the next line if necessary.

- `(HEX number)` prints the given number in hexadecimal.

- `(OCT number)` prints the given number in octal.

- `(BIN number)` prints the given number in binary.

- `(PLUR number)` displays an 's' if the number is greater than 1; otherwise, nothing. This is used for simple plurals, as given in the above example.

11.10.12 Comment Macro Character [7]

The normal comment character (;) allows the programmer to specify single-line comments. Often, a programmer finds it more convenient to have multiline comments, without having to place a special character at the beginning of each line. This facility can be achieved with a read macro.

Define a macro character, !, which introduces a multiline comment. When the LISP reader encounters !, it should ignore all characters until it comes across a left parenthesis in the first column of a line. Here is an example.

!   The comment read macro has been defined in
    my-readtable. LISP is ignoring these lines.

    It is waiting for a left paren in column 1.
    Here it comes now.

(defvar the-answer-to-the-problems-of-the-world nil)
;   The define on the previous line was executed by LISP.

11.10.13   Read-Modify-Write Macros [4*]

Define the following read-modify-write macros: negatef, invertf, upcasef, and
downcasef. They are demonstrated below.

```
> (setf x 5)
5

> (negatef x)
-5

> x
-5

> (negatef x)
5

> (invertf x)
1/5

> x
1/5

> (invertf x)
5

> (setf y "hello")
"hello"

> (upcasef y)
"HELLO"

> y
"HELLO"
```

```
> (downcasef y)
"hello"
```

11.11   Chapter Summary

- The following LISP object type is introduced in this chapter.

  `readtable`

- The syntax of LISP can be modified with macros.

- Macros are created with the `defmacro` special form.

- Macros are useful for creating new control mechanisms, since they allow for selective evaluation of their arguments.

- The backquote read macro allows for selective evaluation of list expressions through the use of its comma and comma-at-sign syntax.

- Macros definitions can employ three additional lambda list keywords: `&body`, `&whole`, and `&environment`. The constant `lambda-list-keywords` is a list of the implementation's available lambda list keywords.

- Macros and functions are not interchangeable. In particular, macros cannot be traced or passed as arguments, whereas functions can.

- Local macros can be defined with the `macrolet` and `symbol-macrolet` special forms.

  ```
  (symbol-macrolet ({(var expansion)}*) {form}*)
  (macrolet ({(name varlist {form}*)}*) {form}*)
  ```

- The predicate `special-form-p` can be used to identify LISP special forms.

- LISP associates symbols with macros definitions, which can be accessed and set by the following function.

  ```
  (macro-function symbol)
  ```

  This function also serves as the predicate for macros.

- For debugging and exploratory purposes, it is often useful to expand macro expressions, using the `macroexpand` and `macroexpand-1` functions.

  ```
  (macroexpand expression)
  (macroexpand-1 expression)
  ```

- Destructuring permits LISP macros to have nested-parameters lambda lists. Functions can employ destructuring with the macro `destructuring-bind`.

- LISP uses readtables to record the method of interpretation for characters. The default is `*readtable*`.

- Macros characters allow the programmer to change LISP's interpretation of individual characters. Readtables are manipulated with the following functions.

```
(copy-readtable readtable)
(readtablep object)
(get-macro-character character &optional readtable)
(set-macro-character character function &optional
                     non-terminating-p readtable)
(set-syntax-from-char to-char from-char
                     [to-readtable [from-readtable]])
```

- The `ignore` declaration advises the compiler not to pay attention to variables that are created but not referenced.

- Read-modify-write macros are defined succinctly with `define-modify-macro`.

Syntactic sugar causes cancer of the semicolon.

◇ ALAN PERLIS, *Epigrams in Programming (1982)*

Chapter 12

Structures

> *Have a place for everything*
> *and keep the thing somewhere else;*
> *this is not advice, it is merely custom.*
>
> ◇ MARK TWAIN, *Collected Works*

> *It is impossible to dissociate language from science or science*
> *from language, because every natural science always involves three things:*
> *the sequence of phenomena on which the science is based;*
> *the abstract concepts which call these phenomena to mind; and*
> *the words in which the concepts are expressed.*
> *To call forth a concept a word is needed; to portray a phenomenon,*
> *a concept is needed. All three mirror one and the same reality.*
>
> ◇ ANTOINE LAURENT LAVOISIER, *Traité Élémentaire de Chimie (1789)*

It is easy to lose sight of the fact that computers do not really manipulate lists or objects or strings or numbers or symbols or even binary digits. The computer only sees one kind of data: voltages. Electricity is the computer's primal world.

Not only is that fact easy to forget, it is absolutely necessary to forget when thinking about writing computer programs. LISP's objects are abstractions, built in a principled way from more primitive elements. These abstractions allow the programmer to specify actions in a clear and concise fashion.

Furthermore, LISP allows the programmer to make her own data abstractions, to create and manipulate new types of data objects. Why would the programmer wish to create an abstraction? For the same reason that the programmer would not want to specify programs in terms of voltage manipulations — for power and clarity of expression.

12.1 Structures

In section 8.4, we defined the `better-zeller` function, which took one argument, a list of the form `(day month year)`.

```
(defun better-zeller (date)
  (let* ((day    (car date))
         (month (cadr date))
         (year  (caddr date))
         (century (truncate year 100))
         (decades (- year century))
         (leap    (cond ((leap-yearp year) 1)
                        (t 0))))
    (zeller day month century decades leap)))
```

This program depends on the fact that the date is represented precisely as a three-element list. However, the *reference* to a piece of data and the *representation* of that data should be separate whenever possible. One way to do this is by defining accessor functions that are specific to the `my-date` data structure, as below.

```
(defun better-zeller2 (date)
  (let* ((day    (my-date-day date))
         (month (my-date-month date))
         (year  (my-date-year date))
         (century (truncate year 100))
         (decades (- year (* 100 century)))
         (leap    (cond ((leap-yearp year) 1)
                        (t 0))))
    (zeller day month century decades leap)))
```

```
(defun my-date-day (d) (car d))
(defun my-date-month (d) (cadr d))
(defun my-date-year (d) (caddr d))
```

All we have done is to define synonyms for the accessor functions used in the previous example. The code should execute exactly as it did before. However, a person looking at the code should find it easier to understand. In fact, the clarity of the names of the new accessor functions make it reasonable to do away with the day and month variables in the `let*` form altogether.

```
(defun better-zeller3 (date)
  (let* ((year    (my-date-year date))
         (century (truncate year 100))
         (decades (- year (* 100 century)))
         (leap    (cond ((leap-yearp year) 1)
                        (t 0))))
```

```
        (zeller (my-date-day date)
                (zeller-month (my-date-month date))
                century decades leap)))
(defun zeller-month (m)
  (if (= m 2) 12
    (mod (+ m 10) 12)))
```

We keep the other variables, year, century, and decades, for purposes of meaning and economy. We also define the zeller-month function to adjust the months to fit the formula, for example, January is 11, February is 12, March is 1, and so forth.

LISP provides a method to implement new data structures, like date, directly, with the defstruct form, demonstrated below.

```
> (defstruct my-date "A date structure" day month year day-of-week)
MY-DATE

> (setf x (make-my-date))        ;  Creates a date, albeit an empty one.
#S(MY-DATE :DAY NIL :MONTH NIL :YEAR NIL :DAY-OF-WEEK NIL)

> (type-of x)                    ;  x is of type MY-DATE.
MY-DATE

> (my-date-p x)
T

> (my-date-day x)
NIL

> (setf (my-date-day x) 1)
1

> (setf (my-date-month x) 9)
9

> (setf (my-date-year x) 1996)
1996

> (my-date-day x)
1

> (my-date-month x)
9
```

```
> (my-date-year x)
1996

> (better-zeller3 x)
0

> (setf (my-date-day-of-week x) 0)
0
```

The arguments to defstruct are not evaluated. Thus, defstruct is not a function, but a macro, with the following basic syntax.

```
(defstruct {name | (name {option}*)} [doc-string] {slot-description}+)
```

The first argument to defstruct is the name of the new data structure, which may include options when given as a list. The second (optional) argument is a documentation string, and the remaining arguments are the names of the components. Defining a structure type has several effects.

- It creates a data structure constructor, make-my-date, which forms its name by adding the prefix make- to the data structure name, my-date.

- It creates a data structure predicate, my-date-p. Structures created with the constructor will answer true to the predicate. The name of the predicate is the data structure name with a -p suffix.

- It creates selector functions for accessing the data:

  ```
  my-date-day
  my-date-month
  my-date-year
  my-date-day-of-week
  ```

- The data structure values are initialized to NIL.

- Data structure values can be specified with the setf form.

The call to better-zeller3 works fine with the revised my-date data structure. The reader should realize that we selected the names of the new accessor functions in better-zeller3 with premeditation. The order of component names in the call to defstruct does not affect the programmer's use of the resulting functions. For example, we could have used the following definition.

```
> (defstruct my-date "Date Structure"  year month
     day day-of-week zodiac-sign)
MY-DATE
```

```
> (setf y (make-my-date))
#S(MY-DATE :YEAR NIL :MONTH NIL :DAY NIL :DAY-OF-WEEK NIL
:ZODIAC-SIGN NIL)

> (setf (my-date-day y) 1)
1

> (setf (my-date-month y) 9)
9

> (setf (my-date-year y) 1996)
1996

> (better-zeller y)
0

> (defvar z (copy-my-date y))
Z

> z
#S(MY-DATE :YEAR 1996 :MONTH 9 :DAY 1 :DAY-OF-WEEK NIL
:ZODIAC-SIGN NIL)

> (eql y z)
NIL

> (equal y z)
NIL

> (equalp y z)
T
```

We have changed the order of the component slots and added `zodiac-sign`, as well. The accuracy of `better-zeller3` is unaffected for dates with the new definition. We also note that `defstruct` has created a copier function, `copy-my-date`, which permits us to create new instances of a structure containing the same information. The resulting copy is not `eql` or `equal` to the old structure instance, but it is `equalp`.

The programmer should appreciate the utility of the abstraction of these data structures. Imagine trying to alter the original explicit list data structure for `my-date` in the manner we just did for the abstract data structure. The programmer would have been forced to rummage through her code to identify all references to days, months, and years. In fact, the programmer who did not use such mnemonic terms might be forced to examine every occurrence of car, cadr, and caddr.

LISP gives you some control over the names of your structure elements and how your structures print. We illustrate some of these options.

```
(defstruct (your-date
              (:conc-name date-)
              (:constructor new-date)
              (:copier another-date)
              (:predicate isa-date?)
              (:print-function
                (lambda (struct stream depth)
                  (declare (ignore depth))
                  (format stream "#<Date ~A/~A/~A>"
                            (date-month struct)
                            (date-day struct)
                            (rem (date-year struct) 100)))))
    day month year)

> (defvar d (new-date))
D

> (date-day d)
NIL

> (setf (date-day d) 1 (date-month d) 2 (date-year d) 1999)
1999

> d
#<Date 2/1/99>

> (isa-date? d)
T

> (defvar d2 (another-date d))
D2

> d2
#<Date 2/1/99>
```

To specify options in a defstruct form, you must first surround the structure name with parentheses and then delimit the option names and values with parentheses. defstruct options include the following.

- :conc-name – The concatenated prefix to use in naming the access functions. In this example, we specify date-, which results in the access function of date-day instead of your-date-day. If the argument to :conc-name is NIL, then no prefix is used. The slot name itself becomes the name of the access function, for example, day instead of date-day.

- :constructor – The name of the constructor function. In this example, we specify new-date instead of the default make-your-date.

- :copier – The name of the copier function. We use another-date instead of the default copy-your-date.

- :predicate – The name of the predicate. We use isa-date? instead of the default your-date-p.

- :print-function – The function used to print instances of the structure. The function must take three arguments: the structure instance, a stream, and a number specifying the depth of the break levels.

One other defstruct option bears mentioning, :include.

```
(defstruct (holiday
             (:include your-date)
             (:print-function
              (lambda (struct stream depth)
                (declare (ignore depth))
                (format stream "#<Holiday (~S) ~A/~A/~A>"
                        (holiday-name struct)
                        (date-month struct)
                        (date-day struct)
                        (rem (date-year struct) 100)))))
  name)

> (defvar h1 (make-holiday))
H1

> (setf (holiday-name h1) "Fourth of July")
"Fourth of July"

> (setf (date-day h1) 4 (date-month h1) 7 (date-year h1) 1999)
1999

> h1
#<Holiday ("Fourth of July") 7/4/99>
```

With :include, we can create a new structure that includes an old structure in its entirety. The holiday structure is a date with a name added to it. The accessor functions for your-date all work with holiday.

12.2 Structures: More Details and Examples

In the holiday example, we saw that structures can clone other structures as components. In fact, they can have recursive components. Here is an example from the domain of baseball.

We shall define a data structure to keep track of baseball games for a league. The pieces of information to record for each game include the following.

- Date of the game

- Name of the home team

- Name of the visiting team

- The final score

- The next home game

Here are the relevant LISP data structures and examples of operations for manipulating structure types.

```
> (defstruct game date home visitor score next)
GAME

> (defstruct score home visitor)
SCORE
```

We create two new structures. defstruct allows us to specify the default initial values for individual items.

```
(defstruct game "A baseball game"
  date
  (home 'bulldogs)
  visitor score next)

(defstruct score
  (home 0)
  (visitor 0))
```

In this case, the default home team is the Bulldogs, and the default initial score is 0-0.

```
> (defvar game1 (make-game))                    ; Creates a game.
GAME1

> (setf (game-date game1) (make-my-date))
#S(MY-DATE :YEAR NIL :MONTH NIL :DAY NIL :DAY-OF-WEEK NIL)

> (setf (game-score game1) (make-score))        ; Creates a score for the game.
#S(SCORE :HOME 0 :VISITOR 0)

> (setf (game-next game1) (make-game))           ; Creates a next game link.
#S(GAME :DATE NIL :HOME BULLDOGS :VISITOR NIL :SCORE NIL :NEXT NIL)

> (setf (game-visitor game1) 'crimson)           ; Names the visiting team.
CRIMSON

> (score-home (game-score game1))
0

> (score-visitor (game-score game1))
0

> (game-home game1)
BULLDOGS
```

We create an instance of the game data structure, which itself contains instances of the date structure, the score structure, and the game structure itself.

Furthermore, using keyword arguments, we can specify initial values of slots when invoking the constructor functions.

```
> (defvar game2 (make-game :home 'mets :visitor 'giants))
GAME2

> game2
#S(GAME :DATE NIL :HOME METS :VISITOR GIANTS :SCORE NIL :NEXT NIL)

> (defvar game3 (make-game :home 'mets :visitor 'giants
        :date (make-my-date :month 8 :day 12 :year 1993)
        :score (make-score :home 3 :visitor 4)))
GAME3

> game3
#S(GAME :DATE #S(MY-DATE :YEAR 1993 :MONTH 8 :DAY 12
        :DAY-OF-WEEK NIL :ZODIAC-SIGN NIL) :HOME METS :VISITOR
        GIANTS :SCORE #S(SCORE :HOME 3 :VISITOR 4) :NEXT NIL)
```

When creating `game2`, we specified initial team values by using the `:home` and `:visitor` keywords, which are the slot names prefixed with a colon. For `game3`, we gave additional initial values for the date and score.

We can write a function for listing the contents of an instance of a date structure.

```
(defun reveal-date (date)
  (mapcar #'(lambda (selector)
              (funcall selector date))
          (list #'my-date-day #'my-date-month #'my-date-year)))

> (setf (my-date-day (game-date game1)) 1)
1

> (setf (my-date-month (game-date game1)) 3)
3

> (setf (my-date-year (game-date game1)) 1996)
1996

> (setf (my-date-day-of-week (game-date game1))
        (better-zeller3 (game-date game1)))
5

> (reveal-date (game-date game1))
(1 3 1996)
```

In this example, we set the date of the big game and then print out the information.

We can now expand on this example to show how various data structures can be combined in programs. We use the game data structure as a component for a system that keeps statistics and calculates league standings.

For each team in the league, we keep track of the number of games won and lost, the winning percentage, and the number of "games behind." The games behind statistic is the standard way of comparing the performance of two baseball teams, based on their respective won and lost records. Here are examples.

```
(defun games-behind (a b)
  (/ (+  (- (team-won b)
            (team-won a))
         (- (team-lost a)
            (team-lost b)))
     2))
```

```
(defun game-average (team)
  (float
    (/ (team-won team)
       (+ (team-won team)
          (team-lost team)))))
```

```
> (defstruct team name won lost average behind)
TEAM
```

```
> (defvar bulldogs (make-team :name 'bulldogs :won 12 :lost 4))
BULLDOGS
```

```
> bulldogs
#S(TEAM :NAME BULLDOGS :WON 12 :LOST 4 :AVERAGE NIL :BEHIND NIL)
```

```
> (defvar crimson (make-team :name 'crimson :won 8 :lost 8))
CRIMSON
```

```
> crimson
#S(TEAM :NAME CRIMSON :WON 8 :LOST 8 :AVERAGE NIL :BEHIND NIL)
```

```
> (game-average bulldogs)
0.75
```

```
> (game-average crimson)
0.5
```

```
> (games-behind crimson bulldogs)
4
```

```
> (games-behind bulldogs crimson)
-4
```

```
> (games-behind crimson crimson)
0
```

games-behind is a comparison predicate. As such, we can use it to rank the teams. Here is a ranking program, which uses the merge sort routine introduced in exercise 6.8.3 on page 199.

```
(defun print-standings (teams)
  (let* ((ranking (msort teams))
         (top-team (car ranking)))
    (labels
```

```
   ((post-stats
          (team)
          (setf (team-average team) (game-average team))
          (setf (team-behind team) (games-behind team top-team))))
    (print-head
          ()
          (format t "~%Team ~12TWon Lost Average Games Behind"))
    (print-stats (team)
               (format t "~%~A ~12T~A ~16T~A ~21T.~A ~29T~A"
                       (team-name team)
                       (team-won team)
                       (team-lost team)
                       (round-off (team-average team))
                       (team-behind team))))
    (mapc #'post-stats teams)
    (print-head)
    (mapc #'print-stats ranking)
    (values))))

;;   round-off converts repeating decimals to standard,
;;   three-digit W/L numbers.
(defun round-off (x)
  (truncate (* x 1000)))

;;   We have entered data for other teams in the league.
> (defvar *league* (list bears lions tigers bulldogs crimson))
*LEAGUE*

> (print-standings *league*)
```

Team	Won	Lost	Average	Games Behind
BULLDOGS	12	4	.750	0
TIGERS	9	6	.600	5/2
CRIMSON	8	8	.500	4
BEARS	7	12	.368	13/2
LIONS	4	14	.222	9

12.3 Generic Functions and Methods

With defstruct, we can easily define a structure for time. To avoid a conflict with the existing Common LISP time object, we use a different name for the structure itself. However, the defstruct options make it possible for us to retain the naming conventions we desire.

```
(defstruct (my-time
              (:conc-name time-)
              (:constructor make-time)
              (:copier copy-time)
              (:predicate time-p))
  (hours 0)
  (minutes 0)
  (seconds 0))
```

The default time is midnight. Another (better) way to represent time is as a single integer giving the number of seconds past midnight. See appendix C.

```
> (defvar x1 (make-time))
X1

> x1                          ;  x1 has the default value of midnight.
#S(MY-TIME :HOURS 0 :MINUTES 0 :SECONDS 0)

> (setf (time-hours x1) 12)
12

> x1                          ;  x1 is reset to noon.
#S(MY-TIME :HOURS 12 :MINUTES 0 :SECONDS 0)
(defun add-time (t1 t2)
  (check-type t1 my-time "a good time")
  (check-type t2 my-time "a good time")
  (let ((new (make-time :hours (+ (time-hours t1)
                                  (time-hours t2))
                        :minutes (+ (time-minutes t1)
                                    (time-minutes t2))
                        :seconds (+ (time-seconds t1)
                                    (time-seconds t2)))))
    (time-normalize new)))

(defun time-normalize (time)
  (check-type time my-time "a good time")
  (cond ((>= (time-seconds time) 60)
         (setf (time-seconds time) (- (time-seconds time) 60))
         (incf (time-minutes time))
         (time-normalize time))
        ((>= (time-minutes time) 60)
         (setf (time-minutes time) (- (time-minutes time) 60))
         (incf (time-hours time))
         (time-normalize time))
```

```
((>= (time-hours time) 24)
 (setf (time-hours time) (mod (time-hours time) 24))
 time)
(t time)))
```

add-time checks the type of its arguments and then creates a new time with hours,
minutes, and seconds that are the sum of the respective slots of its arguments. The
result is normalized to ensure that no minutes have more than 60 seconds, no hours
have more than 60 minutes, and no days have more than 24 hours.

Here is add-time in action.

```
> (defvar x2 (make-time :minutes 30))   ;  Creates a new time.
X2


> x2
#S(MY-TIME :HOURS 0 :MINUTES 30 :SECONDS 0)


> x1                                        ;  This is the old value of x1.
#S(MY-TIME :HOURS 12 :MINUTES 0 :SECONDS 0)


> (defvar x3 (add-time x1 x2))            ;  x3 = x1 + x2
X3


> x3
#S(MY-TIME :HOURS 12 :MINUTES 30 :SECONDS 0)


> (defvar x4 (add-time x3 x3))            ;  x4 = x3 + x3
X4


> x4
#S(MY-TIME :HOURS 1 :MINUTES 0 :SECONDS 0)
```

The comments above indicate that (add-time x1 x2) is x1 + x2. Why not define
add-time to be +? Then we could write: (+ x1 x2).

There could be a problem if we try something like:

Bad Idea ⇒   (defun + (t1 t2) (add-time t1 t2))

LISP warns us not to redefine a system function. If we go ahead, we discover that
the regular definition of + no longer works. That is, we can no longer add numbers.

In fact, it is much worse than that. We cannot even add times, since our
original definition of add-time used the good old + function for adding hours and
minutes and seconds!

Do we give up? Yes. Ha ha ha, just kidding. Of course not. What we want is
to define a version of + that works on time structures and still works for numbers.

```
;;  Saves the old definition of +.
(setf (symbol-function 'old+) (symbol-function '+))

(defun + (x y)
  (cond ((and (time-p x) (time-p y))
         (add-time x y))
        (t (old+ x y))))
```

```
> (+ x1 x2)
#S(MY-TIME :HOURS 12 :MINUTES 30 :SECONDS 0)

> (+ x3 x3)
#S(MY-TIME :HOURS 1 :MINUTES 0 :SECONDS 0)

> (+ 9.0 13)
22.0
```

We can now add times and still use the + function with numbers. What we have done is create a definition for + that behaves differently for different types of arguments. That is, the function will do one thing if the arguments are time instances, and another thing if the arguments are numbers. In fact, the original + function also distinguishes among a variety of numbers, including fixnums, bignums, floats, ratios, and complex numbers.

It is not only useful for a function to behave differently with different types of arguments, it is common. The Common LISP Object System (CLOS) provides a way to create *generic* functions that have separate definitions or *methods* for different types of arguments. Instead of **defun**, we use **defgeneric** to create a generic function and its associated methods. We can use **defgeneric** to define + as a generic function. To avoid conflict, we give the new function the name g+ — *generic plus*.

```
(defgeneric g+ (x y)
  (:method ((x my-time) (y my-time)) (add-time x y))
  (:method (x y) (old+ x y)))
```

```
> (g+ x1 x2)                    ; It adds times.
#S(MY-TIME :HOURS 12 :MINUTES 30 :SECONDS 0)

> (g+ 9 5/3)                    ; It adds numbers.
32/3
```

The principal arguments to **defgeneric** are as follows:

- The name of the generic function, in this case, g+. This could also be a **setf** form, such as (setf g+).

- A number of options, none of which appear here. We discuss these later.

- The lambda list; in this case, just the parameter list, (x y). The keywords &optional, &rest, &key, and &allow-other-keys can be used as well.

- A number of optional method clause lists of the form :method, specialized lambda list, and body of the method.

The specialized lambda list is a list of pairs of the form (argument type). If the argument is not specified with a type, it matches any argument. Thus, the g+ method with arguments (x y) is the default method. The lambda list keywords given above are permitted as well, plus the &aux keyword.

Now, suppose we try to use g+ to add a time to a number? For example, we wish to add 10 seconds to an existing time.

```
> (g+ x1 10)
Error: #S(MY-TIME :HOURS 12 :MINUTES 0 :SECONDS 0)
is an illegal argument to +
  [condition type: TYPE-ERROR]
```

We need to extend our definition to handle the case in which the first argument to g+ is a time and the second argument is a number. We could rewrite our generic definition with an additional method clause:

```
(:method ((x my-time) (y number))
         (add-time x (make-time :seconds y)))
```

This would do the trick. However, suppose that we do not have access to the g+ defgeneric code. It may be part of the system definition. Common LISP permits the incremental definition of methods with the defmethod macro.

```
(defmethod g+ ((x my-time) (y number))
  (add-time x (make-time :seconds y)))

(defmethod g+ ((x number) (y my-time))
  (add-time y (make-time :seconds x)))

> (g+ x1 10)
#S(MY-TIME :HOURS 12 :MINUTES 0 :SECONDS 10)

> (g+ 10 x1)
#S(MY-TIME :HOURS 12 :MINUTES 0 :SECONDS 10)
```

Here we define methods for both cases of times and numbers. By creating new methods on the fly, we can extend existing functions to new structure types.

In fact, we can extend existing functions to *old* types as well.

```
> (g+ "hello " "world.")
Error: "hello " is an illegal argument to +
  [condition type: TYPE-ERROR]
[1]
> (g+ #\a #\b)
Error: #\a is an illegal argument to +
  [condition type: TYPE-ERROR]
[2]
```

What should it mean to add two strings or two characters? It may make sense to
signal an error, as shown here. However, we might also like to interpret addition as
concatenation for strings or characters.

```
(defmethod g+ ((x string) (y string))
  (concatenate 'string x y))

(defmethod g+ ((x character) (y character))
  (format nil "~A~A" x y))

> (g+ "hello " "world.")
"hello world."

> (g+ #\a #\b)
"ab"
```

If the programmer uses `defmethod` to define a method for a function without previously creating the generic function with `defgeneric`, then `defmethod` will create
the function.

```
(defmethod nil+ ((x null) (y null))
  (format nil "This is really useless."))

> (nil+ nil nil)
"This is really useless."
```

Given this feature, `defmethod`, with no type information for its arguments, behaves
like `defun`.

```
(defmethod z (x y)
  (* x y))

> (z 2 3)
6
```

12.4   Multiple Methods

It is possible for more than one method to match a given set of arguments. Consider the following generic function `test-method`.

```
(defgeneric test-method (obj1 obj2)
  (:method ((obj1 integer) (obj2 integer))
           (test-func 'integer 'integer))
  (:method ((obj1 integer) (obj2 number))
           (test-func 'integer 'number))
  (:method ((obj1 number) (obj2 integer))
           (test-func 'number 'integer))
  (:method ((obj1 number) (obj2 number))
           (test-func 'number 'number))
  (:method (obj1 obj2) (test-func 'T 'T)))

(defun test-func (type1 type2)
  (format t "test-method called with types: ~A ~40T~A~%"
          type1 type2)
  (values))

> (test-method 1 2)
test-method called with types: INTEGER   INTEGER

> (test-method 1.0 2.0)
test-method called with types: NUMBER    NUMBER

> (test-method 'one 'two)
test-method called with types: T         T
```

Remember that the type `T` is true for any object. Presumably, the first invocation, with arguments (1 2), matched any of the methods given. In fact, the LISP function `compute-applicable-methods` gives a list of all methods that might apply for the given generic function and argument list.

```
> (compute-applicable-methods #'test-method '(1 2))
(#<STANDARD-METHOD TEST-METHOD (INTEGER INTEGER) @ #x11a9bd6>
 #<STANDARD-METHOD TEST-METHOD (INTEGER NUMBER) @ #x11a9946>
 #<STANDARD-METHOD TEST-METHOD (NUMBER INTEGER) @ #x11a96b6>
 #<STANDARD-METHOD TEST-METHOD (NUMBER NUMBER) @ #x11a9426>
 #<STANDARD-METHOD TEST-METHOD (T T) @ #x11a9196>)
```

We specify the `test-method` function with arguments of (1 2) and see that all the methods apply. The order in which the methods are listed is significant. This is not necessarily the order in which they were defined, but rather the precedence order for selecting methods. The ranking rule is straightforward:

1. Prefer more specific types, for example, INTEGER is more specific than NUMBER.

2. Prefer arguments in left-to-right order, for example, (INTEGER NUMBER) is preferred over (NUMBER INTEGER).

It is possible in LISP to have more than one matching method execute. Using the call-next-method function, the programmer can invoke the next method in the precedence ranking. We modify test-method to use call-next-method.

```
(defgeneric test-method2 (obj1 obj2)
  (:method ((obj1 integer) (obj2 integer))
          (test-func 'integer 'integer)
          (call-next-method))
  (:method ((obj1 integer) (obj2 number))
          (test-func 'integer 'number)
          (call-next-method))
  (:method ((obj1 number) (obj2 integer))
          (test-func 'number 'integer)
          (call-next-method))
  (:method ((obj1 number) (obj2 number))
          (test-func 'number 'number)
          (call-next-method))
  (:method (obj1 obj2) (test-func 'T 'T)))
```

We note there is no "next method" for the last method.

```
> (test-method2 1 2)
test-method called with types: INTEGER   INTEGER
test-method called with types: INTEGER   NUMBER
test-method called with types: NUMBER    INTEGER
test-method called with types: NUMBER    NUMBER
test-method called with types: T         T

> (test-method2 1.0 2.0)
test-method called with types: NUMBER    NUMBER
test-method called with types: T         T

> (test-method2 'one 'two)
test-method called with types: T         T
```

Using call-next-method, the programmer can generalize parts of her program to reflect the hierarchy of the types. call-next-method also has optional arguments, which can be passed to the next method in lieu of the original calling arguments.

In addition to invoking additional methods in type order, LISP programmers can have auxiliary methods invoked *before*, *after*, or *around* the primary method. The programmer may specify an auxiliary method with a *method-qualifier* keyword,

namely, :before, :after, and :around. The keyword is inserted either following
the :method keyword in defgeneric or after the method name in defmethod.

We create a method test-method3 which has primary methods, as well as
before and after auxiliary methods.

```
(defgeneric test-method3 (obj1 obj2)
;;  Primary methods.
  (:method ((obj1 integer) (obj2 integer))
          (test-func3 'primary 'integer 'integer))
  (:method ((obj1 integer) (obj2 number))
          (test-func3 'primary 'integer 'number))
  (:method ((obj1 number) (obj2 integer))
          (test-func3 'primary 'number 'integer))
  (:method ((obj1 number) (obj2 number))
          (test-func3 'primary 'number 'number))
  (:method (obj1 obj2) (test-func3 'primary 'T 'T))
;;  Before methods.
  (:method :before ((obj1 integer) (obj2 integer))
          (test-func3 'before 'integer 'integer))
  (:method :before ((obj1 integer) (obj2 number))
          (test-func3 'before 'integer 'number))
  (:method :before ((obj1 number) (obj2 integer))
          (test-func3 'before 'number 'integer))
  (:method :before ((obj1 number) (obj2 number))
          (test-func3 'before 'number 'number))
  (:method :before (obj1 obj2) (test-func3 'before 'T 'T))
;;  After methods.
  (:method :after ((obj1 integer) (obj2 integer))
          (test-func3 'after 'integer 'integer))
  (:method :after ((obj1 integer) (obj2 number))
          (test-func3 'after 'integer 'number))
  (:method :after ((obj1 number) (obj2 integer))
          (test-func3 'after 'number 'integer))
  (:method :after ((obj1 number) (obj2 number))
          (test-func3 'after 'number 'number))
  (:method :after (obj1 obj2) (test-func3 'after 'T 'T)))

(defun test-func3 (method-order type1 type2)
  (format t "test-method3 ~A called with types: ~A ~40T~A~%"
          method-order type1 type2)
  (values))
```

```
> (test-method3 1 2)
test-method3 BEFORE called with types: INTEGER  INTEGER
test-method3 BEFORE called with types: INTEGER  NUMBER
test-method3 BEFORE called with types: NUMBER  INTEGER
test-method3 BEFORE called with types: NUMBER  NUMBER
test-method3 BEFORE called with types: T  T
test-method3 PRIMARY called with types: INTEGER  INTEGER
test-method3 AFTER called with types: T  T
test-method3 AFTER called with types: NUMBER  NUMBER
test-method3 AFTER called with types: NUMBER  INTEGER
test-method3 AFTER called with types: INTEGER  NUMBER
test-method3 AFTER called with types: INTEGER  INTEGER

> (test-method3 'one 'two)
test-method3 BEFORE called with types: T  T
test-method3 PRIMARY called with types: T  T
test-method3 AFTER called with types: T  T
```

All the before methods are called, in order of most specific to most general. Only the most specific primary method gets called. However, using the function `call-next-method`, the programmer could choose to invoke additional primary methods. All the after methods are called, but in order of most general to most specific.

We next add an *around* method to the existing `test-method3` definition.

```
(defmethod test-method3 :around ((obj1 number) (obj2 number))
  (test-func3 'around 'number 'number))

> (test-method3 1 2)
test-method3 AROUND called with types: NUMBER  NUMBER
```

We note that around methods supersede all before, after, and primary methods. If there are several around methods, the most specific applies.

```
(defmethod test-method3 :around ((obj1 integer) (obj2 integer))
  (test-func3 'around 'integer 'integer)
  (call-next-method))

> (test-method3 1 2)
test-method3 AROUND called with types: INTEGER  INTEGER
test-method3 AROUND called with types: NUMBER  NUMBER
```

We defined a second, more specific around method, using `call-next-method` to trigger the original around method.

We next redefine the original around method to include `call-next-method`.

```
(defmethod test-method3 :around ((obj1 number) (obj2 number))
  (test-func3 'around 'number 'number)
  (call-next-method))
```

```
> (test-method3 1 2)
test-method3 AROUND called with types: INTEGER   INTEGER
test-method3 AROUND called with types: NUMBER   NUMBER
test-method3 BEFORE called with types: INTEGER  INTEGER
test-method3 BEFORE called with types: INTEGER  NUMBER
test-method3 BEFORE called with types: NUMBER   INTEGER
test-method3 BEFORE called with types: NUMBER   NUMBER
test-method3 BEFORE called with types: T   T
test-method3 PRIMARY called with types: INTEGER   INTEGER
test-method3 AFTER called with types: T   T
test-method3 AFTER called with types: NUMBER   NUMBER
test-method3 AFTER called with types: NUMBER   INTEGER
test-method3 AFTER called with types: INTEGER   NUMBER
test-method3 AFTER called with types: INTEGER   INTEGER
```

All the methods get called.

There are several ways of causing errors when using generic functions. First, you may have failed to define a method with the appropriate parameter types. Second, you might invoke `call-next-method` when there is no next method. LISP provides ways to detect and address these situations gracefully. Consider the following generic function.

```
(defgeneric test-method4 (obj1 obj2)
  (:method ((obj1 integer) (obj2 integer))
           (test-func4 'primary 'integer 'integer)))
```

```
(defun test-func4 (method-order type1 type2)
  (format t "test-method4 ~A called with types: ~A ~40T~A~%"
           method-order type1 type2)
  (values))
> (test-method4 1 2)
test-method4 PRIMARY called with types: INTEGER   INTEGER
```

```
> (test-method4 1.0 2.0)
Error: No methods applicable for generic function
       #<STANDARD-GENERIC-FUNCTION TEST-METHOD4 @ #x1069c9e> with args
       (1.0 2.0) of classes (FLOAT FLOAT)
  [condition type: PROGRAM-ERROR]
```

When there are no applicable methods, the function chokes. One solution is to define a primary method for arguments of type T. Another approach is to redefine the generic function `no-applicable-method`, which is called under these circumstances.

```
(defmethod no-applicable-method (func &rest args)
  (format t "~%No method for function: ~S with arguments: ~S~%"
          func args)
  (values))
```

```
> (test-method4 1.0 2.0)
```

```
No method for function: #<STANDARD-GENERIC-FUNCTION TEST-METHOD4 @
                         #x1069c9e> with arguments: (1.0 2.0)
```

Some implementations will warn the programmer who attempts to define `no-applicable-method`. We now choose to define the generic method that invokes `call-next-method`. We once again have a problem, namely, there is no next method.   ⇐ ∞

```
(defmethod test-method4 ((obj1 t) (obj2 t))
  (test-func4 'primary (type-of obj1) (type-of obj2))
  (call-next-method))
```

```
> (test-method4 1.0 2.0)
test-method4 PRIMARY called with types: SINGLE-FLOAT  SINGLE-FLOAT
Error: No next method for method
       #<STANDARD-METHOD TEST-METHOD4 (T T) @ #x1077d7e> of generic
       function #<STANDARD-GENERIC-FUNCTION TEST-METHOD4 @ #x1069c9e>
       with args (1.0 2.0)
  [condition type: PROGRAM-ERROR]
```

We have two solutions. First, we can redefine the generic function `no-next-method`. The first argument for `no-next-method` is of type `standard-generic-function`, and the second argument is of type `standard-method`.

```
(defmethod no-next-method
  ((func standard-generic-function) (meth standard-method) &rest args)
  (format t "~%No next method for function: ~%  ~S
called from method: ~%  ~S
with arguments: ~S~%"
          func meth args)
  (values))
```

```
> (test-method4 1.0 2.0)
test-method4 PRIMARY called with types: SINGLE-FLOAT  SINGLE-FLOAT

No next method for function:
  #<STANDARD-GENERIC-FUNCTION TEST-METHOD4 @ #x1069c9e>
called from method:
  #<STANDARD-METHOD TEST-METHOD4 (T T) @ #x106d626>
with arguments: (1.0 2.0)
```

∞ ⇒   Some implementations will warn the programmer who attempts to define
no-next-method. Second, we can use the predicate next-method-p to check for
the existence of a next method.

```
(defmethod test-method4 ((obj1 t) (obj2 t))
  (test-func4 'primary 't 't)
  (if (next-method-p)
      (call-next-method)))

(defmethod test-method4 ((obj1 symbol) (obj2 symbol))
  (test-func4 'primary 'symbol 'symbol)
  (if (next-method-p)
      (call-next-method)))

> (test-method4 1.0 2.0)
test-method4 PRIMARY called with types: T  T
NIL

> (test-method4 'one 'two)
test-method4 PRIMARY called with types: SYMBOL  SYMBOL
test-method4 PRIMARY called with types: T  T
NIL
```

The predicate next-method-p is the recommended way to control multiple method
calls.

We conclude with one last trick. Instead of specifying a particular *type* for
the method parameters, the programmer can give a particular *value*, using the eql
specification demonstrated below.

```
(defgeneric test-method5 (obj1 obj2)
  (:method ((obj1 integer) (obj2 integer))
           (+ obj1 obj2))
  (:method ((obj1 (eql 3)) (obj2 (eql 4)))
           'seven))
```

```
> (test-method5 1 2)
3

> (test-method5 3 4)
SEVEN

> (test-method5 4 3)
7
```

The second method for **test-method5** is specific to the arguments 3 and 4, in that order.

12.5   Advanced Subjects

The advanced topics for the current chapter are as follows.

- Using Lists as Structures

- Slot Options

- Other **defgeneric** Options

- Method Combination

- Dates and Times

- File System Information

12.5.1   Using Lists as Structures

At the beginning of this chapter, we promoted the use of structures as an alternative to lists, which would separate an object's reference from its representation. However, there may be times when a programmer still wants to use a list representation but wishes to take advantage of some of the other features of **defstruct**. The programmer then can use the **:type** option with **defstruct**. Here is an example.

```
(defstruct (duet (:type list))
  primo
  secundo)

> (setf x (make-duet :primo 'abbott :secundo 'costello))
(ABBOTT COSTELLO)

> x
(ABBOTT COSTELLO)
```

```
> (car x)
ABBOTT

> (duet-primo x)
ABBOTT

> (cadr x)
COSTELLO

> (duet-secundo x)
COSTELLO

> (consp x)
T

> (setf y (copy-duet x))
(ABBOTT COSTELLO)

> (duet-p x)
Error: attempt to call 'DUET-P' which is an undefined function.
   [condition type: UNDEFINED-FUNCTION]
```

Using the :type option, we defined the structure duet to be a list. (It is also possible to specify a vector type, discussed in chapter 14.) We note that car and cadr work just as well as duet-primo and duet-secundo. Also, the predicate consp and the copy function copy-duet both work, while there is no predicate duet-p!

Furthermore, other lists also work with the duet accessors.

```
> (setf y '(martin lewis))
(MARTIN LEWIS)

> (duet-primo y)
MARTIN

> (duet-secundo y)
LEWIS

> (setf (duet-primo y) 'clark)
CLARK

> y
(CLARK LEWIS)
```

If we wish to discriminate between duets and other lists, we can use the :named option.

```
(defstruct (duet2 (:type list) :named)
  primo
  secundo)

> (setf x2 (make-duet2 :primo 'abbott :secundo 'costello))
(DUET2 ABBOTT COSTELLO)

> (duet2-primo x2)
ABBOTT

> (duet2-p x2)
T

> (duet2-p '(duet2 1 2 3 4))
T
```

This is a little better. We get a predicate duet2-p this time and see that the initial slot is set to duet2. However, any list with a car of duet2 satisfies this predicate.

The bottom line is that structures defined by the :type option are not really LISP *structures*. Rather, they are *list* structures. The structure name cannot be used for method definitions or type specification. These structures are just lists. However, lists are a fine and wonderful data type. Using defstruct to create lists may be just what some programmers desire.

One additional feature associated with the :type option is :initial-offset, which allows the programmer to allocate a number of unspecified initial slots with the list structure.

```
(defstruct (duet3 (:type list) (:initial-offset 3))
  primo
  secundo)

> (setf z (make-duet3 :primo 'tom :secundo 'huck))
(NIL NIL NIL TOM HUCK)

> (duet3-secundo z)
HUCK
> (setf (car z) 'twain-boys)
TWAIN-BOYS

> z
(TWAIN-BOYS NIL NIL TOM HUCK)
```

These initial slots can be accessed with the normal list functions.

12.5.2   Slot Options

Two additional options are associated with the slots of a structure: :type and
:read-only.

The programmer can use the :type option to indicate the type of data associated with the given slot. Here, we create a bank account structure requiring that
the bank name be a symbol and the balance be of type number.

```
(defstruct account
  (name nil :type symbol)
  (balance 0 :type number))

> (setf a (make-account))
#S(ACCOUNT :NAME NIL :BALANCE 0)

> (setf (account-name a) "Checking")
"Checking"

> (account-name a)
"Checking"

> (setf (account-balance a) 'overdrawn)
OVERDRAWN

> a
#S(ACCOUNT :NAME "Checking" :BALANCE OVERDRAWN)
```

What is important to note is that our type specifications did not make a nickel's
worth of difference. LISP ignored them. In fact, the language specification indicates
∞ ⇒   that implementations are not obligated to check for slot type data errors. Even if
your dialect does check for slot type errors, you should realize that depending on
this feature means that your code may not be portable to other dialects.

The second slot option is :read-only, which fortunately is not implementation dependent. Here is an example.

```
(defstruct account2
  (name nil :read-only t)
  (balance 0))

> (setf a2 (make-account2 :name 'BCCI))
#S(ACCOUNT2 :NAME BCCI :BALANCE 0)

> (setf (account2-balance a2) 1000000)
1000000
```

```
> (account2-name a2)
BCCI

> (setf (account2-name a2) 'citibank)
Error: (SETF ACCOUNT2-NAME) does not have a function definition
```

If the `:read-only` slot option is followed by a non-NIL value, then the given slot may not be changed after the initial constructor call. Here we set the name to BCCI in the call to `make-account2`. Our subsequent attempt to change the value results in an error.

12.5.3   Other defgeneric Options

As mentioned above, `defgeneric` has a number of options that can appear between the lambda list and the method descriptions as individual lists. Here is a syntactic description of `defgeneric`.

```
(defgeneric function-name lambda-list
    [[ option | {method-description}* ]])

function-name ::= {symbol | (setf symbol)}

lambda-list ::= ( {var}*
                  [&optional {var | (var)}*]
                  [&rest var]
                  [&key {keyword-parameter}* [&allow-other-keys]])

keyword-parameter ::= var | ({var | (keyword var)})

option ::= (:argument-precedence-order {parameter-name}*)
    | (declare {declaration}+)
    | (:documentation string)
    | (:method-combination symbol {arg}*)
    | (:generic-function-class class-name)
    | (:method-class class-name)

method-description ::=
    (:method {method-qualifier}*
             specialize-lambda-list
             [[ {declaration}* | documentation ]]
             {form}*)
```

```
specialized-lambda-list ::=
    ( {var | (var parameter-specializer-name)}*
    [&optional {var | (var [initform [supplied-p]])}*
    [&rest var]
    [&key {specialized-keyword-parameter}* [&allow-other-keys]]
    [&aux {var | (var [initform])}*])

specialized-keyword-parameter ::=
    var | ( {var | (keyword var)} [initform [supplied-p]])

parameter-specializer-name ::= symbol | (eql eql-specializer-form)
```

A lot is going on here. We first note that the function-name component may be
a setf function. Below, we create a person structure and define a generic setf
form for the name. If the function is given a symbol argument, it is converted to a
capitalized string.

```
(defstruct person name age)

(defgeneric (setf name) (val pers)
  (:method ((val symbol) (pers person))
           (setf (person-name pers)
                 (string-capitalize (string val))))
  (:method (val (pers person))
           (setf (person-name pers) val)))

> (setf p (make-person :name "Joe" :age 20))
#S(PERSON :NAME "Joe" :AGE 20)

> (setf (name p) "Mary")
"Mary"

> (setf (name p) 'george)
"George"

> p
#S(PERSON :NAME "George" :AGE 20)

> (fdefinition '(setf name))
#<STANDARD-GENERIC-FUNCTION (SETF NAME) @ #x10792de>
```

Second, we observe that the lambda list does not permit the &aux keyword and
that the &optional variables cannot have default values.

Third, the lambda list of each method must be congruent with the main lambda list, although the method lambda lists may specify optional defaults and the &aux keyword. Below, the generic function bad has three methods, each of which violates the lambda list congruence rule. On this account, the good function is aptly named.

```
(defgeneric bad (a &optional b &rest c)                              ⇐ Bad Idea
  (:method ((a integer) b c) (+ a b))
  (:method ((a string)  &optional b) (concatenate 'string a b))
  (:method ((a symbol)  &rest c) (list a b)))

(defgeneric good (a &optional b &rest c)
  (:method ((a integer) &optional (b 1) &rest c) (+ a b))
  (:method ((a string) &optional (b "one") &rest c)
           (concatenate 'string a b))
  (:method ((a symbol) &optional (b 'one) &rest c) (list a b))
  (:method ((a cons) &optional (b 'one) &rest c &aux (d (cdr a)))
           (list d b)))
```

Fourth, the defgeneric options are as follows.

- (:argument-precedence-order {parameter-name}+) — A keyword followed by the required parameters to the function, specifying the precedence order for method selection. The default is the left-to-right order given in the parameter list.

- (declare (optimize (*qual val*)) — A declaration to optimize the method selection process, where *qual* is either speed or space or both, and *val* is a value appropriate to the given quality. In section 16.4, we discuss the role of declaration in compilation. Note that no other declarations are specified for this option and that this optimize declaration does not affect the performance of the methods themselves, just the selection process. Implementations may add other declarations.   ⇐ ∞

- (:documentation string) — A keyword followed by the documentation string for the generic function.

- (:method-combination symbol {arg}*) — A keyword followed by a symbol specifying the type of method combination for this generic function. Types of method combination are defined with define-method-combination, which is discussed in the next section.

- (:generic-function-class class-name) — A keyword followed by a symbol specifying the class of this generic function. By default, new generic functions belong to the class standard-generic-function. We discuss classes in the next chapter.

- (:method-class class-name) – A keyword followed by a symbol specifying the class of this function's methods. By default, methods belong to the standard-method class. We discuss classes in the next chapter.

It is an error for an option to appear more than once. Here is a limited example. We will explore the other options in more detail later.

```
(defgeneric test-method4 (obj1 obj2)
  (:documentation
      "A test method to demonstrate defgeneric options.")
  (:method ((obj1 number) obj2) (test-func 'number 'T))
  (:method (obj1 (obj2 number)) (test-func 'T 'number))
  (:method (obj1 obj2) (test-func 'T 'T)))

(defgeneric test-method5 (obj1 obj2)
  (:argument-precedence-order obj2 obj1)
  (:documentation
      "A second test method to demonstrate defgeneric options.")
  (:method ((obj1 number) obj2) (test-func 'number 'T))
  (:method (obj1 (obj2 number)) (test-func 'T 'number))
  (:method (obj1 obj2) (test-func 'T 'T)))

(defun test-func (type1 type2)
  (format t "test-method called with types: ~A ~40T~A~%"
          type1 type2)
  (values))

> (documentation #'test-method4 'function)
"A test method to demonstrate defgeneric options."

> (documentation #'test-method5 'function)
"A second test method to demonstrate defgeneric options."

> (test-method4 1 2)
test-method called with types: NUMBER    T

> (test-method5 1 2)
test-method called with types: T              NUMBER
```

∞ ⇒ The first three LISP implementations on which we ran this code did not produce the correct result for the last expression. One signalled a warning that it had not implemented the :argument-precedence-order option. The others used the NUMBER/T method instead of the T/NUMBER method. The correct implementation was Macintosh Common LISP, version 2.0. Caveat programmer.

+	and	append
list	max	min
nconc	or	progn

Table 12.1: Common Method Combination Options

12.5.4 Method Combination

There are four standard types of method combination for generic functions, which are executed in the following order.

1. Around methods, using the keyword `:around`. If present, LISP executes the most specific around method, including `call-next-method` for additional methods, and then returns.

2. Before methods, using the keyword `:before`. All before methods are executed, starting with the most specific.

3. Primary methods (no keyword). The most specific primary method is executed, including `call-next-method` for additional primary methods.

4. After methods, using the keyword `:after`. All after methods are executed, starting with the least specific.

Some implementations provide additional types of method combination, such as listed in table 12.1. These methods use the operator of the same name to collect the results of the applicable methods. Here are examples using and, or, and +.

```lisp
(defgeneric test-method-and (obj1 obj2)
  (:method-combination and)
  (:method and ((obj1 integer) (obj2 integer))
           (test-func6 'integer 'integer obj1))
  (:method and ((obj1 integer) (obj2 number))
           (test-func6 'integer 'number obj1))
  (:method and ((obj1 number) (obj2 integer))
           (test-func6 'number 'integer obj1))
  (:method and ((obj1 number) (obj2 number))
           (test-func6 'number 'number obj1))
  (:method and (obj1 obj2) (test-func6 'T 'T obj1)))

(defun test-func6 (type1 type2 obj)
  (format t "test-method called with types: ~A ~40T~A~%"
          type1 type2)
  obj)
```

```
(defgeneric test-method-or (obj1 obj2)
  (:method-combination or)
  (:method or ((obj1 integer) (obj2 integer))
          (test-func6 'integer 'integer obj1))
  (:method or ((obj1 integer) (obj2 number))
          (test-func6 'integer 'number obj1))
  (:method or ((obj1 number) (obj2 integer))
          (test-func6 'number 'integer obj1))
  (:method or ((obj1 number) (obj2 number))
          (test-func6 'number 'number obj1))
  (:method or (obj1 obj2) (test-func6 'T 'T obj1)))

(defgeneric test-method-+ (obj1 obj2)
  (:method-combination +)
  (:method + ((obj1 integer) (obj2 integer))
          (test-func6 'integer 'integer obj1))
  (:method + ((obj1 integer) (obj2 number))
          (test-func6 'integer 'number obj1))
  (:method + ((obj1 number) (obj2 integer))
          (test-func6 'number 'integer obj1))
  (:method + ((obj1 number) (obj2 number))
          (test-func6 'number 'number obj1))
  (:method + (obj1 obj2) (test-func6 'T 'T obj1)))

> (test-method-and 1 2)
test-method called with types: INTEGER   INTEGER
test-method called with types: INTEGER   NUMBER
test-method called with types: NUMBER    INTEGER
test-method called with types: NUMBER    NUMBER
test-method called with types: T         T
1

> (test-method-and nil 1)
test-method called with types: T         T
NIL

> (test-method-or 1 2)
test-method called with types: INTEGER   INTEGER
1

> (test-method-or nil 1)
test-method called with types: T         T
NIL
```

```
> (test-method-+ 1 2)
test-method called with types: INTEGER   INTEGER
test-method called with types: INTEGER   NUMBER
test-method called with types: NUMBER    INTEGER
test-method called with types: NUMBER    NUMBER
test-method called with types: T         T
5

> (test-method-+ 2 1)
test-method called with types: INTEGER   INTEGER
test-method called with types: INTEGER   NUMBER
test-method called with types: NUMBER    INTEGER
test-method called with types: NUMBER    NUMBER
test-method called with types: T         T
10

> (test-method-+ 1 nil)
test-method called with types: T         T
1

> (test-method-+ nil 1)
test-method called with types: T         T
NIL
```

These methods apply the respective and, or, and + operators on the list of calls to
the applicable methods. The other method combination types listed in table 12.1
have similar behavior.

If your implementation does not support these method combination types, it
is easy enough to define them using the macro define-method-combination.

```
(define-method-combination name [:documentation string]
        [:indentity-with-one-argument boolean]
        [:operator operator])
```

By convention, the name is the same symbol as the operator. The option
:identity-with-one-argument signals the opportunity to optimize the call when
there is only one argument. For example, each of the following forms is equivalent
to x.

```
(+ x)
(min x)
(max x)
(progn x)
(and x)
(or x)
```

We can define all of the method combination types from table 12.1 as follows.

```
(define-method-combination +
  :operator + :identity-with-one-argument t)

(define-method-combination and
  :operator and :identity-with-one-argument t)

(define-method-combination append
  :operator append :identity-with-one-argument nil)

(define-method-combination list
  :operator list :identity-with-one-argument nil)

(define-method-combination max
  :operator max :identity-with-one-argument t)

(define-method-combination min
  :operator min :identity-with-one-argument t)

(define-method-combination nconc
  :operator nconc :identity-with-one-argument nil)

(define-method-combination or
  :operator or :identity-with-one-argument t)

(define-method-combination progn
  :operator progn :identity-with-one-argument t)
```

We can create a new method combination type for strings, which will concatenate the results.

```
(define-method-combination string
  :operator string-append :identity-with-one-argument t)

(defun string-append (&rest arg)
  (if (cdr arg)
      (format nil "~A~A"
              (car arg)
              (apply #'string-append (cdr arg)))
      (car arg)))
```

```
(defgeneric test-method-string (obj1 obj2)
  (:method-combination string)
  (:method string ((obj1 integer) (obj2 integer))
          (test-func7 'integer 'integer obj1))
  (:method string ((obj1 integer) (obj2 number))
          (test-func7 'integer 'number obj1))
  (:method string ((obj1 number) (obj2 integer))
          (test-func7 'number 'integer obj1))
  (:method string ((obj1 number) (obj2 number))
          (test-func7 'number 'number obj1))
  (:method string (obj1 obj2) (test-func7 'T 'T obj1)))

(defun test-func7 (type1 type2 obj)
  (format t "test-method called with types: ~A ~40T~A~%"
          type1 type2)
  obj)

> (test-method-string 1 2)
test-method called with types: INTEGER   INTEGER
test-method called with types: INTEGER   NUMBER
test-method called with types: NUMBER    INTEGER
test-method called with types: NUMBER    NUMBER
test-method called with types: T         T
"11111"

> (test-method-string 1.0 2.0)
test-method called with types: NUMBER    NUMBER
test-method called with types: T         T
"1.01.0"
```

define-method-combination also comes in a more general, harder-to-understand
version, with the following syntax.

```
(define-method-combination name lambda-list
  ({method-group-specifier}*)
  [(:arguments . lambda-list)]
  [(:generic-function generic-function-symbol)]
  [[ {declaration}* | doc-string]]
  {form}*)
```

```
method-group-specifier ::=
  (variable { { qualifier-pattern}+ | predicate}
   [:description format-string]
   [:order order]
   [:required boolean])
```

We can redefine the or method combination, using the long form of the syntax (from [Steele Jr., 1990, page 835]).

```
(define-method-combination or ()
  ((methods (or)))
  `(or ,@(mapcar #'(lambda (method)
                    `(call-method ,method ()))
                 methods)))
```

Here, the method group specifier is (methods (or)), indicating that the variable methods is bound to the list of methods matching the qualifier pattern (or).

The qualifier pattern must be a list or *. If the qualifier pattern is the empty list, it matches any unqualified method. A pattern of * matches all methods, and a regular list matches those methods that have the same method lists, using the * character to match any given item in the list.

The macro call-method takes two arguments: a method and a list of the next available methods. Each invocation of call-macro redefines call-next-method and next-method-p. call-method may appear only in the context of a method combination definition.

12.5.5   Dates and Times

We gave examples in this chapter of structures for dates and times. Common LISP already knows about dates and times. In fact, it has three ways of representing dates and times: universal time, decoded time, and internal time. Universal and internal time can be used to represent both absolute times (a specific time) and relative times (a period of time).

Universal time is given as a non-negative integer representing the number of seconds that have lapsed since midnight, January 1, 1900. That date is time 0. Each day has exactly $86,400$ seconds ($60 * 60 * 24$). The function get-universal-time returns the current time value.

```
> (get-universal-time)
3075381748
```

```
> (get-universal-time)        ; Two seconds later.
3075381750
```

```
> (get-universal-time)        ;  Three seconds later.
3075381753
```

To make sense of this number, we need to decode universal time with the appropriately named function.

```
> (decode-universal-time 3075381748)
28
42
12
15
6
1997
6
T
5
```

The function `decode-universal-time` returns the following multiple values:

- *second* — An integer between 0 and 59, inclusive

- *minute* — An integer between 0 and 59, inclusive

- *hour* — An integer between 0 and 23, inclusive

- *date* — An integer between 1 and 31, inclusive, depending on the month, of course

- *month* — An integer between 1 and 12, inclusive, where January is 1 and December is 12

- *year* — An integer between 0 and 99, inclusive, where the century is assumed to be the one within 50 years of the current date

- *day-of-week* — An integer between 0 and 6, inclusive, where Monday is 0 and Sunday is 6

- *daylight-saving-time-p* — A flag, if non-NIL, indicating that the time reflects daylight saving time

- *time-zone* — A number from −24 to 24, specifying the number of hours west of Greenwich Mean Time

In the above example, the time is 12:42:28 pm, on June 15, 1997, a Sunday, Eastern Daylight Time. `decode-universal-time` has an optional argument specifying a time zone, which defaults to the current time zone.

```
> (decode-universal-time 3075381748 6)
28
42
10
15
6
1997
6
NIL
6
```

The function `get-decoded-time` is equivalent to

```
(decode-universal-time (get-universal-time))
```

```
> (get-decoded-time)
16
46
12
15
6
1997
6
T
5
```

The programmer can also go the other direction, creating a universal time from a decoded time using the function `encode-universal-time`. The arguments to `encode-universal-time` are second, minute, hour, date, month, year, and an optional time-zone specification.

```
> (encode-universal-time 28 42 12 15 6 1997 5)
3075385348
```

Universal time and decoded time are useful for events in the real world. However, inside the computer, there is another real world in which we need to measure events in time units smaller than a second. Common LISP provides *internal time*.

∞ ⇒   The internal time units are implementation dependent and are specified by the constant `internal-time-units-per-second`. The `get-internal-real-time` function returns the current internal time.

```
> internal-time-units-per-second
1000
```

```
> (get-internal-real-time)
76475374530
```

```
> (get-internal-real-time)
76475377683
```

In this implementation, internal time is measured in milliseconds. We define a function `sleep-check`, which gets the internal time before and after running the `sleep` function, which waits a given number of seconds.

```
(defun sleep-check (n)
  (let ((start (get-internal-real-time)))
    (sleep n)
    (values (- (get-internal-real-time) start)
            (get-internal-run-time))))
```

```
> (sleep-check 2)
2006
1266
```

```
> (sleep-check 3)
3008
1266
```

```
> (sleep-check 4)
4005
1283
```

There is a modest overhead of a few milliseconds for `sleep-check`. The function `get-internal-run-time` returns the total CPU time spent since the start of the LISP session, measured in internal time units. The detailed interpretation of this number will vary with implementations. Repeated calls to `get-internal-run-time` ⇐ ∞ should result in a monotonically increasing series.

12.5.6   File System Information

Now that we know about LISP's date conventions, we can access more information about the file system.

LISP allows us to rename and delete files directly, using `rename-file` and `delete-file`. We have previously used `probe-file` to verify the existence of a given file. The `directory` function returns a list of the files in the given pathname.

```
> (probe-file "test.lisp")      ;  Does the file exist?
#p"/server/u18/homes.ai/slade/a/mss/l/test.lisp"
```

```
> (rename-file "test.lisp" "test2.lisp")
#p"/server/u18/homes.ai/slade/a/mss/l/test2.lisp"
#p"/server/u18/homes.ai/slade/a/mss/l/test.lisp"
#p"/server/u18/homes.ai/slade/a/mss/l/test2.lisp"

> (probe-file "test.lisp")
NIL

> (probe-file "test2.lisp")
#p"/server/u18/homes.ai/slade/a/mss/l/test2.lisp"

> (delete-file "test2.lisp")
T

> (probe-file "test2.lisp")
NIL

> (directory ".")
(#p"./l_index.aux" #p"./lll.ind" #p"./l.ps" #p"./log.lisp"
#p"./index.sed" #p"./index" #p"./l_index.tex" #p"./Makefile"
#p"./ll.aux" #p"./ll.idx" ...)
```

LISP permits us to get more information about a file, including its author and date of last modification, using the functions file-author and file-write-date. The latter function returns a date in universal time format.

```
> (with-open-file (out "test1.lisp" :direction :output)
     (print "hello" out))
"hello"

> (with-open-file (out "test2.lisp" :direction :output)
     (print "goodbye" out))
"goodbye"

> (file-author "test1.lisp")
"slade"

> (file-author "test2.lisp")
"slade"

> (setf fwd1 (file-write-date "test1.lisp"))
2994699338
```

```
> (setf fwd2 (file-write-date "test2.lisp"))
2994699385

> (< fwd1 fwd2)
T

> (decode-universal-time fwd1 5)
38              ;  38 seconds
55              ;  55 minutes
15              ;  3 p.m.
24              ;  The 24th
11              ;  of November
1994            ;  1994
3               ;  Thursday
NIL             ;  Not daylight saving.
5               ;  Eastern time zone.
```

We can write a predicate that tells us if one file is newer than another file.

```
(defun newer-file-p (file1 file2)
  (let ((fwd1 (file-write-date file1))
        (fwd2 (file-write-date file2)))
    (> fwd1 fwd2)))

> (newer-file-p "test1.lisp" "test2.lisp")
NIL

> (newer-file-p "test2.lisp" "test1.lisp")
T
```

In chapter 16, we discuss compilation, which converts a LISP source code file into a more efficient object code file. Whenever a programmer makes changes to the source code, she should recompile the source code to produce a new object file. Here is a function that informs the programmer when she needs to recompile a file. We assume that source files have an extension of .lisp and that object files end in .fasl.

```
(defun recompile-p (basefilename)
  (let ((source (format nil "~A.lisp" basefilename))
        (object (format nil "~A.fasl" basefilename)))
    (cond ((not (probe-file source))
           (error "recompile-p: source file does not exist"))
          ((not (probe-file object))
           (error "recompile-p: object file does not exist"))
          (T
           (> (file-write-date source)
              (file-write-date object)))))))
```

```
> (recompile-p "foo")
Error: recompile-p: source file does not exist
[1]
> (recompile-p "test1")
Error: recompile-p: object file does not exist
[2]
> (recompile-p "trtest")          ; trtest.fasl is up to date.
NIL
```

LISP provides access to additional information about the implementation, the site, and the particular machine on which it is running. The global variable *features* provides a list of the specific features for the implementation. The format directives #+ and #-, discussed in section 7.8.2, made use of this information. Additional ∞ ⇒ functions provide further information. The format and values returned by these functions are implementation dependent.

```
> *features*
(:COMPOSER-V2.0 :COMPOSER :CW-MOTIF :CW-X-V2 :CW-X :CLX-MIT-R5
 :CLX-MIT-R4 :XLIB :CLX :HAS-RCSNOTE  ...)
```

```
> (length *features*)
33
```

```
> (lisp-implementation-type)         ; Type of implementation.
"Allegro CL"
```

```
> (lisp-implementation-version)      ; Version number.
"4.1 [SPARC; R1] (4/7/92 13:06)"
```

```
> (long-site-name)                   ; The name of the site.
"austria"
```

```
> (short-site-name)                  ; Possibly shorter name.
"austria"
```

```
> (machine-instance)          ; Machine serial number.
"id: #x5542efd4"

> (machine-type)              ; Generic machine name.
"SPARC"

> (machine-version)           ; Version not specified.
""

> (software-type)             ; Supporting software or OS.
"SunOS"

> (software-version)          ; Version of software.
""
```

As seen from these examples, the programmer should not write code that assumes meaningful values for the above functions.

12.6 Exercises

12.6.1 Sorting Teams [4*]

Modify the `msort` routine from exercise 6.8.3 so that it will sort the baseball teams appropriately in the `print-standings` function defined above.

12.6.2 Generic Sorts [6*]

It probably makes more sense for the `inorderp` function to be a generic function, that behaves differently for different types of data. The beneficial result is that `msort` does not need to be changed when sorting lists of various data types.

```
> (msort '(4 2 5 3 4))
(2 3 4 4 5)

> (msort '(#\w #\b #\t #\p))
(#\b #\p #\t #\w)

> (msort '("one" "two" "three" "four" "five"))
("five" "four" "one" "three" "two")

> (msort '(one two three four five))
(FIVE FOUR ONE THREE TWO)
```

```
> (msort '((1 2 3) (3 4 5) (2 3 4)))
((1 2 3) (2 3 4) (3 4 5))
```

Define inorderp as a generic function that handles a variety of data types, including cons, number, symbol, string, character, and team.

12.6.3 Generic reveal-struct [5*]

We defined a function reveal-date that prints out a date's values as a list. Define a generic function reveal-struct that does the same thing for a variety of data structures, including my-date, my-time, team, and game, as shown here.

```
> (reveal-struct (make-my-date :year 1999 :month 5 :day 23))
(23 5 1999)

> (reveal-struct (make-time :seconds 34))
(0 0 34)

> (reveal-struct (make-team :name 'mets :won 1 :lost 23))
(METS 1 23 NIL NIL)

> (reveal-struct (make-game :visitor 'mars))
(NIL BULLDOGS MARS NIL NIL)

> (reveal-struct (make-game :visitor 'mars :date (make-my-date
    :year 1996 :month 8 :day 13)))
((13 8 1996) BULLDOGS MARS NIL NIL)
```

Note that reveal-struct is recursive.

12.6.4 Score Updates [5*]

Write a function final-score that takes three arguments: a game structure, the final home team score, and the final score for the visitor. The function then posts the scores in the game structure and also updates the team standings as appropriate. Here is an example.

```
> (defvar new-game (make-game :home bulldogs :visitor crimson
    :date (make-my-date :year 1996 :month 5 :day 2)
    :score (make-score :home 15 :visitor 3)))
NEW-GAME

> (reveal-struct new-game)
((2 5 1996) (BULLDOGS 12 4 NIL NIL) (CRIMSON 8 8 NIL NIL)
  (15 3) NIL)
```

```
> (print-standings *league*)        ;  The old standings.
```

```
Team        Won Lost Average Games Behind
BULLDOGS    12   4    750    0
TIGERS       9   6    600    5/2
CRIMSON      8   8    500    4
BEARS        7  12    368    13/2
LIONS        4  14    222    9
```

```
> (final-score new-game 15 3)
END-OF-UPDATE
```

```
> (print-standings *league*)          ;  The new standings.
```

```
Team        Won Lost Average Games Behind
BULLDOGS    13   4    764    0
TIGERS       9   6    600    3
CRIMSON      8   9    470    5
BEARS        7  12    368    7
LIONS        4  14    222    19/2
```

Note that the contents of the game structure include the `team` structures for the home and `visitor` components, instead of simply the names of the teams.

12.6.5 Person Structures [4]

Exercises 3.14.8 and 3.14.9 used association lists and property lists to implement a simple database of facts about people. Write the `make-person` functions again, using structures.

12.6.6 Structured Guessing Game [7]

In section 9.11, we created a general program for binary guessing games. The underlying data representation for the tree of information was property lists.

Rewrite the program, using structures instead of property lists throughout. Note that this exercise will require developing a method for writing structures to a file in a way that can be loaded back into the LISP interpreter.

12.6.7 List Addition [3*]

Extend the definition of the generic addition function `g+` to handle list addition, as demonstrated here.

```
> (g+ '(1 2 3) '(4 5 6))
(1 2 3 4 5 6)
```

12.6.8   &rest Addition [6*]

Our generic addition operator g+ was marvelous and all that, but it was nevertheless slightly deficient. In particular, it could not handle more than (or fewer than) two arguments.

Rewrite g+ to correct for this shortcoming.

```
> (g+ 1 2 3 4 5)
15

> x2
#S(MY-TIME :HOURS 0 :MINUTES 30 :SECONDS 0)

> (g+ x2 x2 x2 x2 x2)
#S(MY-TIME :HOURS 2 :MINUTES 30 :SECONDS 0)

> (g+ x2 37 x2)
#S(MY-TIME :HOURS 1 :MINUTES 0 :SECONDS 37)

> (G+ 'one 'two 'three)
"ONETWOTHREE"

> (g+ #\a #\b #\c #\d)
"abcd"

> (g+ "1" "2" "3" "4")
"1234"
```

You may assume that g+ will have at least one argument and that the arguments will all be of the same type, with the exception of times. However, the first argument will be a time instance if any argument is a time instance.

For extra credit, have your generic function handle mixtures of symbols, strings, and characters.

```
> (g+ 'one "two" #\3)
"ONEtwo3"
```

12.6.9   America's Past Time [6*]

In our efforts to extend time addition to include numbers (for seconds), we forgot something. By adding negative numbers to times, we create non-canonical, that is, unusual, times.

```
> (g+ x2 -30)
#S(MY-TIME :HOURS 0 :MINUTES 30 :SECONDS -30)
```

Modify `time-normalize` so that it does the right thing.

```
> (g+ x2 -30)
#S(MY-TIME :HOURS 0 :MINUTES 29 :SECONDS 30)

> (g+ x2 -3600)
#S(MY-TIME :HOURS 23 :MINUTES 30 :SECONDS 0)
```

12.6.10 Current Time [3*]

Define a function `current-time` that returns the current time as a string, in standard, 12-hour format. No time zone is required.

```
> (current-time)
"04:46:46 pm"

> (current-time)
"04:46:51 pm"
```

12.6.11 Current Date [3*]

Define a function `current-date` that returns the current date as a text string, including the day of the week.

```
> (current-date)
"Friday, September 5, 1997"
```

12.7 Chapter Summary

- Data abstraction is a useful and powerful programming technique. LISP allows the programmer to implement new data structures directly.

- The special form (`defstruct name slots`) creates a new data structure with type `name` and associated operations: a constructor `make-name`, a copier `copy-name`, selectors `name-slot`, and predicate `name-p`.

- Values of structures can be set indirectly through the selectors with `setf` or specified as keyword arguments to the constructor function.

- `defstruct` supports the following options:

    - `:conc-name`, which defaults to the "structure name."

    - `:constructor`, which defaults to `make-` "structure name."

    - `:copier`, which defaults to `copy-` "structure name."

    - `:predicate`, which defaults to "structure name" `-P`.

- :print-function, which takes three arguments: the structure instance, the output stream, and the break-level depth.

- :include, which specifies other structures that become part of the new definition.

- The components of a structure may be any object, including other structures.

- Programmers can define generic functions and associated methods with the functions defgeneric and defmethod.

- More than one method may match a given set of arguments. LISP ranks the methods according from specific to general, in left-to-right order of the arguments. The following function displays these results for a given generic function and argument list.

```
(compute-applicable-methods generic-function arguments)
```

- Using the call-next-method function, the programmer can invoke more than one matching primary method. The predicate next-method-p is useful with call-next-method as are the generic functions:

```
(no-applicable-method generic-function &rest arguments)
(no-next-method generic-function method &rest arguments)
```

- The programmer can define auxiliary methods by specifying a method qualifier: :before, :after, or :around.

- Instead of specifying a particular *type* for the method parameters, the programmer can give a particular *value*, using eql.

- LISP provides three types of time representation: universal, decoded, and internal times. Related functions include the following:

```
(get-decoded-time)
(get-universal-time)
(decode-universal-time universal-time &optional time-zone)
(encode-universal-time sec min hr day mon yr &optional time-zone)
(get-internal-run-time)
(get-internal-real-time)
(sleep seconds)
```

The constant internal-time-units-per-second is implementation dependent.

- LISP gives the programmer access to the file system through several functions.

```
(rename-file oldname newname)
(delete-file filename)
(probe-file filename)
(directory pathname)
(file-author filename)
(file-write-date pathname)
```

- LISP provides a variety of information about the machine and implementation.

```
*features*
(lisp-implementation-type)
(lisp-implementation-version)
(long-site-name)
(short-site-name)
(machine-instance)
(machine-type)
(machine-version)
(software-type)
(software-version)
```

It is better to have 100 functions operate on one data structure than 10 functions on 10 data structures.

◇ ALAN PERLIS, *Epigrams in Programming (1982)*

Chapter 13

Classes and Objects

> *Wordsworth says somewhere that wherever Virgil*
> *seems to have composed 'with his eye on the object,'*
> *Dryden fails to render him. Homer invariably composes 'with*
> *his eye on the object,' whether the object be a moral or a*
> *material one: Pope composes with his eye on his style, into*
> *which he translates his object, whatever it is.*

⋄ MATTHEW ARNOLD, *On Translating Homer (1861)*

> *To find the length of an object, we have to perform certain*
> *physical operations. The concept of length is therefore fixed when*
> *the operations by which length is measured are fixed: that is,*
> *the concept of length involves as much as and nothing more than*
> *the set of operations by which length is determined.*

⋄ PERCY WILLIAMS BRIDGMAN, *The Logic of Modern Physics (1927)*

> *You know my methods, Watson.*

⋄ SIR ARTHUR CONAN DOYLE, *The Memoirs of Sherlock Holmes (1894)*

In the course of this book, we have adopted an implicit view of program execution, namely, that a computer program consists of functions or procedures that manipulate data. This procedural perspective for programming is found in almost all programming languages, and most programmers used to consider it to be the only way one could write programs.

However, there is an alternative to procedural programming, namely, *object-oriented programming*. To understand the difference, first consider the way in which a person might determine the age of a tree by counting its rings. This is a procedural approach. The object, in this case, a tree, is inspected in a specified manner. The procedure entails examination of the object.

Compare this approach with determining the age of a person by asking her how old she is. In this second case, you can rely on several facts. First, people know their own age. Second, people understand requests for personal information. Finally, people can respond to such requests. Trees, for better or worse, fail on all three counts.

In procedural programming, an object is a passive data element which is manipulated by functions. In object-oriented programming, the object plays an active role of responding to requests from other objects.

13.1 Object-Oriented Programming Languages

The precursor of object-oriented programming was the language Simula [Dahl and Nygaard, 1966], developed as an extension to Algol-60. Simula provided a method of describing a collection of processes which could be considered to operate in parallel. Each process contained its own data and could execute actions. The motivation was to simulate complex systems whose components interacted. Simula was built on top of the Algol programming language and permitted the programmer to combine Algol function calls and Simula processes.

The first language to exploit the object-oriented paradigm fully was the Smalltalk language [Goldberg and Robson, 1983], developed in the 1970s at the Palo Alto Research Center of the Xerox Corporation. The Smalltalk philosophy promoted the extreme view that everything in the system should be viewed as objects that send messages to each other. Even simple arithmetic was eventually implemented to conform to this message-passing metaphor. Thus, an expression like "3 + 4" might be interpreted as the number 3 receiving a message of the form "+4", which would mean "answer this message with the sum of your value and the argument 4."

Smalltalk organizes its objects in a class hierarchy, and each class has methods or protocols for answering messages sent to instances of that class. In the example just given, the number 3 would be an instance of the class *SmallInteger*, which itself is a member of the class *Integer*, which is of the class *Number*, which belongs to *Magnitude*, which (finally) is a member of the root class *Object*. The actual method used for addition might differ based on the class of the object. Integer arithmetic may vary quite a bit from floating point arithmetic.

The point is, in Smalltalk, the objects themselves decide how the arithmetic operations would be performed. In procedural languages, the functions make that decision based on the *type* of the objects. The terminology is significant: the words *class* and *type* both refer to categories of objects, but *type* views objects from the perspective of functions, whereas *class* is the object-oriented view.

Unlike Simula and Smalltalk, LISP was not originally designed as an object-oriented programming language. However, LISP has always been extensible, and many researchers have provided object-oriented extensions to LISP. The standard

Concept	Smalltalk	C++	CLOS
class	class	class	class
class instance	object	object	class instance
slot access	selector	member function	accessor / reader
operation	method	member function	method

Table 13.1: Object-Oriented Language Terminology

object-oriented extension to Common LISP is the Common LISP Object System, or CLOS.

Like LISP, the C programming language was also not designed as an object-oriented language. C++ is an object-oriented extension to C. Table 13.1 provides a comparison of object-oriented terms in Smalltalk, C++, and CLOS. For programmers already familiar with C++, appendix C provides a direct comparison between CLOS and C++.

13.2   Object-Oriented Programming in Common LISP

Simula was built on top of Algol. C++ was added to C. Object-oriented programming in LISP lives side-by-side with procedural programming. LISP, like Simula and C++, offers the programmer both alternatives through CLOS.

We have seen the procedural approach in LISP in the preceding chapters. Here is an example of object-oriented programming in LISP, using CLOS. We create a person class for creating objects that can tell us their names and ages.

```
(defclass person ()
  ((name :initarg :name :reader person-name)
   (age  :initform 0 :accessor person-age))
  (:documentation "A simple person class"))
```

Defining a class is similar to defining a structure. The `defclass` macro creates a class. Our example of `defclass` for the `person` class has the following arguments.

- *class-name*: A symbol indicating the name of the new class. In this case, that name is `person`.

- *(superclasses)*: A list of superclass names, each of which is a symbol. A superclass provides a means of *class inheritance* and is similar to the `:include` option in structure definitions. We will discuss superclasses later on. In this case, the `person` class has no superclass, denoted by the empty list: `()`.

- *(slot-specifiers)*: A list of slot specifications, each of which is a list, whose `car` is the slot name, and the remaining items are keyword options, which include the following:

- : initarg — The next keyword argument is used to identify the initial value for this slot when an instance of this class is created. In this example, the keyword :name is used for the name slot.

- : reader — The next argument is the name of a function used to *read* the value of this slot. In this example, the name slot has the reader function person-name.

- : initform — The next value is to be assigned as the default initial value for this slot. In this example, the age slot has an initial value of 0. An : initarg value supersedes an : initform value.

- : accessor — The next value is the name of a function which may be used for both reading and writing values for this slot. In this example, the person-age function can both read and write, that is, set, the value of the age slot.

- (:documentation string): A string providing information about the class.

Thus, our defclass has created the following:

- A person class, with no superclasses and two slots: name and age. The age slot will have an initial value of 0.

- The keyword :name, which identifies initial name values for new instances of the person class.

- The function person-name, which can read the value of a person's name slot.

- The function person-age, which can read and set the value of a person's age slot.

- A documentation string.

We next define some useful functions and methods for the person class.

```
(defgeneric person-p (obj)
  (:documentation "A predicate for the person class.")
  (:method ((obj person)) T)
  (:method (obj) NIL))

(defun make-person (name)
  (make-instance 'person :name name))

(defgeneric age-of (obj)
  (:method ((obj person)) (person-age obj))
  (:method (obj) 'try-carbon-dating))
```

- The predicate `person-p` will return true if its argument is an instance of the person class, and otherwise, will return false.

- The function `make-person` creates a new instance of the `person` class with the given `name`. It calls the generic function `make-instance`, whose first argument specifies the class; the remaining arguments are the optional *initargs* from the slot specifications. In this case, we specify the `:name` initarg.

- The generic function `age-of` which calls `person-age` for instances of the person class and uses a default method otherwise.

We now can try out our new **person** class.

```
> (defvar x (make-person 'pat))      ; Creates a new person.
#<PERSON @ #x11bca2e>

> (person-p x)                       ; x is a person.
T

> (person-p 'x)                      ; 'x is not a person.
NIL

> (person-name x)                    ; Reads the name.
PAT

> (person-age x)                     ; Reads the default age.
0

> (setf (person-age x) 20)           ; Sets the value of age.
20

> (person-age x)
20

> (age-of x)                         ; Tries the generic function.
20

> (age-of 'hills)
TRY-CARBON-DATING

> (setf (person-name x) 'james)      ; We cannot reset the name.
Error: No methods applicable for generic function
```

We get an error in the last example because `person-name` was defined as a `:reader`, not as an `:accessor` like `person-age`.

CLOS provides a generic function `print-object` for printing objects, which is called by the read-eval-print loop. We can define our own `print-object` method for the new `person` class.

```
(defmethod print-object ((object person) stream)
  (format stream "#<PERSON ~A (Age: ~A)>"
          (person-name object)
          (person-age object)))
```

```
> x
#<PERSON PAT (Age: 20)>
```

The behavior of the default `print-object` method can be reproduced or extended by means of the macro `print-unreadable-object`. The term *unreadable* here refers to the LISP reader, not the human one. The macro, which returns the value NIL, has the following syntax.

```
(print-unreadable-object (object stream)
    [:type type] [:identity id] {form}*)
```

The basic macro prints `#<>` but allows other information to appear between the angle brackets. If `:type` is true, then it includes the object's type. If `:identity` is true, then it includes a unique reference for the object, such as a memory address. The forms are evaluated with any output directed to a stream appearing between the angle brackets.

```
> #'+
#<Function + @ #x72c776>
```

```
> (print-unreadable-object (#'+ *standard-output*))
#<>
NIL
```

```
> (print-unreadable-object (#'+ *standard-output* :type t))
#<COMPILED-FUNCTION>
NIL
```

```
> (print-unreadable-object (#'+ *standard-output* :identity t))
#<@ #x72c776>
NIL
```

```
> (print-unreadable-object (#'+ *standard-output* :type t :identity t))
#<COMPILED-FUNCTION @ #x72c776>
NIL
```

```
> (print-unreadable-object (#'+ *standard-output*)
    (format *standard-output* "a really great function."))
#<a really great function.>
NIL

> (print-unreadable-object (#'+ *standard-output* :type t)
    (format *standard-output* "a really great function."))
#<COMPILED-FUNCTION a really great function.>
NIL

> (print-unreadable-object (#'+ *standard-output* :identity t)
    (format *standard-output* "a really great function."))
#<a really great function. @ #x72c776>
NIL
```

The print-object facility makes it possible to have a class specify how its instances are to be printed.

A few other useful functions for classes and objects are class-of, class-name, find-class, and our old friend describe.

```
> (class-of x)                      ;  What is x's class?
#<STANDARD-CLASS PERSON @ #x1162bc6>

> (class-name (class-of x))         ;  What is the name for that class?
PERSON

> (find-class 'person)              ;  What is the class named person?
#<STANDARD-CLASS PERSON @ #x1162bc6>

> (class-name (find-class 'person)) ;  These functions are complementary.
PERSON

> (describe (find-class 'person))   ;  Tell us about the class person.
∞ ⇒  #<STANDARD-CLASS PERSON @ #x1162b26> is the class named PERSON
    of the metaclass STANDARD-CLASS.
    The class is not yet finalized.
    Its direct superclass is STANDARD-OBJECT.
    It has no subclasses.
    Its 2 instance slots are:
      AGE defined in class PERSON.
      NAME defined in class PERSON.
```

Its 6 direct methods are (METHOD PRINT-OBJECT (PERSON T)),
  (METHOD AGE-OF (PERSON)), (METHOD PERSON-P (PERSON)),
  (METHOD (SETF PERSON-AGE) (T PERSON)), (METHOD PERSON-AGE (PERSON)),
  (METHOD PERSON-NAME (PERSON)).
Its documentation is: A person class

```
> (describe x)                          ; Tell us what you know about x.
#<PERSON PAT (Age: 20)> is an instance of
#<STANDARD-CLASS PERSON @ #x1162bc6>:
 The following slots have :INSTANCE allocation:
  AGE    20
  NAME   PAT
```

Just as LISP's print function calls the print-object method, the describe function calls the describe-object method, which we may also modify.

```
(defmethod describe-object ((object person) stream)
  (format stream "This is an instance of the person class~%")
  (format stream "whose name is ~A and age is ~A~%"
          (person-name object)
          (person-age object)))
```

```
> (describe x)
This is an instance of the person class
whose name is PAT and age is 20
```

If we add call-next-method, we get both descriptions.

```
(defmethod describe-object ((object person) stream)
    (format stream "This is an instance of the person class~%")
    (format stream "whose name is ~A and age is ~A~%"
            (person-name object)
            (person-age object))
    (call-next-method))
```

```
> (describe x)
This is an instance of the person class
whose name is PAT and age is 20
#<PERSON PAT (Age: 20)> is an instance of
#<STANDARD-CLASS PERSON @ #x1162bc6>:
 The following slots have :INSTANCE allocation:
  AGE    20
  NAME   PAT
```

The description of x refers to the slots AGE and NAME as having :INSTANCE allocation. This means that each instance of **person** can have different values for these slots. That seems to be a reasonable default.

However, it is also possible to have slots which have the *same* value for each instance. In fact, each instance will share the same slot allocated for the entire class. This type of shared allocation is indicated by the slot specifier keywords :allocation :class in the class definition.

For example, suppose that we want to change the **person** class to include only females. We could use the following definition.

```
(defclass person ()
  ((name :initarg :name :reader person-name)
   (age  :initform 0 :accessor person-age)
   (sex  :initform 'F :accessor sex :allocation :class))
  (:documentation "A person class"))

> x                          ; Pat is still a person.
#<PERSON PAT (Age: 20)>

> (sex x)                    ; Pat is a female.
F

> (class-of x)
#<STANDARD-CLASS PERSON @ #x1162b26>

> (defvar y (make-person 'sam))
Y

> y                          ; Sam is a person.
#<PERSON SAM (Age: 0)>

> (sex y)                    ; Sam is a female.
F

> (setf (sex x) 'M)          ; Changes Pat to a male.
M

> (sex x)
M

> (sex y)                    ; Sam is now a male as well.
M
```

```
> (defvar z (make-person 'lamar))
Z

> (sex z)                    ;  The new person Lamar is male, too.
M

> (describe x)
This is an instance of the person class
whose name is PAT and age is 20
#<PERSON PAT (Age: 20)> is an instance of
#<STANDARD-CLASS PERSON @ #x1162b26>:
 The following slots have :INSTANCE allocation:
  AGE    20
  NAME   PAT
 The following slots have class allocation as shown:
  SEX PERSON    M
```

Several things are going on here. First, we have redefined the **person** class on the fly. That is, our old **person** instance of Pat is now an instance of our redefined **person** class. The new Pat now has a new slot indicating that she is a female.

CLOS automatically converts old class instances to conform to the new class definitions. CLOS is *dynamic*. This is very useful. Most object-oriented languages would require that the programmer start over when redefining classes.

Second, we create another person, Sam, who is a female. However, after we change the sex of Pat to male, we discover that Sam is now a male as well! Also, when we create a new person, Lamar, the default sex is no longer female, but male.

This behavior is a consequence of the shared or class allocation of the **sex** variable. When a class allocated variable is changed, that change is reflected in all instances of the class — both present and future.

13.3 Slot Functions and Macros

It really does not make sense to create a **person** class for which all instances must be either male or female. Instead, we can create a separate **female** class and then use the **change-class** function to make Pat a female once again.

```
(defclass female ()
  ((name :initarg :name :reader person-name)
   (age  :initform 0 :accessor person-age)
   (sex  :initform 'F :reader sex :allocation :class))
  (:documentation "A female class"))
```

```
> (change-class x 'female)
#<FEMALE @ #x1093db6>

> x
#<FEMALE @ #x1093db6>

> (person-name x)
PAT

> (person-age x)
20

> (sex x)
F

> (class-of x)
#<STANDARD-CLASS FEMALE @ #x109ee06>
```

Another approach would be to define the female class to inherit from the person class. We describe inheritance later in this chapter.

CLOS provides a number of functions and generic functions for examining and manipulating the slots of a class instance.

- (slot-value object slot-name) — Reads and writes the value of a given slot

- (slot-boundp instance slot-name) — Indicates whether the specified slot is bound

- (slot-exists-p object slot-name) — Indicates whether the specified slot exists

- (slot-makunbound instance slot-name) — Removes the value of the specified slot

- (slot-missing class object slot-name operation [new-value]) — A generic function that is called when a missing slot is referenced by the given operation

- (slot-unbound class instance slot-name) — A generic function that is called when an unbound slot is referenced

We demonstrate these functions below.

```
> (slot-value x 'name)
PAT

> (setf (slot-value x 'name) 'patty)
PATTY

> (person-name x)
PATTY
```

Note that while **person-name** may not be used with **setf**, **slot-value** may.

```
> (slot-boundp x 'name)          ; Does x have a name?
T

> (setf y (make-instance 'female))
#<FEMALE @ #x10b44d6>

> (slot-boundp y 'name)          ; Does y have a name?
NIL

> (slot-exists-p x 'name)        ; Is there a name slot?
T

> (slot-exists-p x 'nickname)    ; Is there a nickname slot?
NIL

> (person-age y)
0

> (slot-boundp y 'age)           ; Is the age slot bound?
T

> (slot-makunbound y 'age)
#<FEMALE @ #x10b44d6>

> (slot-boundp y 'age)           ; Is the age slot bound now?
NIL

> (slot-value y 'nickname)
Error: The slot NICKNAME is missing from the object
       #<FEMALE @ #x10b44d6> of class
       #<STANDARD-CLASS FEMALE @ #x109ee06>
       during operation SLOT-VALUE
  [condition type: PROGRAM-ERROR]
```

```
Restart actions (select using :continue):
 0: Try accessing the slot again
 1: Return a value
[1]
> :res
```

We can define a slot-missing method to catch this condition. Some implementa-
∞ ⇒ tions will warn the programmer who attempts to define slot-missing.

```
(defmethod slot-missing (class obj name op &optional value)
   (format t "Sorry.  ~S was calling ~S and discovered
there is no slot: ~S in class: ~S~%"
           op obj name (class-name class))
   (if value (format t "Better put ~S somewhere else.~%" value)))
```

```
> (slot-value y 'nickname)
Sorry.  SLOT-VALUE was calling #<FEMALE @ #x1169fce> and discovered
there is no slot: NICKNAME in class: FEMALE
NIL
```

```
> (setf (slot-value y 'nickname) 'joe)
Sorry.  SETF was calling #<FEMALE @ #x1169fce> and discovered
there is no slot: NICKNAME in class: FEMALE
Better put JOE somewhere else.
NIL
```

A similar situation may arise with an unbound slot. The solution is similar as well,
using the generic function slot-unbound.

```
(defmethod slot-unbound (class obj name)
   (format t "Sorry.  Slot: ~s
of object: ~S
in class: ~S is unbound.~%"
           name obj (class-name class)))
```

```
> (person-name y)
Sorry.  Slot: NAME
of object: #<FEMALE @ #x1169fce>
in class: FEMALE is unbound.
NIL
```

∞ ⇒ Some implementations warn the programmer when redefining slot-unbound.
       In addition to slot-value, we can read the values of an instance's slots with
the macros with-accessors and with-slots, which have the following syntax.

```
(with-accessors ({slot-entry}*) instance-form {form}*)
```

```
(with-slots ({slot-entry}*) instance-form {form}*)
```

The only difference between the two macros is the form of the `slot-entry` component, as demonstrated below.

```
(defmethod print-object ((person female) stream)
  (with-accessors
   ((a person-age) (s sex)) person
   (format stream "A female: (~S) (~S)~%" a s)))
```

```
> x
A female: (20) (F)
```

```
> y
A female: (0) (F)
```

The `slot-entry` syntax for `with-accessors` is

```
(parameter accessor)
```

whereas the `with-slots` version is simply the name of the slot itself, for example, the age slot instead of the `person-age` accessor.

```
(defmethod print-object ((person female) stream)
  (with-slots
   (age sex) person
   (format stream "Another female: (~S) (~S)~%"
           age sex)))
```

```
> x
Another female: (20) (F)
```

```
> y
Another female: (0) (F)
```

Both `with-accessors` and `with-slots` can cause problems if one of the slots is unbound. Here is a safe version of `print-object`.

```
(defmethod print-object ((person female) stream)
  (if (some
       #'(lambda (slot) (not (slot-boundp person slot)))
       '(name age sex))
      (format stream "Another female~%")
    (with-slots
     (name age sex) person
     (format stream "Another female: ~S (~S) (~S)~%"
             name age sex))))
```

```
> x
Another female: PATTY (20) (F)

> y
Another female
```

Or, even better.

```
(defmethod print-object ((person female) stream)
  (let ((name (slot-check person 'name))
        (age  (slot-check person 'age))
        (sex  (slot-check person 'sex)))
     (format stream "Another female: ~S (~S) (~S)~%"
             name age sex)))

(defun slot-check (instance slot)
  (if (slot-boundp instance slot)
      (slot-value instance slot)
      (list slot 'unbound)))

> x
Another female: PATTY (20) (F)

> y
Another female: (NAME UNBOUND) (0) (F)
```

The with-slots and with-accessors macros permit changing slot values.

```
(defun add-a-year (female)
  (with-slots (age) female
    (setf age (+ age 1))))

(defun add-another-year (female)
  (with-accessors ((a person-age)) female
    (setf a (+ a 1))))

> (add-a-year x)
21

> x
Another female: PATTY (21) (F)
> (add-another-year x)
22
```

```
> x
Another female: PATTY (22) (F)
```

At this point, we have seen a number of ways to access slots:

- Named accessors, such as `person-name`

- `slot-value`

- `with-accessors`

- `with-slots`

Which one is best? Which one is fastest? Which one is safest?

The speed and efficiency of slot access methods are implementation dependent. It is not uncommon for named accessors and `with-slots` to be implemented in   ⇐ ∞ terms of `slot-value`. However, some implementations may optimize one way or the other. We suggest that the user interested in efficiency issues conduct experiments with her LISP dialect.

As for safety, the named accessors can be defined as read-only, which is a good idea. Then the user can create special write functions which perform type checking, either explicitly using `check-type` or implicitly as a generic function, such as the following.

```
(defclass male ()
  ((name :initarg :name :reader person-name)
   (age  :initform 0 :reader person-age)
   (sex  :initform 'M :reader sex :allocation :class))
  (:documentation "A male class"))

(defun set-name (person name)
  (let ((p (check-type person male))
        (n (check-type name symbol)))
    (setf (slot-value p 'name) n)))

(defmethod set-age ((person male) (age integer))
  (setf (slot-value person 'age) age))

> (setf m (make-instance 'male))
#<MALE @ #x10b74de>
```

```
> (set-name m "Joe")
Error: the value of NAME is "Joe", which is not of type SYMBOL.
  [condition type: TYPE-ERROR]

Restart actions (select using :continue):
 0: supply a new value for NAME.
[1]
> :res

> (set-name m 'joe)
JOE

> (set-age m 49.5)
Error: No methods applicable for generic function
       #<STANDARD-GENERIC-FUNCTION SET-AGE @ #x10b6566> with args
       (#<MALE @ #x10b74de> 49.5) of classes (MALE FLOAT)
  [condition type: PROGRAM-ERROR]

Restart actions (select using :continue):
 0: Try calling it again
[1c]
> :res

> (set-age m 49)
49
```

For the novice programmer, safety and efficiency seem to be always in conflict.
The seasoned programmer understands that safety and efficiency are not merely
compatible, but inseparable.

13.4 A Symbol Generator

The person class example is illustrative. Object-oriented programming can be used
to capture many relationships found in the world. However, as a practical matter,
the most common classes found in object-oriented systems are not flora or fauna,
but computational structures.

There are several related reasons for this. In order to write an object-oriented
system, a programmer must have pertinent knowledge about the target domain.
Programmers know about data structures and control structures. Also, object-
oriented versions of data and control structures have proven very useful. Much of
the original Smalltalk system comprised such classes.

Moreover, these computational classes are generic. They can be applied to
many different domains: circuit simulation, biology, word processing, or tutoring

systems. In our construction metaphor, these computational classes are equivalent to screws, nails, lumber, bricks, and mortar. They are the materials from which many varied artifacts can be created.

We now create such a building block. Below, we define a `symbol-generator` class and use it to create the function `generate-symbol`, which behaves similarly to LISP's gensym.

```lisp
(defclass symbol-generator ()
  ((prefix :initarg :prefix :initform "G" :reader prefix)
   (counter :initform 0 :accessor current-counter)
   (symbol-list :initform nil :accessor symbol-list
                :reader all-symbols)))
```

An instance of the `symbol-generator` class has three components: a `prefix`, which defaults to G; a `counter`, which has an initial value of 0 and an accessor function `current-counter`; and a list of all the symbols generated: `symbol-list`. The last component has an initial value of NIL and both an accessor, `symbol-list`, and a reader, `all-symbols`.

We next define a predicate for symbol generators, a print method, and a constructor function.

```lisp
(defgeneric symbol-generator-p (object)
  (:method ((object symbol-generator)) T)
  (:method (object) NIL))

(defmethod print-object ((object symbol-generator) stream)
  (format stream "#<Symbol-generator: ~A ~D>"
          (prefix object)
          (current-counter object)))

(defun make-symbol-generator (&optional prefix)
  (if prefix
      (make-instance 'symbol-generator :prefix prefix)
    (make-instance 'symbol-generator)))
```

Finally, we define the method for generating the actual symbols.

```lisp
(defmethod generate-symbol ((object symbol-generator))
  (let ((new-symbol
         (read-from-string
          (format nil "~A~A"
                  (prefix object)
                  (current-counter object)))))
    (push new-symbol (symbol-list object))
    (incf (current-counter object))
    new-symbol))
```

The function `generate-symbol` does four things:

1. It creates a new symbol that concatenates the prefix with the current value of the counter, using the LISP function `read-from-string`.

2. It adds this new symbol to the list of symbols.

3. It increments the counter.

4. It returns the new symbol as its result.

We can now take our new class for a test drive.

```
> (defvar x (make-symbol-generator "X"))     ; Creates an instance.
X

> x                                          ; Invokes the print method.
#<Symbol-generator: X 0>

> (current-counter x)                        ; Uses the accessor function.
0

> (prefix x)                                 ; Uses the reader function.
"X"

> (generate-symbol x)                        ; Generates a symbol.
X0

> (all-symbols x)                            ; Gets the list of symbols.
(X0)

> (generate-symbol x)
X1

> (all-symbols x)
(X1 X0)

> (symbol-generator-p x)                     ; Tests the predicate.
T

> (symbol-generator-p 'x)
NIL
```

Everything works pretty well. We add two more methods which return that last symbol generated and reset the symbol generator.

```
(defmethod last-symbol ((object symbol-generator))
  (car (all-symbols object)))

(defmethod reset-counter ((object symbol-generator))
  (setf (symbol-list object) nil)
  (setf (current-counter object) 0))
```

```
> (last-symbol x)              ;  What was the last symbol?
X1
```

```
> (reset-counter x)            ;  Starts over again.
0
```

```
> x
#<Symbol-generator: X 0>
```

```
> (last-symbol x)
NIL
```

One thing to note is that we created new methods after our initial class definition. That is, the definition of a class and its methods are two separate events. This observation is noteworthy only because other object-oriented programming languages often require that a class and its methods be defined simultaneously.

To complete our symbol generator, we shall create a macro for defining symbol generators. The macro, defsymbol-generator, takes advantage of the fact that a symbol in Common LISP can have both a symbol value and a function value. The symbol value is set to the symbol generator object, and the function value is defined as a function that generates symbols using the object.

```
(defmacro defsymbol-generator (name)
  `(progn
     (setf ,name (make-symbol-generator ',name))
     (defun ,name () (generate-symbol ,name))))
```

```
> (defsymbol-generator y)      ;  y is a new generator.
Y
```

```
> y                            ;  y's value is the generator object.
#<Symbol-generator: Y 0>
```

```
> (y)                          ;  (y) is the function call.
Y0
```

```
> (y)
Y1
```

```
> (symbol-generator-p y)          ;  y is a symbol generator.
T
```

```
> (functionp y)                   ;  The symbol value is not a function.
NIL
```

```
> (functionp #'y)                 ;  The function value is a function.
T
```

We observe the object Y being called as a function and being invoked as an argument to methods. This approach permits the programmer to create executable objects.

13.5   Object-Oriented Property Lists

We now define an object that is more complex and more useful: a property list object.

We have used property lists in several places in this volume; however, we have tried to warn the programmer of the problems that can arise from the fact that property lists are global objects. It is difficult for the programmer to maintain control over any global object. We now adopt an object-oriented approach to property lists that allows the programmer to create, manipulate, and control access to multiple property lists.

We give the definitions, with annotation. Then, we give examples. Note that this version of property lists provides more functionality than is normally available.

There is a lot going on, so we shall take it one step at a time. We begin by using defclass to create the property-list class.

```
(defclass property-list ()
  ((plist :initform (empty-plist) :accessor plist)
   (name :initarg :name :reader plist-name)))
```

There are two components in this class: plist, which contains the property list itself; and name, which identifies the property list.

We choose to represent the property list itself as an association list of association lists. The initial value of the plist slot is the result returned by the empty-list function, defined below.

```
(defun empty-plist ()
  (copy-tree '(((()))))))
```

```
(defun make-plist (name)
  (make-instance 'property-list :name name))
```

```
(defgeneric property-list-p (object)
  (:method ((object property-list)) T)
  (:method (object) NIL))
```

The function make-plist creates an instance of a property list with the given name.
property-list-p is the predicate for property lists.

      We now define a method that returns the association list for a given symbol
and adds a new association list if that symbol is not already part of the property
list.

```
(defmethod symbol-lookup ((object property-list) sym)
  (let ((l (assoc sym (plist object))))
    (cond (l (cdr l))
          (t (push (cons sym nil)
                   (cdr (plist object)))))))
```

We can try out what we have defined so far.

```
> (defvar pl (make-plist "PL")) ;  Creates a property list pl.
PL

> (plist pl)                    ;  The initial list is empty.
((NIL))

> (property-list-p pl)          ;  Checks the predicate.
T

> (symbol-lookup pl 'joe)       ;  Adds an entry for Joe.
((JOE))

> (plist pl)                    ;  The list now contains Joe's list.
((NIL) (JOE))
```

Now we add a few more methods.

```
(defmethod all-symbols ((object property-list))
  (mapcar #'car (cdr (plist object))))

(defmethod clear-plist ((object property-list))
  (setf (plist object) (empty-plist)))

(defmethod print-object ((object property-list) stream)
  (format stream "#<Private Property List: ~A>" (plist-name object)))
```

The method all-symbols returns a list of all the symbols for which property lists exist. clear-plist sets the plist back to its initial value. print-object is the standard print method.

```
> (all-symbols pl)                  ; Returns a list of all symbols.
(JOE)

> (clear-plist pl)                  ; Empties the plist.
((NIL))

> (all-symbols pl)
NIL

> pl                                ; Prints the property list object.
#<Private Property List: PL>
```

Now we want to be able to get and put properties on a plist. We define the methods pget and pput and create a setf method for pget.

```
(defmethod pget ((object property-list) sym prop)
  (let ((val-pair (assoc prop (symbol-lookup object sym))))
    (if val-pair
        (cdr val-pair)
      nil)))

(defmethod pput ((object property-list) sym prop value)
  (let ((val-pair (assoc prop (symbol-lookup object sym))))
    (cond (val-pair (setf (cdr val-pair) value))
          (t
           (setf (cdr (assoc sym (plist object)))
                 (cons (cons prop value)
                       (symbol-lookup object sym)))))
    value))

(defmethod (setf pget) (value (object property-list) sym prop)
  (pput object sym prop value))
```

pget is similar to the normal get function. However, note that pget takes an additional argument — the property list object. The normal get implicitly uses a global property list. The pget method can apply to different instances of private property lists.

pput sets new values in the property list. It is used in the setf method for pget. We can now put and get properties.

```
> (pput pl 'iago 'age 'ancient)
ANCIENT
```

```
> (pput pl 'othello 'age 'old-enough-to-know-better)
OLD-ENOUGH-TO-KNOW-BETTER

> (pget pl 'iago 'profession)
NIL

> (setf (pget pl 'iago 'profession) '(management consultant))
(MANAGEMENT CONSULTANT)

> (pget pl 'iago 'profession)
(MANAGEMENT CONSULTANT)
```

Everything seems to fly. We now add a couple of methods for printing out property lists in a "pretty" format. The pp-sym method prints the property list for a given symbol, and pplist pretty prints the lists for all the symbols on the plist. pplist calls pp-sym on all symbol keys in plist.

```
(defmethod pp-sym ((object property-list) sym
                   &optional (s *standard-output*))
  (format s "~%~A" sym)
  (mapc #'(lambda (x)
            (format s "~%~5t~A ~20t~A" (car x) (cdr x)))
        (symbol-lookup object sym))
  (values))

(defmethod pplist ((object property-list)
                   &optional (s *standard-output*))
  (mapc #'(lambda (x) (pp-sym object x s))
        (all-symbols object))
  (values))
```

Note that both pp-sym and pplist take an optional argument to specify the output stream, which has a default value of *standard-output*.

We resume our example with Iago and Othello.

```
> (pp-sym pl 'iago)           ;  Prints Iago's properties.
IAGO
     PROFESSION      (MANAGEMENT CONSULTANT)
     AGE             ANCIENT
```

```
> (pplist p1)                    ;  Pretty prints the whole list.
OTHELLO
      AGE              OLD-ENOUGH-TO-KNOW-BETTER
IAGO
      PROFESSION       (MANAGEMENT CONSULTANT)
      AGE              ANCIENT

> (defvar p12 (copy-tree (plist p1)))
P12

> p12                            ;  p12 is a copy of p1
((NIL) (OTHELLO (AGE . OLD-ENOUGH-TO-KNOW-BETTER))
 (IAGO (PROFESSION MANAGEMENT CONSULTANT) (AGE . ANCIENT)))

> (pput p1 'othello 'profession 'ceo)
CEO

> (pplist p1)                    ;  We have changed p1.
OTHELLO
      PROFESSION       CEO
      AGE              OLD-ENOUGH-TO-KNOW-BETTER
IAGO
      PROFESSION       (MANAGEMENT CONSULTANT)
      AGE              ANCIENT

> (setf (plist p1) p12)          ;  Restores the old plist.
((NIL) (OTHELLO (AGE . OLD-ENOUGH-TO-KNOW-BETTER))
 (IAGO (PROFESSION MANAGEMENT CONSULTANT) (AGE . ANCIENT)))

> (pplist p1)
OTHELLO
      AGE              OLD-ENOUGH-TO-KNOW-BETTER
IAGO
      PROFESSION       (MANAGEMENT CONSULTANT)
      AGE              ANCIENT

> (defvar p13 (make-plist "PL3"))
PL3

> (pput p13 'iago 'age 28)   ;  p13 is a new plist.
28
```

```
> (pput pl3 'othello 'age 42)
42

> (pplist pl3)
OTHELLO
     AGE              42
IAGO
     AGE              28

> (pplist pl)
OTHELLO
     AGE              OLD-ENOUGH-TO-KNOW-BETTER
IAGO
     PROFESSION       (MANAGEMENT CONSULTANT)
     AGE              ANCIENT

> pl
#<Private Property List: PL>

> pl3
#<Private Property List: PL3>
```

This extended example demonstrates the utility and flexibility of an object-oriented approach to data structures.

13.6   Inheritance

One of the main advantages of object-oriented programming is that new classes can be defined as extensions of old classes. For example, we can define a new class, programmer, which is an extension of our earlier person class. For us, a programmer is a person who knows some computer languages.

```
(defclass programmer (person)
  ((languages :initform nil :initarg :languages :accessor knows))
  (:documentation "A programmer class."))

(defun make-programmer (name languages)
  (make-instance 'programmer :name name :languages languages))
```

The function make-programmer creates a programmer with a given name and list of languages.

```
> (defvar joe (make-programmer "Joe" '(pascal lisp)))
JOE
```

```
> (knows joe)                  ;  What languages does Joe know?
(PASCAL LISP)

> (push 'c (knows joe))        ;  Joe has added C to his list.
(C PASCAL LISP)

> (knows joe)
(C PASCAL LISP)

> joe                          ;  Joe prints as a person.
#<PERSON Joe (Age: 0)>

> (setf (person-age joe) 30)
30

> joe
#<PERSON Joe (Age: 30)>
```

CLOS printed Joe by using the `print-object` method for `person` because there
was no method defined for `programmer`. We can add one, though.

```
(defmethod print-object ((object programmer) stream)
  (format stream "#<Programmer ~A (Languages: ~A)>"
          (person-name object)
          (knows object)))
```

```
> joe                          ;  Now Joe prints as a programmer.
#<Programmer Joe (Languages: (C PASCAL LISP))>
```

The general idea of one class borrowing the slots and methods from another class
is called *inheritance.* We say that the `programmer` class inherits from the `person`
class.

The terminology is quite suggestive. Since `programmer` inherits from `person`,
then `programmer` does not have to work as hard. Basically, the same thing happens
with heirs in the real world.

Two other related terms are *superclass* and *subclass.* The `person` class is a
superclass of `programmer`, and `programmer` is a subclass of `person`.[1] We note that
C++ refers to the superclass as the *base class,* and the subclass as the *derived class.*

The principle behind inheritance is also seen in the *semantic network* models
of human memory developed in artificial intelligence in the 1960s [Quillian, 1968].
Quillian and other researchers believed that it was computationally efficient and

---

[1]Just as your friends have suspected.

psychologically appropriate to develop memory models based on hierarchies or networks of information. One of the key relationships in such a model was the *ISA* link. (In exercise 11.10.9, we implemented an ISA hierarchy by using property lists.)

For example, you could represent a mouse with an ISA link to rodent. A rodent would be described as having four legs, and an ISA link to mammal. Associated with mammal would be facts such as mammals have live births, fur, and are vertebrates. These facts do not need to be stored explicitly under mouse or rodent, since they are implicitly available through the ISA links. Thus, the program would be able to deduce that a given mouse has four legs through its link to rodent, and has fur by following the ISA links up to mammal.

Furthermore, if there is a particular amputee mouse, the facts about this mouse's number of legs could be stored explicitly with that instance.

Here is how we can use inheritance to implement this semantic network. We define four classes: vertebrate; mammal, which inherits from vertebrate; rodent, which inherits from mammal; and mouse, which inherits from rodent.

```
(defclass vertebrate ()
  ((backbone :initform T :reader backbone)))

(defclass mammal (vertebrate)
  ((fur  :initform T :accessor has-fur)
   (name :initform "Mammal" :reader animal-name)
   (live-birth :initform T :reader live-birth)))

(defclass rodent (mammal)
  ((legs :initform 4 :accessor legs)
   (name :initform "Rodent" :reader animal-name)))

(defclass mouse (rodent)
  ((name :initform "Mouse" :reader animal-name)))

(defmethod print-object ((object mammal) stream)
  (format stream "#<Mammal ~A>" (animal-name object)))
```

We defined a print method for the mammal class. Both rodent and mouse will inherit this method.

```
> (defvar mickey (make-instance 'mouse))
MICKEY

> mickey                        ;  We have made a mouse.
#<Mammal Mouse>

> (has-fur mickey)
T
```

```
> (defvar ben (make-instance 'rodent))
BEN

> ben                            ; We have made a rodent.
#<Mammal Rodent>

> (legs ben)
4

> (setf (legs mickey) 2)         ; Mickey is a biped.
2

> (legs mickey)
2

> (backbone mickey)              ; Mickey is a mouse of good character.
T
```

With this inheritance mechanism, the programmer could quickly populate the world with vermin. We next create another class for movie stars.

```
(defclass movie-star ()
  ((salary :initform 1000000 :accessor salary)
   (name   :initarg :name      :accessor aka)
   (agent  :initform 'Ovitz   :accessor agent)))

(defun make-movie-star (name)
  (make-instance 'movie-star :name name))

(defmethod print-object ((object movie-star) stream)
  (format stream "#<Movie star: ~A>" (aka object)))

> (defvar grant (make-movie-star "Cary Grant"))
GRANT

> grant
#<Movie star: Cary Grant>

> (salary grant)
1000000

> (agent grant)
OVITZ
```

There is really nothing new here. However, we next create a new class of movie star mice; that is, a class whose members are both mice and movie stars.

```
(defclass mice-stars (mouse movie-star) ())
```

```
> (defvar minnie (make-instance 'mice-stars :name "Minnie" ))
MINNIE
```

```
> minnie                    ;  The name slot is defined twice,
#<Mammal Minnie>            ;  and so is print-object.
```

```
> (agent minnie)
OVITZ
```

```
> (salary minnie)
1000000
```

```
> (aka minnie)
"Minnie"
```

```
> (animal-name minnie)
"Minnie"
```

This is an example of *multiple inheritance* and illustrates some of the associated problems. In particular, multiple inheritance invites ambiguity. In the case of Minnie above, there are two **name** slots and there are two **print-object** methods. CLOS sets both **name** slots to Minnie, as we see by the values returned by **aka** and **animal-name**.

CLOS uses the **mammal** version of **print-object**, based on the rule that prefers methods in a left-to-right order of superclass definition. If we reverse the order of superclasses, we get a different result.

```
(defclass mice-stars (movie-star mouse) ())
```

```
> (defvar tom (make-instance 'mice-stars :name "Tom" ))
TOM
```

```
> tom
#<Movie star: Tom>
```

```
> (compute-applicable-methods #'print-object
                              (list tom *standard-output*))
(#<STANDARD-METHOD PRINT-OBJECT (MOVIE-STAR T) @ #x119f99e>
 #<STANDARD-METHOD PRINT-OBJECT (MAMMAL T) @ #x119c476>
 #<STANDARD-METHOD PRINT-OBJECT (STANDARD-OBJECT T) @ #x847446>)
```

There are three possible print methods for `tom`. One way to handle this situation
is by including an explicit call to the multiple methods.

```
(defmethod print-object ((object movie-star) stream)
  (format stream "#<Movie star: ~A>" (aka object))
  (if (next-method-p) (call-next-method)))
```

```
> tom
#<Movie star: Tom>#<Mammal Tom>
```

Now we get both print methods. As mentioned in the previous chapter, the function `next-method-p` returns true if there is another method available. Then,
`call-next-method` invokes the other method.

It is an error to invoke `call-next-method` if there is no next method.

13.7 Classes as Types, and Types as Classes

The Common LISP Object System was designed to be compatible with the existing
LISP type system. In particular, the following properties obtain.

- Every class has a corresponding type of the same name. The type predicates
  `typep`, `subtypep`, and `type-of` work with classes. For example, the class
  `movie-star` created above is also a LISP type.

  ```
  > (typep tom 'movie-star)
  T
  ```

  ```
  > (subtypep 'mice-stars 'vertebrate)
  T
  T
  ```

  ```
  > (type-of tom)
  MICE-STARS
  ```

- Class names can be used as type specifiers in type declarations and with the
  special form `the`.

  ```
  (defun mouse-spouse (star commoner)
    (declare (type mice-stars star))
    (the movie-star (make-instance 'mice-stars :name commoner)))
  ```

  ```
  > (mouse-spouse tom 'mary)
  #<Movie star: MARY>#<Mammal MARY>
  ```

Here we require that the `star` be an instance of `mice-stars` and that the result returned be of type `movie-star`. By marrying a celebrity, you become one yourself.

- Many of the predefined LISP data types have corresponding class definitions, as listed in Figure 13.1. The numbers in parenthesis refer to the chapter in which that data type is introduced.

- The predefined LISP types can be implemented in three different ways: a *standard class*, as created with `defclass`, a *structure class*, as created with `defstruct`, or a *built-in class*, using a nonextensible implementation.

```
> (class-of tom)
#<STANDARD-CLASS MICE-STARS @ #x11b55de>

> (setf x1 (make-time))
#S(MY-TIME :HOURS 0 :MINUTES 0 :SECONDS 0)

> (class-of x1)
#<STRUCTURE-CLASS MY-TIME @ #x11d8eae>

> (class-of 1999)
#<BUILT-IN-CLASS INTEGER @ #x7a8d96>
```

In our implementation, the LISP type classes are not extensible. This means that you may not create new classes that inherit from the predefined types as superclasses. For example, you cannot define a subclass of integers of strings.

Even though a programmer may not be able to use the predefined types as superclasses, she still may define methods that discriminate based on arguments of the predefined types. Our examples in section 12.3 demonstrated methods whose behavior changed based on their argument types, both predefined and new.

13.8 Initialization Functions

The initial slot values for a class instance can come from several sources. They may be specified with the `:initform` slot option in `defclass`. They may be given as an argument to `make-instance` using the appropriate `:initarg` keyword. `defclass` provides another class option `:default-initargs` for providing default initial slot values. The following two class definitions are equivalent.

```
(defclass person ()
  ((name :initarg :name :reader person-name)
   (age  :initarg :age :initform 0 :accessor person-age)
   (sex  :initarg :sex :initform 'F :accessor sex :allocation :class))
  (:documentation "A person class"))
```

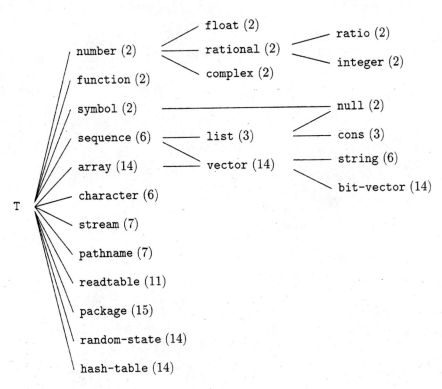

Figure 13.1: CLOS Class Inheritance Hierarchy

```
(defclass person ()
  ((name :initarg :name :reader person-name)
   (age  :initarg :age :accessor person-age)
   (sex  :initarg :sex :accessor sex :allocation :class))
  (:default-initargs :age 0 :sex 'F)
  (:documentation "A person class"))

> (setf x (make-instance 'person :name "Joe"))
#<PERSON @ #x1092dce>

> (setf y (make-instance 'person :name "Jane" :age 20))
#<PERSON @ #x10936e6>

> (person-age x)
0

> (person-age y)
20
```

We can override the :default-initargs values by providing initarg arguments to make-instance.

The Common LISP Object System is like a bank. It has a front-office and a back office. We, the user or customer, usually see only the front office. We deposit money, write checks, use the automatic teller machine, and get statements every month. We deal directly with the front office.

Meanwhile, the back office has to support all the front office operations. The back office keeps of track of how much money we have in our account. The back office credits and debits our account as appropriate and generates the statements that we receive monthly.

We usually deal with CLOS's front office through a few macros and functions, such as defclass, make-instance, and defmethod. However, unlike the bank, CLOS permits us programmers to change the way the CLOS back office works. In fact, we can change the back office to add new front-office features.

One part of CLOS's back office is instance initialization. There are four times at which an object may be initialized.

- Creating an instance, for example, with make-instance

- Reinitializing an instance

- Updating an instance to conform to a redefined class

- Updating an instance to conform to a new class

The instance initialization process is implemented with the following generic functions, for which the programmer can define additional methods. The only standard, front-office function is `make-instance`. The others are not normally called directly by the programmer.

- (make-instance class &rest args) — Creates a new instance of the given class; calls `initialize-instance` with the default initialization arguments

- (initialize-instance instance &rest args) — Assigns initial values to slots; calls `shared-initialize`.

- (reinitialize-instance instance &rest args) — Called to reset values for slots; calls `shared-initialize`.

- (shared-initialize instance slot-names &rest args) — Assigns args to their slots, and for any unbound slots, assigns respective `:initform` values

- (make-instances-obsolete class) — Called when a class is redefined and its previous instances need to be revised;
  calls `update-instance-for-redefined-class`

- (update-instance-for-different-class previous current &rest args) — Called when a class is changed as with `change-class`;
  calls `shared-initialize`

- (update-instance-for-redefined-class instance added-slots discarded-slots property-list &rest args) — Called when a class is redefined as with `defclass`; calls `shared-initialize`

Below, we define `:after` methods for each of the above generic functions to display a message whenever they are called.

```
(defmethod make-instance :after (class &rest args)
   (format t "--> make-instance with
Class: ~A~%" class))

(defmethod initialize-instance :after (instance &rest args)
   (format t "--> initialize-instance with
Instance: ~A~%" instance))

(defmethod reinitialize-instance :after (instance &rest args)
   (format t "--> reinitialize-instance with
Instance: ~A~%" instance))

(defmethod shared-initialize :after (instance slots &rest args)
   (format t "--> shared-initialize with
Instance: ~A~%" instance))
```

```
(defmethod make-instances-obsolete :after (class)
  (format t "--> make-instances-obsolete with
Class: ~A~%" class))

(defmethod update-instance-for-different-class
          :after (previous current &rest args)
  (format t "--> update-instance-for-different-class with
Previous: ~A
Current:  ~A~%" previous current))

(defmethod update-instance-for-redefined-class
          :after (instance added-slots discarded-slots
                    property-list &rest args)
  (format t "--> update-instance-for-redefined-class with
Instance:      ~A
Added-slots:   ~A~%" instance added-slots))
```

Now, we create a new person instance and modify it, revealing the actions of the above generic functions.

```
> (setf z (make-instance 'person :name "Sasha" :age 30))
--> shared-initialize with
Instance: #<PERSON>
--> initialize-instance with
Instance: #<PERSON>
--> make-instance with
Class: #<STANDARD-CLASS PERSON>
--> make-instance with
Class: PERSON
#<PERSON @ #x10aa3a6>
```

Remember that these methods are :after methods. Thus, the order of messages is the reverse of the order of calling. In the preceding example, make-instance calls initialize-instance, which calls shared-initialize.

```
> (person-name z)
"Sasha"

> (setf (person-age z) 33)
33

> (person-age z)
33

> (reinitialize-instance z :name "Alexandra")
```

```
--> shared-initialize with
Instance: #<PERSON>
--> reinitialize-instance with
Instance: #<PERSON>
#<PERSON @ #x10aa3a6>

> (person-name z)
"Alexandra"

> (person-age z)
33

> (sex z)
F
```

We next redefine the person class, which triggers a torrent of initialization action.

```
> (defclass person ()
  ((name :initarg :name :reader person-name)
   (age  :initarg :age :accessor person-age)
   (hair :initarg :hair :accessor person-hair)
   (sex  :initarg :sex :accessor sex :allocation :class))
  (:default-initargs :age 18 :sex 'F :hair 'brown)
  (:documentation "A person class"))

--> shared-initialize with
Instance: #<STANDARD-GENERIC-FUNCTION PERSON-NAME>
--> reinitialize-instance with
Instance: #<STANDARD-GENERIC-FUNCTION PERSON-NAME>
--> shared-initialize with
Instance: #<STANDARD-GENERIC-FUNCTION PERSON-AGE>
--> reinitialize-instance with
Instance: #<STANDARD-GENERIC-FUNCTION PERSON-AGE>
--> shared-initialize with
Instance: #<STANDARD-GENERIC-FUNCTION (SETF PERSON-AGE)>
;; Lots of output deleted at this point.
--> initialize-instance with
Instance: #<STANDARD-EFFECTIVE-SLOT-DEFINITION NAME>
--> make-instance with
Class: #<STANDARD-CLASS STANDARD-EFFECTIVE-SLOT-DEFINITION>
--> make-instances-obsolete with
Class: #<STANDARD-CLASS PERSON>
#<STANDARD-CLASS PERSON @ #x108cf6e>
```

When we try to access our old person, we trigger the update process.

```
> (person-age z)
--> shared-initialize with
Instance: #<PERSON>
--> update-instance-for-redefined-class with
Instance:      #<PERSON>
Added-slots:   (HAIR)
33
```

Next, we define a new class and put our old person in it.

```
> (defclass female ()
  ((name :initarg :name :reader person-name)
   (age  :initarg :age :accessor person-age)
   (hair :initarg :hair :accessor person-hair)
   (sex  :initarg :sex :accessor sex :allocation :class))
  (:default-initargs :age 18 :sex 'F :hair 'brown)
  (:documentation "A female class"))

--> shared-initialize with
Instance: #<STANDARD-CLASS FEMALE>
--> shared-initialize with
Instance: #<STANDARD-DIRECT-SLOT-DEFINITION NAME>
--> initialize-instance with
Instance: #<STANDARD-DIRECT-SLOT-DEFINITION NAME>
--> make-instance with
Class: #<STANDARD-CLASS STANDARD-DIRECT-SLOT-DEFINITION>
;; Lots of output deleted at this point.
--> reinitialize-instance with
Instance: #<STANDARD-GENERIC-FUNCTION (SETF SEX)>
--> initialize-instance with
Instance: #<STANDARD-CLASS FEMALE>
--> make-instance with
Class: #<STANDARD-CLASS STANDARD-CLASS>
#<STANDARD-CLASS FEMALE @ #x10cc766>

> (change-class z 'female)
--> shared-initialize with
Instance: #<STANDARD-EFFECTIVE-SLOT-DEFINITION SEX>
--> initialize-instance with
Instance: #<STANDARD-EFFECTIVE-SLOT-DEFINITION SEX>
--> make-instance with
Class: #<STANDARD-CLASS STANDARD-EFFECTIVE-SLOT-DEFINITION>
--> shared-initialize with
Instance: #<STANDARD-EFFECTIVE-SLOT-DEFINITION HAIR>
```

```
--> initialize-instance with
Instance: #<STANDARD-EFFECTIVE-SLOT-DEFINITION HAIR>
--> make-instance with
Class: #<STANDARD-CLASS STANDARD-EFFECTIVE-SLOT-DEFINITION>
--> shared-initialize with
Instance: #<STANDARD-EFFECTIVE-SLOT-DEFINITION AGE>
--> initialize-instance with
Instance: #<STANDARD-EFFECTIVE-SLOT-DEFINITION AGE>
--> make-instance with
Class: #<STANDARD-CLASS STANDARD-EFFECTIVE-SLOT-DEFINITION>
--> shared-initialize with
Instance: #<STANDARD-EFFECTIVE-SLOT-DEFINITION NAME>
--> initialize-instance with
Instance: #<STANDARD-EFFECTIVE-SLOT-DEFINITION NAME>
--> make-instance with
Class: #<STANDARD-CLASS STANDARD-EFFECTIVE-SLOT-DEFINITION>
--> shared-initialize with
Instance: #<FEMALE>
--> update-instance-for-different-class with
Previous: #<PERSON>
Current:  #<FEMALE>
#<FEMALE @ #x1162c46>
```

∞ ⇒ Different versions of CLOS may implement the initialization methods in other ways,
so your dialect may produce different output for these examples.

   Instead of examining the behind-the-scenes workings of CLOS, we can use the
generic initialization functions for something useful. For example, suppose we want
to keep track of every person. We can create a method for initialize-instance
that posts that information using the person property list.

```
(defmethod initialize-instance :after ((instance person) &rest args)
   (format t "after method for initialize-instance: ~A~%" instance)
   (if (get 'person 'count)
       (incf (get 'person 'count))
       (setf (get 'person 'count) 1))
   (if (get 'person 'instances)
       (pushnew instance (get 'person 'instances))
       (setf (get 'person 'instances) (list instance))))

> (setf p1 (make-instance 'person :name "Moe"))
after method for initialize-instance: #<PERSON>
#<PERSON @ #x107ca6e>
```

```
> (setf p2 (make-instance 'person :name "Larry"))
after method for initialize-instance: #<PERSON>
#<PERSON @ #x107d9b6>

> (setf p3 (make-instance 'person :name "Curly"))
after method for initialize-instance: #<PERSON>
#<PERSON @ #x107e7ee>

> (get 'person 'count)
3

> (get 'person 'instances)
(#<PERSON @ #x107e7ee> #<PERSON @ #x107d9b6> #<PERSON @ #x107ca6e>)

> (mapcar #'person-name (get 'person 'instances))
("Curly" "Larry" "Moe")
```

The various initialization generic functions are quite useful. They are helpful in verifying input and monitoring new data. For example, you could have an initialization function that automatically fills in an age field when a date of birth is given.

13.9 Meta-classes

In CLOS, classes are themselves instances of classes. We refer to these classes which describe classes as *meta-classes*.

By comparison, consider the words in a language. We may view the words as instances of the classes noun, verb, adjective, and so forth. (Some words, such as hand, may belong to more than one class.) The classes themselves, such as noun, belong to the category parts-of-speech, which is a meta-class.[2] CLOS has three standard meta-classes, mentioned earlier in the discussion of types as classes.

- built-in-class – Predefined LISP types, given in Figure 13.1

- standard-class – Classes defined with defclass

- structure-class – Structures defined with defstruct

We can use class-of to identify an object's meta-class.

```
> (class-of nil)
#<BUILT-IN-CLASS NULL @ #x7a8e06>
```

---

[2]The word noun is also an instance of the class noun, demonstrating meta-circularity.

```
> (class-of 42)
#<BUILT-IN-CLASS INTEGER @ #x7a8d96>

> (class-of p1)
#<STANDARD-CLASS PERSON @ #x106a266>

> (defstruct date m d y)
DATE

> (setf d (make-date ))
#S(DATE :M NIL :D NIL :Y NIL)

> (class-of d)
#<STRUCTURE-CLASS DATE @ #x1081c8e>
```

In addition, CLOS provides classes of standard metaobjects.

- standard-object — Subclass of T. It is the direct superclass of standard-class, standard-method, and standard-generic-function.

- standard-method — Default class for methods such as defined with defmethod and defgeneric.

- standard-generic-function — Default class for generic functions, such as defined with defgeneric and defclass.

- method-combination — Superclass for all method combination objects, such as defined with define-method-combination (but not in our standard implementation.)

$\infty \Rightarrow$

```
> (defclass a () () )
#<STANDARD-CLASS A @ #x1069236>

> (typep (make-instance 'a) 'standard-object)
T

> (typep #'make-instance 'standard-generic-function)
T

> (defmethod foo () ())
#<STANDARD-METHOD FOO NIL @ #x106b67e>
```

We now switch to another implementation which supports the method-combination class.

```
> (setf x (define-method-combination + :operator
  + :identity-with-one-argument t))
#<CLOS::STANDARD-SIMPLE-METHOD-COMBINATION 100AA8F8>

> (typep x 'method-combination)
T
```

We could use these classes to redefine various generic functions, such as the print method, for various standard LISP objects, such as methods and generic functions.

CLOS also allows us to extend `standard-class` through inheritance and then to create new classes derived with the `defclass` option `:metaclass`.

Following up on the example from the preceding section, we create a new meta-class for tracking objects. Instead of using a property list to keep the instance information, we define a new meta-class, `tracking-class`, derived from `standard-class`, which has appropriate slots. We then create a `tracked-person` class derived from the `person` class, which specifies `tracking-class` as its meta class.

```
(defclass tracking-class (standard-class)
  ((counter :initform 0)
   (instances :initform nil)))

(defclass tracked-person (person)
  ()
  (:metaclass tracking-class))
```

We now want to have LISP update the `counter` and `instances` slots every time we create a new instance of `tracked-person`. We can define an `:after` method for `make-instance` to handle the update of `counter`.

```
(defmethod make-instance
  :after ((class tracking-class) &rest args)
  (incf (slot-value class 'counter)))

(defun how-many? (obj)
  (how-many-class (class-of obj)))

(defmethod how-many-class ((class tracking-class))
  (slot-value class 'counter))
```

We can now try some examples.

```
> (setf p1 (make-instance 'tracked-person))
#<TRACKED-PERSON @ #x107c94e>
```

```
> (how-many? p1)
1


> (setf p2 (make-instance 'tracked-person))
#<TRACKED-PERSON @ #x107e9c6>


> (how-many? p1)
2
```

It looks like the counter is working fine. Updating the instances is a little trickier. Note that make-instance does not itself know the name of the new instance! We could try something devious, like the following, to try to discover this information.

```
(defmethod make-instance ((class tracking-class) &rest args)
  (let ((new (call-next-method)))
    (pushnew new (slot-value class 'instances))
    new))
```

However, values returned by call-next-method can easily change over the lifetime of the code. The programmer should not vest too much faith in those values.

Here is a better approach. We define a new method for initialize-instance. Just as make-instance did not know the name of the instance, initialize-instance does not know the name of the class. However, we can deduce the class given the instance. We use that information to pass to a new generic function, push-instance, which does the right thing.

```
(defgeneric push-instance (class instance)
  (:method (class instance) nil)
  (:method ((class tracking-class) instance)
           (pushnew instance (slot-value class 'instances))))


(defmethod initialize-instance :after (instance &rest args)
  (push-instance (class-of instance) instance))


(defun show-instances (obj)
  (show-class-instances (class-of obj)))


(defmethod show-class-instances ((class tracking-class))
  (slot-value class 'instances))


> (setf p1 (make-instance 'tracked-person))
#<TRACKED-PERSON @ #x108b1e6>


> (setf p2 (make-instance 'tracked-person))
#<TRACKED-PERSON @ #x108c2be>
```

```
> (show-instances p1)
(#<TRACKED-PERSON @ #x108c2be> #<TRACKED-PERSON @ #x108b1e6>)
```

Suppose we want to track all new classes created with defclass. Assuming that we still have the new method for initialize-instance that calls the generic function push-instance, we can do the following.

```
(defparameter *my-classes*)

(defmethod push-instance :after
  ((class (eql (find-class 'standard-class))) instance)
  (pushnew instance *my-classes*))

> (defclass a () ())
#<STANDARD-CLASS A @ #x1076dae>

> *my-classes*
(#<STANDARD-CLASS A @ #x1076dae>)

> (defclass b () ())
#<STANDARD-CLASS B @ #x107f9ee>

> *my-classes*
(#<STANDARD-CLASS B @ #x107f9ee> #<STANDARD-CLASS A @ #x1076dae>)
```

We can try to do the same thing for structures, using the structure-class meta-class.

```
(defparameter *my-structures* nil)

(defmethod push-instance :after
  ((class (eql (find-class 'structure-class))) instance)
  (pushnew instance *my-structures*))

> (defstruct x ())
X

> (defstruct y ())
Y

> *my-structures*
(#<STRUCTURE-CLASS Y @ #x1098fce> #<STRUCTURE-CLASS X @ #x109479e>)
```

The programmer can deploy the extensible meta-classes as another way to use LISP as a programmable programming language. CLOS's *metaobject protocol*, or MOP, is the topic of the book *The Art of the Metaobject Protocol* [Kiczales et al., 1991], which also discusses how to implement CLOS.

CLOS itself provides a number of back-office functions that are useful for implementing some of the front-office functions and macros.

- `(add-method generic-function method)` – A generic function that destructively adds the given method object to the given generic-function object. Called by `defmethod`.

- `(ensure-generic-function function-name &key)` – Defines a generic function or sets options for a generic function. The available keys include:

  `:lambda-list`
  `:argument-precedence-order`
  `:declare`
  `:documentation`
  `:generic-function-class`
  `:method-combination`
  `:method-class`
  `:environment`

- `(find-method generic-function method-qualifiers specializers &optional errorp)` – For the given generic-function, finds the method that matches the given qualifiers and specializers. Failure to find such a method triggers an error unless `errorp` is NIL. `find-method` itself is a generic function.

- `(function-keywords method)` – A generic function that gets the keyword parameters for the given method.

- `(invalid-method-error method format-string &rest args)` – Called when a method is invoked which is not defined for the given set of arguments. The format string and arguments constitute the output message.

- `(method-combination-error format-string &rest args)` – Called when there is an error in method combination. The format string and arguments constitute the output message.

- `(method-qualifiers method)` – A generic function that returns a list of qualifiers for the given method.

- `(remove-method generic-function method)` – A generic function that deletes the given method object from the given generic function object; the opposite of `add-method`.

These functions make it possible for the user to create her own versions of `defclass` and `defmethod`, as discussed in [Kiczales et al., 1991]. Using programmable metaobjects, the user can extend CLOS and LISP in a number of ways, without resorting to redefining `defclass`. See exercise 13.10.6.

13.10   Exercises

13.10.1   Define Predicate [3*]

We seem to create a predicate for every class we define. Write a `defpredicate` macro that does this task for us, as illustrated below.

```
(defclass building () ((type :initarg :building-type)))

> (setf c (make-instance 'building :building-type 'house))
#<BUILDING @ #x11e1e9e>

> (defpredicate building)
#<STANDARD-GENERIC-FUNCTION BUILDING-P @ #x11b725e>

> (building-p c)
T

> (building-p 'c)
NIL
```

13.10.2   The Empty Property List [4*]

What would have happened if we had defined `empty-plist` as follows?

```
(defun empty-plist ()
  '((())))
```

13.10.3   Removing Property Values [5]

Add a method `premove`, which eliminates a property-value pair from the property list. Here is an example.

```
> (pplist x)
MARY
     AGE        45
JOHN
     SON        JOE
     AGE        199

> (premove x 'john 'age)
199
```

```
> (pplist x)
MARY
      AGE        45
JOHN
      SON        JOE
```

13.10.4   Queue Object [6*]

A queue is a *first-in, first-out* or *FIFO* data structure. By contrast, a stack is a
last-in, first-out or *LIFO* data structure. A queue is like a pipe: items enter at one
end and exit at the other.

We can use lists and objects to implement a queue object. Define the class
queue and the following related methods:

```
(queue-p obj)
(queue-empty-p q)
(enqueue q obj)
(dequeue q)
(q-head q)
(print-object q stream)
```

```
> (setf y (make-instance 'queue))
#<Queue NIL>

> (queue-p y)
T

> (queue-empty-p y)
T

> (enqueue y 1)
(1)

> (enqueue y 2)
(2)

> (enqueue y 3)
(3)

> y                              ;  The queue now has three elements.
#<Queue (1 2 3)>

> (q-head y)
1
```

```
> (dequeue y)                    ;  We remove the first element.
1

> y
#<Queue (2 3)>

> (dequeue y)
2

> (queue-empty-p y)              ;  The queue is not empty.
NIL

> (dequeue y)
3

> (dequeue y)
NIL

> (queue-empty-p y)              ;  The queue is now empty.
T

> (dequeue y)
NIL
```

13.10.5   make-better-plist [5*]

The property list storage and retrieval objects created by `make-plist` require that
the key and property objects be restricted to symbols. In particular, the programmer cannot use lists and strings as retrieval keys or properties.

Write `make-better-plist`, which remedies this deficiency. Here are examples
of its use.

```
> (setf b (make-better-plist))
#<Private property list B>

> (pput b '(things i like) "at the beach" '(sand sun))
(SAND SUN)

> (pput b '(things i like) "in the city" '(movies restaurants))
(MOVIES RESTAURANTS)

> (pput b "things i hate" '(at the beach) '(flies trash))
(FLIES TRASH)
```

```
> (pput b "things i hate" '(in the city) "flies trash")
"flies trash"

> (pplist b)
things i hate
      (IN THE CITY)  flies trash
      (AT THE BEACH)  (FLIES TRASH)
(THINGS I LIKE)
      in the city    (MOVIES RESTAURANTS)
      at the beach   (SAND SUN)

> (pget b "things i hate" '(at the beach))
(FLIES TRASH)

> (setf (pget b '(things i like) "at the beach") 'me)
ME

> (pplist b)
things i hate
      (IN THE CITY)  flies trash
      (AT THE BEACH)  (FLIES TRASH)
(THINGS I LIKE)
      in the city    (MOVIES RESTAURANTS)
      at the beach   ME
```

13.10.6 Meta-Predicates [5*]

In exercise 13.10.1, we defined a macro to make it easier to define predicates for
class objects. Using meta-classes, define a method that will automatically define a
predicate whenever a class is defined. Name the predicate using the standard -P
suffix.

```
> (defclass cat () ())
#<STANDARD-CLASS CAT @ #x1093b5e>

> (setf c (make-instance 'cat))
#<CAT @ #x1099126>

> (cat-p c)
T

> (cat-p 'garfield)
NIL
```

13.11   Chapter Summary

- Object-oriented programming was originally devised in the Simula and Smalltalk programming languages.

- In procedural programming, data objects are manipulated by functions. In object-oriented programming, objects actively engage in computation by sending and responding to messages.

- LISP provides the programmer with a seamless combination of procedural and object-oriented programming.

- Objects are instances of classes created by the `defclass` macro as follows:

```
(defclass class-name superclass-names
  slot-specifiers
  class-options)
```

where

  - `class-name` is a symbol giving the name of the new class.
  - `superclass-names` is a list of zero or more class-names, from which the new class inherits slots and methods.
  - `slot-specifiers` is a list of zero of more slot specifications.
  - `class-options` is zero or more class options.

- Objects of a given class can be created with the `make-instance` generic function:

```
(make-instance class {initarg}*)
```

- CLOS provides a generic method `print-object` for printing objects, which is called by the read-eval-print loop. The programmer can define her own `print-object` methods for new classes, for which she can use the following macro.

```
(print-unreadable-object (object stream)
    [:type type] [:identity id] {form}*)
```

- CLOS provides a generic method `describe-object` for describing objects, which is called by the `describe` function. The programmer can define her own `describe-object` methods for new classes.

- Slot specifications in `defclass` are designated with the following keywords, each of which has associated values:

- :reader is the name of a function for reading the value of the slot.
- :writer is the name of a function for setting the value of the slot.
- :accessor is the name of a function for both reading and setting the value of the slot.
- :allocation is either of the two keywords :instance or :class indicating if the slot's value is set for each instance of the object, or a single value shared by all instances of the class, respectively. The default :allocation is :instance.
- :initarg is the name of the keyword to specify an initial value for this slot by make-instance.
- :initform is the default value for this slot.
- :type is the type specification for the slot.
- :documentation is a documentation string for the slot.

- Class options to defclass include the following:

  - (:default-initargs initarg-list) — Specifies default initial values for slots
  - (:documentation string) — A documentation string for the class
  - (:metaclass class-name) — Specifies a metaclass for the defined class other than the default class standard-class

- Other useful CLOS functions include the following:

```
(class-of object)
(class-name class)
(find-class symbol)
(change-class instance new-class)
```

- CLOS allows the programmer to redefine classes on the fly. CLOS automatically converts old class instances to conform to the new class definitions.

- CLOS provides a number of functions, generic functions, and macros for examining and manipulating a class's slots.

```
;  Functions:
(slot-boundp instance slot-name)
(slot-value object slot-name)
(slot-exists-p object slot-name)
(slot-makunbound instance slot-name)

;  Generic functions:
(slot-missing class object slot-name operation [new-value])
(slot-unbound class instance slot-name)
```

```
;  Macros:
(with-accessors ({slot-entry}*) instance-form {form}*)
(with-slots ({slot-entry}*) instance-form {form}*)
```

- Structures and many LISP types are treated as classes. The programmer can write methods that discriminate based on structures and certain predefined LISP types, as well on classes.

- CLOS provides a number of generic functions to control the process of initializing object instances.

```
(make-instance class {initarg}*)
(initialize-instance instance {initarg}*)
(reinitialize-instance instance {initarg}*)
(shared-initialize instance slot-names {initarg}*)
(make-instances-obsolete class)
(update-instance-for-different-class previous current {initarg}*)
(update-instance-for-redefined-class instance added-slots
        discarded-slots property-list {initarg}*)
```

- The programmer can extend CLOS and LISP expanding the standard-class meta-class and using the defclass option :metaclass.

- CLOS provides a number of functions which the programmer may use to implement her own version of CLOS.

```
(add-method generic-function method)
(ensure-generic-function function-name [[key-options]])
(find-method generic-function method-qualifiers specializers
        [errorp])
(function-keywords method)
(invalid-method-error method format-string {arg}*)
(method-combination-error format-string {arg}*)
(method-qualifiers method)
(remove-method generic-function method)
```

Simplicity does not precede complexity, but follows it.

◇ ALAN PERLIS, *Epigrams in Programming (1982)*

Chapter 14

Vectors and Arrays

> *All are most beautiful, of a thousand shapes,*
> *and all accessible,*
> *and filled with trees of a thousand kinds.*

⋄ CHRISTOPHER COLUMBUS, *Letter to the Sovereigns on the First Voyage (1493)*

> I derived the method I use
> for writing music by tossing coins from the method used in the
> *Book of Changes* for obtaining oracles.

⋄ JOHN CAGE, *A Year From Monday (1963)*

> THEY SAID ONE THING INVOLVING
> SYMBOLS — LINEAR RELATION-
> SHIPS — WHICH MADE ME THINK
> THEY DIDN'T UNDERSTAND. BUT
> THEN THEY SAID SOMETHING ELSE
> — THAT THE SCHOOL'S DAYS OF
> BEING OPEN WOULD BE UNPRE-
> DICATABLY ARRANGED. THE RESULT
> WAS WE HAD A PLEASANT DAY
> TOGETHER.

⋄ JOHN CAGE, *A Year From Monday (1963)*

By this point, the reader has witnessed a broad range of LISP objects that can be manipulated to build programs. We have symbols, numbers, lists, characters, strings, streams, functions, and general objects which can themselves control computations — a diverse array of objects. We now turn our attention to a data

530

structure which serves as the mainstay of many programming languages – the array itself. The simplest array is a one-dimensional, linear array, namely, a vector, which is a basic LISP data type.

In many programming languages, such as FORTRAN or APL, the array is the primary data structure. It is most commonly used for numerical data, often representing matrices. The vector object in LISP can be applied to such linear algebra problems.

A vector is a linear, random-access data structure. The programmer can access any element of a vector directly by specifying that element's location in the vector. It is just as easy to get the last element of a vector as the first.

By contrast, a list is a linear, sequential access data structure. Even if a programmer knows the location of an element in a list, she must still sequentially traverse the list to access the given element. The time required to access an element in a list will be proportional to its distance from the front of the list.

In this chapter, we use vectors in exploring four other programming topics: rectangular arrays, hash tables, random numbers, and lazy evaluation.

14.1   Vectors in LISP

Vectors are similar to lists, and in LISP, they are similarly notated. The function `vector` is a convenient constructor for vectors and is similar to the function `list`. A vector is indicated by a # followed by a list.

```
> '(1 2 3)            ;  The list (1 2 3).
(1 2 3)

> (vector 1 2 3)      ;  The vector #(1 2 3).
#(1 2 3)

> (vector 'alpha '(beta) "gamma" #\D)
#(ALPHA (BETA) "gamma" #\D)


> '#(1 2 3)           ;  The vector #(1 2 3).
#(1 2 3)

> (coerce '(1 2 3) 'vector)
#(1 2 3)

> (coerce '#(1 2 3) 'list)
(1 2 3)
```

The last two examples demonstrate the coercion of a list to a vector, and vice versa.

The basic accessors for lists are `car` and `cdr`. Vectors are referenced with `aref`. The arguments to `aref` are a vector and an index. Vectors in LISP, like strings, are *zero-based*. That is, the elements of a vector of length n are numbered from 0 through $n - 1$.

```
> (setf x '#(0 1 2 3 4))
#(0 1 2 3 4)

> (vectorp x)
T

> (aref x 2)
2

> (aref x 0)
0

> (length x)
5

> (setf (aref x 0) 10)
10

> x
#(10 1 2 3 4)
```

Above, we have created a five-element vector x. The initial value of each element happens to correspond to its respective index. vectorp is the predicate for vectors. The length function gives the number of elements, and aref can be used with setf to change the value of the given element.

It is also possible to find an element of a vector by its contents, without knowing its location. The function position takes two arguments, an object and a vector, and returns the index of the element of the vector, which is eql to the given object. If no such element is found, position returns NIL, as shown here.

```
> (setf x '#(11 12 13 14))
#(11 12 13 14)

> (position 12 x)
1

> (aref x 3)
14

> (position 10 x)
NIL
```

concatenate	copy-seq	count	delete
delete-duplicates	elt	every	fill
find	length	map	merge
mismatch	notany	notevery	nreverse
nsubstitute	position	reduce	remove
remove-duplicates	replace	reverse	search
some	sort	subseq	substitute

Table 14.1: Sequence Functions

```
> (position 12 x :test #'<)          ;  position takes an optional predicate.
2


;  Find the element equal to twice 6:
> (position 6 x :test #'(lambda (x v) (= v (* x 2)))) 
1


> (aref x 1)
12
```

The `:test` keyword for `position` allows the programmer to specify a two-place comparison predicate as an additional argument. (`position obj vec :test #'eql`) is the same as (`position obj vec`). These functions allow one conveniently to search vectors.

For alert readers, some of these vector functions may be *déjà vu* all over again. In fact, vectors, like lists and strings, are *sequences*, and all the sequence functions described in section 6.4 can also be used for vectors. Table 14.1 lists those functions.

We can test drive some of them with vectors.

```
> (reverse x)
#(14 13 12 11)


> x                     ;  reverse is not destructive.
#(11 12 13 14)


> (nreverse x)          ;  nreverse is destructive.
#(14 13 12 11)


> x
#(14 13 12 11)
```

```
> (map 'vector #'1+ x)    ;  Adds 1 to each element of x.
#(15 14 13 12)


> x
#(14 13 12 11)


> (some #'oddp x)         ;  Are any odd numbers in x?
T


> (reduce #'+ x)          ;  Sums the elements of x.
50


> (fill x 100)            ;  Replaces each element with the value 100.
#(100 100 100 100)


> x
#(100 100 100 100)


> (remove-duplicates x) ;  remove-duplicates is not destructive.
#(100)


> x
#(100 100 100 100)


> (delete-duplicates x) ;  delete-duplicates is destructive.
#(100)


> x
#(100)
```

14.2   Two-Dimensional Arrays

The elements of a vector can be any LISP object, including other vectors. We can
create a two-dimensional array out of one-dimensional vectors. Here, we define a
class and associated methods for a two-dimensional, rectangular array object, also
called a matrix.

```
(defclass 2d-array ()
   ((rows :initarg :rows :reader rows)
    (columns :initarg :columns :reader columns)
    (the-array :accessor the-array))
   (:documentation "A two-dimensional array."))
```

```
(defun make-2d-array (x y)
  (let ((new-array (make-instance '2d-array :rows x :columns y)))
    (setf (the-array new-array) (make-array x))
    (dotimes (count x new-array)
            (setf (aref (the-array new-array) count)
                  (make-array y)))))
```

The 2d-array class has three slots: the number of rows, columns, and the array itself. The function make-2d-array sets the values of rows and columns and then creates the array, which is a vector of vectors, using the built-in LISP function make-array.

We next add a predicate and some useful methods for printing and accessing arrays.

```
(defun 2d-array-p (obj)
  (typep obj '2d-array))

(defmethod print-object ((obj 2d-array) stream)
  (format stream "<2d-array (~Ax~A) ~A>"
          (rows obj)
          (columns obj)
          (the-array obj)))

(defmethod 2d-ref ((obj 2d-array) (x integer) (y integer))
  (aref (aref (the-array obj) x) y))

(defmethod (setf 2d-ref) (val (obj 2d-array) (x integer) (y integer))
  (setf (aref (aref (the-array obj) x) y) val))

(defmethod 2d-array-fill ((obj 2d-array) val)
  (map 'vector
       #'(lambda (v) (fill v val))
       (the-array obj)))
```

2d-array-fill will set every array element to a given value. Now, we can try out our creation.

```
> (setf x (make-2d-array 3 4))
<2d-array (3x4) #(#(NIL NIL NIL NIL) #(NIL NIL NIL NIL)
                  #(NIL NIL NIL NIL))>

> (2d-array-fill x 9)
#(#(9 9 9 9) #(9 9 9 9) #(9 9 9 9))
```

```
> (setf (2d-ref x 0 0) nil)
NIL

> x
<2d-array (3x4) #(#(NIL 9 9 9) #(9 9 9 9) #(9 9 9 9))>
```

For safety, we can add bounds checking to our arrays.

```
(defmethod 2d-ref ((obj 2d-array) (x integer) (y integer))
  (assert
    (and (not (minusp x))
         (< x (rows obj)))
    (x)
    "2d-ref error. row value: ~d is out of range (0-~d)"
    x (rows obj))
  (assert
    (and (not (minusp y))
         (< y (columns obj)))
    (y)
    "2d-ref error. column value: ~d is out of range (0-~d)"
    y (columns obj))
  (aref (aref (the-array obj) x) y))

> (2d-ref x 1 1)
9

> (2d-ref x 1 4)
Error: 2d-ref error. column value: 4 is out of range (0-4)

Restart actions (select using :continue):
 0: retry assertion with new value for Y.
[1]
```

At this point, the programmer could specify a new Y value and continue. In the 2d-ref definition, we do not need to use check-type because the generic function dispatch guarantees that the arguments match the type of the parameters. We can use the same bounds-checking code for the setf version of 2d-ref.

In exercises 14.8.4 and 14.8.5, we examine arrays of higher dimensions.

At this point, we need to level with the reader. Common LISP actually provides built-in support for multidimensional arrays. The array is a standard LISP data type. Vectors are a subtype of array, as well as a subtype of sequence.

We can create a two-dimensional array, by using make-array. We note that Common LISP provides a number of constants that indicate the various implementation limits associated with arrays.

∞ ⇒

```
> (setf a (make-array '(3 4)))
#2A((NIL NIL NIL NIL) (NIL NIL NIL NIL) (NIL NIL NIL NIL))

> (arrayp a)
T

> array-rank-limit          ; Upper bound on the number of dimensions.
65536

> array-dimension-limit     ; Upper bound for a single dimension.
16777216

> array-total-size-limit    ; Upper bound for total number of elements.
16777216

> (array-element-type a)    ; The type of element for the given array.
T

> (array-rank a)            ; The number of dimensions for the given array.
2

> (array-dimension a 0)     ; The size of the first (zero-based) dimension.
3

> (array-dimension a 1)     ; The size of the second dimension.
4

> (array-dimensions a)      ; The dimensions of the given array.
(3 4)

> (array-total-size a)      ; The total number of elements for the array.
12

> (array-in-bounds-p a 3 4) ; Predicate to check bounds of array reference.
NIL

> (array-in-bounds-p a 1 2)
T

> (array-row-major-index a 0 0)
0

> (array-row-major-index a 2 3)
11
```

The last two examples indicate that a programmer can consider a multidimensional array as a series of vectors concatenated into one long vector. In this case, the 3 by 4 array a might be thought of as a 12-element vector. The function array-row-major-index performs a translation between the multidimensional references and the vector references. Thus, element $(0,0)$ of a is element 0 of the associated vector, and element $(2,3)$ is element 11 of the vector.

14.3   Hash Tables

The main advantage of vectors over lists is the relative speed of access. Sequential search is usually slower. For example, if you are looking for someone's office in a large building, it is usually not advisable to search through the building room by room. If you know the room number, you can go directly to the right floor and then locate the office. For example, room 408 is probably on the fourth floor. The room number provides information about the number of the floor, thus simplifying the process of locating the room.

Just as a building can be organized with room numbers to correspond to floors, it is possible to use a vector to organize information in a table that can be indexed by keys. Previously, we have used association lists to make tables which are key-indexed. However, association lists are inefficient for large quantities of data because of the sequential search problem.

We can use vectors to implement a key-indexed list by using *hash tables*. The name *hash* comes from the method of generating the table index from the key: the key is chopped up and converted into a number, which in turn is used to specify the element (or *bucket*) in the array for storing the information.

There are many hash methods, as discussed in [Knuth, 1978]. A common technique involves adding up the numerical values of the characters in the key. We shall use LISP's sxhash function, which converts a LISP object into an integer, or *hash code*. Here, we create a hash table for storing ages.

```
> (setf age-table (make-array 10))
#(NIL NIL NIL NIL NIL NIL NIL NIL NIL NIL)

> (sxhash 'john)
13167

> (sxhash 10125466) ;  Numbers can be hashed.
32922

> (sxhash 'mary)
13896

> (setf (aref age-table (mod (sxhash 'john) 10)) '(john 22))
(JOHN 22)
```

```
> (setf (aref age-table (mod (sxhash 'mary) 10)) '(mary 21))
(MARY 21)

> age-table
#(NIL NIL NIL NIL NIL NIL (MARY 21) (JOHN 22) NIL NIL)

> (aref age-table (mod (sxhash 'john) 10))
(JOHN 22)
```

The resulting integer from sxhash is usually a good bit larger than the length of the hash table vector, and an error would result if we used that integer itself as the index. Therefore, we take that integer modulo the size of the table to get a number in the proper range. In this case, since the table is of size 10, the index is just the last digit of the hash code. John goes in bucket 7, and Mary resides in bucket 6.

Note that the last expression shows that information can be retrieved from the table without giving its explicit location. The location is implicit in the key itself. Furthermore, this method of access is generally much quicker than searching through an association list.

The reader may have already noticed a potential problem in this method. What would happen if John and Mary had the same index? That is, their hash codes could have been distinct, but the last digits could have matched. In that case, the second entry would have clobbered the first. They would have hit the same bucket.

There are several methods for handling these collisions. One method is to check for a collision at the time of entry or retrieval. If a collision is found, check the current bucket to see if it matches the specified key. If it does not, try the next bucket in sequence.

Here is a LISP class and related functions and methods for creating hash table objects which implement this collision avoidance strategy.

```
(defclass my-hash-table ()
  ((size :initform 10 :initarg :size :accessor size
         :documentation "size of hash table")
   (table :initform nil :accessor the-table
          :documentation "vector of values"))
  (:documentation "simple hash table class"))

; Predicate for these hash tables.
(defgeneric my-hash-table-p (object)
  (:method ((object my-hash-table)) t)
  (:method (object) nil))
```

```lisp
;   Constructor function.
(defun make-my-hash-table (size)
  (let ((htable (make-instance 'my-hash-table :size size)))
    (setf (the-table htable) (make-array size))
    htable))

(defmethod reveal ((obj my-hash-table))
  (the-table obj))

(defmethod next-number ((table my-hash-table) (number integer))
  (incf number)
  (cond ((= number (size table)) 0)
        (t number)))

(defmethod get-bucket ((table my-hash-table) (number integer))
  (aref (the-table table) number))

(defmethod get-number ((table my-hash-table) key number)
  (cond ((null number)
         (setf number (mod (sxhash key) (size table)))))
  (let ((bucket (get-bucket table number)))
    (cond ((null bucket) number)
          ((eq key (car bucket)) number)
          (t
           (get-number table key (next-number table number))))))

(defmethod table-get ((table my-hash-table) key)
  (cdr (get-bucket table (get-number table key nil))))

(defmethod table-put ((table my-hash-table) key value)
  (setf (aref (the-table table) (get-number table key nil))
        (cons key value)))

> (setf y (make-my-hash-table 10))
#<MY-HASH-TABLE @ #x11b836e>

> (my-hash-table-p y)
T

> (table-get y 'john)
NIL
```

```
> (table-put y 'mary 21)
(MARY . 21)

> (table-put y 'john 39)
(JOHN . 39)

> (table-get y 'john)
39

> (reveal y)
#(NIL NIL NIL NIL NIL NIL (MARY . 21) (JOHN . 39) NIL NIL)
```

We have created a 10-element hash table and have made two entries. We now add another record, which collides with John at index position 7.

```
> (sxhash 'ruth)
17737                          ;  Last digit is 7.

> (table-put y 'ruth 25)
(RUTH . 25)

> (reveal y)
#(NIL NIL NIL NIL NIL NIL (MARY . 21) (JOHN . 39) (RUTH . 25) NIL)
```

We see that Ruth's record was inserted sequentially after John's.

There are many issues involved in designing effective hash tables. The method just given suffers on several counts. First, as the table fills up, the insertion and retrieval rapidly converges to slow, sequential search.

Second, there is no good way to delete items from the table. Removing an item may result in making some other item inaccessible. For example, if you deleted John's entry in the table above, the program would no longer find Ruth.

Finally, the table can fill up. The only way to enlarge the table would be to build a new, bigger table and reenter the existing data in the new table — an expensive proposition. In exercise 14.8.9, we present a method for building extensible hash tables.

LISP actually provides a convenient hash table mechanism. Here is an example.

```
> (setf joe (make-hash-table))
#<EQL hash-table with 0 entries @ #x109b776>

> (type-of joe)               ;  Joe is a hash table.
HASH-TABLE
```

```
> (hash-table-p joe)
T

> (hash-table-count joe)   ;  Joe is empty.
0

> (gethash 'age joe)       ;  gethash retrieves items.
NIL                        ;  The first NIL indicates the result.
NIL                        ;  The second NIL indicates no entry in table.

> (setf (gethash 'age joe) 30)
30

> (gethash 'age joe)       ;  How old is Joe?
30
T

> (gethash 'retired joe)   ;  Is Joe retired?
NIL
NIL                        ;  No entry in the table.

> (setf (gethash 'retired joe) nil)
NIL

> (gethash 'retired joe)
NIL                        ;  Joe is not retired.
T                          ;  The table has an entry for retired.

> (hash-table-count joe)   ;  There are two entries in the table.
2

> (maphash #'(lambda (key value)
               (format t "~%~A~15T~A" key value)) joe)

RETIRED        NIL
AGE            30
NIL

> (maphash #'(lambda (key value)
               (if (numberp value) (incf (gethash key joe)))) joe)
NIL
```

```
> (remhash 'retired joe)   ;  Removes the retired entry.
T

> (maphash #'(lambda (key value) (format t "~%~A~15T~A" key value))
     joe)

AGE            31
NIL

> (remhash 'retired joe)   ;  retired already removed.
NIL

> (clrhash joe)
#<EQL hash-table with 0 entries @ #x109b776>

> (hash-table-count joe)
0
```

There are seven main hash-table functions.

- (make-hash-table &key :test :size :rehash-size :rehash-threshold) produces a table. The keyword options are discussed below.

- (hash-table-p object) is a predicate for hash tables.

- (gethash key hash-table &optional default) is a settable accessor function for hash tables. It is analogous to get. If no entry is found, the default argument is returned if present; otherwise, gethash returns NIL.

- (hash-table-count hash-table) returns the number of entries in the hash table.

- (maphash function hash-table) applies the function to each entry in hash-table, where function has two arguments: an entry's key and value. maphash returns NIL.

- (remhash key hash-table) removes the entry with the given key from the table. remhash returns true if an entry was found, otherwise; false.

- (clrhash hash-table) removes all the entries from the hash table.

LISP's hash tables automatically increase in size as they begin to fill up. The keyword arguments to make-hash-table provide the programmer with greater control over the efficiency and performance of a hash table.

- :test — The test used for comparing keys. The options are the functions
  #'eq, #'eql, or #'equal, or the corresponding symbols eq, eql, or equal.
  The default test is eql.

- :size — The number of initial buckets in the hash-table. For efficiency, LISP
  can increase the size to a larger number, such as a prime number.

- :rehash-size — The amount by which to expand the hash table when it fills
  up. The argument must be a positive number. If the argument is a float, it
  gives the ratio of the new size to the old size. If the argument is an integer,
  it specifies the number of new buckets to add. For example, an argument of
  2.0 would double the size. An argument of 2 would add 2 new buckets.

- :rehash-threshold — A number specifying when to expand the hash table.
  It can be a floating point number between 0 and 1, or an integer between
  1 and the rehash-size. In the latter case, the threshold value is scaled up
  every time the hash table is expanded.

Each of these options has corresponding reader functions, as demonstrated below.
First, we create a hash table z1 with the default values, which are implementation
∞ ⇒   dependent.

```
> (setf z1 (make-hash-table))
#<EQL hash-table with 0 entries @ #x10adcf6>

> (hash-table-test z1)
EQL

> (hash-table-size z1)
65

> (hash-table-rehash-size z1)
101

> (hash-table-rehash-threshold z1)
65
```

We now create a hash table z2 in which we provide arguments for all the keyword
parameters.

```
> (setf z2 (make-hash-table :test #'equal :size 10
        :rehash-size 20 :rehash-threshold 5))
#<EQUAL hash-table with 0 entries @ #x10af26e>

> (hash-table-test z2)
EQUAL
```

```
> (hash-table-size z2)           ;  LISP scaled up the size.
37

> (hash-table-rehash-size z2)
20

> (hash-table-rehash-threshold z2)
5
```

These functions cannot be used with setf. That is, the programmer may specify these values only when creating the hash table.

Hash tables provide an efficient mechanism for storing and retrieving data. We can use hash tables to implement property lists, using a global hash table, *property-list*. We also implement a generic function, pp-props, which pretty prints the elements of the property list, using the with-hash-table-iterator macro.

```
(defvar *property-list* (make-hash-table))

(defun prop-check (node)
  (cond ((gethash node *property-list*))
        (t
         (setf (gethash node *property-list*)
               (make-hash-table)))))

(defun my-get (node property)
  (gethash property (prop-check node)))

(defun (setf my-get) (value node property)
  (setf (gethash property (prop-check node))
        value))

(defun pp-pl ()
  (pp-props *property-list* nil 0))

(defgeneric pp-props (key value indent)
  (:method (key value (indent integer))
           (format t "~%~vT~A:~vT~A"
                   indent key (+ indent 15) value)))
```

```lisp
(defmethod pp-props ((key hash-table) value (indent integer))
  (with-hash-table-iterator
   (get-bucket key)
   (labels
    ((next-bucket
      (bucket &optional bucket-key bucket-value)
      (when bucket
            (pp-props bucket-key bucket-value indent)
            (multiple-value-call #'next-bucket (get-bucket)))))
     (multiple-value-call #'next-bucket (get-bucket)))))

(defmethod pp-props (key (value hash-table) (indent integer))
  (with-hash-table-iterator
   (get-bucket value)
   (labels
    ((next-bucket
      (bucket &optional bucket-key bucket-value)
      (when bucket
            (pp-props bucket-key bucket-value (+ indent 5))
            (multiple-value-call #'next-bucket (get-bucket)))))
     (format t "~%~vT~A:" indent key)
     (multiple-value-call #'next-bucket (get-bucket)))))

> (my-get 'joe 'age)                 ;  Tests it out.
NIL
NIL

> (setf (my-get 'joe 'age) 34)
34

> (my-get 'joe 'age)
34
T

> (setf (my-get 'joe 'height) '(6 2))
(6 2)

> (setf (my-get 'mary 'age) 25)
25
```

```
> (pp-pl)

 JOE:
     HEIGHT:          (6 2)
     AGE:             34
 MARY:
     AGE:             25
NIL
```

We first make *property-list* a global table. The function prop-check is called by both my-get and (setf my-get) to ensure that the given node has been entered as a hash table in the global property list.

The with-hash-table-iterator macro has the following syntax.

```
(with-hash-table-iterator (mname hash-table) {form}*)
```

The mname parameter is a generator macro that produces successive entries from the hash table. It returns three values. The first is a flag, which if false, indicates that there are no more entries in the hash table. If the flag is true, then the second and third returned values are set to the next entry's key and value, respectively. Here is an example in which we check the type of the entry values in a given hash table.

```
(defun check-hash-table-values (ht goodtype)
  (with-hash-table-iterator
   (get-bucket ht)
   (labels
    ((next-bucket
      (bucket &optional key value)
      (when bucket
            (cond ((eq (type-of value) goodtype))
                  (t
                   (format t "~%~A's value (~A) not of type ~A"
                           key value goodtype)))
            (multiple-value-call #'next-bucket (get-bucket)))))
     (multiple-value-call #'next-bucket (get-bucket)))))

(setf age-table (make-hash-table))

(setf (gethash 'joe age-table) 34
      (gethash 'mary age-table) 26
      (gethash 'will age-table) 'twelve)
```

```
> (check-hash-table-values age-table 'fixnum)

WILL's value (TWELVE) not of type FIXNUM
NIL

> (check-hash-table-values age-table 'symbol)

JOE's value (34) not of type SYMBOL
MARY's value (26) not of type SYMBOL
NIL
```

See also `with-package-iterator` in section 15.2.

14.4   Testing Random Numbers

Can a computer flip a coin? Can it make a random choice?

Random numbers are used in a variety of applications in computer programs. Many computer simulations require random data. Other programs require random sampling of input. In exercise 8.7.4, we showed a method of making a deck of cards. How could the computer shuffle the cards? Presumably, if you wrote a bridge or solitaire program, you would not care to be dealt the same hand every time.

In point of fact, computers cannot flip coins. However, they can produce *pseudorandom* numbers. That is, it is possible to specify an algorithm to generate a sequence of numbers that appear to be random, but the algorithm, given the same initial data, will always produce the same sequence of numbers.

Hash functions, such as `sxhash`, share many properties with pseudorandom number generators. The difference is that the hash function always retains its initial state. The pseudorandom number generator uses each new number it produces to determine the next number.

How random is random? There are numerous methods for designing and testing random number generators. These techniques are discussed in [Knuth, 1981]. Here we present a random number generator from [Knuth, 1981] and a function for checking its randomness.

The function `make-random` gets its initial value, or *seed*, from the LISP function `get-universal-time`, which returns the current time as an integer. (We discussed LISP date and time functions in section 12.5.5.) Alternatively, the programmer can specify the seed value as a second argument to `make-random` and thus dispense with the call to `get-universal-time`. The latter method provides the programmer a means of reproducing an exact pseudorandom sequence.

```
(defclass my-random ()
  ((seed :initarg :seed :accessor seed
         :documentation "inital random state")
   (range :initarg :range :accessor range
          :documentation "upper range of random numbers")
   (function :accessor rand-func :documentation "random function"))
  (:documentation "a random number generator class"))

(defun make-random (&optional r s)
  (let* ((initial-range (if r r 100))
         (initial-seed (if s s (mod (get-universal-time) r)))
         (random-object
           (make-instance 'my-random :seed initial-seed
                                     :range initial-range)))
    (make-random-function random-object)))

(defun make-random-function (random-object)
  (let ((modulus 65536)
        (multiplier 25173)
        (incr 13849))
    (setf (rand-func random-object)
          #'(lambda ()
              (let ((range (range random-object)))
                (flet
                 ((coerce
                   (num)
                   (typecase range
                             (integer (floor num))
                             (float (float num))
                             (otherwise num))))
                 (setf (seed random-object)
                       (mod (+ incr
                               (* multiplier (seed random-object)))
                            modulus))
                 (coerce (/ (* (seed random-object) range)
                            modulus))))))
    random-object))
```

The class my-random has three components: a seed, a range, and the actual random number generating function. The function make-random takes optional arguments for the seed and the range, and returns the resulting object. Most of the work is done by make-random-function, which sets the rand-func slot of the object with the magic algorithm. Note that the value returned is coerced to the type of the range. Here are some examples.

```
> (setf x (make-random 10))
#<MY-RANDOM @ #x11af9be>

> (seed x)
5

> (range x)
10

> (funcall (rand-func x))     ;  The function returns a random number
1                             ;  between 0 and 9, inclusive.
5221/16384                    ;  The second value is the rational remainder.

> (funcall (rand-func x))
6
28047/32768

> (setf (range x) 10000.0) ;  We extend the range and choose floats.
10000.0

> (funcall (rand-func x))
6351.3184

> (funcall (rand-func x))
3850.2502
```

Everything seems to be in order. However, we can improve the syntax with the following macro.

```
(defmacro defrandom (name &optional range seed)
   `(progn
     (setf ,name (make-random ,range ,seed))
     (setf (symbol-function ',name) (rand-func ,name))
     ,name))

> (defrandom y 2)
#<MY-RANDOM @ #x11d470e>

> (y)
1
31427/32768

> (y)
0
987/4096
```

```
> (setf (range y) 100.0)
100.0

> (y)
13.990784

> (y)
11.129761
```

With `defrandom`, we can create objects which can also be invoked as functions.

Based on these few pseudorandom samples, we can feel fairly confident that the numbers are coming out at random. However, we can test the generator based on the following observation: if the numbers generated are random, then every number in the range is equally likely to appear. With a large enough sample of numbers, we should expect an equal distribution of all numbers in the range. Here is a program to implement this test.

```
(defun test-rand (randgen trials)
  (let ((testv (make-array (range randgen) :initial-element 0)))
    (labels
      ((trial-run (trials)
                  (cond ((zerop trials) testv)
                        (t
                         (incf (aref testv
                                     (funcall (rand-func randgen))))
                         (trial-run (decf trials)))))))
      (trial-run trials))))

> (test-rand (make-random 10) 100)
#(10 11 7 10 9 8 12 7 16 10)

> (test-rand (make-random 10) 200)
#(20 24 17 24 17 17 18 19 20 24)

> (test-rand (make-random 10) 300)
#(23 28 32 34 32 27 24 31 39 30)

> (test-rand (make-random 10) 1000)
#(104 111 84 100 102 101 104 103 105 86)
```

The `test-rand` function counts the number of times each possible outcome occurs. These results are stored conveniently in a vector, which is returned as the value of the function. In each test case, we generate random numbers between 0 and 9. In the first case, we have 100 trials, which means that we expect each number to occur about 10 times. With 200 trials, we expect about 20 occurrences per number; with 300 trials, we should see around 30 occurrences; and with 1,000 trials, we should observe roughly 100 occurrences.

How can we evaluate the results? Taking the *average* does not tell us anything. The average number of occurrences will be exactly the total number of trials divided by the number of outcomes, that is, 10, 20, 30, and 100, respectively. Even if the random number generator always produced the number 8 each and every trial, this average would be unaffected.

We need a method to judge how much the actual results vary from the predicted results. A standard way of measuring this difference is the *chi-squared* test, which is discussed in [Knuth, 1981] and in most texts on statistics and probability. To compute a chi-squared statistic, we perform the following calculation. For each possible outcome, we subtract the predicted number of occurrences from the observed number of occurrences. This difference is then squared and divided by the predicted number of occurrences. The sum of the resulting values gives the chi-squared statistic.

Here is a program for performing this calculation, where vec is a vector of observed occurrences (such as produced by test-rand), and n is the predicted number of occurrences for each outcome.

```
(defun chi-sq (vec n)
  (let ((total 0))
    (labels
      ((square-dif (x y)
                   (let ((dif (- x y)))
                     (* dif dif))))
      (map 'array
           #'(lambda (v)
               (setf total (+ total (/ (square-dif v n) n))))
           vec)
      (float total))))

> (chi-sq #(10 11 7 10 9 8 12 7 16 10) 10)
6.4

> (chi-sq #(20 24 17 24 17 17 18 19 20 24) 20)
4.0

> (chi-sq #(23 28 32 34 32 27 24 31 39 30) 30)
6.8

> (chi-sq #(104 111 84 100 102 101 104 103 105 86) 100)
6.44
```

A detailed interpretation of a chi-squared test requires referring to a table that indicates how likely a given value is as a function of the number of possible outcomes. In the case of random numbers, the lower the value of the chi-squared statistic, the better — it indicates a more even distribution. It also is affected by the number of samples. Local differences tend to average out in the long run. This is an example of the "Law of Large Numbers," a fundamental precept of statistics. Our samples above do not happen to exhibit this property.

Also, the value of the chi-squared statistic is proportional to the number of possible outcomes. In this case, we have 10 possible outcomes. If we reduce the number of possible outcomes and use the same random number generator, we should get a lower chi-squared value.

```
> (test-rand (make-random 5) 1000)
#(176 216 195 198 215)


> (chi-sq '#(176 216 195 198 215) 200)
5.43


> (test-rand (make-random 2) 1000)
#(501 499)


> (chi-sq #(501 499) 500)        ; Looks too good.
0.004
```

As the reader may have come to expect by now, our discussion of random numbers leads us to reveal that LISP provides a native random number function: `random`. It has a required range argument and an optional seed state argument.

```
> (random 10)                    ; Pick a number between 0 and 9.
4


> (random 10)
3


> *random-state*                 ; Global variable for random seed state.
#S(RANDOM-STATE :SEED 111858210549045)


> (random 10 *random-state*)
9


> *random-state*
#S(RANDOM-STATE :SEED 272903320292921)
```

Every call to `random` resets the associated seed. The programmer can create her own random states by using `make-random-state`, which takes an optional `state` argument. If the argument is omitted or `NIL`, the new state is a copy of the global

random-state. If the argument is another random state, a copy of that state is
returned. If the argument is T, then the new state's seed is derived from the system
clock or some other seemingly random source.

```
> (setf rs (make-random-state))
#S(RANDOM-STATE :SEED 272903320292921)

> rs
#S(RANDOM-STATE :SEED 272903320292921)

> (setf rs2 (make-random-state t))
#S(RANDOM-STATE :SEED 8825948528218340401)

> (setf rs3 (make-random-state rs2))
#S(RANDOM-STATE :SEED 8825948528218340401)

> (random 10 rs2)
7

> (random 10 rs3)
7

> (random 10)
9

> (random 10 rs)
9

> (random-state-p rs)          ;  Predicate for random states.
T

> (type-of rs)
RANDOM-STATE
```

random-state is a regular LISP type. We note that for implementation considerations, LISP does not provide a direct method for resetting the seed of a
random-state.

For the sake of comparison, we shall adapt our test-rand function for LISP's
random function.

```
(defun test-rand2 (range trials)
  (let ((testv (make-array range :initial-element 0)))
    (labels ((trial-run (trials)
                        (cond ((zerop trials) testv)
                              (t
                               (incf (aref testv
                                           (random range)))
                               (trial-run (decf trials)))))))
            (trial-run trials))))

> (test-rand2 10 100)
#(8 12 11 8 8 14 8 9 11 11)

> (chi-sq #(8 12 11 8 8 14 8 9 11 11) 10)
4.0

> (test-rand2 10 200)
#(25 18 21 13 29 17 19 21 17 20)

> (chi-sq #(25 18 21 13 29 17 19 21 17 20) 20)
9.0

> (test-rand2 10 300)
#(32 35 34 31 22 27 30 30 33 26)

> (chi-sq #(32 35 34 31 22 27 30 30 33 26) 30)
4.8

> (test-rand2 10 1000)
#(98 114 93 98 91 118 92 100 87 109)

> (chi-sq #(98 114 93 98 91 118 92 100 87 109) 100)
9.72

> (test-rand2 5 1000)
#(192 183 219 209 197)

> (chi-sq #(192 183 219 209 197) 200)
4.02

> (test-rand2 2 1000)
#(507 493)
```

Range	Trials	make-random	random
10	100	6.4	4.0
10	200	4.0	9.0
10	300	6.8	4.8
10	1000	6.44	9.72
5	1000	5.43	4.02
2	1000	0.004	0.196

Table 14.2: Random Number Chi-Squared Comparison

```
> (chi-sq #(507 493) 500)
0.196
```

Table 14.2 provides a comparison of the chi-sq results for our make-random function and the native LISP random function. Using our qualitative criteria, neither
random number generator is conclusively better than the other.

14.5 Using Random Numbers: Math Quiz

In this section, we present an application for our random number generator which
also allows us to use vectors in two new ways. We create a vector of random number
generators and another set of vectors containing strings to be used as interactive
responses.

The sample program, called prob, is a math drill for subtraction, addition,
and multiplication. It uses the random number generator to choose both the test
numbers and the positive or negative response after the student has replied. Here
are three sample runs — one each for subtraction, addition, and multiplication.

In the first session, the student chooses subtraction problems with numbers
less than 20. Note that the answer is always positive. We underline user input.

```
> (prob '- 20)
How much is 4 minus 1? 3          ;  The student enters 3.
OK.  That's good.                 ;  The program responds.

How much is 14 minus 3? 10
Wrong.  Try again.

How much is 14 minus 3? 11
Of course!  (Why didn't I think of that?)

How much is 9 minus 2? quit       ;  The student terminates the session.
```

```
First tries: 1 correct out of 2.    ; The program prints the score.
```

```
Have a nice day!
```

In the second session, the student selects addition problems with numbers less than 100.

```
> (prob '+ 100)
How much is 21 plus 4? 25
Close enough. (In fact, exactly right.)
```

```
How much is 74 plus 15? 89
OK.  That's good.
```

```
How much is 47 plus 10? q
```

```
First tries: 2 correct out of 2.
```

```
Have a nice day!
```

In the final run, we have multiplication of numbers less than 10.

```
> (prob '* 10)
How much is 2 times 0? 0
OK.  That's good.
```

```
How much is 7 times 1? 7
Yep.  Nice work.
```

```
How much is 4 times 1? 4
Of course!  (Why didn't I think of that?)
```

```
How much is 2 times 2? stop
```

```
First tries: 3 correct out of 3.
```

```
Have a nice day!
```

This program is not profound, but it does illustrate some ways in which vectors and random numbers can be employed. The main underlying structure in this program is a vector of random number generators, produced by the function **make-rand-vector**, given here.

```
(defun make-rand-vector (size)
  (let ((rand-vector (make-array size)))
    (labels
      ((rand-vector-fill (slot)
                       (cond ((= slot size) rand-vector)
                             (t
                              (setf (aref rand-vector slot)
                                    (make-random (+ 1 slot)))
                              (rand-vector-fill (+ 1 slot))))))
      (rand-vector-fill 0))))
```

This function creates a vector of the given size, each element of which is a random number generator whose range is one more than its own index. Thus, executing the generator in element 5 will produce a random number between 0 and 5. We can select our first number from the entire range and then use that number to specify the generator used for the second number. We use this (cumbersome) approach to guarantee that the second number chosen will never be greater than the first. (For another, more efficient means, see exercise 14.8.16.)

Most of the program is taken up with processing the replies. Here is the code for prob.

```
(defun prob (func size)
  (let* ((randv (make-rand-vector size))
         (func-name
          (case func
                ((*) "times")
                ((-) "minus")
                ((+) "plus")))
         (procedure (symbol-function func))
         (right-answers 0)
         (wrong-answers 0))
    (labels ((randsmall (num)
                       (funcall
                        (rand-func
                         (aref randv num))))
             (randbig () (randsmall (- size 1)))
```

```
;  Do not repeat previous problem.
(make-prob (lastbig lastsmall)
             (let* ((big (randbig))
                    (small (randsmall big))
                    (ans (apply procedure (list big small))))
                (cond ((and (= big lastbig)
                            (= small lastsmall))
                       (make-prob lastbig lastsmall))
                      (t
                       (ask-question big small ans t)))))
(print-score
   ()
   (format t "~%First tries: ~A correct out of ~A.~%"
           right-answers (+ right-answers wrong-answers)))
(ask-question
   (big small ans flag)
   (format t "How much is ~A ~A ~A? " big func-name small)
   (let ((resp (read *standard-input*)))
   (cond ((and (numberp resp)
               (= resp ans))
          (cond (flag (incf right-answers)))
          (right-reply)
          (make-prob big small))
         ((member resp '(q qu qui quit stop exit nil ()))
          nil)
         (t
          (cond (flag (incf wrong-answers)))
          (wrong-reply)
          (ask-question big small ans nil))))))
(make-prob 0 0)
  (print-score)
  (format t "~%Have a nice day!~%")
  (values))))
```

The functions right-reply and wrong-reply are both generated as executable functions, using make-reply.

```
(defun make-reply (reply-vector)
  (let ((rand (rand-func (make-random (length reply-vector)))))
    #'(lambda ()
        (format t "~A~%~%" (aref reply-vector (funcall rand))))))
```

```
(setf (symbol-function 'right-reply)
      (make-reply
       '#("Right!"
          "OK.  That's good."
          "Just what I would have said!"
          "Close enough. (In fact, exactly right.)"
          "Great!  Super!  Let's keep going..."
          "Of course!  (Why didn't I think of that?)"
          "Yep.  Nice work.")))

(setf (symbol-function 'wrong-reply)
      (make-reply
       '#("Wrong.  Try again."
          "In a word: no."
          "Not quite right.  One more time."
          "Try again.  You can get it right.")))
```

These functions print randomly selected responses taken from the initial vector of strings.

14.6   Infinite Objects and Lazy Evaluation

How many random numbers can a random number generator produce? Presumably, it can keep cranking out random numbers forever, as long as someone pays the electric bill.

Random number generators are examples of infinite data objects. That is, they *implicitly* represent an infinite amount of data. Even with the dropping costs of disk storage, few programmers opt for an *explicit* representation of infinite data.

Using lambda, we can create an infinite list of integers.

```
(defun integers (n)
  #'(lambda () (incf n)))

> (setf x (integers 0))
#<Interpreted Closure (:INTERNAL INTEGERS) @ #x11db616>

> (funcall x)
1

> (funcall x)
2

> (funcall x)
3
```

```
> (+ (funcall x) (funcall x))
9
```

The argument to `integers` is the initial number in the series. The result is a function which, when evaluated, gives the successive integers. Notice that this object does not contain a list of all the integers; instead, it contains a *method* for generating all the integers. This method for generating integers is an implicit representation of those integers.

The code that generates integers is executed only as needed. The program does not produce the *nth* integer in the series until the first $n - 1$ integers have already been used. At each cycle of evaluation, the function produces two things: a result and a method for producing the next result. This type of delayed execution is termed *lazy evaluation*.

We can implement a more general approach to lazy evaluation with a class `delayed-state`, which we define here with its associated print method and predicate.

```
(defclass delayed-state ()
  ((next
    :initform nil :initarg :next :accessor next
    :documentation "generator function to produce the next value"))
  (:documentation "a class for delayed objects"))

(defmethod print-object ((self delayed-state) stream)
  (format stream "#<Delayed>"))

(defun delayed-p (obj)
  (typep obj 'delayed-state))
```

An instance of `delayed-state` will be a deferred computation. The function to be evaluated in the future is stored in the `next` slot.

We also define a macro `delay` for creating new instances of `delayed-state` and a function `force` to execute the function of a `delayed-state`. We then create a new stream of integers.

```
(defmacro delay (form)
  '(let ((new-state (make-instance 'delayed-state)))
     (setf (next new-state) #'(lambda () ,form))
     new-state))

(defmethod force ((obj delayed-state))
  (funcall (next obj)))

(defun integers2 (n)
  (cons n (delay (integers2 (+ 1 n)))))
```

```
> (setf x (integers2 0))
(0 . #<Delayed>)

> (car x)
0

> (delayed-p (cdr x))
T

> (setf x (force (cdr x)))
(1 . #<Delayed>)

> (car x)
1
```

We define `integers2` to be a recursive function. However, when `integers2` itself
is called, the recursive call is not immediately executed because of `delay`. Instead,
the result is postponed until `force` is applied. We then get another delayed object,
which likewise can be forced to evaluate. The predicate `delayed-p` identifies delayed
objects.

We can define a macro that facilitates this lazy evaluation strategy. We call
it `lazy-pop` and test it out with an odd-number generator.

```
(defmacro lazy-pop (n)
  `(prog1
     (car ,n)
     (setf ,n (force (cdr ,n)))))

(defun odd-numbers (n)
  (cons n (delay (odd-numbers (+ n 2)))))

> (setf x (odd-numbers 1))
(1 . #<Delayed>)

> (lazy-pop x)
1

> (lazy-pop x)
3

> (lazy-pop x)
5
```

```
> x
(7 . #<Delayed>)
```

Another useful application of implicit objects is sparse data structures. Sometimes, a programmer may have a very large data structure that is only minimally populated. For example, a scientific problem may call for a very large two-dimensional array, with only a few dozen non-zero elements. The programmer should not have to allocate the space for the entire array.

One answer to this problem is lazy data structures — data representations that allocate space only when needed. Here is an example using the two-dimensional arrays described at the beginning of the chapter.

```lisp
(defclass lazy-2d-array ()
  ((rows :initarg :rows :accessor rows)
   (columns :initarg :columns :accessor columns)
   (fill-value :initform nil :accessor fill-value)
   (fill-flag :initform nil :accessor fill-flag)
   (the-array :accessor the-array))
  (:documentation "A two-dimensional lazy array."))

;  Makes the top-level array but delays the secondary vectors.
(defun make-lazy-2d-array (x y)
  (let ((new-array
          (make-instance 'lazy-2d-array :rows x :columns y)))
    (setf (the-array new-array) (make-array x))
    (dotimes (count  x new-array)
            (setf (aref (the-array new-array) count)
                  (delay (make-array y))))))

(defun lazy-2d-array-p (obj)
  (typep obj 'lazy-2d-array))

(defmethod print-object ((obj lazy-2d-array) stream)
  (format stream "<lazy-2d-array (~Ax~A) ~A>"
          (rows obj)
          (columns obj)
          (the-array obj)))
```

```
;   Uses type specification on array references.
(defmethod lazy-2d-ref ((obj lazy-2d-array)
                        (x integer) (y integer))
  (assert
   (and (not (minusp x))
        (< x (rows obj)))
   (x)
   "lazy-2d-ref error. row value: ~d is out of range (0-~d)"
   x (rows obj))
  (assert
   (and (not (minusp y))
        (< y (columns obj)))
   (y)
   "lazy-2d-ref error. column value: ~d is out of range (0-~d)"
   y (columns obj))
  (aref (lref obj x) y))


;   Expands the array if needed.
(defmethod lref ((obj lazy-2d-array) (x integer))
  (cond ((delayed-p (aref (the-array obj) x))
         (setf (aref (the-array obj) x)
               (force (aref (the-array obj) x)))
         (if (fill-flag obj)
             (fill (aref (the-array obj) x)
                   (fill-value obj)))))
  (aref (the-array obj) x))


(defmethod (setf lazy-2d-ref)
  (val (obj lazy-2d-array) (x integer) (y integer))
  (setf (aref (lref obj x) y) val))


;   Fills any instantiated vectors.
;   Leaves delayed objects alone but remembers the fill value.
(defmethod lazy-2d-array-fill ((obj lazy-2d-array) val)
  (map 'vector
   #'(lambda (v)
       (cond ((delayed-p v)
              (setf (fill-flag obj) T)
              (setf (fill-value obj) val))
             (t
              (fill v val))))
   (the-array obj)))
```

```
> (setf x (make-lazy-2d-array 3 10))
<lazy-2d-array (3x10) #(#<Delayed> #<Delayed> #<Delayed>)>

> (lazy-2d-array-p x)
T

> (lazy-2d-array-fill x 10)
#(10 10 10)

> x
<lazy-2d-array (3x10) #(#<Delayed> #<Delayed> #<Delayed>)>

> (fill-value x)
10

> (fill-flag x)
T

> (lazy-2d-ref x 2 2)
10

> (setf (lazy-2d-ref x 2 2) 5)
5

> (lazy-2d-ref x 2 2)
5

> (lazy-2d-ref x 2 3)
10

> x
<lazy-2d-array (3x10) #(#<Delayed> #<Delayed>
  #(10 10 5 10 10 10 10 10 10 10))>
```

Lazy evaluation provides a means to create virtual data structures. The program can use these structures in much the same way as fully allocated data structures, but with economies of space and time.

14.7 Advanced Subjects

In this section we present two topics.

- Array Options

- Simple Arrays

14.7.1 Array Options

In addition to a variable number of dimensions, the `make-array` function has seven optional keyword arguments.

- `:element-type` specifies the type for the elements contained in the array.

- `:initial-element` specifies a single value with which to initialize the array.

- `:initial-contents` instead of using `:initial-element`, the programmer can give an explicit nested sequence of values with which to initialize the array.

- `:adjustable`, when given a non-NIL value, indicates that the array's size can be altered after creation. The default value is NIL, that is, no changes are allowed.

- `:fill-pointer`, for one-dimensional arrays (vectors) only, specifies the index of the first inactive cell. If the value is non-NIL, it must be in the range of 0 and the length of the array, or T, which is interpreted as the length of the array.

- `:displaced-to` allows the creation of an array that indirectly indexes another array. The `:displaced-to` value must be an array of the same `:element-type`. This option cannot be used with `:initial-element` or `:initial-contents`.

- `:displaced-index-offset` specifies a non-negative integer to indicate the initial index into the second array used with `:displaced-to`.

Below, we create several arrays, specifying their initial values.

```
> (setf a1 (make-array 5 :element-type 'integer :initial-element 5))
#(5 5 5 5 5)

> (setf a2 (make-array 5 :initial-contents '(a b c d e)))
#(A B C D E)

> (setf a3 (make-array '(2 3) :initial-contents '((a b c) (d e f))))
#2A((A B C) (D E F))
```

Now, we create an adjustable array with a fill pointer.

```
> (setf a4 (make-array 5 :adjustable t :fill-pointer 3
                         :initial-element 1))
#(1 1 1)
```

```
> (adjustable-array-p a4)        ;  Predicate for adjustable arrays.
T

> (adjustable-array-p a3)
NIL

> (array-has-fill-pointer-p a4)  ;  Predicate for fill pointers.
T

> (fill-pointer a4)              ;  Accessor for fill pointers.
3

> (vector-push 2 a4)             ;  Adds an element at the end.
3

> a4
#(1 1 1 2)

> (vector-push 3 a4)
4

> a4
#(1 1 1 2 3)

> (vector-push 4 a4)             ;  No more space at the end.
NIL

> a4
#(1 1 1 2 3)

> (vector-push-extend 4 a4)      ;  Extends the array as needed.
5

> a4
#(1 1 1 2 3 4)

> (vector-push-extend 5 a4)
6

> a4
#(1 1 1 2 3 4 5)
```

```
> (vector-pop a4)                    ;  Removes an element from the end.
5

> a4
#(1 1 1 2 3 4)

> (vector-pop a4)
4
```

The function `vector-push` adds the given element to the end of the array indexed by the fill pointer and increments the fill pointer. `vector-pop` reverses this operation. If the vector is full, `vector-push` returns NIL. However, the function `vector-push-extend` will grow the vector, if needed, to add a new element, using `adjust-array`.

The function `adjust-array` is similar to `make-array` except that it starts with an existing array.

```
> (setf a5 (make-array '(2 3) :initial-element 'a :adjustable t))
#2A((A A A) (A A A))

> (adjust-array a5 '(3 3) :initial-element 'b)
#2A((A A A) (A A A) (B B B))

> (adjust-array a5 '(4 4) :initial-element 'c)
#2A((A A A C) (A A A C) (B B B C) (C C C C))
```

We conclude with an example of displaced arrays.

```
> (setf a6 (make-array '(4 4) :displaced-to a5))
#2A((A A A C) (A A A C) (B B B C) (C C C C))

> a6
#2A((A A A C) (A A A C) (B B B C) (C C C C))

> (setf a7
    (make-array '(3 4) :displaced-to a5 :displaced-index-offset 4))
#2A((A A A C) (B B B C) (C C C C))

> (aref a7 1 1)
B

> (aref a5 1 1)
A
```

```
> (setf (aref a5 1 0) 'z)
Z

> a5

#2A((A A A C) (Z A A C) (B B B C) (C C C C))

> a6
#2A((A A A C) (Z A A C) (B B B C) (C C C C))

> a7
#2A((Z A A C) (B B B C) (C C C C))
```

Array a6 points to a5, and array a7 points to the last three rows of a5. Note that a6 and a7 are not copies of a5. When we change a5, we have also altered a6 and a7.

In section 7.2, we described the macro with-output-to-string, which had the syntax

```
(with-output-to-string (var [string]) {form}*)
```

The optional string variable must have a defined fill pointer.

```
> (setf s1 (make-array 20 :fill-pointer t
                  :initial-element #\0
                  :element-type 'string-char))
"00000000000000000000"

> (setf s2 (make-string 20 :initial-element #\0))
"00000000000000000000"

> (fill-pointer s1)
20

> (setf (fill-pointer s1) 5)
5

> (with-output-to-string (out s1)
    (format out "This is a test"))
NIL

> s1
"00000This is a test"
```

Type	Predicate	simple-array **argument**
simple-bit-vector	simple-bit-vector-p	bit (*)
simple-string	simple-string-p	string-char (*)
simple-vector	simple-vector-p	t (*)

Table 14.3: Simple Array Types and Predicates

```
> (with-output-to-string (out s2)
    (format out "This is a test"))
Error: array does not have a fill pointer
```

14.7.2   Simple Arrays

It may seem strange that the topic of *simple arrays* is discussed in the advanced subjects section. The reason for this placement is that most programmers will never need to pay attention to the difference between an array and a simple array.

A simple array is a standard LISP data type and is specified as one of the following.

```
simple-array
(simple-array [element-type [dimensions]])
```

What makes an array a simple-array is three conditions.

1. The array has no fill pointer.

2. The array is not adjustable.

3. The array is not displaced to another array.

Similarly, if a vector meets the above three conditions, it is a simple-vector. Moreover, if the element-type of a simple-array is either bit or string-char, then the resulting type is specified as simple-bit-vector or simple-string, respectively. These types are summarized in table 14.3.

A bit represents a 0 or 1. We discuss bit-vectors in chapter 16. A string-char is the type for the characters that can be included in a string, which can be tested with the predicate string-char-p.

```
> (type-of #(1 2 3))            ; A simple-array.
(SIMPLE-ARRAY T (3))

> (type-of "1 2 3")            ; A simple-string.
(SIMPLE-ARRAY CHARACTER (5))
```

```
> (type-of #*1010)              ;  A simple-bit-vector.
(SIMPLE-ARRAY BIT (4))

> (typep #(1 2 3) 'vector)      ;  A vector and a simple-vector.
T

> (typep #(1 2 3) 'simple-vector)
T

> (type-of #\a)                 ;  A character and a string-char.
CHARACTER

> (type-of (schar "abcdef" 1))
CHARACTER

> (typep (schar "abcdef" 1) 'string-char)
T
```

The schar function is the same as char, but for simple strings only. It returns a single character from a simple string, as specified by the index in the second argument. The svref function shown below is analogous for simple vectors. As with aref, svref returns a single element from the given simple vector, as specified by the second argument index.

```
> (svref #(1 2 3) 1)            ;  Index is zero-based.
2

> (simple-string-p "abcdef")
T

> (simple-bit-vector-p #*1100)
T

> (simple-vector-p #(1 2 3))
T
```

The hope is that the implementation can be more efficient in creating and accessing the simple sequences. Most applications should benefit from the improvements associated with the explicit use of these simple types.

14.8   Exercises

14.8.1   Expression Drill [4]

Evaluate the following expressions, first by hand, then with the help of the LISP interpreter.

```
(setf x (make-array 10))
(fill x 1)
(position (+ 1 1) #(0 1 2 3 4))
(position (+ 1 1) #(0 1 2 3 4) :test #'<)
(map 'vector #'(lambda (n) (+ n 1)) x)
(setf (aref x 0) (map 'vector #'(lambda (n) (+ n 1)) x))
(- (sxhash 123456789) (sxhash 123456789))
(defun eager-integers (n) (cons n (eager-integers (+ 1 n))))
(eager-integers 0)
```

14.8.2   Tic-Tac-Toe [7]

Using a 3 by 3 two-dimensional array, write a program that plays tic-tac-toe. The program should have the following basic cycle:

1. Determine whether the game is over. If so, stop.

2. Determine whose move it is.

3. If it is the machine's move, select legal move. Otherwise, solicit legal move from opponent.

The program should know both the rules (what constitutes a legal move) and strategy (what constitutes a good move). The program should never lose.

14.8.3   More Tic-Tac-Toe [9]

Modify the previous program for tic-tac-toe. Remove the strategy knowledge and replace it with a function for evaluating and learning new strategies. The program should begin with a random strategy (using the random number generator presented above). The program should notice what succeeds and what fails — both from its own moves and those of its opponent.

The program should learn from its experience. It may be useful to have the program play games with itself to speed up the acquisition of experience.

14.8.4   Three-Dimensional Arrays [5*]

Extend the two-dimensional array class to three dimensions. That is, create a function make-3d-array that takes three arguments, the x, y, and z dimensions of an array, and creates an object analogous to the 2d-array.

```
> (setf d3 (make-3d-array 2 2 2))
#<3d-array (2x2x2)
  #(#(#(NIL NIL) #(NIL NIL)) #(#(NIL NIL) #(NIL NIL)))>

> (3d-array-p d3)
T

> (3d-array-fill d3 8)
#(#(#(8 8) #(8 8)) #(#(8 8) #(8 8)))

> (setf (3d-ref d3 1 1 1) 0)
0

> d3
#<3d-array (2x2x2) #(#(#(8 8) #(8 8)) #(#(8 8) #(8 0)))>
```

14.8.5   n-Dimensional Arrays [6*]

Rather than methodically create special array objects for specific dimensions, we shall solve the problem once and for all, much the way LISP's make-array does. Create a function make-nd-array that takes a variable number of arguments for the dimensions of the array.

Thus, (make-nd-array 2 2 2) would create a three-dimensional array object, and (make-nd-array 2 2 2 2 2 2) would create a six-dimensional array object. The array object should respond to the appropriate methods, including print-object, nd-ref, nd-array-fill, and dimensions-of, which returns the respective dimensions of the array object.

```
> (setf a (make-nd-array '(2 2 2)))
#<nd-array (2 2 2)
  #(#(#(NIL NIL) #(NIL NIL)) #(#(NIL NIL) #(NIL NIL)))>

> (nd-array-p a)
T

> (dimensions-of a)
(2 2 2)

> (nd-array-fill a 0)
#(#(#(0 0) #(0 0)) #(#(0 0) #(0 0)))

> (nd-ref a 1 1 1)
0
```

```
> (setf (nd-ref a 1 1 1) 9)
9

> a
#<nd-array (2 2 2) #(#(#(0 0) #(0 0)) #(#(0 0) #(0 9)))>

> (map-nd-array a #'(lambda (x) (+ x 2)))
#(#(#(1 1) #(1 1)) #(#(1 1) #(1 10))))

> (map-nd-array a #'(lambda (x) (+ x 2)))
#(#(#(2 2) #(2 2)) #(#(2 2) #(2 11))))
```

14.8.6   Hash Tables [3*]

Modify the hash table given previously in this chapter to handle keys other than
symbols. Specifically, it should allow numbers, strings, and lists as keys. Here is
an example.

```
> (setf y (make-my-hash-table 10))
#<MY-HASH-TABLE @ #x11a944e>

> (table-put y '(mary smith) 21)
((MARY SMITH) . 21)

> (table-get y '(mary smith))
21

> (table-put y "Jane Doe" 39)
("Jane Doe" . 39)

> (reveal y)
#(((MARY SMITH) . 21) NIL ("Jane Doe" . 39)
   NIL NIL NIL NIL NIL NIL NIL)

> (table-put y 39 "age of john")
(39 . "age of john")

> (reveal y)
#(((MARY SMITH) . 21) NIL ("Jane Doe" . 39) NIL NIL NIL NIL NIL NIL
   (39 . "age of john"))
```

14.8.7   Searching Hash Tables [4*]

Modify the hash table presented in this chapter to handle the method `table-find`. Given a hash-table object and a value, `table-find` returns the first key in the table that has the specified value, as shown below.

```
> (setf y (make-my-hash-table 10))
#<MY-HASH-TABLE @ #x11b2ff6>

> (table-put y 'mary 21)
(MARY . 21)

> (table-put y 'john 39)
(JOHN . 39)

> (table-find y 21)
MARY

> (table-find y 39)
JOHN

> (table-find y 100)
()
```

14.8.8   Random Hash Tables [2*]

What are advantages and disadvantages of using a random number generator as part of a hashing function?

14.8.9   More Hash Tables [5*]

Above, we created a hash table that handled collisions through sequential search of the hash table itself. Another method is to allow each bucket to contain multiple items and to search each bucket sequentially. Implement a bucket-search hash table, using an association list for the bucket.

```
> (setf h (make-my-hash-table 5))
#<MY-HASH-TABLE @ #x11a49b6>

> (sxhash 'joe)
9309

> (sxhash 'bob)               ;  Joe and Bob have the same hash, mod 5.
8794
```

```
> (table-put h 'joe 20)
20

> (table-put h 'bob 21)
21

> (table-get h 'bob)
21

> (table-get h 'joe)
20

> (reveal h)               ;   Joe and Bob are in the same bucket.
#(NIL NIL NIL NIL ((NIL) (BOB . 21) (JOE . 20)))
```

14.8.10   new-hash [5*]

Write your own version of sxhash. This should be a recursive function that traverses the input, converting it to a number. Here is a sample hash algorithm.

- If the input is an integer, then no change is made.

- If the input is a character, then it returns the ASCII value of that character.

- The empty string hashes to 1.

- The empty list hashes to the magic number 31415926.

- If the input is a symbol, it is converted to a string, which is then hashed.

- If the input is a string, then it returns the sum of the hash value of the first character and twice the hash value of the rest of the string.

- Lists and vectors should be hashed in a manner similar to strings.

Note that embedding changes the hash value.

```
> (new-hash '(a b c))
251327887

> (new-hash '((a b c)))
314159739

> (new-hash '(((a b c))))
376991591
```

14.8.11   Reduced Chi-Squared [3*]

The second argument to the `chi-sq` function is the predicted number of occurrences for each outcome. This value is actually implicitly specified by the first argument, the vector of observed occurrences. Create a new function `chi-sq2` that obviates the second argument, as shown below.

```
> (chi-sq2 #(10 11 7 10 9 8 12 7 16 10))
6.4

> (chi-sq2 #(20 24 17 24 17 17 18 19 20 24))
4.0
```

14.8.12   Generalized Chi-Squared [5*]

We can simulate flipping a coin by using a random number generator with a range of 2. Heads would be 0 and tails would be 1. To simulate the flipping of two coins, we can use two calls to the same generator and then sum the results. Thus, 0 would be two heads, 1 would be one heads and one tails, and 2 would be two tails.

```
(defun coin ()
    (random 2))

(defun two-coins ()
    (+ (coin) (coin)))

> (coin)
0

> (two-coins)
1
```

If we toss two coins, A and B, there are four possible outcomes, with three possible values, as shown here.

	B Heads	B Tails
A Heads	0	1
A Tails	1	2

If we now want to evaluate the effectiveness of our `two-coins` simulator, we must modify our chi-squared program. Previously, we had assumed that all possible values were equally likely. In this case, however, there should be twice as many 1's (one head and one tail) as either 0's or 2's.

Modify the `chi-sq` function to use a vector of expected values as the second argument to allow for varying values of predicted outcomes. The function should still handle the original case of a single integer to represent all expected values.

```
> (setf tc (make-random 3))
#<MY-RANDOM @ #x11d304e>

> (range tc)
3

> (rand-func tc)
#<Interpreted Closure (:INTERNAL MAKE-RANDOM-FUNCTION) @ #x11d3b06>

> (setf (rand-func tc) (symbol-function 'two-coins))
#<Interpreted Function TWO-COINS @ #x1066d46>

> (test-rand tc 100)
#(27 54 19)

> (chi-sq #(27 54 19) #(25 50 25))
1.92

> (chi-sq #(176 216 195 198 215) 200)
5.43
```

The last example shows that the new version of chi-sq produces the same results
as the old one.

14.8.13   Shuffling Cards [5*]

Write a function that permutes the order of a list through a specified number of
two-element swaps.

```
> (shuffle '(1 2 3 4 5 6 7 8 9) 9)
(1 5 4 6 3 2 7 8 9)

> (shuffle '(1 2 3 4 5 6 7 8 9) 200)
(8 1 2 4 9 3 7 5 6)

;; make-deck  is from exercise 8.7.4
> (setf deck (make-deck *ranks* *suits*))
((TEN . CLUBS) (JACK . CLUBS) (QUEEN . CLUBS) (KING . CLUBS)
(ACE . CLUBS) (TEN . DIAMONDS) (JACK . DIAMONDS) (QUEEN . DIAMONDS)
(KING . DIAMONDS) (ACE . DIAMONDS) (TEN . HEARTS) (JACK . HEARTS)
(QUEEN . HEARTS) (KING . HEARTS) (ACE . HEARTS) (TEN . SPADES)
(JACK . SPADES) (QUEEN . SPADES) (KING . SPADES) (ACE . SPADES))
```

```
> (shuffle deck 200)
((QUEEN . DIAMONDS) (JACK . SPADES) (TEN . DIAMONDS) (QUEEN . CLUBS)
(QUEEN . HEARTS) (JACK . CLUBS) (JACK . DIAMONDS) (KING . HEARTS)
(KING . CLUBS) (ACE . CLUBS) (KING . DIAMONDS) (QUEEN . SPADES)
(KING . SPADES) (TEN . HEARTS) (TEN . CLUBS) (ACE . SPADES)
(TEN . SPADES) (JACK . HEARTS) (ACE . DIAMONDS) (ACE . HEARTS))
```

14.8.14 Card Games [8]

Now that we have a deck of cards and a way to shuffle them, we can deal a couple of hands. Write a program that plays your favorite card game. Gin rummy, blackjack, poker, and solitaire games are reasonable choices. Card games can have many subtleties. Even "Go Fishing" proves to be challenging to program well.

14.8.15 Chance Music [6*]

As practiced by composers such as John Cage, music composed at random is termed *aleatoric* music. Write a function music that takes three arguments: a list of pitches, a list of durations, and a positive integer indicating the desired number of notes. It returns a list of the given size containing a random sequence of notes. Here is an example.

```
(defvar *pitches*
        '(a-flat a b-flat b c d-flat d e-flat e f g-flat g rest))

(defvar *durations* '(whole half quarter eighth sixteenth))

> (music *pitches* *durations* 10)
((B-FLAT . HALF) (F . EIGHTH) (D . QUARTER) (B . HALF)
(B-FLAT . HALF) (REST . SIXTEENTH) (G-FLAT . EIGHTH)
(D . QUARTER) (D . QUARTER) (B . HALF))
```

The musically inclined programmer might wish to explore ways of constraining the random composition process to produce music that satisfies rules of tonality, counterpoint, meter, harmony, and/or commercial success.

14.8.16 New Math [4*]

The vector of random number generators used in the math quiz program was both illustrative and inefficient. There really is no need to have a multitude of random number generators to guarantee that subtraction problems never have negative answers. Devise a solution that requires only one random number generator.

14.8.17 Lazy n-Dimensional Arrays [7*]

In exercise 14.8.5, we defined n-dimensional array objects. The space for each array was completely allocated at the time the array was created. This could result in a waste of both space and effort if only a small percentage of the array is actually used.

In this chapter, we saw how to use lazy evaluation to delay the allocation of space in a two-dimensional array. Extend this method to an arbitrary, positive number of dimensions. Here is an example.

```
> (setf x (make-lazy-nd-array '(2 2 2 2 2 2)))
<lazy-nd-array (2 2 2 2 2 2) #(#<Delayed> #<Delayed>)>

> (lazy-nd-array-p x)
T

> (dimensions-of x)
(2 2 2 2 2 2)

> (rank x)
6

> (lazy-nd-ref x '(1 1 1 1 1 1))
NIL

> (lazy-nd-array-fill x 5)
#(5 #(5 5))

> x
<lazy-nd-array (2 2 2 2 2 2) #(#<Delayed> #(#<Delayed> #<Delayed>))>

> (lazy-nd-ref x '(1 1 1 1 1 1))
5

> (setf (lazy-nd-ref x '(1 1 1 1 1 1)) 7)
7

> (lazy-nd-ref x '(1 1 1 1 1 1))
7
```

14.8.18   Executable Data Structures [5*]

Through an extension of array and hash table objects, we can make these data structures executable for reference and storage.[1] Here are some examples.

```
> (setf john (make-hash-table))
#<EQL hash-table with 0 entries @ #x11a0556>

> (make-executable john)
JOHN

> (setf (john 'age) 30)
30

> (john 'age)
30
T

> (setf (john 'sister) 'mary)
MARY

> (john 'sister)
MARY
T
```

Using the macro make-executable, we have made a hash table executable, as both a reader and writer function. The table is a settable accessor function. We can have the same effect with arrays.

```
> (setf xx (make-array '(2 2 2)))
#3A(((NIL NIL) (NIL NIL)) ((NIL NIL) (NIL NIL)))

> (make-executable xx)
XX

> (setf (xx 1 1 1) 'something)
SOMETHING

> (xx 1 1 1)
SOMETHING

> (xx 1 1 0)
NIL
```

---

[1] James Philbin informed the author of this technique for the T dialect of LISP. We have modified it for Common LISP.

```
> xx
#3A(((NIL NIL) (NIL NIL)) ((NIL NIL) (NIL SOMETHING)))
```

We can also use make-executable for lists and strings.

```
> (setf x '(a b c d))
(A B C D)

> (make-executable x)
(SETF X)

> (x 2)
C

> (x 0)
A

> (setf (x 0) 'z)
Z

> x
(Z B C D)

> (setf y "hello")
"hello"

> (make-executable y)
Y

> (y 0)
#\h

> (setf (y 0) #\y)
#\y

> y
"yello"
```

Define make-executable.

14.9   Chapter Summary

- The following LISP object types are introduced in this chapter. Indentation
  indicates subtypes.

```
array
    vector
        bit-vector
hash-table
random-state
```

- Vectors provide an efficient, random-access data structure.

- Vectors in LISP are notated by # followed by a list. For example, #(1 2 3) is a three-element vector.

- LISP provides several functions for vectors.

```
(vector {object}*)
(coerce list 'vector)
(coerce vector 'list)
(aref vector index)
(vectorp object)
```

- Vectors are also sequences, which means that sequence functions can be used with vectors.

- LISP supports multidimensional arrays with the following functions.

```
(array-dimension array number)
(array-dimensions array)
(array-element-type array)
(array-in-bounds-p array)
(arrayp object)
(array-rank array)
(array-row-major-index array {subscript}*)
(array-total-size array)
(make-array dimensions [:adjustable adj] [:element-type et]
    [:fill-pointer fp] [:initial-element ie]
    [:initial-contents ic] [:displaced-to dt]
    [:displaced-index-offset dio])
```

Each implementation establishes the values of the following array constants.

```
array-dimension-limit
array-rank-limit
array-total-size-limit
```

- Hash tables provide an efficient means for implementing key-indexed tables. LISP's **sxhash** is a convenient hashing method.

- LISP provides a built-in `hash-table` type, with the following related functions.

```
(make-hash-table &key :test :size :rehash-size
                 :rehash-threshold)
(hash-table-p object)
(gethash key hash-table [default])
(hash-table-count hash-table)
(maphash function hash-table)
(remhash key hash-table)
(clrhash hash-table)
```

There are four functions for examining the hash-table properties.

```
(hash-table-test hash-table)
(hash-table-size hash-table)
(hash-table-rehash-size hash-table)
(hash-table-rehash-threshold hash-table)
```

- LISP has a macro for iterating through the values in a hash table.

```
(with-hash-table-iterator (mname hash-table) {form}*)
```

- Random numbers are useful in a variety of computer applications, such as simulations and games. Over a large number of trials, a random number generator should produce an even distribution of possible outcomes. The *chi-squared* statistic is an appropriate measure of this distribution. LISP provides the following random number utilities.

```
(random range [state])
*random-state*
(make-random-state [state])
```

- Lazy evaluation provides a method for creating infinite objects and virtual data structures.

- Arrays may be adjustable, in which case the following functions may apply.

```
(adjustable-array-p array)
(array-has-fill-pointer-p array)
(fill-pointer array)
(vector-pop array)
(vector-push object array)
(vector-push-extend object array)
```

When someone says "I want a programming language in
which I need only say what I wish done,"
give him a lollipop.

◇ ALAN PERLIS, *Epigrams in Programming (1982)*

Chapter 15

Scope, Extent, and eval

> *All the vital mechanisms, varied as they are,*
> *have only one object, that of preserving constant*
> *the conditions of life in the internal environment.*
>
> ⋄ CLAUDE BERNARD, *Lessons on Reactions Common to*
> *Animals and Plants (1878)*

> *The first is, that through a vitalizing spirit,*
> *a painting should possess the movement of life.*
> *The second is, that by means of the brush,*
> *the structural basis should be established.*
> *The third is, that the representation should so conform with the objects*
> *as to give their likenesses.*
> *The fourth is, that the coloring should be applied according to their characteristics.*
> *The fifth is, that through organization, place and position should be determined.*
> *The sixth is, that by copying the ancient models should be perpetuated.*
>
> ⋄ HSIETH HO, Concerning the Six Principles of Painting. *Notes Concerning the*
> *Classification of Old Paintings (c. 500)*

> *Who knows what evil lurks in the hearts of men?*
>
> ⋄ LAMONT CRANSTON, The Shadow *(1994)*

Computers do not tolerate ambiguity. When a programmer uses an identifier to refer to a value, there must be exactly one such identifier, and it must have exactly one value. Right? Well, yes and no.

Most programmers write code in which the same identifier is used repeatedly in separate functions. For example, a programmer may use "1st" to identify list

586

arguments, "vec" to identify vectors, and so forth. These identifiers may occur dozens of times in separate functions, but they should never be confused with one another — either by the programmer or by the computer.

The problem of ambiguous reference occurs regularly outside computer programs. How many people do you know named John or Mary or Joe or Jane? A colleague of the author has five different friends named "Stephen." His secretary has learned that the terse message "Stephen called." will be met with bewilderment and frustration.

15.1 Lexical Scoping

The computer should never have to ask "Which Stephen?" or rather "Which vec?" At any given point in a program, there is always a one-to-one relationship between identifiers and values. The programmer's desire to reuse names must be reconciled with this requirement to maintain uniqueness of reference. The answer is for the programmer to control the context of an identifier through its *scope* of reference.

In chapter 5, we discussed the dichotomy of global and local reference. Global variables have indefinite scope — they may be referenced throughout a program. Local variables in LISP normally are *lexically* scoped. That means that the scope of a local variable can be determined by its textual setting at the time it is defined. We have seen that LISP provides a number of ways of creating local variables, such as with defun, let, lambda, and labels. Here are some examples.

```
> (defvar x 0)          ;  x is defined as a global value.
0

> (let ((x 3))          ;  x here is local to this let.
    (let ((x 4))        ;  x here is local to the second let.
      (* x x)))         ;  x is within the scope of the second let.
16

> (let ((x 3))
    (let ((x 4)))       ;  This let expression ends on this line.
    (* x x))           ;  x here is within the scope of the first let.
9

> (let ((y x))          ;  x gets its value here from the global.
    (let ((x 3))
    (let ((x 4)))
    (* y y)))           ;  y got its value from the global value of x.
0
```

There is still room for ambiguity, though.

Bad Idea ⟹   `(defun y (y y) y)`   ; This is ambiguous.

             `(defun z (z) z)`   ; This is confusing, but not ambiguous.

Bad Idea ⟹   `> (let ((x 1) (x 2)) x)` ; This is ambiguous.
             `1`

             `> (y 1 2)`
             `2`

             `> (z 1)`
             `1`

A LISP variable or object has the following attributes.

- *Scope.* If you have a gift certificate for Macy's, you cannot use it at K-Mart, and vice versa. The Macy's gift certificate is good only within the local context or *scope* of Macy's. Cash, presumably, is good everywhere. Cash has *indefinite* scope. Variables, like financial instruments, can vary in scope. The spatial universe of a variable may be either *lexical* or *indefinite*. In the former case, the variable is limited by its local surrounding context, such as a `let` or `lambda`. A variable of `indefinite` scope may be accessed outside of its defining form, such as a `defvar`.

- *Extent.* A gift certificate is not good until it is validated and may expire at a certain date. We generally regard cash as being good in perpetuity. The lifespan of a variable may be either *dynamic* or *indefinite*. A variable of dynamic extent can be referenced any time after it is created up until it dies. An entity of indefinite extent exists so long as it is possible to reference it.

- *Values and bindings.* The association between a variable and its value can be specified in different terms. An association of indefinite scope is a *value*. An association of lexical scope is called a *binding*, though the terms are often confounded. If a variable has no associated value, it is unbound. Functions can also have bindings.

- *Shadowing.* If there is more than one active association for a given variable, the inner lexical binding overrides or *shadows* the other bindings. For example, a global variable may be shadowed by a local variable of the same name.

By combining the different types of scope and extent, we arrive at four major categories.

- *Lexical scope and indefinite extent.* Local variable and function binding fall in this category. It includes bindings created with let, flet, macrolet, and labels.

```
> (let ((z 1))           ;  z is born.
    (+ z                 ;  Uses first z.
      (let ((z 2))        ;  New z is born.
        (+ z z))))        ;  Uses second z.
5

> (let ((z 1))
    (boundp 'z))          ;  Does z have a global value?
NIL

> (let ((z 1))
    (flet ((add-z (n) (+ z n)))
      (add-z 5)))
6

> (flet ((add-2 (n) (+ 2 n)))
    (fboundp 'add-2))     ;  Does add-2 have a global value?
NIL
```

In these examples, add-z, add-2, and all the z's have lexical scope and indefinite extent. The predicates boundp and fboundp test for a symbol's global value or function binding, respectively.

- *Lexical scope and dynamic extent.* The labels in a tagbody or a block name have lexical scope and dynamic extent. Other control forms, including do, do*, dolist, dotimes, prog, and prog*, have implicit tagbody forms.

In the example below, the labels middle and end have lexical scope and dynamic extent.

```
(defun test1 (n)
  (tagbody
   (tagbody
    (if (plusp n) (go end) (go middle))
    middle (setf n 'negative)
    end)
   (go end)
   middle (setf n 'minus)
   end)
  n)
```

```
> (test1 3)
3

> (test1 -3)
NEGATIVE
```

Note that the labels in the inner `tagbody` shadow the labels in the outer `tagbody`.

- *Indefinite scope and indefinite extent.* Constants have indefinite scope and indefinite extent. Examples include T, NIL, and `pi`. The `defconstant` macro creates new constants, and the predicate `constantp` tests for constants.

```
> (constantp nil)
T

> (defconstant inople t)
INOPLE

> (constantp inople)
T

> (let ((pi 0)) pi)
Error: Cannot bind PI -- it is a constant.
  [condition type: PROGRAM-ERROR]
```

It is an error to shadow a constant.

- *Indefinite scope and dynamic extent.* The combination of indefinite scope and dynamic extent is sometimes referred to as *dynamic scope.* Examples of dynamic scope include variables created by `defvar`, variables declared `special`, tags created by `catch`, and variables created by `progv`.

```
> (defvar *var* 1)          ; Creates global variable.
*VAR*

> (let ((var 2))            ; Creates local variable.
    (list *var* var
      (let ((var 3))        ; Shadows local variable.
        var)
      (let ((*var* 4))      ; Shadows global variable.
        *var*)))
(1 2 3 4)
```

```
(defun add-var (n)
  (+ n *var*))

> (add-var 10)
11

> (let ((*var* 2))                ; Shadows the global variable.
    (add-var 10))                 ; Uses the shadow value.
12

> (let ((*var* 2))
    (makunbound '*var*)           ; Removes the shadow binding.
    (boundp '*var*))
NIL

> (boundp '*var*)                 ; The global binding remains.
T

> (makunbound '*var*)             ; Removes the global binding.
*VAR*

> (boundp '*var*)
NIL

> (defun add-q (n) (+ n q)) ; add-q refers to global q.
ADD-Q

> (let ((q 1)) (add-q 10))
Error: Attempt to take the value of the unbound variable 'Q'.
  [condition type: UNBOUND-VARIABLE]

> :res

> (let ((q 1))
    (declare (special q))     ; q now has dynamic scope.
    (add-q 10))
11

> (fboundp 'add-q)
#<Interpreted Function ADD-Q @ #x108d3de>

> (fmakunbound 'add-q)
ADD-Q
```

```
> (fboundp 'add-q)
NIL
```

The functions makunbound and fmakunbound remove a global value or function binding, respectively. The catch special form uses dynamic scope for its tags, such as back, below.

```
(defun catch-test (n)
  (if (plusp n) n (throw 'back 'negative)))
```

```
> (catch 'back (catch-test 1))
1
```

```
> (catch 'back (catch-test 1) 2)
2
```

```
> (catch 'back (catch-test -1) 2)
NEGATIVE
```

The progv special form creates variables of dynamic scope.

```
> (let ((x 100))
    (defun x-times (n) (* x n)))    ; x is local to the closure.
X-TIMES
```

```
> (x-times 5)
500
```

```
> (let ((x 200)) (x-times 5))       ; Cannot rebind the closure's x.
500
```

```
> (defvar y 8)                      ; Creates a global variable.
8
```

```
> (defun y-times (n) (* y n))       ; y has dynamic scope.
Y-TIMES
```

```
> (y-times 5)
40
```

```
> (let ((y 10)) (y-times 5))        ; Local y does not shadow here.
40
```

	Scope	
Extent	lexical	**indefinite**
dynamic	`block` names `tagbody` tags	`special` variables `catch` tags `progv` variables
indefinite	`let` variables `lambda` variables `flet, macrolet` `labels` definitions	`constants` e.g., `pi, nil`

Table 15.1: Scope and Extent

```
> (progv '(y) '(10) (y-times 5))   ; progv creates a dynamic binding.
50

> (progv '(x) '(10) (x-times 5))   ; progv cannot rebind closure's x.
500
```

Table 15.1 presents the four types of scope and extent.

Lexical scope is of great benefit for optimizing compilers. In analyzing the source code, the compiler can determine the precise range of reference for a lexical variable, which makes it possible to generate better code.

However, for years most LISP dialects used dynamic binding, which allowed the programmer to get away with obscure programming habits, such as implicit parameter passing. The LISP programmer can dabble in such debauched practices by using the `progv` form. Here is an example.

In good LISP style, we had previously defined the function `son-of-zeller` (see exercise 2.11.12), which calls the function `zeller`.

```
(defun son-of-zeller (day month year)
  (zeller day month (truncate year 100) (rem year 100)
          (cond ((leap-yearp year) 1)
                (t 0))))
```

```
;  zeller was defined with explicit parameters, like this:
(defun zeller (d m c y l)
    ...
```

However, using `progv`, we can dispense with the explicit passing of parameters. Instead, we can redefine `zeller` to take no arguments, and we can bind exact identifiers before calling `zeller`.

```
(defun son-of-zeller (day month year)                          ⇐ BAD
  (progv '(d m c y l)
         (list day
               month
               (truncate year 100)
               (rem year 100)
               (if (leap-yearp year) 1 0))
         (zeller)))
```

```
; zeller is now defined without any arguments:
(defun zeller ()
   ...
```

The programmer should avoid such usage. It becomes pardonable under rare circumstances, such as in porting large amounts of LISP code from some other dialect that exploits such properties of dynamic scope.

15.2   Packages

The rules of scope and extent effectively resolve ambigous references. If we have a variable X that is defined in several places, any given reference to X should be clear and uniquely bound.

However, there may be times when the programmer might actually want to refer to two different X's at the same time, that is, within the same lexical context. In most languages, she is out of luck. She would need to rename one of the X's. However, LISP provides a remedy: *packages*. Packages are containers for names.

Recall the programmer from chapter 5 who has a cat named George Washington. In LISP terms, the cat's name is in the household pet package. The name of the first president of the United States is part of the American history package. Both names can coexist. In fact, both names could be used in the same sentence, for example, "My cat, George Washington, has wooden teeth, just like President George Washington." Similarly, most Americans can distinguish between Washington state and Washington, D.C.

Packages provide an explicit name space or context for LISP symbols. At any given moment, there is one package which is active, providing the default values for names. The current package is given by the global variable *package*, as shown below.

```
> *package*                        ; What is the current package?
#<The COMMON-LISP-USER package>
```

```
> (packagep *package*)             ; This is the predicate for packages.
T
```

```
> (package-name *package*)        ; Packages have names.
"COMMON-LISP-USER"

> (package-nicknames *package*)   ; Packages can have nicknames, too.
("USER" "CL-USER")

> (type-of *package*)             ; package is a standard LISP type.
PACKAGE

> (package-use-list *package*)    ; What packages does this package use?
(#<The COMMON-LISP package> #<The EXCL package>
#<The CLTL1 package> #<The STREAM package>)

> (package-used-by-list *package*)   ; What packages use this package?
NIL

> (setf plist (list-all-packages))  ; Get all the packages.
(#<The GARBAGE package> #<The HYPERION package>
 #<The CROSS-REFERENCE package> #<The EXCL package>
 #<The SCM package> #<The MULTIPROCESSING package>
 #<The CLIM-UTILS package> #<The EXTENDED-IO package>
 #<The XLIB package> #<The CLOS package> ...)

> (length plist)                  ; There are 41 here.
41
```

Our initial package is named COMMON-LISP-USER and has nicknames USER and
CL-USER. It uses the packages COMMON-LISP, EXCL, CLTL1, and STREAM. That is,
the USER package inherits access to the symbols in those four other packages. Note
the package structure varies with the implementation.   ⇐ ∞

    We now create a new package with the function make-package.

```
> (setf my-package (make-package 'my-package :nicknames '(myp)))
#<The MY-PACKAGE package>

> (setf x 0)                 ; Creates a variable.
0

> (in-package my-package)    ; Changes to the new package.
#<The MY-PACKAGE package>
```

```
> x                           ;  X is in the package USER.
Error: Attempt to take the value of the unbound variable 'X'.
  [condition type: UNBOUND-VARIABLE]
[1]
> :res

> user::x                     ;  Special syntax for referring to other packages.
0

> (setf x 100)                ;  Creates another instance of X.
100

> x
100

> (in-package user)           ;  Return to the USER package.
#<The COMMON-LISP-USER package>

> x                           ;  The default value is from USER.
0

> myp::x                      ;  We can still access the MYP value.
100

> (list x myp::x)             ;  We can get both at once.
(0 100)
```

Symbols have values internal to their respective packages. Using the double colon
"::" syntax illustrated above, we can access these internal values from other packages by prefixing the symbol with its package name or nickname, and two colons.

The programmer can also choose to **export** and **import** a symbol, making it
easier to access within another package.

```
> (make-package 'xxx)         ;  Creates a new package.
#<The XXX package>

> (find-package 'xxx)         ;  Finds a package given its name.
#<The XXX package>

> (intern "X" (find-package 'xxx))
XXX::X
NIL
```

```
> (boundp 'xxx::x)          ;  x has no value yet.
NIL

> (setf xxx::x 0)           ;  Assigns a value to x.
0

> (boundp 'xxx::x)
T

> (find-symbol "X" (find-package 'xxx))
X                           ;  x is internal to XXX.
:INTERNAL

> (export 'xxx::x (find-package 'xxx))
T

> (find-symbol "X" (find-package 'xxx))
X                           ;  Now x is external.
:EXTERNAL

> xxx:x                     ;  Uses a single colon for an exported symbol.
0

> (import 'xxx:x)           ;  Uses import to move a symbol into a package.
NIL

> x
0

> (find-symbol "X")         ;  x is now internal to USER.
X
:INTERNAL

> (unintern 'x)             ;  Remove x from the package.
T

> (find-symbol "X")         ;  It is gone.
NIL
NIL

> (find-symbol "X" (find-package 'xxx))
XXX:X
:EXTERNAL
```

xxx::x	x is internal to XXX
xxx:x	x is exported from XXX
x	x is imported into USER
:x	x is internal to the KEYWORD package

Table 15.2: Package Prefix Syntax for Symbols

```
> (unintern 'x (find-package 'xxx))
T

> (find-symbol "X" (find-package 'xxx))
NIL
NIL

> (list :x)                      ;  An initial colon signifies a keyword.
(:X)
```

The unintern function removes a symbol from a package, which may be specified as an optional second argument. We discuss the find-symbol function below.

Once a symbol has been exported, only a single colon is required with the package name prefix. If the symbol is then imported, no prefix is needed. Keywords are indicated by a single initial colon and are contained in the designated KEYWORD package. These conventions are summarized in table 15.2.

Instead of importing one variable at a time, the programmer can perform a wholesale import with use-package, as illustrated below.

```
> (in-package myp)
#<The MY-PACKAGE package>

> (setf x 5)
5

> (export 'x)
T

> (in-package user)
#<The COMMON-LISP-USER package>

> myp::x
5
```

```
> myp:x
5

> (use-package 'myp)
T

> x                          ;  x is now imported.
5

> (unuse-package 'myp)       ;  We can reverse this process.
T

> x
Error: Attempt to take the value of the unbound variable 'X'.
  [condition type: UNBOUND-VARIABLE]
```

The effect of use-package is to import the external (exported) symbols of the given package. We can reverse this action with unuse-package. Furthermore, we can reverse the export itself with unexport.

```
> (in-package myp)
#<The MY-PACKAGE package>

> (unexport 'x)
T

> (in-package user)
#<The COMMON-LISP-USER package>

> myp:x
Error: The symbol "X" is not external in the MY-PACKAGE package.
  [condition type: READER-ERROR]
```

It is also possible to override imported symbols with the shadow function. Here, we create an actor in MY-PACKAGE and then shadow the imported definition in the USER package. The find-symbol function tells us if a symbol is internal or inherited from another package.

```
> (in-package myp)
#<The MY-PACKAGE package>

> (setf actor 'baldwin)
BALDWIN
```

```
> (export '(actor baldwin))      ; exports both the symbol and value.
T


> (in-package user)
#<The COMMON-LISP-USER package>


> (use-package 'myp)
T


> actor                          ; We inherit the symbol and value.
BALDWIN


> (find-symbol "ACTOR")          ; Identifies source of symbol.
ACTOR
:INHERITED


> (shadow 'actor)
T


> (setf actor 'hanks)            ; The new value does not clobber the old one.
HANKS


> (find-symbol "ACTOR")
ACTOR
:INTERNAL


> myp:actor
BALDWIN


> (import 'myp:actor)            ; Normal import causes an error.
Error: Importing these symbols into the COMMON-LISP-USER
package causes a name conflict: (MY-PACKAGE:ACTOR)
  [condition type: PACKAGE-ERROR]

Restart actions (select using :continue):
 0: Import these symbols with Shadowing-Import.
[1c]
> :res


> (shadowing-import 'myp:actor) ; shadowing-import solves the problem.
T
```

```
> actor
BALDWIN

> (package-shadowing-symbols *package*) ;  Lists all the shadowed symbols.
(ACTOR)
```

The fine distinctions among `export`, `import`, `use-package`, and `shadow` can have the effect of clouding men's minds.

The programmer can also rename packages and delete packages, using functions with appropriate names.

```
> (setf xxx::z 9)                  ;  Creates a variable z.
9

> (rename-package (find-package 'xxx) 'new-xxx-package '(xxx2))
#<The NEW-XXX-PACKAGE package>

> (find-package 'xxx)              ;  The xxx package is history.
NIL

> (find-package 'xxx2)
#<The NEW-XXX-PACKAGE package>

> xxx2::z                          ;  z has a new home.
9

> (delete-package (find-package 'xxx2))
T

> (find-package 'xxx2)
NIL
```

In an effort to provide some order to the process of creating packages, the macro `defpackage` was added to the language. The first argument to `defpackage` is the name of the package, as a symbol or string, followed by any combination of the following keyword options.

- (`:size integer`) specifies the approximate number of symbols to be included in the package. This number is used as a hint to improve the efficiency of the implementation.

- (`:nicknames {name}*`) can be any number of nicknames for the package, as either symbols or strings.

- (:shadow {symbol-name}*) can be any number of symbols that are shadowed in the package.

- (:shadowing-import-from package {symbol-name}*) specifies symbols to be imported and shadowed from the given package into the defined package.

- (:use {package-name}*) specifies other packages used by the new package.

- (:import-from package {symbol}*]) specifies symbols to be imported from the given package into the defined package.

- (:intern {symbol-name}*) specifies symbols to interned in the new package.

- (:export {symbol-name}*) specifies symbols to be exported from the new package.

To avoid conflicts, the options are processed in a specific order:

1. :shadow and :shadowing-import-from

2. :use

3. :import-from and :intern

4. :export

Here is an example.

```
(defpackage "MY-PACKAGE"
  (:size 500)
  (:nicknames "MYP")
  (:use "USER")
  (:export "X"))
#<The MY-PACKAGE package>

> (find-symbol "X" 'myp)
MY-PACKAGE:X
:EXTERNAL

> (boundp 'myp:x)
NIL

> (setf (symbol-value 'myp:x) 0)
0

> (boundp 'myp:x)
T
```

In section 12.3 we discussed how to use generic functions to overload existing LISP functions, such as +. We encountered a naming conflict with the standard functions. Using packages, we solve the problem. Below, we create a new package, myp, which shadows the regular + function. We then create a new generic + function. which concatenates strings.

```
> (defpackage myp (:shadow +))
#<The MYP package>

> (in-package myp)
#<The MYP package>

> (defgeneric + (arg1 arg2)
    (:method (arg1 arg2) (cl:+ arg1 arg2)))
#<STANDARD-GENERIC-FUNCTION + @ #x106a576>

> (defmethod + ((arg1 string) (arg2 string))
  (concatenate 'string arg1 arg2))
#<STANDARD-METHOD + (STRING STRING) @ #x106bbd6>

> (+ 1 2)
3

> (+ "hello " "world")
"hello world"
```

Six more functions are related to symbols and packages.

- (make-symbol print-name) creates a new uninterned symbol with the given print name.

- (copy-symbol sym [copy-flag]) creates a new uninterned symbol with the same print name as the given symbol. If the copy-flag is non-NIL, then the new symbol is bound with the same value, function, and property list as the given symbol. Otherwise, the new symbol is unbound.

- (symbol-name symbol) returns the print name of the given symbol.

- (symbol-package symbol) returns the home package of the given symbol.

- (gentemp [prefix [package]]) creates a new, unique interned symbol. The prefix defaults to T, and the package defaults to the current package. Unlike gensym, the prefix change is local to each call, and the counter cannot be changed.

- (find-all-symbols name) returns a list of all symbols in all packages with the given name.

We exercise these functions below. Note that uninterned symbols print with the prefix #:, and that the symbols returned by **gensym** are unique, even if their print names are not. The symbols returned by **gentemp** are unique and also must have unique print names, because they are interned.

```
> (setf x (make-symbol "new"))
#:|new|

> (setf x2 (copy-symbol x))          ;  x2 is a copy of x.
#:|new|

> x2
#:|new|

> (eq x x2)                          ;  They are different.
NIL

> (boundp x2)                        ;  x2 has no value.
NIL

> (setf y 0)                         ;  Creates y with a value.
0

> (defun y () '(this is y))          ;  Gives y a function binding.
Y

> (setf y2 (copy-symbol 'y t))       ;  y2 is a copy of y.
#:Y

> (symbol-value y2)                  ;  y2 has a value.
0

> (symbol-function y2)               ;  y2 is also a function.
#<Interpreted Function Y @ #x117f21e>

> (funcall (symbol-function y2))
(THIS IS Y)

> (symbol-name x)                    ;  Gets the print name.
"new"

> (symbol-name 'x)
"X"
```

```
> (symbol-package x)              ; Gets the home package.
NIL

> (symbol-package 'x)
#<The COMMON-LISP-USER package>

> (symbol-package 'car)
#<The COMMON-LISP package>

> (setf x (gentemp))             ; Creates a new variable.
T2140

> (symbol-name x)
"T2140"

> (symbol-package x)
#<The COMMON-LISP-USER package>

> (gentemp 'new)                 ; Specifies the prefix for the variable.
NEW2140
NIL

> (gentemp 'new)
NEW2141
NIL

> (gentemp)                      ; Each instance is unique.
T2141
NIL

> (setq x (gensym 0))
#:G0

> (setq y (gensym 0))            ; The names are the same.
#:G0

> (eq x y)                       ; But the values are unique.
NIL

> (find-all-symbols 'symbol)
(SYMBOL :SYMBOL)
```

```
> (find-all-symbols 'actor)
(ACTOR)
```

We close this section with four macros that permit the programmer to process all
the symbols in some or all of the packages.

- (do-symbols (var [package [result-form]]) body)   iterates
  over the symbols in a package, binding var to the next symbol on each
  iteration. The body is an implicit block name nil. do-symbols returns
  result-form as its value or nil.

- (do-external-symbols (var [package [result-form]]) body) iterates over
  the external symbols in a package, binding var to the next symbol on each
  iteration. The body is an implicit block name nil. do-external-symbols
  returns result-form as its value or nil.

- (do-all-symbols (var [result-form]) body) iterates over all the symbols in all packages, binding var to the next symbol on each iteration. The
  body is an implicit block name nil. do-all-symbols returns result-form
  as its value or nil.

- (with-package-iterator (mname package-list types) body) defines the
  mname macro that generates the symbols in the given list of packages of the
  given type(s). Each invocation of (mname) generates the next symbol. The
  types can include :internal, :external, and :inherited. If there is no next
  symbol, (mname) returns NIL. Otherwise, it returns four values: T (indicating
  that there was a symbol), the symbol, the package containing the symbol,
  and a keyword indicating the type of the symbol, for example, :internal.
  (See also with-hash-table-iterator in section 14.3.)

We demonstrate these macros below.

```
> (do-symbols (x my-package) (if (boundp x) (print x)))

ACTOR
*PRINT-LENGTH*
;  — lots of output omitted —
*GENSYM-COUNTER*
NIL

> (do-external-symbols (x my-package) (print x))

ACTOR
BALDWIN
NIL
```

We next define a predicate that answers the eternal question: does a given symbol end in the letter "P"? We then process all the symbols and list those ending with P.

```
(defun lastp (s)
  (eq #\P (char (reverse (format nil "~A" s)) 0)))
```

```
> (lastp 'hello)
NIL
```

```
> (lastp 'lastp)
T
```

```
> (let ((count 0))
    (do-all-symbols (x)
      (if (lastp x) (format t "~%~D: ~A" (incf count) x))))
```

```
1: BCC-PROP
2: R-SIGCONTEXT-SP
; — lots of output omitted —
2329: MAP
2330: MOTIF-FOREGROUND-USER-SPEC-P
NIL
```

Below, we create a function for revealing internal symbols in a given package.

```
(defun reveal-symbol (package count)
  (with-package-iterator
   (next-sym (list package) :internal)
   (dotimes (i (- count 1) (next-sym))
          (if (null (next-sym))
              (return-from nil i)))))
```

```
> (reveal-symbol 'user 1)
T
USER
#<The COMMON-LISP-USER package>
:INTERNAL
```

```
> (reveal-symbol 'user 2)
T
THEN
#<The COMMON-LISP-USER package>
:INTERNAL
```

```
> (reveal-symbol 'user 1000)
23
```

In the last example, we see that there are not $1,000$ internal symbols in the given package.

15.3 Modules

Packages provide a way to organize the symbol namespace, removing ambiguity. LISP provides *modules* as a way to organize packages. A module is a set of one or more files that usually make up one or more packages.

One module may depend on definitions from another module. For example, module A may depend on definitions contained in module B. In LISP terminology, module A *requires* B, and the file or files which constitute module B, *provide* B.

There are three (and only three) module constructs.

- *modules* — A global variable whose value is a list of all modules currently loaded.

- (provide module-name) — A function that adds the given module-name string to the list *modules*, which it returns.

- (require module-name [pathname]) — A function that checks to see if module-name is already loaded, that is, is included in the *modules* list. If so, require returns NIL. If not, require loads the specified file or files.

$\infty \Rightarrow$
```
> *modules*
("CLIM" "COMPOSER" "CLM" "GRAPHER" "PRES-TYPES" "EXTENDED-IO"
"PMACROS" "XCW-MOTIF" "XCLAWS" "XCW"  ...)

> (length *modules*)
32

> (provide "NEW")
("NEW" "CLIM" "COMPOSER" "CLM" "GRAPHER" "PRES-TYPES"
"EXTENDED-IO" "PMACROS" "XCW-MOTIF" "XCLAWS"  ...)

> (require "NEW")
NIL
```

Our LISP starts off with 32 modules. When we execute provide, it adds the new name to the list of modules. If we then require the new module, LISP believes that it is already there and does not need to load any files.

We now shall require a module associated with the following file.

```
;; Beginning of module1.lisp
;; 1. Provide
(provide 'module1)

;; 2. in-package
(in-package my-package)

;; 3. shadow
;; 4. export
;; 5. require
;; 6. use-package
;; 7. import
;; 8. the contents
(defvar x 10)
(defvar y 5)
;; End of module1.lisp
```

The comments in the file indicate the preferred order of statements. In this case, the **provide** statement precedes the **in-package** statement, which comes before the contents of the file. The other options, if present, should appear in the designated order to avoid confusion on the part of the LISP interpreter or compiler.

Violating this order could result in an infinite loading loop. For example, if the **provide** follows a **require**, which in turn loads a file that requires the first file, there is a loop.

We now load the module 1 file, using **require**.

```
> (require 'module1 "module1.lisp")
; Loading /server/u18/homes.ai/slade/a/mss/l/module1.lisp.
T

> (require 'module1 "module1.lisp")
NIL

> *modules*
("MODULE1" "NEW" "CLIM" "COMPOSER" "CLM" "GRAPHER"
"PRES-TYPES" "EXTENDED-IO" "PMACROS"  "XCW-MOTIF" ...)

> (find-symbol "X" 'myp)
MY-PACKAGE::X
:INTERNAL

> myp::x
10
```

```
> myp::y
5

> (boundp 'x)
NIL

> (boundp 'myp::x)
T
```

The module 1 definitions were confined to the MYP package and did not contaminate the default package.

Modules are highly recommended. Their use encourages the programmer to make explicit the dependencies among files and their associated definitions. The provide/require relationships serve to illuminate the global structure of a large software project.

15.4   eval

In the preceding sections, we saw how the same identifier can simultaneously have different values in different packages. This multiplicity of values does not create a conflict because expressions are always evaluated within a specific package.

As the reader may recall, the basic cycle of the LISP interpreter is the read-eval-print loop. That is, expressions are read from the input stream, evaluated, and the results are printed to the output stream. In chapter 7, we encountered **read** and **print**. The remaining member of the central triumvirate is **eval**. Here is how they can be plugged together.

```
(print
 (eval
   (read *standard-input*))
 *standard-output*)
```

eval takes a form as its argument. The eval function can be called directly. Here are examples.

```
> (eval '(car '(a b c d)))
A

> (eval (list '+ 1 2 3))
6

> (eval (append '(* 2) '(3 4)))
24
```

```
> (eval '(setf x 999))
999

> (eval 'x)
999
```

Note that the argument to `eval` is evaluated twice, in effect.

We have stated repeatedly that LISP is extensible. LISP will even let you replace its most fundamental function: `eval`. LISP makes it easy to do this with the global variable `*evalhook*`, which is similar to `*macroexpand-hook*` discussed in section 11.9.4.

This variable is normally NIL. However, when it is non-NIL, it is assumed to be bound to a function that replaces `eval` in the read-eval-print loop.

Here we define a variant of `eval` that echoes and annotates its input and output.

```
(defun my-eval (form &optional env)
   (format t "~%MY-EVAL.  Input form is: ~A~%" form)
   (format t "~%And the answer is: ")
   (eval form))

> (my-eval '(+ 1 2 3))
MY-EVAL.  Input form is: (+ 1 2 3)
And the answer is:
6

> (my-eval '(car (cdr '(a b c))))
MY-EVAL.  Input form is: (CAR (CDR '(A B C)))
And the answer is:
B

> (let ((*evalhook* 'my-eval))        ;  Binds *evalhook*.
    (eval '(car (cdr '(a b c)))))
MY-EVAL.  Input form is: (EVAL '(CAR (CDR '(A B C))))
And the answer is:
B

> (let ((*evalhook* 'my-eval))        ;  Does not need call to eval.
    (car (cdr '(a b c))))

MY-EVAL.  Input form is: (CAR (CDR '(A B C)))
And the answer is:
B
```

LISP provides another global variable, *applyhook*, which allows the programmer to replace the normal apply function with another function of two arguments: a function and a list of arguments. Below, we define the function my-apply, which annotates a call to apply.

```
(defun my-apply (fn args)
   (format t "~%MY-APPLY.___Input args: ~A" args)
   (format t "~%And the answer is: ")
   (apply fn args))

> (my-apply #'+ '(1 2 3))

MY-APPLY.  Input args: (1 2 3)
And the answer is:
6

> (let ((*applyhook* 'my-apply))
     (+ 1 2 3))
MY-APPLY.  Input args: (1 2 3)
And the answer is:
6

> (let ((*applyhook* 'my-apply))
     (+ 1 2 (* 8 9)))
MY-APPLY.  Input args: (8 9)
And the answer is:
MY-APPLY.  Input args: (1 2 72)
And the answer is:
75
```

In the last example, the embedded apply did not get fully annotated. Another approach is to use the function evalhook, which takes three or four arguments:

- The form to be evaluated

- The function to be bound to *evalhook*, or NIL

- The function to be bound to *applyhook*, or NIL

- An optional environment

Using evalhook, we define a more useful function for tracing an execution. Note that recursive evaluations are reflected in additional indentation, using the global variable *indent*.

```
(defvar *indent* 0)

(defun my-eval2 (form &optional env)
  (let ((*indent* (+ *indent* 2)))
    (format t "~%~v@tMY-EVAL2.  Input form is: ~A" *indent* form)
    (let ((answer (evalhook form #'my-eval2 nil env)))
      (format t "~%~v@tAnd the answer is: ~A" *indent* answer)
      answer)))

> (my-eval2 '(car (cdr '(a b c))))

  MY-EVAL2.  Input form is: (CAR (CDR '(A B C)))
    MY-EVAL2.  Input form is: (CDR '(A B C))
      MY-EVAL2.  Input form is: '(A B C)
      And the answer is: (A B C)
    And the answer is: (B C)
  And the answer is: B
B

> (let ((*evalhook* 'my-eval2))
    (+ 1 2 (* 8 9)))

  MY-EVAL2.  Input form is: (+ 1 2 (* 8 9))
    MY-EVAL2.  Input form is: 1
    And the answer is: 1
    MY-EVAL2.  Input form is: 2
    And the answer is: 2
    MY-EVAL2.  Input form is: (* 8 9)
      MY-EVAL2.  Input form is: 8
      And the answer is: 8
      MY-EVAL2.  Input form is: 9
      And the answer is: 9
    And the answer is: 72
  And the answer is: 75
75
```

There is a similar function, `applyhook`, with arguments comprising the function, a list of arguments, plus optional *evalhook* and *applyhook* functions.

```
(defun my-apply2 (fn args)
  (let ((*indent* (+ *indent* 2)))
    (format t "~%~v@tMY-APPLY2.  Input args are: ~A" *indent* args)
    (let ((answer (applyhook fn args nil #'my-apply2)))
      (format t "~%~v@tAnd the answer is: ~A" *indent* answer)
      answer)))
```

```
> (let ((*applyhook* 'my-apply2))
    (+ 1 2 3))

  MY-APPLY2.  Input args are: (1 2 3)
  And the answer is: 6
6

> (let ((*applyhook* 'my-apply2))
    (+ 1 2 (+ 3 4)))

  MY-APPLY2.  Input args are: (3 4)
  And the answer is: 7
  MY-APPLY2.  Input args are: (1 2 7)
  And the answer is: 10
10
```

We now define a more robust tracing eval which permits the programmer to specify the names of those functions to be traced.

```
(defvar *trace-list* nil)

(defun trace-eval (form &optional env)
  (cond ((and (consp form)
              (member (car form) *trace-list*))
         (let ((*indent* (+ *indent* 2)))
           (format t "~%~V@TEvaluating: ~A" *indent* form)
           (let ((answer (evalhook form #'trace-eval nil env)))
             (format t "~%~v@tAnswer: ~A" *indent* answer)
             answer)))
        (t
         (evalhook form #'trace-eval nil env))))

(defun add-trace (fn) (push fn *trace-list*))

> (trace-eval '(+ 1 2 3))
6

> (add-trace '+)
(+)
```

```
> (trace-eval '(+ 1 2 3))
  Evaluating: (+ 1 2 3)
  Answer: 6
6

> (trace-eval '(+ 1 2 (+ 3 4)))
  Evaluating: (+ 1 2 (+ 3 4))
    Evaluating: (+ 3 4)
    Answer: 7
  Answer: 10
10

> (trace-eval '(* 7 8 9))
504

> (trace-eval '(* 7 (+ 2 3)))
  Evaluating: (+ 2 3)
  Answer: 5
35
```

We note that this version does not work with compiled functions.

```
(defun add-2 (n) (+ n 2))

> (trace-eval '(add-2 3))
  Evaluating: (+ N 2)
  Answer: 5
5

> (compile 'add-2)
ADD-2
NIL
NIL

> (trace-eval '(add-2 3))
5
```

We examine compilation in the next chapter.

15.5   eval Example: LISP Workspace

Generally, the programmer does not need to make explicit calls to eval. The regular read-eval-print loop usually provides sufficient functionality. However, there are occasions when the programmer can properly exploit `eval`. We here present a basic example, that of making a workspace.

Some interpreted languages, like APL, provide a convenient mechanism for keeping track of global variables and function definitions. During the course of a programming session, the programmer may have defined or modified several definitions, and created or updated some global variables. In a *workspace*, the computer can keep track of variables and functions so that the programmer can save her work when she is done and later restart her previous session from where she left off. Normal workspace functions include saving a workspace, restoring a workspace, defining new functions, editing function definitions, and creating and modifying global variables.

LISP already allows the programmer to create and modify functions and variables through the interpreter. Editing definitions of functions and variables is discussed in exercise 15.7.4. Here, we present a mechanism for saving and restoring the state of a programming session.

First, we shall look at a sample session. We use the `make-workspace` function, which takes a single filename argument. The workspace expressions will be logged to that file. We will terminate the workspace session with (`save-ws`).

```
> (make-workspace "testfile")
Starting workspace.  End with (save-ws)

WS> pi

3.141592653589793d0
WS> (defvar my-pi 3.14159)

MY-PI
WS> (defun area (r) (* my-pi r r))

AREA
WS> (area 2)

12.56636
WS> (area 3)

28.274311
WS> (setf (get 'joe 'age) 23)

23
```

```
WS> (save-ws)

Workspace saved in file: testfile
END-WORKSPACE
```

Here are the contents of the workspace file, `testfile`.

```
;; workspace file

(DEFVAR MY-PI 3.14159)
(DEFUN AREA (R) (* MY-PI R R))
(AREA 2)
(AREA 3)
(SETF (GET 'JOE 'AGE) 23)
```

This file can be read back into LISP, using `load` to reproduce the final state of the variables and functions. Furthermore, the programmer could edit this file directly to remove those expressions which do not result in side effects, such as the calls to the `AREA` function.

We now present the definition of `make-workspace`.

```
(defun make-workspace (filename)
  (catch 'stop
    (format t "Starting workspace.  End with (save-ws) ~%")
    (let ((stream (open filename :direction :output))
          (ws-prompt "WS> "))
      (flet ((ws-fn? (input)
                (cond ((eq (car input) 'save-ws)
                       (close stream)
                       (throw 'stop nil)))))
        (format stream ";; workspace file ~%")
        (unwind-protect
            (loop
              (format t "~%~A" ws-prompt)
              (let ((input (read *standard-input*)))
                (cond ((listp input)
                       (ws-fn? input)
                       (format stream "~%~A" input)))
                (print (eval input) *standard-output*)))
          (close stream)))))
  (format t "~%Workspace saved in file: ~A~%" filename)
  'end-workspace)
```

Note the use of `unwind-protect`. Without it, an error could terminate execution without saving the workspace file. The `make-workspace` function performs the following.

1. Prints out initial message.

2. Opens an output stream to the given file.

3. Defines a local predicate `ws-fn?` that checks to see if the command `save-ws` was input. If it was, then it closes the output stream and throws control to the `catch` expression.

4. The `loop` clause contains a modified read-eval-print loop. It prints out the special prompt and then reads the input. If the input is a list, then the `ws-fn?` checks the input and the input is copied to the output file. (Nonlist expressions, such as symbols, are not copied to the file because their evaluation does not alter the state of session.) Finally, the input is evaluated, and the results are printed to the standard output.

This example demonstrates how the programmer can insinuate her own code into the read-eval-print loop. Exercise 15.7.3 provides another example.

15.6   eval Exposed

As evidence of the underlying elegance and simplicity of the design of LISP, it is possible to define `eval` in a page or so of LISP code. This basic definition contains the essential components, such as `car`, `cdr`, `cond`, and `eq`, from which more complex functions can be defined.

Our definition of `eval` is both recursive and circular. It is like a dictionary that defines "cat" to be a feline and "feline" to be a cat. For example, we use `cond` in the process of defining `cond`, and even `defun` to define `defun`! The point of the definition is to demonstrate the way in which `eval` works and to show the role of the environment in the process of evaluation.

In this section, we actually present two definitions of `eval`. The first is a minimal version, based on the original definition of LISP. It uses an association list to maintain the bindings between identifiers and values. The second `eval` is closer to Common LISP and uses an object-based environment. Here is `simple-eval`.

```
(defun simple-eval (exp env)
  (cond ((numberp exp) exp)
        ((stringp exp) exp)
        ((characterp exp) exp)
        ((atom exp)
         (simple-env-lookup exp env))
        ((eq (car exp) 'quote)
         (cadr exp))
        ((eq (car exp) 'cond)
         (simple-eval-cond (cdr exp) env))
        (t
         (simple-apply (car exp)
                       (simple-eval-list (cdr exp) env) env))))

(defun simple-env-lookup (id env)
  (cdr (assoc id env)))

(defun simple-eval-cond (exp env)
  (cond ((simple-eval (caar exp) env)
         (simple-eval (cadar exp) env))
        (t (simple-eval-cond (cdr exp) env))))

(defun simple-eval-list (exp env)
  (cond ((null exp) nil)
        (t
         (cons (simple-eval (car exp) env)
               (simple-eval-list (cdr exp) env)))))
```

The algorithm for simple-eval is straightforward. Numbers, strings, and characters evaluate to themselves. Atoms (symbols) return their respective values from the environment. In this case, the environment is just an association list of identifier-value pairs. (Note that the value could be a lambda expression.) A quoted expression passes its argument back without further evaluation. A cond clause is evaluated in the expected fashion — the first test clause is evaluated, and then either the result clause or the remaining conditional clauses are evaluated. If the expression being evaluated does not match any of those categories, then it is assumed to be a function call. In that case, the function is applied to its arguments, which are first evaluated with simple-eval-list.

```
(defun simple-apply (proc args env)
  (cond ((atom proc)
         (case proc
               ((car)    (caar args))
               ((cdr)    (cdar args))
               ((cons)   (cons (car args) (cadr args)))
               ((atom)   (atom (car args)))
               ((eq)     (eq (car args) (cadr args)))
               (otherwise
                (simple-apply (simple-eval proc env) args env))))
        ((eq (car proc) 'lambda)
         (simple-eval (caddr proc)
                 (simple-pairlis (cadr proc) args env)))
        ((eq (car proc) 'defun)
         (simple-apply (caddr proc)
                        args
                        (cons (cons (cadr proc) (caddr proc)) env)))))

(defun simple-pairlis (x y env)
  (cond ((null x) env)
        (t
         (cons (cons (car x) (car y))
               (simple-pairlis (cdr x) (cdr y) env)))))
```

The function `simple-apply` is quite similar to `simple-eval` itself. We have directly defined the primitive functions like `car` and `cdr` inside `simple-apply`. Other functions can be specified in the environment, as shown below. The evaluation of lambda expressions requires the binding of identifiers and arguments with the function `simple-pairlis`, which adds pairs to the front of the environment association list.

The evaluation of `defun` adds the given definition to the environment before applying the function to its arguments. A defun'd function has an identifier in the environment bound to its definition. Thus, `defun` provides a mechanism for recursion. The reader should note that in this version of `eval`, the function definitions are local — they do not persist.

Here are some examples. We first see that numbers, strings, and characters evaluate to themselves.

```
> (simple-eval 9 nil)
9

> (simple-eval "a string" nil)
"a string"
```

```
> (simple-eval #\a nil)
#\a
```

```
;  Symbols get their values from the environment.
> (simple-eval 'x '((x . 5)))
5
```

```
;  The default value for symbols is NIL.
> (simple-eval 'x nil)
NIL
```

```
> (simple-eval '(quote lisp) nil)
LISP
```

```
;  Note that we must specify a value for t.
> (simple-eval '(cond ((eq x 0) t) (t nil))
               '((x . 0) (t . t)))
T
```

```
;  The primitive list methods are built into simple-eval.
> (simple-eval '(car (cdr x)) '((x . (1 2 3))))
2
```

```
> (simple-eval '(car (cons x x)) '((x . "hello")))
"hello"
```

```
;  The heart of function application is the lambda expression.
> (simple-eval '((lambda (n) (car n)) '(a b c)) nil)
A
```

```
;  We can introduce new function names into the environment.
> (simple-eval '(zerop x)
               '((x . 0) (zerop . (lambda (n) (eq n 0)))))
T
```

```
> (simple-eval '(head '(1 2 3))
               '((head . (lambda (n) (car n)))))
1
```

```
;  Or, more succinctly:
> (simple-eval '(head '(1 2 3))
               '((head . car)))
1
```

```
;   Finally, we can define recursive functions.
;   For clarity, we first make the environment a global variable.
> (setf env '((t . t) (null . (lambda (n) (eq n nil)))))
((T . T) (NULL LAMBDA (N) (EQ N NIL)))


;   We next define the last function, and invoke it on a short list.
> (simple-eval
    '((defun last
        (lambda (l)
          (cond ((null (cdr l)) (car l))
                (t (last (cdr l)))))))
      '(1 2 3))
    env)
3
```

To gain a full appreciation of the workings of simple-eval, the reader should enter
the code and trace it during execution. The example evaluation of last resulted
in *38* calls to simple-eval!

We now turn our attention to a more complex eval definition. The primary
difference between cl-eval and simple-eval is the representation of the environment. In cl-eval, the environment is represented as linked objects which can respond to the cl-env-lookup method. Furthermore, the environment distinguishes
between local and global objects.

```
(defun cl-eval (exp env)
  (cond ((or (numberp exp)
             (functionp exp)
             (characterp exp)
             (stringp exp))
         exp)
        ((symbolp exp)
         (value exp env))
        ((consp exp)
         (case
           (car exp)
           ((quote)    (cadr exp))
           ((if)       (cl-eval-if      exp env))
           ((progn)    (cl-eval-progn   exp env))
           ((lambda)   (cl-eval-lambda  exp env))
           ((defun)    (cl-eval-defun   exp env))
           ((setq)     (cl-eval-setq    exp env))
           ((case)     (cl-eval-case    exp env))
```

```
((cond)     (cl-eval-cond    exp env))
((and)      (cl-eval-and     exp env))
((or)       (cl-eval-or      exp env))
((let)      (cl-eval-let     exp env))
(otherwise  (cl-eval-call    exp env)))))))
```

At this point, there is not much difference between `cl-eval` and `simple-eval`. Numbers, functions, characters, and strings are self-evaluating. Symbols return their value from the environment. There are more special cases, but as we shall see, they are generally straightforward.

```
(defun cl-eval-call (exp env)
  (let* ((func (cl-eval (car exp) env))
         (func2 (if (and (consp func) (eq 'lambda (car func)))
                    (cl-eval-lambda func env)
                  func)))
    (apply func2
           (mapcar #'(lambda (arg) (cl-eval arg env))
                   (cdr exp)))))
```

In the function `cl-eval-call`, we use LISP's own `apply` and `mapcar`.

```
(defun cl-eval-if (exp env)
  (if (cl-eval (cadr exp) env)
      (cl-eval (caddr exp) env)
    (cl-eval (cadddr exp) env)))

(defun cl-eval-progn (exp env)
  (cl-eval-sequence (cdr exp) env))

(defun cl-eval-sequence (exps env)
  (cond ((null (cdr exps))
         (cl-eval (car exps) env))
        (t
         (cl-eval (car exps) env)
         (cl-eval-sequence (cdr exps) env))))
```

These definitions are trivial. The reader should note that the termination test in `cl-eval-sequence` is deliberately not `(null exps)`, so as to allow the definition to be properly *tail recursive* — an optimization discussed in the next chapter.

In order to understand most of the remaining definitions, we now present the representation of environments and the mechanism for binding variables. We define a class `environment` that has three slots:

- `id` — the symbol for the name of an object, for example, the variable X or the function `square`

- `contents` — the value associated with the given symbol

- `next` — a pointer to another environment, forming a linked list

We create environments with the `make-environment` function. In addition to arguments specifying the symbol ID, value, and existing environment, the function `make-environment` has a fourth argument: `local?`, which is a flag specifying whether a variable binding is local or global. Local bindings are inserted before the existing environment, and global bindings are inserted after the given environment. By this mechanism, we can control the relative permanence of variable bindings.

　　　We define a `print-object` method for environments, which displays the symbol IDs and values of the linked objects.

```
(defclass environment ()
  ((id :initarg :id :reader env-id)
   (contents  :initarg :contents :accessor env-contents)
   (next :initarg :next :accessor env-next))
  (:documentation "A simple environment class"))

(defun make-environment (id val env local?)
  (let ((new (make-instance 'environment :id id
                              :contents val :next nil)))
    (cond ((and env (not local?))
           (setf (env-next new) (env-next env))
           (setf (env-next env) new))
          ((and env local?)
           (setf (env-next new) env)))
    new))

(defmethod print-object ((env environment) (str stream))
  (format str "~%~A:~10T~A" (env-id env) (env-contents env))
  (if (env-next env) (print-object (env-next env) str))
  (values))
```

Here are the primary functions that manipulate the environment:

- The `cl-env-lookup` method checks to see if the given `id` matches the current environment. If so, that environment object is returned. Otherwise, it checks the next object in the list. If it reaches the end of the list, `cl-env-lookup` optionally creates a new environment. The default method for `cl-env-lookup` returns the object ID itself.

- `env-contents` normally returns the value of an environment object. The default method of `env-contents` returns the function or symbol value of a regular Common LISP object. In this way, we can use existing Common LISP functions, such as `car` and `*`, with `cl-eval`.

- `cl-bind-variables` recursively adds variable bindings to the environment.

- `cl-bind-variable` creates environment objects linked to other environment objects. Note that only local bindings are created in this fashion.

- `value` returns the contents of the environment object returned by the method `cl-env-lookup`.

- `set-value` stores a value in a variable binding, creating it if needed.

Here is the code.

```
(defmethod cl-env-lookup ((env environment) id local? create?)
  (cond ((eq (env-id env) id) env)
        ((env-next env)
         (cl-env-lookup (env-next env) id local? create?))
        (create?
         (make-environment id nil env local?))
        (t nil)))

(defmethod cl-env-lookup (env id local? create?)
  id)

(defmethod env-contents (obj)
  (cond ((fboundp obj)   (symbol-function obj))
        ((functionp obj) obj)
        ((boundp obj)    (symbol-value obj))
        (t obj)))

(defun bind-variables (ids values env)
  (cond ((consp ids)
         (bind-variable (car ids)
                        (car values)
                        (bind-variables (cdr ids)
                                        (cdr values)
                                        env)))
        ((null ids) env)
        (t
         (bind-variable ids values env))))

(defun bind-variable (identifier value env)
  (make-environment identifier value env t))
```

```
(defun value (id env)
  (let ((result (cl-env-lookup env id nil nil)))
    (cond (result (env-contents result))
          (t (env-contents id)))))
```

```
(defun set-value (id env val local?)
  (setf (env-contents (cl-env-lookup env id local? t)) val))
```

We now finish with the code for handling lambda, setq, and defun.

```
(defun cl-eval-lambda (exp env)
  #'(lambda (&rest args)
      (cl-eval-sequence (cddr exp)
                        (bind-variables (cadr exp) args env))))
```

```
(defun cl-eval-setq (exp env)
  (let ((place (cadr exp)))
    (set-value place env (cl-eval (caddr exp) env) nil)))
```

```
(defun cl-eval-defun (exp env)
  (let ((name (cadr exp)))
    (set-value name env
               `(lambda ,(caddr exp) ,@(cdddr exp)) nil)))
```

In exercise 15.7.6, we invite the reader to provide the remaining definitions for cl-eval-cond, cl-eval-or, cl-eval-and, cl-eval-case, and cl-eval-let. Here is cl-eval in action. We first create a new environment, then put cl-eval through its paces.

```
> (setf user-env (make-environment nil nil nil nil))

NIL:      NIL

> (cl-eval 8 user-env)
8

> (cl-eval '(setq x 7) user-env)
7

> (cl-eval 'x user-env)
7

> (cl-eval (quote x) user-env)
7
```

```
> (cl-eval '(quote x) user-env)
X

> (cl-eval '(if nil 1 2) user-env)
2

> (cl-eval '(if t 1 2) user-env)
1

> (cl-eval '(progn x x 3 4 "fhf" (if t 1 2)) user-env)
1

> (cl-eval '(mapcar 1+ (quote (1 2 3))) user-env)
(2 3 4)

> (cl-eval '(apply + (quote (1 2 3))) user-env)
6

> (cl-eval '(defun square (n) (* n n)) user-env)
(LAMBDA (N) (* N N))

> (cl-eval '(square 8) user-env)
64

> (cl-eval '(defun fact (n) (if (zerop n) 1
    (* n (fact (- n 1))))) user-env)
(LAMBDA (N) (IF (ZEROP N) 1 (* N (FACT (- N 1)))))

> (cl-eval '(fact 6) user-env)
720

> user-env              ; Displays the current user environment.

NIL:      NIL
X:        7
SQUARE:   (LAMBDA (N) (* N N))
FACT:     (LAMBDA (N) (IF (ZEROP N) 1 (* N (FACT (- N 1)))))

> (cl-eval '((lambda (x) (* x 5)) 10) user-env)
50
```

15.7   Exercises

15.7.1   Cleaning the Slate [3*]

Write a macro `clean-slate`, which will give you a new, clean package, and `dirty-slate`, which can take you back to your earlier package, as shown below.

```
> (setf x 10)
10

> (clean-slate)

> x
Error: Attempt to take the value of the unbound variable 'X'.
  [condition type: UNBOUND-VARIABLE]
[1]
> :res

> (dirty-slate)
T

> x
10
```

15.7.2   Leaky Workspace [4*]

In the discussion of the workspace in section 15.5, we state:

> Nonlist expressions, such as symbols, are not copied to the file because their evaluation does not alter the state of session.

There are exceptions to this assumption. What is a nonlist expression that can change the state of the workspace?

15.7.3   Making Transcripts [4*]

Modify the `make-workspace` example given in this chapter to simulate LISP's dribble function. What can the built-in function do that this method does not handle?

15.7.4   Workspace Editor [7*]

The workspace function described in this chapter provides the minimum function of capturing the state of a session by logging expressions to a file. However, the `make-workspace` method is indiscriminate in the expressions that it saves. The programmer is usually interested only in definitions of functions and variables.

Another approach to the workspace management problem is to have a method for keeping track of those definitions that are important and, furthermore, making it easier to create and modify those definitions in the first place. One way to provide this functionality is with an interactive editor. Here is an example of one such editor, `wed`. For clarity, we <u>underline user input.</u>

```
> (wed 'fact)
Creating definition of: FACT

WED> ?

?        print help information
car | <  move context down by car
cdr | >  move context down by cdr
del      delete car of current context
exit     save current definition and exit
(exp)    evaluate given expression
find     move context to matching expression
i        insert at current context
p        print current context
pd       print definition
quit     exit editor without saving
rep      replace car of current context
save     save current definition
set      set current definition
subst    global substitution in definition
top      move context to top definition
u        move context up
```

The programmer invokes the workspace editor with the call (`wed 'fact`), and the program responds with the prompt "WED>". The programmer types "?" to produce a list of commands. Synonyms are separated by vertical bars, for example, `car | >`. The session continues.

```
WED> set

Definition: (defun fact (n) (cond ((zero n) 0)
(t (+ n (fact (- nn 1)))))))

WED> exit

Exiting editor.
```

```
> (fact 4)
Error: attempt to call 'ZERO' which is an undefined function.
  [condition type: UNDEFINED-FUNCTION]

Restart actions (select using :continue):
 0: Try calling ZERO again
 1: Try calling CLOS::ZERO instead
 2: Return a value
 3: Try calling a different function
 4: Setf the symbol function of ZERO and call it again
[1]
> :cont 4
enter expression which will evaluate to the function to call: #'zerop
Error: Attempt to take the value of the unbound variable 'NN'.
   [condition type: UNBOUND-VARIABLE]
[1]
```

The programmer gives an initial definition of fact and exits the editor, saving the
definition. When she tests fact, she encounters a couple of errors. She then returns
to the editor to correct the errors.

```
> (wed 'fact)
Modifying definition of: FACT

WED> pd                            ; Prints current definition.

(DEFUN FACT (N) (COND ((ZERO N) 0) (T (+ N (FACT (- NN 1))))))
WED> subst                        ; Global substitution.

Old Expression: nn

New Expression: n

WED> pd

(DEFUN FACT (N) (COND ((ZERO N) 0) (T (+ N (FACT (- N 1))))))
WED> cdr                          ; Moves context down to the cdr.

WED> cdr

WED> cdr

WED> cdr
```

```
WED> p                           ;  Prints current object.

NIL
WED> u                           ;  Too far.  Backs up one.

WED> p

((COND ((ZERO N) 0) (T (+ N (FACT (- N 1)))))
WED> car

WED> p

(COND ((ZERO N) 0) (T (+ N (FACT (- N 1)))))
WED> >                           ;  Synonym for cdr.

WED> p

(((ZERO N) 0) (T (+ N (FACT (- N 1)))))
WED> <                           ;  Synonym for car.

WED> p

((ZERO N) 0)
WED> rep                         ;  Replaces car of current context.

Expression: (zerop n)

WED> p

((ZEROP N) 0)
WED> t                           ;  Moves context to top definition.

WED> p

(DEFUN FACT (N) (COND ((ZEROP N) 0) (T (+ N (FACT (- N 1))))))
WED> save                        ;  Saves current definition.

WED> (fact 3)                    ;  Evaluates given expression.

6                                ;  Looks OK.
WED> (fact 6)                    ;  Hmmm.  Something is wrong here.
```

WED> <u>p</u>

(DEFUN FACT (N) (COND ((ZEROP N) 0) (T (+ N (FACT (- N 1))))))
; We have been adding instead of multiplying.
WED> <u>find</u>   ; Moves directly to the scene of the crime.

Expression: <u>+</u>

WED> <u>p</u>

(+ N (FACT (- N 1)))
WED> <u>del</u>   ; Deletes the old +.

Deleting: +
WED> <u>p</u>

(N (FACT (- N 1)))
WED> <u>ins</u>   ; Inserts the new *.

Expression: <u>*</u>

WED> <u>p</u>

(* N (FACT (- N 1)))
WED> <u>pd</u>

(DEFUN FACT (N) (COND ((ZEROP N) 0) (T (* N (FACT (- N 1))))))
WED> <u>save</u>

WED> <u>(fact 6)</u>   ; Tests it again.
                                     ; Another problem arises.

0
WED> <u>t</u>

WED> <u>find</u>

Expression: <u>0</u>

WED> <u>p</u>

(0)

```
WED> rep                    ;  Replaces 0 with 1.

Expression: 1

WED> p

(1)
WED> pd

(DEFUN FACT (N) (COND ((ZEROP N) 1) (T (* N (FACT (- N 1))))))
WED> save

WED> (fact 6)               ;  Finally.

720
WED> quit

Exiting editor.
```

At long last, we have arrived at the correct definition. We now define a simple constant and then save all our work in a file, using the function save-ws.

```
> (wed 'george-washington)
Creating definition of: GEORGE-WASHINGTON

WED> set

Definition: (defvar george-washington 'cat)

WED> save

WED> exit

Exiting editor.

> *ws-definitions*         ;  A global list of workspace definitions.
(GEORGE-WASHINGTON FACT)

> (save-ws "outfile")

Workspace saved in file: outfile
```

Here are the contents of "outfile".

```
;; workspace file

;; WED definition: GEORGE-WASHINGTON

(DEFVAR GEORGE-WASHINGTON (QUOTE CAT))
;; WED definition: FACT

(DEFUN FACT (N) (COND ((ZEROP N) 1) (T (* N (FACT (- N 1)))))))
```

The exercise is to write the functions wed and save-ws.

15.7.5   standard-simple-env [6]

It is possible to define many LISP functions in terms of the primitive functions given in simple-eval. The reader should create an association list environment containing as many basic LISP list functions as possible. Here are some trivial ones to begin with.

```
(defvar *standard-simple-env*
   '((caar . (lambda (n) (car (car n))))
     (cadr . (lambda (n) (car (cdr n)))))))
```

Other functions would be append, subst, member, assoc, and reverse.

15.7.6   The Rest of cl-eval [7*]

Write the remaining functions to complete the meta-circular definition of cl-eval presented in this chapter. You need to define the following functions.

```
        cl-eval-cond
        cl-eval-case
        cl-eval-or
        cl-eval-and
        cl-eval-let
```

Here are examples of their use.

```
> (defvar e (make-environment nil nil nil nil))
E

> (cl-eval '(cond (nil 1 2) (t 3 4)) e)
4

> (cl-eval '(case 2 ((1) 'one) ((2) 'two) (otherwise 'many)) e)
TWO
```

```
> (cl-eval '(case 3 ((1) 'one) ((2) 'two) (otherwise 'many)) e)
MANY

> (cl-eval '(or (setq x 1) (setq x 2)) e)
1

> (cl-eval 'x e)
1

> (cl-eval '(and (setq x 1) (setq x 2)) e)
2

> (cl-eval 'x e)
2

> (cl-eval '(let ((a 1) (b 2)) (+ a b)) e)
3
```

15.8 Chapter Summary

- The following LISP object type is introduced in this chapter.

  `package`

- The scope and extent of LISP objects fall into four categories.

  - Lexical scope and indefinite extent, for example, local variable and function bindings, such as created with `let`, `flet`, or `labels`
  - Lexical scope and dynamic extent, for example, labels in `tagbody` or a `block` name
  - Indefinite scope and indefinite extent, for example, constants, such as `pi` or `nil`
  - Indefinite scope and dynamic extent, for example, global (special) variables or `catch` tags

- LISP's `progv` special form provides a means for dynamic scoping of variables.

- LISP packages permit the programmer to organize the namespace. Package symbols and functions include the following:

```
*package*
(packagep object)
(package-name package)
(package-nicknames package)
(package-use-list package)
(package-used-by-list package)
(list-all-packages)
(make-package name)
(in-package package)
(export symbol)
(import symbol package)
(use-package package)
(unuse-package package)
(unexport symbol)
(find-symbol string)
(find-package package-name)
(shadow symbol)
(shadowing-import symbol package)
(package-shadowing-symbols package)
(defpackage package {option}*)
(intern string [package])
(unintern symbol [package])
(rename-package package new-name {nickname}*)
(delete-package package)
(make-symbol string)
(copy-symbol symbol [copy-flag])
(symbol-name symbol)
(symbol-package symbol)
(gentemp [prefix [package]])
(find-all-symbols string-or-symbol)
```

- LISP provides several functions for processing symbols in packages.

```
(do-symbols (var [package [result]]) {form}*)
(do-external-symbols (var [package [result]]) {form}*)
(do-all-symbols (var [result]) {form}*)
(with-package-iterator (mname package-list {type}+) {form}*)
```

- The programmer can use modules to manage dependencies among source files. The main module constructs are:

```
*modules*
(provide module-name)
(require module-name {pathname}*)
```

- The `eval` function can be called directly with an expression.

- The programmer can redefine the behavior of `eval`, using the global variables `*evalhook*` and `*applyhook*`, as well as the functions:

```
(evalhook form eval-fn apply-fn [env])
(applyhook fn args eval-fn apply-fn)
```

- We can specify a meta-circular definition of `eval`, implementing the binding environment as an association list or as linked objects.

Making something variable is easy. Controlling duration of constancy is the trick.

◇ ALAN PERLIS, *Epigrams in Programming (1982)*

Chapter 16

Efficiency and Compilation

Efficiency of a practically flawless kind
may be reached naturally in the struggle for bread.
But there is a something beyond — a higher point,
a subtle and unmistakable touch of love and pride beyond mere skill;
almost an inspiration which gives to all work that finish which is almost art
— which is art.

⋄ JOSEPH CONRAD, *The Mirror of the Sea (1906)*

Like Aesop's fox, when he had lost his tail,
would have all his fellow foxes cut off theirs.

⋄ ROBERT BURTON, *Anatomy of Melancholy (1621-1651)*

The late Duchess of Windsor had her motto embroidered on a pillow: "You can never be too rich or too thin." For the programmer, the eternal aphorism is "A program can never be too small or too fast."

In many cases, the programmer is satisfied once her program runs. Period. The question of speed is secondary. After all, computers are fast; therefore, the program must be fast.

This conclusion is illusory. What constitutes a fast program? How long should it take to run? A second? A minute? An hour? For a given problem and set of input, the speed of execution depends on many things: the algorithm, the program itself, the language implementation, and the particular machine.

A discussion of the efficient design of algorithms is beyond the scope of this book. Likewise, we shall not explore machine architecture. In this chapter, we shall first examine some ways to write more efficient LISP code. Then, we shall introduce the major strategy for producing faster programs: compilation.

Copying	Destructive	Arguments
append	nconc	{list}*
butlast	nbutlast	list [n]
intersection	nintersection	list list [[l-options]]
revappend	nreconc	list list
set-difference	nset-difference	list list [[l-options]]
set-exclusive-or	nset-exclusive-or	list list [[l-options]]
sublis	nsublis	alist tree [[l-options]]
subst	nsubst	new old tree [[l-options]]
subst-if	nsubst-if	new pred tree [key]
subst-if-not	nsubst-if-not	new pred tree [key]
union	nunion	list list [[l-options]]

Table 16.1: Copying and Destructive List Functions

16.1 Coding Optimizations: Destructive Functions

There are common list operations which perform extra steps that can often be avoided. In chapter 14, we discussed applications in which vectors provided faster access than lists. List access commonly requires traversing the list, which is usually slower than accessing elements of a vector. Another list inefficiency comes from the copying of list structure. Most list operations that result in a modification to a list make the changes on a copy of the list, not the original list itself. There are good reasons for this extra effort — primarily, safety. If the operation does not result in the intended effect, the programmer still has the old value of the list.

However, copying list structure is expensive, in terms of both time and memory space. We shall see below that the profligate use of space can result in a considerable loss in time spent during memory reclamation.

Therefore, the programmer will occasionally choose to avail herself of *destructive* list operations, which make changes directly to the given list structure, not a copy. (The term *destructive* actually has an inappropriate connotation. Whereas the contents of the data structure may be destroyed, the list itself is *recycled*.) In LISP, these destructive functions are usually indicated by the prefix n. The primary destructive list functions are given in table 16.1. The more general destructive sequence functions are given in table 16.2. The latter functions can apply to lists and other sequences, including vectors and strings. Three additional pairs of copying (nondestructive) and destructive functions for strings, are given in table 16.3.

The following option specifications are used in the tables.

- {list}* — Zero or more lists

- [n] — A non-negative integer

Copying	Destructive	Arguments
remove	delete	item seq [[s-options]]
remove-if	delete-if	pred seq [[s-if-options]]
remove-if-not	delete-if-not	pred seq [[s-if-options]]
map	map-into	result-type func {seq}+
reverse	nreverse	seq
remove-duplicates	delete-duplicates	seq [[s-options]]
substitute	nsubstitute	new old seq [[s-options]]
substitute-if	nsubstitute-if	new pred seq [[s-if-options]]
substitute-if-not	nsubstitute-if-not	new pred seq [[s-if-options]]

Table 16.2: Copying and Destructive Sequence Functions

Copying	Destructive	Arguments
string-downcase	nstring-downcase	string [:start n] [:end n]
string-upcase	nstring-upcase	string [:start n] [:end n]
string-capitalize	nstring-capitalize	string [:start n] [:end n]

Table 16.3: Copying and Destructive String Functions

- [[1-options]] — The three possible keyword arguments, :test, :test-not, and :key

- [key] — The keyword :key with a single argument specifying a key function

- [[s-options]] — The three list keyword options, :test, :test-not, and :key, plus the additional sequence options, :count, :from-end, :start, and :end

- [[s-if-options]] — The same as [[s-options]], but does not include :test or :test-not, which are implicit in -if and -if-not functions

- {seq}+ — One or more sequences

Here are some examples.

```
> (setf x '(1 2 3 4 5))
(1 2 3 4 5)

> (setf y '(6 7 8 9 10))
(6 7 8 9 10)
```

```
> (append x y)              ;  This is the normal append.
(1 2 3 4 5 6 7 8 9 10)

> x                         ;  x is unchanged.
(1 2 3 4 5)

> (nconc x y)               ;  This is the destructive version of append.
(1 2 3 4 5 6 7 8 9 10)

> x                         ;  x has been reused.
(1 2 3 4 5 6 7 8 9 10)

> (reverse x)               ;  This is the normal reverse.
(10 9 8 7 6 5 4 3 2 1)

> x                         ;  x is unchanged.
(1 2 3 4 5 6 7 8 9 10)

> (nreverse x)
(10 9 8 7 6 5 4 3 2 1)

> x                         ;  x is clobbered.
(1)

> y                         ;  So is y.
(6 5 4 3 2 1)

> (map 'list #'1+ y)        ;  map uses a copy.
(7 6 5 4 3 2)

> y                         ;  y did not change.
(6 5 4 3 2 1)

> (map-into y #'1+ y)       ;  map-into reuses an existing structure.
(7 6 5 4 3 2)

> y                         ;  y is clobbered.
(7 6 5 4 3 2)
```

Note the difference in the first arguments of map and map-into. The former takes a sequence type specification, and the latter takes an actual sequence, which is the result returned by map-into.

Destructive operations on sequences and strings are a two-edged sword. They can result in savings of time and space, but they can also result in screwy results. The copying operations are usually safer, but the efficiency-minded programmer may choose to incorporate destructive operations when feasible.

LISP provides a convenient means of measuring the relative costs and benefits of these operations, namely, the `time` macro. Note that `time`'s output is implemen- ∞ ⇒ tation dependent.

To demonstrate the `time` macro, we create two lists of 10,000 elements each, append them, and then reverse the result.

```
> (setf x (make-sequence 'list 10000 :initial-element 'x))
(X X X X X X X X X X ...)


> (setf y (make-sequence 'list 10000 :initial-element 'y))
(Y Y Y Y Y Y Y Y Y Y ...)


> (time (append x y))
cpu time (non-gc) 16 msec user, 33 msec system
cpu time (gc)      0 msec user, 0 msec system
cpu time (total)  16 msec user, 33 msec system
real time  42 msec
space allocation:
 10002 cons cells, 0 symbols, 32 other bytes,
(X X X X X X X X X ...)


> (time (nconc x y))
cpu time (non-gc) 0 msec user, 0 msec system
cpu time (gc)      0 msec user, 0 msec system
cpu time (total)  0 msec user, 0 msec system
real time  5 msec
space allocation:
 2 cons cells, 0 symbols, 32 other bytes,
(X X X X X X X X X ...)


> (length x)              ;  After nconc, x now has 20,000 elements.
20000


> (time (reverse x))
cpu time (non-gc) 50 msec user, 16 msec system
cpu time (gc)      0 msec user, 0 msec system
cpu time (total)  50 msec user, 16 msec system
real time  54 msec
space allocation:
 20001 cons cells, 0 symbols, 32 other bytes,
(Y Y Y Y Y Y Y Y Y ...)
```

Function	Real Time	Cons Cells
(append x y)	42 msec	10002
(nconc x y)	14 msec	2
(reverse x)	54 msec	20001
(nreverse x)	23 msec	1

Table 16.4: Timings for Copying and Destructive Functions

```
> (time (nreverse x))
cpu time (non-gc) 17 msec user, 0 msec system
cpu time (gc)      0 msec user, 0 msec system
cpu time (total)  17 msec user, 0 msec system
real time  23 msec
space allocation:
 1 cons cell, 0 symbols, 32 other bytes,
(Y Y Y Y Y Y Y Y Y ...)
```

The time macro produces various statistics, which we summarize in table 16.4. We note that the destructive functions are at least twice as fast as the copying functions. This increase in speed can be attributed mainly to the fact that the destructive functions require the creation of fewer cons cells. That is, the copying functions need to allocate additional memory in the creation of new list structure from cons cells.

There is an incremental cost every time a new cons cell is allocated. However, the real cost of cons cells is incurred when LISP runs out of free cons cells and has to *garbage collect*.

16.2   GC

GC stands for "garbage collection." This unsavory term denotes the process of dynamic memory reclamation.

In many programming languages, such as C or C++, the programmer must explicitly allocate and deallocate memory. In LISP, memory management is implicit and automatic. Whenever the programmer executes some function that requires memory, LISP provides it without further ado. When LISP's supply of unused memory runs out, LISP must then reclaim memory that it had previously allocated but is no longer in use. This process is known as garbage collection.

Consider an analogy, based on normal college student grooming habits. When a student needs a shirt to wear, she opens a drawer and pulls out a clean t-shirt. The dirty shirts are deposited in various locales, such as the floor, closet, hallway, bathroom, fire escape, or even a hamper. This t-shirt supply system works quite well until the drawer becomes empty. At that point, the student must engage in t-shirt reclamation, also known as doing laundry. The student canvasses her room and environs, locating all t-shirts. Each t-shirt is categorized as either in-use (currently occupied) or free. The unoccupied shirts are collected, washed, and placed back in the drawer, ready for future service.

Memory allocation and reclamation is a similar process, but instead of t-shirts, we have words of computer memory. A typical LISP implementation maintains memory in a *heap*, a data structure for maintaining an unordered collection of objects. Whenever a function, such as cons, requires new memory, LISP allocates some from its heap. This process continues until no free space remains. At that time, garbage collection begins. All previously allocated memory is examined to see if it is currently in use. The memory that is no longer active becomes the new available storage.

The process of garbage collection, like doing laundry, is a slow task with no intrinsic reward. There are two basic ways to avoid garbage collection. First, be very efficient in your use of memory. Techniques such as destructive sequence operations can cut down on memory requirements — just as turning t-shirts inside-out can double their use. Also, the techniques of lazy evaluation, discussed in chapter 14, can be applied to structure allocation to reduce memory requirements.

The second method to cut down on garbage collection is to have lots of memory. The larger the heap, the longer between GCs, but when you do GC, it will take longer. The student with 365 t-shirts might wash them only once each year, $\infty \Rightarrow$ but what a gruesome task. Some LISP implementations use a method of garbage collection that involves copying one heap to another. This means that you actually need *twice* the amount of space as a single heap at the time of garbage collection.

Just as some college students have been known to do their laundry before they run out of clean clothes, some programmers may choose to perform garbage collection before necessity calls. The LISP function gc invokes garbage collection, as shown here.

```
> (time (gc))
cpu time (non-gc) 0 msec user, 0 msec system
cpu time (gc)     666 msec user, 133 msec system
cpu time (total)  666 msec user, 133 msec system
real time  875 msec
space allocation:
 0 cons cells, 0 symbols, 32 other bytes,
```

We note that garbage collection is slow, relative to the other functions we have timed.

The room function provides us with memory usage statistics. The format of $\infty \Rightarrow$ the output is implementation dependent. In general, room with a single argument of nil provides minimum data, room with no arguments provides more data, and room with an argument of T provides verbose output.

In our current implementation, memory is divided into not two, but three areas — one old and two new. The old area contains permanent objects that never get reclaimed (*tenured* objects), and the two new areas are used for creating new objects. When one of the new areas gets full, it is scavenged and copied to the other new area. Objects in the new space get tenured if they hang around long enough (and publish). Here is some output.

```
> (room nil)      ;  We see only one of the new areas.
```

```
area   cons           symbols         other bytes
   (free:used)    (free:used)      (free:used)
New   836:56228       23:739        28400:534256
Old   420:368458      95:35500      513120:5364656
```

```
> (room)          ;  Now we see the second new area, which is empty.
```

```
area  address(bytes)         cons        symbols        other bytes
                        (free:used)   (free:used)     (free:used)
Top #x126e000
New #x1162000(#x10c000)    -----         -----            -----
New #x1056000(#x10c000)    361:56703     23:739        26128:536528
Old #x713740(#x9428c0)     420:368458    95:35500      513120:5364656
Root pages: 84
```

```
> (room t)        ;  We have gc'd! The new areas have switched roles.
```

```
area  address(bytes)         cons        symbols        other bytes
                        (free:used)   (free:used)     (free:used)
Top #x126e000
New #x1162000(#x10c000)    635:9555      209:553       689160:250328
New #x1056000(#x10c000)    -----         -----            -----
Old #x713740(#x9428c0)     308:368570    95:35500      513120:5364656
Root pages: 83
```

```
code   type                            items    bytes
   1: CONS                             377106   3016848 31.8%
  48: (SIMPLE-ARRAY T)                  49054   2452968 25.9%
   8: FUNCTION                          20369   1210864 12.8%
  53: (SIMPLE-ARRAY CHARACTER)          44113   1137008 12.0%
   2: SYMBOL                            36053    865272  9.1%
  60: (SIMPLE-ARRAY CODE)                 513    262208  2.8%
  12: STANDARD-INSTANCE                 14413    230608  2.4%
  15: STRUCTURE                          3093    118792  1.3%
  49: (SIMPLE-ARRAY BIT)                   35    103008  1.1%
```

13:	SYSVECTOR	9	27984 0.3%
64:	SINGLE-FLOAT	2061	16488 0.2%
32:	(ARRAY T)	630	15120 0.2%
10:	HASH-TABLE	183	5856 0.1%
52:	(SIMPLE-ARRAY (UNSIGNED-BYTE 32))	58	2872 0.0%
50:	(SIMPLE-ARRAY (UNSIGNED-BYTE 8))	5	2864 0.0%
65:	DOUBLE-FLOAT	113	1808 0.0%
66:	BIGNUM	165	1720 0.0%
33:	(ARRAY BIT)	34	816 0.0%
67:	RATIO	48	768 0.0%
68:	COMPLEX	17	272 0.0%
59:	(SIMPLE-ARRAY (SIGNED-BYTE 32))	1	88 0.0%
11:	READTABLE	5	80 0.0%
37:	(ARRAY CHARACTER)	1	24 0.0%

```
total bytes = 9474336

> (gc)

> (room)

area  address(bytes)        cons          symbols        other bytes
                          (free:used)    (free:used)     (free:used)
Top #x126e000
New #x1162000(#x10c000)     -----          -----            -----
New #x1056000(#x10c000)    73:10117      209:553       704000:235488
Old #x713740(#x9428c0)    308:368570      95:35500      513064:5364712
Root pages: 83
```

We make several observations.

- Memory addresses are given in hexadecimal, as indicated by the prefix #x.

- The old area is quite large (#x9428c0 bytes) relative to the new areas (#x10c000 bytes). This means that gc is much faster, since the old objects are never examined again.

- Between the first and second calls to room, 475 cons cells were used. ($836 - 361 = 475 = 56703 - 56228$).

- Between the second and third calls to room, a garbage collection was triggered. An additional 112 cons cells were allocated in the old area, possibly through a promotion and tenure decision.

- The verbose version of room reveals that many objects other than cons cells reside in memory. Thus, garbage collection can be triggered by the allocation of objects other than cons cells.

- After our explicit call to gc, the room function again shows that the two new areas have switched roles.

We shall not go into more details of LISP's GC. Garbage collection algorithms can be very complex and must be extremely robust. During garbage collection, it is usually impossible to process errors or interrupt the program. Several classical methods for garbage collection are presented in [Knuth, 1973]. Garbage collection is a significant area of current programming language research. It is hard to find a programming language conference or journal that does not report new results in the area of garbage collection.

The main lesson of garbage collection is that resources are limited. Even with millions of words of memory, a program will eventually run out of storage. The programmer should learn to practice conservation of space and time in her programs. One of the easiest ways to save space and time in LISP is with the compiler.

16.3   Compilation

The LISP compiler is itself a LISP program, albeit a very large one. To invoke the compiler on a function, the programmer calls compile. Here we create an iterative function test1, which we first run interpreted and then compiled.

```
(defun test1 (n)
  (do ((i 0 (+ i 1)))
      ((> i n) i)
      (+ i i)))

> (functionp #'test1)           ;  Is test1 a function?
T

> (compiled-function-p #'test1) ;  Is test1 compiled?
NIL

> (time (test1 1000))           ;  Runs interpreted.
cpu time (non-gc) 183 msec user, 17 msec system
cpu time (gc)     0 msec user, 0 msec system
cpu time (total)  183 msec user, 17 msec system
real time   196 msec
space allocation:
 15031 cons cells, 0 symbols, 64 other bytes,
1001
```

```
> (compile 'test1)              ; Compiles the function.
TEST1
NIL
NIL

> (functionp #'test1)           ; Is test1 a function?
T

> (compiled-function-p #'test1) ; Is test1 compiled?
T

> (compiled-function-p 'test1)  ; The symbol is not compiled.
NIL

> (type-of #'test1)             ; We have a new type.
COMPILED-FUNCTION

> (time (test1 1000))           ; Runs compiled.
cpu time (non-gc) 0 msec user, 0 msec system
cpu time (gc)     0 msec user, 0 msec system
cpu time (total)  0 msec user, 0 msec system
real time  1 msec
space allocation:
 1 cons cell, 0 symbols, 32 other bytes,
1001
```

There is a dramatic performance improvement from compilation — roughly a 200-fold speed-up. The function `compiled-function-p` is the predicate for the type `compiled-function`.

The programmer can also compile lambda expressions, provided as an optional second argument to `compile`.

```
> (setf x (compile nil '(lambda (n) (* n n))))
#<Function (:ANONYMOUS-LAMBDA 93) @ #x109cad6>

> (type-of x)
COMPILED-FUNCTION

> (compiled-function-p x)
T

> (funcall x 9)
81
```

The process of compilation converts a program from a high level language to a machine language or assembly language program to be executed directly. LISP provides not only a compiler but also a convenient way to examine the assembly code, using the function `disassemble`. The output depends on the implementation in general and the target machine language in particular. The following example ⇐ ∞ displays SPARC® assembly language.

```
> (disassemble x)
;; disassembly of #<Function (:ANONYMOUS-LAMBDA 93) @ #x109cad6>
;; formals: N

;; code vector @ #x109c97c:
   0:    save    #x-68,%o6
   4:    move.l  26(%i5),%o7
   8:    add #x8,%o7
  12:    move.l  %o7,26(%i5)
  16:    subcc   #x1,%g3,%g0
  20:    tne #x10,%g0
  24:    taddcctv    %g1,%g0
  28:    move.l  %i0,%o0
  32:    move.l  -601(%g4),%g2    ; *_20P
  36:    move.l  %i0,%o1
  40:    move.l  6(%g2),%o5
  44:    move.l  -2(%o5),%g6
  48:    jmpl    0(%g6),%o7
  52:    xor #x2,%g0,%g3
  56:    jmpl    8(%i7),%g0
  60:    restore %g0,%o0
```

A programmer will usually refrain from compiling functions one at a time. Instead, she will choose to compile an entire file with the `compile-file` function, which takes an argument of the name of the file that contains the source code.

We have created a file called `ctest.cl`, which has the following definitions.

```
;;  generic arithmetic with integer constants
(defun test1 (n)
  (do ((i 0 (+ i 1)))
      ((> i n) i)
      (+ i i)))
```

```
;;  generic arithmetic with float constants
(defun test2 (n)
  (do ((i 0.0 (+ i 1.0)))
      ((> i n) i)
      (+ i i)))
```

We now compile this file and load the resulting object file.

```
> (load "ctest.cl")
; Loading /u18/homes.ai/slade/a/mss/l/ctest.cl.
T
```

∞ ⇒
```
> (compile-file "ctest.cl")
; --- Compiling file /u18/homes.ai/slade/a/mss/l/ctest.cl ---
; Compiling TEST1
; Compiling TEST2
; Writing fasl file "/u18/homes.ai/slade/a/mss/l/ctest.fasl"
; Fasl write complete
#p"/u18/homes.ai/slade/a/mss/l/ctest.fasl"
NIL
NIL
```

```
> (time (test1 1000))    ; Tests speed after compilation.
cpu time (non-gc) 150 msec user, 33 msec system
cpu time (gc)      0 msec user, 0 msec system
cpu time (total)  150 msec user, 33 msec system
real time   191 msec
space allocation:
 15031 cons cells, 0 symbols, 64 other bytes,
1001
```

```
> (load "ctest.fasl")    ; We forgot to load the compiled code!
; Fast loading /u18/homes.ai/slade/a/mss/l/ctest.fasl.
T
```

```
> (time (test1 1000))    ; This looks much better.
cpu time (non-gc) 0 msec user, 0 msec system
cpu time (gc)      0 msec user, 0 msec system
cpu time (total)  0 msec user, 0 msec system
real time   1 msec
space allocation:
 1 cons cell, 0 symbols, 32 other bytes,
1001
```

Function Call	Interpreted (non-GC)	Interpreted (with GC)	Compiled
(test1 10000)	1616	1750	5
(test2 10000.0)	2417	2733	126

Table 16.5: Comparative Execution Times (milliseconds)

```
> (time (test2 1000))
cpu time (non-gc) 50 msec user, 0 msec system
cpu time (gc)      0 msec user, 0 msec system
cpu time (total)  50 msec user, 0 msec system
real time   35 msec
space allocation:
 1 cons cell, 0 symbols, 32080 other bytes,
1001.0
```

Once we load the compiled code, we can execute the functions directly. The answers do not change between interpreted and compiled code, but the speed does. Compiling a program results in two time savings: load time and run time. The object file (.fasl) loads considerably faster than the corresponding source file (.cl). However, the major difference comes at run-time. In table 16.5, we present comparative timings for interpreted and compiled versions of the functions in ctest. These results show that compilation always helps, but that it helps integer arithmetic most dramatically.

The compilation messages can be turned on and off with the two switches *compile-print* and *compile-verbose*, which may also be specified as the keyword arguments :print and :verbose supplied to compile-file. Their effect is illustrated below.

```
> *compile-print*          ; Printing is on.
T

> *compile-verbose*        ; Verbose feedback is on.
T

> (setf *compile-print* nil)  ; Turns off printing.
NIL
```

```
> (compile-file "ctest.cl")
; --- Compiling file /u18/homes.ai/slade/a/mss/l/ctest.cl ---
; Writing fasl file "/u18/homes.ai/slade/a/mss/l/ctest.fasl"
; Fasl write complete
#p"/u18/homes.ai/slade/a/mss/l/ctest.fasl"
NIL
NIL


> (setf *compile-verbose* nil)   ; Turns off verbose feedback.
NIL


> (compile-file "ctest.cl")
#p"/u18/homes.ai/slade/a/mss/l/ctest.fasl"
NIL
NIL


> (compile-file "ctest.cl" :print t)      ; Turns printing on with keyword.
; Compiling TEST1
; Compiling TEST2
#p"/u18/homes.ai/slade/a/mss/l/ctest.fasl"
NIL
NIL


> (compile-file "ctest.cl" :verbose t)
; --- Compiling file /u18/homes.ai/slade/a/mss/l/ctest.cl ---
; Writing fasl file "/u18/homes.ai/slade/a/mss/l/ctest.fasl"
; Fasl write complete
#p"/u18/homes.ai/slade/a/mss/l/ctest.fasl"
NIL
NIL
```

The programmer can also specify an alternative output file by using the keyword argument :output-file followed by a filename.

```
> (compile-file "ctest.cl" :output-file "ctest2.fasl")
#p"/u18/homes.ai/slade/a/mss/l/ctest2.fasl"
NIL
NIL
```

16.4   Optimizations and Declarations

Compilation is a win. The program loads faster and runs faster. However, we are not satisfied. We want to squeeze out more performance. We can achieve this goal by using *declarations* to provide the compiler with more information.

We observed above that integer arithmetic is faster than floating point arithmetic. The programmer can inform the compiler of the type of a variable, using the `declare` special form, and permit the compiler to optimize the resulting code.

Compiling a function without declarations is like hosting a party without RSVPs. Declarations provide the compiler with information that permits greater efficiency in allocating data structures and selecting instructions. RSVPs permit a hostess accurately to plan the menu and order food. It is an error to perform integer arithmetic on a floating point number. It is an error to serve roast beef to a vegetarian.

We add type declarations to our earlier functions, `test1` and `test2`.

```
(defun test1 (n)
  (declare (type integer n i))
  (do ((i 0 (+ i 1)))
      ((> i n) i)
      (+ i i)))

(defun test2 (n)
  (declare (float n i))
  (do ((i 0.0 (+ i 1.0)))
      ((> i n) i)
      (+ i i)))
```

The arguments to `declare` are *declaration specifiers*. In `test1`, we use `type` followed by a data type and a list of typed variables. If the data type is a predefined LISP type, given in table 16.6, then the word `type` can be dropped, as in the `test2` example.

In addition to making data type declarations, the programmer can also help the compiler by explicitly declaring constants with the `defconstant` form. This is analogous to `defvar` for variables, but tells the compiler that the programmer does not intend ever to change the value. Thus, the compiler can substitute the constant's value directly in the code. This optimization technique is called *constant folding*.

There is an analogous declaration for function definitions: `inline`. This declaration tells the compiler that the definition is not likely to change. More to the point, when this function is called by other functions, the code may be directly integrated inline during compilation. Inline functions are also called *open-coded*. Recursive functions cannot be declared `inline`. (See exercise 16.8.2.)

Here is an example that calculates the area of a circle and the volume of a cylinder.

```
(defconstant pi 3.14159)

(defun area (radius) (* pi radius radius))
```

array	hash-table	sequence
atom	integer	short-float
base-character	keyword	signed-byte
bignum	list	simple-array
bit	long-float	simple-bit-vector
bit-vector	nil	simple-string
character	null	simple-vector
compiled-function	number	single-float
complex	package	standard-char
cons	pathname	stream
double-float	random-state	string
extended-character	ratio	symbol
fixnum	rational	t
float	readtable	unsigned-byte
function	real	vector

Table 16.6: Standard Type Specifiers

```
(defun volume (rad height)
  (declare (inline area))
  (* height (area rad)))
```

In this case, the compiler can produce better code because it can assume that the value of `pi` will never change, and the definition of `area` can be directly inserted in the code that calls it in the `volume` function.

It is possible to make global declarations with the `proclaim` function or the `declaim` macro. For example, the programmer might want `area` to be coded inline in all contexts. The following proclamation would achieve that result.

```
> (proclaim '(inline area))
T
```

```
> (declaim (inline area))    ; Macro version of proclaim.
T
```

Note that since `proclaim` is a function, its arguments must be quoted to avoid evaluation, unlike the macro `declaim`. Both `proclaim` and `declaim` should appear globally, not within functions or other expressions.

We describe the other declaration forms.

- (special {variable}*) indicates that the following variables have dynamic scope, as described in chapter 15.

```
(defun f (n)
  (declare (special *z*))
  (+ n *z*))
```

- (ftype (function ({arg-type}*) {result-type}*) {name}*), for the function of the given name, specifies the types of its arguments and its results.

```
(defun f (n)
  (declare (ftype (function (float &optional float)
                           integer float) truncate))
  (truncate n))
```

Here the function truncate is declared to take arguments of a float and an optional float and to return multiple values of type integer and float.

- (notinline {function}*) specifies that the given function should *not* be open-coded. This declaration overrides any previous inline declaration or proclamation.

```
(defun volume (rad height)
  (declare (notinline area))
  (* height (area rad)))
```

Compilation can prevent the programmer from tracing programs which are *tail recursive* (see section 16.6). The programmer can use a notinline declaration to prevent this optimization and permit the function to be traced.

- (ignore {variable}*) tells the compiler that the programmer is aware that certain variables have been created but are never used. Otherwise, the compiler will usually issue a warning.

```
(defun f (n x y)
  (declare (ignore x y))
  (+ n 1))
```

- (optimize {(quality importance)}*) provides general advice to the compiler on the relative priorities of the programmer. The four standard qualities are:

  - compilation-speed — How fast it takes to compile code
  - safety — How careful the program is at run-time, for example, checking for errors
  - space — How much space the program requires, both in terms of the size of the compiled code and the space required at run-time

− speed − How fast the code runs

Some implementations may provide additional qualities. Importance is either   ⇐ ∞
0, 1, 2, or 3. The value of 3 is inferred if the quality appears as a symbol
without parentheses. In the example below, both safety and speed are very
important, whereas size is not.

```
(defun f (n)
  (declare (optimize safety (speed 3) (size 0)))
  (+ n 1))
```

We observe that this optimization may result in conflicts. In code as in
automobiles, safety and speed are generally incompatible.

- (dynamic-extent {item}*), where item can be either a variable name or a
  function, given as (function name) or simply #'name, specifies that the item
  has dynamic extent. (See chapter 15). The compiler may then safely allocate
  this object on the stack. This declaration can result in efficiencies but also
  is fraught with peril. We recommend that the novice avoid this particular
  declaration.

- (declaration {name}*), seemingly redundant, the declaration declaration
  permits the programmer to include implementation-specific declarations in
  portable code. That is, if the programmer's implementation has a declaration
  machine-type, she should use the declaration declaration if she wishes to
  run her code on another, less versatile, implementation. The declaration
  must be globally declaimed (or proclaimed).

```
(declaim (declaration machine-type))
(defun f (n)
  (declare (machine-type ibm-pc))
  (+ n 1))
```

The programmer can add declarations in many contexts other than defun. Table 16.7 provides a list of the special forms and macros that may contain declarations. In all cases, declarations may be introduced at the beginning of the body of
the form.

The special form locally is intended primarily as a means of introducing
local declarations. It is similar to let but does not introduce variable bindings.
The following two forms are equivalent.

```
> (locally
    (declare (inline area))
    (* 5 (area 3)))
141.3716694115407d0
```

defmacro	dotimes
defsetf	flet
deftype	labels
defun	let
do	let*
do-all-symbols	locally
do-external-symbols	macrolet
do-symbols	multiple-value-bind
do*	prog
dolist	prog*

Table 16.7: Special Forms and Macros with Declarations

```
> (let nil
    (declare (inline area))
    (* 5 (area 3)))
141.3716694115407d0
```

We have introduced declarations as a way of improving performance of LISP code. However, that role is merely advisory. Only the special declaration changes the meaning of a program. Declarations provide information. The compiler may choose to ignore that information. Even so, that information is still available to the programmer and serves as another form of documentation.

16.5 Time of Evaluation

To improve the efficiency of our code, we want to decrease the time required to evaluate our code. LISP also provides ways to specify the *time of evaluation* for our code. The special form eval-when is used to control the time of evaluation. There are three, specific evaluation times or situations when an expression might be executed.

- *Execution time.* This is the normal case. The code is executed when the function is called. This situation is specified with the keyword :execute.

- *Compilation time.* The programmer can specify certain code to be evaluated during compilation, using the keyword :compile-toplevel.

- *Load time.* The programmer can specify certain code to be evaluated during loading, using the keyword :load-toplevel.

The following code is from a file, eval-when.lisp, which contains all possible combinations of the eval-when options.

```
(eval-when (:execute)
          (format t "Message one.~%"))

(eval-when (:compile-toplevel :load-toplevel :execute)
          (format t "Message two.~%"))

(eval-when (:compile-toplevel :load-toplevel)
          (format t "Message three.~%"))

(eval-when (:compile-toplevel)
          (format t "Message four.~%"))

(eval-when (:load-toplevel :execute)
          (format t "Message five.~%"))

(eval-when (:compile-toplevel :execute)
          (format t "Message six.~%"))

(eval-when (:load-toplevel)
          (format t "Message seven.~%"))

(eval-when ()
          (format t "Message eight.~%"))
```

We shall now (1) load the source file (:execute situation), (2) compile the file
(:compile-toplevel situation), and then (3) load the compiled file (load-toplevel
situation). (The semi-colon comments are generated by LISP.)

```
> (load "eval-when.lisp")
; Loading /u18/homes.ai/slade/a/mss/l/eval-when.lisp.
Message one.
Message two.
Message five.
Message six.
T
```

```
> (compile-file "eval-when.lisp")
; --- Compiling file /u18/homes.ai/slade/a/mss/l/eval-when.lisp ---
Message two.
Message three.
Message four.
Message six.
; Writing fasl file "/u18/homes.ai/slade/a/mss/l/eval-when.fasl"
; Fasl write complete
#p"/u18/homes.ai/slade/a/mss/l/eval-when.fasl"
NIL
NIL

> (load "eval-when.fasl")
; Fast loading /u18/homes.ai/slade/a/mss/l/eval-when.fasl.
Message two.
Message three.
Message five.
Message seven.
T
```

The eval-when form controls the printing of the various messages according to
the situation in which they are encountered. We note that we never see Message
eight, as there are no circumstances under which its clause is evaluated.

16.6 Tail Recursion

We have seen how the compiler can optimize inline functions by replacing the
function call with the literal code from the function definition. Thus, the definition
of volume that resulted from this substitution was

```
(defun volume (rad height)
  (* height (* 3.14159 rad rad)))
```

Why should this definition be faster than the one that called area? Because there
is a cost to function calls. A function call requires bookkeeping, which uses up time
and memory space. Recursive function calls can be especially expensive.

However, it is possible to limit significantly the recursive function call overhead
under certain circumstances, namely, when the function call is the *last* expression
executed in a given function. Consider the following two definitions of factorial.

```
(defun fact (n)
  (cond ((zerop n) 1)
        (t (* n (fact (- n 1))))))
```

Function Call (length z) = 10000	Allegro CL on SPARC 2	Mac CL on Quadra 800
(r-mapcar #'abs z)	150	stack overflow
(tr-mapcar #'abs z)	67	74
(tr-nmapcar #'abs z)	50	64
(mapcar #'abs z)	50	37

Table 16.8: Comparative Compiled Execution Times (milliseconds)

```
(defun tr-fact (n)
  (tr-fact-aux n 1))

(defun tr-fact-aux (count result)
  (cond ((zerop count) result)
        (t (tr-fact-aux (- count 1)
                        (* result count)))))
```

Both definitions are recursive, but the second one is *tail recursive*. Specifically, the definition of tr-fact-aux calls itself as the last branch of the cond clause. That means that *the value returned by the first recursive call will be the same as the value returned by the last recursive call*. This identity does not hold for the recursive calls in fact because results returned by recursive calls to fact are then multiplied by the current value of n.

Tail recursion is effectively the same as iteration. The compiler can optimize the tail recursion calls into direct jumps. The function call overhead disappears, and the code runs like the wind.

Why should tail recursion make such a difference? Consider an analogy. In chapter 4, we discussed a census taker who had to ask 10 questions at each household. Clearly, it would be best to ask all 10 questions at one time rather than visit each house 10 times — once per question. By not returning to any house a second time, the census taker is saving not only the time required to come back to each house, but also the record-keeping required to keep track of which houses have answered what questions. When the census taker leaves a house, she should not have to return.

So it is with tail recursion. Less overhead results in faster code. Here is another example. We first write a recursive definition of mapcar that takes a function and just one list as arguments. We then write two tail recursive versions; the first one uses reverse and the second uses nreverse, a destructive operation.

```
(defun r-mapcar (proc lst)
  (cond ((null lst) nil)
        (t (cons (funcall proc (car lst))
                 (r-mapcar proc (cdr lst))))))

(defun tr-mapcar (proc lst)
  (tr-mapcar-aux proc lst nil))

(defun tr-mapcar-aux (proc lst result)
  (cond ((null lst) (reverse result))
        (t (tr-mapcar-aux proc (cdr lst)
                          (cons (funcall proc (car lst)) result)))))

(defun tr-nmapcar (proc lst)
  (tr-nmap-aux proc lst nil))

(defun tr-nmap-aux (proc lst result)
  (cond ((null lst) (nreverse result))
        (t (tr-nmap-aux proc (cdr lst)
                        (cons (funcall proc (car lst)) result)))))
```

In table 16.8 we present comparative execution speeds of our functions, compiled with `safety`, `space`, and `speed` set to 1. Tail recursion wins even more than the use of the destructive function `nreverse`.

One of the sources of greatest difference among the many implementations of Common LISP is the quality of the code produced by the compiler. The programmer who is keenly interested in achieving maximum performance from her compiled code is advised to review the compiler documentation specific to her LISP implementation.

This is a book about software. However, programmers should always be mindful that one of the easiest ways to speed up a program is simply to run it on a faster machine. Parallel execution of code is becoming feasible for many applications as well. The silicon gods are benevolent and generous. Every year we witness an increase in processor speed and a drop in price, as illustrated in table 16.9. In two decades, hardware price performance has improved by a factor of $1,000,000$! Is life great, or what?

16.7 Advanced Subjects

At the lowest level, any computer program or data is just bits and bytes. One of the great virtues of LISP is that the programmer can generally ignore the lowest level. LISP encourages the programmer to create abstractions on top of abstractions to distance herself from the bits and bytes.

Year	Machine	Instructions per second	Price	Price per million instructions per second
1975	IBM Mainframe	10,000,000	$10,000,000	$1,000,000
1976	Cray 1	160,000,000	$20,000,000	$125,000
1979	Digital VAX	1,000,000	$200,000	$200,000
1981	IBM PC	250,000	$3,000	$12,000
1984	Sun Microsystems 2	1,000,000	$10,000	$10,000
1994	Intel Pentium PC	66,000,000	$3,000	$45
1995	Sony PCX video game	500,000,000	$500	$1
1995	Microunity set-top box	1,000,000,000	$500	$0.50

Table 16.9: Two Decades of Hardware Price/Performance Progress

However, some programmers have a secret passion for manipulating bits. Sometimes, this desire is motivated by concerns for efficiency. Other times, the programmer may actually be simulating a digital device, such as an integrated circuit, for which bits and bytes are a natural representation.

In either case, LISP provides satisfaction. Bits are represented conveniently in LISP as integers, bit vectors, or bytes. There are extensive functions for handling all types. The advanced topics for the current chapter are as follows.

- Bits of Integers

- Bit Vectors

- Bytes

16.7.1 Bits of Integers

Binary numbers can be entered directly in LISP with the #b prefix. However, numbers normally print as decimal numbers with no prefix, as specified by the values of *print-base* and *print-radix*, respectively.

```
> #b10                    ; Binary 2.
2

> *print-base*            ; *print-base* defaults to base 10.
10

> (setf *print-base* 2)   ; Changes default to base 2.
10
```

```
> 2
10

> *print-radix*
NIL

> (setf *print-radix* t)      ;  Changes default to include radix prefix.
T

> 2
#b10

> -2
#b-10

> (+ -2 -2)
#b-100
```

Negative numbers appear to work fine as binary numbers. This should not be a surprise inasmuch as all numbers are represented internally in binary. However, there is a subtle complication regarding the internal representation of negative numbers.

We are familiar with the not function which returns the opposite value of its argument. The function lognot reverses the bits in its argument, changing 0's to 1's, and *vice versa*.

```
> (not t)                     ;  The opposite of T is NIL.
NIL

> (not nil)
T

> (lognot 1)                  ;  The logical opposite of 1 is -2!
#b-10

> (lognot -2)
#b1
```

What's going on? The answer is that negative numbers are represented using *two's complement* numbers. The two's complement of a number is the logical negation of the bits of the number, plus 1. The reason for using two's complement notation is that arithmetic is easier, namely, that the computer can perform subtraction by using addition!

```
(defun twos-complement (n)
  (+ 1 (lognot n)))
```

```
> (twos-complement 1)           ;  Negative 1 is the two's complement of 1.
#b-1
```

```
> (- 5 3)                       ;  Subtracts 3 from 5.
#b10
```

```
> (+ 5 (twos-complement 3))  ;  Adds 5 with the two's complement of 3.
#b10
```

Given that LISP automatically prints two's complement negative numbers as "normal" numbers, we need a way of revealing the actual bit patterns. Our function binary-to-bits does the trick, taking two arguments: the number to be printed and the *width* of the number in bits. The result is a string giving the underlying bit pattern. (The v format directive is explained on page 218.)

```
(defun binary-to-bits (n width)
  (let ((fstring "~v,'0B"))
    (if (minusp n)
        (flip-bits (format nil fstring width (lognot n)))
        (format nil fstring width n))))
```

```
(defun flip-bits (str)
  (map
   'string
   #'flip-bit
   str))
```

```
(defun flip-bit (char)
  (case char
        ((#\0) #\1)
        ((#\1) #\0)))
```

```
> (binary-to-bits 2 4)
"0010"
```

```
> (binary-to-bits -2 4)
"1110"
```

For positive numbers, binary-to-bits merely prints the regular binary representation, using the ~B format directive. For negative numbers, binary-to-bits takes the logical negation of the number and then prints the opposite of every bit.

Operation	Name	Arguments/Definition
logand	and	{integer}*
logior	inclusive or	{integer}*
logxor	exclusive or	{integer}*
logeqv	equivalence (exclusive nor)	{integer}*
lognand	not-and	(lognot (logand n1 n2))
lognor	nor-or	(lognot (logior n1 n2))
logandc1	and complement of 1st with 2nd	(logand (lognot n1) n2))
logandc2	and 1st with complement of 2nd	(logand n1 (lognot n2)))
logorc1	or complement of 1st with 2nd	(logior (lognot n1) n2))
logorc2	or 1st with complement of 2nd	(logand n1 (lognot n2)))

Table 16.10: Bitwise Logical Operations

We can now use `binary-to-bits` to illustrate LISP's collection of bitwise logical operations.

```
(defun log-test (x y)
  (mapc
   #'(lambda (func)
       (let ((ans (funcall (symbol-function func) x y)))
         (format t "(~A~10T ~B ~B) ~20T=> ~s~%"
                 func x y
                 (binary-to-bits ans 4)))))
   '(logand logior logxor logeqv lognand lognor logandc1 logandc2
           logorc1 logorc2))
  (values))

> (log-test 3 5)
(LOGAND     11 101)  => "0001"
(LOGIOR     11 101)  => "0111"
(LOGXOR     11 101)  => "0110"
(LOGEQV     11 101)  => "1001"
(LOGNAND    11 101)  => "1110"
(LOGNOR     11 101)  => "1000"
(LOGANDC1   11 101)  => "0100"
(LOGANDC2   11 101)  => "0010"
(LOGORC1    11 101)  => "1101"
(LOGORC2    11 101)  => "1011"
```

These operations are summarized in table 16.10. We note that the first four operations can take any number of arguments, while the remaining six require exactly two arguments.

   LISP's boole function provides another means of performing bitwise operations on integers. boole takes three arguments — an operation and two integers
— and returns the result of applying the operation. The operation is actually a
constant — an integer between 0 and 15. We define the function boole-test,
which illustrates all the boole operations, as well as listing the actual values of the
respective operation constants.

```
(defun boole-test (x y)
  (mapc
   #'(lambda (op)
       (let ((ans (boole (symbol-value op) x y)))
         (format t "(boole ~A~20T ~B ~B) ~30T=> ~s   [~B]~%"
                 op x y
                 (binary-to-bits ans 4)
                 (symbol-value op))))
     '(boole-clr boole-set boole-1 boole-2 boole-c1 boole-c2
       boole-and boole-ior boole-xor boole-eqv boole-nand boole-nor
       boole-andc1 boole-andc2 boole-orc1 boole-orc2))
   (values))
```

```
> (boole-test 3 5)
(boole BOOLE-CLR      11 101)  => "0000"   [0]
(boole BOOLE-SET      11 101)  => "1111"   [1]
(boole BOOLE-1        11 101)  => "0011"   [10]
(boole BOOLE-2        11 101)  => "0101"   [11]
(boole BOOLE-C1       11 101)  => "1100"   [100]
(boole BOOLE-C2       11 101)  => "1010"   [101]
(boole BOOLE-AND      11 101)  => "0001"   [110]
(boole BOOLE-IOR      11 101)  => "0111"   [111]
(boole BOOLE-XOR      11 101)  => "0110"   [1000]
(boole BOOLE-EQV      11 101)  => "1001"   [1001]
(boole BOOLE-NAND     11 101)  => "1110"   [1010]
(boole BOOLE-NOR      11 101)  => "1000"   [1011]
(boole BOOLE-ANDC1    11 101)  => "0100"   [1100]
(boole BOOLE-ANDC2    11 101)  => "0010"   [1101]
(boole BOOLE-ORC1     11 101)  => "1101"   [1110]
(boole BOOLE-ORC2     11 101)  => "1011"   [1111]

> boole-set
1

> (constantp boole-set)
T
```

These operations are summarized in table 16.11, and reprised in exercise 16.8.8.

Operation	Result
boole-clr	clear: always 0
boole-set	set: always 1
boole-1	first integer
boole-2	second integer
boole-c1	complement of first integer
boole-c2	complement of second integer
boole-and	AND
boole-ior	inclusive OR
boole-xor	exclusive OR
boole-eqv	equivalence (exclusive NOR)
boole-nand	NOT-AND
boole-nor	NOR-OR
boole-andc1	AND complement of 1st with 2nd
boole-andc2	AND 1st with complement of 2nd
boole-orc1	OR complement of 1st with 2nd
boole-orc2	OR 1st with complement of 2nd

Table 16.11: boole Operation Constants

LISP has a few more binary operations. The predicates logtest and logbitp test for bits. logtest compares two integers and returns true if both numbers have a 1 bit in any of the same positions. The logbitp function checks to see if the bit at a given position in an integer is 1.

```
> (logtest #b1 #b10)        ; Compares bits in 1 and 2.
NIL                          ; None in common.

> (logtest #b11 #b10)       ; Compares bits in 3 and 2.
T                            ; At least 1 in common.

> (logbitp 0 #b10)          ; Is bit 0 set in number 2?
NIL

> (logbitp 1 #b10)          ; Is bit 1 set in number 2?
T

> (logbitp 2 #b10)          ; Is bit 2 set in number 2?
NIL
```

The functions logcount and integer-length provide information about the underlying bit representation of integers. The logcount function returns the number of 1's used in representing positive integers, or the number of 0's used to represent negative integers. The function `integer-length` returns a number indicating how many bits are required to represent the given integer, if positive. Negative integers require one additional bit.

```
> (logcount 2)              ; How many 1 bits?
#b1

> (logcount (lognot 2))     ; (logcount n) = (logcount (lognot n)).
#b1

> (logcount #b10000000)     ; How many 1 bits?
#b1

> (logcount #b-10000000)    ; How many 0 bits?
#b111

> (logcount #b11)           ; How many 1 bits?
#b10

> (integer-length #b1000)   ; How many bits required?
#b100

> (integer-length #b-1000)
#b11
```

We saw above that two's complement arithmetic simplifies subtraction. It is also true that binary numbers simplify multiplication and division, at least by 2. To multiply or divide an integer by 2, you just shift the bits left or right, respectively, using the LISP function `ash` (arithmetic shift). `ash` takes two arguments, the integer and the number of places to shift, where a positive number moves bits to the left, and a negative number moves bits to the right, losing the bits that drop off.

```
> (ash 2 2)
#b1000

> (ash 2 -2)
#b0

> (ash -2 2)
#b-1000

> (ash -2 0)
#b-10
```

The `ash` function is equivalent to the following function, but with much greater efficiency.

```
(defun my-ash (integer count)
  (values (floor (* integer (expt 2 count)))))
```

```
> (my-ash 2 -2)
#b1000
```

```
> (my-ash 2 -2)
#b0
```

16.7.2 Bit Vectors

In addition to binary integers, LISP provides vectors of bits: the `bit-vector`. The same retinue of logical operators that works on integers is also available for bit vectors. Note that with bit vectors, we do not encounter two's complement representation.

Bit vectors are notated with the prefix `#*` followed by a sequence of binary digits. Bit vectors are sequences, which can respond to the regular sequence functions.

```
> #*1001                  ; Bit vectors are self-evaluating.
#*1001
```

```
> (bit-vector-p #*1100)   ; The predicate for bit vectors.
T
```

```
> (typep #*10 'bit-vector) ; bit-vector is a standard type.
T
```

```
> (length #*10101010)
8
```

```
> (every #'zerop #*0000010)
NIL
```

```
> (some #'zerop #*0000010)
T
```

We define the function `bit-test` to demonstrate the use of logical operations on bit vectors.

Operation	Result
bit-and	AND
bit-ior	inclusive OR
bit-xor	exclusive OR
bit-eqv	equivalence (exclusive NOR)
bit-nand	NOT-AND
bit-nor	NOR-OR
bit-andc1	AND complement of 1st with 2nd
bit-andc2	AND 1st with complement of 2nd
bit-orc1	OR complement of 1st with 2nd
bit-orc2	OR 1st with complement of 2nd

Table 16.12: Bit Array Logical Operations

```
(defun bit-test (x y)
  (mapc
   #'(lambda (func)
       (let ((ans (funcall (symbol-function func) x y)))
         (format t "(boole ~A~17T~B ~B)~30T=> ~s~%"
                 func x y
                 ans)))
    '(bit-and bit-ior bit-xor bit-eqv bit-nand bit-nor
              bit-andc1 bit-andc2 bit-orc1 bit-orc2))
  (values))

> (bit-test #*0011 #*0101)
(boole BIT-AND   #*0011 #*0101) => #*0001
(boole BIT-IOR   #*0011 #*0101) => #*0111
(boole BIT-XOR   #*0011 #*0101) => #*0110
(boole BIT-EQV   #*0011 #*0101) => #*1001
(boole BIT-NAND  #*0011 #*0101) => #*1110
(boole BIT-NOR   #*0011 #*0101) => #*1000
(boole BIT-ANDC1 #*0011 #*0101) => #*0100
(boole BIT-ANDC2 #*0011 #*0101) => #*0010
(boole BIT-ORC1  #*0011 #*0101) => #*1101
(boole BIT-ORC2  #*0011 #*0101) => #*1011
```

These operations are summarized in table 16.12. Each of these functions takes an
optional third argument. If it is NIL or omitted, the result is a new array. If the
argument is T, then the result is destructively placed in the first argument. If the
argument is another bit array, then the result is placed there.

Additional bit-array functions include bit-not, which complements the ele-

ments of a bit array, and the `bit` and `sbit` accessor functions. The last two are
analogous to `aref` but specifically for bit arrays and simple bit arrays, in the case
of `sbit`. (As discussed in section 14.7.2, a simple array has no fill pointer and is
not adjustable or displaced to another array.) Both `bit` and `sbit` can be used with
`setf` destructively to change bit-array elements. We demonstrate these functions
below.

```
> (bit-not #*0011)      ;  Logical complement of bit vector.
#*1100


> (bit #*0011 0)        ;  Returns bit in position 0.
0


> (bit #*0011 2)        ;  Returns bit in position 2.
1


> (bit #*0011 4)        ;  There is no position 4.
Error: Index(s) to array function is/are out of the range of the array.
  [condition type: SIMPLE-ERROR]
[1]
> :res


> (sbit #*0011 3)       ;  sbit is like bit for simple bit arrays.
1


> (setf x #*0011)
#*0011


> (setf (bit x 0) 1)
1


> x
#*1011
```

16.7.3   Bytes

Instead of manipulating data bit by bit, the programmer may want to use larger
amounts: bytes. When a programmer thinks of bytes, she usually considers chunks
of 7 or 8 bits, regularly justified. In LISP, the programmer can specify both the
size of bytes and their relative position in a larger group of bits, using the function
`byte`. The first argument to `byte` specifies the size in bits, and the second gives
the starting position for the byte, where bit 0 is the low order (least significant or
rightmost) bit.

```
> (byte 4 0)                    ; Specifies the byte size and position.
(4 . 0)


> (byte-size (byte 4 0))        ; Extracts the size from a specification.
4


> (byte-position (byte 4 0))    ; Extracts the position.
0
```

∞ ⇒
```
> (type-of (byte 4 0))          ; Our byte specification is a cons!
CONS
```

The functions `byte-size` and `byte-position` access the components of a byte specification. In our implementation, `byte`, `byte-size`, and `byte-position` are equivalent to `cons`, `car`, and `cdr`, respectively.

The two primary operations performed with bytes are extracting a byte from an integer (*loading* a byte) and setting a byte field in an integer with a given byte (*depositing* a byte). The functions `ldb` and `dpb` perform these respective operations.

```
> (setf *print-base* 2)
10


> (ldb (byte 4 0) #b111000111)  ; Extracts the first 4 bits.
111


> (ldb (byte 4 4) #b111000111)  ; Gets 4 bits starting at bit 4.
1100


> (ldb (byte 8 0) #b111000111)  ; Extracts the first 8 bits.
11000111
```

The arguments to `ldb` are a byte specification and a number. We observe that leading zeros are suppressed.

The `dpb` function has an initial argument of the new byte, which replaces the existing bits in a copy of the given integer.

```
> (dpb #b1000 (byte 4 0) #b111000111)   ; Replaces the first 4 bits.
111001000


> (dpb #b1000 (byte 4 4) #b111000111)   ; Replaces the second 4 bits.
110000111


> (dpb #b1000 (byte 8 0) #b111000111)   ; Replaces the first 8 bits.
100001000
```

```
> (dpb #b1000 (byte 2 0) #b111000111)    ;  Replaces the first 2 bits.
111000100
```

If the new byte has fewer bits than required, zeros are used. If the new byte has more bits than required, the extra bits are ignored.

The function `deposit-field` is a variant of `dpb`. It uses the second argument byte specification to extract a byte from the first argument and replaces the corresponding byte in a copy of the third argument.

```
> (deposit-field #b11110000 (byte 4 0) #b10101010)
10100000
```

```
> (deposit-field #b11110000 (byte 4 4) #b10101010)
11111010
```

```
> (deposit-field #b11110000 (byte 2 0) #b10101010)
10101000
```

Two variants of `ldb` are `ldb-test` and `mask-field`. They each take two arguments: a byte specification and an integer. `ldb-test` is a predicate that returns true if the byte is non-zero. `mask-field` extracts the specified byte but fills the remaining bits with zeros.

```
> (ldb-test (byte 4 0) #b11110000)
NIL
```

```
> (ldb-test (byte 4 1) #b11110000)
T
```

```
> (ldb-test (byte 4 4) #b11110000)
T
```

```
> (mask-field (byte 4 0) #b10101010)
1010
```

```
> (mask-field (byte 4 2) #b10101010)
101000
```

```
> (mask-field (byte 4 4) #b10101010)
10100000
```

Although Common LISP does not have a type `byte`, there is an `unsigned-byte` type, which corresponds to non-negative integers that can be represented as a two's complement number of n bits.

```
> (typep #b1100 '(unsigned-byte 4))
T

> (typep #b11100 '(unsigned-byte 4))
NIL

> (typep #b11100 'unsigned-byte)
T
```

If 2^n is k, then the following are equivalent type specifications.

```
(unsigned-byte n) ≡ (mod k)
(unsigned-byte n) ≡ (integer 0 k-1)
(unsigned-byte *) ≡ (integer 0 *)
 unsigned-byte    ≡ (integer 0 *)
```

16.8 Exercises

16.8.1 Compilation Experiments [5]

In this chapter, we have discussed a number of ways to write more efficient code. In this exercise, we ask the obstreperous question: *How much more efficient?*

This exercise is open-ended. The reader is asked to design functions that can be implemented in several contrasting ways to produce a range of execution speeds. Appropriate methods to compare would include the following.

- *Multiplication versus addition.* For example, (* x 2) compared with (+ x x).

- *Vectors versus lists.* Rewrite some of the vector code from chapter 14, using lists instead of vectors, and compare the execution speeds of the two versions.

- declare *and* defconstant. Compile programs with and without declare and defconstant declarations. When does it help? How much?

- *Recursive versus iterative.* In section 9.4, we discussed differences between recursive and iterative control mechanisms. Compile functions to test the relative efficiency of these contrasting methods. Finally, write the code in a tail recursive fashion for comparison with the normal iterative and recursive versions.

- labels *versus secondary functions.* The labels form allows the programmer to create local named functions — as does flet with lambda expressions. Compare the efficiency of these approaches with defun'd subfunctions.

The programmer should provide a method for calling the test functions repeatedly, to get an accurate aggregate execution time greater than a few seconds. An obvious way to do this is with the `repeat` macro described in chapter 11. If the programs are executed on time-shared machines, the programmer should take the machine load into account when comparing execution times.

16.8.2   Recursive Inline Functions [3*]

Instead of using tail recursion to reduce the overhead of function calls, why not simply declare recursive functions to be `inline`?

16.8.3   Tail Recursive reverse [4*]

Write a tail recursive version of `reverse`.

16.8.4   Tail Recursive append [4]

Write a tail recursive version of `append`.

16.8.5   Tail Recursive last [4*]

Write a tail recursive version of `last`.

16.8.6   Tail Recursive nth [4]

Write a tail recursive version of `nth`.

16.8.7   Tail Recursive remove-duplicates [4*]

Write a tail recursive version of `remove-duplicates`, described in exercise 4.7.9, page 128.

16.8.8   boola boola [4*]

Assume that the `boole` function did not exist but that all the related constants were available. Write your own version of `boole`.

```
> (my-boole boole-ior 3 5)
7
```

16.9   Chapter Summary

- The following LISP object types are discussed in this chapter.

  ```
  compiled-function
  bit
  bit-vector
  unsigned-byte
  ```

- Most list and sequence functions do not make changes directly on a given structure but instead use a copy. Destructive functions save space and time by recycling the original structure. Destructive list functions include:

```
(nconc {lists}*)
(nbutlast list [n])
(nintersection list list [[options]])
(nreconc list list)
(nset-difference list list [[options]])
(nset-exclusive-or list list [[options]])
(nsublis alist tree [[options]])
(nsubst new old tree [[options]])
(nsubst-if new pred tree [:key key-func])
(nsubst-if-not new pred tree [:key key-func])
(nunion list list [[options]])
```

where [[options]] comprises

[{:test | :test-not} pred] [:key key-func]

- Destructive sequence functions include:

```
(delete item sequence [[options]])
(delete-if pred sequence [[options2]])
(delete-if-not pred sequence [[options2]])
(map-into result-sequence function {sequence}*)
(nreverse sequence)
(delete-duplicates sequence [[options]])
(nsubstitute newitem olditem sequence [[options]])
(nsubstitute-if new pred sequence [[options2]]
(nsubstitute-if-not new pred sequence [[options2]])
```

where [[options]] comprises

[{:test | :test-not} pred] [[options2]]

and [[options2]] comprises

[:count c] [:from-end fe] [:key key-func] [:start sn] [:end en]

- Destructive functions on strings include:

```
(nstring-downcase string [[options]])
(nstring-upcase string [[options]])
(nstring-capitalize string [[options]])
```

where [[options]] comprises

[:start sn] [:end en]

- The `time` macro provides execution timing data.

- LISP performs dynamic memory management, also known as garbage collection. The (gc) function can be invoked explicitly by the programmer.

- The `room` function provides memory usage statistics.

- Compilation produces code that executes faster. The compilation command for a single function is `compile`. The predicate for compiled functions is `compiled-function-p`. The `compile-file` function compiles an entire file.

- The compiler message output is controlled by the switches *compile-print* and *compile-verbose*, and their respective keyword arguments :print and :verbose. The `compile-file` function also uses the :output-file keyword to specify an explicit output file.

- The `declare` form permits the programmer to provide additional information to the compiler. Declaration forms include the following:

```
type
ftype
special
inline
notinline
ignore
optimize (safety, space, speed)
dynamic-extent
declaration
```

Global declarations can be made with the macro `declaim` and the function `proclaim`.

- The `defconstant` form is another method for providing helpful declarations for the compiler.

- The programmer can include declarations in many LISP forms, including the `locally` special form.

- Using `eval-when`, the programmer can specify the time of evaluation as either execution time, compile time, or load time.

- The overhead expense of recursive function calls can be obviated in LISP through the use of tail recursion. The effectiveness of this technique depends on the compiler.

- Another source of efficiency that is sometimes overlooked by us software types is to run on a faster processor.

Optimization hinders evolution.

◇ ALAN PERLIS, *Epigrams in Programming (1982)*

Appendix A

Internet LISP Resources

> *Love that so desires would fain keep her changeless;*
> *Fain would fling the net, and fain have her free.*
>
> ◇ GEORGE MEREDITH, *The Woods of Westermain (1833)*

> *Free soil, free men, free speech. Frémont.*
>
> ◇ ANONYMOUS, *Republican party rallying cry (1856)*

One of the main benefits of LISP is its extensibility. If the language does not fit your needs, you can extend the language.

This text is also extensible. LISP continues to evolve and so will this book, through the Internet. The words in this appendix also appear as a page on the World Wide Web (WWW) at the address, that is, the URL:

```
http://www.prenhall.com/divisions/ptr/
```

Using that entry point, the reader can then gain access to the following resources. (Keeping with Web browser format conventions, we underline text that contains hyperlinks to other Web documents. Clicking is disabled in the print version of this appendix.)

- *Corridenda and Addenda.* Though we have tried to remove mistakes and to include all facets of Common LISP, we assume that alert readers will discover errors of omission and commission. Here we will post such errata for OBJECT-ORIENTED COMMON LISP.

- *Free Speech.* Readers are invited to send comments and suggestions. These may find their way into the *Corridenda and Addenda.*

- *Free Code.* The source code contained in OBJECT-ORIENTED COMMON LISP is available for downloading.

- *Free LISP*. One purpose of this appendix is to help the reader execute the code given in this text. To do that, the reader must have access not only to the code, but also to Common LISP. There are many implementations for sale. Some are available for free. Here we provide information about publicly available Common LISPs.

- *Free Will*. Throughout this book we have focused on the Common LISP programming language. However, despite the lofty intentions of the designers of Common LISP, there is no single Common LISP, but a variety of implementations and dialects. We provide information about LISP dialects, including compatibility code to run the examples in this book.

- *Free Advice*. There are many other Internet resources related to LISP. We provide information about various LISP newsgroups and organizations. We include links to selected online archives of LISP code and lore.

- *Free Documentation*. In violation of one of publishing's ten commandments, Digital Press has made available the complete text of *Common LISP: The Language (Second Edition)* in electronic form. We provide a link to an online edition.

Documentation is like term insurance: It satisfies because almost no one who subscribes to it depends on its benefits.

◇ ALAN PERLIS, *Epigrams in Programming (1982)*

Appendix B

Answers to Selected Exercises

Keep the faculty of effort alive in you
by a little gratuitous exercise every day.

◇ WILLIAM JAMES, *The Principles of Psychology (1890)*

It is better to know some of the questions
than all of the answers.

◇ JAMES THURBER, *Saying*

Most of the answers given in this appendix are definitions of LISP functions. They appear here without comment or annotation. The reader should not assume that this terse manner of presentation be construed as a model to emulate. Rather, the reader should realize that the original exercise cited at each answer elucidates the purpose of the code.

Comments are valuable. Comments are necessary. Comments are a positive force in the universe. Also, if the reader has to rely on this appendix for the answers to the exercises, the least she could do is to write her own comments.

We expect to provide answers to additional exercises via the Internet, as well as improvements and corrections for the published answers. See appendix A for more information.

Exercise 2.11.2 Defining New Functions (p. 59)

```
(defun add2 (x) (+ x 2))

(defun add5 (x) (+ x 5))

(defun double (x) (+ x x))

(defun min-abs4 (a b c d)
  (min (abs a) (abs b) (abs c) (abs d)))

(defun max-abs4 (a b c d)
  (max (abs a) (abs b) (abs c) (abs d)))
```

Exercise 2.11.3 Foreign Function Names (p. 59)

```
(defun ajoutez (x y) (+ x y))
(defun retranchez (x y) (- x y))
(defun hochstmas (x y) (max x y))
(defun multiplizieren (x y) (* x y))
(defun njia-ya-kutokea () (exit))
```

Exercise 2.11.4 Zeller's Congruence (p. 60)

```
(defun zeller (n m c y l)
  (rem
   (+ n
      (truncate
       (- (* m 13/5)
          0.2))
      Y
      (truncate (/ y 4))
      (truncate (/ c 4))
      (- (* 2 c))
      (- (* (+ 1 l)
            (truncate (/ m 11))))
      )
   7))
```

Exercise 2.11.8 cond vs. and/or (p. 61)

Here are three cases in which the and/or version of cond will return different results:

- When there is no expression clause — it should return the value of the predicate.

```
(cond ((predicate x)))
```

- When there are multiple expression clauses — it should return the value of the last expression clause.

```
(cond ((predicate x) (expression-1 x) ... (expression-n x)))
```

- When the predicate is non-NIL, but the value of the expression clause itself is nil.

```
(cond ((predicate x) nil))
```

Exercise 2.11.10 My floor and ceiling (p. 62)

```
(defun my-floor (x)
  (cond ((plusp x) (truncate x))
        ((zerop x) 0)
        ((= x (truncate x))
         x)
        (t (- (truncate x) 1)))))

(defun my-ceiling (x)
  (cond ((minusp x) (truncate x))
        ((zerop x) 0)
        ((= x (truncate x))
         x)
        (t (+ 1 (truncate x)))))))
```

Exercise 2.11.11 Leap Year (p. 62)

```
(defun leap-yearp (year)
  (cond ((zerop (rem year 4))
         (cond ((zerop (rem year 100))
                (cond ((zerop (rem year 400))
                       t)
                      (t nil)))
               (t t)))
        (t nil)))
```

Exercise 2.11.12 Zeller Revisited (p. 63)

```
(defun son-of-zeller (day month year)
  (zeller day month (truncate year 100) (rem year 100)
          (cond ((leap-yearp year) 1)
                (t 0))))
```

Exercise 3.14.1 Name That Tune (p. 106)

All the verse of Emily Dickinson shares the same metric pattern, which is also found in the song, *The Yellow Rose of Texas*. Try it out. (We are confident that few English majors will be reading this book. We are therefore attempting to bring culture and enlightenment to the technologists and scientists who will ultimately control society.)

Exercise 3.14.4 New List Functions (p. 108)

```
(defun no-zeros (lst) (remove 0 lst))

(defun collect-numbers (n lst)
  (cond ((numberp n) (cons n lst))
        (t lst)))

(defvar verb-list '(is am are have has go went gone))
(defun verb-find (sentence)
  (remove nil
          (mapcar #'verb-in sentence)))

(defun verb-in (word)
  (cond ((member word verb-list) word)
        (t nil)))
```

Exercise 3.14.5 Proper List (p. 109)

Note that it is wrong to use endp where improper lists might be found.

```
(defun proper-listp (lst)
  (if (not (listp lst))
      nil
      (not (cdr (last lst)))))
```

Exercise 3.14.6 Last Atom (p. 109)

```
(defun last-atom (lst)
  (if (proper-listp lst)
      (car (last lst))
      (cdr (last lst))))
```

Exercise 3.14.7 Define pairlis (p. 109)

```
(defun my-pairlis (l1 l2)
  (mapcar #'cons l1 l2))
```

Exercise 3.14.8 Association List Personnel File (p. 109)

```
(defun make-person (name age weight sex sign children)
  (pairlis '(name age weight sex sign children)
           (list name age weight sex sign children)))

(defun get-sign (pers)
  (list
    (cdr (assoc 'sign pers))
    '(I knew it)))

(defun get-age (pers)
  (cdr (assoc 'age pers)))

(defun get-children (pers)
  (cdr (assoc 'children pers)))
```

Exercise 3.14.9 Property List Personnel File (p. 110)

```
(defun make-person2 (name age weight sex sign children)
  (put name 'age age)
  (put name 'weight weight)
  (put name 'sex sex)
  (put name 'sign sign)
  (put name 'children children)
  name)

(defun get-sign2 (pers)
  (list (get pers 'sign)
        '(I knew it)))

(defun get-age2 (pers)
  (get pers 'age ))

(defun get-children2 (pers)
  (get pers 'children ))
```

Exercise 3.14.10 More List People (p. 110)

```
(defun get-name+age (x)
  (list x (get x 'age)))

(defun age-of-children (person)
  (mapcar #'get-age+name (get-children2 person)))
```

Exercise 3.14.11 Daughter of Zeller (p. 111)

```
(defun daughter-of-zeller (month day year)
  (nth  (son-of-zeller
         day
         (cadr
          (assoc month
                 '((january 11) (february 12) (march 1)
                   (april 2) (may 3) (june 4) (july 5)
                   (august 6) (september 7) (october 8)
                   (november 9) (december 10))))
         year)
        '(sunday monday tuesday wednesday thursday
                 friday saturday)))
```

Exercise 4.7.3 Making Changes (p. 127)

```
(defun make-change (money)
  (make-change2 money
                '((100 dollar dollars)
                  (50 half-dollar half-dollars)
                  (25 quarter quarters)
                  (10 dime dimes)
                  (5  nickel nickels)
                  (1  penny pennies))))

(defun make-change2 (balance currency-list)
  (cond ((zerop balance) '())
        ((endp currency-list) '())
        ((< balance (caar currency-list))
         (make-change2 balance (cdr currency-list)))
        ((>= balance (* 2 (caar currency-list)))
         (cons (list (truncate balance (caar currency-list))
                     (caddar currency-list))
               (make-change2 (rem balance
                                   (caar currency-list))
                             (cdr currency-list))))
        ((>= balance (caar currency-list))
         (cons (list (truncate balance (caar currency-list))
                     (cadar currency-list))
               (make-change2 (- balance (caar currency-list))
                             (cdr currency-list))))))
```

Exercise 4.7.6 Recursive append (p. 128)

See the definition of my-append2, in section 8.3, on page 280.

Exercise 4.7.9 Recursive remove-duplicates (p. 128)

```
(defun my-remove-duplicates (list)
  (cond ((endp list) nil)
        ((member (car list) (cdr list))
         (my-remove-duplicates (cdr list)))
        (t
         (cons (car list)
               (my-remove-duplicates (cdr list))))))
```

Exercise 4.7.10 Recursive Check Balancing (p. 129)

```
(defun check-book (balance list)
  (cond ((endp list) balance)
        ((atom list) (cons 'error--atom-instead-of-list list))
        ((not (numberp balance))
         (cons 'error--non-numeric-balance balance))
        (t
         (cond ((numberp (car list))
                (check-book (+ balance (car list)) (cdr list)))
               ((and (listp (car list))
                     (numberp (caar list)))
                (check-book (* balance (caar list))
                            (cdr list)))))))
```

Exercise 4.7.11 Recursive NOW Account (p. 129)

```
(defun now-account (balance list)
  (cond ((endp list) balance)
        ((atom list) (cons 'error-atom-instead-of-list list))
        ((not (numberp balance))
         (cons 'error-non-numeric-balance balance))
        (t
         (cond ((numberp (car list))
                (and (< balance 500)
                     (< (car list) 0)
                     (setf balance (- balance .1)))
                (now-account (+ balance (car list)) (cdr list)))
```

```
((and (listp (car list))
      (numberp (caar list))
      (>= balance 500))
 (now-account (* balance (caar list)) (cdr list)))
(t (now-account balance (cdr list)))))))
```

Exercise 4.7.12 Simple Pattern Matcher (p. 130)

```
(defun matchp (pattern list)
  (cond ((and (endp pattern) (endp list)) T)
        ((equalp (car pattern) (car list))
         (matchp (cdr pattern) (cdr list)))
        ((eq (car pattern) '*wild*)
         (cond ((endp list) (endp (cdr pattern)))
               (t (or (matchp (cdr pattern) list)
                      (matchp pattern (cdr list))))))
        (t nil)))
```

Exercise 4.7.13 Count Occurrences (p. 131)

```
(defun count-occurrences (atm lst)
  (cond ((endp lst) 0)
        ((eq atm lst) 1)
        ((atom lst) 0)
        (t (+ (count-occurrences atm (car lst))
              (count-occurrences atm (cdr lst))))))
```

Exercise 4.7.14 Tree Addition (p. 131)

```
(defun tree-addition (n l)
  (cond ((endp l) NIL)
        ((atom l) (+ n l))
        (t (cons (tree-addition n (car l))
                 (tree-addition n (cdr l))))))
```

Exercise 4.7.15 Tree Average (p. 132)

This answer uses `let` to introduce a local variable and to avoid evaluating `leaf-average` twice. See chapter 5 for details.

```
(defun tree-average (num-tree)
  (let ((pair (leaf-average num-tree 0 0)))
    (/ (car pair) (cdr pair))))
```

```
(defun leaf-average (l count total)
  (cond ((endp l) '(0 . 0))
        ((atom l) (cons (+ total l) (+ count 1)))
        (t (add-merge (leaf-average (car l) count total)
                      (leaf-average (cdr l) count total)))))

(defun add-merge (x y)
  (cons (+ (car x) (car y))
        (+ (cdr x) (cdr y))))
```

Exercise 5.7.2 Identifying Local and Global Variables (p. 161)

- *Locals:* n

- *Globals:* x, y, add-to-x (it is a variable with a defined functional value)

Exercise 5.7.3 defvar versus setf (p. 161)

The defvar version of above-average would work, but only once. The variables count and total get set to 0 only the first time, when they are created. The defvar expressions will not set the values of existing variables. The function will not break. It will just not produce reliable results. This is but one way in which global variables can eat you alive.

Exercise 5.7.4 Not for profit (p. 161)

In the expression (* tax-rate revenue), the variable revenue is global, not local. The local value of revenue is not accessible within the scope of the variable declaration clause. This error is comparable to having a function's argument refer directly to a parameter name. To get around this problem, the programmer can use a second let clause.

```
(defun let-profit2 (volume unit-price unit-cost tax-rate)
  (let ((revenue (* volume unit-price))
        (overhead (* volume unit-cost)))
    (let ((taxes (* tax-rate revenue)))
      (- revenue
         (+ overhead taxes)))))
```

Another solution is the special form let*, introduced in chapter 8.

Exercise 5.7.5 Local Variables and Making Change (p. 162)

```
(defun make-change (money)
  (let ((result nil))
    (cond ((>= money 100)
             (setf result
                 (cons (list (truncate money 100) 'dollars)
                       result))
             (setf money (rem money 100))))
    (cond ((>= money 50)
             (setf result
                 (cons (list (truncate money 50) 'half-dollar)
                       result))
             (setf money (rem money 50))))
    (cond ((>= money 25)
             (setf result
                 (cons (list (truncate money 25) 'quarter)
                       result))
             (setf money (rem money 25))))
    (cond ((>= money 10)
             (setf result
                 (cons (list (truncate money 10) 'dime) result))
             (setf money (rem money 10))))
    (cond ((>= money 5)
             (setf result
                 (cons (list (truncate money 5) 'nickel) result))
             (setf money (rem money 5))))
    (cond ((> money 0)
             (setf result
                 (cons (list money 'pennies) result))))
    result))
```

Exercise 5.7.6 Niece of Zeller (p. 162)

```
(defun niece-of-zeller (month day year)
  (let ((days-of-the-week
          '(sunday monday tuesday wednesday thursday
                 friday saturday))
```

```
    (mname (cadr (assoc month
                        '((january 11) (february 12)
                          (march 1) (april 2) (may 3) (june 4)
                          (july 5) (august 6) (september 7)
                          (october 8) (november 9)
                          (december 10))))))
(nth (son-of-zeller day mname year)
     days-of-the-week)))
```

Exercise 5.7.7 Closure Audit Trail (p. 162)

We use a closure to create the global state variables a+count and a+args. We use
a let to return the old values of these variables after they have been reset. We
shall later see that prog1 is the preferred way to perform this latter trick.

```
(let ((a+count 0)
      (a+args nil))
  (defun a+ (x y)
    (push (list x y) a+args)
    (incf a+count)
    (+ x y))
  (defun count+ ()
    (let ((c a+count))
      (setf a+count 0)
      c))
  (defun args+ ()
    (let ((a a+args))
      (setf a+args nil)
      a)))
```

Exercise 5.7.8 Rain Date (p. 163)

```
(defun make-date (month day year)
  (cons month (cons day (cons year NIL))))

(defun date-month (date) (car date))
(defun date-day   (date) (cadr date))
(defun date-year  (date) (caddr date))

(defun (setf date-month) (month date)
  (setf (car date) month))

(defun (setf date-day) (day date)
  (setf (cadr date) day))
```

```
(defun (setf date-year) (year date)
  (setf (caddr date) year))
```

Exercise 5.7.9 Last Chance (p. 163)

```
(defun (setf last) (value object)
  (cond ((eq (last object) (cdr object))
         (setf (cdr object) value))
        (t
         (setf (last (cdr object)) value))))
```

Exercise 6.8.2 String Functions (p. 198)

```
(defun lastchar (string)
  (cond ((string= "" string) string)
        (t
         (elt string (- (length string) 1)))))
```

```
;- Here are three different ways.
(defun capitalize1 (string)
  (coerce (cons (char-upcase (char string 0))
                (coerce (subseq string 1) 'list))
          'string))
```

```
(defun capitalize2 (string)
  (concatenate 'string (string (char-upcase (char string 0)))
               (subseq string 1)))
```

```
;  This method destructively alters string.
(defun capitalize3 (string)
  (setf (char string 0)
        (char-upcase (char string 0)))
  string)
```

```
;; We call this string-equalp to avoid name conflict with string-equal.
(defun string-equalp (s-one s-two)
  (cond ((and (string= "" s-one)    ; Both strings are empty.
              (string= "" s-two))
         T)
        ((or (string= "" s-one)     ; Only one string is empty.
             (string= "" s-two))
         nil)
        ((char=                     ; If the two heads are equal,
          (char-upcase (char s-one 0))
          (char-upcase (char s-two 0)))
         (string-equalp             ; then compare the tails;
          (subseq s-one 1)
          (subseq s-two 1)))
        (t nil)))                   ; otherwise, NIL.

(defun string-lessp (first second)
  (cond ((string= "" first) T)
        ((string= "" second) nil)
        ((char= (char first 0)
                (char second 0))
         (string-lessp (subseq first 1)
                       (subseq second 1)))
        ((char< (char first 0)
                (char second 0))
         t)
        (t nil)))
```

Exercise 6.8.3 Sorting Lists (p. 199)

```
(defun lmerge (a b)
  (cond ((null a) b)
        ((null b) a)
        ((inorderp a b)
         (cons (car a)
               (lmerge (cdr a) b)))
        (t
         (cons (car b)
               (lmerge (cdr b) a)))))
```

```
;    inorderp provides comparison predicates for numbers and characters.
(defun inorderp (a b)
  (cond ((numberp (car a))
         (<= (car a) (car b)))
        ((characterp (car a))
         (char<= (car a) (car b)))))
```

Exercise 6.8.4 Roman Numeral Characters (p. 200)

```
(defun roman-char-to-decimal (str)
  (roman-to-decimal
    (string-to-symbol-list (string-upcase str))))

(defun string-to-symbol-list (str)
  (cond ((string= "" str) nil)
        (t (cons (intern (string (char str 0)))
                 (string-to-symbol-list (subseq str 1))))))
```

Exercise 6.8.5 string-reverse (p. 201)

```
(defun string-reverse (text)
  (coerce (string-reverse2 text 'NIL) 'string))

(defun string-reverse2 (text result)
  (cond ((string= "" text) result)
        (t
          (string-reverse2 (subseq text 1)
                           (cons (char text 0)
                                 result)))))
```

Exercise 6.8.6 Spelling Correction (p. 201)

```
(defun string-swap (string index1 index2)
  (cond ((or (not (stringp string))
             (minusp index1)
             (minusp index2)
             (>= index1 (length string))
             (>= index2 (length string)))
         'error-in-string-swap)
```

```
(t
 (let ((new-string (copy-string string))
       (temp-char (elt string index1)))
   (setf (elt new-string index1)
         (elt new-string index2))
   (setf (elt new-string index2) temp-char)
   new-string))))

(defun string-insert (string new-char index)
  (cond ((or (not (stringp string))
             (not (characterp new-char))
             (not (integerp index))
             (> index (length string))
             (minusp index))
         'error-in-string-insert)
        (t
         (let ((s (copy-seq string)))
           (setf (elt s index) new-char)
           s))))
```

Exercise 6.8.7 Expletive Not Deleted (p. 202)

The fact is that though `delete` is destructive, it still cannot reset the pointer from q to the cons cell (1). Thus, even after the `delete` function executes, q still points to (1), which still points to the list (2 3 4 5). If you are serious about using `delete`, you should probably write something like the following:

```
> (setf q (delete 1 q))
```

which should guarantee that q ends up with the right value.

Exercise 7.9.1 column-print (p. 263)

```
(defun column-print (list indentation stream)
  (cond ((null list)
         (terpri stream)
         (values))
        (t
         (indent (car list) indentation stream)
         (column-print (cdr list) indentation stream))))
```

Exercise 7.9.2 multi-column-print (p. 263)

```
(defun multi-column-print (lst
     &key (columns 1) (width nil) (stream *standard-output*)
     (indent 0))
  (if (not width) (setf width (/ 80 columns)))
  (let* ((num (ceiling (/ (length lst) columns)))
         (lists (split-list lst num))
         (istring (if (zerop indent)
                      "~%~A"
                      (format nil "~~%~~~DT~~A" indent)))
         (fstring (format nil "~~,~DT~~A" width)))
    (multi-list-print lists istring fstring stream)))

(defun multi-list-print (lists istring fstring stream)
  (cond ((null lists) (values))
        (t
         (format stream istring (caar lists))
         (multi-list-print2 (cdar lists) fstring stream)
         (multi-list-print (cdr lists) istring fstring stream))))

(defun multi-list-print2 (lists fstring stream)
  (cond ((null lists))
        (t
         (format stream fstring (car lists))
         (multi-list-print2 (cdr lists) fstring stream))))

(defun split-list (l n)
  (cond ((null l) nil)
        (t
         (mapcar #'reverse (split-list2 l n (make-list n))))))

(defun split-list2 (lst n result)
  (cond ((null lst) result)
        (t
         (let ((count 0))
           (loop
             (unless lst (return result))
             (when (= count n) (return (split-list2 lst n result)))
             (push (pop lst) (nth count result))
             (incf count))))))
```

Exercise 7.9.3 split Command (p. 264)

The left-text and right-text are not printed on the same line.

```
(defun split (left-text right-text stream)
  (flushleft left-text stream)
  (write-spaces stream
                (- (line-length stream)
                   (+ (length left-text)
                      (length right-text)))))
  (write-string right-text stream)
  (values))
```

You can also use some of the special format directives.

```
(defun split (left-text right-text stream)
  (format stream
          (format nil "~~~D<~~A~~;~~A~~>" (line-length stream))
          left-text right-text))
```

Or simply,

```
(defun split (left-text right-text stream)
  (format stream "~V<~A~;~A~>"
          (line-length stream)
          left-text right-text))
```

Exercise 7.9.4 tab Command (p. 265)

```
(defun tab (column stream)
  (cond ((>= (hpos stream) column)
         (terpri stream)))
  (write-spaces (- column (hpos stream)) stream)
  (values))
```

Or, using format,

```
(defun tab (column stream)
  (format stream (format nil "~~~DT" column))
  (values))
```

```
;  Or simply:
(defun tab (column stream)
  (format stream "~VT" column)
  (values))
```

Exercise 7.9.5 Two-Digit Romans (p. 265)

For economy and clarity, we use let to create a local variable.

```
(defun romans (limit n)
  (romans2 limit n 1 nil))

(defun romans2 (limit n count result)
  (if (> count limit)
      result
      (let ((numeral (format nil "~@r" count)))
        (if (= (length numeral) n)
            (push numeral result))
        (romans2 limit n (1+ count) result)))))
```

Exercise 7.9.6 peek-char Problem (p. 265)

It does not return a character. It returns the value of unread-char. It also ignores the type argument.

Exercise 7.9.7 split-fill (p. 266)

```
(defun split-fill (left-text char right-text stream)
  (flushleft left-text stream)
  (repeat-char stream char
               (- (line-length stream)
                  (+ (hpos stream)
                     (length right-text))))
  (write-string right-text stream)
  (values))

(defun repeat-char (stream char count)
  (cond ((zerop count) (values))
        (t (write-char char stream)
           (repeat-char stream char (- count 1)))))
```

Using some wacky format directives, we can write a totally inscrutable version of split-fill.

```
(defun split-fill (left-text char right-text stream)
  (let ((format-string (format nil "~~~D,1,1,'~A<~~A~~;~~A~~>"
                               (line-length stream) char)))
    (format stream format-string left-text right-text)))
```

Or, using format's V parameter, we get something a little better.

```
(defun split-fill (left-text char right-text stream)
  (format stream "~V,1,1,V<~A~;~A~>"
          (line-length stream) char left-text right-text))
```

Exercise 7.9.9 Error in 3-letter-word-p (p. 266)

NIL.

Exercise 7.9.11 File Comparison (p. 267)

```
(defun compare-file (file-1 file-2)
  (let ((stream-1 (open file-1 :direction :input))
        (stream-2 (open file-2 :direction :input)))
    (stream-compare stream-1 stream-2)
    (close stream-1)
    (close stream-2)
    '*end-of-file-compare*))

(defun stream-compare (s-1 s-2)
  (cond
    ((or (not (input-stream-p s-1))
         (not (input-stream-p s-2)))
     (write-string *error-output*
                   "Foul stream in (STREAM-COMPARE)"))
    ((not (listen s-1))
     (cond ((listen s-2)
            (format t "File 1 is shorter than file 2:~%")
            (rest-of-stream 2 s-2)))
     '*END-OF-STREAM-COMPARE*)
    ((not (listen s-2))
     (cond ((listen s-1)
            (format t "File 2 is shorter than file 1:~%")
            (rest-of-stream 1 s-1)))
     '*END-OF-STREAM-COMPARE*)
    (t
     (let ((l-1 (read-line s-1))
           (l-2 (read-line s-2)))
       (cond ((not (string= l-1 l-2))
              (format T "~%1: ~S~%" l-1)
              (format T "2: ~S~%" l-2))
             (t nil))
       (stream-compare s-1 s-2)))))

(defun rest-of-stream (id stream)
  (cond ((listen stream)
         (format t "~D: ~S~%" id (read-line stream))
         (rest-of-stream id stream))))
```

Exercise 7.9.14 More Eliza (p. 271)

The matchp function now returns the response segment matching the *wild* in
the pattern.

```
(defun matchp (pattern list)
  (cond
    ((and (null pattern) (null list)) T)
    ((equalp (car pattern) (car list))
     (matchp (cdr pattern) (cdr list)))
    ((eq (car pattern) '*wild*)
     (cond ((null list) (null (cdr pattern)))
           ((matchp (cdr pattern) list))
           (t
            (let ((result (matchp pattern (cdr list))))
              (if result
                  (cond ((listp result)
                         (cons (car list) result))
                        (t
                         (cons (car list) nil)))
                  nil)))))
    (t nil)))
```

```
;;  Revised to handle echoed input in the response.
(defun fix-reply (match response)
  (cond
    ((member '*wild* response)
     (format t "~%~A~%"
             (combine-match (pronoun-shift match) response))
     t)
    (t
     (format t "~%~A~%" response)
     t)))
```

```
;;  Puts together the echoed input with response.
(defun combine-match (m r)
  (cond ((null r) m)
        ((eq (car r) '*wild*)
         (append m (cdr r)))
        (t (cons (car r)
                 (combine-match m (cdr r))))))
```

```lisp
;;  Association list used for table look-up by pronoun-shift.
(defvar pronoun-alist
  '((me . you) (i . you) (you . i) (am . are)
    (my . your) (mine . your) (your . my)))

;;  Converts first and second person pronouns.
(defun pronoun-shift (match)
  (if (null match)
      nil
    (cons
     (let ((pair (assoc (car match) pronoun-alist)))
       (if pair
           (cdr pair)
         (car match)))
     (pronoun-shift (cdr match)))))

;;  Here is an easier way, using sublis.
(defun pronoun-shift (match)
  (sublis pronoun-alist match))

;;  We have introduced some new patterns and responses.
(defvar *master-script*
  '(((*wild* laundry *wild*)
     (When my clothes get too dirty I just burn them.))
    ((i am *wild*)
     (do you think I care if you are *wild*))
    ((i want you *wild*)
     (why do you want me *wild*))
    ((do you *wild*)
     (why should you care if i *wild*))
    ((this is *wild*)
     (why do you say it is *wild*))
    ((*wild* year *wild*)
     (If I'm lucky I'll graduate before the turn of the century.))
    ((*wild* mother *wild*)
     (Don't make any cracks about my mother.  She's a saint.))
    ((My name *wild*)
     (Glad to meet you.  My friends call me Dr. Death.))
    ((*wild* stereo *wild*)
     (If you touch my turntable I'll rip your lungs out.))
    ((*wild* drugs *wild*)
     (I got some stuff from my vet.  You wanna try it?))
```

```
((No *wild*)
 (Well pardon me for living.))
((*wild* sick)
 (I think this room has lead paint.  It makes you crazy.))
((*wild*) (Really.))))
```

Exercise 7.9.15 Better type and filter (p. 272)

```
(defun better-type (file-name)
  (with-open-file
    (file-stream file-name :direction :input)
    (stream-copy file-stream *standard-output*))
  (values))

(defun better-filter-file (filter input-file output-file)
  (with-open-file
    (in-stream input-file :direction :input)
    (with-open-file
      (out-stream output-file :direction :output)
      (filter-stream filter in-stream out-stream)))
  (values))
```

Exercise 7.9.16 Halloween = Christmas (p. 272)

```
> (= #o31 #10r25)
T
```

Exercise 8.7.2 Mystery Expressions (p. 289)

They each return themselves as their value.

Exercise 8.7.3 More Cryptography (p. 289)

```
(defun new-encode (char1 char2 m)
  (encode char1 (mod (char-code char2) m)))

(defun new-string-encode (string key m)
  (map 'string #'(lambda (ch1 ch2) (new-encode ch1 ch2 m))
       string key))

(defun new-decode (char1 char2 m)
  (decode char1 (mod (char-code char2) m)))
```

```
(defun new-string-decode (string key m)
  (map 'string #'(lambda (ch1 ch2) (new-decode ch1 ch2 m))
       string key))
```

Exercise 8.7.4 Deck of Cards (p. 290)

```
(defun make-deck (ranks suits)
  (apply #'append
         (mapcar
          #'(lambda (suit)
              (mapcar
               #'(lambda (rank)
                   (cons rank suit))
               ranks))
          suits)))
```

Exercise 8.7.5 reverse with labels (p. 291)

```
(defun my-reverse (list)
  (labels
   ((sub-reverse (list result)
                 (cond
                  ((null list) result)
                  (t
                   (sub-reverse (cdr list)
                                (cons (car list) result))))))
   (sub-reverse list nil)))
```

Exercise 8.7.6 Power Set (p. 291)

```
(defun power (lst)
  (cond ((null lst) '(()))
        ((null (cdr lst))
         (list lst '()))
        (t
         (append
          (mapcar #'(lambda (l) (append (list (car lst)) l))
                  (power (cdr lst)))
          (power (cdr lst))))))
```

Exercise 8.7.7 Length Problems (p. 291)

Add a third argument to count-length through which to pass the function itself!
(Thanks to Jim Meehan for this example.)

```
(defun good-length (l)
  (flet
   ((count-length (l n fn)
                  (cond ((null l) n)
                        (t (funcall fn (cdr l) (+ 1 n) fn)))))
   (count-length l 0 #'count-length)))
```

Exercise 9.12.1 Bottles of Beer (p. 327)

Recursion and iteration are two different ways to achieve the same result. A bartender program could use either method.

Exercise 9.12.2 loop Average (p. 327)

```
(defun loop-average (nlist)
  (let ((count 0)
        (total 0))
    (loop
     (cond ((null nlist) (return (/ total count)))
           (t
            (setf total (+ total (car nlist)))
            (setf nlist (cdr nlist))
            (incf count))))))
```

Exercise 9.12.3 Remove String Pairs (p. 327)

```
(defun remove-pairs (str)
  (coerce (r-remove-pairs (coerce str 'list))
          'string))
```

Exercise 9.12.4 More Spelling Correction: Soundex (p. 327)

```
(defun soundex (word)
  (cond ((symbolp word) (setf word (string word))))
  (setf word (remove-pairs (string-upcase word)))
  (soundex-2 (subseq word 0 1) (subseq word 1)))
```

```
;;    Recursive version of soundex-2.
(defun soundex-2 (code word)
  (cond ((or (string= "" word)
             (eql (length code) 4))
         (intern code))
        (t
         (soundex-2 (concatenate 'string code (code-digit
                                                (char word 0)))
                    (subseq word 1)))))

;;  Iterative version of soundex-2.
(defun soundex-2 (code word)
  (do ((code code (concatenate 'string code
                               (code-digit (char word 0))))
       (word word (subseq word 1)))
      ((or (string= "" word)
           (eql (length code) 4))
       (intern code))))

(defun code-digit (character)
  (case character
        ((#\B #\F #\P #\V)            "1")
        ((#\C #\G #\J #\K #\Q #\X)    "2")
        ((#\D #\T)                    "3")
        ((#\L)                        "4")
        ((#\M #\N)                    "5")
        ((#\R)                        "6")
        ((#\S #\Z)                    "7")
        (otherwise                    "")))

(defun tag-word (word)
  (let ((word (cond ((symbolp word)
                     (string word))
                    ((stringp word)
                     (string-upcase word)))))
    (put (soundex word) 'word word)))
```

```
(defun isa-word (word)
   (let ((code-word (get (soundex word) 'word))
         (word (cond ((symbolp word)
                      (string word))
                     ((stringp word)
                      (string-upcase word)))))
     (cond ((equalp word code-word) T)
           ((null code-word)
            "No match at all.")
           (t (format nil "No. How about ~A ?" code-word)))))
```

Exercise 9.12.5 Unwind Protection (p. 329)

```
(catch finish
   (unwind-protect
       (progn
          (step-one 'finish)
          (step-two 'finish))
       (step-three)))
```

Exercise 9.12.6 Binary Game Catch (p. 330)

Nothing. That is, the program would behave the same way. It turns out that the catch in binary is superflous because all calls to functions that call **quit-action** are in the tail position. They are all tail-recursive calls. See chapter 16 for a discussion of tail recursion. The **catch** is still recommended here because a small change to the program could remove this tail recursive property and complicate the termination code.

Exercise 10.6.1 my-error (p. 370)

```
(defun my-error (&rest args)
   (format *error-output* "~%** My error: ")
   (apply #'format *error-output* args)
   (break))
```

Exercise 10.6.2 Buggy fact (p. 370)

The function adds the current number to the result of the recursive call instead of multiplying.

Exercise 10.6.3 bad-length Problem (p. 370)

The function is executing endless calls of (bad-length (cdr ())) because the cdr of the empty list is the empty list itself.

Exercise 11.10.2 swap Macro (p. 414)

```
(defmacro swap (x y)
  `(let ((tmp ,x))
     (setf ,x ,y)
     (setf ,y tmp)))
; Or simply:
(setf (symbol-function 'swap) (symbol-function 'rotatef))
```

Exercise 11.10.3 repeat Macro with a Value (p. 414)

```
(defmacro repeat (n result &body body)
  `(flet ((code () ,@body)
          (result () ,result))
     (let ((n ,n))
       (do ((count n (- count 1)))
           ((<= count 0) (result))
         (code)))))
```

Exercise 11.10.4 repeat with loop (p. 415)

```
(defmacro repeat (n result &body body)
  `(flet ((code () ,@body)
          (result () ,result))
     (let ((count ,n))
       (loop
         (cond ((<= count 0) (return (result)))
               (t
                (code)
                (decf count)))))))
```

Exercise 11.10.5 while Macro (p. 415)

```
(defmacro while (test result &body body)
  `(flet ((test () ,test)
          (body () ,@body)
          (result () ,result))
     (do ()
         ((null (test)) (result))
       (body))))
```

Exercise 11.10.6 until Macro (p. 415)

```
(defmacro until (test result &body body)
  `(flet ((test () ,test)
          (body () ,@body)
          (result () ,result))
     (do ()
         ((test) (result))
         (body))))
```

Exercise 11.10.7 prog1 Macro (p. 416)

One solution is to generate a unique name for the local variable inside the lambda expression.

```
(defmacro my-prog1 (first &body body)
  (let ((var (gensym "PROG1")))
    `((lambda (,var) ,@body ,var) ,first)))
```

Another method is to call a subfunction from the macro. The local variables in the function solve the name conflict problem.

```
(defmacro my-prog1 (first &body body)
  `(*my-prog1 ,first #'(lambda () ,@body)))

(defun *my-prog1 (first body)
  (funcall body)
  first)
```

Exercise 11.10.8 dpsq Macro (p. 416)

The two calls to (pop l) as arguments to put might not be evaluated left to right, and the side effects could result in incorrect code. Here is a safer way. We use do instead of apply for efficiency — avoiding consing the argument list.

```
(defun dps (&rest l)
  (let ((node (car l)))
    (do ((l (cdr l) (cddr l)))
        ((null l) nil)
        (put node (car l) (cadr l)))))

(defmacro dpsq (&body l)
  `(apply #'dps (quote ,l)) )
```

Exercise 11.10.9 ISA Inheritance Hierarchy (p. 417)

```
(defun isa-get (node prop)
  (cond ((get node prop))
        ((get node 'isa)
         (isa-get (get node 'isa prop)))
        (t nil)))
```

Exercise 11.10.10 Data-Driven dpsq Macro (p. 418)

Replace put with ddput in dps.

```
(defun ddput (node prop val)
  (and
    (symbolp node)
    (symbolp prop)
    (progn
      (cond ((isa-get prop '+invert-property)
             (ddput prop val node)))
      (cond ((isa-get prop '+invert-value)
             (*put val prop node)))
      (let ((onto (isa-get prop '+invert-onto)))
        (if onto (ddput val onto node)))
      (cond ((isa-get prop '+multiple-values)
             (add-property node prop val))
            ((and (get node prop)
                  (isa-get prop '+save-property))
             (*put (or (get node 'save-node)
                       (ddput node 'save-node (gensym "SAVE")))
                   prop
                   (get node prop))
             (*put node prop val))
            (t
             (let ((fn (isa-get prop '+lambda-property)))
               (if fn
                   (apply fn (list node prop val))
                   (*put node prop val)))))
      val)))

(defun *put (node prop val)
  (cond (prop
         (setf (get node '+ddprops) (enter (get node '+ddprops) prop))
         (setf (get node prop) val))))
```

```lisp
-(defun add-property (node prop val)
   (*put node prop (enter (get node prop) val)))


(defun enter (l value)
   (adjoin value (if (listp l) l (list l))))


(defun ppp (node)
   (format t "~%~A" node)
   (mapcar #'(lambda (prop)
                     (format t "~%~4T~A ~22T~A" prop (get node prop)))
            (get node '+ddprops))
   (values))


(defmacro pppq (node)
   `(ppp ',node))
```

Exercise 11.10.11 msg Macro (p. 422)

There are a few cases that this version does not handle properly. Note that we use
eval, which is discussed in chapter 15.

```lisp
(defmacro msg (&body body)
   (*msg body))


(defun *msg (body &optional (stream *standard-output*))
   (if (null body)
       ''**value-of-msg**
     (block nil
       (cond
         ((stringp (car body))
          (format stream "~A" (car body)))
         ((numberp (car body))
          (if (plusp (car body))
              (format stream "~A" (make-string (car body)
                                               :initial-element #\space))
            (format stream "~V%" (- (car body)))))
         ((atom (car body))
          (case (car body)
               ((t) (terpri stream))
               (otherwise (format stream "~A" (eval (car body))))))
         ((listp (car body))
          (let ((arg (eval (cadar body))))
            (case (caar body)
                 ((to) (setf stream arg))
```

```
            ((tab)
             (format stream "~VT" arg))
            ((right)
             (format stream "~V<~A~;~A~>"
                     (line-length stream) "" arg))
            ((center)
             (format stream "~V<~A~;~A~;~A~>"
                     (line-length stream) "" arg ""))
            ((hex)
             (format stream "~X" arg))
            ((oct)
             (format stream "~O" arg))
            ((bin)
             (format stream "~B" arg))
            ((plur)
             (format stream "~P" arg))))))
        (*msg (cdr body) stream))))
```

Exercise 11.10.13 Read-Modify-Write Macros (p. 424)

```
(define-modify-macro negatef () -)
(define-modify-macro invertf (&optional (power -1)) expt)
(define-modify-macro upcasef () string-upcase)
(define-modify-macro downcasef () string-downcase)
```

Exercise 12.6.1 Sorting Teams (p. 471)

```
(defun inorderp (a b)
  (not (plusp (games-behind (car a) (car b)))))
```

Exercise 12.6.2 Generic Sorts (p. 471)

```
(defgeneric inorderp (a b)
  (:method ((a cons) (b cons))
           (inorderp (car a) (car b)))
  (:method ((a number) (b number))
           (<=  a b))
  (:method ((a symbol) (b symbol))
           (inorderp (symbol-name a) (symbol-name b)))
  (:method ((a string) (b string))
           (string<= a b))
  (:method ((a character) (b character))
           (char<= a b))
  (:method ((a team) (b team))
           (not (plusp (games-behind (car a) (car b))))))
```

Exercise 12.6.3 Generic reveal-struct (p. 472)

Instead of making `reveal-struct` generic, we have it call a generic function,
`reveal-struct-selectors`.

```
(defun reveal-struct (struct)
  (cond ((reveal-struct-selectors struct)
          (mapcar #'(lambda (selector)
                      (reveal-struct (funcall selector struct)))
                  (reveal-struct-selectors struct)))
        (t struct)))

(defgeneric reveal-struct-selectors (struct)
  (:method ((struct my-date))
          (list #'my-date-day #'my-date-month #'my-date-year))
  (:method ((struct holiday))
          (list #'holiday-name #'date-day #'date-month #'date-year))
  (:method ((struct my-time))
          (list #'time-hours #'time-minutes #'time-seconds))
  (:method ((struct team))
          (list #'team-name #'team-won #'team-lost
                #'team-average #'team-behind))
  (:method ((struct game))
          (list #'game-date #'game-home #'game-visitor
                #'game-score #'game-next))
  (:method ((struct score))
          (list #'score-home #'score-visitor))
  (:method (struct) nil))
```

Exercise 12.6.4 Score Updates (p. 472)

```
(defun final-score (game h-score v-score)
  (setf (score-home (game-score game)) h-score)
  (setf (score-visitor (game-score game)) v-score)
  (cond ((> h-score v-score)
          (incf (team-won (game-home game)))
          (incf (team-lost (game-visitor game))))
        (t
          (incf (team-lost (game-home game)))
          (incf (team-won (game-visitor game)))))
  'end-of-update)
```

Exercise 12.6.7 List Addition (p. 473)

```
(defmethod g+ ((x list) (y list))
  (append x y))
```

Exercise 12.6.8 &rest Addition (p. 474)

```
;; The cases in which all arguments are of the same type.
(defgeneric g+ (first &rest args)
  (:method ((first cons) &rest args)
           (append first (apply #'append args)))
  (:method ((first string) &rest args)
           (format nil "~A~A" first
                     (if args (apply #'g+ args) "")))
  (:method ((first symbol) &rest args)
           (format nil "~A~A"  first
                     (if args (apply #'g+ args) "")))
  (:method ((first character) &rest args)
           (format nil "~A~A"  first
                     (if args (apply #'g+ args) "")))
  (:method ((first my-time) &rest args)
           (add-time first (apply #'resttime args)))
  (:method ((first number) &rest args)
           (old+ first (apply #'old+ args))))

(defun resttime (&rest args)
  (typecase
   (car args)
   (number (add-time (make-time :seconds (car args))
                     (apply #'resttime (cdr args))))
   (my-time (add-time (car args) (apply #'resttime (cdr args))))
   (t (make-time))))
```

Exercise 12.6.9 America's Past Time (p. 474)

```
(defun time-normalize (time)
  (check-type time my-time "a good time")
  (cond ((>= (time-seconds time) 60)
         (setf (time-seconds time) (- (time-seconds time) 60))
         (incf (time-minutes time))
         (time-normalize time))
; Add a check for negative seconds.
        ((< (time-seconds time) 0)
         (setf (time-seconds time) (+ (time-seconds time) 60))
         (decf (time-minutes time))
         (time-normalize time))
        ((>= (time-minutes time) 60)
         (setf (time-minutes time) (- (time-minutes time) 60))
         (incf (time-hours time))
         (time-normalize time))
```

```
;   Add a check for negative minutes.
          ((< (time-minutes time) 0)
           (setf (time-minutes time) (+ (time-minutes time) 60))
           (decf (time-hours time))
           (time-normalize time))
;   Add a check for negative hours.
          ((or (>= (time-hours time) 24)
               (< (time-hours time) 0))
           (setf (time-hours time) (mod (time-hours time) 24))
           time)
          (t time)))
```

Exercise 12.6.10 Current Time (p. 475)

```
(defun current-time ()
  (multiple-value-bind
   (sec min hr day mon yr wd dlp tz)
   (get-decoded-time)
   (declare (ignore day mon yr wd dlp tz))
   (format nil "~2,'0D:~2,'0D:~2,'0D ~A"
           (mod hr 12) min sec
           (if (> hr 11) "pm" "am"))))
```

Exercise 12.6.11 Current Date (p. 475)

```
(defun current-date ()
  (multiple-value-bind
   (sec min hr day mon yr wd dlp tz)
   (get-decoded-time)
   (declare (ignore sec min hr dlp tz))
   (format nil "~a, ~a ~a, ~a"
           (case wd
                 ((0) "Monday")
                 ((1) "Tuesday")
                 ((2) "Wednesday")
                 ((3) "Thursday")
                 ((4) "Friday")
                 ((5) "Saturday")
                 ((6) "Sunday"))
           (case mon
                 ((1) "January")
                 ((2) "February")
                 ((3) "March")
                 ((4) "April")
```

```
                              ((5)  "May")
                              ((6)  "June")
                              ((7)  "July")
                              ((8)  "August")
                              ((9)  "September")
                              ((10) "October")
                              ((11) "November")
                              ((12) "December"))
                 day yr)))
```

You are probably better off using vectors for translating both days and months. See chapter 14.

Exercise 13.10.1 defpredicate (p. 523)

Here are two ways to do it.

```
(defmacro defpredicate (class)
  `(defgeneric ,(read-from-string (format nil "~A-p" class)) (obj)
     (:documentation ,(format nil "Predicate for the ~A class." class))
     (:method ((obj ,class)) T)
     (:method (obj) NIL)))

(defmacro defpredicate2 (class)
  `(defun ,(read-from-string (format nil "~A-p" class)) (obj)
     (typep obj ',class)))
```

Exercise 13.10.2 The Empty Property List (p. 523)

Every property list would be the same. That is, every property list would share the list structure defined in the empty-plist function.

Exercise 13.10.4 Queue Object (p. 524)

```
(defclass queue ()
  ((q-list :accessor q-list :initform nil)
   (q-tail :accessor q-tail :initform nil))
  (:documentation "A simple queue data structure."))

(defmethod print-object ((self queue) stream)
  (format stream "#<Queue ~A>" (q-list self)))

(defpredicate queue)

(defmethod queue-empty-p ((self queue))
  (null (q-list self)))
```

```
(defmethod q-head ((self queue))
  (car (q-list self)))

(defmethod enqueue ((self queue) obj)
  (cond ((null (q-list self))
            (setf (q-tail self) (push obj (q-list self))))
          (t
            (setf (cdr (q-tail self)) (cons obj nil))
            (setf (q-tail self) (cdr (q-tail self))))))

(defmethod dequeue ((self queue))
  (pop (q-list self)))

(defmethod reveal ((self queue))
  (list 'head (q-head self) 'tail (q-tail self)))
```

Exercise 13.10.5 make-better-plist (p. 525)

Substitute all occurrences of assoc in the property list code with assocp, defined
below:

```
(defun assocp (item alist)
  (assoc item alist :test #'(lambda (x obj) (equalp x obj))))
```

Exercise 13.10.6 Meta-Predicates (p. 526)

```
(defgeneric create-predicate (class instance)
  (:method (class instance) nil))

(defmethod create-predicate :after
  ((class (eql (find-class 'standard-class))) instance)
  (let* ((name (class-name instance))
          (pred (read-from-string (format nil "~A-p" name))))
    (setf (symbol-function pred)
          #'(lambda (obj) (typep obj name)))))

(defmethod initialize-instance :after (instance &rest initargs)
  (create-predicate (class-of instance) instance))
```

Exercise 14.8.4 Three-Dimensional Arrays (p. 572)

```lisp
(defclass 3d-array ()
  ((x-dim :initarg :x-dim :accessor x-dim)
   (y-dim :initarg :y-dim :accessor y-dim)
   (z-dim :initarg :z-dim :accessor z-dim)
   (the-array :accessor the-array))
  (:documentation "A three-dimensional array."))

(defun make-3d-array (x y z)
  (let ((new-array
          (make-instance '3d-array :x-dim x :y-dim y :z-dim z)))
    (setf (the-array new-array) (make-array x))
    (dotimes (count-y x new-array)
            (setf (aref (the-array new-array) count-y)
                  (make-array y))
            (dotimes (count-z y new-array)
                    (setf (aref (aref (the-array new-array)
                                      count-y) count-z)
                          (make-array z))))))

(defun 3d-array-p (obj)
  (typep obj '3d-array))

(defmethod print-object ((obj 3d-array) stream)
  (format stream "#<3d-array (~Ax~Ax~A) ~A>"
          (x-dim obj)
          (y-dim obj)
          (z-dim obj)
          (the-array obj)))

(defmethod 3d-ref ((obj 3d-array)
                   (x integer) (y integer) (z integer))
  (cond ((or (minusp x)
             (>= x (x-dim obj)))
         (error "3d-ref -- X value out of range: ~D" x))
        ((or (minusp y)
             (>= y (y-dim obj)))
         (error "3d-ref -- Y value out of range: ~D" y))
        ((or (minusp z)
             (>= z (z-dim obj)))
         (error "3d-ref -- Z value out of range: ~D" y))
        (t
         (aref (aref (aref (the-array obj) x) y) z))))
```

```lisp
(defmethod (setf 3d-ref)
  (val (obj 3d-array) (x integer) (y integer) (z integer))
  (setf (aref (aref (aref (the-array obj) x) y) z) val))

(defmethod 3d-array-fill ((obj 3d-array) val)
  (map 'array
       #'(lambda (d2)
           (map 'vector
                #'(lambda (v) (fill v val))
                d2))
    (the-array obj)))
```

Exercise 14.8.5 n-Dimensional Arrays (p. 573)

```lisp
; Class definition.
(defclass nd-array ()
  ((dimensions-of :initarg :dimensions-of :accessor dimensions-of)
   (the-array :accessor the-array))
  (:documentation "An N-dimensional array."))

; Predicate.
(defun nd-array-p (obj)
  (typep obj 'nd-array))

; Constructor.
(defun make-nd-array (d-list)
  (let ((dim (copy d-list))
        (nd-array (make-instance 'nd-array :dimensions-of d-list)))
    (setf (the-array nd-array) (nd-init nil dim))
    nd-array))

; Print method.
(defmethod print-object ((obj nd-array) stream)
  (format stream "#<nd-array ~A ~A>"
          (dimensions-of obj)
          (the-array obj)))

; General accessor.
(defmethod nd-ref ((obj nd-array) &rest d)
  (dref (the-array obj) d))
```

```
;  Setf method for accessor.
(defmethod (setf nd-ref) (val (obj nd-array) &rest d)
  (setf (dref (the-array obj) d) val))

;  Recursive secondary accessor function.
(defun dref (array dimensions)
  (cond ((null (cdr dimensions))
         (aref array (car dimensions)))
        (t
         (dref (aref array (car dimensions)) (cdr dimensions)))))

;  Recursive setf method for secondary access function.
(defun (setf dref) (val array dimensions)
  (cond ((null (cdr dimensions))
         (setf (aref array (car dimensions)) val))
        (t
         (setf (dref (aref array (car dimensions))
                     (cdr dimensions))
               val))))

;  Recursive secondary constructor function.
(defun nd-init (vector n)
  (cond ((null n) vector)
        ((null vector)
         (nd-init (make-array (car n)) n))
        ((or (= (car n) 0)
             (null (cdr n)))
         vector)
        (t
         (setf (aref vector (- (car n) 1))
               (nd-init nil (cdr n)))
         (nd-init vector (cons (- (car n) 1) (cdr n))))))

;  General mapping method.
(defmethod map-nd-array ((self nd-array) proc)
  (nd-map proc (the-array self) (length (dimensions-of self))))

;  Method for filling array.
(defmethod nd-array-fill ((self nd-array) val)
  (nd-map #'(lambda (v) (fill v val))
          (the-array self) (- (length (dimensions-of self)) 1)))
```

```
;   Secondary mapping function.
(defun nd-map (func obj dim)
  (cond ((zerop dim) (funcall func obj))
        (t
         (map 'vector
           #'(lambda (v) (nd-map func v (- dim 1)))
           obj))))
```

Exercise 14.8.6 Hash Tables (p. 574)

Replace eq with equalp.

Exercise 14.8.7 Searching Hash Tables (p. 575)

```
(defmethod table-find ((obj my-hash-table) value)
    (let ((index
            (position value (the-table obj)
                      :test
                      #'(lambda (m b)
                          (equalp m (cdr b))))))
      (if index
          (car (aref (the-table obj) index))
        nil)))
```

Exercise 14.8.8 Random Hash Tables (p. 575)

The main advantage would be minimizing collisions for insertions. The primary disadvantage would be reducing the odds of ever retrieving data. A random hash table is an example of a write-only data structure.

Exercise 14.8.9 More Hash Tables (p. 575)

```
;   Define the hash table class, same as before.
(defclass my-hash-table ()
  ((size :initform 10 :initarg :size :accessor size
         :documentation "size of hash table")
   (table :initform nil :accessor the-table
          :documentation "vector of values"))
  (:documentation "simple hash table class"))

;   Define the hash table predicate, same as before.
(defgeneric my-hash-table-p (object)
  (:method ((object my-hash-table)) t)
  (:method (object) nil))
```

```
;   Define the hash table constructor, same as before.
(defun make-my-hash-table (size)
  (let ((htable (make-instance 'my-hash-table :size size)))
    (setf (the-table htable) (make-array size))
    htable))

;   Define the hash table reveal function, same as before
(defmethod reveal ((obj my-hash-table))
  (the-table obj))

;   We modify get-bucket to create association lists.
(defmethod get-bucket ((table my-hash-table) key)
  (let ((bucket-number (mod (sxhash key) (size table))))
    (or (aref (the-table table) bucket-number)
        (setf (aref (the-table table) bucket-number)
              (copy-tree '(((()))))))))

;   We use assoc to search the bucket.
(defmethod table-get ((table my-hash-table) key)
  (cdr (assoc key (get-bucket table key) :test #'equalp)))

(defmethod table-put ((table my-hash-table) key value)
  (let* ((bucket (get-bucket table key))
         (entry (assoc key bucket :test #'equalp)))
    (cond (entry
           (setf (cdr entry) value))
          (t
           (setf (cdr bucket)
                 (cons (cons key value)
                       (cdr bucket)))
           value))))
```

Exercise 14.8.10 new-hash (p. 576)

This function can be easily implemented with typecase.

```
(defun new-hash (tree)
  (typecase tree
            (cons (+ (new-hash (car tree))
                     (* (new-hash (cdr tree)) 2)))
            (null 31415926)
            (symbol (string-hash (string tree)))
            (string (string-hash tree))
            (vector (new-hash (coerce tree 'list)))
            (character (char-code tree))
            (integer tree)
            (t (new-hash (error "unhashable leaf: (~s ~s)"
                                'new-hash
                                tree)))))

; Secondary hash function for strings.
(defun string-hash (string)
  (cond ((string= "" string) 1)
        (t
         (+ (char-code (char string 0))
            (* (string-hash
                (subseq string 1)) 2)))))
```

Exercise 14.8.11 Reduced Chi-Squared (p. 577)

```
(defun chi-sq2 (v)
  (let ((n (/ (reduce #'+ v)
              (length v))))
    (chi-sq v n)))
```

Exercise 14.8.12 Generalized Chi-Squared (p. 577)

```
(defun chi-sq (vec exp)
  (cond ((numberp exp)
         (setf exp (make-array (length vec) :initial-element exp))))
  (let ((range (length vec)))
    (labels ((square-dif (x y)
               (let ((dif (- x y)))
                 (* dif dif)))
```

```
((do-next count)
 (cond ((= count range) 0)
       (t
        (+ (do-next (+ count 1))
           (/ (square-dif
                (aref vec count)
                (aref exp count))
              (aref exp count)))))))
 (float (do-next 0))))
```

Exercise 14.8.13 Shuffling Cards (p. 578)

```
(defun shuffle (lst n)
   (let* ((vec (coerce lst 'vector))
          (len (length vec)))
     (do ((count 0 (+ count 1)))
         ((= count n) (coerce vec 'list))
       (let* ((first (random len))
              (second (random len))
              (temp (aref vec first)))
         (setf (aref vec first) (aref vec second))
         (setf (aref vec second) temp)))))
```

Exercise 14.8.15 Chance Music (p. 579)

```
(defun music (pitches durations count)
  (let ((pitch-vec (coerce pitches 'vector))
        (dur-vec   (coerce durations 'vector))
        (note-vec  (make-array count))
        (pitch-length (length pitches))
        (dur-length (length durations)))
    (labels
     ((get-pitch ()
                 (aref pitch-vec (random pitch-length)))
      (get-dur ()
               (aref dur-vec (random dur-length)))
      (get-notes
       (n)
       (cond ((= n count) (coerce note-vec 'list))
             (t
              (setf (aref note-vec n)
                    (cons (get-pitch) (get-dur)))
              (get-notes (+ n 1))))))
     (get-notes 0))))
```

Exercise 14.8.16 New Math (p. 579)

Here are two ways. First, let the small number be some random number modulus the bigger number.

```
(defun prob (func size)
  (labels ((rand (make-random size))
           ((make-prob lastbig lastsmall)
            (let* ((big (rand))
                   (small (mod (rand) big))
                   (ans (func big small)))
    . . .
```

The second way is to choose both numbers at random, then compare them and assign the bigger number to big.

```
(defun prob (func size)
  (labels ((rand (make-random size))
           ((make-prob lastbig lastsmall)
            (let* ((big (rand))
                   (small (rand))
                   (ans (func big small)))
              (cond ((> small big)
                     (SETF ans (abs ans))
                     (exchange big small)))
    . . .
```

Exercise 14.8.17 Lazy n-Dimensional Arrays (p. 580)

```
(defclass lazy-nd-array ()
  ((dimensions-of :initarg :dimensions-of :accessor dimensions-of)
   (rank :initarg :rank :accessor rank)
   (fill-value :initform nil :accessor fill-value)
   (fill-flag :initform nil :accessor fill-flag)
   (the-array :accessor the-array))
  (:documentation "An N-dimensional lazy array."))

(defun make-lazy-nd-array (d-list)
  (let* ((rank (length d-list))
         (new-array (make-instance 'lazy-nd-array
                                   :rank rank
                                   :dimensions-of d-list)))
    (setf (the-array new-array) (lazy-nd-init nil d-list))
    new-array))

(defun lazy-nd-array-p (obj)
  (typep obj 'lazy-nd-array))
```

```lisp
(defmethod print-object ((obj lazy-nd-array) stream)
  (format stream "<lazy-nd-array ~A ~A>"
          (dimensions-of obj)
          (the-array obj)))

(defmethod lazy-nd-ref ((obj lazy-nd-array) d)
  (dref obj (the-array obj) d))

(defmethod dref ((obj lazy-nd-array) array d)
  (cond ((delayed-p (aref array (car d)))
         (setf (aref array (car d))
               (force (aref array (car d))))
         (if (null (cdr d))
             (fill-value obj)
           (dref obj array d)))
        ((null (cdr d))
         (aref array (car d)))
        (t
         (dref obj (aref array (car d)) (cdr d)))))

(defmethod (setf lazy-nd-ref) (val (obj lazy-nd-array) d-list)
  (setf (dref obj (the-array obj) d-list) val))

(defmethod (setf dref) (val (obj lazy-nd-array) array d)
  (cond ((delayed-p (aref array (car d)))
         (setf (aref array (car d))
               (force (aref array (car d)))))
        ((null (cdr d))
         (setf (aref array (car d)) val))
        (t
         (setf (dref obj (aref array (car d)) (cdr d)) val))))

(defun lazy-nd-init (vector n)
  (cond ((null n) vector)
        ((null vector)
         (lazy-nd-init (make-array (car n)) n))
        ((or (= (car n) 0)
             (null (cdr n)))
         vector)
        (t
         (setf (aref vector (- (car n) 1))
               (delay (lazy-nd-init nil (cdr n))))
         (lazy-nd-init vector (cons (- (car n) 1) (cdr n))))))
```

```
(defmethod lazy-nd-array-fill ((obj lazy-nd-array) val)
  (lazy-fill obj (the-array obj) val (cdr (dimensions-of obj)))))

(defmethod lazy-fill ((obj lazy-nd-array) array val d-list)
  (cond ((delayed-p array)
         (setf (fill-flag obj) T)
         (setf (fill-value obj) val))
        ((cdr d-list)
         (map 'vector
              #'(lambda (v) (lazy-fill obj v val (cdr d-list)))
              array))
        (t
         (map 'vector
              #'(lambda (v)
                  (cond ((delayed-p v)
                         (setf (fill-flag obj) T)
                         (setf (fill-value obj) val))
                        (t
                         (fill v val))))
              array))))
```

Exercise 14.8.18 Executable Data Structures (p. 581)

Lists and strings are both handled as sequences.

```
(defmacro make-executable (item)
  `(typecase
     ,item
     (hash-table
      (setf (symbol-function ',item)
            #'(lambda (key) (gethash key ,item)))
      (defun (setf ,item) (val key)
        (setf (gethash key ,item) val))
      ',item)
     (array
      (setf (symbol-function ',item)
            #'(lambda (&rest indices)
                (apply #'aref ,item indices)))
      (defun (setf ,item) (val &rest indices)
        (setf (apply #'aref ,item indices) val))
      ',item)
```

```
(sequence
 (setf (symbol-function ',item)
       #'(lambda (index) (elt ,item index)))
 (defun (setf ,item) (val index)
   (setf (elt ,item index) val)))
(t 'not-an-appropriate-type)))
```

Exercise 15.7.1 Cleaning the Slate (p. 628)

```
(defmacro clean-slate ()
  (let ((package *package*)
        (newpackage (make-package (gensym "PACKAGE"))))
    `(progn
       (defun dirty-slate ()
         (in-package ,package)
         (delete-package ,newpackage))
       (export 'dirty-slate)
       (in-package ,newpackage)
       (import 'dirty-slate)
       (values)
       )))
```

Exercise 15.7.2 Leaky Workspace (p. 628)

The programmer might use a character macro that changes the program's state. Top-level invocations of a macro character would not get written to the file.

```
> (make-workspace "test")
Starting workspace.  End with (save-ws)
WS> (setf x 9)
9
WS> #,(setf x 10)
10
WS> x
10
WS> (save-ws)
Workspace saved in file: test
END-WORKSPACE
```

Here are the contents of file **test**.

```
;; workspace file
(SETF X 9)
```

The expression **#,(setf x 10)** did not get written to the file because the expression was not a list.

Exercise 15.7.3 Making Transcripts (p. 628)

```
(defun my-dribble (filename)
  (catch 'stop
    (format t "Starting transcript.  End with (my-dribble) ~%")
    (let ((stream (open filename :direction :output))
          (ws-prompt "my-dribble> "))
      (flet ((ws-fn? (input)
                     (cond ((eq (car input) 'my-dribble)
                            (close stream)
                            (throw 'stop nil)))))
            (format stream ";; transcript file: ~A ~%" filename)
            (unwind-protect
               (loop
                 (format stream "~%~A" ws-prompt)
                 (format t "~%~A" ws-prompt)
                 (let ((input (read *standard-input*)))
                   (cond ((listp input)
                          (ws-fn? input)
                          (format stream "~%~A" input)))
                   (let ((val (eval input)))
                     (print val stream)
                     (print val *standard-output*))))
               (close stream)))))
  (format t "~%Transcript logged on file: ~A~%" filename)
  'end-transcript)
```

This method does not properly log errors, nor does it handle terminal input and output other than that involved in the read-eval-print loop. For example, the results of most format statements will not make it to the log file.

Exercise 15.7.4 Workspace Editor (p. 628)

```
(defun wed (id)
  (catch 'stop
    (let ((def (get id 'definition))
          (ed-prompt "WED> ")
          (input nil))
```

```
(labels
 ((print-help ()
   (mapcar #'(lambda (str) (format t "~%~A" str))
           '("?        print help information"
             "car | <  move context down by car"
             "cdr | >  move context down by cdr"
             "del      delete car of current context"
             "exit     save current definition and exit"
             "(exp)    evaluate given expression"
             "find     move context to matching expression"
             "i        insert at current context"
             "p        print current context"
             "pd       print definition"
             "quit     exit editor without saving"
             "rep      replace car of current context"
             "save     save current definition"
             "set      set current definition"
             "subst    global substitution in definition"
             "top      move context to top definition"
             "u        move context up" )))
  (myfind (pat tree)
          (cond ((atom tree) nil)
                ((equalp pat (car tree)) tree)
                (t (or (myfind pat (car tree))
                       (myfind pat (cdr tree))))))
  (end-ed ()
          (format t "~%Exiting editor.")
          (throw 'stop nil))
  (save-def (id def)
            (eval def)
            (put id 'definition def)
            (cond ((member id *ws-definitions*) nil)
                  (t (push id *ws-definitions*)))))
 (cond (def
        (format t "Modifying definition of: ~A~%" id))
       (t
        (format t "Creating definition of: ~A~%" id)))
 (let ((context-stack (cons def nil))
       (context def))
   (loop
     (format t "~%~A" ed-prompt)
     (setf input (read *STANDARD-INPUT*))
```

```
(cond
 ((consp input)
  (print (eval input) *standard-output*))
 (t
  (case input
         ((? help) (print-help))
         ((cdr >)  (push context context-stack)
          (setf context (cdr context)))
         ((car <)  (push context context-stack)
          (setf context (car context)))
         ((del)    (format t "~%Deleting: ~A" (car context))
          (setf (car context) (cadr context))
          (setf (cdr context) (cddr context)))
         ((exit)   (save-def id def)
          (end-ed))
         ((find)   (push context context-stack)
          (format t "~%Expression: ")
          (setf context
                (myfind (read *standard-input*) context)))
         ((i ins)  (format t "~%Expression: ")
          (setf (cdr context) (cons (car context)
                                    (cdr context)))
          (setf (car context) (read *standard-input*)))
         ((p)     (pprint context *standard-output*))
         ((pd)    (pprint def *standard-output*))
         ((q quit) (end-ed))
         ((rep)   (format t "~%Expression: ")
          (setf (car context) (read *standard-input*)))
         ((save)  (save-def id def))
         ((set)   (format t "~%Definition: ")
          (setf def (read *standard-input*))
          (setf context def)
          (push context context-stack))
         ((subst)
          (let ((old (progn
                       (format t "~%Old Expression: ")
                       (read *standard-input*)))
                (new (progn
                       (format t "~%New Expression: ")
                       (read *standard-input*))))
            (setf def (subst new old def :test #'equalp)))
          (setf context def))
         ((top t)  (push context context-stack)
          (setf context def))
```

```
              ((u)      (setf context (pop context-stack)))
              (otherwise (format t "~%Unknown command: ~A" input)
                         (format t "~%Type ? for help.~%")))))
      )))))
  (values))

(defvar *ws-definitions* nil)
(defun save-ws (filename)
  (let ((stream (open filename :direction :output)))
    (format stream ";; workspace file~%")
    (mapcar #'(lambda (id)
                (format stream "~%;; WED definition: ~A~%" id)
                (pprint (get id 'definition) stream))
            *ws-definitions*)
    (close stream)
    (format t "~%Workspace saved in file: ~A~%" filename)
    (values)))
```

Exercise 15.7.6 The Rest of cl-eval (p. 634)

```
(defun cl-eval-cond (exp env)
  (cl-eval-cond-aux (cdr exp) env))

(defun cl-eval-cond-aux (exp env)
  (cond ((cl-eval (caar exp) env)
         (cl-eval-sequence (cdar exp) env))
        (t
         (cl-eval-cond-aux (cdr exp) env))))

(defun cl-eval-case (exp env)
  (cl-eval-case-aux
   (cl-eval (cadr exp) env)
   (cddr exp)
   env))

(defun cl-eval-case-aux (key clauses env)
  (cond ((null clauses) nil)
        ((or (eq 'otherwise (caar clauses))
             (member key (caar clauses)))
         (cl-eval-sequence (cdar clauses) env))
        (t
         (cl-eval-case-aux key (cdr clauses) env))))
```

```lisp
(defun cl-eval-and (exp env)
  (cl-eval-and-aux (cdr exp) env))

(defun cl-eval-and-aux (exp env)
  (if (null (cdr exp))
      (cl-eval (car exp) env)
      (if (cl-eval (car exp) env)
          (cl-eval-and-aux (cdr exp) env)
          nil)))

(defun cl-eval-or (exp env)
  (cl-eval-or-aux (cdr exp) env))

(defun cl-eval-or-aux (exp env)
  (cond ((null exp) nil)
        ((cl-eval (car exp) env))
        (t
         (cl-eval-or-aux (cdr exp) env))))

(defun cl-eval-let (exp env)
  (apply
   #'(lambda (&rest args)
       (cl-eval-sequence
        (cddr exp)
        (bind-variables (mapcar #'car (cadr exp))
                        args env)))
   (mapcar #'cadr (cadr exp))))
```

Exercise 16.8.2 Recursive Inline Functions (p. 675)

The inline process would never terminate.

```lisp
;  No inline.
(defun fact (n)
  (if (zerop n) 1
      (* n (fact (- n 1)))))
;  First pass at inline.
(defun fact (n)
  (if (zerop n) 1
      (* n
         (if (zerop (- n 1)) 1
             (* (- n 1) (fact (- (- n 1) 1)))))))
;  etc.
```

Exercise 16.8.3 Tail Recursive reverse (p. 675)

```
(defun tr-reverse (lst)
  (tr-reverse-aux lst nil))

(defun tr-reverse-aux (lst result)
  (cond ((null lst) result)
        (t
         (tr-reverse-aux (cdr lst)
                         (cons (car lst) result)))))
```

Exercise 16.8.5 Tail Recursive last (p. 675)

The normal definition is already tail recursive.

```
(defun tr-last (lst)
  (cond ((null (cdr lst)) (car lst))
        (t (tr-last (cdr lst)))))
```

Exercise 16.8.7 Tail Recursive remove-duplicates (p. 675)

```
(defun tr-remove-duplicates (lst)
  (tr-remove-duplicates-aux lst nil))

(defun tr-remove-duplicates-aux (lst result)
  (cond ((null lst) (reverse result))
        ((member (car lst) (cdr lst))
         (tr-remove-duplicates-aux (cdr lst) result))
        (t
         (tr-remove-duplicates-aux (cdr lst)
                                   (cons (car lst) result)))))
```

Exercise 16.8.8 boola boola (p. 675)

```
(defun my-boole (op int1 int2)
  (case
   op
   ((0)  0)                          ; boole-clr
   ((1)  (lognot 0))                 ; boole-set
   ((2)  int1)                       ; boole-1
   ((3)  int2)                       ; boole-2
   ((4)  (lognot int1))              ; boole-c1
   ((5)  (lognot int2))              ; boole-c2
   ((6)  (logand int1 int2))         ; boole-and
   ((7)  (logior int1 int2))         ; boole-ior
   ((8)  (logxor int1 int2))         ; boole-xor
   ((9)  (logeqv int1 int2))         ; boole-eqv
   ((10) (lognand int1 int2))        ; boole-nand
   ((11) (lognor int1 int2))         ; boole-nor
   ((12) (logandc1 int1 int2))       ; boole-andc1
   ((13) (logandc2 int1 int2))       ; boole-andc2
   ((14) (logorc1 int1 int2))        ; boole-orc1
   ((15) (logorc2 int1 int2))))      ; boole-orc2
```

*In programming, as in everything else, to be in error is
to be reborn.*

◇ ALAN PERLIS, *Epigrams in Programming (1982)*

Appendix C

CLOS and C++

the endeavor, in all branches of knowledge
— theology, philosophy, history, art, science —
to see the object as in itself it really is.

⋄ MATTHEW ARNOLD, *On Translating Homer (1861)*

Plus ça change, plus c'est la même chose.

⋄ ALPHONSE KARR, *Les Guêpes (Janvier, 1849)*

C++ is similar to LISP's CLOS. Both are object-oriented extensions to existing languages, rather than completely new object-oriented languages such as Smalltalk or Eiffel.

In this appendix, we compare the main object-oriented features found in C++ with the Common LISP Object System. We present a sample program written in both languages. The reader who is already familiar with C++ can thereby weigh the differences.

In section 12.3 we defined a structure for time. Here we revisit that problem, with a different solution. We first define a C++ class for time, which has a subclass of periods. In C++ terms, `time` is the base class and `period` is a derived class. Time is represented as the number of seconds after midnight, and periods are represented as the number of seconds from the beginning to the end of the interval. Our class definitions will permit us conveniently to read, write, compare, and perform arithmetic operations on times and periods.

Our C++ example comprises three files: `time.h`, `time.C`, and `timeMain.C`.

C.1 time.h

The header file `time.h` contains some introductory statements followed by the declarations for the `time` and `period` classes. We first see the following.

- *ifndef and define.* The `#ifndef` and `#define` statements check to make sure that this file does not get loaded more than once. The closing `#endif` delimits this context.

- *iostream library.* This standard C++ library needs to be included because we will refer to `ostream` and `istream` classes.

- *Constants.* `seconds_per_day` and `seconds_per_hour` are defined as constants to save the cost of repeated multiplications.

Next, we declare the `time` class, which has the following elements.

- *Member data.* `secs_after_midnight` stores the time value.

- *Member function.* The `hms()` function converts a time value from seconds after midnight into hours, minutes, and seconds, coercing time values to be less than 24 hours. For example, 25 hours becomes 1 a.m.

- *Constructor function.* `time(h,m,s)` creates a new time value from the given hours, minutes, and seconds. The default time is midnight.

- *Overloaded operators.* The `time` class overloads the following operators:

    `<<` – prints a time value to a stream

    `>>` – reads a time value from a stream

    `=` – assigns a time value

    `+` – adds one time to another time

    `-` – subtracts one time from another time

    `<` – compares two time values

The `period` class has the following elements.

- *Constructor function.* `period(time)` creates a new period value from an existing time value.

- *Overloaded operator.* The `period` class overloads only one operator:

    `<<` – prints a period value to a stream

The `period` class inherits all the other `time` class elements.

```
// time.h
#ifndef __time__
#define __time__

#include <iostream.h>
```

```
const long seconds_per_day = 24 * 60 * 60;
const long seconds_per_hour = 60 * 60;

class time {
 protected:
  long secs_after_midnight;
  void hms(long&,long&,long&) const;

 public:
  time(long h = 0, long m = 0, long s = 0);

  friend ostream & operator<<(ostream &, const time &);
  friend istream & operator>>(istream &, time &);

  time operator=(const time & t)
    { secs_after_midnight = t.secs_after_midnight ; return *this; }
  time operator+(const time & t) const;
  time operator-(const time & t) const;
  int operator<(const time & t) const;
};

class period : public time
{
 public:
  period(const time & t) : time(t) {};
  friend ostream & operator<<(ostream &, const period &);
};
#endif
```

C.2 time.C

The file time.C contains the definitions for the time and period member functions.

```
//  time.C
#include "time.h"

//  Constructor for time given hours, minutes and seconds.
//  Truncates times over 24 hours.
time::time(long h, long m, long s)
{
  secs_after_midnight = (h * seconds_per_hour) + (m * 60) + s;
  secs_after_midnight %= seconds_per_day;
}
```

```cpp
//  Converts secs_after_midnight into hours, minutes, and seconds.
void time::hms(long& h,long& m,long& s) const
{
  long tmp;
  h = secs_after_midnight / seconds_per_hour;
  tmp = secs_after_midnight % seconds_per_hour;
  m = tmp / 60;
  s = tmp % 60;
}


//  Prints a time in HH:MM:SS am/pm format.
ostream & operator<<(ostream & os, const time & t)
{
  long hour, minute, second;
  t.hms(hour,minute,second);

  long h = (hour > 12) ? hour - 12 : hour;

  os << h;
  if (minute || second)
    os << ":" << ((minute < 10) ? "0" : "") << minute;
  if (second)
    os << ":" << ((second < 10) ? "0" : "") << second;
  os << ((hour >= 12) ? " pm" : " am");
  return os;
}


//  Inputs a time in hours minutes seconds format.
istream & operator>>(istream & is, time & t)
{
  long h, m, s;
  is >> h >> m >> s;
  t = time(h,m,s);
  return is;
}


//  Adds one time to another time.
time time::operator+(const time & t) const
{
  time nt(0,0,secs_after_midnight + t.secs_after_midnight);
  return nt;
}
```

```
//  Subtracts one time from another time.
time time::operator-(const time & t) const
{
  time nt(0,0,secs_after_midnight - t.secs_after_midnight);
  return nt;
}


//  Compares two times.
int time::operator<(const time & t) const
{
  return (secs_after_midnight < t.secs_after_midnight);
}


//  Prints a period as hour(s), minute(s), and second(s).
ostream & operator<<(ostream & os, const period & p)
{
  long hour, minute, second;
  p.hms(hour,minute,second);
  if (hour)
    os << hour << " hour" << ((hour == 1) ? " " : "s ");
  if (minute)
    os << minute << " minute" << ((minute == 1) ? " " : "s ");
  if (second)
    os << second << " second" << ((second == 1) ? " " : "s ");
  return os;
}
```

C.3   timeMain.C

We now present an example program timeMain.C which uses the time and period
classes and their related member functions.

```
#include "time.h"

void main(void)
{
  time now;
  cout << "Enter current time: (HH MM SS) ";
  cin >> now;
```

```
    int m;
    cout << "Enter a number of minutes: ";
    cin >> m;
    cout << "It is now " << now << endl;
    cout << "In " << m << " minutes it will be "
      << now + time(0,m) << endl;

    time lifeBegins(17,00);
    if (now < lifeBegins)
      {
        cout << "You get off work at " << lifeBegins << endl;
        period p = lifeBegins - now;
        cout << "That is " << p << "from now." << endl;
      }
    else
      {
        cout << "You left work at " << lifeBegins << endl;
        period p = now - lifeBegins;
        cout << "That was " << p << "ago." << endl;
      }
}
```

Below we compile the files, creating an executable named t1. We then run the program; user input is underlined.

```
% CC -o t1 timeMain.C time.C
timeMain.C:
time.C:
% t1
Enter current time: (HH MM SS) 10 30 0
Enter a number of minutes: 25
It is now 10:30 am
In 25 minutes it will be 10:55 am
You get off work at 5 pm
That is 6 hours 30 minutes from now.
% t1
Enter current time: (HH MM SS) 22 22 22
Enter a number of minutes: 5
It is now 10:22:22 pm
In 5 minutes it will be 10:27:22 pm
You left work at 5 pm
That was 5 hours 22 minutes 22 seconds ago.
```

C.4   `time.lisp`

We now present a comparable LISP program. The single file `time.lisp` has the following elements.

- *Constants.* We create the same two constants as in the C++ header file.

- *Classes.* We define the classes `my-time` and `my-period` classes. Note that we avoid using the name `time`, which is already defined in LISP.

- *Constructors.* The functions `make-my-time` and `make-my-period` create instances of the respective classes. Note that we define `make-my-period` as a generic function to get type checking.

- *Generic functions.* The `hms` function decodes a time object. `print-object` is the standard print method. There is no standard input method, so we create a new function, `read-time`. LISP does not encourage new definitions for arithmetic operators, so we define generic versions `g+`, `g-`, and `g<`.

- *Main program.* The function `t1` reproduces the behavior of the `timeMain.C` program.

```
;; time.lisp

(defconstant seconds_per_day (* 24 60 60))
(defconstant seconds_per_hour (* 60 60))

(defclass my-time ()
  ((secs_after_midnight :initarg :sam :reader sam)))

(defclass my-period (my-time) ())

(defun make-my-time
  (&optional (hours 0) (minutes 0) (seconds 0))
  (let ((sam (+ (* hours seconds_per_hour)
                (* minutes 60)
                seconds)))
    (make-instance 'my-time :sam (mod sam seconds_per_day))))

(defmethod make-my-period ((obj my-time))
  (make-instance 'my-period :sam (sam obj)))
```

```lisp
(defmethod hms ((time my-time))
  (let* ((hours (truncate (/ (sam time) seconds_per_hour)))
         (tmp (mod (sam time) seconds_per_hour))
         (minutes (truncate (/ tmp 60)))
         (seconds (mod tmp 60)))
    (values hours minutes seconds)))

(defmethod print-object ((object my-time) stream)
  (multiple-value-bind
    (hours minutes seconds) (hms object)
    (let ((h (if (> hours 12)
                 (mod hours 12)
                 hours)))
      (format stream "~d" h)
      (if (or (not (zerop minutes))
              (not (zerop seconds)))
          (format stream ":~2,'0d" minutes))
      (if (not (zerop seconds))
          (format stream ":~2,'0d" seconds))
      (format stream (if (>= hours 12) " pm" " am")))))

(defun read-time (&optional (stream *standard-input*))
  (let ((h (read stream))
        (m (read stream))
        (s (read stream)))
    (make-my-time h m s)))

(defmethod g+ ((t1 my-time) (t2 my-time))
  (make-my-time 0 0 (+ (sam t1) (sam t2))))

(defmethod g- ((t1 my-time) (t2 my-time))
  (make-my-time 0 0 (- (sam t1) (sam t2))))

(defmethod g< ((t1 my-time) (t2 my-time))
  (< (sam t1) (sam t2)))

(defmethod print-object ((object my-period) stream)
  (multiple-value-bind
    (hours minutes seconds) (hms object)
    (if (not (zerop hours))
        (format stream "~d hour~p " hours hours))
```

```
      (if (not (zerop minutes))
          (format stream "~d minute~p " minutes minutes))
      (if (not (zerop seconds))
          (format stream "~d second~p " seconds seconds)))))

(defun t1 ()
  (let ((now (progn
                (format t "Enter the current time (HH MM SS) ")
                (read-time *standard-input*)))
        (m (progn
             (format t "Enter a number of minutes: ")
             (read *standard-input*)))
        (lifeBegins (make-my-time 17)))
    (format t "It is now ~s~%" now)
    (format t "In ~d minutes it will be ~s~%"
            m (g+ now (make-my-time 0 m)))
    (cond ((g< now lifeBegins)
           (format t "You get off work at ~S~%" lifeBegins)
           (format t "That is ~sfrom now.~%"
                   (make-my-period (g- lifeBegins now))))
          (t
           (format t "You got off work at ~S~%" lifeBegins)
           (format t "That was ~sago.~%"
                   (make-my-period (g- now lifeBegins)))))
    (values)))
```

Below is a transcript of the LISP program in action, with user input underlined.

```
> (t1)
Enter the current time (HH MM SS) 10 30 0
Enter a number of minutes: 25
It is now 10:30 am
In 25 minutes it will be 10:55 am
You get off work at 5 pm
That is 6 hours 30 minutes from now.

> (t1)
Enter the current time (HH MM SS) 22 22 22
Enter a number of minutes: 5
It is now 10:22:22 pm
In 5 minutes it will be 10:27:22 pm
You got off work at 5 pm
That was 5 hours 22 minutes 22 seconds ago.
```

We summarize the major points of comparison.

- *Polymorphism.* Both languages support polymorphism. C++ makes it easier to reuse existing operators through overloading and also has a more flexible parameter structure for the member functions. The lambda list congruence rule in CLOS is more restrictive, though &optional parameters can provide a solution.

  However, C++ has no facilities comparable to CLOS's method combinations, such as :before, :after, and :around methods, as well as call-next-method.

- *Inheritance.* Both languages support multiple inheritance. CLOS gives the programmer more control over inheritance behaviour.

- *Encapsulation.* C++ uses the private: and protected: tags to encapsulate member data and functions. For example, in time.h above, the variable secs_after_midnight and hms function are not directly accessible outside the time class and its children.

  CLOS itself does not support encapsulation, per se. However, LISP provides a number of encapsulation methods including packages and closures.

- *Member function definition.* C++ member functions have to be declared at the time the class is created, namely, compile time. The C++ programmer cannot add a new member function without recompiling the original class definition.

  In CLOS, the programmer can create new member functions at run-time. In fact, the programmer can even redefine the class itself at run-time, after instances of the class have already been created. C++ is static. CLOS is dynamic.

- *Strong typing.* C++, in addition to adding object-oriented constructs to C, also introduced strong typing. The requirement to specify type information in C++ permits the compiler to identify a range of errors that might otherwise go undetected.

  CLOS's generic functions introduce a typing requirement, though not as stringent as that found in C++. LISP in general lets the user make the decision about type checking.

  We note that the C++ template construct has been added to lessen the grip of the strong typing requirement. The introduction of run-time type checking in C++ will continue this trend.

C++ is a major object-oriented programming language today and for the foreseeable future. However, C++ itself has no special object-oriented programming features that make it superior to LISP and CLOS. In fact, given the flexibility of LISP in general, and CLOS's metaobject protocol in particular, it is reasonable to assume that any future developments in object-oriented programming languages will be implemented first as extensions to LISP before making making their way into the C++ world.

Some programming languages manage to absorb change, but withstand progress.

◇ ALAN PERLIS, *Epigrams in Programming (1982)*

Appendix D

ASCII Character Codes

You have suffered worse things;
God will put an end to these also.

◇ VIRGIL, *Aeneid (Book I)*

Perhaps some day it will be pleasant
to remember even this.

◇ VIRGIL, *Ibid.*

We present here a LISP program that prints out the ASCII character codes in decimal (base 10), octal (base 8), and hexadecimal (base 16), as well as the standard readtable entries for each character. Refer to section 11.8 for a discussion of readtables. See page 187 for a definition of the function incr-char.

Finally, we present the output itself for reference.

```
(defun print-ascii-table ()
  (format t "~%Character ~12TDEC ~17TOCT ~22THEX")
  (format t "~27TRead table entry")
  (do ((ch #\null (incr-char ch)))
      ((char> ch #\rubout) (values))
    (print-ascii ch)))

(defun print-ascii (ch)
  (let ((ch-val (char-code ch)))
    (format t "~%~S ~12T~D ~17T~O ~22T~X ~27T~S"
            ch  ch-val ch-val ch-val
            (get-macro-character ch *readtable*))))
```

> (print-ascii-table)

Character	DEC	OCT	HEX	Read table entry
#\null	0	0	0	#<Function READ-TOKEN @ #x73ed26>
#\^a	1	1	1	#<Function READ-TOKEN @ #x73ed26>
#\^b	2	2	2	#<Function READ-TOKEN @ #x73ed26>
#\^c	3	3	3	#<Function READ-TOKEN @ #x73ed26>
#\^d	4	4	4	#<Function READ-TOKEN @ #x73ed26>
#\^e	5	5	5	#<Function READ-TOKEN @ #x73ed26>
#\^f	6	6	6	#<Function READ-TOKEN @ #x73ed26>
#\bel	7	7	7	#<Function READ-TOKEN @ #x73ed26>
#\backspace	8	10	8	#<Function READ-TOKEN @ #x73ed26>
#\tab	9	11	9	NIL
#\newline	10	12	a	NIL
#\vt	11	13	b	#<Function READ-TOKEN @ #x73ed26>
#\page	12	14	c	NIL
#\return	13	15	d	NIL
#\^n	14	16	e	#<Function READ-TOKEN @ #x73ed26>
#\^o	15	17	f	#<Function READ-TOKEN @ #x73ed26>
#\^p	16	20	10	#<Function READ-TOKEN @ #x73ed26>
#\^q	17	21	11	#<Function READ-TOKEN @ #x73ed26>
#\^r	18	22	12	#<Function READ-TOKEN @ #x73ed26>
#\^s	19	23	13	#<Function READ-TOKEN @ #x73ed26>
#\^t	20	24	14	#<Function READ-TOKEN @ #x73ed26>
#\^u	21	25	15	#<Function READ-TOKEN @ #x73ed26>
#\^v	22	26	16	#<Function READ-TOKEN @ #x73ed26>
#\^w	23	27	17	#<Function READ-TOKEN @ #x73ed26>
#\^x	24	30	18	#<Function READ-TOKEN @ #x73ed26>
#\^y	25	31	19	#<Function READ-TOKEN @ #x73ed26>
#\^z	26	32	1a	#<Function READ-TOKEN @ #x73ed26>
#\esc	27	33	1b	#<Function READ-TOKEN @ #x73ed26>
#\^\\	28	34	1c	#<Function READ-TOKEN @ #x73ed26>
#\^]	29	35	1d	#<Function READ-TOKEN @ #x73ed26>
#\^^	30	36	1e	#<Function READ-TOKEN @ #x73ed26>
#\^_	31	37	1f	#<Function READ-TOKEN @ #x73ed26>
#\space	32	40	20	NIL
#\!	33	41	21	#<Function READ-TOKEN @ #x73ed26>
#\"	34	42	22	EXCL::READ-STRING
#\#	35	43	23	#<Function READ-DISPATCH-CHAR @ #x740fe6>
#\$	36	44	24	#<Function READ-TOKEN @ #x73ed26>
#\%	37	45	25	#<Function READ-TOKEN @ #x73ed26>
#\&	38	46	26	#<Function READ-TOKEN @ #x73ed26>
#\'	39	47	27	EXCL::READ-QUOTE
#\(	40	50	28	EXCL::READ-LIST

```
#\)          41    51    29    EXCL::READ-RIGHT-PAREN
#\*          42    52    2a    #<Function READ-TOKEN @ #x73ed26>
#\+          43    53    2b    #<Function READ-TOKEN @ #x73ed26>
#\,          44    54    2c    #<Function COMMA-MACRO @ #x739716>
#\-          45    55    2d    #<Function READ-TOKEN @ #x73ed26>
#\.          46    56    2e    #<Function READ-TOKEN @ #x73ed26>
#\/          47    57    2f    #<Function READ-TOKEN @ #x73ed26>
#\0          48    60    30    #<Function READ-TOKEN @ #x73ed26>
#\1          49    61    31    #<Function READ-TOKEN @ #x73ed26>
#\2          50    62    32    #<Function READ-TOKEN @ #x73ed26>
#\3          51    63    33    #<Function READ-TOKEN @ #x73ed26>
#\4          52    64    34    #<Function READ-TOKEN @ #x73ed26>
#\5          53    65    35    #<Function READ-TOKEN @ #x73ed26>
#\6          54    66    36    #<Function READ-TOKEN @ #x73ed26>
#\7          55    67    37    #<Function READ-TOKEN @ #x73ed26>
#\8          56    70    38    #<Function READ-TOKEN @ #x73ed26>
#\9          57    71    39    #<Function READ-TOKEN @ #x73ed26>
#\:          58    72    3a    #<Function READ-TOKEN @ #x73ed26>
#\;          59    73    3b    EXCL::READ-COMMENT
#\<          60    74    3c    #<Function READ-TOKEN @ #x73ed26>
#\=          61    75    3d    #<Function READ-TOKEN @ #x73ed26>
#\>          62    76    3e    #<Function READ-TOKEN @ #x73ed26>
#\?          63    77    3f    #<Function READ-TOKEN @ #x73ed26>
#\@          64    100   40    #<Function READ-TOKEN @ #x73ed26>
#\A          65    101   41    #<Function READ-TOKEN @ #x73ed26>
#\B          66    102   42    #<Function READ-TOKEN @ #x73ed26>
#\C          67    103   43    #<Function READ-TOKEN @ #x73ed26>
#\D          68    104   44    #<Function READ-TOKEN @ #x73ed26>
#\E          69    105   45    #<Function READ-TOKEN @ #x73ed26>
#\F          70    106   46    #<Function READ-TOKEN @ #x73ed26>
#\G          71    107   47    #<Function READ-TOKEN @ #x73ed26>
#\H          72    110   48    #<Function READ-TOKEN @ #x73ed26>
#\I          73    111   49    #<Function READ-TOKEN @ #x73ed26>
#\J          74    112   4a    #<Function READ-TOKEN @ #x73ed26>
#\K          75    113   4b    #<Function READ-TOKEN @ #x73ed26>
#\L          76    114   4c    #<Function READ-TOKEN @ #x73ed26>
#\M          77    115   4d    #<Function READ-TOKEN @ #x73ed26>
#\N          78    116   4e    #<Function READ-TOKEN @ #x73ed26>
#\O          79    117   4f    #<Function READ-TOKEN @ #x73ed26>
#\P          80    120   50    #<Function READ-TOKEN @ #x73ed26>
#\Q          81    121   51    #<Function READ-TOKEN @ #x73ed26>
#\R          82    122   52    #<Function READ-TOKEN @ #x73ed26>
#\S          83    123   53    #<Function READ-TOKEN @ #x73ed26>
#\T          84    124   54    #<Function READ-TOKEN @ #x73ed26>
```

#\U	85	125	55	#<Function READ-TOKEN @ #x73ed26>
#\V	86	126	56	#<Function READ-TOKEN @ #x73ed26>
#\W	87	127	57	#<Function READ-TOKEN @ #x73ed26>
#\X	88	130	58	#<Function READ-TOKEN @ #x73ed26>
#\Y	89	131	59	#<Function READ-TOKEN @ #x73ed26>
#\Z	90	132	5a	#<Function READ-TOKEN @ #x73ed26>
#\[	91	133	5b	#<Function READ-TOKEN @ #x73ed26>
#\\	92	134	5c	NIL
#\]	93	135	5d	#<Function READ-TOKEN @ #x73ed26>
#\^	94	136	5e	#<Function READ-TOKEN @ #x73ed26>
#_	95	137	5f	#<Function READ-TOKEN @ #x73ed26>
#\'	96	140	60	#<Function BACKQUOTE-MACRO @ #x74477e>
#\a	97	141	61	#<Function READ-TOKEN @ #x73ed26>
#\b	98	142	62	#<Function READ-TOKEN @ #x73ed26>
#\c	99	143	63	#<Function READ-TOKEN @ #x73ed26>
#\d	100	144	64	#<Function READ-TOKEN @ #x73ed26>
#\e	101	145	65	#<Function READ-TOKEN @ #x73ed26>
#\f	102	146	66	#<Function READ-TOKEN @ #x73ed26>
#\g	103	147	67	#<Function READ-TOKEN @ #x73ed26>
#\h	104	150	68	#<Function READ-TOKEN @ #x73ed26>
#\i	105	151	69	#<Function READ-TOKEN @ #x73ed26>
#\j	106	152	6a	#<Function READ-TOKEN @ #x73ed26>
#\k	107	153	6b	#<Function READ-TOKEN @ #x73ed26>
#\l	108	154	6c	#<Function READ-TOKEN @ #x73ed26>
#\m	109	155	6d	#<Function READ-TOKEN @ #x73ed26>
#\n	110	156	6e	#<Function READ-TOKEN @ #x73ed26>
#\o	111	157	6f	#<Function READ-TOKEN @ #x73ed26>
#\p	112	160	70	#<Function READ-TOKEN @ #x73ed26>
#\q	113	161	71	#<Function READ-TOKEN @ #x73ed26>
#\r	114	162	72	#<Function READ-TOKEN @ #x73ed26>
#\s	115	163	73	#<Function READ-TOKEN @ #x73ed26>
#\t	116	164	74	#<Function READ-TOKEN @ #x73ed26>
#\u	117	165	75	#<Function READ-TOKEN @ #x73ed26>
#\v	118	166	76	#<Function READ-TOKEN @ #x73ed26>
#\w	119	167	77	#<Function READ-TOKEN @ #x73ed26>
#\x	120	170	78	#<Function READ-TOKEN @ #x73ed26>
#\y	121	171	79	#<Function READ-TOKEN @ #x73ed26>
#\z	122	172	7a	#<Function READ-TOKEN @ #x73ed26>
#\{	123	173	7b	#<Function READ-TOKEN @ #x73ed26>
#|	124	174	7c	#<Function READ-TOKEN @ #x73ed26>
#\}	125	175	7d	#<Function READ-TOKEN @ #x73ed26>
#\~	126	176	7e	#<Function READ-TOKEN @ #x73ed26>
#\rubout	127	177	7f	#<Function READ-TOKEN @ #x73ed26>

If your computer speaks English, it was probably
made in Japan.

◇ ALAN PERLIS, *Epigrams in Programming (1982)*

Appendix E

References

You will find it a very good practice
always to verify your references, sir.

◇ MARTIN JOSEPH ROUTH, *From* J. W. Burgon, *Memoir of Dr. Routh (1878)*

The reason why so few good books are written is,
that so few people that can write know anything.

◇ WALTER BAGEHOT, *Literary Studies (1853)*

[Bogen, 1973] Bogen, R., et al. (1973). Macsyma user's manual. Technical report, MIT Project MAC.

[Camerson and Rosenblatt, 1991] Camerson, D., and Rosenblatt, B. (1991). *Learning GNU Emacs*. O'Reilly and Associates, Sebastopol, CA.

[Charniak et al., 1987] Charniak, E., Riesbeck, C., McDermott, D., and Meehan, J. (1987). *Artificial Intelligence Programming, Second Edition*. Lawrence Erlbaum Associates, Hillsdale, NJ.

[Church, 1941] Church, A. (1941). *The Calculi of Lambda Conversion*. Annals of Mathematics Studies Number 6. Princeton University Press, Princeton, N.J.

[Dahl and Nygaard, 1966] Dahl, O., and Nygaard, K. (1966). Simula – an algol-based simulation language. *Communications of the ACM*, 9(9):671–682.

[Foderaro and Sklower, 1992] Foderaro, J., and Sklower, K. (1992). The FRANZ lisp manual. Technical report, University of California, Berkeley.

[Franz Inc., 1988] Franz Inc. (1988). *Common LISP: The Reference*. Addison Wesley, Reading, MA.

[Goldberg and Robson, 1983] Goldberg, A., and Robson, D. (1983). *Smalltalk-80: The Language and Its Implementation.* Addison-Wesley, Reading, Mass.

[Greenblatt, 1974] Greenblatt, R. (1974). The LISP machine. Working Paper 79, MIT Artificial Intelligence Laboratory, Cambridge, MA.

[Griss and Hearn, 1981] Griss, M., and Hearn, A. (1981). A portable LISP compiler. *Software Practice and Experience*, 11:541–605.

[Hofstadter, 1979] Hofstadter, D. R. (1979). *Gödel, Escher, Bach: An Eternal Golden Braid.* Vintage Books, New York.

[Kernighan and Plauger, 1976] Kernighan, B., and Plauger, P. (1976). *Software Tools.* Addison-Wesley, Reading, Mass.

[Kernighan and Ritchie, 1988] Kernighan, B., and Ritchie, D. (1988). *The C Programming Language.* Prentice Hall, Englewood Cliffs, NJ, second edition.

[Kiczales et al., 1991] Kiczales, G., des Rivières, J., and Bobrow, D. (1991). *The Art of the Metaobject Protocol.* MIT Press, Cambridge, MA.

[Knuth, 1973] Knuth, D. (1973). *The Art of Computer Programming, Volume 1: Fundamental Algorithms.* Addison-Wesley, Reading, Mass.

[Knuth, 1978] Knuth, D. (1978). *The Art of Computer Programming, Volume 3: Sorting and Searching.* Addison-Wesley, Reading, Mass.

[Knuth, 1981] Knuth, D. (1981). *The Art of Computer Programming, Volume 2: Seminumerical Algorithms.* Second Edition. Addison-Wesley, Reading, Mass.

[McCarthy, 1981] McCarthy, J. (1981). History of LISP. In Wexelblat, R., editor, *History of Programming Languages*, chapter IV, pages 173–197. Academic Press, New York.

[McCarthy et al., 1962] McCarthy, J., Abrahams, P., Edwards, D., Hart, T., and Levin, M. (1962). *The LISP 1.5 Programmer's Manual.* MIT Press, Cambridge, MA.

[Meyer, 1988] Meyer, B. (1988). *Object-oriented Software Construction.* Prentice Hall, Englewood Cliffs, NJ.

[Moon, 1974] Moon, D. (1974). MacLISP reference manual. Technical report, MIT Project MAC, Cambridge, MA.

[Newell et al., 1964] Newell, A., Tonge, F., Feigenbaum, E., Jr., B. G., and Mealy, G. (1964). *Information Processing Language-V Manual.* Prentice Hall, Englewood Cliffs, NJ, second edition.

[Norvig, 1992] Norvig, P. (1992). *Paradigms of Artificial Intelligence Programming: Case Studies in Common LISP.* Morgan Kaufmann.

[Perlis, 1982] Perlis, A. (1982). Epigrams in programming. *ACM SIGPLAN.*

[Plauger, 1992] Plauger, P. (1992). *The Standard C Library.* Prentice Hall.

[Quillian, 1968] Quillian, M. (1968). Semantic memory. In Minsky, M., editor, *Semantic Information Processing*, pages 227–353. MIT Press, Cambridge, MA.

[Steele and Gabriel, 1993] Steele, G., and Gabriel, R. (1993). The evolution of lisp. *ACM SIGPLAN Notices*, 28(3):231–270. The Second ACM SIGPLAN History of Programming Languages Conference (HOPL-II).

[Steele Jr., 1990] Steele Jr., G. L. (1990). *Common LISP: The Language.* Digital Press, Burlington, Mass., second edition.

[Steele Jr. and Sussman, 1978] Steele Jr., G. L., and Sussman, G. J. (1978). The revised report on scheme: A dialect of lisp. AI Memo 452, MIT Artificial Intelligence Laboratory.

[Stroustrup, 1986] Stroustrup, B. (1986). *The C++ Programming Language.* Addison Wesley, Reading, MA.

[Sussman and Steele Jr., 1975] Sussman, G. J., and Steele Jr., G. L. (1975). Scheme: An interpreter for extended lambda calculus. AI Memo 349, MIT Artificial Intelligence Laboratory.

[Teitelman, 1974] Teitelman, W. (1974). InterLISP reference manual (first revision). Technical report, Xerox Palo Alto Research Center, Palo Alto, CA.

[Teitelman, 1978] Teitelman, W. (1978). InterLISP reference manual (third revision). Technical report, Xerox Palo Alto Research Center, Palo Alto, CA.

[Weinreb and Moon, 1981] Weinreb, D., and Moon, D. (1981). LISP machine manual, third edition. Technical report, MIT Artificial Intelligence Laboratory, Cambridge, MA.

[Weizenbaum, 1966] Weizenbaum, J. (1966). Eliza - a computer program for the study of natural language communications between man and machine. *Communications of the Association for Computing Machinery*, 9(1).

The best book on programming for the layman is Alice in Wonderland; *but that's because it's the best book on anything for the layman.*

◇ ALAN PERLIS, *Epigrams in Programming (1982)*

Index

The secret of being a bore is to tell everything.

◇ VOLTAIRE, *Sept Discours en Vers sur l'Homme (1738)*

Items in (typewriter font and parentheses) or undelimited-symbols are Common LISP names. For convenient reference, functions, macros, and special forms are given with their normal arguments, for example, (cons object object). The following additional markings are used to provide more specific identification of LISP fauna.

CONSTANT	constants
DECLARATION	declaration specifier
FORM	special forms
GENERIC	generic functions
KEYWORD	keywords
LAMBDA KEYWORD	lambda list keywords
MACRO	macros
SETF	setf accessor functions
TYPE	data type
TYPE SPECIFIER	type specifier
VARIABLE	global variable

Items in *[slant font and square brackets]* are names of functions, macros, and classes given as examples or exercises in the text. Generally, they are not the same as LISP system names. Discretionary arguments are notated with the syntax described in section 2.9.

Computation has made the tree flower.

◊ ALAN PERLIS, *Epigrams in Programming (1982)*